Classic Movie Fight Scenes

Classic Movie Fight Scenes

75 Years of Bare Knuckle Brawls, 1914–1989

GENE FREESE

McFarland & Company, Inc., Publishers

Jefferson, North Carolina

LIBRARY OF CONGRESS CATALOGUING-IN-PUBLICATION DATA

Names: Freese, Gene Scott, 1969– author.
Title: Classic movie fight scenes : 75 years of bare knuckle brawls,
1914–1989 / Gene Freese.
Description: Jefferson, North Carolina : McFarland & Company, Inc.,
Publishers, 2017 | Includes bibliographical references and index.
Identifiers: LCCN 2017031381 | ISBN 9781476669434
(softcover : acid free paper) ∞
Subjects: LCSH: Hand-to-hand fighting in motion pictures. | Motion
pictures—United States—History—20th century.
Classification: LCC PN1995.9.H295 F74 2017 | DDC 791.43/655—dc23
LC record available at https://lccn.loc.gov/2017031381

BRITISH LIBRARY CATALOGUING DATA ARE AVAILABLE

ISBN (print) 978-1-4766-6943-4
ISBN (ebook) 978-1-4766-2935-3

Front cover: John Wayne as Tom Dunson and Montgomery Clift
as Matt Garth in *Red River*, 1948 (United Artists/Photofest)

Printed in the United States of America

McFarland & Company, Inc., Publishers
Box 611, Jefferson, North Carolina 28640
www.mcfarlandpub.com

Table of Contents

Preface

I have been interested in movie fights as long as I can remember. As a youngster, they appealed to my own sense of athleticism and identification of heroic role models overcoming adversity. It's easy to cheer John Wayne when he gives a bad guy what he deserves on the chin.

Fight scenes tap into macho attitudes and red-blooded male sensibilities. In the early 1980s, cable television began showing movies day and night. The first I recall was *Any Which Way You Can* (1980) featuring Clint Eastwood's highly anticipated slugfest with William Smith. HBO showed that often and I watched it a dozen or more times. The monumental exchange of punches was mesmerizing.

I sought out John Wayne and Victor McLaglen's epic brawl in *The Quiet Man* (1952). That led to Wayne and Randolph Scott's famous battle in *The Spoilers* (1942). Bruce Lee and Chuck Norris in *Way of the Dragon* (1972) created excitement in martial arts. Charles Bronson taking on Robert Tessier and Nick

Dimitri in *Hard Times* (1975) was bare-knuckle nirvana. The famous Sean Connery–Robert Shaw train fight in *From Russia with Love* (1963) delivered the goods, and the legend of the no-holds-barred fight between Rod Taylor and William Smith in *Darker Than Amber* (1970) stirred further interest in the subject.

While there have been books dedicated to stage combat training and fight scene choreography, there hasn't been a book examining fight scenes themselves in detail. This will be the first. Fight scenes have been around since the early days of silent film and their evolution merits historical interest.

The filming and presentation of fight scenes changed in the 1990s with advances in computer technology so I chose 1989 as a cut-off date for this project. In researching the book, I viewed the films in question and exhausted everything written and commented on or about these scenes and the participants by the studios, the press and the filmmakers.

Introduction

Throughout recorded history there has been an outlet for man's competitive nature in either sport or war. Something innate within man's psychological wiring forces him to prove himself not only to others but to himself in battle. It might be showing off for the opposite sex to attract a mate. It might be natural selection, as only the strongest of a species can survive. It could be a cathartic need to act out violent tendencies and let off steam. It might be vanity fueled by testosterone and adrenaline. Technology has offered advantages in the form of advanced weaponry, but the primitive standby remains brawn against brawn. Who hits the hardest? Who can take a punch and stay on his feet? Who is the toughest? In some ways, it's the measure of a man.

From the advent of storytelling on film, many a Third Act has pitted the antagonist against the protagonist in some form of violent conflict resolution. Sometimes this involves a gunfight, a knife fight or a sword duel. Most often it's an old-fashioned bare-knuckle brawl with Hollywood ignoring the damage a fist can do to a face outside a trickle of blood from the mouth or nose. In the land of movie play-acting, the participants struggle to a pre-determined outcome, with the best fights having structure and an emotional context between the characters. Customarily the characters are on equal footing in regard to skill level and psychologically equipped to see a battle to its end. The fight is well-rehearsed, and the choreography practiced like a dance routine. Yet it remains a forum for the real individual

to assert his manhood. It's an ego trip in a profession famous for egos. Sometimes the actors have the requisite background: former boxers, wrestlers or martial artists who landed in movies because of their look or skill. They are the proverbial last guy you'd like to meet in a dark alley. Usually it's all artifice.

The best choreographed fights are the ones that have something extra and provide an intense edge. It's possible the stars involved are doing their own stunts. Maybe they brought a boosted energy to the proceedings, which can drag on for days to capture what lasts a handful of minutes on screen. Perhaps the actors involved truly dislike one another and play extra rough for the cameras. Hollywood tough guys have been known to get carried away while throwing fake punches that on occasion become all too real. Sometimes it's the emotion of the character or the urgency of the situation. Oftentimes it's the location that makes a fight interesting. It might be a raging river, a high cliff or a pit of mud. Even then, it takes pros behind the camera in the form of the director, fight coordinator and cameraman to capture it all correctly. Editors and music conductors have the ability to make a fight noteworthy in post-production. Mostly it's the brawlers themselves: Hollywood he-men going mano a mano to discover the toughest fighter in the land of make-believe. Or at least, other guys wearing their clothes while pretending to be them.

Stunt doubles keep the stars out of physical danger and the investors' insurance companies happy. In the early days of Hollywood, little effort was made to disguise this fact. Occasionally the stunt double and star were so obviously mismatched as to lend an air of comedy to the proceedings. In retrospect, early fights could look comical. Stuntmen often improvised quickly with pulled punches, open-handed slaps to the shoulder, and old-fashioned wrestling in the dirt. Action was captured with a static camera placement and hope for the best. Still there were good fights from the silent era, most notably in *The Spoilers* (1914) with William Farnum and Tom Santschi exchanging actual damage-inducing blows. They were among a handful of actors from this period who were unafraid to take lumps. "Reel fights must be real," I.E. Eubanks wrote in *Motion Picture* magazine in 1917. "Good fighting is good acting."

The brawling buddy picture originated with Edmund Lowe and Victor McLaglen's Quirt and Flagg characters in Raoul Walsh's *What Price Glory* (1926) and *The Cock-Eyed World* (1929). They punched their way through several films together into the sound era, often at odds over a woman. The Quirt and Flagg concept was adopted by a variety of co-stars over the years. Choreographed fight routines entered the picture in the early 1930s as did attention to a cinematographer's camera placement and angle. Efforts were made to suggest that the stars were engaging in all the action even when they weren't.

Two men are credited with the change in filming philosophy. They are actor John Wayne and his stunt double and frequent co-star Yakima Canutt. Wayne became a star because he could throw a great screen punch and could "sell" his partner's blow effectively. For example, a Wayne right cross with Canutt rolling

his head to the opposite side looks like a solid hit with correct camera placement even if the punch misses by several inches. This is because the movie camera has no depth perception. Likewise, a straight Wayne right could pull up an inch short of Canutt's jaw, but if the stuntman were to throw his head straight back with proper timing, this too looks like a devastating punch. The same effect could be had with the camera shooting at the back of Canutt's shoulder. The new movie punches differed from a real boxer's punch: The movie blows were exaggerated roundhouse punches the camera couldn't miss. While boxers throw short, straight-on punches, movie fighters severely telegraph blows for the camera and the audience, paying strict attention to never violate an imaginary 180-degree viewing plane. This new technique came to be known as the Pass System. Sound effects (originally a mallet striking a grapefruit) and editing could give the appearance of a punch connecting, and audiences would never know the blow missed by a good six inches. The possibilities seemed limitless. The B-western fight team of Bob Steele and Charlie King quickly picked up on the new

Yakima Canutt (left) and John Wayne are credited as the architects of the choreographed fight scene. Here they fight in Monogram's *Paradise Canyon* (1935).

technique, cementing their tremendous popularity with audiences. Stunt coordinators and gaffers began to specialize in putting together fight routines. Directors and second-unit teams took pride in thrilling audiences with fisticuffs on film. The modern screen fight was born, and it lasted over 50 years.

The cut-off to realism arrived in the 1990s with the increasing reliance on MTV-style flash cuts, shaky cameras, computer graphics (CGI) and wire work. Combatants were flying across the screen in all kinds of improbable ways, and oftentimes faster than the naked eye could see or comprehend. Typical "old school" fights might have a dozen or more edits; the new fights could have hundreds, seeking to provide a disorienting adrenaline rush to the audience. Overhead wires and harnesses were attached to legs and hips and assisted in creating fancy martial art moves with no basis in reality. Digitally enhanced artistry could put an actor's head on a cartoon image's body. Action didn't necessarily have to happen for it to appear to happen. Once again, the possibilities seemed endless, even if the results often bordered on the ridiculous and the impossible for fight scene purists.

What's more, the combatants no longer seemed to be real-life tough guys, but too often model-types who had been put on strict diets and spent three months in the gym with a cycle of hormone enhancers to artificially pump up the muscles. Stunt doubles and gaffers who created some of the screen's greatest moments did so in anonymity for years. In the new era, not only were the stuntmen and coordinators given on-screen credit, but so were the actors' personal trainers, bodyguards and special groomers. Modern studio budgets could spend millions of dollars in time and resources to create the big screen illusion these men could handle themselves in a fight. However, one senses they'd be lost without their entourages, cell phones, designer clothes and café lattes. The new action stars were not veterans of world wars, survivors of economic Dust Bowl Depression, or whiskey-drinking men whose idea of a "gym workout" was to put on the gloves and punch one another in the face for an afternoon. They were soft no matter how hard they appeared on screen.

But with the emergence of cable television, Internet, and DVDs, new audiences can easily rediscover those 75 glorious years of realistic roughhousing from men of action. Here they are, complete with fight description, significance, behind-the-scenes stories of legend and lore, and biographies on the actors and stuntmen who made their reputations as tough guys during the silent and sound era.

Charlie King (left) and Bob Steele were quick to pick up the new fighting technique in B-westerns like Supreme's *Brand of the Outlaws* (1936).

The Fights

WILLIAM FARNUM VS. TOM SANTSCHI in *The Spoilers* (1914)

Colin Campbell directed this ambitious 1898 Gold Rush story for Selig Polyscope. This silent is renowned for its legendary climactic two-man fight which *Stage Combat* calls "the brawl to end all brawls." *Variety* labels it "one of the classic brawls of filmdom," while *Films and Filming* claims it "set a standard in ruggedness which is said to remain unequaled." The landmark fight, totally improvised, was filmed over the course of one continuous hour, leaving both the exhausted protagonist and antagonist bloody, beaten men. *Classics of the Silent Screen* declares that it "created an understandable sensation," elaborating that "legends about its merits, and tales about the savagery of the famous fight scene, have been enabled to grow without the counterbalance of critical analysis." A 110-minute version of the groundbreaking film was distributed in 1916. Surviving incomplete prints show a choppy brawl lasting barely over two minutes. Legend would have one believe the original cut lasted up to ten times longer. It was so notorious that single reels of the fight were passed around Hollywood for years for interested parties to view.

The husky actors agreed to make some physical contact in a cramped interior set but quickly became carried away in the heat of battle. Farnum, a 215-pound six-footer, had mentioned that he was contracted to begin another film in a week and asked the 6'1", 218-pound Santschi to avoid hitting him in the face. However, one of Santschi's first punches landed on Farnum's nose, breaking it. A bleeding Farnum immediately decided that Santschi did it on purpose and responded in kind. Director Campbell kept the camera running. For the rest of the extended fight, the two exchanged damaging uppercuts, tearing and clawing savagely at one another's faces. At one point, a real book-case collapsed on the two staggering men. Santschi fell on a typewriter, injuring his back. There were no breakaway props, stunt doubles or pulled punches. It was all done for real with their shirts literally ripped to shreds. When Farnum cinched in a painful hammerlock wrestling hold, Santschi broke character and begged him to let go. By the time cameraman Harry G. Gerstad stopped filming, Santschi had lost three teeth, bruised his ribs and sprained a thumb. Farnum had suffered a broken nose, a fractured hand, damaged his ribcage and sustained a blood clot on his cheek that nearly killed him. The justifiably famous brawl sent both men to the hospital. Farnum claimed he was never the same physically after this fight. Ironically, the two actors became friends, convalescing together at a Turkish bath where they received massages to soothe their aching muscles.

"Fighting" Bill Farnum became cinema's first tough guy, realizing he needed to match emotion to the struggle. For training, he studied the scientific wrestling holds of popular grappler Frank Gotch and applied them to his screen endeavors. His follow-up films *Fighting Blood* (1916), *When a Man Sees Red* (1917), *The Broken Law* (1918), *Wolves of the Night* (1919) and *The Man Hunter* (1919) all featured mammoth fights that tried to emulate or better his *Spoilers* battle. Publicity claimed a Farnum fight was "worth going miles to see." Santschi became an in-demand heavy, fighting Mitchell Lewis in *Code of the Yukon* (1918) and *Frivolous Sal* (1925), Frank Mayo in *The Plunderer* (1919) and William S. Hart in *Cradle of Courage* (1920). Both original combatants were recruited as technical advisors for the first re-filming of the *Spoilers* tale occurring between Milton Sills and Noah Beery in 1923, a fight sequence that took five days to film. They repeated the behind-the-scenes assignment for the 1930 version that saw Gary Cooper and William "Stage" Boyd face off. Not to be outdone by the youngsters, Farnum and

Santschi staged another lengthy go-round for *Ten Nights in a Barroom* (1931).

The *Spoilers* fight was based on a legendary real battle between two miners that author Rex Beach witnessed in Alaska. Beach took a full nine pages describing the fight in his 1905 novel, pitting the characters Glenister and McNamara against one another over mining rights. In the movie, dialogue cards show Farnum announcing, "I'm going to kill you with my bare hands," and claim-jumping Santschi responding, "I'd like to feel your throat." In addition to the 1923 and 1930 remakes, the picture received its most famous reimagining with John Wayne and Randolph Scott in 1942 *(see entry)*. The story received additional mileage in 1955 with Jeff Chandler and Rory Calhoun in the lead roles (see entry). Once again, the fight was the main attraction. Kent Taylor and Nils Asther did a low-budget off-shoot of the brawling story in *Alaska* (1944).

See: Bodeen, DeWitt. "The Farnum Brothers: Dustin and William." *Films in Review*. November, 1983; Franklin, Joe. *Classics of the Silent Screen: A Pictorial Treasury*. Secaucus, NJ: Citadel, 1960; Owen, K. "Tom Santschi, Battler." *Photoplay*. August, 1916.

WILLIAM S. HART vs. BOB KORTMAN in *The Narrow Trail* (1917)

Early western star William S. Hart achieved fame for producer Thomas Ince portraying realistic, true-to-life cowboys who habitually drank, gambled, fought and hung out with saloon girls. Astride his Pinto named Fritz, he became known as the "good" bad man, redeemed at picture's end by the heroine after fighting far worse men than himself. Although Hart was already 50 when he debuted in films, *True West* claimed that he was "well capable of handling himself in physical combat." Standing 6'1" and weighing 184 pounds, Hart kept fit working out with noted boxing trainer Billy Delaney. Hart's rough-edged fights were fan favorites. He took special pride in mixing it up on screen without a double, determined to put on a good show for the audience while taking on as much punishment as he doled out. Despite suffering broken ribs after being kicked by a horse, he fought Leo Willis in *O'Malley of the Mounted* (1921), only to learn that the film was ruined and that the scene needed to be reshot.

One actor who matched up well slugging with Hart was Bob Kortman. Six feet tall and 188 pounds, the menacing-looking Kortman was equally willing to draw blood and get bruised and became Hart's favored on-screen opponent. In addition to their three-minute Barbary Coast dive brawl in Lambert Hillyer's *The Narrow Trail*, they fought tooth-and-nail in *The Whistle* (1920). Kortman is knocked out twice in *The Narrow Trail* fight, with Hart taking on a half-dozen thugs between Kortman's KOs. Paramount Artcraft publicity declared that "for sheer spectacular features [their fight] has no parallel in screen battles." French writer Jean Cocteau wrote effusively about the fight, calling it "a little masterpiece," while film historian William K. Everson compared the fight favorably to *The Spoilers*, claiming that classic 1914 battle "pales beside some of the brawls Hart staged, particularly one in *The Narrow Trail*."

See: Everson, William K. *The Hollywood Western*. Secaucus, NJ: Carol, 1992; "Great Hart Picture is *The Narrow Trail*." *Artcraft Advance*. October 8, 1917; Hart, William S. *My Life East and West*. New York: Houghton Mifflin Co., 1929; La Roche, Pete. "William S. Hart." *True West*. June, 1971; O'Hara, Kenneth A. "A Story of Fists and Films." *The Movie Magazine*. July, 1915.

DOUGLAS FAIRBANKS vs. WALLACE BEERY in *The Mollycoddle* (1920)

Foppish expatriate Douglas Fairbanks heads to his native Arizona to become a cowboy, toughening up to the point that by picture's end he is able to take on diamond smuggler Wallace Beery in an extended two-minute brawl that became known within the industry as "the two-mile fight" due to the geographic distance it covered. The men fight in a tree, fall through a roof, battle across a Hopi Indian village, tumble down a steep embankment, and go over a waterfall before Beery succumbs. It was one of the most brutal fights of the silent era in large part because of Beery's forcefulness. At one point the men smash through an adobe wall. The *Tulsa Daily World* called it "the most sensational fight scene ever staged for a motion picture," while the *New York Times* wrote that this concluding sequence "outdoes anything of the kind."

United Artists publicity called it "the most red-blooded scene of [Fairbanks'] screen career" and declared, "Fairbanks stages his greatest fist fight." The 5'8", 150-pound actor was renowned for performing his own elaborate stunts to showcase his graceful athleticism and proficiency in boxing and jujitsu. He trained with professional wrestler Bull Montana and worked out the intricacies of the physical action ahead of time with stunt ace Richard Talmadge. In the case of *The Mollycoddle*, it was Talmadge performing the 15-foot leap from a cliff into the tree. Fairbanks had already sprained his wrists and broken two fingers performing action in the film. The studio, however, continued to maintain to the viewing public that Fairbanks was never doubled. Upon completing the fistic action, Fairbanks revealed, "It was the toughest fight I ever had." Harry Thorpe and William McGann ably handled the outdoor cameras for director Victor Fleming.

See: "At the Theatres." *Evening Herald*. February 18, 1923; Fairbanks, Douglas. "The Big Adventure." *Boys' Life*. June, 1928; Vance, Jeffrey, and Tony Maietta. *Douglas Fairbanks*. Berkeley: University of California Press, 2008.

RICHARD BARTHELMESS VS. ERNEST TORRENCE in *Tol'able David* (1921)

Courageous display of grit, determination and intestinal fortitude from Inspiration Pictures and director Henry King. It is in fact a David and Goliath story of young, slightly built Virginia mailman Richard Barthelmess besieged for six minutes by raging, murderous fugitive Ernest Torrence in a backwoods shack. Towering over Barthelmess, the leering Torrence has stolen his mail, killed his dog, caused his father's fatal heart attack and crippled his brother. He's even made unwanted advances toward Barthelmess' girlfriend Gladys Hulette, Both men lose family members at the hands of the other, and it's a violent fight to the finish the *Los Angeles Times* labeled "thrilling" and *Photoplay* called "the greatest fight we have seen since *The Spoilers*." It's primitive desperation to the extreme with no punches thrown in the savage hand-to-throat action. The 6'4" Torrence brutally slams the 5'9" Barthelmess against the walls until the little guy jumps onto Torrence's body and strangles the giant to the floor. Both exhausted men vie for a gun to determine the outcome.

Barthelmess didn't use a double when he is flung against a door and bounces back into Torrence's arms in a medium shot. The best moment comes when cinematographer Henry Cronjager gets his camera in close on the terrifying Torrence, one of the best villains of the silent era. King creates further suspense by having editor Duncan Mansfield cut away to Hulette's desperate run for help, then linger on the open shack door waiting for the fight's survivor to emerge. *The Parade's Gone By* called it "a brilliantly edited fight scene," while *Motion Picture Daily* remarked that the scene was "handled with superb skill." The classic film was remade as a talkie in 1930 with Richard Cromwell and Noah Beery. The original 1921 fight sequence gained infamy for being the picture shown on a movie theater screen in the cult horror movie *The Tingler* (1959).

See: Brownlow, Kevin. *The Parade's Gone By*. Berkeley: University of California Press, 1968.

GEORGE O'BRIEN VS. FRED KOHLER in *The Iron Horse* (1924)

This epic John Ford transcontinental rail story from Fox Film Corporation concerns the 1862 joining of the Union Pacific and Central Pacific rail lines. Two-fingered heavy Fred Kohler uses Cheyenne Indians to divert the rail builders onto land he owns for personal profit. Buckskin-clad young hero George O'Brien is out to stop him, unaware they have a long history with one another. Kohler subordinate Cyril Chadwick, fiancé of O'Brien's childhood sweetheart Madge Bellamy, tries shooting O'Brien in the back; leading to a rousing three-minute bare-knuckle match in a crowded saloon where the brawny lad's toughness is put on display. By picture's end he's facing off against the evil Kohler as the Cheyenne storm the rail workers around them. O'Brien finds extra fighting spirit when he realizes Kohler is the same man who viciously killed his father many years earlier. When Kohler comes at him with a pick-axe, O'Brien lifts the heavy in the air and body slams him to the ground. After a battle that sees both men's shirts torn off, O'Brien chokes the life out of Kohler. The *San Francisco Chronicle* wrote, "George O'Brien stages what has been proclaimed the greatest fistfight ever filmed," while *Variety* added that Ford "puts his story over on the screen with a lot of punch."

Ironically, it was Ford who landed in a real fistfight on the set with his brother Edward O'Fearna. O'Brien had to pull them apart. Ford stages the climactic fight in an open-air log cabin on the Wadsworth Nevada desert location, with the combatants centered in a frame-within-a-frame doorway shot from Ford's cinematographer George Schneiderman. The composition was one the auteur would return to throughout his career. Ford also films his action from multiple angles and distances, creating a level of excitement seldom seen on the screen. Both men swing furious punches into the air between them with the occasional fist thudding onto an arm or a shoulder. Ford thrillingly intercuts the fight with the Indian battle going on around them. The six-foot, 200-pound Kohler was in fact missing a thumb and digits on his right hand, the result of a mining accident. This never interfered with his ability to be a convincing screen puncher. He was considered one of the best fighting heavies of the silent era. The well-matched Kohler and O'Brien continued to clash in *Hard Rock Harrigan* (1935), *Painted Desert* (1938) and *Lawless Valley* (1938), but *Iron Horse* remains the best of their hard-socking struggles.

O'Brien, six feet tall and 198 pounds, was a light heavyweight boxing champion while in the U.S. Navy and entered films as a stuntman. He owed his stardom to Ford casting him in *Iron Horse,* during which O'Brien won many female admirers when revealing his muscular torso. Ford would only cast O'Brien after he'd proved himself in a tough grappling audition with Kohler. Ford was impressed enough that he had O'Brien square off against Victor McLaglen the following year in a realistic street brawl for *The Fighting Heart* (1925), a film that's considered lost.

O'Brien took pride in doing his own fights. In his youth he received boxing instruction from Gentleman Jim Corbett and weight-trained long before it became trendy in Hollywood. He worked out regularly with pro wrestler Al Baffert. O'Brien became a popular B-western star who always featured a big fight in his films in which he showed off his athleticism against heavies such as Ward Bond, Harry Woods and Frank Hagney. *Variety* once claimed, "O'Brien looks better in a scrap than any other film land cowpoke." His best fights came against Tom Santschi in *Honor Bound* (1928), Weldon Heyburn in *The Gay Caballero* (1932), Noble Johnson in *Mystery Ranch* (1932), William Hall in *Windjammer* (1937) and Harry Cording in *Marshal of Mesa City* (1939).

See: Coons, Robbin. "No Doubles Take Risks for George O'Brien." *Gettysburg Times.* November 11, 1932; "Film Fights Declared to be Real Battles." *Los Angeles Times.* April 5, 1925; Menefee, David W. *George O'Brien: A Man's Man in Hollywood.* Albany, GA: BearManor, 2009.

THE HAVANA CAFE BRAWL in *HER MAN* (1930)

Al Sherman of *The Morning Telegraph* called the mass Havana saloon scrum that concludes this early talkie version of *Frankie and Johnny* "the most stirring fight sequence I have ever seen in motion pictures." Although commenting on its staginess, the *New York Times* tagged it "a prodigiously energetic brawl," while the *Oakland Tribune* referred to it as "one of the fiercest and most convincing waterfront brawls that the screen has produced." The *Oregonian* described it as "a big free-for-all fight that makes the audience stand up and yell." Director Tay Garnett pulls out all the stops in having a bar full of toughs led by heavy Ricardo Cortez descend upon two-fisted star Phillips Holmes as he tries to make off with café singer Helen Twelvetrees. Holmes fights off the horde admirably until his sailor buddies arrive for a massive four-minute tilt. Everyone grabs a chair as a weapon as bodies are tossed to and fro. Holmes, his shirt torn to shreds, uses an overturned table as a weapon and a shield. Finally, a Holmes punch sends Cortez backward into his own knife.

The film's leading man, the forgotten Holmes (listed at six feet and 155 pounds) is impressively reminiscent of a wiry young Kirk Douglas. The 6'1" Cortez, a former amateur boxer, is an appropriately fierce foil. The two go toe to toe, with Cortez burying a series of body shots into Holmes' midsection. Garnett set a boisterous standard he tried to live up to with the screen brawls he directed in *Seven Sinners* (1940) and *Wild Harvest* (1947) (see entries). Garnett and cameraman Edward Snyder are especially innovative for the time period with their varied action set-ups and multiple angles, while editors Joseph Kane and Doane Harrison maintain a ferocious visual pace. When he became a director, Kane demonstrated great skill staging fights. Harold Stine and Earl A. Wolcott's synching is especially impressive for an early sound film.

Garnett populates the scene with stuntmen and professional fighters the likes of Frank Hagney, Harry Wilson, Chuck Hamilton, Chuck Sullivan, Joe Rivers, Joe Silver, Abe Attell and Sailor Vincent. More than a dozen professional athletes from three different sports took part, as well as USC football players George Dye, George Templeton, Bill Armstead and Bill Emmons. Scrappy former baseball pro Mike Donlin plays the bartender. Even B-western cowboy star Tom Tyler is in there. Veteran stunt actor Pat Harmon, playing a drunk, claimed involvement in more than 1000 screen battles through the 1920s. Co-writer Garnett wanted to inject some levity into the chaotic violence. Throughout the story he had hard-luck comedy-relief character James Gleason repeatedly drop a coin into a slot machine without a payoff. In the midst of the brawling, Gleason is knocked into the slot machine, which rains coins down upon his head.

One important change with the advent of sound: The projection speed of film became standardized at 24 frames per second so audio could be easily understood. Silent movies had been shot at varying speeds on hand-cranked cameras, typically averaging 18 fps (frames per second). In regard to action scenes, this created fast, jerky body motions when played back at normal speed. Therefore, silent movie fights appear unnatural. The new 24 fps standard smoothed action out, making punches look much more realistic. This created several areas of experimentation. Directors and cinematographers began playing around with camera and shutter speeds, realizing they could film fights slowly and safely in real time but play it back on screen so it would look relatively normal. This method of filming is called undercranking. However, when actors or stuntmen performed their fight routines punching at regular speed, under-cranked film created comically fast movements upon playback. Under-cranking at the rate of 22 fps worked best to liven up fights without making them look too ridiculous.

See: "Noted Athletes Are Starred in *Her Man*." *Berkeley Daily Gazette*. November 26, 1930; Tasker, Yvonne. *The Action and Adventure Cinema*. New York: Routledge, 2004.

BUCK JONES VS. LOUIS HICKUS in *Border Law* (1931)

Former Texas Ranger Buck Jones is searching south of the border for the killer of his brother, and ex-prizefighter Louis Hickus is a prime suspect. Stinging from an insult, Hickus challenges Jones to a fight. The men have an unusually formal two-minute Mexican cantina knuckle-buster, both doffing their shirts for the fistic action that sees Jones knock the bigger man clear off his feet and spin him through the air with the power of his right hook. The actors fight to contact throughout, pounding away at one another's arms, chests, ribs and shoulders. Several times the fight realistically goes to the floor. Jones' final knockout punch is delivered straight into the camera. There's some evidence of an awareness of the direction fights would take. None of the powerful haymakers to the jaw land on Hickus but are the result of decep-

tive camera angles and editing. The Louis King–directed B-western boasts superior lens work throughout from L.W. O'Connell. Sound technician Glenn Rominger and editor Otto Meyer create excitement with the crowd noise and reaction shots.

Columbia publicity trumpeted, "There is a fist-fight sequence that is said to reach the high peak of thrill-dom," as they distributed articles on Jones' pugilistic skill. *Film Daily* praised the film for "a couple of good fights that carry a kick," and *Variety* claimed the brawling action "grips the average adult attention." Jones biographer Buck Rainey called *Border Law* "a real dust stirrer, with enough gunfights and brawls to make action fans forgive the implausibilities of the script." Columbia remade the same story three years later with Jones starring as *The Fighting Ranger* (1934). He once again shed his shirt to fight heavy Ward Bond.

Breaking into the film business as a stuntman, Jones was a popular action star from the days of silent films into the early sound era. Sturdy, masculine and courageous at 5'10" and 175 pounds, the former boxer performed his own fights on screen against such tough hombres as Ward Bond, Harry Woods and Fred Kohler. Jones favored the old-style movie punch-ups, freely punching his opponent's arms and shoulders while demanding they do the same to him. He had a great deal of pride and didn't want anyone pulling their punches in a Buck Jones fight. Even into middle age, he sported muscular arms and remained remarkably fit and agile. He worked out with Olympic gymnast turned boxing trainer Frank Merrill. During the making of *Black Aces* (1937), Jones and his stuntmen took on a group of drunken, unruly miners on location in a real brawl that became known in the industry as "The Battle of Kernville."

See: "New Film Reveals Jones as Pugilist." *Kingsport Times*. November 22, 1931; Rainey, Buck. *The Life and Films of Buck Jones: The Sound Era*. Waynesville, NC: World of Yesterday, 1991.

WALLACE BEERY VS. GEORGE RAFT in *The Bowery* (1933)

Raoul Walsh directed this robust slice of 1890s New York City life featuring the memorable real-life characters Chuck Connors (Wallace Beery) and Steve Brodie (George Raft), a Quirt and Flagg set of rivals who laid down wagers and brawled over everything from girls to the boxers they managed. Raft's masked fighter turns out to be bare-knuckle legend John L. Sullivan (portrayed by the director's brother George Walsh, a silent movie tough guy). Much of the highly offensive film is played as broad comedy with Beery raising his fists at the slightest provocation. At one point, a Chinese laundry is on fire and the stars pit their fire-fighting brigades against one another in a massive street brawl over who'll put out the fire and save the screaming laundrymen. Among the brawling firemen are stunt actors Pat Harmon, Frank Mills and Harry Tenbrook. Real professional boxers populate the scene, including Phil Bloom, Kid Broad, Pueblo Jim Flynn, Joseph Glick, Jack Herrick, Joseph Herrick, Al McCoy, Frank Moran and Abe Hollandersky.

Issues come to a head between the main characters at the climax after Raft's alleged dive off the Brooklyn Bridge wins him Beery's saloon. They battle out their differences on a fog-enshrouded barge with a throng of spectators eagerly awaiting the outcome. 20th Century publicity declared that Walsh insisted his actors not pull their punches for the sake of realism. *Variety* called the finale fight "an exciting interlude," while the *New York Times* noted that the audience in the theater was "quite enthusiastic" over the clash. After screening the final brawl, in which a bloodied but victorious Beery rows to shore, a boxing promoter contacted Beery about putting on a fight with professional heavyweight champ Max Schmeling. Beery had no interest in that match-up.

The Bowery garnered lasting notoriety for the actual animosity existing between the mismatched stars. It was common of the era to work out a short series of punches thrown at the arms and shoulders beforehand so the actors could appropriately plan their reactions and roll with the blows. Raft, 5'7" and 160 pounds, claimed that in setting up the fight, the 6'1", 235-pound Beery asked to throw the first punch. Beery promptly sucker-punched Raft on the jaw, momentarily knocking him out. When Raft came to, the former professional lightweight boxer attacked Beery's bulging midsection with a flurry of punches before crew members pulled them apart. Walsh claimed that attempting to direct the two leads "was like trying to keep the peace between a lion and a tiger." Much of the 90-second fight for Barney McGill's camera is an overhead shot of stunt doubles Sailor Vincent and Harvey Parry. Editor Allen McNeill cut in close-ups of the stars pounding away at one another.

Beery was known to work "stiff" in fights and barely hold back. The former elephant trainer with the self-described face "like an old squash" knocked out Clark Gable for several minutes on *Hell Divers* (1932) when he failed to pull a punch. Beery, who played the toughest con in the joint in *The Big House* (1930) and won a Best Actor Oscar as a broken-down boxer in *The Champ* (1931), felt he had a tough guy reputation to uphold for the cameras. One of his best pals was former champion boxer Jack Dempsey. Future champ Joe Louis termed Beery the best battler in the film business. To play a wrestler in *Flesh* (1932), Beery was taught submission holds by pro grappler Count Rossi.

In a screen career comprising over 250 battles, two of his best showcases came in *The Mollycoddle* (1920) and *Stand Up and Fight* (1939) (see entries). Beery fought Tom Kennedy in *We're in the Navy Now* (1926), George Bancroft in *Old Ironsides* (1928), John Gilbert in *Way for a Sailor* (1931), Frank Hagney in *The Champ* (1931), Ward Bond and Nat Pendleton in *Flesh* (1932), John Barrymore in *Grand Hotel* (1932), Alan Hale in *A Message to Garcia* (1936), Warner Baxter in *Slave Ship* (1937), Dennis O'Keefe in *Bad Man of Brimstone* (1938), Chester Morris in *Thunder Afloat* (1939), Douglas Fowley in *20 Mule Team* (1940), Barton MacLane in *Barnacle Bill* (1941), Dick Curtis in *Jackass Mail* (1942), Jerome Cowan in *The Bugle Sounds* (1942), Reginald Owen in *Salute to the Marines* (1943), J. Carrol Naish in *Bad Bascomb* (1947) and Jimmie Dundee in *The Mighty McGurk* (1947).

See: "*Bowery* Screens Famous Pugilists." *Times-Picayune*. December 3, 1933; Katchmer, George A. *Eighty Silent Film Stars*. Jefferson, NC: McFarland, 1991.

JOHN WAYNE VS. YAKIMA CANUTT in *The Lucky Texan* (1934)

Six-foot-four, 200-pound John Wayne and 6'3", 210-pound Yakima Canutt worked out fight routines on several early 1930s quickies under the Monogram–Lone Star banner. They were assisted on some of these films by stuntmen Eddie Parker and Allen Pomeroy. Occasionally Canutt doubled Wayne. Sometimes it was Parker. Often the former USC football player Wayne did his own fights with one of the stuntmen as his opponent. Wayne was wise during this period to work one on one with top stuntmen who could effectively sell the power of his blows and build him up as a convincing screen fighter for audiences to cheer on. Stuntmen prefer to work fights with fellow stuntmen; trained professionals who will maintain distance, keep a loose fist, and are unlikely to lose their bearings in a fight routine. Actors will rush fights and inadvertently make contact. If a mistake is made, stuntmen can start over. If a mistake is made with an actor resulting in an injury, it can cause a production delay and cost the stuntman his job and reputation. It's a testament to Wayne that stuntmen considered him like one of their own. Canutt claimed Wayne was as good if not better at doing screen fights than any stuntman he knew. They fought one another in *Riders of Destiny* (1933), *Sagebrush Trail* (1933), *The Lucky Texan* (1934), *Randy Rides Alone* (1934), *West of the Divide* (1934), *'Neath the Arizona Skies* (1934), *Dawn Rider* (1935), *Paradise Canyon* (1935) and *Pals of the Saddle* (1938).

In *The Lucky Texan*, Wayne has a memorable match-up with Canutt in the entertaining climax. Hero Wayne jumps from a horse onto a railcar to exchange blows with Canutt, then "bulldogs" the gold mine–robbing villain to the ground. Producer Paul Malvern erred in having one stuntman on the set in the form of Canutt. He could double Wayne making the jump from the horse, but that meant somebody needed to double Canutt playing the bad guy on the railcar. The problem was solved when Wayne exchanged wardrobes with Canutt and doubled him being jumped on. So for this one stunt Canutt became Wayne and Wayne became Canutt. After switching wardrobes again, they punch it out in the dust with Wayne emerging victorious via a flurry of haymakers. When doubling an actor, Canutt used a specially designed hat with a tightened wire brim that wouldn't come off. It kept his facial features hidden or disguised when the action became hot and heavy.

Though it may now be seen as dated and hokey, the fight choreography and alternating camera angles looked more realistic and exciting than anything that had come before. *Hollywood Corral* wrote, "The fights are admittedly perpetrated with more dash than the average western of the period, but there is little evidence that Wayne and Canutt had come upon any great innovation as yet." Ironically, Canutt came up with the Pass System because Wayne's hard punches were leaving his arms and shoulders black and blue, and he was tiring of the constant pain. However, there was a pressing need for improved safety standards in the industry and extensive rehearsal to improve the overall product. B-western cowboy star Buck Jones had

recently been hospitalized with fractured ribs, skull and back after stuntman Joe Bonomo erred in throwing a heavy chair into him during a wing-it bar brawl in *The Deadline* (1932). In 1928, *Collier's* wrote, "Every actor-fighter is covered with honorable scars of battle." Wayne and Canutt showed that needn't be the case.

Through repeated practice, Wayne and Canutt learned to effectively "travel" with one another across a set during a faked fight while maintaining balance and never making contact. Wayne would throw a punch at Canutt's eye level. Canutt would react and back up a step as Wayne glided forward for the next punch; they were always aware of the camera's placement. The result was a knockout in terms of audience response for Wayne, and Canutt earned the reputation of an innovative stunt coordinator. They both moved on to bigger and better material, far beyond the quickie B-westerns turned out by this film's director Robert N. Bradbury, whose contributions to the technical side of the fight scene shouldn't be ignored. Bradbury's camera operator Archie Stout gained a sterling reputation for filming second unit action scenes.

Wayne, known as "Duke," was determined to set himself apart from other cowboy heroes by showing a character who wasn't afraid to fight dirty and gave as good as he got. In later years, he incorporated generous doses of humor into his fights, but in these early oaters the emphasis was on realism and letting the audience know he was doing all the fighting stunts. Wayne based his fighting style on heavyweight boxing champ Jack Dempsey, studying newsreels of the fighter he admired to learn to position his hands and arms effectively. He had a strong stance and, upon delivering a punch, looked confident that it was damage-inducing. His wide signature roundhouse punch became known in the business as a "John Wayne." Wayne benefitted from his long arms and keen sense of camera awareness which allowed audiences to see his punches and their powerful effect through the full range of motion. When Wayne drew his arm back with elbow up for a blow, it looked like the person on the receiving end was done for. With age and added weight, his already formidable presence became overwhelming on a theater screen. Boxing trainer Ralph Volkie claimed that Wayne had the biggest closed fist he'd ever seen and the most devastating right hand knockout punch since Joe Louis. In Volkie's estimation, Wayne could have been a successful professional boxer. To give an idea of how iconic his punch became, Wayne's fist-print was literally put into the cement outside Grauman's Chinese Theatre. In the late 1960s, he did a special strobe sequence project for photographic artist Phil Stern, showing the viewer what it was like to be on the receiving end of the famous John Wayne punch.

There are notable John Wayne fights in *Seven Sinners* (1940), *The Spoilers* (1942), *In Old California* (1942), *Pittsburgh* (1942), *The Lady Takes a Chance* (1943), *Tall in the Saddle* (1944), *Dakota* (1945), *Angel and the Badman* (1947), *Red River* (1948), *The Quiet Man* (1952), *Big Jim McLain* (1952), *Hondo* (1953), *The Wings of Eagles* (1957), *The Barbarian and the Geisha* (1958), *North to Alaska* (1960), *Donovan's Reef* (1962), *McLintock!* (1963), *The Sons of Katie Elder* (1965), *El Dorado* (1967), *The War Wagon* (1967), *Hellfighters* (1968), *The Undefeated* (1969), *Chisum* (1970), *The Cowboys* (1972) and *Brannigan* (1975) (see entries). Fights of interest came against Allen Pomeroy in *Blue Steel* (1934), Eddie Parker in *The Star Packer* (1934), Reed Howes in *Dawn Rider* (1935), LeRoy Mason in *Texas Terror* (1935), Moroni Olsen in *Adventure's End* (1937), Ward Bond in *The Shepard of the Hills* (1941), Ray Milland in *Reap the Wild Wind* (1942), Albert Dekker in *In Old Oklahoma* (1943), Harry Woods in *Tycoon* (1947), Rosanno Brazzi in *Legend of the Lost* (1957), Stuart Whitman and Lee Marvin in *The Comancheros* (1961), Victor French in *Rio Lobo* (1970), Tom Hennesy, Christopher Mitchum and his own son Patrick Wayne in *Big Jake* (1971) and Al Lettieri in *McQ* (1974). During the making of *Blood Alley* (1955), Wayne took a break from filming a fight to do a public service announcement for Christmas Seals to combat tuberculosis. On a 1966 episode of *The Lucy Show*, "Lucy and John Wayne," the star appeared in a cowboy saloon brawl with veteran bad guy Morgan Woodward.

See: "Duke Reveals Health Secret." *Ottawa Journal.* September 14, 1968; Handsaker, Gene. "Hollywood Sights and Sounds." *Prescott Evening Courier.* November 18, 1948; "John Wayne Had Calibre of Heavyweight Champ." *Morning Record.* January 9, 1967; Price, Michael. "Tall in the Saddle." *Chicago Tribune.* May 3, 1992.

HENRY FONDA VS. CHARLES BICKFORD in *The Farmer Takes a Wife* (1935)

Henry Fonda made his film debut as a simple farm boy in this well-received Victor Fleming–directed 20th Century-Fox film about workers on the Erie Canal. Fonda had played the part successfully on Broadway, but the studio wanted the already established Gary Cooper or Joel McCrea for their movie version. The 6'1", 175-pound Fonda is ridiculed for his cowardice by 6'1", 190-pound bully Charles Bickford, but then Fonda stands up for himself in a violent two-minute fistfight on the edge of a canal in front of cheering, betting hordes. Bickford thinks he's going to have an easy time with the rube and doesn't even take a pipe from his mouth until he suffers his first knockdown. It's a realistic battle with both actors doing the majority of the fighting. After a tough exchange of blows, Fonda emerges victorious when he knocks Bickford into the waterway. He gains Bickford's respect as well as female lead Janet Gaynor. *Esquire* termed

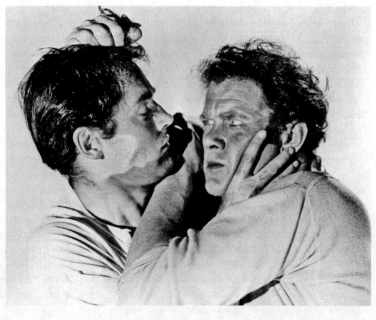

Henry Fonda (left) and Charles Bickford fight dirty in Fox's *The Farmer Takes a Wife* (1935).

it "a good windup fight sequence," and The *New York Times* added, "Charles Bickford brawls and carouses splendidly as the bully." *The Farmer Takes a Wife* was remade in 1953 with Dale Robertson and John Carroll fighting between two barges in the final reel.

When the principal actors worked on their portion of the fight on the Fox back lot, Bickford was blinded by the glare of a Klieg light and miscalculated a punch, landing a crushing haymaker on Fonda's chin that crumpled the star into unconsciousness. On the next take, Fonda claimed to be blinded by the same light and socked Bickford between the eyes. For the next week, Bickford had a walnut-sized lump on his forehead. Fonda later broke a bone in his right hand when he punched Bickford in his barrel chest. Fonda kept going despite the pain until the take was in the can, earning the applause of the cast and crew for his toughness. Ernest Palmer was behind the camera and Harold Schuster edited.

Yakima Canutt was assigned as a double but faced ridicule from fellow stuntman Jack Stoney. The latter fought professionally and had been working for the big studios for the past decade as a top stuntman. Stoney was upset that the studio had sent a "cowboy" out to do a fight. At this time, stuntmen had one or two specialties and stuck to them. They didn't need a broad range of skills as competition in the industry had not reached its zenith. Stoney opted to ad-lib instead of choreograph and neglected to pull all his punches. Canutt in turn let his own fists fly to contact. After a handful of takes, both went full-bore until director Fleming was frantically yelling "Cut!" By the time the dust settled, Canutt had proven himself to be the fight specialist, and Stoney saw the error of his ways. The two became friends, and Canutt's reputation as a "fight man" was solidified with the major studios.

Gruff character actor Bickford, a former dockworker, lumberjack and World War I veteran, had a real-life tough guy reputation. Quick with his fists and fearless, he regularly sparred in the boxing ring with heavyweight champion Gentleman Jim Corbett. Hollywood legend maintains that the combative Bickford punched out director Cecil B. DeMille during production of *Dynamite* (1929), causing many directors to live in fear of him. While making *East of Java* (1935), Bickford ill-advisedly eschewed the use of a stunt double and wrestled a lion on screen, and nearly lost his life. He survived, but the heavy scars on his neck ruined his days as a leading man.

Bickford fought John Miljan in *The Sea Bat* (1930), Victor McLaglen in *Under Pressure* (1935), Randolph Scott in *High, Wide and Handsome* (1937), Barton MacLane in *The Storm* (1938), Wayne Morris in *Valley of the Giants* (1938) (see entry), Bob Burns in *Our Leading Citizen* (1939), Dick Foran in *Riders of Death Valley* (1941), Bruce Cabot and Dana Andrews in *Fallen Angel* (1945), Robert Ryan in *The Woman on the Beach* (1947), Stephen McNally in *Johnny Belinda* (1948) and Alan Ladd in *Branded* (1950). In *Pride of the Marines* (1936), Bickford was cast as the Armed Services' boxing champion. *Gangs of New York* (1938) saw Bickford playing two roles and fighting himself on screen!

See: Bickford, Charles. *Bulls, Balls, Bicycles, and Actors.* New York: P.S. Eriksson, 1965; Coons, Robbin. "Hollywood Sights Sounds." *State Times Advocate.* December 9, 1935; "Henry Fonda Gets Broken Finger in Battle on Barge." *Omaha World Herald.* May 15, 1935.

JAMES CAGNEY VS. FRED KOHLER in *Frisco Kid* (1935)

Inspired by the oft-told brawl in *The Spoilers*, this Warner Bros. film contains James Cagney's greatest screen fight. In the pages of *The Spectator*, noted writer Graham Greene called it "the most brutal and convincing I can remember seeing on the screen." The *New York Times* termed it "monumental" while the *Los Angeles Times* called it "terrific." *The Sunday Morning Star* said it was "disturbingly realistic."

Director Lloyd Bacon staged the spirited affair in a San Francisco waterfront saloon between Cagney and Fred Kohler, here playing a white slave trader named Shanghai Duck. The husky Kohler has a hook for a hand and uses it to his advantage, adding an extra element of danger to the proceedings. The two actors went at each other so ferociously that Cagney worried about his adversary's health when Kohler was too exhausted to rise from the floor. Cagney's concern was well-founded. Kohler succumbed to heart disease less than three years later at the age of 49. The six-foot, 230-pound actor was one of the top ruthless, sneering bad guys of silent film, often opposing the likes of George O'Brien, Tom Mix and George Bancroft.

Pro boxer turned movie stuntman Chick Collins doubles Kohler in a few spots, while Cagney's stuntman is Harvey Parry. As the doubles fought it out in front of 240 extras, Cagney rode cinematographer Sol Polito's camera crane and Kohler sat on the sidelines reading a book. When it came time for the principals to shoot the close-ups, Cagney sprained an ankle dodging Kohler's hook on the first of five days of filming on the fight. Another brief delay was caused by a group of visitors to the set. When Cagney and Kohler began punching one another and Kohler fell against a table, a female visitor let out a piercing scream, necessitating the set be redressed and the sequence shot anew. In all, there were four tables broken, half a dozen chairs smashed, and several glasses shattered. Cagney injured his shoulder and elbows and suffered several skin abrasions. Kohler, who outweighed Cagney by nearly 80 pounds, cut a forearm. As if fighting Kohler weren't enough of a challenge, Cagney also tangles with imposing heavy Barton MacLane. Makeup artist Perc Westmore was responsible for the fake blood seen in the film.

Much has been made of Cagney's height, with estimates pegging him at 5'5" with a typical weight of 155 pounds. To his credit, Cagney favored fighting big guys on screen to show how tough he was. He had been an amateur boxer, finishing as a runner-up for the New York state title as a lightweight. Because of his early dance training, he bounced across the screen in fights with a fantastic

energy seldom seen from the usual lumbering giants. Since he often played anti-heroes, it wasn't atypical for Cagney to throw the first punch in a fight, and if his opponent didn't go down, there'd be a flurry of fists to follow. He was literally full steam ahead as evidenced by his fistic freak-out against the prison guards when he learns of the death of his beloved mother in *White Heat* (1949). Cagney never worried about blocking out a fight. He simply instructed his opponents to swing for his head, and he'd make them miss by ducking inside their blows.

Cagney stayed in shape with boxing, judo and weightlifting. He often sparred with former pro boxer Mushy Callahan at the gym on the Warner lot. Fight trainer Callahan claimed Cagney could hold his own in the professional ring. In regard to the judo, Cagney became a black belt in the art (he was the first movie actor to accomplish this feat). Whenever Cagney had a big fight, he trained with his stunt double Parry, a former boxer. The two lived on a houseboat docked off Catalina Island and spent several weeks swimming, running and sparring in the ring as if they were training for a real boxing match. Parry called Cagney pound for pound the hardest puncher of any actor in Hollywood.

There are notable Cagney fights in *The Oklahoma Kid* (1939) and *Blood on the Sun* (1945) (see entries). Fights of interest came against Donald Cook in *The Public Enemy* (1931), George Raft in *Taxi!* (1932) and *Each Dawn I Die* (1939), Duke York in *Footlight Parade* (1933), Pat O'Brien in *Here Comes the Navy* (1934) and *Devil Dogs of the Air* (1935), Robert Barrat in *The St. Louis Kid* (1934), Edward Pawley in *"G" Men* (1935), Joe Sawyer in *Great Guy* (1937), Duke Green and Chick Collins in *Something to Sing About* (1937), Alan Hale in *The Fighting 69th* (1940), Bob Steele in *City for Conquest* (1940), Dennis Morgan in *Captain of the Clouds* (1942), Bill Henry in *Johnny Come*

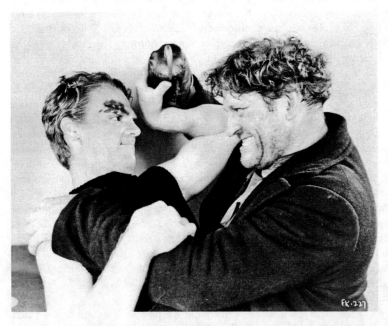

James Cagney (left) and Fred Kohler put on a memorable battle in Warner Bros.' *Frisco Kid* (1935).

Lately (1943), Ward Bond in *Kiss Tomorrow Goodbye* (1950), Alan Hale, Jr., in *The West Point Story* (1950), Dan Dailey in *What Price Glory* (1952) and Stephen McNally in *Tribute to a Bad Man* (1956).

See: Callahan, Mushy. "Films Make Actor-Boxer Look Good." *Pittsburgh Post-Gazette.* July 6, 1939; "Film Battle Lasts Week." *Los Angeles Times.* November 26, 1935; "Sock in Hollywood." *Des Moines Register.* July 21, 1940.

HENRY FONDA vs. FRED MACMURRAY in *The Trail of the Lonesome Pine* (1936)

Henry Hathaway's beautifully filmed Hatfields and McCoys–inspired family feud is highlighted by a hectic three-minute brawl that begins as a two-man fight between Henry Fonda and interloper Fred MacMurray for the hand of female lead Sylvia Sidney. The two combatants join forces when the bad guys Robert Barrat, Bob Kortman and Philip Barker arrive. The fight becomes a wild melee in and around a small mountain town's makeshift structures. Paramount publicity touted it as "one of the fiercest screen battles ever waged" with a half dozen participants seeking medical care after two entire days devoted to fighting. Fonda received a real-life black eye when he was accidentally struck by MacMurray. The entire movie was made on location in and around Cedar Lake near Big Bear, California, literally up in the clouds for many scenes. It was the first outdoor film to be made in Technicolor with cinematographer Howard Greene behind the camera and Robert C. Bruce lending assistance.

MacMurray was marketed as "the fistic champion of films" because for a three-year run all his films featured at least one or two fight sequences. Ironically, most modern audiences know him best from mild-mannered roles in Walt Disney films and the mid–1960s TV sitcom *My Three Sons*. MacMurray was surprisingly muscular and at 6'3" and 185 pounds makes for a stalwart leading man. He played football at Carroll College, and legend has it he was the inspiration for artist Charles Clarence Beck's rendition of the comic superhero Captain Marvel. MacMurray's career went in a decidedly different direction from action star, a testament to his range and abilities as an actor. He more than holds his own here in the fights.

MacMurray trained with pro boxer John Indrisano to portray a pugilist in *Invitation to Happiness* (1939). Fights of interest came against Anthony Quinn in *Swing High, Swing Low* (1937), Sterling Hayden in *Virginia* (1941), Robert Preston in *New York Town* (1941), Peter Whitney in *Murder, He Says* (1945), Bruce Cabot in *Smoky* (1946), Roy Roberts in *Borderline* (1950), Ward Bond in *The Moonlighter* (1953), Charlton Heston in *The Far Horizons* (1955), Jeffrey Hunter in *Gun for a Coward* (1957), Skip Homeier in *Day of the Bad Man* (1958) and Alan Baxter in *Face of a Fugitive* (1959).

The principals are doubled by the top stuntmen in the business, Yakima Canutt and Richard Talmadge. The latter staged the action and recruited his real brothers Otto and Victor Metzetti to fill the ranks. The stuntmen put on a show. Much of the action was ad-libbed on the spot because at this point, Talmadge preferred not to routine fights out. He was known as a free swinger. In his early days, he rarely choreographed fight action, preferring to make it up on the fly with his experienced brothers. They'd fight in a huddle with their chins buried into their chests for protection, directing punches toward the shoulder. Each man awaited Talmadge's cue for them to take a knockdown blow. Once again Canutt was earning his stripes with his peers, especially when Talmadge didn't hear the director call "Cut" and accidentally split Canutt's lip. It was all right with Canutt as he knew they had great footage in the can. The fighting became so hectic that Otto Metzetti was found knocked unconscious beneath the rubble of a porch that had collapsed.

Fonda possessed a quiet strength of character that helped overcome a natural physical awkwardness in fights. He slugged his way through many early assignments as a man who had to rely on his fists for his own survival. The U.S. Navy veteran seemed real in every endeavor and audiences believed him. Fights of interest came against Charles Bickford in *The Farmer Takes a Wife* (1935) (see entry), Joe Sawyer in *Slim* (1937), George Raft in *Spawn of the North* (1938), Barton MacLane in *Wild Geese Calling* (1941), Jack Carson in *The Male Animal* (1942) and Roy Jenson in *The Red Pony* (1973). He fought alongside Glenn Ford in a humorous brawl in *The Rounders* (1965) with both veteran actors able to handle enough action for the camera to move in close.

See: "MacMurray: Film's Fistic Champ." *Pittsburgh Press.* May 31, 1936; "Screen Battle Puts Actors on Sick List." *Hartford Courant.* March 8, 1936.

Bob Steele vs. Charlie King in *Last of the Warrens* (1936)

This low-budgeter from director Robert N. Bradbury and Supreme Pictures sees 5'5", 150-pound cowboy star Bob Steele tangling with 5'8", 200-pound Charlie King in a small western town. Bad guy King is intercepting Steele's mail so the town will think he's dead, and that's nearly reason enough for "Battling Bob" to put a major hurt on him. The slow-talking King has beat up and shot Steele's dad, made overtures to Steele's girlfriend, and has sent henchmen to make trouble for Steele. The 52-minute film takes its time getting around to the inevitable fisticuffs but at last Steele announces, "I'm going to break you with my bare hands." King and Steele unload nearly a minute of non-stop punches onto each other's chins until King curls up in a heap on the floor. It might not be their greatest fight together but it is representative of the quality of high-octane action they were able to perform.

In the same way that John Wayne worked regularly with Yakima Canutt on fisticuffs, Steele worked with King on more than 25 films and nearly 30 fights. One of their best came in *Lightnin' Crandall* (1937). Interestingly, King shows up as a stunt double for fellow bad guy Harry Woods in *Westward Bound* (1944), giving him one more crack at fighting Steele. B-western writer Mario DeMarco referred to the pair as "the slugger and the boxer, a perfect match." Author William C. Cline concurred: "The particular sight of the light-weight, ring-trained Steele absorbing the licks of the heavier brawler and then so deftly overpowering his brute strength with boxing prowess was a crowd-pleaser for several years." *Western Clippings* calls their fights "legendary screen battles we all eagerly anticipated."

The actors carefully worked over their fights until they had the distance and timing down perfect, with King throwing his head back in time to Steele's repetitive jabs. The two often filmed their fisticuffs later in the day after a liquid lunch, giving them the spirit to tear the set apart. That spirit is on display here, as the fight is an excellent example of their enthusiasm. It's been said that heavyweight boxing champion Joe Louis was inspired in his training by the brawling of Steele and King. Veteran action director Bradbury was in actuality Steele's real father, so extra care was put into the fight scenes as they guaranteed Steele's immense popularity with audiences.

A former amateur boxer, Steele reigned as a cowboy star well into the 1940s. He preferred fighting from a boxing stance and would jump in the air to bring a blow crushing down on his opponent's jaw for his final signature knockout punch. Steele was noted for his resiliency and ability to take punishment. He'd get knocked down or staggered by an opponent's punch, often bouncing on one foot to maintain his balance, but he'd fight back until the opposition could take no more. Steele did all his own fights with his fistic skills held in high enough esteem by the major studios to obtain him jobs fighting Lon Chaney, Jr., in *Of Mice and Men* (1939), James Cagney in *City for Conquest* (1940) and Humphrey Bogart in *The Big Sleep* (1946). He had an especially good fight with veteran heavy William Haade in *Exposed* (1947) and performed memorably with Audie Murphy in *Drums Across the River* (1954) (see entry). On TV's *The Rebel*, Steele fought Nick Adams in the episodes "Judgment" (1959) and "In Memoriam" (1960).

See: DeMarco, Marco. *The Photo Story of Battling Bob Steele*. Self-published, 1981; Nareau, Bob. *The Films of Bob Steele*. Self-published, 1997.

The Prison Brawl in *Nancy Steele Is Missing!* (1937)

Large-scale movie brawls such as the prison riot in *Nancy Steele Is Missing!* inevitably end up mixing several qualified stuntmen with dozens of less than qualified extras. Some of these rough-hewn extras were known as "bump men." They typically made $15 a day for engaging in fisticuff action, more than double the unskilled extra. Many "bump men" aspired to be elevated to higher stunt pay. However, the actual experienced stuntmen on a film looked down on them and thought they took unnecessary risks in hopes of impressing a director. The most opportunistic of extras were known to position themselves so actors or stuntmen who had just taken a punch would collide into them on camera, giving them a valid reason to seek higher pay. Some studios tried getting away with filling a fight with inexpensive "bump men," ultimately paying the price as inferior action made it to the screen. The size of this riot scene required there be an intermingling of stuntmen and extras, and *The Milwaukee Sentinel* felt the resulting prison break action was "staged expertly." 20th Century-Fox employed nearly three dozen experienced stuntmen, 100 bump men and an additional 400 extras running away from the fight. Among the skilled stuntmen were Yakima Canutt, Harvey Parry, Oscar "Dutch" Hendrian, Gordon Carveth, Chick Collins, Roger Creed, Duke Green, Billy Jones, Otto Metzetti, Victor Metzetti, Pat McKee and Bobby Rose.

Anti-hero Victor McLaglen starts the fight in the prison's mess hall by throwing a loaf of bread at John Carradine, at which point mass mayhem breaks loose among the convicts for cinematographer Barney McGill's camera. Cups and assorted kitchenware fly everywhere. Director George Marshall gave strict orders that only stuntmen were allowed to hurl chairs at one another. He'd immediately call "Cut!" if any extra picked up a chair. Veteran stuntman Harvey Parry became angered when his forehead was cut by a plate haphazardly thrown by an extra. Parry went after the man, only to be engaged midway to his target by fellow stuntman Duke Green. The extra escaped a real on-screen thrashing.

The friction between stuntmen and overly ambitious extras continued for the next several years with cost-conscious studios always looking to save a buck. Tensions reached a head during a brawl scene on the otherwise inconsequential naval comedy *Everything's Ducky* (1961). An extra wrecked a barroom set while showing off, creating a delay that prompted star Mickey Rooney to walk off the film until more qualified stuntmen were brought in for the fight. During the wait, stuntmen Loren Janes and Richard Geary began discussing the idea of a stunt coordinator hiring from a fraternal organization of qualified performers with an emphasis on professionalism and safety. This led to the formation of the Stuntmen's Association of Motion Pictures which resulted in less power for a film's production manager or assistant director to hire and assign stunts from the extra ranks.

See: "Bump Men Play Rough in Picture." *Seattle Daily Times.* March 24, 1937; "Path to Hollywood Glory Carved in Fracture Fame." *Springfield Republican.* February 7, 1937; Setlowe, Rick. "Biz's Fall Guys Join Hands." *Variety.* December 5, 1996.

VICTOR MCLAGLEN VS. PRESTON FOSTER in *Sea Devils* (1937)

Coast Guard members Victor McLaglen and Preston Foster are at odds with one another throughout the course of *Sea Devils,* an entertaining multiple fight punch-up that sees Foster romancing McLaglen's daughter Ida Lupino against the elder man's wishes. One of their battles is on an iceberg! Whenever they call a truce to shake hands, one of them takes the opportunity to land a sucker punch. There are enough minutes between the fights for audiences to catch their breath. By the end of director Ben Stoloff's film, the stars join forces for the common good, but they have inflicted plenty of bruises on one another. This was the case for the tough guy actors, who elected to do much of their on-screen action for the cameras of Joseph August and J. Roy Hunt. Several punches landed, and both visited RKO's infirmary to deal with assorted nicks and scrapes from their overenthusiastic brawling. Publicity compared it to the original *Spoilers,* declaring that the fights were "far more realistic and nerve-tingling than any other currently seen upon the screen." *The Motion Picture Review* wrote, "There are enough blows to afford vicarious joy to fight-loving men."

McLaglen, 6'3" and 240 pounds, was a fight scene legend with a real background as a professional prizefighter in Canada where he was re-

Preston Foster prepares to break a chair over Victor McLaglen in RKO's *Sea Devils* (1937).

gional champ. He once fought heavyweight champion Jack Johnson to a draw in an exhibition and also engaged fellow champ Jess Willard. Although he held his own in these encounters, they convinced him his talents were less than world-caliber. A World War I veteran, McLaglen did win the British Army heavyweight boxing championship. He also wrestled professionally, taking on all comers as a traveling circus attraction. Concurrently, his showman brother Leopold McLaglen distributed jujitsu and bayonet fighting manuals for the British Army but ran afoul of Vic for occasionally fighting under his name in various territories.

Brought to the United States to portray the title boxer in *The Beloved Brute* (1924), the real Victor McLaglen became known for movie fights after battling George O'Brien in *The Fighting Heart* (1925). He worked with Edmund Lowe in many popular Quirt and Flagg pictures beginning with *What Price Glory* (1926) and *The Cock-Eyed World* (1929) that saw them regularly facing off. Audiences came to expect fights in a McLaglen picture, even after he won a Best Actor Oscar as the star of John Ford's *The Informer* (1935). McLaglen could work "stiff" in fights and often failed to properly pull his mighty knockout punches. He did a one-man fight with a dozen stuntmen on *The Magnificent Brute* (1936) and left more than a few professional fall guys nursing wounds. Stuntmen typically put in for extra hazard pay whenever working a fight with the ham-fisted McLaglen.

Other notable fights include *She Wore a Yellow Ribbon* (1949) and *The Quiet Man* (1952) (see entries). Fights of interest came against Donald Crisp in *The River Pirate* (1928), Robert Armstrong in *A Girl in Every Port* (1929), Frank Hagney in *Captain Lash* (1929), Charles Bickford in *Under Pressure* (1935), William Hall in *The Magnificent Brute* (1936), Brian Donlevy in *Battle of Broadway* (1938), Brian Aherne in *Captain Fury* (1939), Nelson Eddy in *Let Freedom Ring* (1939), Jon Hall in *South of Pago Pago* (1940), Sammy Stein in *Powder Town* (1942), John Payne in *Strictly Dynamite* (1942), George Montgomery in *China Girl* (1942) and Chester Morris and Tom Kennedy in *Rough, Tough, and Ready* (1945). On TV he fought Richard Boone in the 1958 *Have Gun, Will Travel* episode "The O'Hare Story" and Clint Eastwood in the 1959 *Rawhide* episode "Incident of the Shambling Man."

See: "An Epic Set-To." *Richmond River Herald.* February 18, 1938; "Fight Scenes Bring Thrills to Melodrama." *Seattle Daily Times.* March 14, 1937; McLaglen, Victor. *Express to Hollywood.* London: Jarrolds, 1934; "Medical Help Needed by Two Film Fighters." *Chicago Tribune.* November 7, 1936.

TEX RITTER VS. CHARLIE KING in *Riders of the Rockies* (1937)

As Bob Steele had his preferred fight partner in film after film, B-western singing cowboy Tex Ritter also favored the rotund roughhousing of his pal Charlie King. Ritter fought King a total of 23 times on screen, with their best battle coming in *Riders of the Rockies* (1937). *Western Clippings* includes it among the "great screen fights," while Mario DeMarco wrote the realistic fights were "the highlight of the early Ritter films." *The Filming of the West* claims this fight was "the most bloodcurdling of their eleven fights at Grand National." Both men draw blood in the roughhousing, and Ritter's famous hair gets plenty mussed. The three-minute cantina brawl features many upended tables and a tense, realistic struggle for a pistol. A highlight comes when Ritter puts a headlock on King and flings him across the floor. Every time the audience thinks the fight is over, the two charge at one another and begin swinging again. Yakima Canutt worked on the film, but the surprisingly athletic Ritter does the entire fight.

Veteran fight man King carefully tutored the 6'2", 180-pound Ritter in the art of screen fighting and found an enthusiastic opponent. It has been said that the heavy-drinking, fun-loving King often woke Ritter in the middle of the night to go over the next day's fight work. Ritter obliged, knowing full well a King fight was the highlight of any B-western. Unfortunately for King, when Ritter or Steele went on a publicity tour to put on fight displays for the fans, they used stuntman Jack O'Shea. Because of King's drinking, he couldn't be trusted on the road. Nevertheless, King was well-liked by all those who worked with him.

See: Bond, Johnny. *The Tex Ritter Story.* New York: Chappell Music Co., 1976; DeMarco, Mario. *Tex Ritter and Fred Scott: The Singing Buckaroos of the Movies.* Self-published, 1988.

THE TAXI CAB BRAWL in *BIG CITY* (1937)

Big City (aka *Skyscraper Wilderness*) is noted for the gimmick casting of real boxers and wrestlers for a climactic waterfront war between rival taxi cab companies. As if there wasn't enough going on plot-wise, director Frank Borzage has leading lady Luise Rainer giving birth during the melee. Like many in Hollywood during this time, Borzage was a fight fan. Among the boxers cast in the MGM pic were former heavyweight champs Jack Dempsey and Jim Jeffries, former light heavyweight champ Maxie Rosenbloom, former welterweight champs Jackie Fields and Jimmy McLarnin, lightweight Joe Rivers, heavyweight contenders George Godfrey and Neal Clisby, and Australian Olympic standout Rex "Snowy" Baker. The professional wrestling lineup includes Man Mountain Dean, Bull Montana and Gus Sonnenberg, while judo masters Tasuke Hagio and Don Sugai Matsuda were added for good measure. USC quarterback Cotton Warbutton, Olympic runner Frank Wykoff, and Olympic decathlete turned pro football standout Jim Thorpe round out the fighting cast. The group of athletes are recruited on screen by Spencer Tracy from Dempsey's New York City restaurant. George B. Seitz handled the second unit direction for the brawl on location. Much of the action is played tongue-in-cheek. *Argus* called it an "uproarious comic brawl," while *The Sydney Mail* found it "one of the screen's liveliest mass fight sequences."

Guinn "Big Boy" Williams and experienced stunt actors Bud Geary, Harry Wilson and Frank Hagney took on the parts of cab drivers, as did familiar tough mugs Lew Harvey, James Flavin and Jack Pennick. The casting call for extras: "Only tough guys wanted." There weren't many established stunt pros clamoring for the assignment. While professional wrestlers were accustomed to enhancing the theatricality of their performance, boxers were trained to make contact. Nobody wanted to catch a famous Dempsey punch on the chin. A 190-pound six-footer, the Manassa Mauler's punching power was legendary. Native American Thorpe, six feet tall and 210 pounds, was also known to pack a powerful punch and was a much feared bar fighter. Professional wrestler Man Mountain Dean broke his leg during filming. He subsequently did all his screen fighting while supported against a post.

See: Dumont, Herve. *Frank Borzage: The Life and Times of a Hollywood Romantic.* Jefferson, NC: McFarland, 2006; "Luise Rainer and Spencer Tracy Have Leading Roles." *San Jose News.* September 23, 1937; "Theatre Gossip." *Evening Independent.* October 30, 1937.

Bob Livingston vs. Yakima Canutt in *Heart of the Rockies* (1937)

The enduringly silly, good-natured Three Mesquiteers entries from director Joseph Kane and Republic Pictures mixed comedy and western action. The films benefited greatly from having Yakima Canutt on hand to ramrod the stunts and portray henchmen. Kane and cinematographer Jack Marta also distinguished themselves with their handling of fights. *Heart of the Rockies* is a far more serious entry and boasts two lengthy and spectacular battles between hero Bob Livingston, a 180-pound six-footer, and bearded villain Canutt. The first is an intense, knock-down drag-out affair around a lakeside cabin, and the second is a running shot stretching from the driver's seat to the tongue of a moving covered wagon. There are no process shots here, it was all done for real. Canutt was becoming a seasoned pro at these dangerous moves. The studio would simply hand him screenplays with blank segments stating, "See Yakima Canutt for action." Although his regular double Duke Taylor worked on the film, Livingston did all his own stunts for the cabin fight, which was filmed in the San Jacinto Mountains near Lake Hemet. The star was proud of the brawl and credited Canutt with teaching him how to picture-fight. For the wagon battle, Taylor and stuntman Kenny Cooper stood in for Livingston.

Kane was expert at shooting action and had one of the largest personal film libraries consisting of more than 100 fight scenes dating back to the 1914 *Spoilers.* He'd show his film combatants favorites to inspire them before shooting. On *Heart of the Rockies,* the camera follows the fighters fluidly and from multiple angles. It took a full day to film the three-minute brawl at the cabin, a near eternity in the world of quickie B-westerns. Canutt emerged with a minor injury to his elbow, but undying respect from his fellow stuntmen for putting on a great screen fight under the conditions. *Western Clippings* terms it "one of the best fights in B-westerns," and author Merrill McCord calls it "a well-executed and exciting affair and could be compared with what are probably considered to be the greatest fist fights in the history of film."

See: McCord, Merrill. *Brothers of the West: The Lives and Films of Robert Livingston and Jack Randall.* Bethesda, MD: Alhambra, 2003; "New Film Boasts Rough and Ready Fight Sequence." *The*

News and Eastern Townships Advocate. March 8, 1951.

CHARLES STARRETT VS. DICK CURTIS in *The Old Wyoming Trail* (1937)

Cowboy hero Charles Starrett (6'2", 190 pounds) and hulking villain Dick Curtis (6'3", 220 pounds) squared off against one another in more than 15 Columbia films from 1937 through 1940. Starrett took to calling their assembly line run-ins "the never-ending fight," joking that a feature film could have been made of their battles alone. *The Old Wyoming Trail* from director Folmer Blangsted is perhaps the best known of their bruising encounters with publicity comparing the dynamite action to the original *The Spoilers*. The *Richmond Times Dispatch* called it "a sensational screen fight," while *Western Clippings* declares it "probably the best of all the Starrett-Curtis bare-knuckle brawls." The battle received nice press for a B-film, particularly in a photo spread and write-up in the 1957 coffee table book *The Movies*. Stuntman Ted Mapes was on hand to double Starrett, but the cowboy star was able to do the majority of his own fight work with perennial villain Curtis.

Starrett played football at Dartmouth College and later became beloved by B-western fans as the Durango Kid. He noted that former wrestler Curtis, who carried the moniker "The Meanest Man in the West," was well-coordinated for his imposing size and had good reflexes. In all their fights together, they never once suffered an injury. Initially the cameramen sped up their fights from 24 frames per second to 22, but their timing became so good together they were able to stage them successfully at normal speed. One of their best fights came in a burning cabin in *Riders of Black River* (1938).

See: DeMarco, Mario. *Charles Starrett: The Durango Kid, Gallant Defender.* Self-published, 1982; Griffith, Richard, and Arthur Mayer. *The Movies: The Sixty-Year Story of Hollywood and Its Effect on America.* New York: Simon & Schuster, 1957; "Hot Fist Fight." *Cumberland Evening Times.* June 24, 1938.

WAYNE MORRIS VS. CHARLES BICKFORD in *Valley of the Giants* (1938)

Lumberjacks battle it out in rich Technicolor among the redwoods of California in this scenic Warner Bros. outing from director William Keighley. Beefy blond Wayne Morris is the hero, going against nefarious Charles Bickford in a film full of fight action. During the climax, the two have a solid one-minute brawl on a rocky ledge overlooking a dam that's about to be dynamited. The fight is aided immensely by the work of stunt doubles Wes Hopper and Fred Graham, who do all the dangerous ledge shots for Sol Polito's camera. A heavy bed of moss on the rocks gives them some padding for their falls. Publicity called it "a terrific battle" and revealed that studio executives were comparing the climactic fight to the early versions of *The Spoilers*, then regarded as the benchmark for all two-man fights. Morris and Bickford come to blows earlier in the picture as well, with Bickford getting the upper hand on that occasion. In the climactic fight, Bickford lost his footing and

Alan Hale (left) and Wayne Morris charge into a saloon fray in Warner Bros.' *Valley of the Giants* (1938).

took a 30-foot fall into the Van Duzen River. He was pulled out by stuntman Don Turner.

Early in the film, there's an action-packed saloon fight where Morris comes to the aid of Alan Hale against a barroom full of henchmen the likes of Harry Cording, Lew Harvey and Dick Purcell. The minute-and-a-half battle royal took five days to film and exposed thousands of feet of film for editor Jack Killifer to sift through. The 6'2", 220-pound Hale proves to be an energetic centerpiece in the blistering action as he demolishes everything in his path. Even in scenes of violence, the hearty Hale kept a gleam in his eye that lent a comic touch to the proceedings. Stuntmen employed in the 20-man lumberjack brawl include Graham, Hopper, Turner, Sol Gorss, Gil Perkins, Cliff Lyons, Buster Wiles, Bob Perry and fight coordinator Sailor Vincent.

The stunt work is solid throughout, with beautiful locations in Eureka, California, making the otherwise routine film pleasant to look at. Many of the action scenes (including the main two-man fight) were intercut into the 1952 film *The Big Trees* (1952). *The Hollywood Reporter* wrote, "It's one good struggle after another from the first line of dialog to the last fight between hero and villain on the edge of a cliff." *The Repository* called the scuffles "a couple of the swellest fights ever recorded by the camera," while *The Oregonian* declared the saloon skirmish "one of the greatest film fights ever seen."

Six-foot-two, 200-pound Wayne Morris, fresh off playing a boxer in *Kid Galahad* (1937), angered several stuntmen working on the film when he insisted on doing his own fighting during the saloon brawl. Stuntmen could become highly agitated when an actor dipped into their potential earnings, and they gave Morris a rougher time than they'd have one of their own. The brash Morris, reputedly a football star at Los Angeles City College, was sporting a slightly discolored eye on the train trip to the northern California location and was more than willing to hand over fight duties from that point on. Nevertheless, studio trainer Mushy Callahan rated Morris one of the strongest punchers among actors. He accidentally knocked out tough steelworker William Haade for real filming in the ring and played power-punching boxers in *The Kid Comes Back* (1938) and *The Kid from Kokomo* (1939). Fights of interest came against Humphrey Bogart in *Men Are Such Fools* (1938), Rod Cameron in *Stage to Tucson* (1950), Preston Foster in *The Tougher They Come* (1950) and *The*

Big Gusher (1951), Alan Hale, Jr., in *Arctic Flight* (1952) and Mickey Simpson in *Star of Texas* (1953). Morris served as an ace pilot for the U.S. Navy in World War II.

See: "Alan Hale Gets Two-Fisted Jobs." *Boston Globe.* June 13, 1939; Callahan, Mushy. "Films Make Actor-Boxer Look Good." *Pittsburgh Post-Gazette.* July 6, 1939; Carroll, Harrison. "Behind the Scenes in Hollywood." *Victoria Advocate.* June 12, 1938; Kahn, Alexander. "Film Stunt Men Mad at Mr. Morris." *Pittsburgh Press.* July 8, 1938; "Movie Acting Often Strenuous." *Murray Pioneer and Australian River Record.* December 15, 1938.

PETER LORRE VS. LEON AMES in *Mysterious Mr. Moto* (1938)

The 20th Century-Fox Mr. Moto series was notable in fight lore as one of the first to showcase the Japanese martial art of jujitsu, thrilling audiences with the way the pint-sized Asian detective (played by German actor Peter Lorre) could manhandle any number of big ugly brutes. The fifth of eight films, *Mysterious Mr. Moto* is the best Moto for fighting. There's a major 90-second saloon brawl in a Limehouse causeway tavern, The Blue Peter, midway through the film that leaves nearly every participant unconscious. Highlights include a waiter climbing a light fixture to escape and a couple of overhead crane shots from cinematographer Virgil Miller. These camera angles were normally avoided in fight action because it was too easy for the audience to spot missed punches from above. Lorre flips henchman John Rogers over the counter before making his escape with Karen Sorrell as the bar descends into chaos. Director Norman Foster disguised himself as a hoodlum for the fight and does a walk-through before bartender Cecil Weston cuts off the power. The fast-paced climax in a dusty attic sees Lorre battle villainous assassin Leon Ames for a full minute of head-first dives and hip tosses over a hole in the floor.

Publicity falsely claimed that Lorre was a jujitsu expert, supposedly having trained with Professor Haiku Watsutu. In reality, Lorre didn't know martial arts and rarely if ever became involved in action scenes, preferring to let stunt doubles Harvey Parry or Johnny Kascier take over. In this film, it's Parry who handles all the fights. He also shows up as a fighter in the saloon brawl started by Frank Hagney and Allen Pomeroy. Other stuntmen involved in the brawling include Sailor Vincent, Chick Collins, Billy Jones, Bobby Rose, Jack

Woody, Barney O'Toole and Harry Wilson. During the fighting, Parry was accidentally knocked cold by a punch from U.S. Navy boxing champion Vincent, who has a humorous bit as a drunk who wakes up from his stupor throwing punches.

See: Berlin, Howard M. *The Complete Mr. Moto Film Phile: A Casebook.* Berkeley Heights, NJ: Wildside, 2005; "Theatres." *Winnipeg Tribune.* November 18, 1938; Youngkin, Stephen D. *The Lost One: A Life of Peter Lorre.* Lexington: University Press of Kentucky, 2005.

Robert Taylor vs. Wallace Beery in *Stand Up and Fight* (1939)

Robert Taylor (left) and Wallace Beery square off in MGM's *Stand Up and Fight* (1939).

A forgotten MGM release, director W.S. Van Dyke's *Stand Up and Fight* has rarely been seen on TV because of its depiction of blacks as slaves. Set in the 1850s, the plot pits railroad man Robert Taylor versus blustery, scheming stagecoach owner Wallace Beery as free slaves in the North are kidnapped and resold to the South. *Cue* called it a "bang-up, brawling melodrama from start to finish," while *Variety* noted, "It holds a sock almost every 100 feet of film." Taylor biographer Lawrence J. Quirk wrote, "Van Dyke extracted every possible value out of [the fights], staging them for electric, well-paced results." Two realistic and exciting fistfights occur between the stars, with lots of jostling and little hint of pre-planned choreography. There is no musical accompaniment. Taylor takes a great pounding from the much larger Beery in the first encounter, with Beery challenging him, "Stand up and fight!" Taylor manages to triumph in the second fistfight, a crowd-pleasing one-minute battle in a heavy snowfall. Taylor bleeds and bruises but refuses to back down, even when Beery starts hitting him over the head with a tree branch. When Taylor stands over a beaten Beery, he says, "Come on! Stand up and fight!" Beery admits defeat, blaming the altitude, and the two reach an alliance and share a drink. As was typical of Beery's carefully established screen image, in the end he turns out to be a lovable cuss with a soft heart.

MGM was inundated with letters of concern from female fans who were worried about the damage done to Taylor's famous face. The studio had to reassure fans that Beery struck no real blows upon Taylor's treasured visage. The stars liked one another and had a good time throwing fake snowballs at the crew when the cameras weren't on. The final fight in a foot of manufactured snow was filmed simultaneously by three cameras. Cinematographer Leonard Smith placed two on platforms and positioned one at eye level to capture the action at different angles. The combatants and their uncredited stunt doubles tore up the set. At one point, Beery initiated a kick to the head that caught Taylor unaware. Director Van Dyke was quick to step in and call a break so an on-set nurse could examine Taylor whenever Beery became too rough.

MGM became determined to toughen the image of their good-looking star. They placed Taylor on a weightlifting program with physical trainer Don Loomis and had him spar with boxing trainer Mickey Cianci for the prizefight picture *The Crowd Roars* (1938). The training paid off and a newly muscled 5'11", 175-pound Taylor was able to handle action scenes convincingly throughout his career. After service with the U.S. Navy during World War II, he worked regularly with Golden Gloves champ Terry Robinson.

Fights of interest came against Griffith Jones in *A Yank at Oxford* (1938), George Sanders in *Her Cardboard Lover* (1942), Van Heflin in *Johnny Eager* (1942), John Hodiak in *Ambush* (1949), James Millican in *Devil's Doorway* (1950), Stewart Granger in *All the Brothers Were Valiant* (1953),

Alan Hale, Jr., and George Raft in *Rogue Cop* (1954) (see entry), Carlos Thompson in *Valley of the Kings* (1954), Alan Hale, Jr., in *Many Rivers to Cross* (1955), Jack Lord in *Tip on a Dead Jockey* (1957), Lee J. Cobb in *Party Girl* (1958), Henry Silva in *The Law and Jake Wade* (1958) and Richard Devon in *Cattle King* (1963). On his TV series *The Detectives* (1959–1962), he engaged in a judo exhibition with Bruce Tegner in 1960's "Karate."

See: Quirk, Lawrence J. *The Films of Robert Taylor.* Secaucus, NJ: Citadel, 1975; "Robert Taylor and Wallace Beery Stage All-in Scrap." *The Queenslander.* February 22, 1939; Wayne, Jane Ellen. *Robert Taylor: The Man with the Perfect Face.* New York: St. Martin's, 1989.

JAMES CAGNEY VS. HUMPHREY BOGART in *The Oklahoma Kid* (1939)

Top screen gangsters James Cagney and Humphrey Bogart are absurdly miscast in cowboy garb as they face off at the climax of this Cherokee Strip western for director Lloyd Bacon. Nevertheless, it's a match-up made in classic cinema heaven, even if the stuntmen step in for much of the action and editor Owen Marks gets overly aggressive with the scissors. Composer Max Steiner provides a pulse-pounding score for the fist-slinging. Graham Greene called it "a magnificent slug feast" in *The Spectator,* while *Commonweal* praised the "bang-up fights." The *Morning Herald* labeled it "one of the greatest fight scenes ever seen on the screen." According to *The Western: From Silents to the Seventies,* "It was fast, vigorous action all the way, complete even to the last-reel fist fight in the saloon."

In the Warner Bros. film, black hat Bogart lynches Cagney's father, setting up the dynamic final action lensed by cinematographer James Wong Howe. The minute-and-a-half fight begins as Cagney opens a second story door and steps out with guns drawn into the Territory Saloon. Bogart is waiting and hits him over the head with a breakaway chair. The two exchange punches and fall down a staircase onto the empty bar floor, where they fight vigorously with fists and broken bottles until Bogart, going for a gun,

is shot by Cagney's mortally injured brother Harvey Stephens. Cagney's double Harvey Parry sprained his wrist taking the stair fall.

Making matters especially interesting, there was no love lost between the two stars. Bogart, still a few films away from superstardom, had become tired of playing second fiddle to Cagney and let his displeasure be known. The two shared dinner at the restaurant Chasen's before filming, ostensibly to discuss the film and iron out any hard feelings. The dinner didn't last long enough for drinks, suggesting that animosity remained. Once on the set, Bogart thought Cagney looked foolish and announced, "In that ten gallon hat, you look like a mushroom." Cagney saved his reply for the fight, where he had far greater experience than Bogart and could take delight in seeing his co-star hit the floor. Bogart's tough guy act proved to be just that. When all was said and done and shooting wrapped, Cagney commented, "When it came to fighting, Bogart was about as tough as Shirley Temple."

U.S. Navy veteran Bogart's reputation as a two-fisted star was curious. Five-foot-eight and 150 pounds, he was given judo training by June Tegner for *Tokyo Joe* (1949), but when it came to fights he usually handed over the majority of action to stunt doubles. In real life he talked tough and made people think he could handle himself but rarely resorted to blows. On occasion in nightclubs such as the Trocadero and the Mocambo, he took a swing at someone who was pushing him. Stuntman Harvey Parry called Bogart an expert at the

James Cagney is about to be clobbered by a chair-wielding Humphrey Bogart in Warner Bros.' *The Oklahoma Kid* (1939).

sneak punch. Bogart's wife Mayo Methot was known to jump into a fray to keep him from the action. She was as hard-drinking as Bogie, and the two became known in Hollywood as the Battling Bogarts during their brief and tenuous time together. She stabbed him in the back and even shot him. After seeing him with two Mayo-related black eyes, stuntman Buster Wiles suggested the two should book Madison Square Garden for one of their fights.

On screen he came across as a world-weary cynic, staying on his feet after absorbing a Barton MacLane punch in *The Maltese Falcon* (1941) and withstanding a Victor Sen Yung judo flip in *Across the Pacific* (1942). Bogart had fights of interest against Lyle Talbot in *Big City Blues* (1932), Joe Sawyer in *San Quentin* (1937), Wayne Morris in *Men Are Such Fools* (1938), George Brent in *Racket Busters* (1938), Edward G. Robinson in *Brother Orchid* (1940), Eddie Albert in *The Wagons Roll at Night* (1941), Sol Gorss in *All Through the Night* (1942), Joe Downing in *The Big Shot* (1942), Fred Graham in *Passage to Marseille* (1944), Bob Steele and Jack Perry in *The Big Sleep* (1946), Clifton Young in *Dark Passage* (1947), Barton MacLane in *The Treasure of the Sierra Madre* (1948) (see entry), Teru Shimada and Hideo Mori (aka Howard Kumagai) in *Tokyo Joe* (1949), John Derek in *Knock on Any Door* (1949) and Jack Lambert and Ted DeCorsia in *The Enforcer* (1951).

See: "Bogart Learns Judo from Woman Expert." *Pittsburgh Press.* March 16, 1949; Meyers, Jeffrey. *Bogart: A Life in Hollywood.* New York: Fromm International, 1999; "Sock in Hollywood." *Des Moines Register.* July 21, 1940.

THE SALOON BRAWL in *DODGE CITY* (1939)

The blueprint for all barroom brawls, this rip-roarer from director Michael Curtiz employed several rough and tumble actors (Guinn "Big Boy" Williams, Bruce Cabot, Alan Hale, Victor Jory, Ward Bond and Douglas Fowley) and three dozen of Hollywood's top stuntmen as the North takes on the South in the famous frontier town. Everything that would become a western cliché is here, including a chair thrown into the mirror behind the bar, several men crashing through the front window, and whiskey bottles and chairs smashed over heads. The only thing missing in this legendary fight is the film's heroic star Errol Flynn. The melee was deemed too dangerous by the stu-

dio to allow Warner's top star to participate, although Flynn does throw Fowley (doubled by Buster Wiles) through a barbershop window later in the film. There's plenty of humor mixed with the sprawling action courtesy of Williams, who is showcased at his grinning best. He nearly steals the film thanks to his amicable, punched-up performance.

Dodge City was a huge hit, and stock footage from this donnybrook was used for many years in other Warner Bros. films such as *Frontier Days* (1945) and *Cattle Town* (1952), as well as the TV series *F Troop* (1965–1967). Every western saloon showdown on film and television ultimately tried to measure up. Robert Buckner's script used the Civil War as a motivating force between the combatants, but it became a point of humor in subsequent films that every saloon cowboy seemed willing to join a fray no matter the reason or cost. Blake Edwards' *The Great Race* (1965) and Mel Brooks' *Blazing Saddles* (1974) famously spoofed the battle.

Film Daily called the *Dodge City* donnybrook "probably the most exciting mob fight scene ever filmed," while *Newsweek* termed it "extra-special." *Variety* remarked that it contained "some of the dandiest melee stuff screened," and *The Hollywood Reporter* weighed in with, "No show in this reviewer's memory has ever crammed so much punch and drama into one scene as the free-for-all brawl in the Gay Lady saloon." According to the *Pittsburgh Post-Gazette*, "Never have the movies produced such a tumultuous display of wholesale bone-cracking," and *The Stanford Daily* said, "It beats any of the fight scenes ever filmed." *Blazing West* tags it "the wildest, wooliest mass saloon fight of them all." Film historian/critic Leonard Maltin identifies it as "the granddaddy of all barroom brawls," and *Western Clippings* calls it "spectacularly staged." *USA Today* ranks it among the Top 10 movie fights of all time, writing that it is "slickly choreographed, almost operatic."

Bodies fly right and left. Furniture is smashed. Tables are overturned. Broken bottles explode on walls. Men and shelves are lassoed and brought down. It's shoulder-to-shoulder, wall-to-wall fighting for nearly four solid minutes at the Gay Lady Saloon (actually Stage 16 as designed by art director Ted Smith). The fight took a week for Curtiz and Sol Polito to film at a budgeted cost of $75,000. Some reports placed the fight's final cost as high as $112,500. Among the highlights are stuntmen Duke Green, Harvey Parry and Sol

Gorss crashing through a staircase (for which they were each paid $485), Green going headfirst through a breakaway window, and Buster Wiles and Hurley "Red" Breen flying off a second floor balcony onto a half a dozen men. Among the 105 stuntmen and brawling atmosphere players present were Yakima Canutt, Cliff Lyons, Fred Graham, Gil Perkins, Don Turner, Jack Stoney, Sailor Vincent, Allen Pomeroy, Paul McWilliams, Reed Howes, Pat Flaherty, Glenn Strange, Ralph Sanford, Herbert Holcombe, Jack Williams, George "Tex" Bloom, Bud Osborne, Chick Collins, Ben Corbett, Chet Brandenburg and trick roper Sam Garrett.

Mention should be made of the props involved in such a scene. The breakaway movie glass found in window panes and whiskey bottles is called candy glass. It's also known as sugar glass and is just that: sugar baked until it takes on the appearance of glass with none of the latter's heaviness or danger. In later years, a form of light plastic replaced candy glass. Breakaway chairs and tables are commonly made of light balsa wood or yucca, a pliable wood that's mostly hollow. They are held together by glue instead of potentially dangerous nails and are lightly scored to break easily on impact. This is how actors and stuntmen can withstand the punishment of falling through furniture or having it broken over their head. Even then, it takes skill to learn to administer and take the blows effectively to avoid injury. A properly prepared chair must be swung at full force to ensure that it breaks fully and looks good for the camera. Swinging a chair too softly can hurt a target if it doesn't break. Hitting someone with the seat must be avoided as that's the heaviest area and edges can be painful. Breakaways could sometimes lead to humorous moments on the set. Often an actor or stuntman became caught up in the heat of the moment and gripped a prop too tightly, having it fall apart in their hands.

While on location, star Flynn decided that he was going to discover who was the toughest of his co-stars. Having once come out on the losing end of a fight with Victor Jory, Flynn put former USC football player Ward Bond up to testing the U.S. Coast Guard boxing champ. Jory promptly broke Bond's nose. Suitably impressed, Flynn next told "Big Boy" Williams that Jory had his girlfriend in his hotel room. An irate Williams broke down Jory's door and was promptly hit several times and placed in a headlock. The struggle attracted the police, who were set to arrest the two until Jory convinced them they were play-acting despite the broken door. Realizing he had been set up by Flynn, Williams made amends and split a bottle of gin with Jory.

Six-foot-two, 230-pound Williams played football at Texas Normal University and served with the U.S. Army in World War I. He entered films as a stuntman. By the 1930s, "Big Boy" was a much-in-demand studio supporting player and enthusiastic low-budget B-western star. He could play good guys, bad guys and comedic foils with equal aplomb. Often he was cast as boxers, football players or U.S. Marines. He became known for his powerful physique and was a legendary figure in old-time Hollywood as a drinking buddy of Flynn and John Wayne. He had the reputation of being one of filmdom's toughest men. Williams was convincing in his action scenes and enjoyed performing his own fisticuffs on screen even into his later years. He packed a mighty punch.

Williams had notable fights

Guinn "Big Boy" Williams (right) throws a punch during the famous saloon brawl in Warner Bros.' *Dodge City* (1939).

in *Big City* (1937), *The Desperadoes* (1943) and *Station West* (1948) (see entries). Fights of interest came against J. Gordon Russell in *Trail of Hate* (1922), Randolph Scott in *Heritage of the Desert* (1933), Dick Alexander in *Cowboy Holiday* (1934), George Raft in *The Glass Key* (1935), Frank Hagney and Maxie Rosenbloom in *Kelly the Second* (1936), Jack Holt in *North of Nome* (1936), Pat Flaherty in *End of the Trail* (1936), Herman Brix in *Flying Fists* (1937), Frank Hagney in *Wise Girl* (1937), Ward Bond and William Haade in *Pardon Our Nerve* (1938) and Dana Andrews in *Swamp Water* (1941). He greatly impressed viewers busting heads alongside Roy Rogers in a comic brawl in *Cowboy and the Senorita* (1944). On late 1950s TV, a still-tough Williams knocked out Clint Walker with one punch on *Cheyenne* and fought James Arness in the 1957 *Gunsmoke* episode "Skid Row."

See: Rainey, Buck. *The Strong Silent Type.* Jefferson, NC. McFarland, 2004; Vieira, Mark A. *Majestic Hollywood: The Greatest Films of 1939.* Philadelphia: Running Press, 2013.

MARLENE DIETRICH VS. UNA MERKEL in *Destry Rides Again* (1939)

George Marshall's western contains what remains the most famous female vs. female fight ever captured on film. Legendary German actress Marlene Dietrich and Una Merkel go at it as ferociously as any pair of men in the Bloody Gulch's Last Chance Saloon as they fight over a pair of pants to the tune of composer Frank Skinner's energetic score. Universal's publicists called it "an epochal fist-fight." They slap, punch, kick, wrestle, scratch, bite and pull one another's hair until James Stewart resorts to pouring a bucket of water on them to cool them off. This unleashes Dietrich's fury on him, as she throws everything but the kitchen sink at Stewart. Even a banjo is used as a weapon. In the climax, Dietrich's Frenchy leads other female cast members into the saloon armed with rolling pins to take on Brian Donlevy's bad guys.

Variety called the Dietrich-Merkel fight "outstanding," while *The Adelaide Advertiser* termed it "one of the best screen brawls we have ever seen." The *New York Times* wrote, "We thought the battle between Paulette Goddard and Rosalind Russell in *The Women* was an eye-opener; now we realize it was just shadow-clawing." *The Big Damn Book of Sheer Manliness* calls it "the greatest cat fight ever," and *Legendary Westerns* includes it among the top screen scraps.

The Dietrich-Merkel match-up, a riotous tooth-and-nail catfight lasting over two minutes, took five days to film. Dietrich was adamant about doing as much of her own fighting as possible on screen, and dished it out to Stewart as well as Merkel. Co-star Merkel realized Dietrich wasn't pulling punches and opted to do her own fighting as well. In reality, Dietrich whispered to Merkel throughout the fight to make sure she was okay even as she was stomping on her toes with French heels. Both actresses became carried away in the moment in front of Hal Mohr's camera, coming away with scrapes, bruises and even splinters. A first aid station was set up off the soundstage for injuries. Pioneering stuntwoman Helen Thurston filled in for Dietrich when the action became too heavy. Publicity claimed the stars did all their own stunts in one continuous take and were presented with champagne toasts by their stunt doubles and applause from the cast and crew. Stuntman Duke York coordinated the action.

The film was loosely remade as *Frenchie* (1950) with Shelley Winters and Marie Windsor and again as *Destry* (1954) with Mari Blanchard and Mary Wickes. They were all shown the Dietrich-Merkel battle as a point of reference. Other female match-ups of interest include Penny Singleton and Ann Miller in *Go West, Young Lady* (1941), Arlean Whelan and Katy Jurado in *San Antone* (1953), Joan Crawford and Mercedes McCambridge in *Johnny Guitar* (1954), Peggie Castle and Betty Brueck in *Jesse James' Women* (1954), Angie Dickinson and Lyla Graham in *The Return of Jack Slade* (1955), Beverly Garland and Allison Hayes in *Gunslinger* (1956), Coleen Gray and Randy Stuart in *Star in the Dust* (1956), Nancy Kovack and Sally Starr in *The Outlaws Is Coming* (1965) and stuntwoman Polly Burson and Barbara Werle (doubled by Julie Ann Johnson) in *Gone with the West* (1969). The Aliza Gur–Martine Beswick gypsy fight in *From Russia with Love* (1963) is perhaps the most famous outside the western genre. On TV, Barbara Stanwyck took on Julie Adams in the 1968 *Big Valley* episode "The Emperor of Rice." Unfortunately, researching additional female catfights inevitably leads into a maze of underground fetish films or outright pornography amidst the legitimate efforts. *Destry Rides Again* will be the sole entry here for girl-on-girl fighting, a subject that undoubtedly warrants its own volume for those interested parties.

See: Anderson, Nancy. "Una Merkel Loved Second Fiddle." *Beaver County Times*. December 5, 1978; "Glamor Girl Swings Fist in Western." *Pittsburgh Press*. October 4, 1939; "This Is a New High in Movie Roughhouse." *Life*. October 9, 1939.

VICTOR JORY VS. TOM TYLER in *The Light of Western Stars* (1940)

This fine adaptation of a Zane Grey western features an interesting role reversal as frequent screen villain Victor Jory is cast as the roguish hero and Tom Tyler, who made his name as a strong cowboy hero, is the shady sheriff who takes Jory on in a wild one-minute saloon brawl. Director Lesley Selander builds tension between the men when Tyler slaps Alan Ladd for dancing with his girl. A gentleman's wager solves that showdown, but after Ladd is killed it's no-holds-barred as Jory stares Tyler down with perhaps the most intensely cold eyes the screen has ever seen. The two actors have a great dialogue exchange before Tyler goes for his gun. Jory instinctively knocks it away, and all hell breaks loose.

No stunt doubles were used, and it's a fierce and realistic struggle as the men spend as much time wrestling on the floor as they do connecting with punches. This is how real fights often develop as opposed to punches traded back and forth. Many of their falls look unrehearsed and spontaneous, with furniture occasionally getting in the way as chairs are thrown and tables overturned. The way their bodies twist and turn against one another, it's a wonder they both weren't in need of chiropractic care when all was said and done. Tyler tries to smash Jory with a whiskey bottle, but Jory lands a knockout punch that puts Tyler out on his feet. Tyler's vacant, glassy-eyed face is one of the cinema's most memorable fight-dazed expressions, perfectly captured by cameraman Russell Harlan. Jory lands two more punches before Tyler drops for good.

When the scene wrapped, the crew gave the men a standing ovation. The fight, saved until the last day of shooting in case the participants sustained

black eyes, boasts great sound effects and no intrusive music, with only choppy editing from Sherman Rose a drawback to perfection. Jory and Tyler also fought in *Riders of the Timberline* (1941). The 6'2", 200-pound Tyler was an amateur boxer who entered films as a stuntman. An AAU weightlifting champion, he earned his bones in B-westerns fighting ubiquitous heavies Charlie King, Dick Alexander, Harry Woods and Slim Whitaker in film after film. One of his best fights came against Rod Cameron in *Boss of Boomtown* (1944).

Six-foot-one, 190-pound Victor Jory boxed in Golden Gloves and fought professionally. He held British Columbia and U.S. Coast Guard boxing and wrestling championships, played football at Fullerton Junior College and worked as a circus strongman. He habitually squeezed cork grips to maintain his forearm strength and could tear apart two decks of cards stacked together. He was widely regarded as one of the toughest men in Hollywood. When Jory hit someone for real, they stayed down. He favored doing his own fights though they resulted in an assortment of bruises, slashes and minor broken bones. Jory had heroic leads in the serials *The Green Archer* (1940) and *The Shadow* (1940) but became best known as a foil to Hopalong Cassidy in B-westerns.

Jory had notable on-screen fights in *Dodge City* (1939), *Hoppy Serves a Writ* (1943) and *The Kansan* (1943) (see entries). Fights of interest came against James Dunn in *Sailor's Luck* (1933), LeRoy

FAVORITE FILMS Presents

ZANE GREY'S The LIGHT of WESTERN STARS

Starring ALAN LADD · RUSSELL HAYDEN · VICTOR JORY · IO ANN SAYERS · NOAH BEERY Jr.

Victor Jory presses Tom Tyler against a bar counter in Paramount's *The Light of Western Stars* (1940).

Mason in *Smoky* (1933), Dewey Robinson in *Too Tough to Kill* (1935), Cecil Perry in *Men with Whips* (1936), George Bancroft in *Hell-Ship Morgan* (1936), George Raft in *I Stole a Million* (1940), Dennis Morgan in *River's End* (1940), Russell Hayden in *Knights of the Range* (1940), Dennis O'Keefe in *Girl from Havana* (1940), Richard Dix in *Buckskin Frontier* (1943), Joel McCrea in *South of St. Louis* (1949), Randolph Scott in *Canadian Pacific* (1949), Sterling Hayden in *Flaming Feather* (1952), Vaughn Moore in *Toughest Man in Arizona* (1952) and Glenn Ford in *The Man from the Alamo* (1953). On TV he played a San Diego cop in the syndicated *Manhunt* (1959–1961), squaring off against Jim Davis in the 1961 episode "Kidnapped."

See: Chapman, Mike, and Bobby J. Copeland. *The Tom Tyler Story*. Newton: Culture House, 2005; Thomas, Bob. "Victor Jory Specializes in Movie Fight Scenes." *Toledo Blade*. June 14, 1948.

CLARK GABLE VS. SPENCER TRACY in *Boom Town* (1940)

This popular MGM entry stars screen giants Clark Gable and Spencer Tracy as oil field wildcatters. They become rich and go bust throughout the course of the picture while fighting over Claudette Colbert and Hedy Lamarr, from the muddy streets of Texas to the high rises of New York City. Director Jack Conway keeps events moving as the two nearly come to blows more than once for Harold Rosson's camera. Screenwriter John Lee Mahin provides five fights. In one humorous but highly unbelievable exchange with husky mugs Frank Hagney, Olin Francis and Malcolm Walte, Gable and Tracy compete to see who can knock their opponent the furthest across the saloon floor. The inevitable fight between the stars is set in a locked Manhattan office, and it's a humdinger full of pithy one-liners and challenges as they belt one another over the furniture. The office and its contents are demolished by their actions. Editor Blanche Seward offers too many close-up shots of the stars waiting either to throw a punch or take one. Tighter snipping would have helped the flow of the fight.

Six-foot-one, 205-pound Gable and five-foot-nine, 170-pound Tracy co-starred in *San Francisco* (1936) and liked working together. They even stepped into the boxing ring to good-naturedly spar with one another on screen. By the time of *Boom Town,* however, U.S. Navy veteran Tracy was tired of not getting the girl on screen and let his displeasure be known on the set. This came through in his performance with Gable continually referring to him on screen as "Shorty." As tensions rise between the characters, Tracy punches Gable before they are broken up. By the last act, the audience is geared up to see these two men go at it behind closed doors. MGM publicity declared the fight "spine-tingling" and "nothing short of sensational." Hollywood columnist Sheilah Graham called it "a terrific fistic fight." The *Evening-Independent* termed it "the champion fighting picture," and the *New York Times* labeled it "a bang-up fist fight."

A notable mishap occurred while Gable battled Tracy's double George DeNormand (legend says

Spencer Tracy takes a big punch from Clark Gable in MGM's *Boom Town* (1940).

it was Tracy). DeNormand accidentally hit Gable with a roundhouse right that split the star's lip and created a large bruise. Worse, the blow broke Gable's dentures and he had to be away from the set for more than a week. The delay in Gable's return cost the production a reported $50,000, significant at the time. Full of remorse, director Conway was replaced by Victor Fleming, who completed the fight with stuntmen. Gable's double Joe Hickey finished the fight with DeNormand. Tracy flatly refused to take part in extended movie fights for the rest of his career, though he was coaxed into action for *Bad Day at Black Rock* (1955) (see entry). In real life, Tracy garnered a reputation as a brawler who came to blows multiple times with director William Wellman.

The rough-hewn, robust Gable was a former oil field roughneck and Oregon lumberjack. He reigned as an MGM star for over 20 years and was known in the industry as "The King," commanding attention with his presence and animal magnetism in such films as *Mutiny on the Bounty* (1935) and *Gone with the Wind* (1939). Studio publicity played up his punching power when he supposedly flattened stuntman Allen Pomeroy during the making of *Cain and Mabel* (1936). Promoters tried to lure him into the boxing ring with Max Baer, but Gable had more sense. Gable was confident enough in his real-life fighting skills to face down his Irish drinking buddy Jack Doyle, a 6'5" contender for the heavyweight crown. Gable later trained with former Golden Gloves champ and World War II hand-to-hand combat instructor Terry Robinson. Gable served with the U.S. Army Air Corps during the war as an aerial gunner.

He had movie fights of interest against William Boyd in *The Painted Desert* (1931), Wallace Beery in *Hell Divers* (1931), Franchot Tone in *Mutiny on the Bounty* (1935), Edgar Kennedy in *San Francisco* (1936), Pat Flaherty in *Parnell* (1937), Albert Dekker in *Strange Cargo* (1940) and *Honky Tonk* (1941), Tom Tully and Frank Hagney in *Adventure* (1945), Richard Rober in *Any Number Can Play* (1949), Raymond Burr in *Key to the City* (1950), Broderick Crawford in *Lone Star* (1952) (see entry), and Mel Welles in *Soldier of Fortune* (1955). Gable took part in a mass stuntman brawl in *Across the Wide Missouri* (1951).

See: "Film Calendar." *Brooklyn Daily Eagle.* October 13, 1940; Graham, Sheilah. "Accidents Do Happen—Even to Movie Stars." *Toledo Blade.* March 18, 1951; Marsh, W. Ward. "One Moment, Please!" *Plain Dealer.* September 25, 1940.

GARY COOPER VS. FORREST TUCKER in *The Westerner* (1940)

William Wyler's *The Westerner* pits lanky cowboy drifter Gary Cooper against Walter Brennan's Judge Roy Bean (an Oscar-winning performance), a worthy mental opponent with questionable morals and the law on his side. Cooper vs. the aged Brennan physically was a mismatch the audience wouldn't buy. The film was in need of a credible physical threat to Cooper among the homesteading farmers upon whom cattleman-friendly Brennan was applying pressure. Looking for a suitable young actor to play a sympathetic heavy and match up with Cooper in a subplot over leading lady Doris Davenport, the film's producer Samuel Goldwyn stumbled across the husky Forrest Tucker. At nearly 6'5" and 215 pounds, Tucker was more than the studio had bargained for. In addition to his physical attributes, he was a capable actor who could call Cooper "a snake and a liar" and look like he meant it. After those words are uttered, both men slowly undo their gun belts, fully aware they are about to tear into one another. It's hero Cooper who surprises the audience by throwing the first punch.

Tucker had a boxing background and proved especially good at fights, a requirement for this film's one minute of dust-covered, knee-buckling fisticuffs which *The New York Sun* termed "the toughest fist-fight filmed since the silent *The Spoilers*." The strapping Tucker was concerned he might hurt the 6'3", 180-pound Cooper because he had so much weight on him. However, Cooper entered films as a stuntman and boxed recreationally on the side. He worked on the 1930 version of *The Spoilers* with boxer Sailor Vincent and could handle himself in a movie fight. When Cooper accidentally connected with a punch, he was immediately apologetic to the film newcomer. Cooper took a fall during the nine-hour battle that banged up his knee, and he had to have water drained from it during the remainder of the picture.

The fight was shot on location near Tucson, Arizona, in a real horse corral. Wyler and cinematographer Gregg Toland obtained long shots of stunt doubles doing the fight but abandoned them for close-up action cut together by Daniel Mandell. The makeup department applied bruises and sufficient dust and straw to the men's heads to accentuate their rolling around in the dirt. Off-camera, a giant fan blew Fuller's Earth across the screen and into their faces. *The Western: From Silents to the Seventies* praised the intentional clumsiness of the fight between a cowboy and a farmer, writing that the action content was "unusually well-handled" and didn't reek of a typical stunt fight. To even out their height difference on screen, Tucker wore flat-heeled boots while Cooper had on built-up heels. Toward the end, Wyler ingeniously resorted to filming the men's shadows battling on the ground.

Cooper had a reputation as a superb technical actor possessing the physical ability to consistently hit his marks and perform repetitive action take after take. He was a real cowboy but also possessed expert comic timing. In *Mr. Deeds Goes to Town* (1936), he drops Douglass Dumbrille and three other men with a single punch! He had notable fights in *Saratoga Trunk* (1945), *Cloak and Dagger* (1946), *High Noon* (1952) and *Man of the West* (1958) (see entries). He had other fights of interest against William "Stage" Boyd in *The Spoilers* (1930), Henry Wilcoxon in *Souls at Sea* (1937), William Haade in *Sergeant York* (1941), Dana Andrews in *Ball of Fire* (1941), Warren Hymer in *Meet John Doe* (1941), Ray Teal and Lane Chandler in *Along Came Jones* (1945), Larry Chance in *Distant Drums* (1951), Lon Chaney in *Springfield Rifle* (1952), Cameron Mitchell in *Garden of Evil* (1954), Charlton Heston in *The Wreck of the Mary Deare* (1959) and Eric Portman in *The Naked Edge* (1959).

Forrest Tucker (left) and Gary Cooper stage one of the screen's dustiest fights in United Artists' *The Westerner* (1940).

See: "Forrest Tucker Talks of Hit." *New York Sun.* 1940; "90 Second Tussle Takes Nine Hours." *Detroit Free Press.* April 11, 1940.

THE CAFÉ FIGHT in *SEVEN SINNERS* (1940)

Seven Sinners was Universal's answer to Warner Bros.' *Dodge City* brawl. It employed over 30 stuntmen and took director Tay Garnett and first assistant Phil Karlson ten days to shoot the fistic acrobatics between sailors and waterfront thugs in a South Seas island café designed by art director Jack Otterson. Editor Ted Kent cut cameraman Rudolph Mate's footage together at a breakneck pace with Hans Salter and Frank Skinner's fitting score providing the background energy for the dizzying action. The *New York Times* called it "simply magnificent," while the *St. Petersburg Times* opined it was the "wildest brawl any camera has ever filmed." The *Los Angeles Times* wrote, "Practically the biggest café fight in history gives the production an action impact that is unrivaled," and *Commonweal* called it "a new high in slug fests." *Newsweek* said it offered "a screen high in mass mayhem" and *The Mercury* termed it "the most complete and thorough rough-and-tumble the screen has seen tis [*sic*] for many a long day." The *Hollywood Reporter* described it as "a tremendous climax which offers the wildest, most uproarious, spine-tingling, free-for-all brawl which ever has reached the screen." *USA Today* included it in the Top 10 all-time movie fights.

John Wayne starts the action by confidently taking on a dozen thugs before Broderick Crawford arrives with reinforcements. Even leading lady Marlene Dietrich throws a few punches. There's plenty of humor mixed in with the flying fists to keep things light and entertaining. Producer Joe Pasternak called it the best fight ever put on film and granted Garnett two extra days of production time. The mostly bloodless finished product lasts six minutes with stars Wayne, Crawford, Billy Gilbert, Mischa Auer and villain Oscar Homolka doing many of their own stunts. Crawford received a concussion after taking a flower pot over the head. Standing out among the heavies was 6'2", 215-pound Frank Hagney, who singles out Crawford for a one-on-one, then goes off a balcony with him. Hagney had been the Australian boxing champ and was a longtime sparring partner for heavyweight champ Jack Johnson.

Among the stunt aces working on the film were Dave Sharpe, Duke Green, Gil Perkins, Eddie Parker, Ken Terrell, Jimmy Fawcett, Tom Steele, Fred Graham,

Oscar Homolka (left) and John Wayne exchange haymakers in Universal's *Seven Sinners* (1940).

Harvey Parry, Eric Alden, Mike Lally, Bud Wolfe, Carey Loftin, Bobby Rose, Ted Billings, Loren Riebe, Louis Tomei, Harry Wilson, Chick Collins and Richard Talmadge. Even the director Garnett shows up as a drunken sailor who gets involved. The stuntmen were hurled over balconies, thrown through doors and windows, smashed into mirrors, tossed down stairs, slammed against walls and splayed on top of furniture. There were 24 tables broken, 72 chairs crushed, and a bar, a pool table, and a staircase demolished.

It was a virtual *tour de force* for Dave Sharpe as he showed up as six different characters in the fight. He and Jimmy Fawcett take a 25-foot balcony fall onto a table. He's catapulted ten feet through the air, landing on his belly on a low-hanging beam. Wayne smashes him through a door, flips him from a stage onto a breakaway table, and heaves him upside down into a wall of shelves. Sharpe even completes a stunt Duke Green began for Wayne, being jettisoned from a chandelier. Wayne's assigned double Eddie Parker wasn't considered good working at heights. Most of the stuntmen were under contract for $35 a day, but Sharpe was making an extra $250 per take for each of his spectacular leaps and falls. At the fight's conclusion, the audience must suspend disbelief at the comic sight of unconscious bodies literally hanging motionless from the Seven Sinners Cafe's rafters and light fixtures.

Broderick Crawford, a 240-pound six-footer, played football at the Dean Academy and dabbled as a professional fighter. He joined the U.S. Navy before embarking on an acting career. He re-upped during World War II and served as a combat instructor for the U.S. Army Air Force. Best known as the star of TV's *Highway Patrol* (1955–1959), he had a reputation as one of Hollywood's heaviest drinkers. Often he'd be approached by someone in a bar who wanted to see how tough he was. When the police came to break it up, Crawford tussled with them and made headlines. He had his nose broken seven times. The worst came in a Mexican cantina and involved a beer bottle smashing his beak. Most weekends Crawford brawled for fun with pal Lon Chaney, Jr. The two would as soon fight with each other as they would strangers.

Crawford was proud of his tough guy rep and enjoyed doing the bulk of his fights, even if others were wary of tangling with him. He rushed through dialogue and had a similar approach when it came to roughhousing with his fellow actors. Notable fights include *North to the Klondike* (1942), *Sin Town* (1942) and *Lone Star* (1952) (see entries). There were more fights of interest against Joel McCrea in *Woman Chases Man* (1937), Pat O'Brien in *Slightly Honorable* (1939), George Raft in *Broadway* (1942), Rod Cameron in *The Runaround* (1946), John Ireland in *Cargo to Capetown*

(1950), Neville Brand in *The Mob* (1951) and John Derek in *The Last Posse* (1953).

See: Krebs, Albin. "Broderick Crawford; Oscar-Winning Tough." *New York Times.* April 27, 1986; "Tay Garnett Sparing of Bloody Makeups." *Spokane Daily Chronicle.* October 15, 1940; "Thirty Stuntmen Used in Fight Scenes." *Los Angeles Times.* December 13, 1940.

VICTOR MATURE VS. BRUCE CABOT in *Captain Caution* (1940)

"A veritable melee of manliness" screamed the film's publicity as Victor Mature engages Bruce Cabot in a full minute of fierce hand-to-hand combat for the hand of leading lady Louise Platt.

Produced independently by Hal Roach and directed by Richard Wallace, the rollicking action film is set during the War of 1812 and pits not only the two principals against one another, but also a host of shipboard battles between British sailors and pirates using swords and cutlasses. Cabot gives a charismatic performance as the opportunistic villain who deems Mature's chin worthy of his fist. Richard Talmadge was stunt coordinator and second unit director with stuntmen Otto Metzetti, Victor Metzetti, Tom Metzetti, James Dime, Bud Geary, George Suzanne, Carl Mudge, William Sundholm, Jack Perry, Constantine Romanoff and Ethan Laidlaw doubling actors and filling out the ranks of the battling seamen. Mature also engages in a bare-knuckle boxing match with brutish professional wrestler Jules Strongbow.

The main fight took three days to film in 90 degree heat with Mature losing seven pounds and Cabot dropping five. Both men had boxing backgrounds, yet considered the struggle to be their most strenuous bout of endurance. Cabot suffered a two-inch gash on his scalp when he was hit by a belaying pin during the battle. The two fought all over the 200 feet of space on the *Olive Branch* ship for Norbert Brodine's camera. Thick synthetic fog blanketed the wet deck as the men struggled from port to starboard in a fight the *Pittsburgh Press* said "made the famous brawl in *The Spoilers* look like a game of patty-cake." The *Sydney Morning Herald* wrote, "Many fist fights have been seen on the screen but few to equal that between Captain Caution and Bruce Cabot."

Audiences took to the husky (6'3", 205-pound) Mature. who bared his beefy chest in film after film. Two of his most notable assignments came in the Biblical epics *Samson and Delilah* (1949)

and *Demetrius and the Gladiators* (1953) as the title strongmen. Mature fought in Golden Gloves tournaments as a youth and played a boxer in *Footlight Serenade* (1942). However, the U.S. Coast Guard veteran was quick to hand over the more strenuous activities to his stunt doubles throughout his Hollywood career. Mature fought Brad Dexter in *The Las Vegas Story* (1952), Don Haggerty and Karl Davis in *Gambling House* (1952), Vincent Price in *Dangerous Mission* (1954) and Peter Whitney in *The Last Frontier* (1956).

See: "Daring Action Is Highlight of Big Epic of Sea." *Herald-Journal.* October 20, 1940; McKay, James. *The Films of Victor Mature.* Jefferson, NC: McFarland, 2013; "Movie Scrap Real Brawl!" *Pittsburgh Press.* July 7, 1940.

GEORGE RAFT VS. EDWARD G. ROBINSON in *Manpower* (1941)

Despite the participation of director Raoul Walsh, *Manpower* is a standard Warner Bros. melodrama about power linemen and the frictions that develop when a girl enters the story. It's more notorious for the real animosity existing between stars George Raft and Edward G. Robinson, which resulted in fisticuffs and newspaper headlines. Plenty of punch-ups punctuate the picture as the hot-headed Robinson takes swings at Ward Bond and John Kelly. Raft is cool and handy with his fists, willing to stick up for his friend whenever Robinson gets out of line over unsavory comments about his girlfriend Marlene Dietrich. Raft shows off his superior fighting skill in a nightclub brawl with Barton MacLane. He later takes on loudmouth Dick Wessel in a diner. Walsh, who debuted in films as a stuntman, especially enjoyed staging action and fights.

Inevitably the two leads come to blows over Dietrich in a climactic two-minute sequence atop a transformer in a driving rainstorm. The *New York Times* called the battle "suspenseful" and "titanic." Stuntmen Allen Pomeroy and Duke Green earn their pay for the elevated fight work (all done on a controlled studio set for cinematographer Ernest Haller's camera), commanding $800 apiece for the brawl. Buster Wiles doubled Alan Hale as a fellow lineman who tries to stop the wrench-swinging Robinson, who incorrectly believes Dietrich has been cheating on him with his friend Raft. Raft mostly defends himself and ultimately must try to save Robinson after the latter loses his footing and dangles perilously from the end of a safety belt.

Ralph Dawson's editing and Adolph Deutsch's score add to the suspense.

It's safe to say Robinson and Raft came from two different strata of society. The short, chunky Robinson was highly cultured in the arts and looked down on any type of physical activity, while Raft was a boxer with scant education and mob ties. Raft often felt he was spoken down to by Robinson and didn't take well to Robinson's many acting pointers. Dietrich created additional tension, entertaining both men socially during filming. At some point, tempers flared on Stage 11. Co-stars Bond and Hale pulled the men apart before Raft could do too much damage, but there were enough reporters present that day to get accounts and pictures to the public. It was the first fight Robinson had ever been in his life. For Raft, it was probably his first that week. Raft seemed to catch the most flak, and his career began to go downhill in the ensuing years. Years later the two actors made light of their feud at social functions to the delight of audiences.

Raft boxed professionally in an undistinguished career spanning 17 fights. He made more impact once he hit Hollywood, with one of his first screen fights coming against James Cagney in *Taxi!* (1932). He scored that same year playing Paul Muni's deadly bodyguard in the gangster classic *Scarface* (1932). Raft was quick to react with real punches when provoked and needed to be pulled apart from Wallace Beery while filming a fight in *The Bowery* (1933) (see entry). In 1943 he punched out Peter Lorre during the making of *Background to Danger* after Lorre blew smoke in his face during a scene. To stay in shape, Raft sparred regularly with Mushy Callahan, stuntman Joe Gray and middleweight contender Carmen Barth.

He had movie fights of interest against "Big Boy" Williams in *The Glass Key* (1935), Henry Fonda in *Spawn of the North* (1938), William Holden in *Invisible Stripes* (1939), Victor Jory in *I Stole a Million* (1940), James Cagney and Joe Downing in *Each Dawn I Die* (1939), William Haade in *They Drive By Night* (1941), Broderick Crawford in *Broadway* (1942), Bern Hoffman in *Nocturne* (1946), George Macready in *Johnny Allegro* (1949) and Robert Taylor in *Rogue Cop* (1954) (see entry).

See: "Allen Pomeroy." *Catholic Digest.* November 1947; "Fighting Is Film Motto for Raoul Walsh in *Manpower.*" *Montreal Gazette.* August 8, 1941; "Robinson & Raft Stage Impromptu Fight on Set." *Life.* May 12, 1941.

BRODERICK CRAWFORD vs. LON CHANEY in *North to the Klondike* (1942)

Significant weight gets thrown around in this climactic, nearly three-minute grunt-and-groaner, set in the Klondike but filmed on picturesque Big Bear, California, locations. Some feel it's one of the best rough'n'tumble fights ever put on film, and it's easy to see why. Man against man surrounded by dangerous elements is always enticing. Broderick Crawford and Lon Chaney were both large, heavy-framed men who elected to film as much without doubles as they could. They were aware this act would take work away from a pair of stuntmen, so they demanded that Universal pay their assigned doubles $75 apiece; the men would then take a seat to watch the actors do their own fight. Chaney takes wild bumps as he crashes onto tables and eats dirt hitting the ground. Both men take in smoke from a broken stove, and Crawford (in a close-up) is hit over the head with a bottle that left a real lump. The extended fight stretches from a saloon, onto the patio, off a bridge and into a creek before Crawford drags Chaney out. The stuntmen were used for the bit where they crash through the cabin window and likely the long shot of the two going off the bridge. Editor Ted Kent conceals their identities well. *Variety* labeled it "spectacular," while *Photoplay* called it "the best screen fight you've seen in many a day." The *Spokane Daily Chronicle* wrote, "It is doubtful if any battle since that memorable one in *The Spoilers* has surpassed this spectacularly bruising and mauling conflict between the two fist-flailing giants." *Western Clippings* honors it among their "great screen fights."

Universal had the stars coached by boxing expert Frankie Van in preparation for their screen confrontation, and improbable publicity emphasized that no punches were pulled. The fights were filmed first over four days; Crawford accidentally chipped one of Chaney's front teeth. Chaney elected to do the rest of his part with the imperfection, feeling it made his character appear nastier. Chaney knocked Crawford out for real when they were fighting in the water and Crawford's foot slipped, placing his jaw directly in the path of a Chaney blow. The impressive fight provides a rousing finish to director Erle C. Kenton's film. Crawford and Chaney also battled in *Badlands of Dakota* (1941), with Chaney again coming out the loser.

In real life, the participants were good friends and drinking buddies. Legend has it they once destroyed a dressing room when they became carried away tussling together. Between camera set-ups, they played a violent game of rock, paper, scissors in which the loser took a hard slap to the face. Wardrobe and makeup were constantly on their toes to cover the real blood shed by the stars. Personnel at Universal took to calling the duo "The Monsters" in regard to their behavior. Chaney famously portrayed the Wolf Man, the Frankenstein Monster, Dracula and the Mummy while at the studio, which might have contributed to his nickname. He and Crawford drank together at Foster's Bar and were the originators of the "Shin Kicking Club." They were also members (alongside John Wayne and Ward Bond) of the macho "Slap Club." Between drinks, the men would good-naturedly kick one another with cowboy boots. One thing the two had in common was the part of huge simpleton Lennie in *Of Mice and Men*. Crawford had scored on Broadway in the part, while Chaney played the part on film to critical acclaim.

Six-foot-two, 230-pound Chaney entered films as a stuntman and relished doing his own fight work. He claimed to have choreographed many of his own brawls although he had a reputation for becoming over-enthused and out of control in the heat of battle. Many actors were wary of working with him for fear he'd accidentally belt them. His best fights came against Tom Tyler in *Cheyenne Rides Again* (1937), Bob Steele in *Of Mice and Men* (1939), Claude Rains in *The Wolf Man* (1941), Marc Lawrence in *Eyes of the Underworld* (1942), Bela Lugosi in *Frankenstein Meets the Wolf Man* (1943), Randolph Scott in *Albuquerque* (1948), Lloyd Bridges in *16 Fathoms Deep* (1948), John Payne in *Captain China* (1950) (*see entry*), Gary Cooper in *Springfield Rifle* (1952) and Cornel Wilde in *Passion* (1954).

See: Chapman, John. "Looking at Hollywood." *Chicago Tribune*. October 17, 1941; Graham, Sheilah. "The Gadabout of Hollywood." *Milwaukee Journal*. May 16, 1943; "Hollywood Tough Guy Lon Chaney Likes Nothing Better Than Rough Fight Scene." *St. Petersburg Times*. June 19, 1949.

Broderick Crawford drops Lon Chaney, Jr., to the ground in Universal's *North to the Klondike* (1942).

Tyrone Power vs. George Sanders in *Son of Fury* (1942)

Reviewing this period piece about a young man seeking his birthright, *The New Yorker* noted that it contained "some of the meanest fist fights in a long time." *Variety* called the fights "among the best ever screened." Those are fair assessments as villain George Sanders hits star Tyrone Power as he takes off his coat. Early in the 20th Century-Fox film, dandy aristocrat Sanders teaches his nephew Power how to be a man by fighting dirty, then flogging him. Power toughens up while sailing the South Seas. At the end of the episodic costume picture, the two meet again and Power asks to continue his education. This time he's a match for the older man, and the two have a furious brawl all over Sanders' stateroom. They go over furniture, upend tables and smash mirrors. Sanders puts Power into a headlock and flings him onto a collapsing table. Power emerges triumphant as Sanders lies bloody and beaten at the one-minute mark. As Power slowly makes his way to the door, Sanders rallies and the incredible fight goes on for another 30 seconds, backed by Alfred Newman's dramatic score. This time Power puts Sanders out for good.

The fight took four days to film. The action was originally diagrammed by director John Cromwell, but the actors and stuntmen deviated and ended up having a more traditional "old school" brawl. Initially each faked punch was photographed individually with great precision by cinematographer Arthur C. Miller, which would have been a chore for editor Walter Thompson to cut back and forth. It's likely that approach would have been too disconcerting for the audience to absorb. The end product is largely the efforts of the stuntmen, giving the fight a proper feel for the set and surrounding props. Sanders' double Jack Stoney broke a hand in the fight. Sanders, an interscholastic heavyweight boxing champ at Brighton College, also has a bare-knuckle match with pro wrestler Louis Bacigalupi in a different part of the movie.

Power (six feet, 170 pounds) and Sanders (six-three, 215 pounds) appeared in several films together. They had fights in *The Black Swan* (1942) and *Solomon and Sheba* (1959), where U.S. Marine Corps pilot Power showcased his fencing skill to great effect. The latter fight had tragic consequences: It was cold in Madrid, Spain, when this swashbuckling duel scene was shot and Power became tired. He retreated to his dressing room where he died of a massive heart attack at age 44. Close friend Sanders was devastated, as were the rest of the cast and crew. Yul Brynner was brought in to take over Power's role (Power can still be spied in long shots in the finished film). Power's best fights came against Peter Graves in *The Long Gray Line* (1955) and Richard Egan in *Untamed* (1955).

See: Gill, Ted. "There's Art in Preserving Hero's Face in Film Fisticuffs." *The Sun.* January 25, 1942; Sanders, George. *Memoirs of a Professional Cad.* Metuchen, NJ: Scarecrow, 1992.

Kane Richmond vs. Ken Terrell and Duke Green in *Spy Smasher* (1942)

Republic Pictures' greatest action serial comes thanks to the sure-handed direction of William Witney, the competency of cameraman Reggie Lanning, the fast-paced editing of Tony Martinelli and Edward Todd, and the incredible fighting acrobatics of stuntman Dave Sharpe, who doubles star Kane Richmond as he takes on nefarious Nazis for 12 exciting chapters. Sharpe was heading the Republic stunt team and is matched especially well with stuntmen Ken Terrell and Duke Green. Terrell and Green fly and tumble in their fights nearly as incredibly as Sharpe, and the result is some of the greatest fights ever put onto film. With hats securely fastened to their heads to help conceal their identities, Witney's energetic stuntmen became legendary with their non-stop flying fists and judo throws. *Films in Review* called the fights "a spectacular achievement," and author William C. Cline wrote that the *Spy Smasher* fight choreography "set the standard for the remainder of the serial era."

It's amazing that these ballets of violence were performed on low budgets with minimum chance for retakes. The highlights are Sharpe's fight with Terrell in a tower and Sharpe's fight with Green on a lumber platform. Green makes a 20-foot staircase jump onto Sharpe, only to be jettisoned another 30 feet onto a table. Other stuntmen working fights on the film as henchmen or doubles include Tom Steele, Duke Taylor, John Daheim, Gil Perkins, Jimmy Fawcett, Bud Wolfe, Loren Riebe, Carey Loftin, Eddie Jauregui, Bert LeBaron, Louis Tomei, Bill Wilkus and Yakima Canutt. They are all at the top of their game. Cline wrote that this group "staged some of the most incredible rough and tumble brawls ever seen on the serial screen."

Director Witney became an important figure in the filming of action and kinetic fight scenes. An assistant and second unit director at Mascot in the early 1930s, he moved to Republic when they absorbed that outfit and became one of Hollywood's youngest directors with a solid reputation for efficiency and visual flair. His quick and able shooting style was perfectly suited to the fly-by-the-seat-of-the-pants Republic serials of the late 1930s, and he developed an innovative technique for handling fights. He studied Busby Berkeley musicals to see how the dance segments were broken apart and decided to do the same with his fights. All his varied camera shots were afforded two minutes of concentrated action before changing set-ups. His stuntmen (nicknamed "The Cousins") were given a rest and were able to go all-out for every brief series of punches instead of tiring during an extended routine which could become sloppy. Witney hated seeing stuntmen lose their place in front of the camera or begin looking for someone to hit as a long fight progressed. Now they had time and energy to perfect their moves.

Witney looked for another edge as he regularly under-cranked the camera to 22 frames per second. When it was played back at the normal speed of 24 frames per second, it made the combatants and their punches look amazingly quick. Sometimes this method was a safety precaution as well. If the stuntmen were in a dangerous location, they could slow their movements down so as not to lose their footing. When the sped-up fight action was combined with Mort Glickman's relentlessly driving score ("V for Victory" from Beethoven's 5th Symphony), it produced edge-of-the-seat excitement for young Saturday matinee audiences.

See: Cline, William C. Serials-ly Speaking: Essays on Cliffhangers. Jefferson, NC: McFarland, 2000; Nevins, Francis M. "Ballet of Violence: The Films of William Witney." Films in Review. November 1974.

JOHN WAYNE vs. RANDOLPH SCOTT in The Spoilers (1942)

Nothing like this magnificent battle had been seen on screen before, and The Spoilers set the benchmark for every two-man fight that came after it. The Hollywood Reporter called previous versions of the fight "prelims by comparison to the bruising punishment John Wayne and Randolph Scott inflict on each other." The Los Angeles Times termed it "spectacular" while the New York Times called it

"a lulu." Time labeled it "a beaut." Newsweek said it was "a brawl guaranteed to give even Joe Louis the fainting vapors," and the Ottawa Citizen anointed it "the greatest slugfest in movie history." The Daily News wrote, "It puts to shame any fight you've ever seen anywhere at any time between two mad men and is the film's redeeming feature." Stage Combat calls it "a truly great example of the barroom brawl," while Legendary Westerns ranks it one of the top screen fights. The Best of Universal calls it "a true classic of well-choreographed, extended barroom brawling that has never been equaled." Action Films ranks it among the best fights ever, as does USA Today. The Manly Movie Guide says it is "one of the most celebrated fistfights in film history," and The Big Damn Book of Sheer Manliness calls it "a mythic match-up." It remains one of the all-time greats, both in technical ambition and big star gusto. Wayne and Scott slug away for over five exhausting minutes, battering one another into bloody, ripped-shirt pulps. Wayne is knocked down a total of 30 times, while Scott hits the floor 31 times. It's been reported there was animosity existing between the stars, and not all the punches were pulled.

Six-three and 190 pounds, Randolph Scott was career-savvy and originally wanted the leading role of Glennister. Co-star Marlene Dietrich, who was having an affair with Wayne, intervened on Wayne's behalf with the studio to land him the more heroic role. Veteran cowboy star Scott was unaccustomed to playing villainy and managed to negotiate second billing behind Dietrich. Wayne is incredibly billed third, and his pride was hurting over that. Both men were in real pain by the time the fight concluded. Wayne could sometimes get carried away with the intensity of his on-screen fighting and connected with too many blows. Scott responded in kind when Wayne began throwing his weight around. In at least one take, the fight briefly turned real before they could be separated by the nearly 30 stuntmen comprising the crowd. Both men suffered cuts and contusions, and Scott injured a hip when Wayne knocked him into a prop. The biggest blow proved to be a Scott punch that damaged Wayne's nose. Wayne was upset over this contact. Except for the scripted dialogue in their immediate follow-up Pittsburgh (1942), Wayne wouldn't speak to Scott again for another decade. The two made amends in the 1950s.

The Lawrence Hazard–scripted action begins in a hotel bedroom where the two have words over Dietrich, spills onto the hallway balcony, and hits every nook and cranny of the giant Northern Saloon set designed by Oscar-nominated art director Jack Otterson before crashing through a window and finishing on the muddy streets of Nome. The fight took five days to film on the Universal lot and involved an unheard-of 15 cameras and a seven-ton crane. It's one of the first times actors throw punches directly into the camera for effect. Director Ray Enright let noted second unit specialist "Breezy" Eason handle much of the action with Clarence Kolster cutting it together at an especially fast pace to maintain continuity and keep the lengthy battle interesting for the viewer. Hans J. Salter provided the enthusiastic musical backing in post-production. Sound director Bernard Brown's effects also merit special mention. From top to bottom, it's a fine collective achievement.

Throughout the fight, it's mostly Wayne and Scott battling away. Doubles Eddie Parker and Allen Pomeroy are apparent in long shots and in the more daring stunts. These include a banister leap, a stair fall, tumbles onto and over the bar, and crashing through glass. They are visible for an extended period during the ambitious crane shot when a stovepipe is knocked loose and falls onto the combatants. Stand-in Jack Parker and stuntman Gil Perkins also stepped in for Scott. Eddie Parker and Pomeroy mapped out the master plan for the fight, but rushes showed some footage to be overly speeded-up by Milton Krasner's camera. It had to be reshot. Eddie Parker was, however, off on another assignment so Pomeroy ran through

the fight again with Wayne for the inserts that replaced the unusable footage. The main stuntmen were paid $150 a day, over five times the basic rate. The original (1914) version of the *Spoilers* fight cost $5000 to film and was shot in 60 minutes. The Wayne-Scott version cost ten times that money.

See: Chapman, John. "Looking at Hollywood." *Chicago Tribune*. February 21, 1942; "Film Fight Makes Cinema History." *Dayton Review*. August 5, 1943; *The Spoilers* pressbook; Wagoner, Ronald W. "Death Recalls Most Fervid Film Battle." *Berkeley Daily Gazette*. April 11, 1931.

RICHARD ARLEN VS. BUSTER CRABBE in *Wildcat* (1942)

Hollywood stuntmen once voted former amateur boxer Richard Arlen the best puncher in the movie business, having logged 200 fake fights for the camera against such foes as Buddy Rogers in *Wings* (1927), William "Stage" Boyd in *Gun Smoke* (1931), Bruce Cabot in *Let 'em Have It* (1935) and Reed Hadley in *The Return of Wildfire* (1948). The fistic champion of filmdom received fan letters urging him to take on heavyweight Joe Louis in a real bout. However, Arlen broke both his hands punching to contact in silent films and was smart enough to avoid getting into the ring with a pro. In director Frank McDonald's low-budget *Wildcat*, the 5'11", 170-pound Arlen is paired against a 185-pound six-footer, Buster Crabbe. The latter was a local boxing champion while a teenager in Hawaii so throwing punches came easily to both men. In this story, con man Arlen enters the oil business only to meet his match in female lead Arline Judge as he tries to go straight. Crabbe shows up as his rival and the two have a lively 90-second exchange of haymakers that Hollywood columnist Erskine Johnson called "one of the most realistic in movie fight history."

William Ziegler's editing is choppy, but the stars are commended for doing all their own stunts. They fling coffee pots and chairs, go over tables, pound one another against the side of a building, and roll in the dirt with little regard for keeping their profiles fresh for Fred Jackman, Jr.'s camera. Arlen later said he considered actors

Randolph Scott (left) and John Wayne stage one of the screen's most famous fights in Universal's *The Spoilers* (1942)

who didn't do their own fights to be sissies. The action-packed quickie is over in under 70 minutes, so the fight registers strongly. *Wildcat* was produced for Paramount by the frugal team of Bill Pine and Bill Thomas. They were known as "The Dollar Bills." Showing up on the set, they were dismayed to find the stars rehearsing their fight for 20 minutes of production time with no cameras rolling. Pine half-jokingly suggested Arlen should knock over a light and they could film 500 feet of dark film and simply add sound effects.

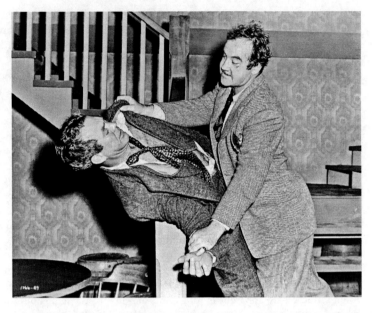

Ward Bond (left) and Broderick Crawford put on a furious fight in Universal's *Sin Town* (1942).

Multi-sport athlete Crabbe excelled at the University of Hawaii before transferring to USC so he could train for the Olympics in swimming. At the 1932 Los Angeles Olympic Games, he took Gold. Crabbe entered films as a stuntman but was soon starring in popular serials as Tarzan, Flash Gordon and Buck Rogers. These typed him, and he languished in B-westerns throughout the 1940s staging countless fights with Glenn Strange, Charlie King, Jack Ingram, Kermit Maynard, Frank McCarroll and John Cason. Crabbe's best battles came against Randolph Scott in *To the Last Man* (1933), Gene Autry in *Colorado Sunset* (1939) and Johnny Weissmuller in *Swamp Fire* (1946) and *Captive Girl* (1950).

See: "Best Film Puncher Title Goes to Arlen." *Pittsburgh Post-Gazette*. June 8, 1942; Coons, Robin. "Cut-Rate Duo Finds Success in Quick Style." *Port Arthur News*. March 1, 1942; Johnson, Erskine. "Screen Chats." *Shamokin News Dispatch*. December 18, 1943; Vermilye, Jerry. *Buster Crabbe: A Biofilmography*. Jefferson, NC: McFarland, 2008.

BRODERICK CRAWFORD VS. WARD BOND in *Sin Town* (1942)

Coming fast on the heels of *The Spoilers* was another slam-bang western fight that, despite its minute-and-a-half brevity, was even more relentlessly violent. Universal publicity termed it "the most vicious second-for-second fistic melee of all time." The *New York Times* called it "undoubtedly the most hectic cinema donnybrook since *The Spoilers*," while *Variety* labeled it "a dilly of a rough and tumble battle." *The Showmen's Trade Review* announced, "There's a brawl between Brod Crawford and Ward Bond that runs the famous one in *The Spoilers* a close second," and *Universal Sound Westerns* terms it "an impressive knockdown, drag-out fistfight." *Western Clippings* includes it on their list of great screen fights.

The 1910 oil boom story made use of *Spoilers* director Ray Enright, who filmed the crushing action with three of D.P. George Robinson's cameras running simultaneously. The entire fight between anti-hero Crawford and bad guy Bond was allegedly done in one take barely lasting more than 20 seconds. Enright was so concerned about the safety of his actors that he stopped filming. He reasoned that with the multiple cameras, he had more than enough footage for Edward Curtiss to piece together a usable fight. Any further takes would have endangered his actors, who were too wound up for their own good. They appear to be doubled for the climactic fall from a stairwell onto a poker table. The action demolished art director Jack Otterson's parlor set. The men landed together in a corner of the bar with several chairs, overturned tables and a splintered three-walled booth left in the wake of their destruction. Interestingly, it's Bond who emerges as the fight's winner in this cheaters cheat cheaters tale. Many years later, the fight was referenced in *A Little Romance* (1979) with Crawford playing himself and recalling the movie in which he punched Ward Bond in the gut.

Ward Bond, a six-foot-three 220-pounder, played football at USC and dabbled in amateur boxing. One of his first movie assignments was taking a punch from Spencer Tracy in *Up the River* (1930). A larger-than-life presence, he excelled at playing exaggerated brutes and was often called upon to provide powerful fighting skills against Buck Jones and Ken Maynard in B-westerns. The boisterous Bond was best friends with John Wayne and a John Ford stock player who found his way into many classic films. In the 1940s, a badly broken leg severely hindered his mobility. Even then, he held a reputation as a good fight man and remained a top name when it came to being a screen heavy. Bond loved doing fight scenes because he felt as an actor it gave him a wonderful opportunity to react in a scene. He became a TV star on the early days of *Wagon Train* (1957–1960) and on publicity tours staged fights for audiences with stuntman Lennie Geer.

Notable fights include *Dodge City* (1939), *Gentleman Jim* (1942), *Tall in the Saddle* (1944) and *Canyon Passage* (1946) (see entries). Fights of interest came against Buck Jones in *The Sundown Rider* (1933), *Fighting Ranger* (1934) and *The Crimson Trail* (1935), Ken Maynard in *Western Courage* (1935) and *Cattle Thief* (1936), Barton MacLane in *Prison Break* (1938), John Garfield in *Dust Be My Destiny* (1939), John Wayne in *The Shepherd of the Hills* (1941), Dana Andrews in *Swamp Water* (1941), James Cagney in *Kiss Tomorrow Goodbye* (1950), Robert Ryan in *On Dangerous Ground* (1951), Fred MacMurray in *The Moonlighter* (1953) and Lee Van Cleef in *Gypsy Colt* (1954). He took part in a bar brawl alongside Gary Cooper in *Sergeant York* (1941). Bond was Captain Flagg to Pat O'Brien's Sgt. Quirt in John Ford's 1949 stage version of *What Price Glory*.

See: "Fight Biggest Feature of *Sin Town*." *St. Petersburg Times*. December 24, 1942; "Movies Held Over for Shows Today." *Herald Journal*. January 2, 1943; "The Old Wagonmaster Gets Rolling." *TV Guide*. April 11, 1959.

JOHN WAYNE VS. ALBERT DEKKER in *In Old California* (1942)

Between their monumental brawls in this film and the following year's *In Old Oklahoma* (1943), it seemed John Wayne and Albert Dekker were poised to fight it out in every state of the union for Republic Pictures. The two-minute western saloon brawl here is a show-stopper, but ultimately fails to live up to the legend that the *Spoilers* fight was becoming. The Duke is cast as a discredited Sacramento pharmacist who can bend a silver dollar between his fingers. He butts heads with crooked saloon keeper Dekker in an effort to make the latter admit to his wrongdoing in framing him. Dekker is motivated to fight by the attention his girl Binnie Barnes has shown toward Wayne. Great punches are thrown with plenty of furniture broken, including a chair onto Dekker's unidentified stunt double. This was the first film in which Fred Graham doubled Wayne, and he takes a great fall with Dekker's double off a balcony into a piano. The *Seattle Daily Times* called it "a devastating barroom brawl." William C. McGann directed with Jack Marta behind the camera.

There were real political overtones in the match-up between Wayne and the 6'3", 240-pound Dekker, a former amateur boxer and football player for Bowdoin College. Wayne was developing his sense of Republican ideas while Dekker was a die-hard and vocal Democrat. He'd serve as a Democratic assemblyman for the state of California from 1945 to 1946. Dekker came dangerously close to blows with Wayne's pal Ward Bond while making the 1949 stage version of *What Price Glory*. No doubt Wayne and Dekker relished the opportunity to roughhouse with one another. Dekker fought Clark Gable in *Strange Cargo* (1940) and *Honky Tonk* (1941), Joel McCrea in *Reaching for the Sun* (1941), Robert Preston in *Wake Island* (1942) and Bill Elliott in *Wyoming* (1947) (see entry).

Stuntman Fred Graham doubled John Wayne throughout the 1940s and was nicknamed "Slugger" for his fight prowess. Action director William Witney called Graham the best when it came to screen brawling, and B-western writer Boyd Magers named him "one of the greatest 'fight' men ever in the film business." Graham would emerge from B-western bits into small character heavies requiring him to punch it out with the stars. He'd say a few lines and slug away. In this capacity, he had memorable battles against Humphrey Bogart in *Passage to Marseille* (1944), Robert Preston in *Tulsa* (1949), Robert Ryan in *The Woman on Pier 13* (aka *I Married a Communist*) (1949), Joel McCrea in *The San Francisco Story* (1952), Arthur Kennedy in *Rancho Notorious* (1952), Rod Cameron in *Fort Osage* (1952) and Jock Mahoney in *Overland Pacific* (1954). Graham's presence in a brawl as actor or double enlivened the proceedings and always added a sense of professional polish.

See: Andrews, Bart. "Fred Graham: Super Stuntman." *Falling for Stars*. Vol. 1 #7. September–October 1965; Sherman, Sam. "Albert Dekker Rides." *Wildest Westerns*. #6. August 1961.

ERROL FLYNN VS. SAMMY STEIN in *Gentleman Jim* (1942)

Errol Flynn is perfectly cast as 1890s heavyweight champion Gentleman Jim Corbett, the bridge between old-style bare-knuckle brawlers and gloved scientific boxers who utilized footwork and jabs under the new Marquess of Queensberry rules. A cocky up-and-comer, Corbett has his eyes set on legendary champ John L. Sullivan (Ward Bond) but must first make a name for himself as he rises up through the ranks in sometimes unsanctioned bouts. The highlight of Raoul Walsh's entertaining film is an illegal wharf bout on a barge against the fearsome Joe Choynski (Sammy Stein), a bruiser who beat Corbett when they were younger. Choynski's manager throws his gloves into the bay and outfits him with illegal mitts he guarantees will cut Corbett. Makeup artist Perc Westmore applied the blood and bruising. The five-minute battle features knockdown after knockdown and a spill into the bay before Choynski goes down for the count. The police arrive to roust the crowd, who begin jumping into the water to escape.

Cinematographer Sid Hickox shot the wharf action utilizing five cameras on an expansive Warner Bros. soundstage created by art director Ted Smith. The *Sea Wolf* ship is moored in the background with a huge tank of water the size of a football field simulating San Francisco Bay. Technical advisor Mushy Callahan trained Flynn for six weeks before filming and had him perfect Corbett's signature left jab. Despite his pugilistic skill, Flynn was prevented from serving in the military during World War II because of a diagnosed "Athlete's Heart." He was allowed to film the boxing sequences for a minute at a time and claimed to have suffered a mild heart attack while making this film. Because of the star's physical restrictions, Freddie Steele, a middleweight champ reputed to be one of the era's hardest punchers, stood in for him in the long shots. Close-ups of Corbett's footwork were of Callahan's feet. Sammy Stein connected with the punch that sent Flynn's stuntman Paul Stader into the water. An angry Stader climbed back into the ring and began connecting with his own punches until Walsh said "Cut!" The six-foot, 205-pound Stein, a professional wrestler and football player, appeared in 40-odd films, always as wrestlers or tough mugs.

The climactic boxing match with Bond's Sullivan in New Orleans was shot on Stage 22 with 500 extras in attendance. Steele once again doubled in long shots with pro wrestler Ed "Strangler" Lewis doubling Bond. Lewis also appears as a bare-knuckle fighter. Wrestlers and boxers Frank Sexton, Frank Hagney, Mike Mazurki, Jack Roper, Wee Willie Davis, Pat McKee, Jack Herrick and Frank Moran have bit parts, as does Art Foster as English boxer Jack Burke. Walsh cast them because their bulky physiques best resembled the old-time bare-knuckle boxers. Pro boxer Roper had fought Flynn in *The Perfect Specimen* (1938). He knocked Flynn out more than once during sparring sessions, even leaving the star unconscious for over two hours. When Roper became too docile in the ring for fear of hurting Flynn, the star whacked Roper between the legs to raise his dander. Roper promptly knocked Flynn out again on instinct. Flynn wears Bond

Sammy Stein takes a punch from Errol Flynn during their wild wharf fight in Warner Bros.' *Gentleman Jim* (1942).

down after 21 rounds and captures the championship, ushering in a new era in boxing. There's an especially well-acted scene between the two men when Bond hands over the championship and Flynn acknowledges the legendary fighter. Ironically, Corbett is shown to come from a family of brawlers. A running gag has him going bare-knuckled against his husky brothers Pat Flaherty and James Flavin while pop Alan Hale referees and onlookers declare, "The Corbetts are at it again!"

Variety called all the fight scenes "excellent" while *Magill's Survey of Cinema* announced, "The fights in *Gentleman Jim* are beautifully choreographed instead of being gory contests of survival; they are like fencing matches with skillful feinting, parrying, and riposting." The *New York Times* called the film "a fight fan's delight," while *Newsweek* wrote, "Raoul Walsh stages the frequent fight sequences for all their potential excitement and with genuine appreciation for the footwork, brainwork, and jolting left hook that made Corbett one of the greatest fighters in boxing history."

Six-foot-two, 190-pound Flynn, an amateur boxer in New South Wales, claimed *Gentleman Jim* was his own favorite film. The charismatic Flynn's penchant for fisticuffs was well known around Hollywood, as was his engaging personality. It wasn't uncommon for Flynn to come to blows with a perceived rival and soon be sharing drinks with his new pal. Flynn didn't always win his fights. He lost a bare-knuckle brawl with Victor Jory at a fancy Hollywood party and was dropped by Olympic medal winner Jim Thorpe in a bar. Both men became close friends with the actor. Flynn's most legendary fight came against director John Huston in David O. Selznick's garden in 1945. The lengthy brawl over actress Olivia de Havilland lasted anywhere from ten minutes to an entire hour. It made all the trades as Flynn broke Huston's nose and three of his ribs, requiring overnight hospitalization and several stitches for both men.

As a screen fighter, Flynn was polished and poised, displaying an uncommon grace of movement for a big man. In addition to his boxing background, he had judo training with Sego Murakami and extensive fencing instruction with Fred Cavens, Ralph Faulkner, Paddy Crean and Bob Anderson. Most of the swashbuckling Flynn's notable film confrontations came with an epee or sword in hand in classics such as *Captain Blood* (1935), *The Adventures of Robin Hood* (1938) and *The Sea Hawk* (1940). He had fistfights of interest against Barton MacLane in *The Prince and the Pau-*per (1937) and *Silver River* (1948), Douglas Fowley in *Dodge City* (1939) (see entry), Van Heflin in *Santa Fe Trail* (1940), Arthur Kennedy in *They Died with Their Boots On* (1941), Craig Stevens in *Dive Bomber* (1941), Paul Kelly in *San Antonio* (1945), Ian MacDonald in *Montana* (1950), Raymond Burr and Howard Chuman in *Mara, Maru* (1952), Michael Ross in *Against All Flags* (1952) and John Dennis in *Too Much, Too Soon* (1958).

See: Gronsky, Norman K. *Let's Feel the Wind While We May: An Oral History of People Who Knew Errol Flynn.* Soho, 2011; "Wrestlers Are the Best Movie Fighters." *The Milwaukee Journal.* August 23, 1942.

GEORGE BRENT VS. BRUCE CABOT in *Silver Queen* (1942)

George Brent (6'1", 185 pounds) and Bruce Cabot (6'1", 200 pounds) fight over Nevada City mining rights and gambling debts incurred by society gal Priscilla Lane. It's a standard western from director Lloyd Bacon that did garner Oscar nominations for Victor Young's score and the set decoration of Ralph Berger and Emile Kuri. Cameraman Russell Harlan shot the fight, and Sherman Rose cut the action together. The film's publicists compared this climactic brawl to the real epic bare-knuckle battle between John L. Sullivan and Jake Kilrain.

This is far from an organized affair, as the combatants break saloon chairs, tables and glassware in their effort to emerge victorious. Both actors incurred minor injuries. The *Los Angeles Times* wrote of the fight, "Like the recent one in *The Spoilers*, [it's] full of sound if not fury," while *The Milwaukee Sentinel* said that the fight "rivals the memorable bout in *The Spoilers.*" The *Schenectady Gazette* offered, "The best thing in the film is the final battle of fisticuffs between Cabot and Brent, a battle staged as redundantly as everything else in the production, but played with ardor and abandon and wholly satisfying to watch."

Cabot played football at the University of the South, worked as a sparring partner in the squared circle, and was a bouncer at the Coconut Grove Bar before starring in the adventure classic *King Kong* (1933) where he did many of his own stunts. Most of his career was spent as a sinister screen-villain, with time out during World War II to serve with Army Intelligence. Cabot was a drinking crony of both John Wayne and Errol Flynn and had a reputation as a man who could be quick with his fists. He and Flynn occasionally came to blows even when they were close friends. Cabot was still throwing movie punches over 25 years later.

Notable fights include *Dodge City* (1939), *Captain Caution* (1940), *Hellfighters* (1968), and *The Undefeated* (1969) (see entries). Other fights of interest came against Richard Arlen in *Let 'em Have It* (1935), Robert Barrat in *The Last of the Mohicans* (1936), Glenn Ford in *My Son Is Guilty* (1939), Marc Lawrence in *Homicide Bureau* (1939), John Carroll in *Pierre of the Plains* (1942), Charles Bickford in *Fallen Angel* (1945), Fred MacMurray in *Smoky* (1946), Bill Elliott in *The Gallant Legion* (1948), Forrest Tucker in *Rock Island Trail* (1950) and Dale Robertson in *Law of the Lawless* (1964).

See: Parish, James Robert, and William T. Leonard. *Hollywood Players, the Thirties.* New Rochelle, New York: Arlington, 1976; "*Silver Queen* Here This Week." *Deer Park Union.* June 6, 1943.

RANDOLPH SCOTT VS. JOHN WAYNE in *Pittsburgh* (1942)

Following the success of *The Spoilers*, Universal again teamed Marlene Dietrich, Randolph Scott and John Wayne for director Lewis Seiler's modern Pennsylvania mining tale. The catch is that Wayne is the good guy who has turned bad with enterprising greed, and it's a role his fans didn't care for. Screenwriter Kenneth Gamet does a fine job building tension between the male friends over Dietrich until the inevitable climax. The highlight is another lengthy battle between Scott and Wayne in a darkened mine shaft, but it falls short of *The Spoilers'* lofty standards because of the limitations of the claustrophobic setting. Scott biographer Robert Nott writes, "The fight will forever be compared to the one in *The Spoilers*, which is both unfortunate and accurate. It's not a bad fight." The brawl is now remembered as one of the few fights Wayne lost. Consider it Scott's revenge for taking such a beating in *The Spoilers*. Ace stuntmen Allen Pomeroy and Eddie Parker returned to double the stars, with Gil Perkins and Fred Graham pitching in. The moment when Pomeroy swings a shovel into a pillar and the blade goes flying over a ducking Parker's head is perhaps the most expertly timed and dangerous-looking stunt ever captured on film.

In the three-minute showcase, there's a plethora of head-snapping punches and some nearly homicidal actions. The *Richmond Times Dispatch* called it "a classic for unbridled viciousness." Scott swings a mean-spirited shovel, and Wayne tries to crush him with chunks of coal as they forget they were good-humored friends at the film's beginning. The best moment occurs as they battle on an open elevator rising to the surface. Wayne falls back and a wooden fence is broken, crushed against the side of the jutting wall of rock rapidly flying by Robert De Grasse's camera. A moment later, Wayne is nearly decapitated but he moves away in the nick of time. The segment is excitingly edited by Paul Landres and backed by Hans Salter's suspenseful score. Scott gets the better of Wayne in the fight. Dietrich is injured in a descending elevator, and the men come to their senses. The *Washington Evening Post* declared, "The movie would have been nigh ridiculous if blasting fists had not been written generously into the script."

Universal publicity played up the fight, describing it as "a terrific fistic battle" and "one of the most violent fistfights ever staged for the screen." Scott initiated one blow that knocked Wayne back so hard the latter lost his balance and stumbled into Dietrich, knocking them both over and leaving her with real bruises. Still upset over the busted nose he suffered in the *Spoilers* fight, Wayne went on record as saying he didn't think Scott was much of an actor. Scott responded by calling Wayne uncouth and ungentlemanly. Wayne didn't care for losing a screen fight now that he was creating his popular screen image. He wouldn't even let his own children see him in this role.

A Southern gentleman, Scott carried himself with dignity and came away from his lengthy Hollywood career a legendary cowboy star. He served his country with the 2nd Trench Mortar Battalion during World War I. He had ambitions of playing professional football but was injured on the field at the Georgia Institute of Technology. The notoriously reclusive Scott was at home in westerns and became a tight-lipped, slim-hipped stalwart of the genre. He starred in many early 1930s Zane Grey adaptations for director Henry Hathaway, where a stuntman wasn't always required. Scott was able to handle all the action demands. He kept in shape working with boxing trainer Mickey Cianci. Ironically, Scott claimed he had never been in a real-life fistfight. This didn't stop him from throwing some of the screen's most convincing punches. Scott brought a consistent emotional tone to his men of action. They were of strong moral fiber, stood their ground, and fought for what they believed in. Audiences embraced him.

Notable fights include *The Spoilers* (1942), *The Desperadoes* (1943), *Abilene Town* (1946), *Coroner Creek* (1948), *Return of the Bad Men* (1948), *Santa Fe* (1951), *Man in the Saddle* (1951), *Hangman's Knot* (1952), and *A Lawless Street* (1955) (see entries). Other fights of interest came against Fred Kohler in *Wild Horse Mesa* (1933), Noah Beery in *Man of the Forest* (1933), Buster Crabbe in *To the Last Man* (1933), "Big Boy" Williams in *Heritage of the Desert* (1933), Robert Barrat in *Village Tale* (1935), Charles Bickford in *High, Wide, and Handsome* (1937), Grant Withers in *The Gunfighters* (1947), Lon Chaney in *Albuquerque* (1948), Victor Jory in *Canadian Pacific* (1949), Frank Fenton in *The Doolins of Oklahoma* (1949), John Ireland in *The Walking Hills* (1949), Lou Nova, Gregg Barton and Michael Ross in *Fighting Man of the Plains* (1949), Jim Davis in *The Cariboo Trail* (1950), Forrest Tucker in *The Nevadan* (1950), David Brian in *Fort Worth* (1951), Mickey Simpson in *Carson City* (1952) and *Tall Man Riding* (1955), Lex Barker in *Thunder Over the Plains* (1953), Lee Marvin and Ernest Borgnine in *The Stranger Wore a Gun* (1953), Robert Keys in *The Bounty Hunter* (1954) and Leo Gordon in *Ten Wanted Men* (1955) and *7th Cavalry* (1956).

See: "Dietrich's Famous Legs Bruised in Fight Scene." *Omaha World Herald.* September 25, 1942; *Pittsburgh* pressbook.

WILLIAM BOYD VS. VICTOR JORY in *Hoppy Serves a Writ* (1943)

Perhaps the most enduringly popular of all the B-western characters was William Boyd's Hopalong Cassidy. Boyd made 66 films as the heroic black-suited do-gooder, and one of the staples of the series was a good old-fashioned fistfight. Boyd often matched up with character actor Victor Jory, whom he fought in *Wide Open Town* (1941), *Colt Comrades* (1943) and *Bar 20* (1943). Their best fight was in director George Archainbaud's *Hoppy Serves a Writ*, and it's arguably the best fisticuffs in the entire series. *Variety* called it "a lusty barroom fight," while the *New York Post* noted, "The hand-to-hand encounters find Boyd struggling through a vast and gratifying amount of shattered furniture." *Hollywood Corral* said the movie's highlight was "a bruising slugging session between Boyd and Victor Jory," and *Western Clippings* anoints it among their "great screen fights."

There's fine tension built between Boyd and Jory during a card game that sees Jory fold on a winning hand. When he discovers Boyd bluffed him with a pair of deuces, the fight is on.

Boyd and Jory go over tables and chairs and up a staircase for two minutes in a wild battle that makes fine use of many saloon props. The choreography is awkward, but the unrehearsed nature tends to make it more realistic. The men slip and slide with only the sound of their boots hitting the floor and fists hitting face audible on the soundtrack. Unfortunately, cinematographer Russell Harlan is unable to consistently get proper filming angles. A few obviously missed punches are scored as hits, and Boyd's stunt double (either Ted Wells or Frosty Royce) is all too apparent at key times. Jory does the entire fight and takes wild bumps. Robert Mitchum, making his film debut, is in the background watching the action as one of Jory's thugs.

The character of Hopalong Cassidy exemplified the ideal cowboy role model for children. He didn't drink or smoke and he didn't fight dirty when it came to taking on the bad guys. Differences were settled with words before fists and fists before guns. He never threw the first punch, but he nearly always threw the last as he tried to set filmdom's dark hearts on a righteous path. Young audiences wouldn't see Hoppy biting, kicking, scratching or eye-gouging. There would be no rabbit punches to the back of an opponent's neck, and when a bad guy hit the floor the fight was over in Hoppy's mind. It wasn't sporting to hit a fellow when he was down. It was akin to shooting someone in the back. Kids of the 1930s and '40s learned their morals from virtuous clean fighters and straight shooters such as Hopalong Cassidy, the Durango Kid, Gene Autry and Roy Rogers.

A 180-pound six-footer, Boyd toiled at several hard-scrabble jobs as a young man, among them lumberjack, miner and oil field worker. He became a star in Cecil B. DeMille silent films despite a head of prematurely whitened hair. Boyd was a good actor but wasn't an athlete or fond of horses. He was quick to let stunt doubles take over action scenes. Some fans complained that Boyd was borderline inept as a screen fighter, but that didn't stop him from being in a bunch of them. A handful were decent depending on the opponent and production value. Boyd didn't particularly like doing extended fights. He felt, because of his star status, that if he punched a bad guy once, it should be sufficient for them to stay on their back. Boyd fought

Alan Hale in *Skyscraper* (1927), Spencer Tracy in *Sky Devils* (1931), Addison Richards in *The Eagle's Brood* (1935), Morris Ankrum in *Pirates on Horseback* (1941), Tom Tyler in *Riders of the Timberline* (1941), Robert Mitchum in *False Colors* (1943) (see entry) and Douglass Dumbrille in *Lumberjack* (1944). He battled several stuntmen in *Santa Fe Marshal* (1940).

See: Agnew, Jeremy. *The Creation of the Cowboy Hero: Fiction, Film and Fact.* Jefferson, NC: McFarland, 2015; Nevins, Francis. *The Films of Hopalong Cassidy.* Waynesville, NC: World of Yesterday, 1988.

THE SALOON BRAWL in *The Desperadoes* (1943)

The saloon brawl is afforded a comic touch in Charles Vidor's *The Desperadoes*, Columbia's first Technicolor film. The *New York Times* called it "a straightaway sock-'em and shoot-'em western," but the *Los Angeles Times* recognized it as "one of the most hilarious barroom brawls ever staged." Randolph Scott and Glenn Ford star as friendly rivals, but Scott doesn't participate in the slugfest against bad guy Bernard Nedell and his accomplices Glenn Strange, Ethan Laidlaw and Slim Whitaker. Ford's buddy "Big Boy" Williams is given center stage as the most rambunctious fighter. He doles out head butts and cartoon-like fist poundings to any who get in his way. Bartender Billy Jones is the one who bears the brunt of "Big Boy"'s attacks.

Movie fight veteran Reed Howes is on hand as a waiter, and even Charlie King is supposedly in there somewhere. Nervous saloon keeper Irving Bacon gets the majority of laughs as he tries to save his liquor inventory with little success. A poker game continues unabated as fists fly and bottles smash all around. However, Ford and Nedell's fighting is serious throughout, like they're in a different movie as cut together by Gene Havlick.

Richard Talmadge served as the fight's technical director with Ford doing the majority of his own fighting for George Meehan's camera. Due to the war effort, such saloon brawl staples as balsa wood and resin glass were in high demand. Therefore the *Desperadoes* brawl employed real chairs and actual bottles and glasses, so the principal actors and stuntmen had to be extra careful when they were using props as weapons. Future western director Budd Boetticher was the assistant to Vidor, who demanded that Boetticher throw a chair into the melee. But the chair hit star Ford, and Boetticher was fired by Vidor. Williams threw a chair so hard at 6'5", 220-pound Glenn Strange that it stuck in the wall after sailing over his head. Vidor chastised Williams for damaging the set. Williams threatened with tongue-in-cheek to pick up a horse and throw it at Vidor if he didn't let up on his demands. Vidor wasn't about to test Williams' legendary strength. Williams suffered his first real injury doing a screen fight when he broke a rib in the tussle.

Ford, 5'11" and 165 pounds, was a Coast Guard veteran and served with the Marine Corps during World War II. He was one of the best horsemen in Hollywood, fast with a gun, and consistently put on a good fight. Half of his Hollywood films were westerns, and he was made an honorary member of the Stuntmen's Association. Ford worked closely with stunt doubles Robert "Buzz" Henry and Bill Hart so he could do the majority of his own screen fights for the camera. At MGM he worked out with boxing trainer Terry Robinson to keep his reflexes sharp. His characters were quick to throw a punch and carried themselves with a brash confidence, often displaying the hint of a smirk in

Bernard Nedell takes a beating from Glenn Ford in Columbia's *The Desperadoes* (1943).

knowing the damage they could do when under-estimated. On film, Ford's fists were always getting him into or out of trouble.

Fights of interest came against Bruce Cabot in *My Son Is Guilty* (1939), Ian MacDonald in *The Adventures of Martin Eden* (1942), Pat O'Brien in *Flight Lieutenant* (1942), Joe Sawyer in *Gilda* (1946), William Holden in *The Man from Colorado* (1948), John Ireland in *Mr. Soft Touch* (1949), Lloyd Bridges in *The White Tower* (1950), Victor Jory in *The Man from the Alamo* (1953), Sean McClory in *Plunder of the Sun* (1953), Chris Alcaide in *The Big Heat* (1953), Vic Morrow in *Blackboard Jungle* (1955), Mickey Shaughnessy in *The Sheepman* (1958), Charles McGraw in *Cimarron* (1960), Arthur Kennedy in *Day of the Evil Gun* (1968) and David Carradine in *Heaven with a Gun* (1969). He brawled alongside Henry Fonda in *The Rounders* (1965). As host of the 1979 TV special *When the West Was Fun,* Ford demonstrated in a saloon brawl how to break a chair over stuntman Jock Mahoney's back.

See: Ford, Peter. *Glenn Ford: A Life.* Madison:

University of Wisconsin Press, 2011; Marsh, W. Ward. "*Desperadoes* Goes to Utah for Real Background." *Plain Dealer.* March 21, 1943.

ROBERT RYAN VS. MIKE MAZURKI in *Behind the Rising Sun* (1943)

This propagandist film from director Edward Dmytryk is an early look at the debate of who'd prevail in a fight between a boxer and a martial artist. Judo represents the Japanese style of fighting while boxing represents the American way. The fight was based on an actual pre–World War II incident in which the American Naval boxer won. Lensed by esteemed cinematographer Russell Metty, the Robert Ryan–Mike Mazurki fight consumed nearly ten minutes of screen time, unheard-of at the time, with Ryan prevailing with a mighty knockout punch to Mazurki's jaw. The pro–Axis Argentinines were so impressed, they cut the fight out and ran it as a special short. *Time* called the fight "as savage as anything in the history of screen roughhouse," while *Motion Picture Daily*

American boxer Robert Ryan goes up against Japanese judoka Mike Mazurki (on floor) in RKO's *Behind the Rising Sun* (1943).

said it was "exciting and certainly different." The film's director proudly proclaimed it "a beautifully choreographed battle between two superior athletes." *Variety* called it "a rouser" and the *Pittsburgh Post-Gazette* wrote, "It is a grim, grisly affair, which makes that fabled encounter in *The Spoilers* look like a pink tea by comparison."

Sinewy 6'4", 190-pound Ryan, a college boxing champ, plays U.S. boxer Lefty O'Doyle. He is recruited by a serviceman pal on a bet to represent the Americans against towering judoka Mazurki. (Mazurki was a professional wrestler who looked little like a man of Japanese persuasion.) The two actors went all-out for three days of filming, with both dropping nearly ten pounds apiece through water loss under the hot lights. Since the RKO film required Ryan to wear boxing gloves, both men agreed to pull as few punches as possible. Mazurki largely used pulls, grabs, monkey flips, chops, kicks, eye gouges, arm-locks, bear-hugs and chokeholds while Ryan jabbed and body punched away at an opponent who outweighed him by nearly 50 pounds. Mazurki even uses the old-time pro wrestling airplane spin. The fight was done under the supervision of John Indrisano, a student of judo. Mazurki later commented that Ryan impressed him with his boxing ability. He felt Ryan was the lone actor who could have had a successful heavyweight boxing career. Ryan took pride in performing his own fights, He kept in lean shape with regular gym workouts and sparring. Many rank Ryan's on-screen boxing match with real boxer Hal Baylor in *The Set-Up* (1949) as one of the best choreographed ring fights committed to celluloid.

While studying at Dartmouth College, Ryan played football and won the National Collegiate Heavyweight Boxing Championship. He was undefeated in the ring but lost enthusiasm for athletics. His father talked him out of turning professional, convincing him that all boxers were washed up by the time they were 30. Ryan did, however, fight once professionally for money under an assumed name. Among the manly professions he toiled at during the Great Depression were sandhog, coal-stoking seaman, miner, cowboy, union bodyguard and loan collector. When World War II reached its zenith, Ryan enlisted in the Marines and became a drill instructor at Camp Pendleton. He was one of the big screen's most dependable character leads, appearing in such high-testosterone fare as *Bad Day at Black Rock* (1955), *The Professionals* (1966), *The Dirty Dozen* (1967) and *The Wild Bunch* (1969).

As a screen fighter, Ryan was a consummate pro who put in the required training time with the stuntmen to master a fight routine and its required footwork. They afforded him a tremendous amount of respect and were glad he kept his distance when doing fights. He had a reputation of being able to hit like a mule and could have done serious damage to anyone unfortunate enough to step in front of one of his punches. One of his first screen roles was boxing Richard Denning in *Golden Gloves* (1940), and Denning had to reportedly get x-rays, as he was convinced that Ryan's body punches had broken his ribs. Ryan once had a political argument during a dinner with John Wayne and invited his fellow actor to step outside to settle their differences. Wayne wanted no part of a real fight with Ryan and quickly made amends. Ryan's characters meant business, and he approached fight scenes with a dead seriousness that came across the screen.

Notable fights include *Return of the Bad Men* (1948), *City Beneath the Sea* (1953) and *Day of the Outlaw* (1959) (see entries). Fights of interest came against Harry Woods in *Trail Street* (1947), Charles Bickford in *The Woman on the Beach* (1947), Michael Harvey in *Berlin Express* (1948), Willard Parker in *The Secret Fury* (1950), Ward Bond in *On Dangerous Ground* (1951), Robert Preston in *Best of the Badmen* (1951), Raymond Burr and James Arness in *Horizons West* (1952), William Lundigan in *Inferno* (1953), Brian Keith in *Alaska Seas* (1954), Wayne Rogers in *Odds Against Tomorrow* (1959), Richard Burton in *Ice Palace* (1960) and Stewart Granger in *Crooked Road* (1965). On TV, Ryan fought Robert Fuller in the 1964 *Wagon Train* episode "The Bob Stuart Story." Ryan's skill at screen fights came in handy for co-star Montgomery Clift's fight with Mike Kellin in *Lonelyhearts* (1958). Clift, dealing with a myriad of emotional and chemical problems, accidentally hit Kellin and became so distraught that he was unable to finish the scene. Ryan stepped in as Clift's stuntman, donning his shirt and jacket to throw the necessary punch at Kellin for the cameras.

See: "Plenty Fight in Movie Set-To." *Baltimore Sun.* May 30, 1943.

WILLIAM BOYD VS. ROBERT MITCHUM in *False Colors* (1943)

Hollywood's favorite symbol of virtuosity Hopalong Cassidy takes on notorious bad boy Robert

Mitchum in a one-minute slugfest in director George Archainbaud's *False Colors*. Boyd comes to the aid of sidekick Andy Clyde, whom bully Mitchum has in a nose-lock for taking too close an interest in his card game. It's a one-sided fight as Boyd knocks Mitchum all over a saloon and sends him over the bar a bloodied and embarrassed mess. Russell Harlan gets in on the action with his camera so the audience can feel the blows. Mitchum does the entire fight without the aid of a double, erroneously thinking that only the star merited the benefit of a stuntman. Boyd uses Ted Wells or Frosty Royce for the long shots. Archainbaud was blessed with the vision to edit

William Boyd's Hopalong Cassidy puts a hurt on bad guy Robert Mitchum in United Artists' *False Colors* (1943).

in-camera as he filmed so the fight footage was nearly complete by the time it reached post-production. Boyd fights bad guy banker Douglass Dumbrille to climax the film, and in a couple of brief glimpses it looks like it may even be Mitchum taking the falls for Dumbrille.

Broad-shouldered and barrel-chested, the 6'1", 205-pound Mitchum epitomized cool as a sleepy-eyed film noir tough guy. He gave off a vibe of reluctance to undertake any action called upon, yet he was a natural athlete who looked smooth and effortless in all physical activity. His varied background laid the foundation for a powerful physique and handy athleticism. He had tramped across the country as a teen and tried his hand at being a longshoreman, stevedore, quarry worker, ditch digger, bar bouncer and tank town boxer who brawled his way through more than 20 loosely organized bouts. By 1942–1943 he was replacing a dead stuntman in the Hoppy series. Naturally he was expected to learn the art of screen fighting to earn his pay. Boyd and Mitchum also tangled in *Hoppy Serves a Writ* (1943), *Colt Comrades* (1943) and *Riders of the Deadline* (1943). Another physical role that attracted early attention came as a Marine Raider taking on the Japanese in fierce hand-to-hand combat in *Gung Ho!* (1943).

Mitchum was a legendary drinker and marijuana smoker. A photographic memory allowed

him to keep odd hours and still arrive on the set knowing his lines and technical cues. He had tremendous screen presence and the know-how to mimic the way real punches were thrown depending on the scenario. He had vast experience to draw from. He sometimes landed in saloon scrapes, where he emerged victorious because of a penchant for not fighting by any set of pre-established rules. The Hollywood Stuntmen's Association voted him the actor they'd most like on their side in a barroom brawl. In the early 1950s, Mitchum broke the jaw of heavyweight boxing contender Bernie Reynolds in a bar fight. In the late 1950s, he bested a trio of Marines in a Caribbean brawl. In Ireland, he cleaned out a pub with fellow actor Richard Harris. The fisticuffs all became part of Mitchum lore. On screen, Mitchum throttled Frank Sinatra in *Not as a Stranger* (1955) and unleashed a vicious karate chop to Jacques Aubuchon's face in *Thunder Road* (1958), giving an indication to the type of unconventional striker he was in a real fight.

Notable fights include *Lone Star Trail* (1943), *Blood on the Moon* (1948), *His Kind of Woman* (1951), *Second Chance* (1953), *Cape Fear* (1962), *El Dorado* (1967) and *The Good Guys and the Bad Guys* (1969) (see entries). Fights of interest came against Harry Woods in *Nevada* (1944) and *West of the Pecos* (1945), John Rodney in *Pursued* (1947), Steve Brodie in *Out of the Past* (1947),

William Holden in *Rachel and the Stranger* (1948), William Bendix in *The Big Steal* (1949), Eddie Parker in *The Racket* (1951), Brad Dexter in *Macao* (1952), Arthur Kennedy in *The Lusty Men* (1952), Rory Calhoun in *River of No Return* (1954), Jack Lemmon in *Fire Down Below* (1957), Chuck Roberson in *The Wonderful Country* (1959), Stanley Baker in *The Angry Hills* (1959), Jack Kelly in *Young Billy Young* (1969), Jan-Michael Vincent in *Going Home* (1971), Bill Saito in *The Yakuza* (1975), Richard Egan in *The Amsterdam Kill* (1977), Richard Boone in *The Big Sleep* (1978) and Asher Brauner in the TV movie *One Shoe Makes It Murder* (1982). Mitchum also partook in screen brawls in *Till the End of Time* (1946) and *The Sundowners* (1960). In *The Red Pony* (1949), he had an extended fight with professional wrestler Wee Willie Davis. It was cut out by Republic as too brutal for audiences interested primarily in the John Steinbeck story.

See: Gefen, Peark Sheffy. "Mitchum the Ambassador." *Montreal Gazette*. December 13, 1983; Seymore, James. "Rough, Tough, & Rowdy: Robert Mitchum." *People*. February 14, 1983.

THE BEER HALL BRAWL in *A Lady Takes a Chance* (1943)

The John Wayne starrer *A Lady Takes a Chance* is a fun little film. The comedy is good-natured and appealing as two-fisted modern-day cowpoke Wayne romances big city girl Jean Arthur while on a bus trip across the west. Early on in the William A. Seiter–directed film, Arthur finds herself in a situation all too familiar to the rodeo man: a beer hall brawl. RKO publicity hailed it "the wildest bar fight ever filmed," and *The Big Damn Book of Sheer Manliness* includes it among the screen's best barroom brawls. It's not of that magnitude, but it's entertainingly enacted. *The Boston Globe* found that the movie contained "nicely choreographed stunt work," while *Variety* remarked the fight was "done with finesse that distinguishes it from the series of similarly staged sequences in westerns."

The frenetic fight begins when a drunk Don Costello throws a sucker punch and Wayne clobbers him with a beautiful roundhouse. The drunkard falls into a chair that collapses and slides across the floor. Mass mayhem ensues as diving, flying, colliding bodies fill the screen for Frank Redman's camera. Highlights include Wayne ducking a three-person dive and Allan Pomeroy flipping onto and breaking a table. Wayne does all the ac-

tion, although Fred Graham was on the film as his double. Graham can be spotted as one of the bar fighters. Other stuntmen include George DeNormand, Bud Geary, Jack Stoney, Sailor Vincent, Ray Jones, Artie Ortega, Mike Lally, Bobby Barber, Jack O'Shea and Richard Talmadge; the latter also coordinated the action. Wayne and Arthur escape at the minute-and-a-half mark by jumping out a second story window into a bale of hay. Robert Aldrich served as an assistant director.

There was a fantastic story released to the press about Arthur's involvement in the fight. As a young woman in New York City, she was nearly run over by a speeding taxi, pulled to the pavement from harm's way by a local actor. After recovering from her injuries, she sought the actor out to thank him. When she visited his talent agency, she was "discovered" there by agents and put on the path to Hollywood. Whether by design or coincidence, the actor assigned in this film to pull her out of the way of a flying chair was Charles Winninger, the same actor who had saved her in New York.

See: "In Hollywood." *Trenton Evening Times*. March 1, 1943.

THE SALOON BRAWL in *Lone Star Trail* (1943)

Reliable screen fighter Johnny Mack Brown takes on tough newcomer Robert Mitchum in this quickie from director Ray Taylor about a recent parolee trying to clear his name. Outside the presence of soon-to-be-star Mitchum playing a bad guy, it's a standard Brown cowboy flick complete with obligatory 90-second saloon brawl. B-western enthusiasts consider this to be one of the genre's better fights, though the focus isn't on Brown against Mitchum. Co-star Tex Ritter lends a pair of fists as henchmen Jack Ingram and Eddie Parker become involved in the brawling. Brown exchanges more punches on a staircase with Ingram than he does with Mitchum. The highlight is undoubtedly the hero delivering punches while sitting astride Mitchum on the bar counter. The climax has Brown once again fighting Mitchum and dress heavy George Eldredge. Tom Steele doubled Mitchum with Carl Matthews doubling Brown. The action is well-choreographed and appropriately energetic in both fights.

According to *The Best of Universal*, the film is "well remembered by western buffs thanks to the savage barroom brawl between Brown and a young villain named Robert Mitchum." It's included among the "great screen fights" in *Western Clippings*, and Mitchum biographer Alvin H. Marill writes that the fight "still ranks among the very best in the eyes of B-western enthusiasts." *Hollywood Corral* adds, "There was a tremendously vicious, realistic barroom scrap, with Brown making his punches appear to land solidly, and sporting cuts and bruises at the conclusion, something rare in these antiseptic low-budget westerns."

In the early 1940s, Ritter was often paired with Brown at Universal in the two-star format in such films as *The Old Chisholm Trail* (1942), *Little Joe, the Wrangler* (1942) and *Raiders of San Joaquin* (1943). Capitalizing on the success of the Universal hit *The Spoilers* (1942), the duo often had a fight with one another before joining forces to take on the villains. The studio hoped to bring in fans of both these complimentary talents: those who liked fighting and those who preferred singing cowboys. Other pairings of this nature consisted of Wild Bill Elliott and Ritter and Charles Starrett and Russ Hayden.

Johnny Mack Brown, 5'11" and 190 pounds, was an All-American football player at the University of Alabama and a 1926 Rose Bowl standout. He was a popular big screen cowboy noted for his fighting ability. Western stuntmen claimed that Brown had the best punch in the business. His signature move was to place one hand behind the bad guy's head and pull him into his approaching fist. His films featured at least one fistfight, and Brown had good ones against heavies Charlie King, Dick Alexander, Harry Cording, Dick Curtis and Roy Barcroft. Fans liked how he'd never start a barroom brawl but always finished it. He'd dust off his hat, reposition it on his head, and order a sarsaparilla from the barkeep. Fights of interest came against Yakima Canutt in *Branded a Coward* (1935), William Farnum in *Between Men* (1935), Harry Woods in *West of Carson City* (1940), Frank Hagney in *Boss of Hangtown Mesa* (1942), Marshall Reed in *Trailin' Danger* (1947) and *Oklahoma Justice* (1951) and Pierce Lyden in *Whistling Hills* (1951).

See: Copeland, Bobby J. *Johnny Mack Brown: Up Close and Personal.* Madison, NC: Empire, 2005.

TOM STEELE VS. DALE VAN SICKEL in *The Masked Marvel* (1943)

Former stuntman Spencer Gordon Bennet was one of the best directors of the serial genre, cranking them out for Republic while relying on cameraman Reggie Lanning and a talented group of stuntmen headed by Tom Steele and Dale Van Sickel. These two stunters became so integral to the studio that Republic began casting their leading men based on their resemblance to the stuntmen. Ace stuntman Steele literally has the leading role in *The Masked Marvel*, although he went without credit to lend mystery to the fedora-clad character who takes on Japanese spies with little more than his two flying fists and Mort Glickman's energetic background score. Beneath the mask, he's one of four lookalike characters played by Rod Bacon, David Bacon, Bill Healy and Richard Clarke, but Steele makes the role his own with a tour de force action performance. Serial fans think of no one other than the great screen fighter Steele in the part. In his excellent serial retrospective *In the Nick of Time*, William C. Cline writes, "*The Masked Marvel* holds a place as one of the finest mystery serials released, because of the outstanding work by its team of able stuntmen, headed by the lanky Steele."

The non-stop action becomes slightly disorienting after a while, but never stops being entertaining. Editors Wallace Grissell and Earl Turner cut back and forth between multiple fights occurring at the same time at different locations. Stuntmen play characters who are killed in one chapter only to show up as another character in a later chapter. Steele and Van Sickel square off several times during the serial's 12 chapters, as Van Sickel plays three characters and doubles more. Steele even manages to have two fights with himself playing additional characters. Ken Terrell plays three characters and doubles villain Johnny Arthur in the climactic fight. Other stuntmen filling out the thug ranks include Fred Graham, Allen Pomeroy, Eddie Parker, Bud Geary, John Daheim, Duke Green, Carey Loftin and George Suzanne.

Steele insisted that Republic schedule one fight a day to keep the quality high. Often times he paired up with the stockier Van Sickel, who doubled the villains in outstanding fights with Steele seen in *G-Men vs. the Black Dragon* (1943), *Secret Service in Darkest Africa* (1943), *The Tiger Woman* (1944), *Zorro's Black Whip* (1944), *The Purple Monster Strikes* (1945), *Manhunt on Mystery Island* (1945) and *The Crimson Ghost* (1945). They worked countless westerns at Republic, then the dynamic duo moved over to Columbia to stage fights for the serial *Bruce Gentry* (1949). Other films they worked on together as a fight team include *Thunder in the Pines* (1948), *Day the World*

Ended (1956), *Flesh and the Spur* (1957) and *Cattle King* (1963).

See: Mallory, Michael. "Tom Steele." *Filmfax.* April-May 1992; Mallory, Michael. "Tom Steele: King of the Cliffhangers." *Starlog.* #137, December 1988; Mathis, Jack. *Republic Confidential: The Studio.* Self-published, 1999.

The Saloon Brawl in *The Kansan* (1943)

United Artists tried to match the epic Warner Bros. western *Dodge City* (1939) with a three-and-a-half-minute fight in the town of Broken Lance, Kansas. Harold Shumate and Frank Gruber's script presents wall-to-wall action featuring stalwart marshal Richard Dix and good bad guy Victor Jory clashing with Douglas Fowley and Albert Dekker's small army of heavies. A little levity is present as heavyset character player Eugene Pallette uses a belly bump to take out foes. This was a move popularized by Andy Devine in other films. Actor Jack Norton also gets laughs as a drunk continually knocked over during the skull-cracking melee, though his musical cues are too obvious. Composer Gerard Carbonara was Oscar nominated for this film. Set decorator Emile Kuri filled the cavernous saloon, which features appropriately rounded edges on the bar and tables to lessen the likelihood of actors or stuntmen being injured on a sharp angle.

Combatants swing from chandeliers, fall from balconies and tumble down stairs. Even the dance hall girls become involved. As can be expected, a chair is thrown into the mirror behind the bar. It is standout action on a small-scale budget capably directed by George Archainbaud and photographed by Russell Harlan. *Motion Picture Herald* called it "a saloon brawl of unusual dimensions and ferocity," while *Western Clippings* deems it "the wildest free-for-all saloon brawl outside of *Dodge City.*" The *New York Times* wasn't as impressed, remarking there were too many "haymakers that wouldn't have stunned a fly." Stuntmen include John Daheim, Jack Stoney, Lew Morphy, Cliff Parkinson, Ralph Bucko and Frank McCarroll. Stunt actors Glenn Strange, Rod Cameron and Pierce Lyden have parts and might be participating somewhere in the background of the massive brawl.

Rugged Richard Dix, six feet tall and 180 pounds, enjoyed success in both silents and talkies in fare such as *Cimarron* (1931), for which he was Oscar-nominated. Having come from an athletic background in his native Minnesota, he was an adept action actor, portraying prizefighters in *The Shock Punch* (1925) and *Knockout Reilly* (1927). He broke ribs boxing real heavyweight contender Jack Renault in the latter. Trainer Jimmy De Forest insisted Dix could have had a successful ring career as a light-heavy. Dix had notable screen brawls with George Siegmann in *Manhattan* (1924), Matthew Betz in *Shooting Straight* (1930), Fred Kohler in *West of the Pecos* (1935) and Skelton Knaggs in *The Ghost Ship* (1943). By the 1940s he was on the downside of his career but still made a fine leading man.

The same filmmakers also released the western *Buckskin Frontier* (1943) with Dix and Jory squaring off in the climax.

See: "A Real Fighter." *Pittsburgh Press.* March 20, 1927; Dix, Robert. *Out of Hollywood.* Chatsworth, CA: Ernest, 2009; "Richard Dix Injured." *Reading Eagle.* February 18, 1927.

John Wayne vs. Ward Bond in *Tall in the Saddle* (1944)

Tall in the Saddle, an entertaining John Wayne western from RKO and director Edwin L. Marin, is highlighted by a 30-second punch-up between Wayne and crooked judge Ward Bond in the latter's office. *Western Clippings* considers this one of cowboy cinema's "great screen fights." It was Wayne and Bond's fourth screen battle, the others occurring in *Conflict* (1936), *A Man Betrayed* (1941) and *The Shepherd of the Hills* (1941). The latter fight in a sheep pen is the longer and better, but *Tall in the Saddle* is more widely known. The USC football teammates throw great punches at one another for Robert De Grasse's camera with the lone drawback being the fight's brevity, not its ferocity. Bookcases are turned over and a chair goes flying out a window onto the street below while composer Roy Webb capably fills the soundtrack with a cacophony of strings and horns. Bond is knocked through a door and onto a bed as Wayne emerges triumphant. Doubles Fred Graham and Allen Pomeroy contribute solid work when called upon. Significant fight footage was left out by editor Philip Martin.

There's a climactic fight alongside a bridge with Harry Woods (doubled by Fred Graham) that repeatedly knocks down co-star Gabby Hayes to comic effect. Ben Johnson briefly doubles Wayne in this scene for a jump off a wagon and through a fence. It's been said that no actor's face met Wayne's fists on film more than veteran heavy Woods. The burly Woods specialized in playing cruel, sneering bad guys, and his size and demeanor made him an effective opponent for Wayne even if Woods often turned the action over to the stuntmen. Welcome touches of humor are displayed in the Woods fight, but it's the Wayne-Bond exchange that audiences remember.

The personal relationship between Wayne and Bond was built on macho posturing and roughhousing over drinks. They regularly hurled insults and sarcasm at one another on the set to the point some thought they'd really come to blows. That was part of the daily repartee the two had been carrying on for over 15 years. They were taken in by John Ford in the late 1920s and became regular guests on the director's fishing yacht *Araner*. They were familiar faces at the Hollywood Athletic Club, where they sparred with one another in the boxing ring, took steam baths to sweat out the booze, lifted weights and imbibed more spirits at the club's lounge. Wayne and Bond formed a fraternity of sorts with other hard drinkers Johnny Weissmuller, Preston Foster and Bruce Cabot and called themselves "The Young Men's Purity Total Abstinence and Snooker Pool Association" in jest.

All the drink occasionally landed them in trouble. Wayne and Bond had a challenge with one another at the Athletic Club that evacuated all the gym members and had the actors paying for several hundred dollars in damages after they punched holes in all the doors. They were both suspended from the gym for a year. Another time they roughhoused in the middle of director Frank Capra's living room and destroyed the carpet. A legendary story had Bond betting Wayne he couldn't knock him off a newspaper with a punch. When Wayne took the bet, Bond put a newspaper down in a doorway, stood on it, then closed the door while laughing heartily. Wayne allegedly put his fist through the door and connected with

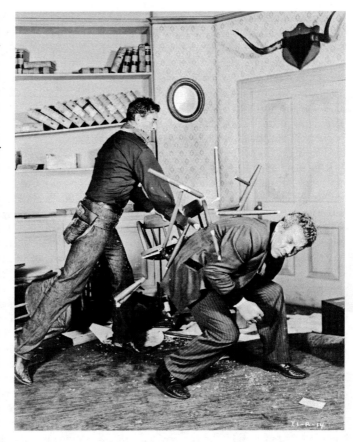

John Wayne smashes a chair across Ward Bond's back in RKO's *Tall in the Saddle* (1944).

Bond's jaw, winning the bet. At personal appearances and benefits, Wayne and Bond enacted a corny fight routine where Wayne pinched Bond's cheek and tweaked his nose. Wayne later did that same routine on film to Big John Hamilton in *McLintock!* (1963).

See: Bond, Ward. "The Duke and I." *Motion Picture.* June 1951.

ALLAN "ROCKY" LANE VS. ROY BARCROFT in *Corpus Christi Bandits* (1945)

Allan "Rocky" Lane was called "America's Fighting Cowboy" and it's a title he took pride in. Lane and top Republic bad guy Roy Barcroft made 38 films together and wound up fighting one another in most of them, including such titles as *Stagecoach to Denver* (1946), *Code of the Silver Sage* (1950) and *Desert of Lost Men* (1951). Their fights were noted for their brutality, and Wallace Grissell's

Corpus Christi Bandits features one of their more furious fights. Lane wins the Lone Star Saloon from crooked owner Barcroft in a poker game, and the latter refuses to give up his property without a fight. Barcroft goes for his gun which Lane improbably avoids by fanning a deck of cards in his face. For the next two minutes they brawl wildly over every square inch of the set. A generic backing score from musical director Richard Cherwin has no bearing to the action.

Cinematographer Bud Thackery filmed many fights on Republic serials and worked well with stuntmen. However, Thackery had little to do here other than capture the thrilling action in a basic wide shot. Tom Steele doubled liberally for Lane while Eddie Parker doubled Barcroft going over tables and against the bar until Lane delivers a final knockout blow. The Republic film fights were choreographed by Steele and/or Dale Van Sickel with *Blazing West* declaring them "some of the best brawls ever put onto film." The stunt doubles performed in a master shot with two or three cameras capturing the action from different angles in the morning. After lunch, the prop men redressed the set and Lane and Barcroft did everything but the hardest stunts so editor Charles Craft could cut close-ups in appropriately. Lane also fights Kenne Duncan atop a stagecoach during the exciting climax, a scene marred by the too obvious process shots taken on a soundstage.

Not everyone enjoyed working with the perfectionist Lane, but former oil field roughneck Barcroft was a professional who tolerated any ego. Nevertheless the 6'2", 240-pound Barcroft occasionally had to send a message to the star, especially when Lane became carried away in his quest for realism. Barcroft claimed the 6'1", 190-pound Lane sometimes neglected to pull punches and found humor in damage he had done. Lane once hit Barcroft wrong with a breakaway chair, landing the edge of the seat and nearly knocking Barcroft unconscious. In response, Barcroft let his body go limp when Lane had to lift him off the saloon floor. Every so often, Barcroft gave Lane a light pop in the jaw to remind him to tone it down. Lane's signature move, often performed during fights, was an all-out dive and roll directly into the camera. Outside of Barcroft, Lane most often fought Dick Curtis and stunt actors Dale Van Sickel, Ted Mapes and Lane Bradford. One of his best fights came against Mickey Simpson in *Leadville Gunslinger* (1952).

See: Alexander, Linda. *I Am Mr. Ed: Allan "Rocky"*

Lane Revealed. Albany, GA: BearManor, 2014; Brooker, John. "Roy Barcroft Interview." *Western Clippings.* #81. January-February 2008; Thornton, Chuck. *Allan "Rocky" Lane: Republic's Action Ace.* Madison, NC: Empire, 1990.

SUNSET CARSON VS. ROY BARCROFT in *Santa Fe Saddlemates* (1945)

When he wasn't fighting Allan Lane, Roy Barcroft was putting in time against 6'6", 200-pound Sunset Carson. The two close friends made half a dozen films together during Carson's brief Republic cowboy reign. *Santa Fe Saddlemates* is their best match-up, a lengthy skirmish in the tradition of *The Spoilers* that begins in a speeding wagon bed and ends in a livery stable. Thomas Carr was the director, but Yakima Canutt handled the second unit stunt direction. Ben Johnson and Carol Henry doubled Carson while Fred Graham doubled Barcroft in the climax. The fight was the lone time Barcroft was hurt in the business, when Carson accidentally fell on him and twisted his knee. Barcroft was forced to miss a couple of days work. The two fought again, most notably in *Alias Billy the Kid* (1946).

Santa Fe Saddlemates is full of fights, opening with Carson making his way into an office by slugging it out with henchmen Fred Graham, George Magrill and Bill Nestell. He knocks Graham into a barrel and sends Magrill down a flight of stairs. These battles turn out to be a test for the undercover assignment he's about to take on. *Western Clippings* calls this one of the "great screen fights," while *Hollywood Corral* labels the movie "the fightin'est horse opera seen for many a moon." Carson also has a saloon brawl with henchman Bud Geary, who remains Carson's opposition until Barcroft is revealed to be the real heavy.

Rodeo champion Carson had no idea how to picture fight but began working with Tom Steele and Dale Van Sickel to learn the ropes. His films were especially heavy on action, and Carson's fistfights became crowd-pleasers. Although limited as an actor, he proved to be a highly capable screen fighter. Unfortunately, he fell afoul of Republic boss Herbert Yates and was soon unemployed. Carson remained popular with the public and spent a good portion of the 1950s making personal appearances.

See: Copeland, Bobby J. *Sunset Carson: The Adventures of a Cowboy Hero.* Madison, NC: Empire, 2007.

JAMES CAGNEY VS. JOHN HALLORAN in *Blood on the Sun* (1945)

Billed as the mightiest fight of James Cagney's career, this energetic David vs. Goliath judo confrontation is the best opportunity to see Cagney show off his martial arts skill, even if there's liberal use of his stunt double for all the upending and table-smashing. The double is most likely veteran stuntman Harvey Parry, who had judo training and claimed he worked on all Cagney's films. Always aware of camera placement, the double buries his face into his shoulder at opportune times to conceal his identity. Cagney was in there for a great deal of the Frank Lloyd–directed action, so much so he suffered an ear infection from all the rough-housing and head-cuffing. Set in 1920s Tokyo, *Blood on the Sun* is notable as one of the first American films to prominently display the art of judo being used by a Caucasian. Judo slowly began to emerge on screen as American soldiers returned from World War II and incorporated the hand-to-hand combat skills they picked up in the service.

Today the fight may seem hokey with overly melodramatic Miklos Rozsa music and sometimes rushed choreography. The movie is an entertaining programmer based on a real pre–World War II incident, and the final two-minute fight in a waterfront shack remains the United Artists film's selling point. It's a treasure for Cagney fans featuring a multitude of judo tosses, chops, wristlocks and a rear chin-lock. Ippon Seoi Nagi (one-armed shoulder throw), Harai Goshi (sweeping hip throw), Ogoshi (large hip throw), Tomoe Nagi (monkey flip), Ukemi (safe fall) and Kesa Gatema (controlled side hold) are featured, and Cagney's technique is sound. Cagney held a black belt in judo and wanted a chance to show off his skill on film as well as introduce the Japanese art to a broader audience.

Cagney's regular judo partner John Halloran was his opponent in this film. Cagney received additional instruction from pro wrestler Abe Stein (aka actor Aaron Saxon). Cagney spent six weeks specifically training for this fight, which took two days to film on a houseboat anchored on the set of a General Service Studios water tank. In the end, a tenacious Cagney prevails with a flurry of boxing punches that knocks the much larger Halloran through a wall and into the water. The fight was symbolic of America prevailing over the Japanese while beating them with their own skill to boot.

The *New York Times* gushed that the fight was "a beauty," while the *Los Angeles Times* wrote, "The climax … is quickened by Cagney's combination judo-and-fists battle with John Halloran." *Time* opined that Cagney "uses judo to thrilling and protracted effect," and *Life* claimed that the film was "mainly notable for a quantity of fist fighting, judo, stabbing, shooting and hari kari that for sheer luxuriance and international variation has seldom been matched in a single picture." *The American Martial Arts Film* calls it "[o]ne of the first and most intense displays of martial arts in an American film," while *Action Films* ranks it among the screen's best fights and tagged it as "an awesome achievement."

Judo black belt Halloran made his film debut in *Blood on the Sun*, looking as Oriental as any towering U.S. citizen born in Argentina could expect to be given the circumstance. His real name was Jack Sergel (aka Sergil) and he was a former Los Angeles police sergeant with backgrounds in boxing, wrestling and knife fighting. He was forced to resign from the force at the outset of World War II when the FBI investigated him because his

Japanese villain John Halloran takes a punch from American judoka James Cagney in United Artists' *Blood on the Sun* (1945).

favorite sport was the Asian art of judo. Such was the imperialist hysteria of the time. He adopted John Halloran as a stage name in light of publicity in the Los Angeles newspapers. Ironically, the Marine Corps retained his services as a judo instructor. Sergel appeared in several films and taught Edmond O'Brien judo for the Cagney film *White Heat* (1949).

Cagney became so enthused with judo that he had a dojo built in his home. He trained regularly with 5th degree black belt master Ken Kuniyuki, who postwar became the Cagney family's live-in butler. Outside of *Blood on the Sun,* one of the best showcases for Cagney's judo came in the espionage film *13 Rue Madeleine* (1946). In 1950, there was a real judo battle at the Cagney home between the masters Kuniyuki and Sergel after a domestic disturbance. The police arrested Kuniyuki after his estranged wife felt threatened and Cagney's wife called for Sergel's help. Sergel emerged victorious and detained Kuniyuki until the police arrived. James Cagney wasn't home.

See: "Cagney Home Scene of Judo Battle." *Prescott Evening Courier.* March 9, 1950; Chapman, John. "He's Never Lost a Fight." *Los Angeles Times.* March 16, 1947; "Star Learns Judo for Screen Role." *Toledo Blade.* July 23, 1945.

JOHN WAYNE VS. MIKE MAZURKI in *Dakota* (1945)

This one had all the makings of a legendary brouhaha as John Wayne slugs it out with 6'4", 240-pound professional wrestler Iron Mike Mazurki. Publicity called it "the screen fight to end all screen fights." However, what made the screen is a disappointment. The fight is over with too quickly, and bits are staged off-screen or in complete darkness. It seems odd not to put these heavy-handed tough men front and center for an all-out punchfest. It's still a serviceable display of two fight giants butting heads, but it could have been so much more. A combination of factors likely played into what ultimately made the screen and what did not. First and foremost, both actors were injured during the fight. In addition, director Joseph Kane may have been toeing the line for Republic and run into budget and time constraints. Stunt coordinator–second unit director Yakima Canutt was likely eyeing the staging of the impressive prairie fire finale over his umpteenth fight scene. The Walter Scharf music score is standard, but memorable bits still occur.

No moment is more infamous than the Wayne punch through Mazurki's hat. During their fight, Wayne pulls Mazurki's hat over his face and buries his fist into the material. Unfortunately, Wayne buried his fist too deeply, misjudging the space between the hat and Mazurki's proboscis. The punch broke Mazurki's nose. Wayne recounted that it was one of the few movie punches he threw in error (forgetting a punch that injured actor Victor Kilian's eye in 1942's *Reap the Wild Wind*). Mazurki didn't seem to mind, as he had already broken the nose numerous times in the wrestling arena. Still, the damage had been done and needed to be covered up. Wayne's normal double Fred Graham stepped in to double Mazurki, though he was several inches shorter. Wayne injured his shoulder in the tussle and had to step out of the action. Canutt took over for Wayne. Considering that Canutt and Graham were two legends of the movie fight game, the fight still could have amounted to more. Their sudden presence was hidden by cameraman Jack Marta's lighting choice and editor Fred Allen's splicing. Wayne and Mazurki do unleash a few big blows for their fans. Wayne also tangles with Cliff Lyons, Jack Roper and Graham, who gets his front teeth knocked out for his trouble. *Variety* concluded, "Action isn't always robust, but there are a number of knock-down fights to help carry it along."

Gravel-voiced Mazurki was Hollywood's resident goon heavy for decades. He had the market cornered on dimwitted thugs in classic film noir such as *Nightmare Alley* (1947) and *I Walk Alone* (1948) where he was called upon to rough up stars Tyrone Power and Burt Lancaster, respectively. His most notable assignment came as the towering Moose Malloy in *Murder, My Sweet* (1944), where he made quick work of Dewey Robinson. Sporting a 52" chest and a 21" neck, former professional football and basketball player Mazurki found his true calling as a wrestler, becoming one of the biggest names in the mat business as a bad guy. In the 1930s, Mae West employed him as a bodyguard and introduced him to Hollywood. During a 35-year wresting career, he competed in approximately 5000 matches around the world, taking on such notables as Ed "Strangler" Lewis, Lou Thesz, Primo Carnera and Gorgeous George.

Notable fights include *Behind the Rising Sun* (1943), *Night and the City* (1950), *Davy Crockett—King of the Wild Frontier* (1955), *Donovan's Reef* (1963), *4 for Texas* (1963), *Seven Women* (1966) and *The Wild McCullochs* (1975) (see entries). Fights of interest came against Barton MacLane in *The Spanish Main* (1945), Sammy Stein in *The French Key* (1945), Morgan Conway in *Dick Tracy* (1945), Victor Mature in *Samson and Delilah* (1949), Charlton Heston in *Dark City* (1950), Stewart Granger in *The Light Touch* (1951), Rod Cameron in *The Man Who Died Twice* (1958) and *Requiem for a Gunfighter* (1965), and Roddy McDowall in *The Adventures of Bullwhip Griffin* (1967). He fought TV's toughest men such as Richard Boone on *Have Gun—Will Travel,* Dan Blocker on *Bonanza,* Charles Bronson on *The Travels of Jamie McPheeters* and William Smith in a bare-knuckle ring on the 1965 *Laredo* entitled "Pride of the Rangers." Mazurki's karate fight with Lee Marvin in the 1959 *M Squad* episode "Decoy in White" was especially noteworthy, as was his fight with Mike Connors in the 1960 *Tightrope* episode "Long Odds." On 1969's *Land of the Giants* episode "Giants and All That Jazz," he duked it out with boxing champion Sugar Ray Robinson. One of Mazurki's highest profile assignments came as a craggy senior citizen punching out Rod Stewart in the 1984 music video "Infatuation." VH1 humorously voted him one of ten actors who could take a folding chair to the face.

See: Clary, Patricia. "Strenuous Life of Husky Actor." *Avalanche-Journal.* September 23, 1945; Lousararian, Ed. "Mike Mazurki: Mean Only on Screen." *Wildest Westerns.* #1, 1998; Scheuer, Philip K. "Former Matman Likes Hollywood Atmosphere." *Los Angeles Times.* April 15, 1945.

The Trainyard Brawl in *Saratoga Trunk* (1945)

Set in 19th century New Orleans, *Saratoga Trunk* boasts a huge climactic brawl for possession of the Saratoga rail line, and it's fought with clubs and gun butts. A collision between two trains punctuates the action handled by second unit director Don Siegel and expertly photographed by Ernest Haller. Max Steiner provides dramatic backing music to the spirited melee while Perc Westmore's makeup unit worked round the clock to apply the required bruises and blood. Star Gary Cooper squares off against Frank Hagney, who is so mean he strikes midget Jerry Austin with a shovel. Although the shovel was a breakaway model and Harry Monty was present as a stunt double, director Sam Wood was particularly concerned about Austin. He was less worried about Cooper, who was an old hand at doing movie

fights. Cooper, playing a Texan, is easily identifiable throughout the two-minute fight due to wearing a white ten gallon hat (which becomes a weapon). *The New Yorker* commented, "Mr. Cooper conducts himself in assorted brawls with dour and impressive competence."

Ted Mapes and Slim Talbot were on hand as doubles, but their presence was minimized by Cooper's willingness to partake in the chaotic action and Ralph Dawson's expert, fast-paced cutting. Harvey Parry and Allen Pomeroy headed up the fight planning, with the bodies from both sides colliding head-on like the two trains. Stuntmen and tough guy actors Lane Chandler, Glenn Strange, Ethan Laidlaw, Sailor Vincent, Dale Van Sickel, Duke Green, Cliff Lyons, Buster Wiles, Paul Stader, Benny Corbett, Bobby Rose, Bob Reeves, Leo Anthony, Al Lloyd, Chet Brandenburg, Jack Tornek and boxer Freddie Steele all contributed to the brawling action. New York–based stuntman Bob Oran and other eastern stuntmen were also recruited for the film, which was lensed during the summer of 1943. Because of a shortage of stuntmen, a national call was put out for at least 50 men with fighting experience. In all, over 175 stuntmen were used. In addition, nearly 70 extras were upped from $10.50 a day to $35 for the two weeks it took to film the battle on Stage 9 at Warner Bros. Approximately 4500 balsa wood pickaxes, shovels and railroad ties were used as prop weapons. In the end, 27 men were taken to the hospital. Most were the inexperienced extras who didn't know the tricks of the trade such as distance and timing. Among the professionals, Cliff Lyons pulled Duke Green away from fiery debris in front of a blazing railroad engine just in time to avoid serious injury. Warner Bros. liked to recycle footage of the train crash and snippets of the brawl, used for the episode "The Brasada Spur" on the TV series *Maverick.*

Composer Max Steiner was known in Hollywood circles as "the Father of Film Music." He was a pioneer when it came to adding musical accompaniment to enhance a film. Unlike studio-hired musicians who simply inserted their original compositions into a soundtrack, Steiner waited until the film was fully edited and near completion to add the music of his full 100-piece orchestra. He was able to tailor his music specifically for the film itself in tempo. He measured every cue on screen to the split second with his score rising and falling in perfect time to the action and drama on screen. In time, Hollywood filmmakers discovered that fights were able to play effectively without any music at all. Sound effects and the labored breathing and grunting of the combatants was more than enough. However, the prolific orchestrator Steiner's scores never failed to add an extra something to fight action.

See: Foster, Ernest. "Midget Jerry Austin Thinks He's Jack the Giant Killer." *Pittsburgh Press.* August 1, 1943; "Gary Cooper Ex-Stuntman." *Oregonian.* February 10, 1946; Wilson, Elizabeth. "Hollywood Hardpans." *Liberty.* October 20, 1945; Yolen, Will. "New York Develops Stuntmen for Television and Pictures." *Spokane Daily Chronicle.* March 21, 1950.

JOHN MILLS VS. STEWART GRANGER in *Waterloo Road* (1945)

Waterloo Road contains one of the classic fights of British cinema. The *Sydney Morning Herald* termed it "as exciting a brain-versus-brawn episode as has appeared in any film for a long time," while *British Film Noir Guide* says, "*Waterloo's* highlight is a nicely staged fight scene." Co-star Stewart Granger considered it the toughest fight he'd ever done, as he battles it out with soldier John Mills over the latter's unfaithful wife Joy Shelton. Granger inadvertently took a fist to the stomach while Mills was accidentally hit on the chin, although both men tried to remain as calm as possible in blocking out the fight moves. It took seven days to film the action with the combatants going up and down a staircase, over bannisters, and into windows above the Amusement Arcade. Much of the fight was filmed amidst broken glass on the floor. What's more, it was occurring during a German air bombing raid, adding to the heightened drama from director-writer Sidney Gilliat's scenario. Former British lightweight boxing champ Dave Crowley was the fight arranger, training the actors two weeks beforehand to pull their punches an inch short of the chin so the fight wouldn't need to be filmed over the shoulder by cinematographer Arthur Crabtree.

Stewart Granger, 6'2" and 195 pounds, was playing a slick boxer and hated the idea that his character could lose a fight to a smaller man. Granger didn't think it made sense for him to be chinned, and most tended to agree. Granger biographer Don Shiatch wrote that the fight "teeters on the edge of farce" because of this physical discrepancy. Mills stood roughly 5'7" and barely tipped the scales at 140 pounds. He did have a background in boxing. The fight turns corny when

Mills pulls Granger's jacket down over his arms so Granger can't defend himself. The plot twist explaining Mills' superiority involves a fake medical condition for Granger that turned out to be all too real. The husband and remorseful wife are reunited by film's end. In real life, both actors were discharged from the British military due to ulcers.

Best known as the swashbuckling star of *Scaramouche* (1952) and *The Prisoner of Zenda* (1952), Granger's best slugging showcases were *Soldiers Three* (1951) and *North to Alaska* (1960) (see entry). He was proud of his sportsman background at Epsom College and would place his boxer's hands before studio executives as a deterrence to miscasting if he thought a part was too milquetoast for his liking. To stay in shape, he stepped into the ring to spar with pro light heavyweight boxing champ Freddie Mills. Fights of interest came against Mike Mazurki in *The Light Touch* (1951), Howard Petrie in *The Wild North* (1952), Robert Taylor in *All the Brothers Were Valiant* (1953), Fred Graham, Dale Van Sickel and Terry Wilson in *The Last Hunt* (1956), Arch Johnson in *Gun Glory* (1957) and Robert Ryan in *Crooked Road* (1965).

See: Carroll, Harrison. "Dirty Fighting Common on TV but Not in Movies." *Boston Daily Record.* March 11, 1953; Ellis, James. "Sir John Mills." *Metro.* October 27, 2009; Keaney, Michael F. *British Film Noir Guide.* Jefferson, NC: McFarland, 2008; Shiach, Don. *Stewart Granger: The Last of the Swashbucklers.* London: Aurum Press, 2005.

RANDOLPH SCOTT VS. JACK LAMBERT in *Abilene Town* (1946)

This brisk western from director Edwin L. Marin and screenwriter Harold Shumate has laconic Randolph Scott cast as a marshal trying to keep peace between warring factions of cattlemen and homesteaders. Into the fray steps scowling hired gun Jack Lambert, and it becomes inevitable the two are going to have a rousing confrontation. The *Prescott Evening Courier* called this fight "one of the most furniture-wrecking hand-to-hand battles on screen record." When the back-and-forth action ends after 90 seconds, Scott wipes the sweat from his forehead with a gloved hand and sighs in relief. Resourceful actors such as Scott preferred wearing gloves during fights to add extra protection to their own hands. Unfortunately, the use of stunt doubles is painfully evident. Editor Otho Lovering would have been wise to break away from the stuntmen and incorporate varied close-ups of Scott and Lambert. Normally reliable Archie Stout also could have set up better camera angles, but time and budget were constraining factors. It's an entertaining fight, but it could have been done better.

When insufficient fight footage was provided to the editor, special effects technician Linwood Dunn was brought in to fix any obvious gaffes in post-production. Dunn had an optical printer and was able to blow up the footage and split the screen. By slightly delaying one side of the whole image, he could correct any errors in timing between a punch and an actor's reaction. A swing and a miss could look like a solid hit to the naked eye. A legend in the business for his work on Orson Welles' *Citizen Kane* (1941), Dunn used his optical printer and special matte work on many Oscar-nominated films.

Six-foot-one, 210-pound Jack Lambert, a former boxer and *True Crime* cover model, once spoke contemptuously of actors who claimed to the press and fans to have done their own stunts during fights with him. But he too was sometimes doubled when a finished product hit the screen. In *Abilene Town* it is possible Lambert may have done run-throughs of the fight with the star's stunt double, only to have both stuntmen work a master shot when Lambert wasn't on the set. Most stars were hesitant to engage the squint-eyed Lambert in fisticuffs because he looked so menacing and they were aware of his threatening screen image.

Notable fights include *99 River Street* (1953), *Kiss Me Deadly* (1955) and *Day of the Outlaw* (1959) (see entries). Fights of interest came against Burt Lancaster in *The Killers* (1946), Ralph Byrd in *Dick Tracy's Dilemma* (1947), Rod Cameron in *River Lady* (1948) and *Brimstone* (1949), George Montgomery in *Belle Starr's Daughter* (1948), Roy Rogers in *North of the Great Divide* (1950), Humphrey Bogart in *The Enforcer* (1951), James Stewart in *Bend of the River* (1952), Brian Keith in *Chicago Confidential* (1957) and Ken Curtis in *Freckles* (1960). As a regular on *Riverboat* (1959–1961), Lambert often fought alongside series star Darren McGavin. One of his best TV fights came against Preston Foster in the 1954 *Waterfront* episode "Cap'n John's Dilemma."

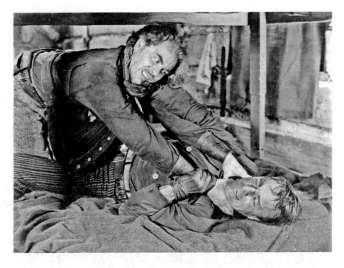

Jack Lambert goes for Randolph Scott's throat in United Artists' *Abilene Town* (1946).

See: Eyman, Scott. *Five American Cinematographers: Interviews with Karl Struss, Joseph Ruttenberg, James Wong Howe, Linwood Dunn, and William H. Clothier.* Metuchen, NJ: Scarecrow, 1987.

DANA ANDREWS VS. WARD BOND in *Canyon Passage* (1946)

Film noir tough guy Dana Andrews' best fight came against bullying thief Ward Bond in Jacques Tourneur's scenic 1850s Oregon-set western *Canyon Passage* (1946). It's a brutal and bloody minute-and-a-half encounter in the Golden Nugget Saloon that Ernest Pascal's screenplay had the whole community itching to see, including leading lady Susan Hayward. The much smaller Andrews dominates the big man with his quickness and superior fighting skills. Not only is there a great exchange of punches, but store owner Andrews is a hero unafraid to fight dirty. He uses a knee, breaks a chair and cracks a bottle over Bond's head, allowing the split cranium to bleed red in glorious Technicolor for Edward Cronjager's camera. Bond is unable to see and punches a wooden post before realizing he is defeated, a moment well played.

Universal's publicity machine touted this as "the greatest fight scene ever shown," and the *Toledo Blade* declared it "one of the most brutal fight scenes ever filmed, a bar-room brawl to top them all." The *New York Times* agreed: "The slaughter is something to behold," while *Commonweal* labeled it "a slug-fest as brutal as movies have ever offered." The *Pittsburgh Post-Gazette* wrote, "When Mr.

Andrews and Mr. Ward Bond come to blows in a barroom brawl the crunch and crackle blow the roof off."

Stuntman Fred Graham does portions of the fight for Bond, while Andrews is doubled by Dale Van Sickel in seamless editing by Milton Carruth. Both Andrews and Bond sought medical attention after too many punches made contact. Andrews struck Bond with a mighty blow that split his lip open, so not all the blood was coming from makeup artist Jack Pierce. During the remainder of the filming, Bond had trouble eating solid foods because he kept tearing the stitches from his lip. He was forced to go on a liquid diet until the wound healed. Bond and Andrews also fought one another in *Swamp Water* (1941).

Dale Van Sickel is the spitting image of Andrews, which enhances the believability of the fight scene. Even with the camera directly on Van Sickel, the audience still buys that it is Andrews they are seeing. When casting a stunt double for a fight sequence, it's important to find someone of similar looks, build and stature. However, it's not a necessity. Wigs, lifts, camera angles and efficient editing can fool the audience easily enough, especially in the days before home video and the ability to pause and rewind. A stunt double may be a few inches shorter or taller, but if his opponent is the same ratio of height as the actor he is doubling, the audience is unable to tell the difference. The best stunt doubles manage to bring something

extra to the show and have great camera awareness. When seen in profile, they subtly raise a shoulder and bury their chin into their chest, making it more difficult to view their face. They learn to match an actor's movements on set and are able to pick up exactly where an actor left off in a particular cut. More importantly, they realize they are not only doubling an actor but a character placed in a situation. They are telling and selling a story to the audience as much as the actors. Stuntman tricks such as slicked-back hair, water in the mouth or Fuller's Earth in the hand let loose at the point of impact can greatly sell the force of movie blows.

Five-foot-ten and 175 pounds, Andrews, formerly a football player for Sam Houston State, was well-cast as a sturdy two-fisted sort. He moved with confidence in his physical abilities and came by his toughness honestly. During the Depression, he had found jobs as a ditch digger, gas pumper and truck driver. The real-life brother of equally rough-hewn actor Steve Forrest, Andrews became the archetypal trenchcoated 1940s film hero after starring as a tough detective in the noir classic *Laura* (1944). He can lay claim to throwing one of the big screen's most perfectly realized knockout punches against Ray Teal in *The Best Years of Our Lives* (1946). His greatest fight, however, came against alcohol, which ultimately affected his career as a leading man.

Andrews had notable fights in *Where the Sidewalk Ends* (1950) and *Strange Lady in Town* (1955) (see entries). Fights of interest came against Gary Cooper in *Ball of Fire* (1941), Vincent Price in *Laura* (1944), Charles Bickford in *Fallen Angel* (1945), Louis Jourdan in *No Minor Vices* (1948), Ray Teal in *Edge of Doom* (1950), David Farrar in *Duel in the Jungle* (1954), Richard Webb in *Three Hours to Kill* (1954), Rex Reason in *Smoke Signal* (1955), Henry Brandon in *Comanche* (1956), Ted DeCorsia in *Enchanted Island* (1958), Kelly Thordsen in *The Fearmakers* (1958), Roger Torrey and DeForest Kelley in *Town Tamer* (1965) and Lyle Bettger and John Agar in *Johnny Reno* (1966).

Ward Bond (left) and Dana Andrews engage in a brutal slugfest in Universal's *Canyon Passage* (1946).

See: Carroll, Harrison. "Behind the Scenes in Hollywood." *The Dispatch.* December 6, 1945; Fujiwara, Chris. *Jacques Tourneur: The Cinema of Nightfall.* Jefferson, NC: McFarland, 1998.

GARY COOPER VS. MARC LAWRENCE in *Cloak and Dagger* (1946)

This World War II spy thriller from Warner Bros. features a tremendously effective battle to the death between Gary Cooper and a knife-wielding Nazi henchman Marc Lawrence in a building's entryway. Upon its release, *Commonweal* dubbed it "terrifically brutal," while *Esquire* called it "hair-raising." *Variety* found it "a high moment of thrill." Cooper astutely wraps a jacket around his arm to protect his vital arteries and is able to knock Lawrence's knife away. Set in Italy, the flavorful local tenor music from the outside street provided by orchestrator Max Steiner is the only thing heard over the desperate grunts of the eye-gouging, shin-kicking, foot-stomping and finger-bending combatants. It's one of the first times heightened, melodramatic studio music wasn't dubbed in during post-production, and the film is much better off for it. Judo chops, arm-bars and a monkey flip (Tomoe nage) are displayed before Cooper chokes Lawrence out. Makeup artist Perc Westmore provided the fake blood coming from Lawrence's mouth. The finger-bending is especially brutal and likely a first of its kind on the big screen. Up to this point, the Production Code Administration prohibited any kicking or choking on screen.

Afforded a single line of description in the Albert Maltz–Ring Lardner, Jr., script, the 90-second fight took over four days to complete. Director Fritz Lang and camera operator Sol Polito captured the action in close-up and it's superbly cut together by Christian Nyby. In all, there are 26 shots with an average length of three seconds. Cooper was bothered by a bad hip and back, but the demanding Lang coaxed him into doing the entire fight. Stuntmen Eddie Parker and Don Turner were on hand to double the ailing star, but it's all Cooper in the finished product save perhaps for a single shot. The 5'10", 175-pound Lawrence, a serpentine menace for years on the big screen, was an admirer of Cooper and apologized throughout the fight for having to stick his fingers into the star's mouth.

World War II changed the way fights were depicted on film. Fights became more lethal and realistic; with filmmakers unafraid to show blood or wrenched limbs. War veterans had been exposed to hand-to-hand combat skills and the Asian fighting arts. Popular self-defense books were published such as boxing champion Jack Dempsey's *How to Fight Tough,* which he co-wrote with fellow Coast Guard self-defense instructor Barney Cosneck. The latter had distinguished himself as a Big Ten wrestling champion at the University of Illinois before turning pro on the mat. He followed his Dempsey collaboration with the book *American Combat Judo.* W.E. Fairbairn's *Get Tough* and *All-In Fighting* were other popular teaching tools, detailing how to prevail in close-quarter combat. The ensuing generation of stuntmen and big screen tough guys, many war veterans themselves, were all exposed to this material and began incorporating these moves into their fights. Judo chops and throws proved adaptable enough for film cameras to capture without too much head-scratching.

See: Lawrence, Marc. *Long Time No See: Confessions of a Hollywood Gangster.* Riverwood, 1997; McElhaney, Joe. *A Companion to Fritz Lang.* Bognor Regis: John Wiley & Sons, 2014.

ROY ROGERS VS. DAVID SHARPE in *Bells of San Angelo* (1947)

The King of the Cowboys meets the Crown Prince of Stuntmen in William Witney's *Bells of San Angelo,* a climactic battle *Western Clippings* includes among its "great screen fights." This action-packed Republic outing ushered in a new tougher era for a Roy Rogers film, replete with brutal and graphic violence. It's the first Rogers film to show bloody noses, and the 5'10", 170-pound cowboy star takes a beating throughout. He gives as good as he gets, and the memorable two-minute climax occurs against bad guys John McGuire and David Sharpe on a rocky cliff in Nevada's Valley of Fire. Joe Yrigoyen doubled Rogers, while Sharpe handled his own action, offering impressive leaps and falls among the jagged rocks and hard terrain. Rogers' dogs take care of McGuire so the star can concentrate on handling the athletic Sharpe. The two had an earlier fight at the Monarch Mine, but in that encounter Sharpe had his men hold Rogers down. Sharpe also fought Rogers in *Susanna Pass* (1949), and the stuntman often faced off against him while doubling other actors. *The A to Z of Westerns in Cinema* declared, "Some of the best fistfights in B-westerns occur in these late Rogers films."

Witney instructed Sharpe and Yrigoyen to perform their fight in an exaggerated slow-motion for Jack Marta's camera. Given the perilous nature of their footing on the rocky ledges, he didn't want the men to lose their balance and risk falling. When screen cowboys fought on rocky surfaces, they often used specially made boots with rubber tennis shoe soles for better traction. Witney shot the slowed-down movements at 14 frames a second. In the finished film, the action played out at nearly normal speed. It's a shame Witney, an action master on the fly, wasn't able to move in for a few more gritty close-ups. Much of the fight is filmed from a distance as Witney was protective of Rogers.

Rogers had many good fistfights committed to celluloid over the years. He was never afraid to mix it up and handled a great deal of the fisticuffs. Ironically, in his early films, fights were avoided because of his slight frame. As he filled out physically Rogers proved to be a most adept action star and publicity began trumpeting his famous right hook. Frequent director Witney became determined to toughen up Rogers' image and make his fights more realistic. That was fine with the obliging Rogers, who was known to willingly turn his back to the camera during fight blocking to give face-time to supporting players or stunt actors so they'd have a chance to be seen. Rogers' first screen fight was versus Gene Autry in *The Old Corral* (1936). When he lost, Autry made him sing.

Rogers had fights of interest came against William Haade in *Song of Texas* (1943) and *My Pal Trigger* (1946), Dick Curtis in *Song of Arizona* (1946), Brad Dexter in *Heldorado* (1946), Charles McGraw and Fred Graham in *On the Old Spanish Trail* (1947), Roy Barcroft in *Springtime in the Sierras* (1947), Bob Livingston in *Grand Canyon Trail* (1948), House Peters, Jr., and Wade Crosby in *Under California Stars* (1948), Clayton Moore in *The Far Frontier* (1949), Greg McClure in *The Golden Stallion* (1949), Jack Lambert in *North of the Great Divide* (1950), Grant Withers in *Spoilers of the Plains* (1951) and Fred Graham in *Heart of the Rockies* (1951). On *The Roy Rogers Show* (1951–1957) he fought all the era's western black hats. He even stepped into the boxing ring with Charles Bronson in 1952's "Knockout." On the 1983 and 1984 nostalgic episodes of *The Fall Guy*, entitled "Happy Trails" and "King of the Cowboys," he was still punching out bad guys Marshall Teague and Michael Pataki.

See: Nevins, Francis M. "Ballet of Violence: The Films of William Witney." *Films in Review*. November 1974; Rothel, David. *The Roy Rogers Book*. Madison, NC: Empire, 1987.

THE SALOON BRAWL in *Angel and the Badman* (1947)

As producer-star of this entertaining Republic western, John Wayne wasn't about to disappoint the many fans who had come to expect thrilling fisticuffs in his films. There's a two-minute saloon scrum here that had the *Beach Morning Journal* claiming, "Enough furniture is smashed in the traditional barroom brawl to furnish a season's kindling for a cabin colony." *Movie Westerns* declared it "a terrific fight." The throwdown was in place to balance out the otherwise talky romance seen between reformed gunman Wayne and Quaker girl Gail Russell. Much of the fight is in a light-hearted vein as Wayne and Lee

Villain Dave Sharpe (left) and cowboy hero Roy Rogers struggle on rough terrain in Republic's *Bells of San Angelo* (1947).

Dixon run afoul of the beefy Baker brothers (Eddie Parker, Jack Stoney, Wade Crosby and Pat Flaherty) whom Wayne pushes through to get to the bar. They are all soon exchanging punches. Fred Graham doubles Wayne in the long shots. Other stuntmen in the Yakima Canutt–coordinated action include John "Bear" Hudkins, Joe Yrigoyen, Loren Riebe, Henry Wills, Sid Davis and Ken Terrell, who steals the show with a fall from the balcony onto a gambling table. Canutt and veteran cinematographer Archie Stout help first-time director James Edward Grant immeasurably in the staging of the brawl. Much of the movie was filmed on location in Sedona, Arizona, but the saloon sequence was done at Republic. The movie was remade for TV in 2009 with a toned-down bar brawl and Lou Diamond Phillips in Wayne's part.

Six-foot-two and 220 pounds, character actor Pat Flaherty, playing one of the Baker brothers, was a Marine captain with a background in competitive boxing and wrestling. He played professional football for the Chicago Bears and made more than 250 Hollywood films, specializing in bit part tough guys. He joked that in most parts the screenplay simply called for him to be knocked down. At one time or another, most of the industry's leading men had put him on his backside. He shows up for fights in *Dodge City* (1939) and *Gentleman Jim* (1942) (see entries).

When it came to staging fights, Yakima Canutt, Richard Talmadge, Allen Pomeroy, David Sharpe and Harvey Parry were emerging as the top men in the business. During this period, they were typically referred to as ramrods or stunt gaffers. In addition to providing the doubles and background stuntmen, they were responsible for blocking out the action with the cameraman while devising the proper angles to capture the brawling in the most effective manner. This often entailed extensive rehearsal and fine-tuning if production time and budget allowed. They typically worked out and negotiated the cost of a fight scene for the production manager or assistant director so as not to hurt a film's bottom line. Fights were standard fare for most stuntmen and they received a flat rate, but a fall such as Ken Terrell took from the balcony paid out at a much higher rate for the stunt performer.

See: Ray, Bob. "Sports Soldier of Fortune Making Good as an Actor." *Los Angeles Times.* September 8, 1940; Reid, John Howard. *Movie Westerns: Hollywood Films the Wild, Wild West.* Lulu, 2005.

BILL ELLIOTT VS. ALBERT DEKKER in *Wyoming* (1947)

Republic Pictures moved popular B-western star Bill Elliott into their higher-budgeted films and made him the anti-hero of *Wyoming*. He plays a cattle baron battling homesteaders in a film *Variety* praised for its "fine fisticuffs." Albert Dekker tries to muscle in and profit off the feud, drawing the ire of Elliott when he murders his friend Gabby Hayes. Director Joseph Kane and second unit helmsman Yakima Canutt stage an energetic one-minute saloon brawl between the two that's straight from the *Spoilers* handbook. In fact, the encyclopedic book *The Western* said the fight "is comparable to the one that is the high point of all three versions of *The Spoilers*." *Western Clippings* agreed, calling it "a terrific battle darn near equal that of *The Spoilers*." Elliott biographer Gene Blottner called the fight "well-choreographed and one of the finest to be brought to the screen," while the *New York Times* labeled it "a pip of a knockdown drag-out donnybrook."

While it has nowhere near the epic length of *The Spoilers*, it's a memorable fight in its own right. Dekker hurls a bottle at Elliott's head to start the action, prompting Elliott to fight dirtier than what is accustomed for a wholesome cowboy star. He bites, thumbs, kicks and gouges Dekker to gain an advantage. Elliott's screen trademark became announcing that he was "a peaceable man" before erupting into violence to vanquish a foe. Elliott was occasionally doubled and often assisted by veteran stuntman Tom Steele, ensuring that his fights were top-notch. In *Wyoming*, Ben Johnson doubles Elliott and Fred Graham doubles Dekker. Both stuntmen are clearly visible save for cinematographer John Alton's close-ups of the principals. Arthur Roberts' editing achieves an appropriate balance.

Bill Elliott, 6'1" and 180 pounds, embraced the cowboy genre and worked studiously on perfecting his riding, fast draws and fights. He was an enthusiastic screen puncher whose fisticuffs were often the highlight of his films. Fights of interest came against Jack Roper in *North from the Lone Star* (1941), Bud Geary in *Mojave Firebrand* (1944), Glenn Strange and LeRoy Mason in *San Antonio Kid* (1944), Dick Curtis in *Wagon Wheels Westward* (1945), William Haade in *Phantom of the Plains* (1945), Bruce Cabot in *The Gallant Legion* (1948), Forrest Tucker in *The Last Bandit* (1949), Roy Barcroft in *The Savage Horde* (1950) and Lane Bradford in *The Forty-Niners* (1954).

See: Blottner, Gene. *Wild Bill Elliott: A Complete Filmography*. Jefferson, NC: McFarland, 2007; Copeland, Bobby J. *Bill Elliott: The Peaceable Man*. Madison, NC: Empire, 2000.

VAN JOHNSON VS. JIM DAVIS in *The Romance of Rosy Ridge* (1947)

A well-made, little-known backwoods story from director Roy Rowland, *The Romance of Rosy Ridge* is set in post–Civil War Missouri, with tempers between the North and South flaring up. Yankee stranger Van Johnson draws the ire of Jim Davis when he begins courting Janet Leigh. The film is full of atmospheric musical set pieces, but the best sequence is a rough two-minute fight in the blackened remains of a burnt-out cabin between Johnson and Davis. The open air fight is preceded by an exciting foot chase through the woods with Johnson in pursuit, until Davis realizes that Johnson doesn't have a gun. At that point it's a bruising bare-knuckle match-up where the perceived soft Johnson gets to show his mettle. Johnson was known for romantic roles, and MGM was trying to toughen his image with this film. Davis' boot in his face was a step in the right direction.

Cinematographer Sidney Wagner had little experience shooting fights, but the sequence as edited by Ralph Winters comes off superbly. Winters felt it was easiest to cut scenes of movement together as eye level didn't have to match from shot to shot. Terry Wilson doubled Johnson during

much of the fight, with Jack Sterling subbing for Davis. Winters establishes a fine mix of close-ups of the principals with longer shots of the stuntmen, while George Bassman merits praise for his suspenseful backing music. A few days of filming were lost when Johnson ran into poison oak during the chase. In all, the fight consumed seven days of the production schedule and the crew erupted in applause when it was finished. The movie was filmed on location in Santa Cruz, California, and Kennedy Meadows in the High Sierras.

Six-foot-two and 200 pounds, Jim Davis had a long career as a movie and television tough guy. He could play the two-fisted hero but was more often cast as a vicious villain. The Missouri-born Davis was an oil field roughneck and a football player at William Jewel College before serving with the Coast Guard. He was a convincing screen fighter who had no problem dialing up the emotional intensity needed for his characters when they sprang into action. Davis starred as the TV western detective Matt Clark in *Stories of the Century* (1954–1955), tangling with guest stars such as Leo Gordon and Slim Pickens. He was still throwing punches nearly 25 years later as patriarch Jock Ewing on the popular series *Dallas* (1978–1981). He squared off against Robert Wilke in the 1979 episode "The Dove Hunt."

On the big screen, Davis fought Rod Cameron in *Brimstone* (1949), *The Sea Hornet* (1951) and *Woman of the North Country* (1952), Randolph Scott in *The Cariboo Trail* (1950), Kirk Douglas in *The Big Sky* (1952), Charlton Heston in *The President's Lady* (1953), John Derek in *The Outcast* (1954), George Barrows in *The Outlaw's Daughter* (1954), Ben Cooper in *Duel at Apache Wells* (1957), Lee Van Cleef in *The Badge of Marshal Brennan* (1957), John Hart in *Wolf Dog* (1958), Don Megowan in *Lust to Kill* (1958), Leo Gordon in *Noose for a Gunman* (1960), John Ireland in *Fort Utah* (1967) and James Caan in *Comes a Horseman* (1978). On TV, he battled Lee Marvin on *M Squad*, Rod Cameron on *Coronado 9*, Robert Fuller on *Laramie* and Chuck Connors on *Branded*. His 1968 fight with James Arness in the *Gunsmoke* episode "The Railroad" is one of the small screen's best. A two-man brawl with Dan Blocker in

Van Johnson takes a big right cross from Jim Davis in MGM's *The Romance of Rosy Ridge* (1947).

the 1965 *Bonanza* episode "Lothario Larkin" is also of note, as is his punch-up with Blocker and Jan-Michael Vincent in 1968's "The Arrival of Eddie."

See: "At the Broadway." *Council Bluffs Nonpareil.* February 8, 1948; Winters, Ralph E., and Laurie Holz. *Some Cutting Remarks: Seventy Years a Film Editor.* Landham, MD: Scarecrow, 2001; Whitney, Dwight. "The Cut-Rate John Wayne Changes His Luck." *TV Guide.* February 17, 1979.

ALAN LADD VS. ROBERT PRESTON in *Wild Harvest* (1947)

A brawling buddy picture from director Tay Garnett about wheat harvesting crews is highlighted by plenty of comic-laced fisticuffs. There's a three-minute brawl between rival crews which the *Hartford Courant* called "a barroom brawl to end all barroom brawls." The *Los Angeles Times* admitted that the fight "has its moments of amusement, if not of special excitement," but complained, "It is too much the sort of thing that has been viewed in barroom conflicts ere this." Later there's a two-minute one-on-one battle between stars Alan Ladd and Robert Preston in the back of a bar over female lead Dorothy Lamour, who has pitted the friends against one another. Both fights take time out for Preston's humorous search for a lost tooth, a gag borrowed from Alan Hale in *Skyscraper* (1928). The technical credits are strong with John F. Seitz behind the camera and Billy Shea and George Tomasini cutting the action.

According to Paramount publicity, the dance hall brawl employed 42 stuntmen with 22 returning from Garnett's famous brawl-fest *Her Man* (1930) (see entry). Ladd, Preston, Lloyd Nolan, Anthony Caruso and their men wrap belts around their fists to take on a chair-wielding crew comprised of veteran villains Frank Hagney, Bob Kortman, Harry Wilson, Frank Moran, Constantine Romanoff and Fred Gra-

ham. Stuntman Graham doubled Preston crashing a table in the later fight. Buster Wiles and Jimmy Dundee were the film's fight arrangers. Some of the $100-a-day stuntmen working the fight were Sailor Vincent, John Indrisano, Charlie Regan, Gordon Carveth, Pat Lane, Bud Wolfe, Chick Collins, Chuck Hamilton, Chuck Sullivan, Stubby Kruger, James Cornell and Kermit Maynard.

One of the brawl's recurring laughs comes from Harry Wilson, a 210-pound former pro wrestler who was known to have the ugliest face in the movies. Handsome Harry, as he was called, spends the entire fight trying to climb over a banister and enter the fray. Looking "two sheets to the wind," he's continuously knocked back over the rail by Ladd, Preston and Nolan. Ladd also punches out shaggy-haired, raspy-voiced Frank Moran. The 6'1", 200-pound Moran was a professional boxer who twice fought for the heavyweight crown, going the distance against Jack Johnson in 1914 and Jess Willard in 1916. One of the Great White Hopes, he nearly upset Johnson with the concussive power in his right hand, which he called Mary Anne because she was such a knockout.

Ladd told reporters there was so much fighting in *Wild Harvest* that he was throwing punches in his sleep and was especially sore from being stretched out during the sequence in which he swung from an iron bar and kicked his opponents. Ladd does some of his own acrobatics, but uses a double for a bottom-first leap from a crossbeam

Alan Ladd blocks a Robert Preston punch in Paramount's *Wild Harvest* (1947).

into the fray and when he goes through a glass door in the Preston fight. At a wrap party, Ladd was confronted by a drunken Bakersfield local who was itching for a fight with the movie tough guy. Five-foot-five, 150-pound Ladd tried to humor the man by asking the crew members to obtain his stature-adding planks so he could stand up to the man. (Ladd was extremely conscious of his small size. It was common on Ladd films for him to stand on boards to put him up to eye level with co-stars.) Preston had enough of the local blowhard and intervened on his friend's behalf, roughly escorting the man to the door.

The handsome Ladd became Paramount's top male lead playing two-fisted tough guys throughout the 1940s though he was undersized and prone to illness and physical maladies. He briefly served in the Army during World War II but was discharged due to an ulcer and a double hernia. Although he used a core group of professional stuntmen, Ladd tended to suffer many injuries. Several times he injured his hands or back. He fractured his nose on *Captain Carey, USA* (1950) and broke four ribs on *Saskatchewan* (1954). Nevertheless he was a cool and composed screen fighter. Audiences believed him as a tough man of action. He studied judo for his role in the spy drama *O.S.S.* (1946).

Notable fights include *Shane* (1953), *Drum Beat* (1954) and *The Carpetbaggers* (1964) (see entries). Fights of interest came against William Bendix in *The Glass Key* (1942), Sheldon Leonard in *Lucky Jordan* (1942), Walter Sande in *The Blue Dahlia* (1946), Charles Bickford in *Branded* (1950), Dan Riss and Jack Webb in *Appointment with Danger* (1951), Arthur Kennedy in *Red Mountain* (1951), Anthony Caruso in *The Iron Mistress* (1951) and *The Big Land* (1957), Stanley Baker in *Hell Below Zero* (1954), Hugh O'Brian in *Saskatchewan* (1954), Rod Taylor in *Hell on Frisco Bay* (1955), Lloyd Nolan in *Santiago* (1956), Ernest Borgnine in *The Badlanders* (1958), Don Murray in *One Foot in Hell* (1960), Sidney Poitier in *All the Young Men* (1960) and Gilbert Roland in *Guns of the Timberland* (1960).

See: "Boxers Play Part in Movie." *San Diego Union.* August 3, 1947; Robinson, Johnny. "If One Must Fight, It Is Best to Fight Your Friends—At Least in Films." *Lewiston Evening Journal.* July 6, 1957; Thomas, Bob. "Alan Ladd Just Naturally Gravitates Toward Violence." *Pasadena Independent.* August 31, 1958.

HUMPHREY BOGART AND TIM HOLT vs. BARTON MACLANE in *The Treasure of the Sierra Madre* (1948)

The one-minute Tampico cantina fight over lost wages in director John Huston's multiple Oscar-winning classic *The Treasure of the Sierra Madre* was praised for its brutal realism, with producer Henry Blanke claiming it was the most exciting fight he ever saw. *The Big Damn Book of Sheer Manliness* considers it "one of the most realistically painful" fights of all time. It wins points for showing the desperate measures man must resort to in a violent struggle. Down on their luck south of the border, drifters Humphrey Bogart and Tim Holt are forced to double-team the much larger Barton MacLane, a welshing employer who establishes his bad guy credentials when he smashes a whiskey bottle across Holt's face. There's leg-grabbing, kicking, kneeing and headlocks featured as the two men overpower MacLane, who admits, "I'm licked, boys. I'm licked."

The fight took five days to film on Warners' Stage One with a smattering of Mexican extras drinking in the background beneath slowly moving ceiling fans. Huston shot from both low and high angles, giving his actors free rein in making suggestions for blocking out the fight and setting up the shot with cinematographer Ted McCord. Sound effects maestro Robert Lee does a superb job synching the punches to the action. Huston stressed there should be no post-production music from orchestrator Max Steiner and the staging and editing must offer a seamless transition between the doubles and stars. For all the skill and care put into the fight, the doubles are still obvious. As good as Huston was at creating compositions and editing in his head, putting together an extended movie fight for the screen wasn't something he often did. It's likely he didn't leave Owen Marks enough to work with, although the fight was trimmed down to meet the censor's requirements. Harvey Parry was in charge of stunts, but it's not Parry subbing for Bogart. Pro boxer turned stuntman Fred Palmer worked on *Sierra Madre* and is likely doubling Bogart. Dave Sharpe is apparent doubling for Holt and landing a punch on the chin of MacLane's unidentified double.

The stoutly built Holt looked to be a couple of inches shorter than his publicized 5'11" height and 165 pounds. At any rate, the World War II bombardier could legitimately ride and fight, having grown up on the western film sets of his actor dad Jack Holt. As an RKO western star, Tim did many of his own stunts. His pictures saved the fights for the last day of filming in case any injuries were incurred to the star's face. From the action in his films, Holt suffered several broken bones, although he wore gloves to protect his hands. He tangled with Steve Brodie in *Thunder Mountain* (1947) and *Arizona Ranger* (1948). Fights of interest came against Eddie Dew in *Riding the Wind* (1942), Robert Bray in *Stagecoach Kid* (1949), John Doucette in *Border Treasure* (1950) and John Pickard in *Trail Guide* (1952).

Six-foot-one, 215-pound Barton MacLane's specialty was getting beaten up on screen. The Wesleyan University football player was 0–87 in screen fights by his own count. He wasn't a poor fighter in real life. Once during location filming in the Pacific Northwest, MacLane was followed around by a lumberjack who kept trying to egg him into a fight. MacLane put the man in his place. Such occurrences were commonplace for actors who played tough heavies. Another time MacLane was accosted without provocation by a pair of professional wrestlers in a hotel bar. They wrapped him up in finishing holds because they were simply intrigued to test his real toughness versus that of his screen image.

MacLane fought Randolph Scott in *Man of the Forest* (1933), George Brent in *Stranded* (1936), *God's Country and the Woman* (1937) and *Gold Is Where You Find It* (1938), Errol Flynn in *The Prince and the Pauper* (1937) and *Silver River* (1948), Charles Bickford in *The Storm* (1938), Ward Bond in *Prison Break* (1938), Gene Autry in *Melody Ranch* (1940), Wallace Beery in *Barnacle Bill* (1941), Henry Fonda in *Wild Geese Calling* (1941), Humphrey Bogart in *The Maltese Falcon* (1941), Pat O'Brien in *Secret Command* (1944), Mike Mazurki in *The Spanish Main* (1945), Lawrence Tierney in *San Quentin* (1946), John Carroll in *Angel in Exile* (1948) and Leif Erickson in *Captain Scarface* (1953). In *The Kid Comes Back* (aka *Don't Pull Your Punches*) (1938), MacLane vied with Wayne Morris for the heavyweight boxing championship.

See: DeMarco, Mario. *Republic's Wild & Woolly Western Heroes, Heroines, Heavies & Side-kicks.* Self-published, 1982; Meyers, Jeffrey. *John Huston: Courage and Art.* New York: Crown Archetype, 2011; "Outdoors in Texas." *Kerrville Daily Times.* November 20, 1959; Rothel, David. *Tim Holt.* Madison, NC: Empire, 1994; *The Treasure of the Sierra Madre* DVD special features.

DENNIS O'KEEFE VS. JOHN IRELAND in *Raw Deal* (1948)

Stylish Anthony Mann direction and John Alton photography overcome a so-so story in this well-regarded example of film noir. In Mann's black-and-white world, the visual composition of a scene has a far more lasting effect than either character or plot. Anti-hero Dennis O'Keefe escapes jail and vows revenge against Raymond Burr, a former associate who framed him. A pair of women complicate matters, as does Burr's torpedo John Ireland. O'Keefe and the vicious Ireland have a 90-second fight in Tom Fadden's spookily lit taxidermy shop with animal heads looming in the shadows. The men push their fingers into each other's face, and O'Keefe forces Ireland's cheek into a deer antler, requiring the makeup expertise of Ern Westmore for the resultant wound. As Ireland is momentarily dazed, O'Keefe struggles with Fadden and actress Marsha Hunt draws a gun. Notable is the presence of hard-hitting sound effects and the lack of orchestrator Paul Sawtell's musical intrusion until the end. It's highly effective.

Stuntmen Carey Loftin and John Daheim doubled O'Keefe and Ireland, though excellent editing by Alfred DeGaetano conceals their use. Six-foot-three leading man O'Keefe received his start in the business as a stuntman. Both O'Keefe and Ireland were athletic enough to do much of this fight routine. Mann biographer Jeanine Basinger calls the fight "a visually exciting episode." The film concludes with a dramatic struggle between O'Keefe and the imposing Burr in a burning house. Both men are injured from gunshots. Yet it's the O'Keefe-Ireland match-up that audiences remember because of Mann's execution.

Six-one and 200 pounds, Ireland was a competitive swimmer once hired by a water carnival to wrestle a dead octopus. His husky physique made him a convincing two-fisted presence, but Ireland never hesitated to use a stuntman in fights. Nevertheless, he participated in his share both as cynical hero and brutal antagonist. While few could be considered standout battles, the majority of his fights were better than average against an array of interesting opponents. Possessing unconventional looks, Ireland lent tough support to several superior westerns, including *My Darling Clementine* (1946), *Red River* (1948) and *Gunfight at the O.K. Corral* (1957). Even in middle age, he was still sufficiently rugged enough to portray a gladiator in *Spartacus* (1960).

Ireland fought Randolph Scott in *The Walking Hills* (1949), Glenn Ford in *Mr. Soft Touch* (1949), Broderick Crawford in *Cargo to Capetown* (1950), Burt Lancaster in *Vengeance Valley* (1951), Lloyd Bridges in *Little Big Horn* (1951), Lawrence Tierney in *The Bushwhackers* (1952) and *The Steel Cage* (1954), James Craig in *Hurricane Smith* (1952), Rod Cameron in *Southwest Passage* (1954), Chris Alcaide in *Gunslinger* (1956), John Russell, Scott Brady and Jim Davis in *Fort Utah* (1967) and Howard Keel in *Arizona Bushwhackers* (1968). On TV he fought Burt Reynolds on *Riverboat,* Clint Eastwood on *Rawhide,* Chuck Connors on *Branded,* Michael Landon on *Bonanza* and Fess Parker on *Daniel Boone.*

See: Alvarez, Max. *The Crime Films of Anthony Mann.* Jackson: University Press of Mississippi, 2013; Basinger, Jeanine. *Anthony Mann.* Middletown: Wesleyan University Press, 2007; "John Ireland; Played Tough Guys in Movies, TV Shows." *Los Angeles Times.* March 22, 1992.

ROD CAMERON VS. JEFF YORK in *Panhandle* (1948)

Panhandle is an interesting Lesley Selander–directed western presented in sepia-tone. Its highlight, according to the *Los Angeles Times,* was a saloon brawl that starts with dandy young bad guy Blake Edwards (who had a hand in co-writing the script) coming on tough to Rod Cameron at the bidding of town boss Reed Hadley. The stalwart hero knocks Edwards into the lower panel of the Last Frontier bar stand, then hurls a pistol into his belly. Burly henchman Jeff York steps in to sock Cameron in the jaw. The next two minutes of brawling has been compared to *The Spoilers* (1942). The fight has all the requisite broken chairs and jagged bottles, moving the *Lewiston Morning Tribune* to call it "worth the price of admission" and *The Nebraska State Journal* to declare it "the most exciting since *The Spoilers.*" The *Dallas Morning News* claimed this "peach of a fight will keep the customers on the edges of their seats." *Western Clippings* calls it "one of the best screen brawls in westerns."

The savage action culminates with both men crashing through the saloon's plate glass window and falling off the back of a wagon. These street shots were done at the Monogram Ranch near Newhall, California. Stuntman Dick Crockett oversaw the fight action and plays a character who fires a shotgun into a chandelier, bringing it crashing down into the center of the bar. There's liberal use of stunt doubles Bob Morgan and Terry Wilson during the bulk of the action, but the stars become involved in taking noteworthy bumps for the close-ups. Otho Lovering cut the action together.

Cameron considered the *Panhandle* fight to be his best and most demanding, joking that for a significant amount of time he was still finding lumps on his head while combing his hair. He was amazed that he and York didn't break any bones. Cameron and York had another brutal fight in *Short Grass* (1950). The 6'4", 230-pound York was a Golden Gloves and collegiate boxing champion at San Jose State under both his real name Granville Owen Scofield and the far tougher sounding ring name Glen Owens. In 88 amateur and professional fights, he lost twice and was never knocked out. He quit boxing after breaking his hand. On a 1955 episode of the TV show

Rod Cameron prepares to smash Jeff York with a chair in Allied Artists' *Panhandle* (1948).

You Were There, York played boxer John L. Sullivan to Pat Conway's Gentleman Jim Corbett. York became best known for playing the colorful Mike Fink, comically brawling alongside Fess Parker in Disney's "Davy Crockett and the River Pirates" in 1956. The two teamed up again to fight Johnny Rebs in *The Great Locomotive Chase* (1956).

Rod Cameron, 6'5" and 215 pounds, was a construction worker and semi-pro football player before breaking into films as a stuntman. He was quickly elevated to the role of two-fisted leading man in the Republic serials *G-Men vs. the Black Dragon* (1943) and *Secret Service in Darkest Africa* (1943), where he put on great slugging matches with the studio's top stuntmen. The rugged Cameron studied judo with Ken Kuniyuki to aid his on-screen fighting techniques, and his size and athleticism made him a believable tough guy. With age and increasing fame, Cameron began to hand over the bulk of his stunt work to fight doubles. This proved especially true after he suffered a broken nose fighting Andrew Faulds in *Passport to Treason* (1956).

He had fights of interest against Tom Tyler in *Boss of Boomtown* (1944), Sheldon Leonard in *Frontier Gal* (1945), Broderick Crawford in *The Runaround* (1946), Dan Duryea and Jack Lambert in *River Lady* (1948), Marshall Reed in *Stampede* (1949), Jim Davis and Jack Lambert in *Brimstone* (1949), Don Castle in *Strike It Rich* (1949), Wayne Morris in *Stage to Tucson* (1950), Jim Davis in *The Sea Hornet* (1951) and *Woman of the North Country* (1952), Fred Graham in *Fort Osage* (1952), Forrest Tucker in *Ride the Man Down* (1952) and *San Antone* (1953), John Ireland in *Southwest Passage* (1954), John Russell in *Hell's Outpost* (1955) and Mike Mazurki in *The Man Who Died Twice* (1958) and *Requiem for a Gunfighter* (1965). Cameron headlined three TV series: *City Detective* (1953–1955), *State Trooper* (1956–1959) and *Coronado 9* (1960–1961), where he faced tough guy guests Leo Gordon and Jim Davis. As a guest star, Cameron had a memorable fight with Lorne Greene in the 1966 *Bonanza* episode "Ride the Wind."

See: "Cameron Always Found

in Fight." *Omaha World Herald.* July 3, 1949; Wilson, Ivy Crane. *Hollywood in the 1940s: The Stars Own Stories.* New York: Frederick Ungar, 1980.

RANDOLPH SCOTT VS. FORREST TUCKER in *Coroner Creek* (1948)

Director Ray Enright's violent western was a significant departure from the inoffensive by-the-numbers product Randolph Scott was turning out. It was deemed shocking and mean-spirited as Scott single-mindedly pursues the killers of his bride-to-be, willing to stoop to their level of dirty tactics to exact his revenge. Filmed on picturesque Sedona, Arizona, locations by Fred Jackman, Jr., it's now considered one of Scott's best films from that period. The highlight is the vicious, nearly five-minute battle with henchman Forrest Tucker near a creek bed. There's strong stunt doubling from Jock Mahoney and Al Wyatt as the men torpedo into one another with tremendous fury and bring down a building's porch. Tucker knocks Scott out with a knee to the face, but Scott revives in a biting, head-butting rage when he realizes Tucker has broken his hand while he was unconscious. Scott even punches Tucker with his broken hand twice! He returns the bone-crunching favor by stomping his boot down on Tucker's hand. It was quite the un-heroic action for the day, a disturbing piece of business leaving audiences with an uneasy feeling in their stomachs.

Randolph Scott (left) and Forrest Tucker stage a bloody fight in Columbia's *Coroner Creek* (1948).

Columbia publicity emphasized the fight scene and presence of blood displayed in glorious Cinecolor. The studio was experimenting with what they termed "subjective sound," where the audience was able to hear the bone-breaking action through Scott's own involvement. On location, Scott wore a microphone under his neckerchief recording the fight as he experienced it. The experiment didn't catch on. Scott and Tucker squared off again in *The Nevadan* (1950) in a collapsing mine. In this superior western, Jock Mahoney and Bob Morgan doubled the leads. Scott biographer Robert Nott called the *Coroner Creek* fight "one of the best staged brawls in western film history," while *Variety* remarked that the fisticuffs "have rarely been matched on the screen." *Six Gun Law* claims it is "a savage five minutes summing up *Coroner Creek's* underlying air of viciousness."

A football player at George Washington University and an amateur boxer in the Army, 6'5", 215-pound Forrest Tucker was a leading figure in movie fights, either as antagonist or protagonist. For a time, he was considered a low-budget version of John Wayne at Republic. Most of his pictures featured at least one instance of Tucker gritting his teeth and rearing back his fist for a knockout punch. He had notable fights in *The Westerner* (1940), *The Big Cat* (1949), *Chisum* (1970) and *The Wild McCullochs* (1975) (see entries). Fights of interest came against Bruce Bennett in *Honolulu Lou* (1941), Gregory Peck in *The Yearling* (1946), William Bishop in *Adventures in Silverado* (1948), Bill Elliott in *The Last Bandit* (1949), John Wayne in *Sands of Iwo Jima* (1949), Bruce Cabot in *Rock Island Trail* (1950), John Payne in *Crosswinds* (1951), Victor Jory in *Flaming Feather* (1951), Edmond O'Brien in *Warpath* (1951), John Russell in *Fighting Coast Guard* (1951), Scott Brady in *Montana Belle* (1952), Rod Cameron in *Ride the Man Down* (1952) and *San Antone* (1953), Archie Duncan in *Trouble in the Glen* (1954), Frank Lovejoy in *Finger Man* (1955) and Jason Robards and Norman Wisdom in *The Night They Raided Minsky's* (1968).

On TV's *Gunsmoke* he had memorable battles with Robert Wilke in 1967's "The Cattle Barons" and James Stacy in 1972's "Yankton." One of Tucker's most colorful roles came in 1970 as the boozing and brawling Sergeant Holly in the *Gunsmoke* episode named after his character, in which he slugged down as much liquor as he did bad guys. Tucker played another entertaining character in repeat performances as river pirate Joe Snag

on *Daniel Boone*, squaring off with Fess Parker and comically fighting bad guys as if he were swatting flies in 1967's "The Battle of Sidewinder and Cherokee" and 1968's "The Return of Sidewinder." Tucker had a bare-knuckle match with Denny Miller in the 1974 *Dusty's Trail* episode "John T. Callahan."

See: Clary, Patricia. "New Movie Has Savage Fights." *State Times Advocate.* August 1, 1949; Kendall, John. "Forrest Tucker: Stage, TV & Film Star Dies." *Los Angeles Times.* October 27, 1986; Lewis, Jack. "Life & Times of Forrest Tucker." *Guns of the Old West.* #38, 2004.

RANDOLPH SCOTT VS. ROBERT RYAN in *Return of the Bad Men* (1948)

Pushing 50, Randolph Scott was yielding increasingly to the use of stunt doubles for his action scenes. Though he could still throw a great screen punch, it was common knowledge at this time of his career Scott was allowing his double Jock Mahoney to do a great deal of his action. Scott didn't mind throwing fists at the camera for close-ups, but was hesitant he'd catch one in the mouth during too much give-and-take. It became a running gag for Scott, with everpresent *Wall Street Journal* in hand, to ask the director how he looked on screen immediately after Mahoney put in the rough work. As a result, most of his recent fights failed to measure up to the lofty standards of his John Wayne brawls. *Coroner Creek* (1948) was the exception. That film's director Ray Enright, who helmed *The Spoilers* in 1942, seemed able to coax Scott into giving something extra for the cameras.

Return of the Bad Men features an outlaw congregation with the Younger brothers, the Daltons, Billy the Kid and Robert Ryan's Sundance Kid all present for the action. Scott's climactic deserted saloon brawl with Ryan is one of the best of his later efforts and remains an underrated gem. Cinematographer Roy Hunt creates a great shadowy black-and-white mood in the ghost town, and Paul Sawtell's dramatic score is a perfect complement. The action is well-cut by Samuel Beetley. *Motion Picture Magazine* declared, "Not since the famous fight scene in *The Spoilers* has such a brawl been staged," while *Six Gun Law* refers to it as "a bruising three-minute fistfight."

The actors are well-matched physically and perform the entire fight save for a few dangerous bits where Mahoney and Paul Stader step in. An especially impressive balcony fall onto a table high-lights the action. Scott and Ryan trained for weeks in anticipation of the fight. In the end, Ryan ran over into starting another picture and couldn't risk damaging his face in the fight, necessitating Stader's presence. The stars put great action onto the screen as a chair, a beer keg and a broken bottle are mixed in with the haymakers. The brawl ends with a desperate Ryan going for his gun and a shot being fired.

See: "Scott, Ryan Training for Their Film Fight." *Pittsburgh Post-Gazette*. June 20, 1947; "Stars Fight Own Battles." *Advocate*. August 29, 1948.

John Wayne vs. Montgomery Clift in *Red River* (1948)

John Wayne had one of his best character roles as tyrannical cattle driver Tom Dunson in Howard Hawks' sweeping western *Red River*. Credit must go to Oscar-nominated screenwriter Borden Chase for putting the drama in motion. Wayne kills those who threaten to leave his epic cattle push and clashes with adopted son Montgomery Clift over his crazed leadership. His anger reaches a boiling point when Clift assumes command of the drive. Wayne swears he will kill the young man. En route to their showdown in Abilene, a deter-mined Wayne trades bullets with Clift's friend John Ireland, but not even a bullet wound can keep him from exacting his revenge as Dimitri Tiomkin's score rises to the occasion. What fol-lows moved *The A to Z of Westerns in Cinema* to hail it "one of the greatest fight scenes in the history of westerns." *Legendary Westerns* in-cludes it among the most memo-rable cowboy fights. *The Manly Movie Guide* lists it as one of the best western showdowns. *Life* termed it "an unusually ferocious fight."

Devastating punches are thrown into Clift's jaw before the young man summons up the guts to fight back. This pleases Wayne im-mensely. They trade eye-opening blows for nearly a minute until Joanne Dru fires a gun and brings them to their senses. The happy resolution between the men and Dru rang false with many viewers, especially in light of Ireland's

wounded body a few feet away. Wayne was origi-nally supposed to die from Ireland's bullet. Nev-ertheless, the film as a whole is considered one of Hollywood's all-time classics. Cliff Lyons was stunt coordinator. Sid Davis briefly doubled Wayne taking a fall while Richard Farnsworth stunted for Clift. Davis was Wayne's stand-in for over a decade. On rare occasions he performed a stunt for Wayne, such as happened on location in Elgin, Arizona, for *Red River*. Wardrobe man Jack Miller had backup costumes available in case the actors' clothing became torn or unusable through repeated takes.

Hawks' greatest concern in staging this emo-tional and physically demanding scene was that New York actor Clift wouldn't be able to pull off the fight believably. He was deemed too fragile and uncoordinated. His stunt double Farnsworth had already been earning his pay for the horse riding shots, but Hawks didn't want to rely on doubles any more than he had to during the fight. The di-rector claimed his own arms became tired trying to show Clift how to throw punches correctly. Clift was a slightly built 5'9" and 150 pounds. Wayne was a 6'4", 240-pound screen fight legend. Wayne was similarly concerned that the fight wouldn't work and would appear to the audience as an in-credible mismatch. Hawks opted to keep the scene short and have Russell Harlan shoot from low an-gles to play down the size difference between the two men. The greatest equalizer was the decision to have Wayne wounded by Ireland's gun imme-

Joanne Dru looks on as John Wayne (left) and Montgomery Clift bat-tle in United Artists' classic western *Red River* (1948).

diately before the fistfight. It was felt that if Wayne was incapacitated, audiences would accept that Clift could knock the giant down. Wayne still wasn't convinced. Despite the compromises, *Chicago Tribune* writer Mike Royko still found it a "ridiculous notion that delicate Montgomery Clift would get in a knock down fistfight with the Duke and hold his own." According to *The Making of the Great Westerns*, the scene works: "Perhaps Clift's ignorance of the subject aided the true-to-life look of the fisticuffs."

The theatrically trained Clift's sensitive features and vulnerable nature contrasted remarkably with Wayne. Clift was everything Wayne's man's man wasn't, including being a liberal Democrat and a closet homosexual. Clift had been rejected by the Army for chronic diarrhea and was plagued by dysentery, colitis and an assortment of allergies. To deal with his insecurities, he was a heavy alcohol and pill user and spent hours on his therapist's couch. Yet the Method actor could convey intensity when called for on the big screen. Wayne agreed to put all their differences aside before filming for the good of the motion picture. The film sat on the shelf for over a year while United Artists and Monterey Productions haggled over a distribution deal. Shortly before the release, there was another problem: a lawsuit from Howard Hughes, who claimed the climax was too close to his 1943 film *The Outlaw* with the Clift character refusing to draw his gun. Hawks had worked on developing *The Outlaw* for Hughes and filmed at least part of it without credit. A compromise was reached and 24 seconds of the *Red River* fight was excised before the film's release by Hughes and editor Christian Nyby.

Red River was remade as a 1988 TV movie with James Arness and Bruce Boxleitner playing the main roles.

See: Bosworth, Patricia. *Montgomery Clift: A Biography*. New York: Open Road, 2012; "Montgomery Clift." *Life Magazine*. August 16, 1948; Royko, Mike. "Well, Pilgrim, There's Reason for Many Movie Uprising." *Chicago Tribune*. March 19, 1997.

ROBERT MITCHUM VS. ROBERT PRESTON in *Blood on the Moon* (1948)

A moody black-and-white noir-western, *Blood on the Moon* features cattlemen against homesteaders with hired gun Robert Mitchum turning on bad guy employer Robert Preston for the love of Barbara Bel Geddes. Their dimly lit, claustrophobic two-minute knockdown, drag-out barroom battle drew blood and avoided the usual fight clichés by having the principals largely slug it out *sans* acrobatic doubles. Scenarist Lillie Hayward and Harold Shumate work from a dark Luke Short novel that benefits from giving the men a long history with one another, deepening the character motivation for the fight. Director Robert Wise wanted the combatants to enthusiastically go at it, with the winner being as bloodied and exhausted as the loser. Mitchum and Preston perfectly understood what he was looking for and brought a healthy dose of brutal realism to the scene. Intentional misses as well as hits occur as both stagger for sure footing. Editor Samuel Beetley leaves the errant swings in per former editor Wise's specifications. There's excellent use of perfectly timed sound effects from Foley artists John Cass and Terry Kellum, while Roy Webb's pulsing music score rises and falls dramatically with each shift of power.

Critics weren't used to seeing such gritty themes in a cowboy picture and were confused. In response to the violent nature of the Mitchum-Preston clash, the *New York Times* wrote that the bruising fistfight "ought to settle most savage instincts," and *Variety* added that the film was "loaded with suspense wallop." *The New York Sun* critic wrote, "Mitchum and Preston stage one of the most vicious screen fights I've yet had the horror to witness." Overlooking the rest of the classic film's merits, the *Hollywood Citizen News* said, "The fistfight is about the best thing *Blood on the Moon* has to offer." Over the years, the film and the fight began to build in reputation. Wise biographer Robert C. Keenan felt that the fight "constitutes the high point of *Blood on the Moon*," while Mitchum biographer Lee Server added that it was "the film's most memorable sequence." In his film location book on Sedona, *Arizona's Little Hollywood*, Joe McNeill wrote that the fight "is still one of the most brutally realistic bare-knuckle brawls ever filmed."

The fight took three days to record on a shadowy RKO soundstage. Wise was pleased, calling it "the most distinctive scene in the whole film." Cinematographer Nicholas Musuraca was a master of film noir lighting, and his stamp is clearly evident. The fight occurs halfway through the film as tension builds between the two men. Mitchum tips over a table and dives over chairs to engage Preston. When gunman Tom Tyler appears at the door, Mitchum fans his pistol in Tyler's direction, then throws the gun to knock out the overhead light. In semi-darkness Mitchum and Preston trade several punches and smash into walls and every chair and table in the bar. Mitchum even slices his hand open on a piece of broken glass. One of the best bits has Preston smashing a bottle with deadly intentions inches above Mitchum's head. With his long hair flying, Mitchum gets atop Preston and lands five unanswered punches to end the fight.

Sensationalistic publicity claimed that Mitchum had been having problems breathing properly due to the lingering effects of a broken nose he suffered during his boxing days. He

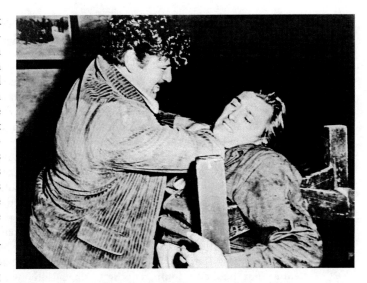

Robert Preston (left) and Robert Mitchum stage one of the screen's most realistic fights in RKO's *Blood on the Moon* (1948).

was considering having an operation to alleviate the condition. During his fight with Preston, he was clobbered on his nose. When the swelling had gone down, Mitchum could now breathe easier. Mitchum did injure a knuckle during the melee, requiring a visit to the studio medical staff, and both men unintentionally stepped on one another's toes and caused minor abrasions. The uncredited doubles are likely Ted Mapes and Clem Fuller, who both have bit parts. Preston's double appears far more than Mitchum's. The stuntmen clashed with Wise over the staging of the action. They wanted to do a more traditional stunt fight. Wise won out, and the stuntmen barely appear in the finished film. The fight has taken its rightful place in the annals of cinematic history. It's one of Mitchum's best.

Five-foot-ten, 190-pound Robert Preston, as an amateur boxer, had won many trophies for his pugilistic talents. A Paramount talent scout initially balked at signing him because he thought Preston, with his husky frame, looked too much like a professional wrestler. During World War II, Preston was a physical instructor with the Army Air Corps and boxed in his squad's heavyweight division. In Hollywood he specialized in playing charming villains, occasionally toplining as a B-movie hero. He was as comfortable performing song and dance routines as he was fisticuffs for the screen. That didn't always translate to real life. In 1952 the charismatic, multi-talented star of stage and screen was sucker punched and attacked by

half a dozen men in New York as he was leaving a restaurant. One of the assailants was Joseph Scarlato, a professional boxer in the lightweight division. Preston lost three teeth, suffered bruises to his face, and needed 20 stitches sewn into his lower lip.

He had fights of interest against Lloyd Nolan in *King of Alcatraz* (1937), Joel McCrea in *Union Pacific* (1939), Preston Foster in *Moon Over Burma* (1940), Fred MacMurray in *New York Town* (1941), William Bendix and Albert Dekker in *Wake Island* (1942), Alan Ladd in *Wild Harvest* (1947) (see entry) and *Whispering Smith* (1948), Gregory Peck in *The Macomber Affair* (1947), Fred Graham in *Tulsa* (1949), Robert Sterling in *The Sundowners* (1950), Robert Stack in *My Outlaw Brother* (1951) and Robert Ryan in *Best of the Badmen* (1951).

See: "Actor Tells of Attack." *The Times-News.* January 29, 1952; "Big Bob Preston Feels Like Bird Just Released from Gilded Cage." *Indianapolis Star.* January 18, 1948; "Black Eyes in Film Fight to Be Real." *Hartford Courant.* May 2, 1948; Emery, Robert J. *The Directors: Take One.* New York: Allworth Press, 2002.

CORNEL WILDE VS. LOUIS BACIGALUPI in *Road House* (1948)

This tense, effective Jean Negulesco film noir is set in a smoke-filled Wisconsin bowling alley called Jefty's Road House where bouncer Cornel

Wilde and mentally unhinged owner Richard Widmark vie for the affections of torch singer Ida Lupino. Wilde, a framed ex-con, shows the lengths he'll go to in order to protect her when he stands up to a bullying drunkard who tosses Lupino against the bar. The huge troublemaker is as wide as he is tall and was played by 6'4", 300-pound Louis Bacigalupi, a professional wrestler who once carried the reputation in the ring as the meanest man in Los Angeles County. In real life, Bacigalupi was a gentle giant who repaired musical organs and was concerned when Lupino injured her back and neck. The climactic fight was also not without injury, as Wilde accidentally caught Widmark with an uppercut to the jaw. John Indrisano was fight coordinator and noir stylist Joseph LaShelle the black-and-white cinematographer.

20th Century-Fox publicity compared the minute-long fight to *The Spoilers,* claiming it rivaled the classic in "savage intensity." This fight must set a record for broken glass as the bar top is cleared and bottles are thrown and smashed throughout. At first Wilde seems overmatched by the giant and he even resorts to jumping on his back. He quickly changes tactics and uses quickness to elude Bacigalupi's attacks, wearing the big man down. Bacigalupi takes especially effective falls, tripping directly into the camera positioned on the floor. Wilde gets the upper hand with a chokehold and bangs Bacigalupi's head against the floor until the police arrive. The *Evening Courier* called it "a peachy fight."

Cornel Wilde (6'1", 175 pounds) was a member of the 1936 U.S. Olympic fencing team after having starred in the sport at City College of New York. The athletic actor was in his element as a swashbuckling star. He undertook specialized boxing and judo training for fistfights weeks ahead of a film schedule. Wilde had solid fights with Barton MacLane in *The Walls of Jericho* (1948), Steve Cochran in *Operation Secret* (1952), Lon Chaney in *Passion* (1954) and Mickey Shaughnessy in *Edge of Eternity* (1959). His fights to the death against native warriors hunting him across the South African savannah in *The Naked Prey* (1966) were especially desperate and primal.

See: Donati, William. *Ida Lupino: A Biography.* Lexington: University Press of Kentucky, 2013; "Wilde Took to Road to Train for Fast, Furious Film Fights." *Ellensburg Daily Record.* October 10, 1949.

DICK POWELL VS. GUINN "BIG BOY" WILLIAMS in *Station West* (1948)

"You're too little to make that big a mistake," "Big Boy" Williams tells undercover government agent Dick Powell after the smaller man throws a drink in his face and pops him in the jaw. Williams leads Powell into the dimly lit western street for what he believes will be an easy whooping in front of the entire town of Rock Pass. It doesn't work out that way. Powell more than holds his own in a tense two-minute knee-buckling battle. It's a nicely choreographed, realistic fight highlighted by a Powell arm-bar allowing him to pummel a defenseless Williams. "Big Boy" gets out of the arm-bar with a bear-hug, but Powell's punches wear the bigger man down. Williams collapses onto a hitching post to the astonishment of the citizens, who were laying odds against Powell. No clichéd sound effects occur, and Powell insisted on wearing realistic makeup showing the results of his battle throughout the remainder of the film. As it wasn't filmed chronologically, the result was that Powell and Williams wore bruises weeks before they did the fight scene.

Dick Powell, 5'11" and 185 pounds, was a musical comedy star who abruptly decided to change his career path and become a cynical tough guy when he played Raymond Chandler's detective Philip Marlowe in *Murder, My Sweet* (1944). It seemed unlikely casting, but Powell knew what he was capable of as an actor. He was accepted as one of the noir genre's stars, and Sidney Lanfield's *Station West* was an attempt to bring noir to a western setting. It's an atmospheric, superior film distinctively lensed in black-and-white shadows by Harry J. Wild and edited by Frederic Knudtson. Screenwriters Frank Fenton and Winston Miller created punched-up dialogue working off a Luke Short story. The fight serves the purpose of impressing saloon owner Jane Greer, whom Powell suspects of being involved in the murder of two soldiers.

The brisk picture is best remembered for the two-man brawl. It wasn't for lack of effort on the participants' part. Powell lost 13 pounds and Williams lost 17 pounds training for the fight. Powell also dislocated his wrist and broke a finger performing the action. *The Joplin Globe* wrote, "The dramatic highlight of *Station West* is a terrific knock-down and drag-out fight," while *Western Stars* called it "a real rough-and-tumble battle of brains vs. brawn." *Variety* labeled it "terrific," while

Western Clippings includes it among their "great screen fights."

See: Clary, Patricia. "Bare-Knuckle Fighter Cannot Stay Pretty, Moviegoers Claim." *Long Beach Press Telegram.* April 24, 1948; "Slugfest." *Western Stars.* #1, November 1948; "Train for Film Fight." *Pittsburgh Post-Gazette.* October 16, 1947.

GENE AUTRY VS. JOCK MAHONEY in *Rim of the Canyon* (1949)

Public cowboy #1 Gene Autry engages in one of his best fistfights against stuntman Jock Mahoney (billed as Jock O'Mahoney) in a ghost town's dilapidated hotel lobby in this solid B-western from veteran action director John English and Columbia Pictures. The setting is dusty and falling apart, allowing Mahoney the opportunity to rip a staircase dowel off its mooring and bash Autry with it. Mahoney makes the two-minute fight worthy with his outstanding leaping ability and willingness to fall off staircases and roll over tables with Autry's double Joe Yrigoyen. Mahoney, his long hair flying, smashes Autry with three chairs during the fight. Autry contributes solid punches in the close-ups for cinematographer William Bradford, wearing Mahoney down. Autry manages a chicken-wing hold on a downed Mahoney before being cracked over the head by Walter Sande. *The Filming of the West* calls it "a fabulous fight."

In the climax, Autry's double Sandy Sanders leaps from a tree limb and bulldogs Mahoney off his horse, and the two have another fight. The 6'4" Mahoney towered over Autry but made sure to keep his knees bent every time they were in the camera frame together. Mahoney and Autry fought again in *Cow Town* (1950), and stock footage of their *Rim of the Canyon* fight made it into Autry's *The Old West* (1952). Mahoney so impressed Autry with the smoothness of his delivery and his physical skills that Autry, who was also a TV producer, starred him in the popular TV series *The Range Rider* (1950–1953). That series employed the talents of D.P. William Bradford, who worked with Mahoney to put on many of the small screen's greatest and most influential fights. Director John English, a former editor, worked as a co-director on Republic serials with William Witney, developing and perfecting the fragmentary method of filming the modern fight scene.

Audiences embraced the 5'9", 180-pound Autry. Many contemporaries pondered his success, noting that he was short, out of shape, balding, couldn't ride, couldn't fight, couldn't do gun tricks, and wasn't all that special as a singer or guitar player. "I don't have to do any of that stuff," Autry said. "I'm Gene Autry." Autry learned screen fighting from Yakima Canutt and made it a point to fight men on screen who were bigger than he was, so that his heroic characters wouldn't be perceived as bullying. Enough props were thrown in to break up the monotony of a toe-to-toe slugfest and keep it visually interesting. Autry also chose western veterans who had a knack for staging fisticuffs. They'd sometimes talk their way through a fight, knowing their voices would not be heard by the time the movie reached theater screens. Autry wore gloves to protect his hands and usually handed over his fights to stunt doubles, but he had a few good tussles. He joked that he fought more rounds than boxing champ Jack Dempsey, but in reality his fights hardly stack up next to those of Roy Rogers.

Autry had fights of interest with Roy Rogers in *The Old Corral* (1936), George Chesebro in *Red River Valley* (1938), Buster Crabbe in *Colorado Sunset* (1939), Barton MacLane, Horace MacMahon and Joe Sawyer in *Melody Ranch* (1940), William Haade in *Heart of the Rio Grande* (1942), John Cason in *The Big Sombrero* (1949), Hugh O'Brian in *Beyond the Purple Hills* (1950), Kenne Duncan and Alan Hale, Jr., in *The Blazing Sun* (1950), Harry Lauter in *Whirlwind* (1951), Kenne Duncan in *Texans Never Cry* (1951), Dickie Jones and Don Harvey in *The Old West* (1952) and Fred Krone in *The Last of the Pony Riders* (1953). On *The Gene Autry Show* (1950–1956), he kept action heavies the likes of Harry Lauter and Gregg Barton employed with regularity.

See: Hurst, Jack. "Autry Rides Again." *Chicago Tribune.* March 20, 1987; Magers, Boyd. *Gene Autry Westerns.* Madison, NC: Empire, 2007.

PRESTON FOSTER VS. FORREST TUCKER in *The Big Cat* (1949)

Grizzled Depression-era characters Preston Foster and Forrest Tucker have a long-standing feud that erupts into a frenzied all-or-nothing three-minute battle in this Phil Karlson film about a mountain lion on the loose in southern Utah. There's decent location work and W. Howard Greene color photography for a low-budgeter, but the real draw here is the outrageous hatred between these two men as enacted by the stars. Their fight is an especially intense and brutal affair, full of face-gouging, hair-pulling, head-pounding action. They use whatever advantage they can lay their hands on, including the chain Tucker uses to whip Foster. The fight goes down a hillside and into a river where the combatants pound one another's heads into logs. When a dazed Foster tries to steady himself on a log, Tucker jumps on it, forcing the end into Foster's face. Editor Harvey Magner intercuts the fight with the men's kids breaking into a battle of their own, showing that this fight is going to carry on into the next generation. Paul Sawtell's score is typically accomplished. Legendary makeup artists Jack Pierce and Ern Westmore applied the fake blood.

Variety called it "one of the best fistic brawls seen in a long time," while critic Leonard Maltin labeled it "one of the best and longest fistfights in film history." Tough guys Foster and Tucker are game for much of the Wasatch Mountain action, although unidentified doubles take a few of the bigger tumbles and a Tucker somersault down the hill. The actors were in waist-deep water in Hoosier Lake for several days and fighting at a significant altitude, which further sapped them of strength. The actors spent five minutes at a time in the water with the crew providing them steaming cups of tea upon their exit. Besides being cold, no injuries were incurred by the two pros. However, Foster jokingly told the press that screenwriters were always finding ways for him to be bashed around on screen.

Six-foot-two, 210-pound Foster was known as a man that could handle himself in a scrap. The former railroad cop once beat three men in a dockside brawl, and early in his career dabbled as a professional wrestler. Foster carried a tough guy rep even into his Hollywood career where he gained brief leading man stardom as a blacksmith turned gladiator in *The Last Days of Pompeii* (1935). His penchant for brawling caused trouble when he was sued by a motorist who allegedly ran him off the road near Mint Canyon. Foster cornered the man and knocked out three of his teeth. During World War II, Foster served in the Coast Guard.

Notable fights include *Sea Devils* (1937) and *Law and Order* (1953) (see entries). Fights of interest came against Edward G. Robinson in *Two Seconds* (1932), John Carroll in *Muss 'Em Up* (1936), Randolph Scott in *20,000 Men a Year* (1939), Robert Preston in *Moon Over Burma* (1940), Douglas Fowley in *Café Hostess* (1940), Robert Montgomery in *Unfinished Business*

(1941), Noel Madison in *Secret Agent of Japan* (1942), Horace McMahon in *Roger Touhy, Gangster* (1944), John Hodiak in *The Harvey Girls* (1946), William Bishop in *Thunderhoof* (1948), Tom Tyler in *I Shot Jesse James* (1949) and Wayne Morris in *The Tougher They Come* (1950) and *The Big Gusher* (1951). On TV, Foster was the two-fisted Cap'n John on *Waterfront* (1954–1956), squaring off against guests such as Jack Lambert.

See: "Big Cat Shows Brutal Fight." *Medicine Hat News.* September 26, 1956; "The Big Cat." *Camden News.* August 13, 1949; "Preston Foster Dies; Starred as Brawler." *Milwaukee Sentinel.* July 15, 1970.

SCOTT BRADY vs. JOHN RUSSELL in *The Gal Who Took The West* (1949)

"The roaring story of the West's wildest feud," cried the Universal ads for this Frederick De Cordova film. Yvonne DeCarlo's presence in this family squabble pits brothers Scott Brady and John Russell against one another in a *Spoilers*-inspired battle that *Western Clippings* includes among its "great screen fights." Tensions come to a head at the climax when the two knock one another all over the inside of the Clarence Brown Ranch in Calabasas for an action-packed minute and a half. Brady and Russell throw punches with bad intentions, but its stunt doubles Jock Mahoney and Guy Teague who make the fight truly special with their flips over banisters, railings and furniture. Sofa chairs and cushions serve as launching pads for Mahoney's trademark leaps as well as effectively soft landing areas for the well-choreographed falls. DeCarlo watches the men with pride, knowing she caused the fisticuffs. In real life, DeCarlo became highly enamored with Mahoney, and the two were engaged to be married. Cinematographer William H. Daniels, composer Frank Skinner and editor Milton Carruth contribute admirably to the action scene. Brady and Russell battled each other later the same year in the crime drama *Undertow* (1949).

Scott Brady, born Gerard Tierney, was 6'3", 210 pounds and, in real life, the brother of legendary screen tough Lawrence Tierney. Brady was a light-heavyweight boxing champion in the Navy as well as a lumberjack and wasn't one to be messed with. Like his brother, Brady could throw back the booze and earned a reputation as one of Hollywood's best barroom brawlers. However, he didn't resort to his brother's near-lunatic escapades while under the influence and was liked by those he worked with. Over the years, Brady tired of Tierney's constant troubles, leading to strained relations. Issues came to a head in the 1960s when the brothers had a fistfight with one another. Brady was said to have come out better in that exchange and the two rarely spoke with one another from that point on.

The strapping Brady was a believable movie fighter with good reactions and a wallop of a knockout punch, first displayed when he played a boxer in *In This Corner* (1948). He had a distinctive fighting method: When facing the camera, he'd zing straight crosses past each of his opponent's ears. Fights of interest came against Forrest Tucker in *Montana Belle* (1952), Joseph Cotten in *Untamed Frontier* (1952), Alan Hale, Jr., in *The Law vs. Billy the Kid* (1954), Neville Brand in *Mohawk* (1956), Barry Sullivan in *The Maverick Queen* (1956), Leo Gordon in *The Restless Breed* (1957), Clint Eastwood in *Ambush at Cimarron Pass* (1958), Rory Calhoun in *Black Spurs* (1965), John Ireland in *Fort Utah* (1967) and Robert Stiles in *$* (1971). On his western TV series *Shotgun Slade* (1959–1961), he fought professional wrestlers Bern Hoffman and Count Billy Varga in the 1960 episodes "The Fabulous Fiddle" and "The Smell of Money." As a TV guest star, Brady had a solid fight with John Gavin in the 1963 *Alfred Hitchcock Hour* "Run for Doom."

See: Folkart, Burt A. "Ruggedly Handsome Star of Westerns Was 60: Movie Tough Guy Scott Brady Dies." *Los Angeles Times.* April 18, 1985; *The Gal Who Took the West* pressbook.

THE QUINCANNON BRAWL in *She Wore a Yellow Ribbon* (1949)

One of director John Ford's corniest scenes is nonetheless a memorable set piece showcasing the blustery brawling of an aging but still potent Victor McLaglen. The humorous fight is set to the familiar Irish tune of "Garyowen" from one of Ford's favored composers, Richard Hageman. Occurring midway through the film, it manages to liven up what until this point had been a slow-paced Frank Nugent–scripted western colorfully shot in Ford's picturesque Monument Valley by Oscar-winning cinematographer Winton C. Hoch and second unit cameraman Archie Stout. Editor Jack Murray does a solid job with the pacing, keeping the mood light despite the violence. *Variety* called the fight

"the roughest, yet most hilarious seen on the screen in months," while the *New York Times* praised "the brash bravado of the barrack-room brawl." Tap Gallagher wrote, "Speed makes Victor McLaglen's hammy barroom brawl one of Ford's best friendly fights." However, many critics found it silly. Ford biographer Ronald L. Davis wrote, "Victor McLaglen's brawl in the company store goes on and on, more roughhouse than humorous, almost to the point of becoming ludicrous." Ford chronicler Bill Levy called it "an over-the-top brawl that has been a guilty pleasure for generations of audiences."

Cavalry commander John Wayne allows Sgt. Quincannon (McLaglen) some fun before his hitch is up. Admonishing McLaglen not to drink, he sends him to the company bar to do just that, then orders soldier Michael Dugan to gather his men and throw McLaglen in the stockade. Behind bars, McLaglen won't be in danger of encountering Indians on a final patrol. Dugan and troopers Fred Graham, Mickey Simpson, Fred Kennedy and Billy Jones have their work cut out for them in a brawl lasting three minutes with a time-out for all to down a toast to Wayne. Ford's camera-cute fight often delves into slapstick, with the punch-drunk soldiers occasionally swinging at one another as McLaglen sits on the bar and drinks his favorite Irish whiskey with bartender Francis Ford. It's only the tongue-lashing of Mildred Natwick that sends McLaglen to the guard house. She even berates the soldiers: "Eight of you picking on one poor man."

"Only seven, ma'am," McLaglen says as he marches off. Cliff Lyons coordinated the action.

All the soldiers were stuntmen with the exception of former boxer Mickey Simpson as the sledge-carrying blacksmith. The original fight choreography called for Simpson's face to be buried in a sack of flour. To prepare, he was wadding up tissue to stick in his nose so he wouldn't inhale the flour into his lungs. John Ford told him he wouldn't need the tissue as the choreography was going to change. He now wanted Simpson to simply back up across the bar and sit down, his character wanting no further part of McLaglen's fists. It's a nice touch. Among the stuntmen, Graham stands out with a variety of falls. Legend has it that McLaglen, in his early 60s here, wasn't always able to pull his punches appropriately. It's apparent he still could pack a powerful punch if he were to land one.

See: Davis, Ronald L. *John Ford: Hollywood's Old Master.* Norman: University of Oklahoma

Press, 1995; Gallagher, Tap. *John Ford: The Man and His Films.* Berkeley: University of California Press, 1986; Levy, Bill. *Lest We Forget: John Ford's Stock Players.* Albany, GA: BearManor, 2013.

JOHN PAYNE VS. LON CHANEY in *Captain China* (1950)

Disgraced sea captain John Payne takes passage on the ship of a former underling in an effort to prove his worth in a routine Lewis R. Foster–directed drama highlighted by a terrific four-minute fight. Payne discovers that the new captain Jeffrey Lynn gave false testimony in regard to his (Payne's) previous command, as did crew member Lon Chaney, who had locked him in his quarters. Tensions erupt in a gigantic and bloody fistfight between Payne and Chaney, which ends when Lynn points a gun at both men. Publicity played up the battle, and there was even a comic book tie-in to the film that focused on the fistfight. Chaney's character was called "the most murderous menace

John Payne (right) and Lon Chaney, Jr., clash in Paramount's *Captain China* (1950).

who ever sailed the seven seas." Fred Graham worked on the film as a fight double, as did Charles Regan. They take several great falls on the ship's deck. *Variety* praised the film as having "several good rough and tumble sequences," while the *Adelaide News* described it as "the most heartfelt screen fight for months." Chaney biographer Don G. Smith wrote, "The Chaney-Payne fight is one of the film's high points, but it doesn't rise above Lon's confrontation with Crawford in *North to the Klondike.*"

The fight took five days to complete on the Paramount lot and not without damage to both stars, who did much of the action for John Alton's camera. Chaney's lips required two stitches when he inadvertently hit himself in the mouth with his own fist while taking a fall on the ship's deck. In addition to injured ribs, he ripped open the top of his ear. Payne injured three of his own ribs when he was heaved against a ship's mast and needed to spend three days under a doctor's care. He also chipped an elbow and broke a finger. Payne proudly talked about doing their own stunts on the publicity trail. Editor Howard Smith did an exceptional job cutting the fight action together.

Six-foot, 185-pound Payne spent time as a professional boxer and wrestler before entering films playing pugilists in *Kid Nightingale* (1939), *Tin Pan Alley* (1940) and *Footlight Serenade* (1942). Once in Hollywood, he worked with Mushy Callahan and kept fit sparring with pro heavyweight Jack Roper. Whenever hitting a new town on the publicity trail, his first order of business was finding a local gymnasium where he could work out. An Army Air Corps veteran, he was a convincing screen fighter and excelled in adventure films and noir titles where he had to punch his way out of trouble. Payne's characters often ended up bloodied, broken and bandaged by picture's end.

Notable fights include *Kansas City Confidential* (1952) and *99 River Street* (1953) (see entries). Fights of interest came against

Victor McLaglen in *Strictly Dynamite* (1942), Dan Duryea in *Larceny* (1948) and *Rails into Laramie* (1954), Sterling Hayden in *El Paso* (1949), Sonny Tufts in *The Crooked Way* (1949), Forrest Tucker in *Crosswinds* (1951), Dennis O'Keefe in *Passage West* (1951), Willard Parker in *Caribbean* (1952), Ronald Reagan in *Tennessee's Partner* (1955), Leo Gordon in *Santa Fe Passage* (1955), William Bishop in *The Boss* (1956) and John Smith in *Rebel in Town* (1956). On his western series *The Restless Gun* (1957–1959), Payne fought Dan Blocker in 1957's "Jody." Makiong a 1957 TV guest appearance, Payne staged a fight with the host of *The Tennessee Ernie Ford Show*.

See: "How to Be a TV Cowboy." *TV Guide*. January 18, 1958; Ingram, Frances. "John Payne: Living Out the Dream." *Classic Images*. June 2011; Nichols, Harmon W. "Star Travels to Promote New Movie for Paramount." *Spokane Daily Chronicle*. January 18, 1950.

STANISLAUS ZBYSZKO VS. MIKE MAZURKI in *Night and the City* (1950)

This classic film noir from director Jules Dassin stars Richard Widmark as a low-level London fight promoter who latches onto Greco-Roman wrestler Stanislaus Zbyszko and his young charge Ken Richmond with empty promises of restoring their pure technique to the ring. Mike Mazurki, a drunken wrestling rival under the control of promoter Herbert Lom, continually taunts Zybysko and Richmond at the gym at Widmark's opportunistic urging. Lom is in fact Zybysko's real son and the emotional manipulations of both promoters have dire consequences. During a training session, Mazurki crosses the line and all hell breaks loose between the two men as Widmark and others futilely try to pull them apart in the ring. This is what's known in theatric wrestling circles as a "shoot," or a real match in the ring where the predetermined outcome is ignored. No cheering public is present, only panicked witnesses in the gym. It's a fight to the death, with actual wrestling arm-bars, chokes and

bear-hugs intending to hurt and maim. The tense struggle lasts four entire minutes of sweaty positioning as each man tries to crush the other's spine. The aged Zbyszko emerges victorious but falls over dead from the exertion. *Variety* called the fight "one of the most exciting bouts ever glimpsed on the screen," while *Time* labeled it "an agonizingly filmed grudge fight." *New York Times* critic Bosley Crowther was so turned off by the back-breaking action that he wrote, "If any more cruel repulsive picture of human brutishness than this is ever screened, this writer has no desire to see it."

The 5'8", 260-pound Zbyszko was a Polish-born professional wrestler active through the 1920s. The bearish grappler was the European heavyweight king and twice crowned the world heavyweight champ. He acquitted himself surprisingly well in the role, giving a realistic and heartfelt performance in the powerful dramatic scenes. In addition to playing the heavy in the picture, Mazurki served as the technical advisor and blocked out the wrestling action. His assistants

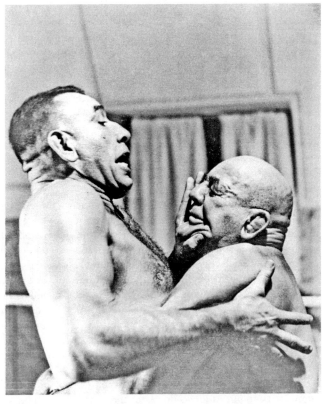

Mike Mazurki (left) and Stanislaus Zbyszko "shoot" a wrestling match in 20th Century–Fox's *Night and the City* (1950).

were Walter Magnee and Mickey Wood, a London-based self-defense and physical training expert who had been the lightweight wrestling champ of Britain. The latter managed the firm "Tough Guys Limited" which provided stuntmen for European-based films.

Mazurki had squared off in the ring against legends like Lou Thesz and "Strangler" Lewis, but said publicly that Zbyszko might have been the toughest man he ever faced. Mazurki pegged Zbyszko's age in his 70s during filming and said the senior wanted to work out every day. They spent three months training and three weeks shooting the action with seven of Max Green's cameras. Every move Mazurki made, Zbyszko countered strategically. When Mazurki tried to take Zbyszko down for real, he couldn't pin him. Mazurki's ribs needed to be taped up every evening from the power of Zbyszko's bear-hug. Despite this dose of reality, Mazurki picked up a few pro match-ups during his time in England for extra money.

See: Danko, Walter W. "Mike Mazurki: Star Athlete." *Ukrainian Weekly*. December 26, 1950; Dowd, Kathy. "An Interview with Mike Mazurki." *The Wrestling News*. March 1975.

DANA ANDREWS VS. NEVILLE BRAND in *Where the Sidewalk Ends* (1950)

This is an effective Otto Preminger–directed, Ben Hecht–scripted film noir with Dana Andrews in top-notch form as a rough-edged cop taking down criminal Gary Merrill to cover his own missteps. Andrews brazenly enters Merrill's Turkish Baths with the intention of pinning the beating death of war hero Craig Stevens on him, but Merrill smells a set-up. When Andrews gets out of line and smacks Merrill in the steam room in front of his t-shirted hoods, top tough Neville Brand steps in with a sadistic smile to trade punches with the anti-hero police detective. Joseph LaShelle gets his camera in close for the action, with the sound of the men's shoes clicking on the floor overriding everything else on the soundtrack. It's a tense 45-second struggle with Brand going for the throat until Andrews breaks the hold and knocks Brand away. Merrill's hoods Bob Evans and Lou Nova step in, Evans laying Andrews out with a right cross.

Former light heavyweight boxer Evans' punch connected and put Andrews down for the count. This was a legitimate danger whenever real boxers were hired for fights. They had spent their entire careers throwing punches to land as opposed to stuntmen who were trained to miss, and Evans was called on to run into the action and deliver his punch on the fly. Andrews ended up with two black eyes and what is known in boxing circles as a butterfly nose: a cut to the bone. He missed a total of 12 days of filming, costing 20th Century-Fox over $45,000 in total costs to pay off contracted players. A sorrowful Evans became physically ill, knowing the errant punch likely cost him future work.

Andrews was lucky it wasn't the 6'3", 210-pound Nova who made contact as he was a legitimate heavyweight contender. For that matter, actor Brand earned a reputation as a man who was often unable to hold back in fights. He looked like he enjoyed mixing it up as a malicious grin crossed his face whenever he was about to punch someone. As a decorated soldier, Brand killed over 200 Germans in World War II and was haunted by his actions. Brand drank heavily with pal Lee Marvin, and the two were in and out of brawls up and down the Pacific Coast Highway. None of this stopped the 5'11", 190-pound Brand from being hired to perform in fights.

His best bouts came against Broderick Crawford in *The Mob* (1951), Leo Gordon in *Gun Fury* (1953) (see entry), George Montgomery in *The Lone Gun* (1954) and *Badman's Country* (1958), Rory Calhoun in *Raw Edge* (1956), Scott Brady in *Mohawk* (1956), James Mason in *Hero's Island* (1962), Robert Conrad in the TV movie *The Adventures of Nick Carter* (1972) and Don Stroud in *Scalawag* (1973). His TV western *Laredo* (1965–1967) was full of scuffles, with the best saloon brawl coming when Brand fought alongside Peter Brown and William Smith in 1965's "Rendezvous at Arillo." As a TV guest, Brand fought Brian Keith in the 1959 *Zane Grey Theatre* episode "Trouble at Tres Cruces" and Dan Blocker in the 1960 *Bonanza* episode "The Last Viking."

See: "Butterfly Nose for Dana Andrews." *Trenton Evening Times*. February 21, 1950; Heffernan, Harold. "Occupational Hazards Are Numerous in Hollywood." *Toledo Blade*. March 8, 1950; "Neville Brand; Tough-Guy Actor, Decorated War Hero." *Los Angeles Times*. April 18, 1992.

JOEL MCCREA VS. JOHN RUSSELL in *Saddle Tramp* (1950)

This solid little western stars Joel McCrea as one of his most amiable cowpokes, trying to raise a pal's orphans while caught in a cattle-thieving ranch war. For all his laid-back niceties, when push came to shove McCrea could swing it with the best of them. The action-filled climax sees him take on crooked foreman John Russell in a bruising two-minute slugfest that leaves both men worse for wear. The furiously paced fight, which begins in a cabin but goes up and down a hillside, took over three days to rehearse and 13 hours to film the principals. The two stars did a good deal of fistic action, and at day's end both wished they had turned over more to their stunt doubles. McCrea suffered scratches and a bruised cheek. According to Universal publicity, it was the toughest screen fight of McCrea's career.

John Russell (left) has "chin music" played on him by Joel McCrea in Universal's *Saddle Tramp* (1950).

The stunt work is excellent, with Bob Morgan doubling McCrea and Sol Gorss doubling Russell. The fight benefits from fine editing from Frank Gross and a punchy music score. There's a series of quick close-ups of the men landing punches to one another's face. Argentinian-born director Hugo Fregonese was mystified by the western genre and traditional cowboy slugfests in which more than a dozen knockout blows were delivered without so much as a hat being knocked off. Working from Harold Shumate's script, he tried to the best of his abilities to make McCrea a less than traditional movie cowboy by having him not wear a gun. The only one he handles, he uses as a club in the fight. Russell was a late replacement in the villain role for Lawrence Tierney. *Last of the Cowboy Heroes* calls it "a realistic brawl ... the film's action highlight," while *Six Gun Law* refers to it as "a lively climax."

An excellent equestrian, 6'3", 200-pound Joel McCrea started in Hollywood as a riding double. He became the embodiment of Hollywood's Golden Age as a tanned outdoorsman at the Santa Monica Beach Club. Scenes of action came easily enough for the Pomona College frosh football player, who displayed an effective boxing jab against pro wrestler Ivan Linow in a bare-knuckle match in *The Silver Horde* (1930). In *The Sport Parade* (1932), McCrea starred as an amateur wrestling champion thrown into the world of professional grappling, once again opposite the much larger Linow. He was a solid screen fighter much respected by Hollywood stunt artists. They never minded doing medium shots with him. When Bob Hoy accidentally clipped him on *Border River* (1954), McCrea took the blame for being in the wrong place. As the film's star, he could easily have squashed a promising young stuntman's career.

McCrea fought Broderick Crawford in *Woman Chases Man* (1937), Robert Preston, Robert Barrat and Harry Woods in *Union Pacific* (1939), Albert Dekker in *Reaching for the Sun* (1941), Anthony Quinn in *Buffalo Bill* (1944), Lloyd Bridges in *Ramrod* (1947) and *Wichita* (1955), Victor Jory in *South of St. Louis* (1948), Fred Graham in *The San Francisco Story* (1952), Pedro Armendariz, Jr., in *Border River* (1954), Murvyn Vye and Race Gentry in *Black Horse Canyon* (1954), Brad Dexter in *The Oklahoman* (1957), Barry Kelley in *The Tall Stranger* (1957), Don Haggerty in *The Gunfight at Dodge City* (1959) and Ron Starr in *Ride the High Country* (1962).

See: Carroll, Harrison. "Joel McCrea Puts All in Screen Fight." *Boston Daily Record.* June 17, 1958; MacPherson, Virginian. "Saddle Up, Western Fans!" *Milwaukee Journal.* April 8, 1950; "13 Hours of Fighting." *Sydney Morning Herald.* November 30, 1950.

RANDOLPH SCOTT vs. JOCK MAHONEY in *Santa Fe* (1951)

An exciting minute-and-a-half fight atop a moving train's flatcar highlights this fine Randolph Scott Columbia western directed by Irving Pichel, who is surrounded by Scott's customarily efficient production team. Kenneth Gamet wrote the script pitting outlaw interests out to stop the building of the Santa Fe rail line with Scott emerging as the company's protector. Cinematographer Charles Lawton, Jr., contributes great exterior shots during the fight, while Paul Sawtell's score is stirring if overly familiar. Editor Gene Havlick's cutting is top-notch considering the dizzying changes going on behind the scenes. It's a show for the stuntmen all the way.

Scott goes fist to fist with henchman Jock Mahoney, the great stuntman who doubled Scott in such films as *Coroner Creek* (1948) and *The Nevadan* (1950). Here Mahoney gets the chance to step up and play Scott's main opponent. He still winds up doubling Scott within the same fight. He also doubles Scott in an earlier barroom fight with villain Roy Roberts (doubled by Eddie Parker).

To open the picture, Scott knocks Mahoney into a wheelbarrow and promptly deposits him into a ditch, but it's the train battle everyone remembers with *Last of the Cowboy Heroes* opining, "Scott (or his double) does have a neat fistfight with Jock Mahoney on a moving train, in which our hero loses his gun—a nice, realistic touch." *Six Gun Law* calls this fight "a hardboiled highlight."

Mahoney served as stunt coordinator and does a fine job setting up the thrilling train action. Logs slip off the train as Mahoney swings a pickaxe at Scott's head and real scenery rushes past. Mahoney wound up doubling Scott when Scott's original stuntman Bob Morgan expressed concerns at slipping off the train onto a dangerous stretch of

rocks. This necessitated the stuntmen to switch outfits, with Mahoney doubling Scott and Morgan now doubling Mahoney, who takes the fall off the train. He manages to cling to the side of the flatcar before pulling himself up and resuming the fight as the stuntmen once again switched outfits. Mahoney was back in his own clothes in time to be clubbed by Scott's pistol and fall off the train and roll down a hill. The timing of the fall was slightly off and Mahoney bounced down a path that had not been cleared of rocks. Still, he emerged unscathed.

Six-foot-four, 200-pound University of Iowa football player and Marine fighter pilot Jock Mahoney became an important figure in fight scene history. As a stuntman he quickly distinguished himself as one of the greatest in the business with his all-around athleticism and leaping ability. Mahoney had effortless balance and moved with the grace of a big cat in action scenes. He threw a great screen punch and could sell others' blows for the camera by creating great space between himself and the ground as he launched into the air with arms and hair flying. While making the TV series *The Range Rider* in the early 1950s, Mahoney perfected the art of combat against multiple opponents coming from all directions.

Mahoney emphasized timing in his fights and was extremely camera-savvy. The smoothness with which he and *Range Rider* fight partner Dick Jones worked in their innovative fight choreography is legendary. It spawned an entire generation of play-fighting children to become professional stuntmen. No prop was safe as the two could demolish a set with unique and well-planned precision. They put on a superb fight with one another in 1953's "Jimmy the Kid," with Jones playing the lookalike title outlaw. In 1952's "Indian War Party," Jones stepped in to double Rodd Redwing for a thrilling fight with Mahoney atop a fallen redwood tree. On the publicity trail, the duo thrilled live audiences with their exciting fight routines at fairs and rodeos and even took their fight to *The Ed Sullivan Show* in 1953.

Notable Mahoney fights include *Coroner Creek* (1948), *Rim of the Canyon* (1949), *The Gal Who Took the West* (1949), *Joe Dakota* (1957) and *Tarzan the Magnificent* (1960) (see entries). Fights of interest came against Fred Graham in *Overland Pacific*

Randolph Scott delivers a crushing blow to Jock Mahoney aboard a flatbed train in Columbia's *Santa Fe* (1951).

(1954), Lane Bradford in *Showdown at Abilene* (1956), Anthony Dexter in *Three Blondes in His Life* (1961), Leo Gordon in *Tarzan Goes to India* (1962), Woody Strode in *Tarzan's Three Challenges* (1963) and Fernando Poe, Jr., in *Walls of Hell* (1964). On his New Orleans–based series *Yancy Derringer* (1958–1959), he fought Mickey Simpson in "Wayward Warrior" and battled James Foxx atop a pool table in "Thunder on the River." As a TV guest, Mahoney had standout fights with Buddy Baer in the 1958 *Wagon Train* episode "The Dan Hogan Story," Eric Fleming in the 1961 *Rawhide* episode "Incident of the Phantom Bugler" and Ron Ely in the 1966 and 1967 *Tarzan* episodes "The Deadly Silence" and "Mask of Rona."

See: Lewis, Jack C. "Ultimate Stuntman." *Guns of the Old West.* November 2006; "Pow! But Not in the Kisser." *TV Guide.* February 23, 1963.

ROBERT MITCHUM'S YACHT FIGHT in *His Kind of Woman* (1951)

Notorious behind-the-scenes maneuvering distinguished the enjoyably tongue-in-cheek mystery *His Kind of Woman* as RKO head Howard Hughes became obsessed with Robert Mitchum's climactic fight. Mitchum was originally to tangle with henchmen on the bridge of a yacht, emerge victorious and take Jane Russell in his arms. That's how original director John Farrow shot the film, but in watching the first cut Hughes became convinced it needed to be bigger and better, including a total recasting of the main villain. Richard Fleischer was brought in to direct the new climax, with Hughes personally overseeing the writing and blocking of the action. Mitchum wouldn't have just one fight. He'd have an ongoing battle with many henchmen all over the yacht, taking a break only to be tortured at gunpoint. The yacht needed to be built to exact specifications to handle all the action. The process dragged on for months, and Mitchum became so peeved at his treatment he had a legendary blow-up at the end of filming.

Fleischer began filming with Hughes' eventual choice for the bad guy Robert Wilke replacing actor Howard Petrie. After having much of the part in the can, Hughes decided he preferred Raymond Burr as the heavy. Fleischer had to restart everything. For three whole months, a shirtless Mitchum spent every day being slugged, knocked around, tied up, beaten down, belt-whipped, boiler-steamed and hit in the head by pipes. Hughes perversely insisted that henchman Anthony Caruso's fist be shown going deep into Mitchum's belly. Mitchum continued to oblige. Hughes decided he wanted Mitchum's character to be given a drug with a hypodermic needle, with a close-up of the skin being penetrated. Mitchum flatly refused. Coming on the heels of his famous pot bust, he didn't want audiences to think he was into needles. Hughes instead devised new beatings for his star. Caruso punched Mitchum with a brass belt buckle rolled over his fist. At one point, Burr knocked Mitchum's head against a pipe so hard he was rendered unconscious. Fleischer was forced to re-film the scene, because somehow the blow didn't look realistic enough. Through it all, Mitchum kept on showing up for his daily whooping. The rough cut of the new ending lasted an hour and 20 minutes by itself and posed a great challenge for editors Frederic Knudtson and Eda Warren due to its bizarre shifts in tone and the need to assemble the footage per Hughes' specifications.

The best battle occurs early on in the yacht's wheelhouse with stuntmen Dale Van Sickel and Gil Perkins, where Mitchum manages to land several significant licks. Mitchum busts them up in sharply edited footage that Fleischer and Harry J. Wild captured with a hand-held camera. There's a fine backward stair fall done by Mitchum's double Paul Stader, who served as stunt coordinator. Mitchum is nabbed and the extended torture scene occurs before he once again breaks free and starts swinging at Burr, Caruso and stuntmen Van Sickel and Sol Gorss. Comic-relief Vincent Price and the Mexican police arrive by boat to save the day in a massive brawl topside involving 28 stuntmen. These include Bud Wolfe, John Daheim, Charles Horvath, Ken Terrell, Art Dupuis, Chuck Hamilton, Al Murphy and Mitchum's stand-in Boyd Cabeen.

The movie had been filming for more than a year. Late one afternoon, Fleischer thought he could wrap the film with one final shot of Mitchum struggling with his captors. An exhausted Mitchum gave Fleischer the okay for the late shooting, but by the time the set was dressed Mitchum had imbibed too much vodka in his dressing room and was in a lousy mood. Being led into the ship's salon by stuntmen Van Sickel and Gorss, Mitchum flung them to the floor. Another shot was called for, and Mitchum again improvised in a rough manner. By the third try the stuntmen were replying in kind and Fleischer had a full-scale fight on his hands. Mitchum turned his fury onto the set itself, smashing walls, putting his fists through doors, and cursing Hughes and the neverending movie. By the next morning, Mitchum was remorseful. But the set needed to be rebuilt, adding to the lengthy production schedule.

Mitchum biographer Damien Love wrote, "Mitchum's final beatings are extraordinarily brutal," while Lee Server acknowledged, "Only Anthony Mann's brutal noirs contained anything to match the sadistic fury of Fleischer's and Hughes's belt buckle and hypodermic melee." The *New York Times* called it "the crudest, cheapest kind of sensationalized violence." The film became symbolic of what Mitchum with tongue in cheek termed his typical 1950s "gorilla picture." For 90 minutes he is beaten on the head by "gorillas" until they become so exhausted they collapse on top of him. At this point the female lead searches through the unconscious thugs until she finds Mitchum, lifts him to his feet, and declares him the hero. They kiss, and the credits begin. Ironically enough, in *White Witch Doctor* (1953) Mitchum has to fight a man in a gorilla outfit.

See: Love, Damien. *Robert Mitchum: Solid, Dad, Crazy.* London: B.T. Batsford, 2002; "28 Stuntmen Required for Mass Movie Brawl." *Chicago Tribune.* June 10, 1951.

RANDOLPH SCOTT VS. JOHN RUSSELL in *Man in the Saddle* (1951)

An above-average Randolph Scott western from director Andre DeToth, *Man in the Saddle* benefits from picturesque High Sierra locations and one of the era's best fights. First off, the Scott and John Russell characters hate each other with a passion. Screenwriter Kenneth Gamet, a veteran of several of Scott's films, knew how to pit two men against one another until they clash violently. The two cowboys are at odds over Ellen Drew, with jealous paramour Russell tracking Scott and Drew to a mountain cabin alongside the Portals Waterfalls (a 300-foot stretch of falls 9400 feet above sea level in Lone Pine, California). There he and Scott have a true knockdown drag-out brawl that literally brings the entire cabin crashing to the ground as they take out vital support beams with all the angry punching and kicking. The Charles Lawton, Jr.–photographed action spills outside into the high mountain scenery, where they slide through snow and mud while continuing to slug it out along a waterfall. There are tumbles over bushes, jumps off ledges and wrestling on the ground as Scott fights in a blind rage. Russell hops on his horse to escape after Scott is momentarily knocked out. Scott comes to and uncharacteristically tries to shoot the fleeing Russell.

The fight takes up approximately two and a half minutes of screen time, and an incredible effort is put in by the anonymous stuntmen. Bob Morgan appears to be doing the bulk of the doubling for Scott, although at different times during the extended battle at least two other stuntmen double for the star. It was a challenge for editor Charles Nelson to keep Scott's overall lack of participation hidden. There's also an impressive 200-foot rolling fall which publicity claimed was done by accident by female lead Drew. She luckily emerged with mere scrapes and bruises. The 52-year-old Scott spent a day at the falls doing the fight, finding the high altitude left him short of breath. *The Western* terms the extended brawl "memorable," while *The Filming of the West* refers to it "as the high point of the picture."

Six-foot-four and 185 pounds, John Russell was an athlete at UCLA before distinguishing himself as a Marine during World War II. Carved from granite, Russell effectively played both heroes and villains until he landed his defining role as Marshal Dan Troop on the TV western *Lawman* (1958–1962). The taciturn Russell's best *Lawman* fight was a bare-knuckler against Mickey Simpson in 1960's "Samson the Great," with both combatants realistically hurting their hands with punches. Russell kept in tip-top condition at Vince's Gym and excelled at action scenes, especially on the TV adventure series *Soldier of Fortune* (1955–1957) where he tangled with the likes of Leo Gordon, Claude Akins, Woody Strode and Lee Van Cleef.

Notable Russell fights include *The Gal Who Took the West* (1949) and *Saddle Tramp* (1950) (see entries). Fights of interest came against Gregory Peck in *Yellow Sky* (1948), Jerome Courtland in *The Barefoot Mailman* (1951), Forrest Tucker in *Fighting Coast Guard* (1951) and *Hoodlum Empire* (1952), Rod Cameron in *Hell's Outpost* (1955), Rory Calhoun in *Apache Uprising* (1966) and John Ireland in *Fort Utah* (1967). His fight with Clint Eastwood in *Honkytonk Man* (1982) was cut from the final print. Russell fought Jock Mahoney in a nostalgic 1982 *Simon and Simon* episode entitled "Rough Rider Rides Again."

See: "He Has All the Expression of a Rock." *TV Guide.* July 28, 1959; "Star Affected by Altitude." *Oregonian.* January 21, 1952; "Thrilling Fight Scenes in Film." *Rocky Mount Evening Telegram.* January 20, 1952.

CLARK GABLE VS. BRODERICK CRAWFORD in *Lone Star* (1952)

MGM's Clark Gable western concerns the fight for independence in Texas. It remains best known for the climactic battle between the heavy-drinking stars. Gable and Broderick Crawford have a stand-out exchange of fists over both the state and Ava Gardner, their boozy off-screen reputations sparking a disappointing script from Borden Chase. The fight is excitingly created by stunt gaffer Gil Perkins, D.P. Harold Rosson and editor Ferris Webster with the robust action standing out from the otherwise pedestrian Vincent Sherman direction. The real stars of the fight are stuntmen George Robotham and Phil Schumacher. Robotham performs a leap from a porch to take Schumacher off a horse, and later offers an impressive backward flip in place of Gable. *Western Clippings* includes this among their "great screen fights," while *The Herald* anointed it "as hair-raising an affair as has been seen in many a month." *The Spokesman Review* wrote that this Gable-Crawford fight "belongs to the screen's roster of bigger and better scraps."

Before filming the fight, Gable and Crawford were dining in a private room at Chasen's Restaurant. They became inebriated to the point where they decided to stage a run-through for the producer. The two demolished the room, but after the brouhaha good-naturedly paid for all the damages. The restaurant owner had special boxing glove cufflinks made for the actors commemorating the occasion. William Farnum from the original *Spoilers* has a bit part. Between takes, Gable sought out Farnum's advice on screen fisticuffs. By the end of the battle, both actors were bruised and shaken, with Crawford suffering a cut on his arm. Publicity declared that *Lone Star* featured more fighting than any other Gable film.

See: "Day's Best Hollywood Story." *Toledo Blade*. July 2, 1951; "Double Lives Dangerously." *The Mercury*. November 21, 1951; *Lone Star* press-book; "This Fight Really Hurt." *San Diego Union*. September 16, 1951.

CHARLES MCGRAW VS. DAVID CLARKE in *The Narrow Margin* (1952)

When RKO head Howard Hughes screened this film, made in 1950 by director Richard Fleischer from an Earl Felton screenplay, he was so taken by the tense, efficient quickie that he considered shelving it and remaking it as an A-picture with Robert Mitchum and Jane Russell in the leads instead of husky, gravel-voiced Charles McGraw and Marie Windsor. (In 1990, the movie *was* remade with Gene Hackman and Anne Archer in the leading roles.) The original tale of a tough cop protecting a mob moll on a train includes a 45-second fight in a compartment: McGraw vs. henchman David Clarke. It predates the similar battle in *From Russia with Love* (1963) and stacks up impressively next to its more famous counterpart. McGraw biographer Alan K. Rode calls it "a terrific fight scene."

Stunt coordinator John Daheim choreographed the close-quarters brawl, which was shot with a hand-held camera by cinematographer George Diskant. No stunt doubles appear in the finished cut, a novel accomplishment for the day. Windsor was slightly shook up when Clarke pushed her down and she missed the padding of the seat. The most memorable moment has McGraw delivering the sole of his shoe into the camera. The stone-faced McGraw, usually seen as a character actor but here cast as the trenchcoated lead, is reminiscent of Mickey Spillane's Mike Hammer. McGraw's as tough as they come in this type of film. The 5'10", 170-pound actor, a former boxer and Army veteran, was known for getting into barroom scrapes. He famously started the fight that saw pal Robert Mitchum kayo heavyweight contender Bernie Reynolds in Colorado.

Notable McGraw fights include *Joe Dakota* (1957) and *Spartacus* (1960) (see entries). Fights of interest came against Roy Rogers in *On the Old Spanish Trail* (1947), James Arness, Lex Barker and Keith Andes in *The Farmer's Daughter* (1947), John Ericson in *The Cruel Tower* (1956) and Glenn Ford in *Cimarron* (1960). On TV's *The Adventures of the Falcon* (1954–1955), McGraw was globetrotting man of action Mike Waring. As a TV guest, he fought Robert Horton on *Wagon Train*, George Maharis on *Route 66*, Doug McClure on *The Virginian* and Jan-Michael Vincent on *Bonanza*.

See: Oliver, Wayne. "McGraw Has Background for Falcon." *Reading Eagle*. February 8, 1955; Weaver, Tom. "Memories of Cat Women." *Starlog*. #222, January 1996.

THE SALOON BRAWL in *Cripple Creek* (1952)

The extended three-minute saloon brawl in this Ray Nazarro Columbia western pits undercover heroes George Montgomery and Jerome

Courtland against gold-smuggling bad guys John Dehner, Don Porter, Chris Alcaide, Zon Murray and Sandy Sanders. While they fight on the second floor, mayhem breaks out on the first over a poker game with a gaggle of stuntmen including Tom Steele, Dale Van Sickel, Ken Terrell, Eddie Parker, Boyd "Red" Morgan, Bob Morgan, Bob Reeves, Leroy Johnson and Jack Stoney duking it out. Al Wyatt can be spied doubling for leading man Montgomery on the balcony. Stuntman-actor Sanders performs the highlight fall from the second floor to the first and Alcaide does a flip into the wall. It's frenetically paced with heightened musical accompaniment from Mischa Bakaleini-koff. Several of the punches thrown are too obvious misses. William V. Skall was the D.P. and Richard Fantl was responsible for the editing. *Motion Picture Herald* praised the film for having "some of the best fisticuffs seen in a western."

Six-three and 180 pounds, character actor John Dehner surprisingly does his own stunt fighting against the second floor banister railing. His participation greatly adds to the effectiveness of the fight. Dehner often played distinguished and sophisticated brain heavies and dress heavies, but he was capable as a dog-ass action heavy when called upon. On the 1960 TV series *The Westerner*, he had outstanding comic fights with Brian Keith. Henchman Chris Alcaide was hired partly for his ability to do his own screen fighting as well as appear menacing. A 6'2", 200-pound Army veteran and Golden Gloves boxer, Alcaide was a bouncer

at the Hollywood Palladium. Although he looked like he was born to dole out punishment, what landed him a ton of work in the 1950s was his ability to throw his own body around in reaction to being hit. He memorably sold a Glenn Ford punch in *The Big Heat* (1953) by heaving himself backward after an uppercut and was soon working regularly as ill-fated torpedoes. Leading men liked an actor who could make them look tough. A back injury limited Alcaide's physical activity and cut his career short.

George Montgomery, 6'2" and 195 pounds, was a collegiate boxer at the University of Montana, holding the title of Northwest Champ. He originally journeyed to California to train with former heavyweight champ Jim Jeffries. Upon arriving in Hollywood in the late 1930s, his first work was as a stuntman. The ruggedly handsome Montgomery made a fine action hero and handled the bulk of his own screen fighting through the next two decades. At home in westerns, he impressed audiences playing modern detective Philip Marlowe in *The Brasher Doubloon* (1947), in that he took a memorable sap beating from stunt thugs Jack Stoney and Ray Spiker. While serving with the Army in World War II, Montgomery built a boxing ring for the troops.

Montgomery fought Kane Richmond in *Riders of the Purple Sage* (1942), Victor McLaglen in *China Girl* (1942), Kent Taylor in *Bomber's Moon* (1943), Greg McClure in *Lulu Belle* (1948), Jack Lambert in *Belle Starr's Daughter* (1948), Sheldon Leonard in *The Iroquois Trail* (1950), Douglas Kennedy in *The Texas Rangers* (1951), Neville Brand and Robert Wilke in *The Lone Gun* (1954), Alan Hale, Jr., and Robert Wilke in *Canyon River* (1955), Leo Gordon in *Robbers' Roost* (1955) and *Black Patch* (1957), Charles Horvath in *Pawnee* (1957), Neville Brand in *Badman's Country* (1958), Lane Bradford in *The Toughest Gun in Tombstone* (1958), Emile Meyer in *King of the White Stallions* (1958) and House Peters, Jr., in *The Man from God's Country* (1958). On his western TV series *Cimarron City* (1958–1959), he fought Don Megowan in 1958's "Beast of Cimarron." As a guest star, Montgomery portrayed Gentleman Jim Corbett in a 1957 *G.E. Theatre*

Zon Murray takes a mighty punch from George Montgomery in Columbia's *Cripple Creek* (1952).

and fought Lee Van Cleef in 1958's *Wagon Train* episode "The Jesse Cowan Story."

See: Fagen, Herb. *White Hats and Silver Spurs.* Jefferson, NC: McFarland, 1996; Kleiner, Dick. "Show Beat." *Park City Daily News.* August 2, 1964; MacPherson, Virginia. "Realistic Cinematic Brawl Proves Ex-Stuntman Montgomery Can Take It." *Toledo Blade.* September 11, 1946.

GARY COOPER VS. LLOYD BRIDGES in *High Noon* (1952)

The politically controversial *High Noon*, a classic Hollywood western shot in stark black-and-white by director Fred Zinnemann and his D.P. Floyd Crosby, goes against cowboy convention by featuring a good guy fighting a good guy. Carl Foreman's Oscar-nominated screenplay presents an abbreviated yet memorable one-minute confrontation between newlywed lawman Gary Cooper and his deputy Lloyd Bridges, smarting at being passed up for the job of Cooper's replacement. Bridges is an atypical villain; a friend suffering from petty jealousy and not above delivering a sucker punch. He tries to get Cooper out of town before the arrival of four outlaws who will be gunning for him, but Cooper balks at being pushed around. Best Actor winner Cooper is at his best playing Marshal Will Kane. He is the epitome of the underdog hero, a stubborn man of principle who faces down dangerous opposition alone when no one else will help him or only get in his way. It's a less-than-subtle swipe at Hollywood blacklisting and the House Un-American Activities, which was grabbing headlines in what many within the industry considered a Communist witch hunt.

Heading up Hollywood's own Motion Picture Alliance for the Preservation of American Ideals were John Wayne and Ward Bond. Wayne famously labeled *High Noon* as Un–American. He hated the idea of the town all but abandoning Cooper. Ironically, Wayne was offered the chance to star in *High Noon* but was disgusted by Foreman's script and turned it down. Wayne and Howard Hawks later made *Rio Bravo* (1959) as a response to *High Noon*. Wayne and Cooper had been casual friends for many years, but Wayne let his dis-

pleasure with Cooper for taking the role be known. Somehow Cooper cajoled Wayne into agreeing to accept the Best Actor Oscar for him at the Academy Awards should he win. Cooper did just that, and Wayne followed through on the promise that he never thought he'd have to keep. Elmo Williams and Harry Gerstad received an Oscar nomination for their editing, while composer Dimitri Tiomkin won the award for his score.

Cooper told the press this was his toughest screen fight. Both Cooper and Bridges are game for the fight action, sensing the project's quality. Though he was bothered by an ulcer and a bad back, Cooper was prodded into performing much of the fight, despite the presence of longtime stunt stand-in Slim Talbot. Likewise, Bridges eschewed the use of Don Turner in the finished product, lending added realism to the scene. Especially effective are the shots where the fighters roll beneath the horse's legs, creating an extra element of danger. Nevertheless, *Mad Magazine* did a parody of this fight in which they specifically found humor in the presence of stunt doubles for the stars.

Another humorous moment occurred while filming the fight in a real Sonoran barn. Bridges' young son Beau was above the action in the hayloft under strict orders not to utter a peep. Lloyd explained that the fight was all choreographed and that no one would be hurt. But Beau wasn't prepared to see his dad doused with a bucket of water in the face and let out a loud laugh, necessitating that part be filmed again. The elder Bridges was

Gary Cooper (left) and Lloyd Bridges battle in United Artists' western classic *High Noon* (1952).

highly upset, fearing he could be fired from the production for having his boy on the set and ruining the take. Cooper alleviated Bridges' fears by inviting the father and son out to lunch.

Six-one and 190 pounds, Bridges was a UCLA athlete and Coast Guard veteran who started off fighting cowboy star Charles Starrett in B-westerns. As the star of the Universal serial *Secret Agent X-9* (1945), a young Bridges had his sleeves rolled up ready for action. On more than one occasion he was cast as a boxing champion. His greatest claim to fame was playing the aquatic adventurer Mike Nelson on TV's *Sea Hunt* (1958–1961), enacting more underwater fights than any other actor in Hollywood. Sometimes Bridges' Nelson fought on land or on boat decks, even performing judo moves while still wearing his swim fins! Modern audiences remember him best as the gruff comic Navy man Tug Benson, punching out both Efrem Zimbalist, Jr., in *Hot Shots!* (1991) and Saddam Hussein (Jerry Haleva) in *Hot Shots! Part Deux* (1993). Further spoofing his established tough guy image, Bridges played the geriatric fitness trainer Izzy Mandelbaum on TV's *Seinfeld* (1997).

Fights of interest came against Joel McCrea in *Ramrod* (1947) and *Wichita* (1955), Lon Chaney in *16 Fathoms Deep* (1948), Steve Brodie in *Home of the Brave* (1949), John Hoyt in *Trapped* (1949), Glenn Ford in *The White Tower* (1950), Frank Lovejoy in *The Sound of Fury* (1951), John Ireland in *Little Big Horn* (1951), Spencer Tracy in *Plymouth Adventure* (1952), Robert Keys in *Wetbacks* (1955), Lance Fuller in *Apache Woman* (1955), Earl Holliman in *The Rainmaker* (1956), Rory Calhoun in *Ride Out for Revenge* (1957) and Tommy Lee Jones in *Blown Away* (1994). On his western *The Loner* (1965–1966), he fought Mike Mazurki in 1966's "Pick Me Another Time to Die" and even tangled with his own son Jeff Bridges in 1965's "The Ordeal of Bud Windom." As a TV guest, Lloyd fought Edward Binns and Dale Van Sickel in the 1958 *Zane Grey Theatre* episode "Wire."

See: Bubbeo, Daniel. "Fast Chat: New Business for Beau Bridges." *Newsday.* January 12, 2012; Hopper, Hedda. "Looking at Hollywood." *Chicago Tribune.* July 11, 1951.

JOHN WAYNE VS. VICTOR MCLAG-LEN in *The Quiet Man* (1952)

The sprawling, comedic donnybrook in John Ford's *The Quiet Man* remains the most highly touted match-up in cinema history. *Action Superheroes* ranks this clash of titans among the greatest screen fights, as does *Action Films,* the *Toronto Star* and *USA Today. The Big Damn Book of Sheer Manliness* calls it a "spectacular fistfight." *The Boxing Filmography* declares it "arguably the greatest fist fight outside of a ring in film history." *The Hollywood Reporter* called it "a stirring brawl that manages to be thrilling and uproariously funny at the same time." *Newsweek* described it as "one of the grandest free-for-alls ever sprawled across the screen." Irish author Steve Farrell calls it "the greatest good-natured fight in Hollywood history." Every subsequent two-man battle fell under its shadow.

Ford's labor of love took him nearly a decade to bring to the screen, but it became an instant classic, full of colorful Irish atmosphere and memorable performances from the entire cast. It inspired the 1961 Broadway play *Donnybrook,* with Art Lund and Philip Bosco playing the roles John Wayne and Victor McLaglen made famous on the big screen. *The Missouri Traveler* (1958), *The Wild McCulluchs* (1975) and *Any Which Way You Can* (1980) all borrowed heavily from *The Quiet Man.* Multiple nominations were doled out at Oscar time, with Ford earning Best Director and cinematographers Winton C. Hoch and Archie Stout winning for their sumptuous visuals and deft camerawork. Composer Victor Young provides the perfect musical accompaniment with the lilting "The Rakes of Mallow" playing in the background.

Frank Nugent's script involves prizefighter Sean Thornton (Wayne) returning home to Inisfree after killing Jack Roper in the ring. This has left him reluctant to fight. He immediately runs afoul of local bully Will Danaher (McLaglen) while at the same time falling for the hulking man's sister Maureen O'Hara. The locals wait in eager anticipation for the inevitable showdown, all the while laying odds and wagers. When Wayne is denied his legal dowry after the two are married, O'Hara urges her man to take a stand. At first Wayne refuses, but O'Hara is prepared to board a train and leave unless he does. This leads to Wayne famously pulling her off the train and dragging her across a field to deposit her in front of McLaglen. The two men begin unloading one big punch after another, brawling across the town before an expanding crowd, fighting in bales of hay and beside a river, and settling into Cohan's Pub, where they pause for a Guinness (and McLaglen spits out a tooth). Then it's back to the fight. Side bits include Ward

Victor McLaglen (left) and John Wayne exchange "Irish caresses" in one of cinema's best-known fights in Republic's *The Quiet Man* (1952).

Bond's Father Lonergan abandoning his treasured fishing pole to excitedly hop a fence to view the fight and Francis Ford literally rising from his death bed to attend. At several humorous points, locals throw buckets of water on the combatants, whether they need it or not. In another memorable moment, the two squabble over the use of Marquess of Queensberry Rules, abandoning them as quickly as they agree to them. In the end, the quiet man Wayne emerges victorious, restoring his lost pride and gaining acceptance within the community.

Plenty of laughs and tremendous roundhouse punches occur in front of picturesque green scenery. The fight took four days to film on the grounds of Ashford Castle in Cong, County Mayo; additional bits were lensed back at Republic. Cohan's Pub was a local grocery store. Wayne and McLaglen did almost the entire fight, and the two never laid a hand on one another. Ford's son Patrick did the fall into the river for the nearly 65-

year-old McLaglen, while local Irish heavyweight boxing champ Mairtin Thornton was used for long shots. Director Ford was so taken with the real boxing champ that he changed Wayne's character's name from Sean O'Brien to Sean Thornton. Wayne's stand-in Joe Mellotte donned McLaglen's clothing and did a take crashing through the door of Cohan's, a sequence reshot back in the States. At Republic, stuntmen Bob Morgan and Terry Wilson set up and executed the door-crashing finale in the pub. Wayne ran through fight rehearsals with supporting player Ward Bond, taking McLaglen's place. Stuntmen Bert LeBaron, Brick Sullivan, Billy Jones, Bobby Rose, Slim Hightower and Fred Kennedy populate the crowd of onlookers, hired both to break into their own fight and catch the actors if they were in danger of taking too rough a fall. For the most part, it's Wayne and McLaglen trading blow after blow for nearly ten minutes of entertaining screen time.

Ford was legendary for being hard on his actors

and crew to capture what he wanted on screen. He spared no one's feelings, and *The Quiet Man* was no exception. By all accounts McLaglen was an easygoing, mild-mannered man, but one evening Ford manipulated him by severely criticizing his acting in front of McLaglen's son Andrew. The next day the fight was scheduled, giving McLaglen an entire night to stew over Ford's comments and arrive in the proper frame of mind Ford wanted. Ford would also not bow down to Republic head Herbert Yates. When Yates demanded the film be under two hours, Ford presented an early screening that ended as the much anticipated fight was set to begin. Ford got his way, although some of the fight was cut to bring down the film's overall length. In 1954, the fight was spoofed in comic form by *Panic* magazine under the title "The Quite-a-Man."

It's one of Wayne's most famous roles. However, Ford considered casting Robert Ryan in the part.

See: Farrell, Steve. "Those Fighting Irish and Their Good-Natured Fights on Film." Irish American Cultural Institute Essay; Gibbons, Luke. *The Quiet Man.* Cork: Cork University Press, 2002; McNee, Gerry. *In the Footsteps of* The Quiet Man. New York: Random House, 2012.

GENE EVANS VS. CHARLES HORVATH in *Park Row* (1952)

In a single long take, cult writer-director Samuel Fuller's camera moves in and out of a violent fight as tough newspaper editor Gene Evans takes on a rival newspaper's hired thug. The scene benefits from a realistic depiction of the historic 1886 Park Row district of New York City which Fuller captured with a specially built four-story set. Incidentally, former journalist Fuller financed the independent film himself. Evans' strong-willed character Phineas Mitchell is fighting on principle, defending his own ideas and integrity. Words are his greatest weapon, but he proves here that his fists can do in a pinch against heavy Charles Horvath. Burly World War II hero Evans, recipient of a Purple Heart and the Bronze Star, stood 6'1" and although slimmed down for the rare lead role was no lily. He had been a bouncer and carried a reputation as a bar fighter. Fuller biographer Lee Server writes, "The script is so tightly written that every barroom brawl seems to lead directly to another great moment in journalism."

Fuller raised star Evans' curiosity when blocking out the lengthy fight, telling him how he'd roll under a wagon and continue fighting. Evans surveyed the scene and asked, "What wagon?" Fuller replied, "The wagon that will be coming down the street." Luckily, fellow combatant Horvath was an experienced stuntman and saw to it Fuller's vision was realized with safety for all concerned. In the finale, cinematographer Jack Russell's camera gets in close as Evans repeatedly bashes a bloodied Horvath's head against a statue of Benjamin Franklin. Fuller garnered a reputation for shooting especially vigorous fights. The elaborate *Park Row* tracking shot was one of Fuller's own personal favorites, and Martin Scorsese called it an influence on his own style.

Six-three and 220 pounds, Horvath played football at Brown University and was a judo champion in the Marines. He literally wrote their self-defense manual and had a reputation as one of Hollywood's toughest men. Superb at conveying menace, Horvath was often called on to fight film leads including Burt Lancaster in *His Majesty O'Keefe* (1954), George Montgomery in *Pawnee* (1957), Yul Brynner in *The Brothers Karamazov* (1958), Jeff Chandler in *Man in the Shadow* (1958) and Jim Brown in *Kenner* (1969). On TV, he made the rounds of all the shows. His most memorable fights came against Clint Walker in the 1956 *Cheyenne* episode "The Law Man," Rod Taylor in the 1960 *Hong Kong* episode "Freebooter," William Smith in the 1966 *Laredo* episode "Last of the Caesars, Absolutely" and Robert Conrad in the 1965 *Wild Wild West* episode, "The Night of the Glowing Corpse."

See: "Charles Horvath, Top TV Stuntman Risks Neck Often." *Van Nuys Valley News* December 1, 1967; Oliver, Myrna. "Gene Evans; Actor Known for Tough Guy Roles." *Los Angeles Times.* April 3, 1998; Weaver, Tom. *Science Fiction and Fantasy Film Flashbacks.* Jefferson, NC: McFarland, 2004.

JOHN WAYNE VS. HAL BAYLOR in *Big Jim McLain* (1952)

John Wayne and James Arness portray Communist hunters for the House Un-American Activities Committee, on assignment in beautiful Hawaii in this seldom seen, campy slice of Warner Bros. propaganda from director Edward Ludwig and screenwriter James Edward Grant. As they close in on the hidden infiltrators, Arness is sapped and killed by burly Commie thug Hal Baylor and Wayne's ire is raised. Wayne, as the title character Big Jim, wipes the walls with all involved. The 30-

second climactic fight places the odds at seven to one, with the already formidable Baylor joined by Robert Keys, Peter Whitney, Jay Woolsey, Web Overlander, Alan Napier and professional wrestler Lucky Simunovich. Wayne doesn't hesitate in taking them all on, until the Hawaiian police arrive. Publicity photos show Baylor landing a punch on Wayne that's not in the film, suggesting that the fight was trimmed. For European release, the villains were turned into drug dealers through creative dubbing. The 6'2, 195-pound Keys was a former Marine and star football player at Tulane.

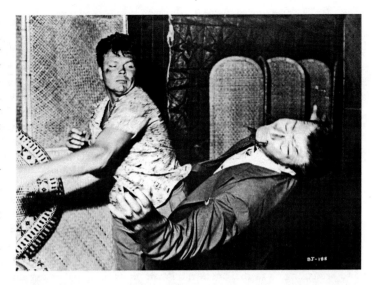

Hal Baylor sends John Wayne reeling in Warner Bros.' Big Jim McLain (1952).

The fight was done in an outside pavilion on location in Honolulu, and there was none of the customary Hollywood props available such as breakaway chairs, tables or glasses. There wasn't even a stuntman or a gaffer to coordinate the fight. This made director Ludwig ill at ease, but producer-star Wayne assured him he had done so many fights there'd be no danger to the participants. Wayne coordinated the fight, and when all the dust had settled there were no injuries. The best moment comes when Wayne upends loudmouth Baylor with a big punch, as he did during a previous confrontation when Baylor made the mistake of grabbing his shirt. On both occasions, Baylor sells the blow terrifically and goes tumbling backwards end over end. Andrew McLaglen served as the second unit director and Archie Stout was behind the camera. The Los Angeles Herald Examiner found it to be "a walloping good movie." Variety praised the "slam-bang fistfight," but Time complained, "The action in the foreground is implausible and fumblingly filmed." The New York Times came away with the impression that according to Wayne, "the best medicine for a cowardly Communist is a sock in the nose."

Six-four, 210-pound Baylor was a professional boxer and California heavyweight champ under the name Hal Fieberling. An in-demand screen heavy, he put on many great fights without the need for a stuntman. Baylor worked often in fight scenes because producers favored a man who could convincingly do his own action. They didn't

have to pay a stuntman, and it saved time. They could move in closer with the camera and it improved continuity when it came time to cut the film. The former Marine's boxing match with Robert Ryan in The Set-Up (1949) is a classic. After he loses in the ring, he has his pals hold Ryan down so he can later beat him in a back alley.

Baylor fought Robert Mitchum in River of No Return (1954), Tab Hunter in The Burning Hills (1956) (see entry), Montgomery Clift in The Young Lions (1958), Henry Silva in Johnny Cool (1963) and Claude Akins in Timber Tramps (1975). Whenever Baylor showed up on TV, it meant a fight was likely to ensue. He battled Clint Walker on Cheyenne, Richard Boone on Have Gun—Will Travel, Chuck Connors on The Rifleman and Dan Blocker on Bonanza. The stand-out was a one-on-one with Walker in the 1956 Cheyenne episode "Lone Gun." In the bare-knuckle ring, he fought John Smith in 1959's Laramie episode "Bare Knuckles," Van Williams in 1964's Temple Houston episode "Ten Rounds for Baby," Larry Pennell in 1966's Big Valley episode "The Price of Victory" and Victor French in 1970's Bonanza episode "An Earthquake Named Callahan." One of his best TV fights came against Wayne Rogers in the 1961 Stagecoach West episode "The Big Gun." On the 1959 Maverick episode "The Sheriff of Duck 'n' Shoot," Baylor did a comic fight with diminutive stuntman Harvey Parry.

See: Anderson, Bob. "And in This Corner." Trail Dust Magazine. Winter 1995; Anderson, Bob.

"The Winner and Still the Champ." *Trail Dust Magazine.* Spring 1996; "John Wayne Heads *Big Jim McLain* Free for All." *Bonham Daily Favorite.* October 19, 1952; "New Image for Hal Baylor: He Gets Girl." *Daily Herald.* October 27, 1969.

JOHN PAYNE VS. LEE VAN CLEEF AND NEVILLE BRAND in *Kansas City Confidential* (1952)

Action director Phil Karlson delivers hard-hitting violent crime noir with John Payne as an anti-hero muscling in on the perpetrators of a heist for which he was the unintentional fall guy. Crooked cop Preston Foster, mastermind of the job, employs hoods Neville Brand, Lee Van Cleef, and Jack Elam to pull off the caper. All wear masks and are strangers to their cohorts. Payne finds Elam and assumes his place to put the pressure on the others, with Foster monitoring the action and developing an appreciation for Payne's prowess with his brain and his fists.

Dismissed at the time, the film is now regarded as the toughest of the brutal noirs with George Diskant responsible for the adroit and atmospheric black-and-white camerawork. The *New York Times* was particularly put off by the brutality, calling it "an uncommon lot of face slapping, stomach punching and kicking in the groin."

United Artists publicity played up Payne's prowess as a man of action. Fights galore occur, with the principal actors doing all their own stunt work. Elam had ribs cracked when he was hit too hard by the leading man. Payne has four confrontations with Van Cleef. However, the only time the menacing Van Cleef gets the upper hand is when borderline psychotic Brand helps out. The two classic screen toughs surprise Payne in his swim robe and knock him around for 20 intense seconds before leading lady Coleen Gray arrives to save him from the dire predicament. The final fight occurs between Van Cleef and Payne on a yacht, with the two struggling over a gun as Foster and Brand lie bleeding. Payne and Van Cleef also have confrontations in *Rails into Laramie* (1954) and *The Road to Denver* (1955). Van Cleef and Brand start a saloon fight with one another on the 1979 nostalgic special *When the West Was Fun.*

Lee Van Cleef, 6'2" and 190 pounds, was a Navy veteran and one of the top villains of 1950s cinema. He looked mean and had a reputation as a bar fighter, although he was adamant that he never started fights. He no doubt ended a few. The lean, well-muscled Van Cleef was a solid fight man who was able to do a great deal of his own action for the screen. He famously drew on John Wayne in *The Man Who Shot Liberty Valance* (1962) only to be clobbered over the head. His first screen fights came against Jock Mahoney on TV's *The Range Rider.* On the TV western *Buffalo Bill, Jr.,* Van Cleef had a great mixer with Dick Jones in 1955's "Boomer Bill." Another top fight occurred with Ty Hardin in the 1960 *Bronco* episode "Yankee Tornado."

Van Cleef had fights of interest against Phil Carey in *The Nebraskan* (1953), Ward Bond in *Gypsy Colt* (1954), Sean McClory in *I Cover the Underworld* (1955), Jim Davis in *The Badge of Marshal Brennan* (1957), Sterling Hayden in *Gun Battle at Monterey* (1957), Jock Mahoney in *Joe Dakota* (1957) (see entry), Gerald Mohr in *Guns, Girls, and Gangsters* (1959), Jim Brown in *El Condor* (1970) and Stuart Whitman in *Captain Apache* (1971). Van Cleef improbably starred as an aging ninja in the short-lived TV series *The Master* (1984), once again taking on Jock Mahoney in "A Place to Call Home." Most of the show's run was spent going against actual expert Sho Kosugi as Van Cleef's arch-nemesis. Ironically, it was Kosugi who doubled Van Cleef for his martial arts kicks.

See: Boisson, Steve. "Phil Karlson: No Holds Barred." *Filmfax.* #110, 2006; *Kansas City Confidential* pressbook; Malloy, Mike. *Lee Van Cleef: A Biographical, Film and Television Reference.* Jefferson, NC: McFarland, 2005.

RANDOLPH SCOTT VS. LEE MARVIN in *Hangman's Knot* (1952)

Hangman's Knot is a solid if unspectacular Randolph Scott western from writer-director Roy Huggins. It is best known for giving an early look at bad guy Lee Marvin, with *The Hollywood Reporter* noting that Marvin "stages a whale of a fight." This top villain meets Scott's gallant fists after unwisely coming on to Donna Reed in a cabin. Scott and Marvin knock one another all over the furniture for nearly two minutes. Marvin sends Scott rolling into the fireplace, but it's largely Scott dominating the bad guy until the bully can barely stand on his two feet. Clumsy editing from Gene Havlick mars the fight, as does the obvious use of doubles Al Wyatt and Bob Morgan. Still, it's a solid fight put on by two of the era's top stuntmen (*Seattle Daily Times:* "[It's] violent enough to make even strong men shudder").

Columbia publicity played up Scott's popularity as a screen brawler, suggesting that local athletic establishments hand out "Randolph Scott Trophies" to their top boxers and wrestlers as a promotional tie-in. The highlight of the battle has Marvin giving up at the one-minute mark, only to take a cheap shot at Scott which begins the fight anew. In real life, veteran screen puncher Scott didn't trust movie newcomer Marvin or his penchant for throwing down booze. He found him to be too wild and undisciplined, fearing that Marvin wouldn't properly pull his

Lee Marvin takes a big right from Randolph Scott in Columbia's *Hangman's Knot* (1952).

punches for the scene. Scott agreed only to close-ups of himself throwing punches at Charles Lawton, Jr.'s camera. That's the chief reason for the heavy use of stuntmen Wyatt and Morgan. Marvin gradually earned Scott's trust and was asked to work on *The Stranger Wore a Gun* (1953) and *Seven Men from Now* (1956).

Six-three, 190-pound Marvin earned a Purple Heart as a Marine fighting at Saipan and is synonymous with on-screen mayhem. He had a wealth of real experience in violent matters from which to draw from and picked up judo moves for the movies from his stunt pals. Later he received Shotokan karate instruction from Enoeda Keinosuke and paid Bruce Lee $150 an hour for training in Jeet Kune Do. Marvin was a notorious drinker and bar fighter, with his success in the latter depending on his frame of mind, level of intoxication and what he was drinking. Nevertheless, the rangy actor moved with the grace of a big cat and affected an air of dangerous menace. He often exploded into action like a coiled spring and was able to close ground quickly on an opponent. Audiences tended to live vicariously through Marvin's tough guy characters and their doling-out of pain. They feared Marvin as an unpredictable villain and later embraced him as a battle-hardened anti-hero.

Notable fights include *The Wild One* (1953), *The Missouri Traveler* (1958), *Donovan's Reef* (1963), *Point Blank* (1967), *Emperor of the North*

(1973) and *Shout at the Devil* (1976) (see entries). Fights of interest came against John Wayne in *The Comancheros* (1961), Toshiro Mifune in *Hell in the Pacific* (1968), Michael Conrad in *Monte Walsh* (1970), Gregory Walcott in *Prime Cut* (1972) and Robert Culp in *The Great Scout and Cathouse Thursday* (1976). On TV, Marvin fought Martin Milner on the 1961 *Route 66* episode "Mon Petit Chou," robot boxer Chuck Hicks on the 1963 *Twilight Zone* episode "Steel" and Ricardo Montalban in the 1963 *Dick Powell Theatre* episode "Epilogue." Milner broke Marvin's nose with an errant punch, but Marvin shrugged it off and said it improved his looks. On his own series *M Squad* (1957–1960), Marvin's fight with Mike Mazurki in 1959's "Decoy in White" was particularly fierce, with Marvin resorting to palming his handcuffs and delivering a series of devastating heart punches to fell Mazurki. Marvin's stuntman pals made him an honorary member of the Stuntmen's Association.

See: *Hangman's Knot* pressbook; Klein, Doris. "Lee Marvin Tells Secrets of Filming Movie Fights." *Reading Eagle*. September 26, 1962; "The Man for Vicaries." *Time*. 1965.

THE BAMBOO BAR BRAWL in *City Beneath The Sea* (1953)

Carefree deep sea divers Robert Ryan and Anthony Quinn become caught up in the hunt for sunken treasure in the lost Jamaican city of Port Royal, submerged under the sea. Outside the colorful scenery and diving footage, one of this entertaining Budd Boetticher–directed Universal film's highlights is a spirited two-minute brawl inside a bamboo bar involving Quinn and a group of never-do-wells who are coming on to a lady. Seen-it-all-before Ryan remains detached in the balcony with the men's girlfriends Mala Powers and Suzan Ball and nonchalantly watches his partner in action. Finally, he removes his jacket and leaps onto the floor, finishing Quinn's fistic work in a tidy ten seconds. Ryan told reporters that character and on-screen action mattered far more than romantic leading man stardom when it came to his choice of film roles.

Stunt coordinator Paul Stader doubles Ryan for the impressive leap into the fray, while George Robotham does an excellent job as Quinn's double. Cinematographer Charles P. Boyle and editor Edward Curtiss feature plenty of smashed chairs and nicely cut camera angles. The two-fisted opposition is represented by stuntmen Duke Taylor, Chuck Hamilton, Fred Zendar and former heavyweight boxer Thomas Garland. The stuntmen were glad for the work as business had been slow with penny-pinching studios turning to the use of black-and-white stock action footage already in the studio vaults. Luckily for the stunt pros, films were increasingly being made in color.

Director Boetticher was a tough guy. He played football at Ohio State and had been both a boxer and a professional bullfighter. The former Marine had a knack for filming action, particularly in the western genre, and was often able to coax his leading actors into doing more for the camera than they normally would. His late 1950s Randolph Scott westerns are classics. One of Boetticher's more interesting fights came in a locked sanitarium between Richard Carlson and pro wrestler Tor Johnson in Behind Locked Doors (1948). A decade later, this scene was reworked on the 1959 Peter Gunn TV episode "See No Evil" with Johnson beating up star Craig Stevens in a padded cell. Boetticher went on record as saying the toughest men in Hollywood during his era were Jack Palance, Robert Mitchum and Robert Ryan.

Six-foot-two and 195 pounds, Anthony Quinn once earned five to ten dollars a fight as a sparring partner for towering heavyweight Primo Carnera. He quit boxing after being floored in his seventeenth fight, although he famously returned to the ring to play the aging Mountain Rivera in Requiem

for a Heavyweight (1962). Quinn had a few off-set altercations that made the news and enjoyed partaking in movie fights, logging notable efforts against Fred MacMurray in Swing High, Swing Low (1937), Bing Crosby in Waikiki Wedding (1937), Cornel Wilde in The Perfect Snob (1941), Joel McCrea in Buffalo Bill (1944), Gregory Peck in The World in His Arms (1952), Jeff Chandler in East of Sumatra (1953), Peter Graves in The Naked Street (1955), Peter Whitney in Man from Del Rio (1956), Ray Milland in The River's Edge (1957), Jack Palance in Barabbas (1961), H.B. Haggerty in Dream of Kings (1969) and Victor French in Flap (1970).

See: Binder, David. "Budd Boetticher, Director Whose No-Frills 50's Westerns Became Classics, Dies at 85." New York Times. December 1, 2001; "City Beneath the Sea." Courier-Gazette. April 2, 1953; Marill, Alvin H. The Films of Anthony Quinn. Secaucus, NJ: Citadel, 1975; Thomas, Bob. "Stunt Business Lags." Trenton Evening Times. May 2, 1952.

ALAN LADD VS. BEN JOHNSON in Shane (1953)

George Stevens' classic range war western features Alan Ladd in his signature role. He plays the understated, buckskin-clad drifter who becomes a heroic father-figure to Brandon de Wilde at the expense of the boy's real dad Van Heflin. There are plenty of character-building moments in A.B. Guthrie's Oscar-nominated screenplay, an adaptation of Jack Schaefer's novel. Tensions mount between the men over the boy and mother Jean Arthur until Ladd and Heflin end up furiously brawling with one another in a dark long shot on a Paramount studio set. Ladd, whom we learn is a gunfighter with many notches on his belt, heads off to face down the cruel hired gun Jack Palance. The Ladd-Heflin battle, however, doesn't come close to matching an earlier two-man fistfight in a saloon between Ladd and a grizzled, chaps-wearing cowboy played by Ben Johnson. Writer Richard Jensen calls this "an iconic moment of western film." The Big Damn Book of Sheer Manliness cites it as one of the best barroom brawls in screen history, and Legendary Westerns includes it among the best cowboy fights. Johnson is excellent as the heavy who develops a conscience once Ladd earns his respect. The fight itself is a contrast in styles, with Johnson throwing John Wayne haymakers while Ladd delivers shorter blows in more

Alan Ladd floors Ben Johnson during the famous saloon brawl in Paramount's *Shane* (1953).

effective combinations. The fight is one of *Shane's* many indelible scenes, with *Newsweek* noting of its nuance, "A barroom brawl, although in the required tradition of outrageous mayhem, is given that added touch of plausibility."

The cocksure Johnson ridicules Ladd for ordering soda pop. Ladd promptly orders two whiskeys. The first is tossed onto the shirt of a surprised Johnson, with the second going into his face along with Ladd's fist. The blow knocks Johnson back ten feet into the general store. Johnson rises with a smile, wiping makeup artist Wally Westmore's stage blood from his mouth; an image permanently etched into western fans' minds. The two circle one another cautiously, feinting blows to make the other commit. Stevens has opted not to use any background music, making the fight all the more effective. Both combatants land several blows, though Johnson captures too much air with his. Ladd wears him down, dancing over the fallen bully before landing a last punch as Johnson tries to rise up. Johnson's half-dozen cohorts move in

on Ladd, but Heflin comes to his aid and the viewer is treated to a spirited free-for-all. The two men successfully fight back to back as Johnson quietly slips out of the saloon, a beaten man. The *Ellensburg Daily Record* proclaimed that *Shane* boasted "the longest, bloodiest rough-and-tumble fistfight that has ever been presented on celluloid," while the *Toledo Blade* reviewer noted that it contained "the most brutally realistic cinematic brawl these eyes have seen in many years of movie-going."

The Ladd-Johnson fight took three weeks to prepare and a full two days to film with the director seeking a combination of myth and reality. Assisted by stunt coordinator John Indrisano, Stevens walked each actor through the fight, detailing blow by blow how he wanted the action to proceed, at what pace, and from what angle. Logistically, it was difficult to shoot not only because of the cumbersome Technicolor cameras and the many different positions, but due to the size difference between the men. Ladd was 5'5" while

Johnson was nearly 6'3" and had a good 70 pounds in his favor. Stevens and second unit director Fred Gill expertly manipulated the scene with Oscar-winning D.P. Loyal Griggs' camera placement, needing to take into account Ladd's well-worn shoe lifts and hidden planks. Johnson had to be careful not to knock Ladd off his platform when he was throwing his punches. Much of the film is shot from Brandon de Wilde's point of view on the floor, with the audience hearing blows and watching the boy's reactions. He memorably cracks the candy stick in his mouth in synch with the last big punch.

Paramount and Stevens had the film in post-production for nearly two years. The superb William Hornbeck editing keeps one from noticing the huge disparity between the men, as does Griggs' shooting through chair legs and beneath tables to partially obscure the use of doubles for Ladd and Heflin. USA Today noted, "Every angle in this brilliantly edited classic is the right one," and they included it among the Top 10 all-time fights. Publicity compared it to The Spoilers, and Ladd told the press that former stuntman Johnson was the toughest man he ever fought.

Johnson's background came in handy. He did all his own stunts, although he did knock himself dizzy when he flew through the swinging doors and hit his head. Ladd is doubled by Russ Saunders, Heflin by Wayne Burson. The combatants in the brawl are Henry Wills, Steve Raines, Bill Cartledge, Jack Sterling, Chick Hannan and Lucky Brown. There have been claims that Clayton Moore of The Lone Ranger worked on this fight under the name Rex Moore during the period when he left the TV show, but that hasn't been substantiated. Moore doesn't mention it in his autobiography.

Heflin became carried away during the clash and knocked out a stuntman. He had rehearsed in a gym with the men for more than a week but forgot the choreography when the cameras began to roll; this is one of the primary reasons that stuntmen prefer working with their experienced brethren. Heflin ducked into a punch that split his lip. Overcome with a flash of anger, he hit the stuntman and punched another. Some blood seen on Heflin's chin was his own from the lip injury. He needed eight stitches and was ordered home for five days until he healed.

The stunt crew had no such problem with the highly regarded Johnson. The rodeo champion was one of their own before being discovered by John Ford while working on Fort Apache (1948). The director groomed Johnson for stardom, but the latter wouldn't let himself be bullied by Ford on the set and was soon back on the rodeo circuit. His performance in Shane guaranteed him a lifetime of western work. Johnson was cowboy-tough, often serving as director Sam Peckinpah's protector on south-of-the-border filming adventures. He also commanded respect and was known to grab men around the neck who had the temerity to swear around a lady, setting them on a future path of good manners. Nobody messed with Ben Johnson. He had fights of interest with Dane Clark in Fort Defiance (1951), Don Haggerty in Wild Stallion (1952), Larry Chance in Fort Bowie (1958), James Drury in Ten Who Dared (1960), Charles Gray in Junior Bonner (1972) (see entry) and Roy Jenson in The Red Pony (1973). On television, he had major fights with Richard Boone in the 1960 Have Gun—Will Travel episode "The Race" and James Arness in the 1963 Gunsmoke episode "Quint-cident."

See: Jensen, Richard D. Ben Johnson: The Nicest Fella. Bloomington, IN: IUniverse, 2010; "Historic Film Fight in The Spoilers Has a Rival in Shane." The World's News. August 15, 1953; Johnson, Erskine. "One-Punch Van Heflin Kayoes Stunt Man in Movieland Brawl." Trenton Evening Times. October 1, 1953.

RONALD REAGAN VS. PRESTON FOSTER in Law and Order (1953)

It's odd seeing the future president of the United States Ronald Reagan getting down and dirty in a bust-up with Preston Foster in this Nathan Juran–directed western from Universal-International. Foster, a cruel villain with a metal hand, blames former lawman Reagan for his deformity. Reagan wants to settle down with Dorothy Malone in Cottonwood, Arizona, but must face down Foster when he threatens to burn down the town. It's an energetic and surprisingly violent fight trimmed by censors because of its bloodiness. The action goes under horses and wagons, onto a sidewalk, and into a general store during its spirited two minutes. As if his iron fist were not enough, Foster uses a concealed derringer and a jug to hit Reagan and tries to do additional damage with a hatchet and a pitchfork. Reagan keeps pounding on Foster with his own fists as they knock down shelves and crash through a window for Clifford Stine's camera. Foster leaps onto an

open buckboard to escape, but Reagan knocks him
off. Foster meets a grisly end as he falls into the
path of a stagecoach. The excellent stunt work was
done by Jack Young and Carl Andre, with Ted
Kent splicing the exhilarating action together. The
Dallas Morning News labeled the brawl "magnificent."

The 6'1", 185-pound Reagan was a lifeguard and
a football player at Eureka College before signing
a Warner Bros. contract and playing two-fisted
government agent Brass Bancroft in the B-films
Secret Service of the Air (1939), *Code of the Secret
Service* (1939) and *Smashing the Money Ring* (1939).
The studio announced that Reagan had one fight
for every thousand feet of film shot. While serving
stateside with the First Motion Picture Unit during World War II, Reagan worked alongside Oren
Haglund, who trained combat cameramen in the
art of judo and self-defense. Reagan also served
with the First U.S. Cavalry. Westerns like *Law and
Order* helped solidify his reputation as a tough
Hollywood cowboy when he took office as president of the United States in 1981.

Fights of interest came against Zachary Scott in
Stallion Road (1947), Grant Withers in *Tropic
Zone* (1953) and John Payne in *Tennessee's Partner*
(1954). On TV he fought Leo Gordon in the 1958
Death Valley Days episode "No Gun Behind His
Badge" and Scott Marlowe in the 1961 *Zane Grey
Theatre* episode "The Long Shadow." Of course
his greatest battle was the Cold War game of wits
against Communism and he prevailed over the So-
viet Union's leader Mikhail Gorbachev, ultimately
bringing down the Berlin Wall in 1989.

See: McGivern, Carolyn, and Fred Landesman.
Ronald Reagan in Hollywood. Cork: Reel, 2005;
Vaughn, Stephen. *Ronald Reagan in Hollywood:
Movies and Politics.* Cambridge: Cambridge Uni-
versity Press, 1994.

RICHARD WIDMARK VS. RICHARD KILEY in *Pickup on South Street* (1953)

Pickup on South Street is superbly filmed noir
from iconoclastic director Samuel Fuller, an ex–
World War II infantryman who began scenes by
firing a pistol. That toughness is evident in what
many consider his best film. Richard Widmark
stars as a brash, anti-heroic pickpocket who becomes embroiled in a Communist plot when he
lifts Jean Peters' purse containing important microfilm. The film is so tough that Widmark knocks

out Peters with a fist to the jaw and revives her
with beer in the face. Bad guy Richard Kiley beats
up Peters before the men ultimately turn their fists
on one another in a subway for a climax that the
Dallas Morning News called "terrifying." *The Hollywood Reporter* praised the film for its "gritty,
hard-hitting, brutal realism," while noir expert
Eddie Muller wrote, "Love scenes or fight scenes,
Fuller gave them all the lurid gusto of someone
born to the crime beat."

Fuller shot from a high angle, utilizing long, extended takes emphasizing swift camera movement
around the physical action. There's tremendous
energy and rhythm to the perfectly paced fight, all
done on a Fox studio set with a crowd of shocked-
looking extras. The action begins in a men's room,
spills into the subway's ticket area and over turn-
stiles, before leaving the platform and ending on
the tracks where Widmark pounds Kiley into unconsciousness. At one outlandish point, Widmark
drags Kiley down a flight of stairs with the latter's
head banging off each step. The Breen Office ob-
jected to such violence as knees and kicks, although a turnstile to the gut and the infamous stair
sequence survived into the final cut. The only neg-
ative is the often too obvious use of stuntmen, although both actors are involved in a lot of the action. In fact, the 5'11", 175-pound Kiley injured his
neck in this fight and was bothered by it the rest
of his career. John "Bear" Hudkins served as Widmark's double. The film was remade with a South
African backdrop as *The Cape Town Affair* (1967),
with James Brolin and John Whitely slugging it
out down a long staircase.

Richard Widmark, 5'9" and 165 pounds, played
collegiate football at Lake Forest but was denied
military service due to a perforated eardrum. In
real life he abhorred violence, but his early on-
screen image seemed built on rugged action and
dastardly deeds, with films like *Kiss of Death*
(1947) leaving audiences hating him. His on-
screen tough guy rep even led to his Jim Bowie
character in *The Alamo* (1960) briefly tangling
with John Wayne. Widmark usually let doubles
step in for extended fights, perhaps stemming from
being clobbered unconscious when Jack Palance
hit him over the head with a real gun making *Panic
in the Streets* (1950). Widmark was also injured in
a screen tussle on *Garden of Evil* (1954) with Gary
Cooper and Cameron Mitchell.

Fights of interest came against Cornel Wilde in
Roadhouse (1948) (see entry), Richard Boone in
Red Skies of Montana (1952), Bert Freed in *Take*

the High Ground (1953), Robert Wagner in Broken Lance (1954), William Campbell in Backlash (1956), Timothy Carey in The Last Wagon (1956), Rip Torn in Time Limit (1957), Tom Drake in Warlock (1959), Harry Carey, Jr., and Ken Curtis in Two Rode Together (1961), Kirk Douglas in The Way West (1967) and John Saxon in Death of a Gunfighter (1969).

See: Day, Crosby. "Everyone Wants That Microfilm." Orlando-Sentinel. March 2, 2003; Holston, Kim. Richard Widmark: A Bio-Bibliography. Westport, CT: Greenwood, 1990; Muller, Eddie. Dark City: The Lost World of Film Noir. New York: St. Martin's, 1998.

CHARLTON HESTON vs. JACK PALANCE in *Arrowhead* (1953)

One of the more realistic hand-to-hand combat fights put to film features an interesting match-up between cavalry scout Charlton Heston and fearsome Apache leader Jack Palance. As children, the two were blood brothers, but now Heston hates all Indians, including the Eastern-educated Palance. The fight to the death is novel in that no punches are thrown. It's all grappling down a rocky hillside as tracked by Ray Rennahan's camera, and neither actor uses a stuntman. This is especially impressive considering Palance does the fight shirtless. Palance suffered multiple cuts and bruises from the rugged terrain.

The injuries didn't dampen Palance's odd sense of humor. He lifted the strapping Heston over his head and refused to put him down. Palance enjoyed Heston's profane protests. The tense 90-second struggle ends with Heston breaking Palance's neck. Henry Wills ran the stunts in the Charles Marquis Warren–directed film, going after a Non–Hollywood style fight. Editor Frank Bracht mixes medium shots with close-ups, never straying from the central action, while Paul Sawtell's score effectively emphasizes the top dramatic moments. However, the fight could have benefitted dramatically from a few well-placed punches. Heston also fights Robert Wilke.

Six-three and 205 pounds, Charlton Heston was an Army Air Corps veteran as a B-25 gunner during World War II. He was noted for his physical preparation before undertaking films, working so closely with the professional stuntmen that he was accepted into their fraternal organization as an honorary member. When engaging in a fight, the stalwart actor's jaw was clenched nearly as tightly as his fists. The majority of his fights come across as a realistic physical struggle for his characters. Few actors could play fatigue as convincingly in an action scene. By the end of a fight, Heston was usually spent and breathing heavily, but he packed enough of a punch to frequently come out the winner. He studied judo with Leo Leonard at Bottner's Gym in New York City. Ironically, his first movie punch was off the mark, breaking Mike Mazurki's nose on Dark City (1950).

Notable fights include The Big Country (1958) and Beneath the Planet of the Apes (1970) (see entries). Fights of interest came against Pat Hogan in Pony Express (1953), Jim Davis in The President's Lady (1953), Chris Alcaide in Bad for Each Other (1953), Alan Reed in The Far Horizons (1955), Gary Cooper in The Wreck of the Mary Deare (1959), Richard Harris in Major Dundee (1965), Bruce Dern and Roy Jenson in Will Penny (1968), Joe Canutt in Planet of the Apes (1968), James Brolin in Skyjacked (1972), Chuck Connors in Soylent Green (1973) and James Coburn in The Last Hard Men (1976). He traded comic punches with Brian Keith in The

Charlton Heston (left) and Jack Palance fight to the death in Paramount's *Arrowhead* (1953).

Mountain Men (1980) and memorably cleared out a bar in *Touch of Evil* (1958).

See: "Actors Will Do Anything." *Screenland Plus.* 1952; Kitzmiller, Chelley. "Jack Palance: The Black Knight of the Purple Sage." *Wildest Westerns.* Special, 2005; "Stunts Earn New Nickname for Charlton Heston." *San Diego Union.* January 30, 1957.

ROBERT MITCHUM VS. JACK PALANCE in *Second Chance* (1953)

This RKO 3-D action programmer pits a dream pairing of tough ex-heavyweight palookas against one another in a novel setting that studio publicity called "breathtaking."

Prizefighter Robert Mitchum has wandered off to South America after killing a man in the ring. He still boxes but is reluctant to throw his killer right. He gets wrapped up in all kinds of intrigue as he protects Linda Darnell from hit man Jack Palance. Rudolph Maté's film is most notable for the suspenseful one-minute climactic fight with Palance aboard an endangered cable car high in the Andean mountains. Frayed cables are on the verge of snapping as Mitchum and Palance go blow to blow with one another on the outside observation post while hanging precariously by a thread. Palance goes hurtling to his death from a Mitchum right hand. Mitchum biographer Alvin H. Marill called it a "sensational climax."

Mitchum, who trained with Ralph Volkie for the fight sequences, also takes on California heavyweight boxing champ Abel Fernandez in the ring. Mitchum had fought many tank town fights while Palance was a professional boxer. Paul Stader coordinated a combination of studio and location work with George Robotham doubling Mitchum and Bob Morgan doubling Palance. The stars did much of the fighting, but not without incident. They knew going in that they needed to fight to contact because of D.P. William Snyder's 3-D cameras. Palance was a Method actor who worked into a huffing, puffing rage before fights. According to Mitchum, the stuntmen warned him there was a high probability Palance's punches wouldn't be pulled. With the first overzealous punch to ring aside his head, Mitchum buried his fist deep into Palance's gut. Mitchum claimed that Palance threw up his lunch. Another version made the rounds from director Maté, who claimed that Palance knocked Mitchum out with a blow to the head. In at least one interview, Mitchum said Palance flattened him for a full count. Whatever the case,

Mitchum and Palance had no further problems with one another during the fight routine, although they made their presence in Mexico known with their extracurricular activities including a brawl with a Mexican general at La Reforma.

Jack Palance, 6'3" and 210 pounds, was raised in a Pennsylvania coal mining community, escaping via an athletic scholarship to play football at the University of North Carolina. He boxed professionally under the ring name Jack Brazzo, scoring a 15–1 record with 12 knockouts. During World War II he served with the Army Air Force and trained to be a B-24 bomber pilot. Publicity maintained that he survived a fiery plane crash, and the resulting plastic surgery explained his taut facial features. Palance was well-built, strong and moved like a jungle cat. He had a reputation as an aggressive man who liked brawling; many actors feared doing fights with him. He studied Kenpo karate with Ed Parker and Okinawa-Te with Bob Wall.

Notable fights came against Charlton Heston in *Arrowhead* (1953) (see entry), Jeff Chandler in *Sign of the Pagan* (1954) and *Ten Seconds to Hell* (1959), Lee Marvin in *I Died a Thousand Times* (1955), Rex Reason in *Kiss of Fire* (1955) and Anthony Quinn in *Barabbas* (1961). Palance was a brawling adventurer in *Kill a Dragon* (1967) and fought alongside Bud Spencer in the Spaghetti Western *It Can Be Done, Amigo* (1972). On TV, Palance won an Emmy playing aging boxer Mountain McLintock in a 1956 *Playhouse 90* version of *Requiem for a Heavyweight*. On his series *Bronk* (1975–1976), he had battles against William Smith, Denny Miller and Steve Sandor.

See: "Actors' Brawl Wins Stuntman's Accolade." *Chicago Tribune.* August 30, 1953; "Palance Punches Too Realistic." *Oakland Tribune.* November 8, 1955; *Second Chance* pressbook.

ROBERT STACK VS. PETER GRAVES in *War Paint* (1953)

B-western action vet Lesley Selander's *War Paint* benefits from cinematographer Gordon Avil's fantastic Death Valley location camerawork. It was filmed in vivid Pathecolor and a rugged cast featured Robert Stack, Peter Graves, Charles McGraw and Robert Wilke. A cavalry troop traveling on foot begins bickering among themselves as they trek further into the desert and are picked off by renegade Indian brave Keith Larsen. The film is notable for the novelty of pairing future straight-faced *Airplane!* (1980) co-stars Robert Stack and Peter Graves in the climactic one-and-a-half-minute fight along a formidable 90-degree mountain slope; United Artists publicity described the fight as "an amazing battle on the ledges." The *Ames Daily Tribune* commented, "When they get around to giving out Academy Awards for realistic, spine-tingling man-to-man fights they'll have to give serious consideration to the Robert Stack–Peter Graves crusher in *War Paint.*" Stack also fights Robert Wilke.

The six-foot, 180-pound Stack and the 6'3", 200-pound Graves both look fit and agile. Stack was a gunnery sergeant with the Navy during World War II and trained with boxer Mushy Callahan. He is best remembered as no-nonsense G-man Eliot Ness on TV's *The Untouchables* (1959–1963). Graves served with the Air Force and starred as undercover agent Jim Phelps on *Mission: Impossible* (1967–1973). Both act out the dusty life-or-death struggle with appropriate strain and grimace. Their stuntmen are to be commended for the great leaps, rolls and tumbles along the rocky cliffs and stark wasteland, making this fight picturesque and unique. Bill Catching doubled Stack; the star was one of the rare actors to acknowledge and praise his stuntman. Credit must be given to John F. Schreyer who cut the exciting action together seamlessly.

Stack's most memorable screen fight was comically taking on Hari Krishnas and other annoying people handing out pamphlets at the airport in the disaster spoof *Airplane!* (1980). Stack's methodology is simply to punch his way through the gauntlet. On a more serious note, he fought Rock Hudson in *Written on the Wind* (1956). Graves' best fights came against Rory Calhoun in *Rogue River* (1951), Dane Clark in *Fort Defiance* (1951), Anthony Quinn in *The Naked Street* (1955), Tyrone Power in *The Long Gray Line* (1955), Timothy Carey in *Bayou* (1957), Chuck Connors in *Death in Small Doses* (1957), and George Kennedy in *The Ballad of Josie* (1967).

See: Pollak, Michael. "Peter Graves, *Mission: Impossible* Star, Dies at 83." *New York Times.* March 14, 2010; Stack, Robert, and Mark Evans. *Straight Shooting.* New York: MacMillan, 1980; *War Paint* press-book.

John Payne vs. Brad Dexter in *99 River Street* (1953)

99 River Street is a fast-moving, underrated film noir from director Phil Karlson with publicity promising "battering-ram violence" and "brutal savagery." The ads screamed, "It hits you right in the teeth!" In addition to hard-hitting action, it's one of star John Payne's best roles. He plays a brooding and bitter prizefighter turned taxi driver. He lost a championship fight against Hal Baylor because of a cut and now laments over footage of the bout to the displeasure of his former showgirl wife Peggie Castle. The plot twists and turns as Payne must clear his name after jewel thief Brad Dexter kills Payne's estranged wife. Payne is the chief suspect in the eyes of the police. A highlight remains the climactic 90-second fight on a ship's deck and gangplank with Dexter. A wounded Payne is haunted by editor Buddy Small's intercut flashbacks to his fight with Baylor but summons the strength to keep fighting until the police arrive. The *Daytona Beach Morning Journal* called it "a terrific fistfight," while *Film Noir Guide* termed it "a knockout climax."

Director Karlson stages the action well and gets excellent black-and-white camerawork from Franz Planer. Payne and Dexter conduct their fight in menacing shadows. The boxing footage is well coordinated by John Indrisano. The final fight is arguably not even the best one: Earlier, Payne had a nifty 30-second exchange with Jack Lambert in an apartment during which the tables are neatly turned. The scene begins with Lambert repeatedly judo chopping Payne's neck as he brutally questions him, thinking he's merely a nosy cab driver. Payne sees an opening and unleashes his boxing skills on the thug. Stuntman Bob Morgan can be spied in a medium shot exchanging punches with star Payne before falling backwards over a chair. To Lambert's credit, the camera changes and it's the actor who takes a flip for the camera and rises.

Six-foot-two, 200-pound Brad Dexter was a Golden Gloves champ and a member of the USC boxing team. He served with the Army Air Force during World War II and nixed offers to go pro in the ring. Nevertheless, he liked sparring with professional boxers at the Main Street Gym in Los Angeles until RKO ended that activity in the early 1950s. They wanted him to save himself for movie dust-ups with Robert Mitchum in *Macao* (1952) and Victor Mature in *The Las Vegas Story* (1952). Dexter was later one of *The Magnificent Seven* (1960). On TV, he battled Ty Hardin on *Bronco*, John Vivyan on *Mr. Lucky* and Troy Donahue on *77 Sunset Strip.* His best fight came against Richard Boone in the 1958 *Have Gun—Will Travel* episode "24 Hours at North Fork."

See: Keaney, Michael F. *Film Noir Guide*. Jefferson, NC: McFarland, 2003; Lousararian, Ed G. "Brad Dexter: Screen Tough Guy Remembers *The Magnificent Seven*." *Wildest Westerns*. #1, 1998; *99 River Street* pressbook.

JOHN WAYNE VS. LEO GORDON in *Hondo* (1953)

One of John Wayne's most popular western vehicles was helmed by director John Farrow on location in Mexico with writer James Edward Grant adapting Louis L'Amour's story for the screen. Wayne, as scout Hondo Lane, comes across Geraldine Page and her young son in dangerous Apache territory. He later runs into loutish Leo Gordon at an Army encampment. Wayne doesn't realize that Gordon is Page's husband, but the latter has heel written all over him when he tries to kick Wayne's dog. The two come to blows in a barroom, with Wayne proving his skill as a fighter by dispatching Gordon with an economy of punches. Although it's considered a good screen match-up, Gordon never lands a punch. The fight is so one-sided that Wayne has time to hit fellow scout Ward Bond, humorously claiming he knows him too well to trust him. Realizing he's no match for Wayne, Gordon goes for his gun and "Duke" promptly knocks him clean out the saloon door with a big right hand. As classic as the film is, Farrow and his film cutter Ralph Dawson could have gone to more trouble to edit in close-ups of Gordon's punches and reactions. Perhaps have him land a punch. Cliff Lyons coordinated the action with Archie Stout serving as the cameraman.

Wayne's regular stuntman Chuck Roberson doubles Gordon and is on-screen as much as the actor in the fight, rolling over a table, taking a chair hit and going out the door. Wayne was reluctant to trade punches with the inexperienced movie fighter Gordon. As the action began, Gordon grabbed Wayne's shirt collar and got a reprimand from Wayne. He next let loose a punch that was too straight and aimed at Wayne's chin. Again Wayne chastised him and showed Gordon how to wind up and throw a movie punch. Gordon noted that he could have hit Wayne three times before Wayne's fist reached its destination. Wayne felt more comfortable doing the fight with his trusted pal Roberson, considering newcomer Gordon's background. When Wayne later shoots Gordon, he again took Gordon to task for falling forward instead of backward. Gordon calmly lifted his shirt to display an old bullet wound and informed Wayne when he was shot in the belly in real life, he fell forward. This silenced Wayne and earned Gordon the star's grudging respect. Because of his size and toughness, Gordon squared off with Wayne again in *The Conqueror* (1956) and *McLintock!* (1963).

Leo Gordon (6'2", 220 pounds) was a boxing champion in the Army and a real tough guy who had served time in prison. Legend has it that the former construction worker with the face like a clenched fist was one of the most feared men behind the San Quentin walls. Don Siegel, director of *Riot in Cell Block 11* (1954), described him as "the scariest man I ever met." In that film, Gordon frightened audiences as he led the revolt and pounded on the guards. Gordon dedicated himself to reading and became a prolific screenwriter and family man. When he began his career in Hollywood, most co-stars were reluctant to do fights with him due to the realism he brought to such scenes. He had a reputation for mixing it up, occasionally offering a stiff shot to the belly to test a screen opponent's mettle. William Shatner, star of *The Intruder* (1962), is a shining example of an actor who ended up with Gordon's palm around his throat. Facing Leo Gordon in a fight was a

Rayford Barnes watches Leo Gordon make the mistake of grabbing John Wayne's shirt in Warner Bros.' *Hondo* (1953).

rite of passage for Hollywood's toughest leading men.

Gordon had notable fights in *Gun Fury* (1953), *The Yellow Mountain* (1954), *Red Sundown* (1956) and *The Night of the Grizzly* (1965) (see entries). Fights of interest came against Randolph Scott in *Ten Wanted Men* (1955) and *7th Cavalry* (1956), George Montgomery in *Robbers' Roost* (1955) and *Black Patch* (1957), John Payne in *Santa Fe Passage* (1955), Scott Brady in *The Restless Breed* (1957), Jeff Chandler in *Man in the Shadow* (1958), Rory Calhoun in *Apache Territory* (1958), Steve Cochran in *The Big Operator* (1959), Jim Davis in *Noose for a Gunman* (1960), Jock Mahoney in *Tarzan Goes to India* (1962), Lino Ventura in *The Dictator's Guns* (1965), Tab Hunter in *Hostile Guns* (1967) and Barry Sullivan in *Buckskin* (1968).

On TV, he squared off with Clint Walker on *Cheyenne* in especially rugged fights, the most noteworthy coming in 1962's "Vengeance Is Mine." He literally made the rounds of TV, menacing the heroes on many of the major shows. Special mention should be made of fights with Ronald Reagan in 1958's *Death Valley Days* episode "No Gun Behind His Badge," Robert Fuller in 1960's *Laramie* segment "Ride into Darkness" and Ron Ely in 1966's *Tarzan* episode "The Circus." Tough as ever, Gordon played a boxer tired of being forced to take dives in the 1960 *Untouchables* episode "Head of Fire: Feet of Clay." On the 1965 *Get Smart* episode "School Days," he engages in judo with Bruce Tegner. In 1979, he played an aging wrestler who grapples with Merlin Olsen on the *Little House on the Prairie* episode "The King Is Dead."

See: *Hondo* DVD special features; "Leo Gordon, 78, Villain of Westerns in Films and on TV." *New York Times*. January 6, 2001; Lousaraian, Ed. "Leo Gordon: An Actor Who's Good at Being Bad." *Wildest Westerns*. #2, 1999.

MARLON BRANDO VS. LEE MARVIN in *The Wild One* (1953)

Based on a real incident where outlaw motorcyclists took over the town of Hollister, California, Laslo Benedek's *The Wild One* became famous as one of star Marlon Brando's early signature roles, influencing a generation of lost youth. He plays leather-jacketed biker Johnny, a societal rebel who clashes with Chino, leader of a rival gang. Chino is played by Lee Marvin in glorious loose-limbed fashion. He towers over Brando and commands the attention of Hal Mohr's camera. Marvin based his skuzzy biker on an actual outlaw named Wino Willy of the Booze Fighters, and his scene-stealing performance impressed real bikers. Hell's Angels president Frank Sadilek sought out Marvin's vest and wore it to club meetings. It was passed down to famed Angels leader Sonny Barger. The force of Marvin's realistic portrayal made Brando's conflicted, mumbling leather-clad boy look ridiculous by comparison.

After plenty of build-up, the two have a center-of-the-town three-minute fight over a racing trophy. Brando pushes Marvin to the ground, and the latter merely smiles. "I love you, Johnny," Marvin says before trying a sneak attack. Unfortunately, the use of stunt doubles Dave Sharpe and Tom Steele by stunt coordinator Carey Loftin for an overwhelming portion of the action (including Marvin's character crashing through a store window) undermines the fight. Sharpe is a great stuntman, but he's unconvincing as Brando. It's one of the more obvious cases of stunt doubling ever seen in an otherwise famous film, yet *The Spokesman Review* declared, "Lee Marvin's street fight with Brando is one of the high points of the film for slug-it-out action that looks authentic."

Brando and Marvin were at odds on *The Wild One* in a competitive sense over their opposing acting styles. Brando was into his internalized Method acting and gave little for co-stars to work off. Marvin realized Brando's focus was on a cigarette butt lying on the ground. Marvin kicked it away, eliciting curses from the disrupted star. Combat veteran Marvin enjoyed needling Brando about being 4-F for Korea. To add further contrast, Brando rode a British Triumph on screen and in real life. Marvin rode a Harley Davidson. The real bikers and stuntmen aligned with Marvin and his manly nature, snickering over Brando's costume and his postured sensitivity. Marvin could drink excessively off-screen and carry it over into his colorful character. Brando became worried that Marvin was stealing the picture. Marvin, on the other hand, didn't appreciate the pull Brando had with the director or the star's many close-ups.

When Benedek told the two actors he wanted them to do their own fight, they clashed with great gusto for a lone take. Brando tried to be as rough as possible to prove his own manhood, with the larger and tougher former Marine Marvin only losing because the script dictated that was the thing to do. Punches are thrown back and forth and even a few judo movements are employed. When the single take of them rolling around on the ground was in the can, Marvin improvised with an upraised finger for Brando's benefit. The two later had a laugh over all of this, but at the time it added to the tension reaching the screen. Some thought the two might really come to blows. Benedek's hesitance to push the issue further with another take resulted in the abundant footage of the stuntmen's fight routine once the film reached Al Clark's editing room.

Five-foot-nine, 165-pound Brando played football at Shattuck Military Academy but was rejected from military service because of a knee injury. He emphasized his physical presence with weightlifting and boxing workouts. He liked to informally spar backstage while doing *A Streetcar Named Desire* on Broadway, playing the uncouth Stanley Kowalski. He famously went on one night with a bloody broken nose. Legend says it was an errant punch from understudy Jack Palance, but it was more likely a stagehand. Brando scored big in the 1951 movie version of *Streetcar* and became top dog in the industry. Notable fights include *On the Waterfront* (1954), *Guys and Dolls* (1955) and *The Chase* (1966) (see entries). Fights of interest came against Ray Teal in *The Men* (1950), Slim Pickens and Timothy Carey in *One-Eyed Jacks* (1961) and Hans Christian Blech in *Morituri* (1965).

See: Kanfer, Stefan. *Somebody: The Reckless Life and Remarkable Career of Marlon Brando*. London: Faber & Faber, 2011; Zec, Donald. *Marvin: The Story of Lee Marvin*. New York: St. Martin's, 1980.

ROCK HUDSON VS. PHIL CAREY in *Gun Fury* (1953)

Location is everything as pacifistic Civil War veteran Rock Hudson and psychotic bad guy Phil Carey battle over Donna Reed among jagged red rocks in picturesque Sedona, Arizona. The two-minute fight was shot at the foot of the formidable Bell Rock, one of the great western sites for color moviemaking. Rattlesnake wranglers were on hand to clear the area before filming, and the stalwart actors are stunt-doubled extensively on horseback and foot by Al Wyatt and Bob Morgan as they fall and roll around the ground. Director Raoul Walsh and D.P. Lester White shot the Columbia film in the 3-D process, with Carey (6'4", 205 pounds), a former Marine, throwing a tree stump and a small boulder directly into the camera for effect. The *Los Angeles Daily News* wrote, "The audience is constantly on the edge of its collective seat waiting for the next knife, rock or fist to come

flying from the screen." According to Hudson biographer John Mercer, "The film is action-packed, with many shootouts and fights, all of which the actor executes convincingly."

Several minor fistic exchanges pepper the film, most notably between outlaws Leo Gordon, Neville Brand and Lee Marvin. Behind the scenes, tough guy Gordon intrigued director Walsh. The Irving Wallace-Roy Huggins script called for fellow bad guys Marvin and Brand to wake Gordon from a slumber and rough him up. Walsh told Marvin and Brand he didn't want them to pull their punches on Gordon for the scene. Gordon sensed what was going on and proceeded to beat the tar out of the two battle-tested war heroes. Brand and Gordon reminisced about this exchange years later when they were staging another fight together on the TV western *Laredo*.

Strapping 6'5", 215-pound Rock Hudson was a Navy veteran prior to being signed to a Universal contract. He learned to box from Frankie Van for *Iron Man* (1951), and many of his films featured fights. Hudson was an effective movie fighter, especially imposing on the silver screen thanks to his huge frame. He also had a high pain tolerance, once accidentally tearing open his hand when throwing a punch at the camera. He simply had it taped up and returned to work. Many stars would have missed several work days for such an injury. Hudson's hand turned out to be broken.

Notable fights include *Giant* (1956) and *The Undefeated* (1969) (see entries). Fights of interest came against Henry Brandon in *Scarlet Angel* (1952), Steve Cochran and Hugh O'Brian in *Back to God's Country* (1953), Hugh O'Brian in *Seminole* (1953), Rex Reason in *Taza, Son of Cochise* (1954), Robert Stack and John Larch in *Written on the Wind* (1956), Sidney Poitier in *Something of Value* (1957), Kirk Douglas in *The Last Sunset* (1961) and George Peppard in *Tobruk* (1967). In the 1972 *McMillan and Wife* TV episode "Terror Times Two," Hudson fought himself using creative camera angles and longtime stunt double George Robotham.

See: Mercer, John. *Rock Hudson*. London: Palgrave MacMillan, 2015; "Star Breaks Hand During Fight." *Sarasota Herald Tribune*. February 13, 1981.

AUDIE MURPHY VS. RUSSELL JOHNSON in *Tumbleweed* (1953)

Tumbleweed is an entertaining B-western featuring decorated war hero turned cowboy star Audie Murphy trying to clear his name after he's unfairly labeled a deserter. Interestingly, this was a match-up of war heroes, though many were unaware of co-star Russell Johnson's impressive military record. Most audiences came to know him as the mild-mannered Professor on TV's *Gilligan's Island*, but here he makes an effective heavy and is game for the fist-flying, boot-kicking action. The 5'10, 165-pound Johnson and the 5'8", 145-pound Murphy perform much of the action, including a great deal of tricky climbing along California's Vasquez Rocks. Stuntmen Dave Sharpe and Bill Williams doubled for the toughest parts. Johnson had additional run-ins with Murphy in *Column South* (1953) and *Ride Clear of Diablo* (1954).

The nearly three-minute fight starts with an impressive bulldog and ends with Johnson falling to his death from the top of a cliff. It's exciting, but a couple of missteps keep it from being a truly great fight. A tell-tale Virgil Vogel editing mistake occurs when Johnson kicks out from Murphy near the end. Johnson raises his left leg, but the film cuts to a long shot of stunt double Williams kicking Sharpe with his right leg. Another of Murphy's punches obviously misses Johnson, but he still reacts. Director Nathan Juran was noted for doing a minimum of takes. These are minor quibbles for an otherwise handsomely produced Universal film. Juran and cameraman Russell Metty move in close among the rocks for great shots, and it's preceded by a thrilling horse chase and a stirring musical score. Murphy accidentally connected with Johnson and split his lip open.

Russell Johnson reacts to a big punch from Audie Murphy in Universal's *Tumbleweed* (1953).

When he joined the Army at age 16, an undernourished Audie Murphy stood 5'5" and weighed barely 110 pounds. The young Texan was initially rejected by the military but became its most highly decorated soldier for his unparalleled courage in combat. He killed more than 240 Germans and made the cover of *Life* magazine as a Congressional Medal of Honor winner. Hollywood saw potential and Universal signed him to a contract.

Murphy undoubtedly suffered from Post-Traumatic Stress Disorder. He had a hair-trigger temper and a chip on his shoulder. Given his background, many considered him to be the most dangerous man in Hollywood. He slept with a gun underneath his pillow and made the news numerous times for getting into real fights. Late in his career, he was acquitted of attempted murder charges after beating up a 6'1", 195-pound dog trainer. Murphy boxed regularly at Terry Hunt's Athletic Club with director Budd Boetticher and welterweight pros Art Aragon and Joey Barnum. They all complimented him on his tenaciousness and fearlessness. He studied judo with Ken Kuniyuki and Kenpo karate with Ed Parker.

Despite his lack of size, Murphy was a gutsy on-screen fighter who liked to throw punches and get dirty. When it made sense within the framework of a fight, he occasionally incorporated real and effective ground fighting techniques such as armbars and wristlocks. Stuntmen were not fond of doing fights with him because he could get carried away with action and not pull punches. However, audiences took to this underdog hero who feared no man. They believed this tough little guy could take down the giants.

Fights of interest came against Mike Ragan and Henry Wills in *Gunsmoke* (1953), Bob Steele in *Drums Across the River* (1954) (see entry), William Pullen in *Ride Clear of Diablo* (1954), Henry Silva in *Ride a Crooked Trail* (1958), James Best in *Cast a Long Shadow* (1959), Peter Breck in *The Wild and the Innocent* (1959), Barry Sullivan in *Seven Ways from Sundown* (1960), Rex Holman and Walter Sande in *The Quick Gun* (1964), Darren McGavin in *Bullet for a Badman* (1964), L.Q. Jones in *Apache Rifles* (1964), Kelly Thordsen in *Gunpoint* (1966), Aldo Sambrell in *The Texican* (1966) and Kenneth Tobey in *40 Guns to Apache Pass* (1967). On TV, Murphy fought Robert Redford in the 1961 *Whispering Smith* episode "The Grudge."

See: "Audie Dislikes Pulling Punches." *Deseret News*. January 9, 1949; Larkins, Bob, and Boyd Magers. *The Films of Audie Murphy*. Jefferson, NC: McFarland, 2009.

AUDIE MURPHY VS. BOB STEELE in *Drums Across the River* (1954)

Legend has it that after his career as a B-western star ended, Bob Steele resorted to becoming a stunt double for Audie Murphy. Steele does indeed show up in many small roles in Murphy films, but that was because Murphy liked and idolized the former cowboy hero. *Drums Across the River* contains one of Steele's better heavy roles opposite Murphy and an exciting 90-second fight grappling around a campfire. Murphy is doubled here by stuntman Dave Sharpe for a fall over a log and the fire while Steele appears to do the entire fight. He later had to seek medical treatment because Murphy, carried away, connected in the heat of the moment. It's possible that since Sharpe and Steele had worked together for several years, they blocked out the fight routine together, with Steele stepping in for Murphy at that early point while Sharpe worked out Steele's character's action with second unit cameraman Harold Lipstein. During the fight, Murphy accidentally caught an elbow to the neck area. The studio doctor checked on him and told the star he might be unable to move his head by morning. Murphy spent the night wrapping his neck in hot towels and by the morning was able to resume filming. Such injuries were part of being a Universal cowboy star and an occupational hazard Murphy accepted.

The Nathan Juran–directed film sees Murphy trying to clear his name while fighting Indians and outlaws including Lyle Bettger, Hugh O'Brian, Ken Terrell, James Anderson, Gregg Barton and Lane Bradford. It's regarded as one of Murphy's best westerns with tech credits fine across the board. Henry Mancini and Herman Stein provide the stirring score with Virgil Vogel's editing entirely competent. Prolific pulp fiction writer John K. Butler's screenplay is efficiently plotted with plenty of action scenes. All the talent went on to bigger assignments and wider acclaim. Murphy biographer Bob Larkins calls it "one of the best screen fights in all of Audie's westerns." According

to *Six Gun Law*, "Murphy's renowned fistfights were over-vigorous to the point of punishing."

See: Murphy, Audie. "Things I Don't Tell My Wife." *Screen Life*. May 1954.

THE BARN-RAISING BRAWL in *Seven Brides for Seven Brothers* (1954)

This popular, glossy MGM musical focuses on seven backwoods brothers in 1850s Oregon who resort to two-fisted courtship of the ladies in town. The centerpiece barn-raising features four competitive groups vying to complete the building. Intentional carpentry mistakes continuously plague the Pontipee brothers' group until they decide to fight back during a two-minute triumph of slapstick timing and intricate choreography involving planks, ladders, 2 × 4s, crossbeams and window frames. *Magill's* found the fight "as precisely choreographed as any of the dances," while *Variety* called it "a rousing sequence." *American Cinematographer* termed it "a spectacular free-for-all." Dance choreographer Michael Kidd and assistant Alex Romero had vital input, but the stunt coordinator for the brawling action was John Indrisano. He squares off against top-billed Howard Keel in the melee. Veteran MGM editor Ralph Winters cut the fight and dance sequences together superbly to Adolph Deutsch's score, including the horrified reaction shots of Keel's new wife Jane Powell. Winters received an Oscar nomination.

Director Stanley Donen and cinematographer George Folsey shot the fight with two cameras running simultaneously, one in CinemaScope and one in normal aspect ratio. A 23,000-square-foot MGM soundstage was used, with dressing rooms, makeup and lighting equipment temporarily moved outside to give the participants enough room to freely dance and fight. A quarter of a million watts were required to light the scene. The athletic actors and dancers cast as the redheaded Pontipee brothers did their own stunt fighting, keeping their stuntmen opponents on their toes for any mistimed punches. Six-foot-four, 195-pound Howard Keel could handle himself in a fight and was joined by Jeff Richards, Russ Tamblyn, Tommy Rall, Marc Platt, Matt Mattox and Jacques d'Amboise. Tamblyn was 5'9", but his gymnastic background allowed him great moments in both the dancing and fighting scenes. He also did his own screen fighting in *High School Confidential!* (1958) and *Satan's Sadists* (1969). The toughest brother, 6'2", 200-pound Jeff

Richards, has a fight against town suitors Terry Wilson, George Robotham and Russ Saunders and stacks them up in an unconscious pile. Those stunt actors work the barn-raising brawl alongside Dale Van Sickel, John Daheim, Charles Horvath, Bud Wolfe, Henry Wills, Tom Steele, Reg Parton, Sol Gorss, Fred Kennedy, Clint Sharp, Frank Mc-Grath, Leroy Johnson, Carl Pitti, Carl Saxe, Roger Creed and Al Jackson. In the budget western *Waco* (1966), Keel and Richards fight one another.

See: Keel, Howard, and Joyce Spizer. *Only Make Believe: My Life in Show Business.* Fort Lee, NJ: Barricade, 2005; Knowles, Mark. *The Man Who Made the Jailhouse Rock: Alex Romero, Hollywood Choreographer.* Jefferson, NC: McFarland, 2013; "Stage Holds Big Farm." *Oregonian.* August 5, 1954.

Robert Taylor vs. George Raft and Alan Hale, Jr., in *Rogue Cop* (1954)

Unusually dark by MGM standards, this bad cop drama from director Roy Rowland features Robert Taylor in one of his best roles. He's a cop on the take who tries to protect his brother Steve Forrest from gangster George Raft. When Raft has Forrest killed, Taylor is out for revenge. Along the way he beats up hit man Vince Edwards and, most impressively, Raft and his beefy bodyguard Alan Hale, Jr., in a brutal one-minute fistfight in Raft's apartment. "No punches pulled!" exclaimed the ads. The bulk of the action comes against Hale, playing Raft's torpedo, a former boxer. Taylor calls him a stumblebum who fought fixed fights and proves it to him. Furniture is upended and lamps are broken as they fight along the bar and over a couch. At one point, Taylor throws a drink in Hale's face. Taylor finishes the fight with a spinning double axe-handle to the throat that knocks the wind out of Hale. Dale Van Sickel choreographed the fight and doubled Taylor. Cinematographer John F. Seitz received an Oscar nomination for his excellent camerawork. Taylor and Hale had another fistfight the following year in *Many Rivers to Cross* (1955).

Young actor Edwards was so proud of being in a well-produced MGM film that he called his mother in Brooklyn and excitedly told her to go to the local movie house to see him in *Rogue Cop.* His mother did so only to be dismayed at the pummeling her son received from the star. Though she knew it was all make-believe, she couldn't bear to see her boy thrashed around and knocked over a collapsing bed frame. She immediately called Edwards and told him she could never watch him be beaten like that again. Taylor had been her favorite movie star, but he wasn't any longer. *Variety* wrote, "Rowland makes the most of a number of violent fight sequences and the customers of this type drama will like them best."

A dead ringer for his character actor father, 6'2" 225-pound Alan Hale, Jr., is best known for playing the beleaguered Skipper on TV's *Gilligan's Island* (1964–1966). The husky Coast Guard veteran was often called upon to provide menace on screen though he had a hearty laugh and great smile. Hale did a great deal of his own fight work on TV shows such as *Gene Autry, The Range Rider, Cheyenne, Bronco, M Squad,* and *Shotgun Slade.* One quality Hale possessed was the ability to believably soften his heavies. They often ended up joining the protagonists after they were bested in fisticuffs. With age he put on considerable weight and began playing more comedic characters.

Hale fought Gene Autry in *The Blazing Sun* (1950), Dan Duryea in *The Underworld Story* (1950), James Cagney in *The West Point Story* (1950), Wayne Morris in *Arctic Flight* (1952), Scott Brady in *The Law vs. Billy the Kid* (1954), George Montgomery in *Canyon River* (1955) and Cameron Mitchell in *All Mine to Give* (1957) (see entry). He had leading TV roles as the two-fisted title spy in *Biff Baker, USA* (1952–1954) and the tough train engineer in *Casey Jones* (1957–1958). As a guest he memorably went toe to toe with James Arness in the 1966 *Gunsmoke* episode "Champion of the World."

See: Carpozi, George. *Vince Edwards: A Biography of Television's Dr. Ben Casey.* New York: Belmont, 1962; Whitney, Dwight. "He's Still Selling Vacuum Cleaners." *TV Guide.* June 11, 1966.

Kirk Douglas vs. Umberto Silvestri in *Ulysses* (1954)

This Italian-made costume epic based on the adventures of the Greek poet Homer's *Odyssey* hero was a departure for a pre–*Spartacus* Kirk Douglas. The serious actor is running around clad in only a loincloth, but he manages to give an energetic and memorable performance as the amnesiac Ulysses journeys from Troy to Ithaca over the course of ten years. Popular worldwide, the film opened the door to a flood of mythical gladiator films.

Most viewers remember the bearded Ulysses

for his fighting ability. Here he takes on Umberto Silvestri in a two-minute Greco-Roman wrestling exhibition in Phaecia featuring takedowns, escapes, leg scissors and an inverted pile-driver that finishes off Silvestri. The latter, a Mediterranean champion, competed as a light-heavyweight in the Olympic Games. Both men assist one another in their fast-paced wrestling moves for Harold Rosson's camera, never dwelling on a single hold to maintain the audience's attention. For the final pile-driver, Silvestri held himself in a handstand until director Mario Camerini gave the cue for action. Silvestri also donned makeup to portray the one-eyed cyclops Polyphemus that Douglas outwits. In the action-packed climax, Douglas kills villain Anthony Quinn to rescue his patient wife Silvana Mangano from amorous suitors.

Five-foot-nine and 175 pounds, Douglas competed in wrestling for St. Lawrence University before earning money professionally as a carnival wrestler. The Navy veteran scored as a tenacious boxer in *Champion* (1949), training for the part with Mushy Callahan. Full of kinetic energy, Douglas had an especially aggressive personality and was often lambasted by peers and the press for having a giant-sized ego. He was a talented athlete who enjoyed mastering skills such as judo. He tried to perform as many stunts as possible, approaching each role the way a professional athlete would an event. He was spry and agile well into his later years, appearing alongside Burt Lancaster in *Tough Guys* (1986) and comically throwing punches at Sylvester Stallone from his deathbed in *Oscar* (1991). As a screen fighter, however, Douglas garnered a reputation for being overly enthusiastic and inadvertently making contact with opponents. Walter Matthau claimed Douglas busted his jaw with a punch in *The Indian Fighter* (1955).

Notable fights include *Man Without a Star* (1955), *Spartacus* (1960), *Lonely Are the Brave* (1962) and *The War Wagon* (1967) (see entries). Fights of interest came against Burt Lancaster in *I Walk Alone* (1948), James Anderson in *Along the Great Divide* (1951), John Archer in *The Big Trees* (1952), Fred Graham in *The Big Sky* (1952), Robert Wilke in *20,000 Leagues Under the Sea* (1954), Tony Curtis in *The Vikings* (1958), Earl Holliman in *Last Train from Gun Hill* (1959), Walter Matthau in *Strangers When We Meet* (1960), Rock Hudson in *The Last Sunset* (1961), Hal Needham and Dean Smith in *In Harm's Way* (1965), Richard Harris in *The Heroes of Telemark*

(1965), Richard Widmark in *The Way West* (1967), Hank Garrett in *A Lovely Way to Die* (1968), Don Stroud in *Scalawag* (1973) and David Janssen in *Once Is Not Enough* (1975). On the 1983 TV special *Celebrity Daredevils,* Douglas put on a fight for the audience.

See: "An Eye for a Cyclops." *Life.* September 21, 1953; Burton, Ron. "Actor Kirk Douglas Is Film Colony's Top Judo Expert." *Terra Haute Tribune.* November 4, 1956.

MARLON BRANDO VS. LEE J. COBB in *On the Waterfront* (1954)

Elia Kazan's Academy Award–winning classic about union struggles among East Coast longshoremen starred Marlon Brando as ex-prizefighter Terry Malloy. His Oscar-winning performances is considered to be one of cinema's greatest. The engrossing drama builds to a superbly shot confrontation on the Hoboken, New Jersey, shipyard docks between Brando and mob boss Johnny Friendly (Lee J. Cobb). Credit must go to Budd Schulberg's script for the effective conflict created between the characters. Brando calls the six-foot, 190-pound Cobb a "cheap, lousy, dirty, stinking mug!" and charges toward him, but Cobb deftly sidesteps him and trips Brando to the sound of Leonard Bernstein's pulsating score. Cobb uses every dirty tactic in the book to gain an advantage, but Brando begins to overwhelm him with body shots. Cobb calls for four of his thugs to step in and give Brando one of filmdom's most savage beatings, topping the previous year's mauling of Brando by the townspeople in *The Wild One* (1953). No one was better than Brando at suggesting they had the living snot kicked out of them. His bloody, exhausted walk up the pier in front of the longshoremen is one of filmdom's most indelible moments.

Cobb, Kazan and Schulberg had named names in front of HUAC. While Brando didn't agree with their actions, he made peace with them and moved forward in the role. Kazan wasn't sure he'd enjoy the same gentle treatment from the many longshoremen populating the cast as extras. He hired several ex-professional boxers and pro wrestlers to play bit parts and serve as protection. Among them were Abe Simon, Tony "Two-Ton" Galento, Tami Mauriello, Don Blackman, Mike O'Dowd and Tiger Joe Marsh. Nobody touched Kazan.

Roger Donoghue, a recently retired middleweight boxer, was hired as a trainer and technical advisor when an early screenplay draft included scenes in the ring. Brando had boxed in his youth and sparred with Rocky Graziano while appearing on Broadway in *A Streetcar Named Desire*. Donoghue put him to work at Stillman's Gym and accompanied him on regular jogs through Central Park. He was impressed with Brando's level of concentration and quick learning, suggesting he could have been successful in the ring with proper training. Donoghue was nearly a champion, but quit the fight game after killing a ring opponent. Donoghue is often credited with feeding Schulberg the famous line Brando gives to brother Rod Steiger in the back of the car, "I could have been somebody. I could have been a contender." After *Waterfront*, Donoghue trained James Dean for a proposed biopic on his (Donoghue's) life. It was cancelled with Dean's death.

In a local bar, Kazan spotted boxer William Ramoth (he used the ring moniker Billy Kilroy) and noticed a striking resemblance to Brando. It so happened Ramoth had come to the set to visit his friend Tony Galento. A Golden Gloves champ

Lee J. Cobb trips Marlon Brando in Columbia's classic *On the Waterfront* (1954).

and All-Service middleweight champ in the Navy, Ramoth had recently given up the ring after paralyzing another boxer. He was hired as Brando's stuntman for the fight and launched a second career as a boxing technical advisor and double. Another local character, Joseph "Cowboy" Lucignano, was recruited to double Cobb in the fight, which *Action Films* includes among their all-time greatest.

See: Martin, Douglas. "Roger Donoghue, 75, Boxer and Brando's *Waterfront* Trainer, Dies." *New York Times*. August 25, 2006; Schwartz, Jordan. "Kilroy Was Here: The Story of Boxer and Stuntman Billy 'Kilroy' Ramoth." *Bleacher Report*. February 23, 2009.

ALAN LADD VS. CHARLES BRONSON in *Drum Beat* (1954)

Set in the 1870s, *Drum Beat* is a solid Delmer Daves western based on historical fact. It places peace negotiator Alan Ladd on the Oregon-California border where he negotiates with the local Modoc Indians but runs into problems with renegade warrior Charles Bronson. Due to Hollywood's Red Scare, it was the first film where Charles Buchinski used the surname Bronson, and it's a breakthrough performance. The *New York Times* called the chiseled Bronson "the most muscular Indian ever to have brandished a rifle before a camera," while the *Los Angeles Times* said he was "only slightly less than sensational." Because of producer-star Ladd's fragile star ego, Bronson's forceful portrayal made him uncomfortable. So did an early altercation in which Bronson hits Ladd with a rifle butt. Bronson did that action too effectively, making contact and injuring Ladd's ribs.

The film was shot by J. Peverall Marley in Arizona's Slide Rock State Park near Sedona. The picturesque location benefits the climactic hand-to-hand combat, where Bronson and Ladd fight along a river's edge and into a sweeping current. Warner Bros. publicity called it "one of the liveliest brawls of Ladd's career." Stunt doubles Paul Baxley and Bob Hoy tumble and slide down the ledges of the red rocks and into the water chute, although Ladd and Bronson are visible throughout much of the action. Temperatures were reported to have gone upwards of 100 degrees, extremely hot for the thin air and the nearly 5000-foot elevation. Prior to the fight, the actors were given a physical exam by Dr. Norman D. Whitney, who presided over Arizona's Boxing Commission. Publicity stressed the elements and likened the on-screen battle to a prizefight. The men trained and rehearsed for three weeks before cameras rolled. There was such a build-up that cast members Anthony Caruso, Marisa Pavan and Audrey Dalton stayed on at the location at their own expense to witness it.

The climactic fight began and ended on a Warner Bros. soundstage, but what came between was filmed in five different locations 25 miles apart that covered two Arizona counties. The set-up had Bronson firing a rifle at Ladd from a concealed location beneath the ridge. The shot where Ladd pushes a boulder to flush Bronson from his hiding place was filmed in Coconino County. The action switched to Yavapai County's Oak Creek and Slide Rock location for the bulk of the battle. The bit with Ladd sliding on his boots and firing his guns was filmed at yet another location. Both Ladd and Bronson wound up with minor scrapes and abrasions from the rocks. Editor Clarence Kolster was tasked with matching continuity and putting it all together cohesively. He succeeded.

Five-eight and 170 pounds, Charles Bronson grew up in the Pennsylvania coal mines, escaping

Alan Ladd (with hat) and Charles Bronson tangle on Slide Rock in Warner Bros.' *Drum Beat* (1954).

a bleak future there via his World War II military service. The muscular, granite-faced Bronson boxed in the Army and kept tremendously fit, displaying one of Hollywood's greatest whipcord physiques into his fifties when he finally attained superstardom. He worked out one hour every day and his bulging biceps were the envy of many a film fan. Although Bronson wasn't tall, few who encountered him doubted his ability to handle himself in a fight. He was quick and tightly coiled, moving with athletic assurance. He was also a quiet loner, giving off a tough guy vibe few dared to mess with. Because he was agile and had good timing, he could do a fight as well as many stuntmen. He threw rapid-fire crosses that looked like they were aimed with bad intentions; his opponents needed to be on their toes and quick with their reactions. The stone-faced Bronson looked deadly serious when he was in a screen fight. He also fought dirty, even when he was a leading man, mixing in kicks and effective streetfighting techniques. In the 1970s he trained in Gosoku-ryu karate with Tak Kubota. They spar briefly with one another in *The Mechanic* (1972).

Notable fights include *A Thunder of Drums* (1961), *Farewell, Friend* (1969), *Red Sun* (1971), *Hard Times* (1975), *Breakheart Pass* (1976) and *Caboblanco* (1980) (see entries). Fights of interest came against Paul Picerni in *House of Wax* (1953), Dewey Martin in *Tennessee Champ* (1954), Archie Savage in *Vera Cruz* (1954)., Richard Jaeckel in *When Hell Broke Loose* (1958), Richard Burton in *The Sandpiper* (1965), Robert Redford in *This Property Is Condemned* (1966), Gerry Crampton and Terry Richards in *The Dirty Dozen* (1967), Anthony Quinn in *Guns for San Sebastian* (1968), Tony Curtis in *You Can't Win 'Em All* (1970), Al Lettieri in *Mr. Majestyk* (1974), Paul Mantee in *Breakout* (1975), Robert Englund and Jeff Goldblum in *St. Ives* (1976), Thomas F. Duffy in *Death Wish II* (1982) and Gavan O'Herlihy in *Death Wish III* (1985).

On his action-packed TV series *Man with a Camera* (1958–1960), Bronson played crime photographer Mike Kovac. The series featured some of the best-choreographed fights for the period with Bronson even utilizing judo. His best one-on-ones came against Johnny Seven in

1960's "The Picture War" and Lawrence Tierney in that same year's "Hot Ice Cream." On the western *The Travels of Jamie McPheeters* (1963–1964), he played young Kurt Russell's mentor, tangling with Mike Mazurki in 1964's "The Day of the Lame Duck." As a TV guest, Bronson portrayed boxers on *The Joe Palooka Story, The Roy Rogers Show, Crusader, M Squad* and *One Step Beyond*. He had memorable fights with David Janssen in the 1957 *Richard Diamond, Private Detective* episode "The Pete Rocco Case," Richard Boone in the 1958 *Have Gun—Will Travel* episode "The Man Who Wouldn't Talk," Michael Landon in the 1964 *Bonanza* episode "The Underdog" and George Kennedy in the 1965 *Virginian* episode "The Nobility of Kings."

See: "Doc Okays Actors for Fight Scene." *Times-Picayune.* December 19, 1954; "Fight Worth Price." *Oregonian.* December 26, 1954; Latham, Bill. "What's Another Cracked Rib to Tough Alan Ladd?" *Boston Daily Record.* July 20, 1954.

HOWARD DUFF VS. LEX BARKER in *The Yellow Mountain* (1954)

Pre-release publicity played up this two-man gold fever western brawl, trumpeting it as the next coming of *The Spoilers*. Director Jesse Hibbs, former star halfback at USC, devoted three days to the filming of the fight. He invited the press onto his Universal set to watch leading men Howard Duff and Lex Barker throw punches at one another and prove their toughness as they fight it out over leading lady Mala Powers. It's one of those Quirt and Flagg brawling buddy pictures where the two mend their differences to take on real villain Leo Gordon.

The centerpiece brawl opening the film is novel in the sense that when others try to break them apart, the two men temporarily turn their fists against the interlopers before again taking aim at one another's jawline. As for any comparison to *The Spoilers,* the eventual product is underwhelming despite the destruction of much bric-a-brac furniture during the roughly 60 seconds of fist-slinging action. Stuntmen trying to stop the two include Eddie Parker, Jack Stoney and Sol Gorss.

Lex Barker, 6'4" and 210 pounds, had spent the past five years playing Tarzan at RKO. Howard Duff, a 190-pound six-footer, was the voice of private detective Sam Spade on the radio. Both actors emerged with an assortment of bumps and bruises as Hibbs convinced them to forgo stunt doubles

for much of the action so he could move George Robinson's camera in close. Barker told the press that being Tarzan on a back lot jungle was like going to Sunday school in comparison to this grueling fight. Unfortunately, the actors lack the visual fluidity an accomplished pair of well-practiced stuntmen bring to the master shot. As a result, the scene is choppy with Edward Curtiss forced to create the continuity in bits and pieces of usable footage.

The role of the Foley artist in a fight scene should be discussed. A Foley artist is the technician responsible for adding the appropriate sound effects to the on-screen action during post-production. The term is named after veteran Universal sound artist Jack Foley. *The Yellow Mountain* had Jack Foley himself coming up with the fight's sound effects. After a rough cut was assembled, he was given the fight footage to enhance the action. He used an old standby for Barker's fist hitting Duff's face: In his studio, he held up a large ham and let an assistant punch it to perfectly simulate the sound of a fist hitting flesh. The moment when Duff is dropped by a Barker punch proved to be challenging for Foley. For this effect, he decided to drop a large mail bag filled with a dozen pairs of shoes to the floor from a ten-foot height. It worked like a charm.

Barker was a football and track athlete at Fessenden and the Phillips-Exeter Academy before serving with the Army in Sicily during World War II. Despite his athleticism, he had a reputation for sometimes forgetting fight choreography in the middle of a scene. In the 1960s he achieved significant Euro-western acclaim playing Karl May's fictional character Old Shatterhand, so named for his great punching power. Barker fought Charles McGraw and Sol Gorss in *The Farmer's Daughter* (1947), Henry Kulky in *Tarzan's Magic Fountain* (1949), Anthony Caruso in *Tarzan and the Slave Girl* (1950), Larry Chance in *Battles of Chief Pontiac* (1952), Randolph Scott in *Thunder Over the Plains* (1953) and Stephen McNally and Myron Healey in *The Man from Bitter Ridge* (1955).

See: Archerd, Armand. "Lex Barker Finds Civilized Roles Just as Tough as Old Jungle Ones." *Beaver Valley Times.* August 21, 1954; "Big Fight Scene Has New Slant." *Portland Oregonian.* April 4, 1954; Johnson, Erskine. "Hollywood Today." *Shamokin News-Dispatch.* June 4, 1954; "Screen Actors Stage Real Brawl." *San Diego Union.* April 12, 1954.

SPENCER TRACY VS. ERNEST BORGNINE in *Bad Day at Black Rock* (1955)

This classic suspense-mystery from director John Sturges was notable as one of the first Hollywood studio films to feature martial arts being used by a Caucasian. Spencer Tracy's brief judo demo on bullish Ernest Borgnine in a Black Rock café is as shocking to the audience as it is to the film's dumbfounded characters, among them chief villain Robert Ryan and goon Lee Marvin. The scene shows the power of martial arts. Here a one-armed senior citizen regarded as a cripple by all those he encounters annihilates a young and powerful opponent without so much as breaking a sweat. The 5'9", 215-pound Borgnine was defining his career as a slimy, gap-toothed heavy with a sadistic mean streak, and audiences feared this new screen monster with the 17" neck and 49" chest. No one thought Tracy had a chance going into the fight, even the star.

Borgnine approached Sturges with concerns about the scene. He wasn't sure it was believable for him to be beaten by one-armed Tracy. Sturges agreed it might be problematic. Borgnine has taken credit for suggesting the use of judo, though stunt coordinator John Indrisano had a background in the self-defense tactic. Bruce Tegner, the 1949 California State Judo Champ and a self-defense trainer of the Armed Forces' Military Policemen, was consulted for his expertise, verifying that Tracy's chop to the larynx could kill Borgnine, and certainly take the wind out of him. Despite the brevity of the action, it's regarded as one of cinema's greatest scenes. Sturges credits this to the tension-filled build-up in Millard Kaufman's script that makes the audience identify with Tracy and root for Borgnine's downfall. It's also an important character-revealing moment, opening up all types of mystery into Tracy's background and training. Both actors are superb in their roles.

The script called for the fight to end after the first blood-inducing blow, a violent heel of the hand to Borgnine's nose; but Sturges wanted more moves including a knee to the face. Borgnine con-

Lee Marvin (seated) and Robert Ryan watch Spencer Tracy surprise Ernest Borgnine with a judo flip in MGM's classic *Bad Day at Black Rock* (1955).

cealed a sponge in his hand and squeezed it after the knee blow, producing the blood above his lip. Sturges knew the Production Office and the Catholic Legion of Decency would raise a stink at that degree of violence so he avoided close-ups and shot in full frame with minimal cuts. He needed Borgnine to recover enough for the fight to climax with the heavy going backward out the café door. Despite Sturges' attempts to involve his star in the action, Tracy was doubled by stuntman Carey Loftin. Tracy didn't like doing fights, allegedly because of his own tendency to get carried away in such moments. He was afraid he might accidentally hurt someone. Certainly his advancing age played into the decision for a double, whose identity is kept hidden by superb staging by cinematographer William C. Mellor. However, Sturges was concerned that Loftin wasn't an appropriate double. Loftin was a highly regarded automotive specialist, but he proved a capable fight man after being bulked up in costume. Borgnine was doubled for the final judo flip by professional football player turned boxer Teddy Pavelec.

During filming, Sturges had fun at Borgnine's expense. Throughout rehearsals he left the screen door unlatched and had mattresses on the ground for Borgnine's fall. When it came time to film the scene, Sturges locked the door and removed the pads. Borgnine wasn't prepared for the resistance, adding to his sense of shock captured by the camera as he plummets to the bare ground. He was angry until he realized that the director was responsible and that it improved the scene. *Colliers* called *Bad Day at Black Rock* "one of the greatest fights since Tom Santschi and William Farnum were matched in *The Spoilers*." According to *Chasing Dragons: An Introduction to the Martial Arts Film*, "It is a brilliant sequence, executed with style and precision by the director and cast." *Action Films* ranks it among the best movie fights ever.

A former truck driver and construction worker, Navy veteran Borgnine became a surprise Best Actor Oscar winner for *Marty* (1955). Despite the prestige, he remained best utilized as a bad guy and enjoyed working on fights. When he was playing heavies, he often took on a sadistic gleam in his eye as he was about to dole out punishment. Few will forget his performance as "Fatso" Judson in *From Here to Eternity* (1953) and his knife fight with Montgomery Clift. The explosive Borgnine had a mercurial reputation early in his career, but he grew into a professional who was well-liked by film crews.

Notable fights include *Chuka* (1967), *The Split* (1968), *Emperor of the North* (1973) and *Convoy* (1978) (see entries). Fights of interest came against Randolph Scott in *The Stranger Wore a Gun* (1953), Sterling Hayden in *Johnny Guitar* (1954) and *The Last Command* (1955), Alan Ladd and Anthony Caruso in *The Badlanders* (1958), Vincent Barbi in *Pay or Die* (1960), Peter Finch in *The Flight of the Phoenix* (1965), Jim Brown and Patrick McGoohan in *Ice Station Zebra* (1968) and Warren Vanders in the TV movie *Twice in a Lifetime* (1974). On his enjoyable comic military series *McHale's Navy* (1964–1966). he fought George Kennedy and Ron Soble. As a TV guest, Borgnine fought Paul Sorensen in the 1960 *Zane Grey Theatre* episode "A Gun for Willie" and played an aging pro wrestler in the 1982 *Magnum P.I.* episode "Mr. White Death."

See: Guild, Leo. "Borgnine Always Itching for a Fight." *Pittsburgh Press.* May 6, 1966.

KIRK DOUGLAS VS. RICHARD BOONE in *Man Without A Star* (1955)

This lusty and boisterous King Vidor western finds Kirk Douglas cast as a footloose cowpoke tangling with ranchers over the use of barbed wire. Douglas rides, sings, plays the banjo, performs gun tricks and ultimately uses his fists against sadistic ranch foreman Richard Boone in the violent climax. Screenwriter Borden Chase built appropriate tension between the two men, primarily over who's most appropriate for beautiful ranch owner Jeanne Crain. After Boone has his men beat a drunken Douglas in the street, the star has a personal score to settle. A crackling fight, shot in California's Conejo Valley, it begins with Douglas bulldogging Boone off his horse. The two Alpha males wrestle amidst the barbed wire, trading several crisp, well-choreographed punches. Boone tries to use both a pickaxe and sledgehammer to his advantage, but Douglas knocks the bigger man out onto the barbs. The *Motion Picture Herald* called it "a forthright, hard-hitting and tightly written picture."

Cameraman Russell Metty offers typically deft movement in the fight while taking advantage of the natural beauty of the surrounding environment. A minor continuity problem occurs as Douglas' lost hat mysteriously reappears then disappears from his head during the exchange of punches. Stuntman Jack Young doubled Douglas and Fred Carson took the bulldog fall for Boone. Douglas called this one of his most physically demanding roles. *Man Without a Star* was recycled by Universal for an episode of *The Virginian* guest starring Brian Keith. It was remade in 1969 as *A Man Called Gannon* with Tony Franciosa taking on the Douglas role.

Richard Boone (6'2", 200 pounds) was an intercollegiate light-heavyweight boxing champ at Stanford University who continued to compete while serving with the Navy in World War II. He briefly considered a career as a pro until seeing Joe Louis work out in a New York gym. Boone determined he could never be the best and decided to become an actor. As a screen fighter, he was realistically rough, occasionally fought dirty, and nobody in the business looked better smashing a bottle over another man's head. Best known as the cultured gunfighter Paladin on *Have Gun—Will Travel* (1957–1963), Boone felt fight scenes fell in line with the demands of an actor playing a tough part. Director Andrew McLaglen ranked him on par with John Wayne when it came to screen fisticuffs. Although Boone could do all his own

fights, he increasingly gave young stuntman Hal Needham the chance to double him.

Boone fought Richard Widmark in *Red Skies of Montana* (1952), Rory Calhoun in *Way of a Gaucho* (1952), Peter Lawford in *Kangaroo* (1952), Van Johnson in *Siege at Red River* (1954), George Montgomery in *Robbers' Roost* (1955), Kerwin Mathews in *The Garment Jungle* (1957), Mickey Simpson in *Rio Conchos* (1964) and Robert Mitchum in *The Big Sleep* (1978). On *Have Gun— Will Travel*, he fought martial artist Fuji Nozawa in 1957's "The Hatchet Man" and 1962's "Coming of the Tiger" and stepped into the bare-knuckle ring to take on Hal Baylor in 1958's "The Prize Fight Story." His best fights came against Charles Bronson in 1958's "The Man Who Wouldn't Talk," Ben Johnson in 1960's "The Race," Denny Miller in 1960's "Saturday Night," Roy Barcroft in 1961's "Long Weekend" and Richard Jaeckel in 1962's "The Predators." As a TV guest, a grizzled Boone battled Stuart Whitman in 1967's *Cimarron Strip* episode "The Roarer." On a 1961 episode of *The Ed Sullivan Show,* Boone staged a fight with stuntmen Hal Needham and Chuck Couch.

Richard Boone is knocked into barbed wire by Kirk Douglas in Universal's *Man Without a Star* (1955).

See: Levy, Charles J, "Boone Says Oater Stars Do Have to Be Actors." *Norwalk Hour*. February 11, 1961; Rothel, David. *Richard Boone: A Knight Without Armor in a Savage Land*. Madison, NC: Empire, 2000.

DANA ANDREWS VS. ROBERT WILKE in *Strange Lady in Town* (1955)

Set in 1880s Santa Fe, New Mexico (but filmed at Old Tucson Studios in Arizona), this Mervyn LeRoy western concerns the upheaval caused by the arrival of Eastern doctor Greer Garson. She fights bigotry and prejudice while the men fight one another over her. Dana Andrews and beastly heavy Robert Wilke nearly take one another's heads off in a spirited two-minute brawl. Beginning inside a mission with Wilke brandishing a knife, the fight moves outdoors where they swing a spade and hatchet at one another. An excellent Dimitri Tiomkin score emphasizes the fight's high points, with wardrobe and makeup contributing torn clothing and bloody faces by fight's end. Cameraman Harold Rosson captures the location scenery well, and the rough fight routine is energetically and professionally staged. *The Great Bend Daily Tribune* wrote of Andrews, "He is thoroughly believable in the part and the fierce fight he has with one of the plug-uglies in the pic turns this into the type of role he does best." *Variety* said the fight was "all that the most avid fan could ask for."

A champion high diver, 6'3", 210-pound Wilke began his career as a stuntman in B-westerns. Thanks to his bullish build and unhandsome mug, Wilke played dozens of snarling henchmen throughout the 1940s opposite Bill Elliott, Sunset Carson, Charles Starrett and Tim Holt. He was often cast for his physicality and punching ability with many a battle ending with him landing on his backside. His best fights came versus Edmond O'Brien in *Cow Country* (1953), George Montgomery in *The Lone Gun* (1954) and *Canyon River* (1955), Kirk Douglas in *20,000 Leagues Under the Sea* (1954), Sterling Hayden in *Shotgun* (1955), Clayton Moore in *The Lone Ranger* (1956) (see entry) and James Stewart in *Night Passage* (1957). Most viewers will remember him on the wrong end of James Coburn's knife in *The Magnificent Seven* (1960). Wilke had a bare-knuckle match with Gene Barry in the 1958 *Bat Masterson* episode "The Fighter" and fought Dale Robertson in the 1960 *Tales of Wells Fargo* episode "The Wade Place." His battle with Forrest Tucker in the 1967

Gunsmoke episode "The Cattle Barons" ignited one of the biggest mass street brawls ever seen on the show. In 1979 he faced Jim Davis in the *Dallas* episode "Dove Hunt."

See: "Robert Wilke Was Villain in Scores of Films." *Los Angeles Times*. April 1, 1989.

BURT LANCASTER VS. WALTER MATTHAU in *The Kentuckian* (1955)

Burt Lancaster made his directorial debut on this 1820s frontier saga, scripted by A.B. Guthrie and shot on location in Owensboro, Kentucky. It's notable for a three-and-a-half-minute fight with whip-wielding villain Walter Matthau, a guy so dastardly that he gets his guffaws while supervising the whipping of Lancaster's son by another child. The bare fists vs. bullwhip scenario provides a memorable opportunity for Lancaster to showcase his athleticism. He dives away time and again trying to elude the crack of Matthau's whip, then launches himself into the air off a tree stump. When Matthau loses his advantage, the fight becomes a standard bout of fisticuffs in which a bloodied, ripped-to-shreds Lancaster ultimately triumphs despite Matthau throwing dirt in his eyes. Charles Horvath was on hand to double Lancaster in the long shots while former B-movie cowboy star Whip Wilson stood in for Matthau during scenes requiring skill with the bullwhip. The 6'3", 180-pound Matthau was a boxing coach for the Police Athletic League and claimed one professional fight to his credit. The former Army Air Corps gunner even boasted that at age ten, he had beaten Rocky Graziano in a street fight. It was Matthau's film debut. He considered his casting was due to his basset-hound face accentuating star Lancaster's handsome features.

It would be Lancaster's only crack at directing, and some of the choreography during the fight seems rushed. It had to have been a challenge to oversee the action and be the main participant. Too many of Lancaster's charges at Matthau look off the mark, a likely result of misguided Ernest Laszlo camera placement and slight discrepancies in timing between Lancaster and Matthau. During the fight, Lancaster instructed Wilson to sting him enough to make it look convincing, resulting in slight cuts across his shoulders. In some markets, the scene was trimmed of any bit where the whip tore into Lancaster's flesh. Biographer David Fury felt that the scene came across as "unnecessarily brutal." Despite the violence, United Artists publicity played up the bullwhip fight. Bernard Herrmann's score is suitably dramatic and George Luckenbacher edited with an eye toward keeping the audience on the edge of their seats.

Although the set-up may now seem novel, both Whip Wilson and Lash LaRue had been staging thrilling whip fights in B-westerns for several years. Republic had been putting out serials ranging from *Zorro's Black Whip* (1944) to *Man with the Steel Whip* (1954). Tyrone Power and Richard Egan had a whip vs. whip fight the same year in *Untamed* (1955). On TV's *The Range Rider,* Jock Mahoney and Robert Wilke put on what was arguably a better choreographed fists vs. whip fight in the 1951 episode "Western Fugitive." Nevertheless, some reviewers were mightily impressed by Lancaster's scene. The *New York Times* noted that Lancaster "is best when he is bucking and brawling in his sportiest athletic style," while *Times Daily* called it "one of the most exciting fights in cinema history."

Six-foot-one and 180 pounds, Lancaster was renowned for his circus background and ability to do a great deal of his own stunt work. He attracted immediate attention playing the doomed boxer in his debut film *The Killers* (1946). At Warner Bros., he trained under the instruction of Mushy Callahan at the studio gym, even stepping into the ring with wrestler Gorgeous George for a 1948 charity match. In real life, he was known for rages and tantrums, garnering a reputation for behind-the-scenes fist-slinging with producers, directors and co-stars. Despite his abundant athleticism, Lancaster had few truly outstanding or protracted on-screen fistfights. He was still punching away alongside fellow senior Kirk Douglas in *Tough Guys* (1986).

Fights of note came against Hume Cronyn in *Brute Force* (1947), John Hodiak in *Desert Fury* (1947), Mike Mazurki in *I Walk Alone* (1948), Paul Henreid in *Rope of Sand* (1949), John Ireland and Ted De Corsia in *Vengeance Valley* (1951), John Dehner in *Ten Tall Men* (1951) and *Apache* (1954), Mike Ragan in *Jim Thorpe—All American* (1951), Chuck Connors in *South Sea Woman* (1953), Charles Horvath in *His Majesty O'Keefe* (1954), Tony Curtis in *Trapeze* (1956), Charles Horvath, Saul Gorss and John Daheim in *Elmer Gantry* (1960), Audie Murphy and John Saxon in *The Unforgiven* (1960), Ossie Davis in *The Scalphunters* (1968) (see entry) and Ed Lauter in *The Midnight Man* (1974).

See: Edelman, Rob, and Audrey Kupferberg. *Matthau: A Life.* Lanham, MD: Taylor Trade, 2002; Fishgall, Gary. *Against Type: The Biography of Burt Lancaster.* New York: Scribner, 1995; Fury, David. *The Cinema History of Burt Lancaster.* Minneapolis: Artists' Press, 1989; *The Kentuckian* pressbook.

FESS PARKER VS. MIKE MAZURKI in *Davy Crockett, King of the Wild Frontier* (1955)

Popular frontier folk hero Davy Crockett gets the Disney treatment in a Norman Foster film that originally aired on television as a multi-part episode of *The Wonderful World of Disney.* Fess Parker, 6'5" and 210 pounds, effectively dons the famous coonskin cap and engages in a rough 'n' tumble, no-holds-barred bout of fisticuffs with Mike Mazurki as his foe Bigfoot Mason. It's an old-fashioned 90-second fight that unfortunately suffers from poor editing and an overly melodramatic George Bruns music score. Nevertheless, a couple of good moments occur, such as Mazurki throwing dirt in Parker's eyes, kicking him in the back and knocking him through a fence. Ultimately Parker lands a series of punches and a final short left that knocks Mazurki dizzy.

It was shot on location in Cherokee, North Carolina, and no stuntmen were brought in for either actor. Parker did the fall through a split-rail fence twice without the aid of stunt pads. On his second go-through, he borrowed the camera blanket and attached it to his hindquarters to soften the blow. Publicity played up Mazurki's veteran tough guy presence, noting that he could rip open a tomato can with his bare hands. In real life, Parker and Mazurki got along fabulously and worked hard to make their fight a memorable one. Parker relied heavily on Mazurki's experience to choreograph their moves. Mostly he opted to let Mazurki throw him around like a rag doll. Parker accidentally clipped Mazurki a couple of times on the jaw and ended up with a lump on his head from the fence rail.

Disney publicity claimed the film contained "some of the most dangerous fight scenes ever filmed." Parker also has a fight along the Oconaluftee River with Pat Hogan as Chief Red Stick of the Creek Indians. Both actors did their own stunts, working out their fight routine so Parker would throw a fake tomahawk at Hogan who'd move out of the way. In the heat of battle, Hogan moved the wrong way and took a tomahawk blow to the head, knocking him out. At one point, Hogan has Parker pinned against a tree, and Parker gives a grin. Parker thought it was a silly piece of business, but audiences loved that fun-loving aspect of the Crockett character.

Navy veteran Parker's most notable fight came off-screen in 1946 and contributed to a facial scar on the left side of his cheek. He was involved in an auto accident in Texas and had an argument with the other driver. The man pulled a knife and stabbed Parker in the face, with the blade breaking off against Parker's jawbone. This prompted the normally mild-mannered Parker to lay a serious beating on the man. He forced the man to drive him to the hospital for treatment. On film he took part in a bar brawl in *Battle Cry* (1955) and fought alongside Jeff York in both *Davy Crockett and the River Pirates* (1956) and *The Great Locomotive Chase* (1956). He also fought Jeff Chandler in *The Jayhawkers!* (1959) and Hoyt Axton in *Smoky* (1966). On TV's *Daniel Boone* (1964–1970), he faced bare-knuckle boxer Maxwell Reed in 1965's "Cry of Gold," Aldo Ray in 1965's "The Trek," Leif Erickson in 1966's "River Passage" and Forrest Tucker in 1967's comic "The Ballad of Sidewinder and Cherokee." As a TV guest, Parker fought Gene Barry in the 1964 *Burke's Law* episode "Who Killed WHO IV?"

See: Chemerka, William R. *Fess Parker: Frontier*

Hero. Albany, GA: BearManor, 2011; Watts, Steven. *The Magic Kingdom: Walt Disney and the American Way of Life.* Columbia: University of Missouri Press, 2001.

RALPH MEEKER VS. PAUL RICHARDS in *Kiss Me Deadly* (1955)

Arguably the most popular books of the post–World War II period were Mickey Spillane's sex- and violence-heavy Mike Hammer stories. The ex–GI private eye was first brought to the big screen in 1953 with Biff Elliot playing the hard-hitting character in *I, the Jury.* For *Kiss Me Deadly,* Ralph Meeker took on the role. He's near-perfect as the sadistic, cocksure Hammer. He's so tough, he takes on knife-wielding thug Paul Richards with a bag of popcorn in a crisp fight clocking in slightly under a minute. When Richards attacks, Meeker throws the popcorn in his face and begins pounding him with his fists long past the point an audience is used to seeing a hero punish a villain. Meeker repeatedly smashes Richards' head against a concrete wall, then knocks the assailant down a long flight of stone steps with a big right cross. Stuntman Fred Krone takes the fall for Richards, shot effectively at L.A.'s Bunker Hill with a wide angle lens by director Robert Aldrich and cinematographer Ernest Laszlo. Carl Saxe served as Meeker's double with Michael Luciano cutting the action together superbly by alternating between close-ups and medium shots. At the outset of the scene, composer Frank De Vol builds significant tension during a tracking shot of Richards following Meeker with knife in hand; while all the while a nonchalant Meeker is aware of his presence.

The Production Code balked at the scripted version of this scene, as Meeker was also to knee and kick Richards and slug him after his body had gone limp. The kneeing and kicking were removed, but Aldrich fought to keep the head-banging. A compromise was reached in which all but one of the five slams are heard and not seen.

Mike Mazurki (left) and Fess Parker battle in *Davy Crockett, King of the Wild Frontier,* a 1955 "feature" made from episodes of Walt Disney's TV series.

Aldrich focused on the delight Meeker took in the act, which was still unsettling. *The American Martial Arts Film* notes, "One of the film's highpoints comes when Hammer is being followed, and savagely beats a thug at his own game using a mix of martial arts and boxing." Among more fights and beatings, Jack Lambert is coldcocked with one Meeker punch in a pool cabana. Later, he and Jack Elam team up to give the Hammer character one of his trademark beatings on a Malibu beach. Hammer will use his deadly .45 for further encounters.

Overlooked upon its release, Aldrich's film found great popularity with the French New Wave, leading to its sustained cult status among fans of stylish L.A. noir. Robert Bray played the Hammer role in *My Gun Is Quick* (1957) and Darren McGavin was cast in the 1958–1959 TV series *Mike Hammer*. Spillane himself took on the role of Hammer in *The Girl Hunters* (1963), engaging in a fight with stuntman Larry Taylor. Armand Assante played him in a 1982 version of *I, the Jury*. In the mid–1980s, Stacy Keach became strongly identified with the part on another TV series, but for many, Ralph Meeker is the quintessential callous Spillane private eye.

Six-one and 185 pounds, Ralph Meeker was a Navy veteran and judo instructor who excelled at playing cruel, swaggering tough guys brimming with self-confidence. One of his earliest roles saw him step into the boxing ring in *Glory Alley* (1952) after he trained with John Indrisano. Meeker quickly learned to yield much of his action over to stunt doubles after breaking a tooth fighting collegiate wrestling champ Jonathan Cott in *Code Two* (1953). He did deck Joe Turkel with a mighty punch in *Paths of Glory* (1957). On the syndicated TV series *Not for Hire* (1959–1960), Meeker starred as a tough Army investigator, Sgt. Steve Dekker.

Fights of interest came against James Whitmore in *Shadow in the Sky* (1952), James Stewart in *The Naked Spur* (1953), John Smith in *Desert Sands* (1955), Christopher George in *The Devil's Eight* (1969) and Gregory Peck in *I Walk the Line* (1970). As a TV guest, he fought Steve McQueen on *Wanted—Dead or Alive*, Tom Tryon on *Texas John Slaughter*, Ron Ely on *Tarzan* and

Cameron Mitchell on *The High Chaparral*. His best fight came against Wayne Maunder in the 1967 *Custer* episode "Glory Rider."

See: Folkart, Burt A. "Played Tough Guys and Villains: Ralph Meeker." *Los Angeles Times.* August 6, 1988; Prince, Stephen. *Classical Film Violence: Designing and Regulating Brutality in Hollywood Cinema, 1930–1968.* New Brunswick, NJ: Rutgers University Press, 2003.

JEFF CHANDLER VS. RORY CALHOUN in *The Spoilers* (1955)

The classic fight from Rex Beach's novel got its first color treatment with Jeff Chandler and Rory Calhoun assuming the roles made famous in 1942 by John Wayne and Randolph Scott in this slick but routine Universal western. John Wayne publicly ridiculed this version as inferior to his own, but it remains a decently realized slugfest afforded a grand and epic staging. It's muddier than its predecessor and at four minutes nearly as lengthy. Much of the basic fight choreography remains the same. Director Jesse Hibbs was determined to present a straightforward and stand-up fight, with no gimmicks such as the use of chains or breakaway chairs. However, there is a thrown spittoon.

Real-life friends Chandler and Calhoun were game for the action. Chief doubles Bob Morgan and Chuck Roberson earned their pay, with great table smashes. In such instances, the legs of the

Rory Calhoun (left) and Jeff Chandler take a crack at the famous fight scene in Universal's *The Spoilers* (1955).

table are scored so they will collapse upon impact and lessen the resistance for the appropriately padded stuntmen. The effect on camera looks fantastic. The fight took five days for the principals to film on Universal's Stage 14. The injury list was far shorter than the movie's predecessors. One of the stuntmen broke a finger, Chandler bruised his knees and Calhoun hurt one hand.

Variety commented, "Such punishment you won't believe but it is fun to watch and well-staged," while *Film Bulletin* wrote that the brawl was "carried off with all the rousing flourish of its predecessors." *The Hollywood Reporter* described it as "a bang-up fight ... which director Jesse Hibbs does not allow to go overboard." The *Los Angeles Herald Examiner* agreed: "The much-touted brawl has been kept within bounds ... but still packs plenty of wallop." *Harrison's Reports* said, "The fight more than matches any of the others both in violence and in length," and *Western Clippings* added, "The big fight isn't Wayne and Scott, but still well-staged."

With his rugged build and premature head of salt and pepper hair, 6'4", 215-pound Jeff Chandler was one of the more physically capable and believable leading men of the 1950s. He once joked that many of the screenplays he was offered required him to have a fistfight every ten pages. An excellent athlete, he turned down college football scholarships and offers to play on the gridiron professionally. Instead he entered the Army's Cavalry division during World War II. At Universal, he was given boxing instruction for *Iron Man* (1951) by Frankie Van.

Chandler fought Jay Silverheels in *The Battle at Apache Pass* (1952), Jim Bannon in *War Arrow* (1953), Anthony Quinn in *East of Sumatra* (1953), Lyle Bettger in *The Great Sioux Uprising* (1953), Jack Palance in *Sign of the Pagan* (1954) and *Ten Seconds to Hell* (1959), Leo Gordon and Charles Horvath in *Man in the Shadow* (1958), Richard Denning in *The Lady Takes a Flyer* (1958), Jacques Bergerac in *Thunder in the Sun* (1959), Fess Parker in *The Jayhawkers!* (1959) and Roger Torrey in *The Plunderers* (1960).

See: Carroll, Harrison. "New Version of *Spoilers* Puts on Fight Scene." *Boston Daily Record*. March 2, 1955; Mosby, Aline. "Famed *Spoilers* Fisticuffs Return but with Doubles." *Omaha World Herald*. February 27, 1955; Wells, Jeff. *Jeff Chandler: Film, Record, Radio, Television and Theater Performances.* Jefferson, NC: McFarland, 2005.

James Stewart vs. Arthur Kennedy in *The Man from Laramie* (1955)

In 1950, James Stewart made the Anthony Mann western *Winchester '73* and changed the course of his career the moment he grabbed Dan Duryea and forced his head onto a bar top. No longer was the 6'3", 160-pound Stewart the gangly, drawling wimp of Hollywood. Now he was a two-fisted action star, and director Mann brought out his edgy toughness in film after film.

In *The Man from Laramie,* Stewart is out to find the gunrunner responsible for his brother's death. In doing so, he and Arthur Kennedy have a rematch of their 1952 *Bend of the River* fight, with Alex Nicol thrown in to make it even more difficult for the star. It's far superior to the previous film's fisticuffs and was Stewart's personal favorite among his westerns. Shot in CinemaScope, it was also director Mann and Columbia's most brutal. People still offer commentary on the violence as Mann's hero shows himself every bit as capable of the villain's extremes. "Rough viewing for the timid," said *Variety,* "But straight actions fans will like it." *Legendary Westerns* includes it among the top brawls in a cowboy film, and *The Making of the Great Westerns* called it "a rough fight that recalls the battles of the various *Spoilers* westerns."

Stewart is lassoed and dragged through smoldering coals and later has his hand shot at close range by Nicol. In between these violent events, he marches memorably enraged across a western street in a fantastic tracking shot from cinematographer Charles Lang before laying into mama's boy Nicol. When ranch foreman Kennedy intervenes, Stewart slugs him as well. Kennedy is an even match, and the two roll underneath horses and crash through a fence while wrestling among scattering cows for a full minute of dust-covered action until interrupted by land baron Donald Crisp. It's a tough battle filmed on location in Santa Fe, New Mexico, with Mann shooting from low angles to emphasize the clear blue skies above the men at the fight's outset. By the conclusion, his camera is on top of them as they roll on the ground. The opening is scored in suspenseful fashion by George Duning, but for the bulk of the fight there's only the sound of the mooing cattle. Stewart insisted upon doing many of his own stunts, and Kennedy accidentally connected with Stewart's mouth. Stuntman Bill Catching doubled Stewart during the toughest bits with Jack Young subbing for the 5'10", 165-pound Kennedy. Editor William Lyon does a fantastic job concealing the use of the stuntmen.

During World War II, Stewart became much-decorated as a pilot, earning an Air Medal, a Distinguished Flying Cross, the Croix de Guerre and seven Battle Stars. At 138 pounds, he was initially deemed too skinny for the service. In the late 1930s, MGM's physical trainer Don Loomis managed to put 20 pounds of temporary muscle on him with weight workouts. By the 1950s, his frame had filled out and he became adept at doing his own fights, particularly in a string of classic westerns. His long, looping punches were often thrown slightly off-balance, giving them a certain authenticity absent in the traditional cowboy hero. Audiences identified with his unease. The Stuntmen's Association made him an honorary member of their fraternal organization.

Fights of interest came against Stephen McNally in *Winchester '73* (1950), Will Geer in *Broken Arrow* (1950), Jack Lambert in *Bend of the River* (1952), Dan Duryea in *Thunder Bay* (1953), Robert Ryan and Ralph Meeker in *The Naked Spur* (1953), Raymond Burr in *Rear Window* (1954), Robert Wilke in *Night Passage* (1957), John Wayne in *The Man Who Shot Liberty Valance* (1962), Kelly Thordsen and Lane Bradford in *Shenandoah* (1965), Jack Elam and Brian Keith in *The Rare Breed* (1966), Jack Elam in *Firecreek* (1968) and John Dehner in *The Cheyenne Social Club* (1970).

James Stewart (left) and Arthur Kennedy get tough with one another in Columbia's *The Man from Laramie* (1955).

See: *The Man from Laramie* pressbook; Thomas, Tony. *A Wonderful Life: The Films and Career of James Stewart.* Secaucus, NJ: Carol, 1997.

THE LIVE TV BRAWL in *It's Always Fair Weather* (1955)

A lavish, entertaining MGM CinemaScope musical, *It's Always Fair Weather* concludes with a zany four-minute show-stopping slugfest between a trio of cynical ex–G.I. hoofers (Gene Kelly, Dan Dailey and Michael Kidd) and gangster Jay C. Flippen's hoods (Sol Gorss, Terry Wilson and John Indrisano) during the filming of a live TV show entitled *Midnight with Madeline*. The hoofers have been lured onto the show by Cyd Charisse as part of a reunion in hopes of recapturing their lost magic from years ago. The disengaged dancers use their dormant athletic skill to make the thugs look silly and force a public confession of their illicit activities. In effect, the dancers place joy and spontaneity back into their lives with this fight. Stanley Donen directed the slapstick action, which *MGM's Greatest Musicals* calls "a spectacular free-for-all brawl."

A common criticism of movie fights is their unrealistic nature; the slick and entertaining choreography found in *It's Always Fair Weather* is abundantly guilty. Staged film combat is akin to a dance routine or fistic ballet. Footwork and balance is especially important. Seldom do the fighters ever emerge broken, bloodied, black and blue, or with injuries of any lasting effect. In Hollywood, they stand toe to toe slugging it out with roundhouse punches that would fell or exhaust any normal man. MGM musicals are entertainment on a grand scale. To a degree, so are movie fights. *It's Always Fair Weather* presents them both to advantage. Gene Kelly (5'9", 165 pounds) was front and center as the acrobatic star of *The Three Musketeers* (1948) and was showcased during the entertaining fight in *Singin' in the Rain* (1952). The dancer's work in action scenes was an early influence on martial arts superstar Jackie Chan.

See: Fordin, Hugh. *MGM's Greatest Musicals.* New York:

Doubleday, 1975; Yudkoff, Alvin. *Gene Kelly: A Life of Dance and Dreams*. New York: Back Stage, 1999.

RANDOLPH SCOTT VS. DON MEGOWAN in *A Lawless Street* (1955)

Sheriff Randolph Scott faces giant-sized Don Megowan in this standard Joseph H. Lewis western. Scott had earlier killed Megowan's brother Frank Hagney in self-defense. Although Megowan is aware that Hagney was a hired gunman, his solemn bitterness turns to fury after Scott tries to give Hagney's widow the "dirty" money the gunman was carrying. The two trade haymaker after haymaker in the vigorous three-minute saloon fight until their faces are bloody and their shirts are torn. Megowan attempts to slam Scott against a post and bear-hug him into submission, but the star proves resilient. Scott wears the big man down as the fight stumbles into the street. Scott is about to throw another punch but sees Megowan is offering no defense so holds back. The two men ultimately resume their previous friendship and Megowan becomes an important ally against the real bad guys. Kenneth Gamet was responsible for creating the believable misunderstanding between acquaintances and made the fight an important plot point. During the battle, Scott injures his gun hand and is unable to use it when the next hired gun Michael Pate shows up.

Columbia publicity called the Megowan fistfight the most spectacular of Scott's career. That might reek of hyperbole, but it's in his career top ten. The *Los Angeles Times* was sufficiently impressed to declare the fight "almost on par with the famous one from *Shane*," while *Six Gun Law* refers to it as "spectacular." Scott believed a solidly staged fight was one of the key ingredients to success when it came to scoring with moviegoers, and the visceral experience in a darkened theater was something they'd remember for years. However, *A Lawless Street* has too many strikes against it to make it truly memorable including Paul Sawtell's unobtrusive yet hardly noteworthy background score. The fight is fluidly lensed by cameraman Ray Rennahan, but Gene Havlick's editing is choppy, no doubt to hide the extensive use of Scott's stuntman Al Wyatt.

Don Megowan does the bulk of the fight himself. There weren't many stuntmen around who could believably double him. He stood 6'6" and weighed over 250 pounds. Thanks to his size and fighting prowess, the former USC football player and Army boxing champion duked it out with TV's Clint Walker (*Cheyenne*) and James Arness (*Gunsmoke*). Megowan was a perfect fight partner for he-men of the day. He fought George Montgomery in the 1958 *Cimarron City* episode "Beast of Cimarron," Richard Boone in the 1959 *Have Gun—Will Travel* "First, Catch a Tiger," Dan Blocker in the 1959 *Bonanza* "The Magnificent Adah" and Chuck Connors in the 1960 *Rifleman* "Seven." Each was a show-stopper. On film he had notable brawls in *Gun the Man Down* (1956) and *The Devil's Brigade* (1968) (see entries). Fights of interest came against Jim Davis in *Lust to Kill* (1958), John Cason in *Snowfire* (1958), Mike Henry in *Tarzan and the Valley of Gold* (1966) and Isaac Hayes in *Truck Turner* (1974).

See: Burton, Ron. "Good Fight Can Make Movie." *The News*. September 9, 1953; "Championship Fight." *News and Eastern Townships Advocate*. May 24, 1956; Weaver, Tom. "Don Megowan: Coolest Father in the World." *Classic Images*. March 2013.

THE HAVANA CLUB BRAWL in *Guys and Dolls* (1955)

In this Damon Runyon gangster story–musical, Marlon Brando is improbably cast as gambler Sky Masterson. He's out of his element warbling tunes and seems more at home when throwing punches in a frenzied Cuban nightclub after female lead Jean Simmons starts a jealous fight with Larri Thomas. John Indrisano coordinated the frantic 60 seconds of fistic action, with Oscar-nominated Harry Stradling behind the camera shooting Joseph White's colorful set. Stuntman Paul Baxley was on hand to double Brando, but the star lobbied to do much of his own fighting, including getting hit by a bass fiddle and dodging thrown chairs. The first punches are overly stagey, but a rhythm develops that nicely compliments the Mambo dance number choreographed by Michael Kidd that precedes it. The *Saturday Review* called it "a marvelous brawl."

Former heavyweight boxing champ Jack Dempsey visited the set and had a hand in teaching Simmons how to throw a punch. The fight called for 50 extras and 13 stunt professionals. Among the stunt performers are Larry Duran, Eddie Saenz, John Daheim, Gil Perkins, Dick Crockett, Harvey Parry, George Robotham, Polly Burson, Lila Finn,

Helen Endicott, Suzanne Ridgeway and Mary Ann Hawkins. Director Joseph L. Mankiewicz decided to double the order for breakaway furniture and props, making it the largest ever assembled for a single fight scene. There were 160 chairs, 40 tables, 300 bottles and 1000 glasses ordered. Frank Sinatra, who co-stars as Nathan Detroit, wanted Brando's Masterson role. There was friction between the leads, and they spent the subsequent years bad-mouthing both one another and this film.

See: Bacon, James. "Goldwyn Sets Precedent in *Guys, Dolls.*" *Reading Eagle.* May 29, 1955; "Scene in *Guys and Dolls* Actually Breaks Them Up." *The Miami News.* May 29, 1955; Thomas, Bob. "Jean Simmons Very Happy Dancing in *Guys and Dolls.*" *Pittsburgh Post-Gazette.* June 30, 1955.

CLAYTON MOORE VS. ROBERT WILKE in *The Lone Ranger* (1956)

This colorful Warner Bros. feature version of the popular TV series showcases plenty of two-fisted action on Kanab, Utah, locations bookended by the iconic "William Tell Overture" theme. The Stuart Heisler–directed film is full of tremendous stunt falls and slides down rocky ledges, well-lensed by Edwin DuPar and superbly edited together by veteran film cutter Clarence Kolster. The memorable climax pits masked hero Clayton Moore against bad guy Robert Wilke in an interesting battle of two 1934 World's Fair performers turned stuntmen actors. Here they yield a decent part of the action to their doubles, allowing for one of the screen's greatest bulldog stunts where one man dives off his horse onto another and takes him to the ground. Some sources say it's Al Wyatt, while Moore's autobiography says it was his series stuntman Bill Ward. At any rate, Moore's stunt double bulldogs Wilke's double Bob Morgan alongside a dangerously steep ledge, and the two go tumbling down the cliff together and the fistfight commences at the bottom. It's a truly impressive stunt. The doubles are sharply edited and cross-cut with the principals pounding away on each other for a great screen fight. Moore also battles aggressive Indian brave Michael Ansara, while the Ranger's sidekick Tonto (Jay Silverheels) fights an entire town of main heavy Lyle Bettger's henchies. *Variety* declared, "Some of the fight sequences staged are thrillingly rugged." Moore proudly stated that the film contained "one of the great fight scenes in western movies."

In his youth, 6'1", 185-pound Clayton Moore worked with the Flying Behrs trapeze act. His gymnastic ability aided his entrance into Hollywood, where he was schooled in fight techniques by Tom Steele and Dave Sharpe at Republic. He served with the Army Air Force during World War II, before making a name as an athletic serial hero and B-western villain who did the bulk of his own screen battles. He fought the likes of Charles Starrett, Allan Lane, Gene Autry and Jock Mahoney, always putting on a spirited show. In the serial *G-Men Never Forget* (1947), a heroic Moore fought Roy Barcroft and John Crawford. In *Kansas Pacific* (1953), he battled Sterling Hayden.

On the *Lone Ranger* series (1949–1957), Moore regularly engaged heavies such as Lane Bradford, Mickey Simpson, Mike Ragan and Hal Baylor in fisticuffs. His biggest battle came against former heavyweight boxing champion Max Baer in 1957's "The Law and Miss Aggie." In the feature film *The Lone Ranger and the Lost City of Gold* (1958), he fought Bill Henry.

See: Moore, Clayton. *I Was That Masked Man.* Dallas, TX: Taylor, 1996.

RORY CALHOUN VS. ROBERT MIDDLETON in *Red Sundown* (1956)

Some of the actors who do their own fights are ex-athletes who retain an air of rough-hewn fitness. They are often physically capable of performing the required action and have a sense of pride about their abilities. They want the audience to know it's them fighting on screen. *Red Sundown* leading man Rory Calhoun fits that bill and establishes his tough guy credentials early on with a one-punch knockdown of bad guy Leo Gordon. With stuntman Chuck Roberson's blessing, Calhoun does all his own fights for William Snyder's camera in this above-average Jack Arnold Universal western. What is surprising is that character actor Robert Middleton doesn't fit that criteria. He is heavyset and not known for partaking in action scenes. Yet he too does all his own one-minute fight with Calhoun, and the two put on a blistering saloon brawl that's the film's highlight. It's notable for its lack of a music score, relying on the sound of breaking glass, cracking wood and fists on chins. Editor Edward Curtiss cut the fight together superbly. The *Toledo Blade* exclaimed, "For those who like fistic combat there is a rock and roll bare-knuckle brawl," while *Western Clippings* calls the fight "one of the best ever from the period."

Six-foot-three, 195-pound Calhoun toiled at many rugged professions including lumberjack, firefighter, miner, cowboy and boxer before being cast as Gentleman Jim Corbett in *The Great John L* (1945). He spent part of his youth in a reformatory and did a stint in prison, giving him a definite bad boy image. Yet he proved to be a heroic leading man with many of his roles requiring physical action, at which he was superb. He was a natural choice to fight Jeff Chandler in the 1955 version of *The Spoilers* (see entry). Whenever he was in a fistfight, his hair became mussed and believable determination painted his face. Calhoun developed a pronounced twisting follow-through that effectively sold the power of his punches. The Stuntmen's Association made him an honorary member.

Calhoun fought Guy Madison in *Massacre River* (1949), Dan Dailey in *A Ticket to Tomahawk* (1950), Peter Graves in *Rogue River* (1951), Richard Boone in *Way of a Gaucho* (1952), Robert Mitchum in *River of No Return* (1954), Charles Drake in *Four Guns to the Border* (1954), Stephen McNally in *A Bullet Is Waiting* (1954), Neville Brand in *Raw Edge* (1956), Max Baer in *Utah Blaine* (1957), Chuck Connors and Vince Edwards in *The Hired Gun* (1957), Lloyd Bridges in *Ride Out for Revenge* (1957), Leo Gordon in *Apache Territory* (1958), John Larch and Russell Johnson in *The Saga of Hemp Brown* (1958), Scott Brady in *Black Spurs* (1965) and John Russell in *Apache Uprising* (1966). On his western TV series *The Texan* (1958–1960), he had a big fight with Mort Mills in 1960's "Thirty Hours to Kill." As a guest, he fought Andrew Duggan in the 1970 *Lancer* episode "The Rivals."

See: Scott, Vernon. "Rory Calhoun Got Into Films on His Good Looks, Not Talent." *Spokane Daily Chronicle.* November 3, 1980; "Smile When You Say That, Pardner." *TV Guide.* January 31, 1959.

THE RACETRACK BRAWL in *The Killing* (1956)

Director Stanley Kubrick put himself on the map with this classic heist picture lensed by Lucien Ballard. Cerebral anti-hero Sterling Hayden recruits a crew to take the gambling proceeds from a racetrack, utilizing the bald-headed real-life professional wrestler Kola Kwariani as a distraction. The six-foot, 250-pound Kwariani fights over half a dozen cops and a few bartenders, losing his shirt in the process to the accompaniment of Kubrick's emphasis on the sounds of shoes and bodies thudding onto the floor. He flips two cops at the same time and takes a bottle over the head that barely fazes him. The police are able to drag him away, but Hayden's ruse has worked. Kwariani knew Kubrick from playing chess in a Greenwich Village club, and some have compared Hayden's moves in the film to an elaborate chess game. Kwariani died in 1980 after engaging in a brawl with five delinquents who tried to mug the 77-year-old.

Stuntmen Harvey Parry, John Hudkins, Gil Perkins, Wally Rose, Eddy Saenz, Don Turner, Fred Graham, Sol Gorss and Fred Gabourie worked the fight with Kwariani. Comedian Rodney Dangerfield supposedly appears in the sequence as an extra. After the Kwariani brawl, leading man Hayden makes off with the loot, but not before he is confronted by racetrack guard Gorss. Hayden sends Gorss sprawling with a monumental punch, one so big that in real life Hayden threw his back out delivering it. The verdict was a slipped disc, and production was immediately halted as the star was now laid up in traction. An emergency call was placed to stuntman Bob Morgan, who was on his honeymoon with actress Yvonne DeCarlo in Las Vegas. The producers knew Morgan had worked with Hayden before and looked enough like him to fill in for long shots so the film could get back into production. Hayden ultimately made it back on his feet and finished out the role.

Six-five and 210 pounds, Hayden was a ship's captain and sailed around the world several times as a young man. During World War II, he joined the Marines and was active with the O.S.S. in Yugoslavia, winning a Silver Star for his valor. Paramount promoted photos of Hayden boxing at the studio gym and advertised him as "the blond Viking God." As a movie fighter, he was impressive. With his imposing size, he could throw a believable blow with leverage and panache. Many of his fights were one-punch knockouts. He was excellent as the two-fisted hooligan who turns out the lights on Ray Teal in the crime classic *The Asphalt Jungle* (1950).

Hayden fought Fred MacMurray in *Virginia* (1941), John Payne in *El Paso* (1949), Victor Jory in *Flaming Feather* (1952), James Arness in *Hellgate* (1952), Edmond O'Brien in *Denver and Rio Grande* (1952), Reed Hadley and Clayton Moore in *Kansas Pacific* (1953), Philip Reed in *Take Me to Town* (1953), Ernest Borgnine in *Johnny Guitar* (1954) and *The Last Command* (1955), Gene

Barry in *Naked Alibi* (1954), William Bishop in *Top Gun* (1955), Zachary Scott and Robert Wilke in *Shotgun* (1955), David Brian and Howard Petrie in *Timberjack* (1955), Lee Van Cleef in *Gun Battle at Monterey* (1957) and Sheb Wooley in *Terror in a Texas Town* (1958).

See: Grasso, John. *The Historical Dictionary of Wrestling.* Lanham, MD: Scarecrow Press, 2014; Nashawaty, Chris. "One Tough Guy You Need to Know: Sterling Hayden." *Entertainment Weekly.* March 4, 2007; "Sterling Hayden Hurt; Substitute Halts Honeymoon." *Seattle Daily Times.* November 23, 1955.

TAB HUNTER VS. EARL HOLLIMAN AND SKIP HOMEIER in *The Burning Hills* (1956)

Director Stuart Heisler's western about a young cowpoke looking for the killer of his brother boasts an outstanding climactic fight. It was shot in CinemaScope by Ted McCord along rocky cliffs above the Kern River near Bakersfield, California. The stunt doubles for combatants Tab Hunter and Skip Homeier roll over bushes and down crevices, before tumbling off a ledge into the river. In the close-ups, Hunter and Homeier wore wetsuits underneath their costumes and were tied with safety lines around their waists so they wouldn't be swept away by the currents. Allen Pinson is one of the brave stuntmen. Cutter Clarence Kolster does a good job concealing the stuntmen's identities and keeping the pace hopping. The *New York Times* claimed the fight was "a bout that rivals anything done in that famed barroom brawl scene from *The Spoilers.*"

Tab Hunter, a 170-pound six-footer, didn't escape injury. He wound up with skinned arms and a greater appreciation for the energy needed to engage in a movie fight. He told the press he had never been so exhausted in his life. He also thrashes Hal Baylor and has a fight in a barn with Earl Holliman, who goes after Hunter with a hay hook and a leather strap. It's a well-choreographed and spirited two-minute exchange, and once again Pinson can be spied as a double. Heisler shot the action with his principals in one take using three cameras; one on the floor, one on a boom and one in the rafters. Composer David Buttolph punctuates the action in short dramatic bursts. *Western Clippings* includes both main battles among their "great screen fights." The Holliman fight contained a humorous moment behind the scenes: While

they were in a clinch, Holliman broke up the crew when he said to Hunter, "Kiss me quick!"

Navy veteran Earl Holliman (six feet, 175 pounds) portrayed a boxer in *Tennessee Champ* (1954) and was comfortable throwing movie punches throughout the remainder of his career as a supporting player and occasional leading man. He is best known as Angie Dickinson's tough but caring counterpart on the popular TV series *Police Woman* (1974–1978). As the star of the western series *Hotel de Paree* (1959–1960), his fights routinely injected humor to lighten the mood. His best fight came against Mark Richman in 1959's "Return of Monique." In "The Lucky Punch," a 1963 episode of the rodeo drama *The Wide Country* (1962–1963), he knocked out boxing champion Bruce Yarnell in a barroom brawl

Holliman had notable fights in *Armored Command* (1961) and *The Sons of Katie Elder* (1965) (*see entries*). Fights of interest came against Lloyd Bridges in *The Rainmaker* (1956), Kirk Douglas and Brad Dexter in *Last Train from Gun Hill* (1959), Jerry Lewis in *Visit to a Small Planet* (1960), George Maharis in *A Covenant with Death* (1967) and Clifton James in *The Biscuit Eater* (1972). As a TV guest, he fought Tim Matheson in the 1974 *Police Story* episode "Fingerprint."

See: Hunter, Tab, and Eddie Muller. *Tab Hunter Confidential: The Making of a Movie Star.* Chapel Hill, NC: Algonquin, 2006; "Inside Hysteria." *TV Guide.* February 16, 1963; "Screen Battle in One Big Take." *Pittsburgh Press.* July 26, 1956.

ROCK HUDSON VS. MICKEY SIMPSON in *Giant* (1956)

The fight between Rock Hudson and diner owner Mickey Simpson comes out of nowhere in George Stevens' Texas epic *Giant*, but it's an important moment for the previously prejudiced Hudson character. He's taking a stand for something, stepping up for an old Mexican man being refused service by the bigoted Simpson. It's a memorable fight thanks to the powerhouse punches, inventive camera angles and the song "Yellow Rose of Texas" playing in the background courtesy of the film's orchestrator Dimitri Tiomkin. *Variety* noted, "Fight footage catches some of the raw power of the brawl in *Shane*," while *Time* praised the fight, saying it was "worked over with a care for the meanings beneath the meanings on the surface: something that Hollywood almost never takes the time for." *Stage Combat* calls it "one of the truly great fist fights captured on film," and *Burns, Falls, and Crashes* refers to it as "a piece of pure stunt poetry." *USA Today* ranks it among the Top 10 all-time movie fights.

The most notable aspect of the two-and-a-half-minute fight was how it shocked movie audiences when lead actor Hudson didn't emerge victorious. In fact, he's knocked around the diner by Simpson's big uppercuts and measured right crosses for most of the fight, to the horror of his wife Carroll Baker. Hudson, whose character is in his 50s, puts up a game fight, but he is overmatched. This is the moment when Hudson lands the loudest punch courtesy of sound recorder Earl Crain, giving the audience hope their underdog will prevail. It's a fleeting hope, as Simpson's big right fist is sent straight into William C. Mellor's camera for a knockout blow. Director Stevens wished to show it can ultimately be unrewarding to take the side of the underdog.

Simpson was a late replacement for actor Gregory Walcott in the role of Sarge. Walcott was on another movie and was forced to give up the part. Stunt coordinator Paul Stader rehearsed the actors and stuntman Troy Melton for a full week before shooting began at Warner Bros. Stader would double Hudson if need be. In the finished product, both actors end up doing almost the entire fight, which was Stevens' intention. The fight took an incredible three weeks for Stevens to prepare and

shoot because it was covered from every angle, giving his editor William Hornbeck plenty of options. The diner set was built by Ralph Hurst to accommodate Stevens' vision, with walls and ceilings continuously being moved by the technical crew.

Six-foot-five and 240 pounds, Mickey Simpson was the heavyweight boxing champion of New York City and spent time as a construction worker and lumberjack. He joined the Navy during World War II and met director John Ford at the Hollywood Canteen while with the Shore Patrol. He was later a bouncer at the Florentine Gardens while taking on small acting parts. His size and boxing background landed him many jobs requiring fight action. There were few stuntmen big enough to convincingly double him, so Simpson requested extra stunt pay for fights and routinely received it. Some co-stars thought he was slow and clumsy and didn't like doing fights with him.

Simpson fought Johnny Weissmuller in *Tarzan and the Huntress* (1947), Victor McLaglen in *She Wore a Yellow Ribbon* (1949) (see entry), Jock Mahoney in *Roar of the Iron Horse* (1951), Allan Lane in *Leadville Gunslinger* (1952), Randolph Scott in *Carson City* (1952) and *Tall Man Riding* (1955), Wayne Morris in *Star of Texas* (1953) and Richard Boone in *Rio Conchos* (1964). On TV, he stepped into the bare-knuckle ring against Jock Mahoney in the 1952 *Range Rider* episode "Fight Town" and 1959's *Yancy Derringer* episode "Wayward Warrior," as well as John Russell in the 1960 *Lawman* episode "Samson the Great." He fought Clayton Moore on *The Lone Ranger,* Clint Walker on *Cheyenne,* Richard Boone on *Have Gun— Will Travel,* David Janssen on *Richard Diamond, Private Detective,* Craig Stevens on *Peter Gunn,* Chuck Connors on *The Rifleman,* Ty Hardin on *Bronco,* James Garner on *Maverick* and Edd Byrnes on *77 Sunset Strip.*

See: "*Giant* Fight Finds Hero as Loser." *Greensboro Daily News.* November 1, 1956; "Staging of Fight Scene Adds Emotional Tension to *Giant.*" *Amarillo-Globe Times.* January 14, 1957.

Mickey Simpson is knocked backward by Rock Hudson in Warner Bros.' classic *Giant* (1956).

James Arness vs. Don Megowan in *Gun the Man Down* (1956)

This well-performed, tension-filled western from director Andrew McLaglen has anti-hero James Arness tracking former partners in crime Robert Wilke and Don Megowan and girlfriend Angie Dickinson. The minor revenge film was shot after the first season of the long-running TV series *Gunsmoke* and plays like a black-and-white TV episode, though it was written by Burt Kennedy and shot by the esteemed William H. Clothier. There's not much budget or action until a one-minute battle between the tallest men in the movies. Publicity played up the men's height: Arness stood 6'7" while Don Megowan was 6'6". Both perform all their own stunt work. The match-up is doubly intriguing since Arness had famously played the title alien in *The Thing from Another World* (1951) while Megowan donned the Gill Man costume for *The Creature Walks Among Us* (1956).

There's no musical accompaniment, only the sound of fists connecting. An impassioned Arness pulls Megowan off a horse, lands huge punches, kicks a gun from his hand and pins him under an overturned wagon to learn the whereabouts of Wilke. Arness corners Wilke in a box canyon, and the latter puts up no fight. Arness merely drills him with six punches. It's anti-climactic as the main match-up is the earlier battle with Megowan, which Clothier keeps in medium shots to show the full image of the men's long arms winding up and slinging punches coordinated by Jack Young. The two giants fought again in the 1960 *Gunsmoke* episode "Big Tom" with Arness a surrogate fighter for the ailing title character. Big Tom was an over-the-hill prizefighter portrayed by none other than Wilke. The episode was directed by Victor McLaglen's son Andrew, a member of the University of Virginia's boxing team. The younger McLaglen, who stood 6'7", was the assistant director on *The Quiet Man* (1952). He liked filming fights so much that his crews good-naturedly nicknamed him "The Sadist."

World War II infantry veteran James Arness was a capable screen fighter and threw punches with a mighty follow-through. The 235-pounder was especially good at delivering a fast and powerful backhand. Even as his weight climbed into the 260-pound range in the late 1960s, he still presented a formidable challenge to any opponent. He started his career with a brawl against Charles McGraw in *The Farmer's Daughter* (1947), boxed Jeff Chandler in *Iron Man* (1951) and fought Robert Ryan in *Horizons West* (1952) and Sterling Hayden in *Hellgate* (1952). However, it's his *Gunsmoke* fights that fans remember. The confrontation with William Smith in 1972's "Hostage" is heralded as one of the best match-ups ever done for television. The battle with Jim Davis in 1968's "The Railroad" has a great buildup and payoff as they slug throughout the town and take a time-out from exhaustion. The fight with John Anderson in 1958's "Buffalo Man" was shown for years at USC Film School to teach prospective editors how to assemble such a scene. In 1970, he had a big fight with frequent guest star Victor French in "Kiowa." Other great battles came in the 1972 episodes "Sarah" and "The River" with Arness slugging it out with Michael Lane and Roger Torrey. The brawl with pro boxer Buddy Baer in 1957's "Never Pester Chester" was another standout against a huge and worthy opponent. Sometimes the audience couldn't wait for Arness to plant his fist on a bad guy's jaw. There was perhaps no more satisfying fight than Arness duking it out with smug rapist Ben Johnson in 1963's "Quint-cident." In the late 1950s, Arness went on a promotional tour staging fights with stuntman Al Wyatt. On a 1958

Don Megowan is felled by James Arness in United Artists' *Gun the Man Down* (1956).

Ed Sullivan Show. he put on a fight with stuntman Bob Morgan.

See: Arness, James, and James E. Wise, Jr. *James Arness: An Autobiography.* Jefferson, NC: McFarland, 2012; "Giant McLaglen Directs Softly." *Sunday Independent.* July 31, 1961; *Gun the Man Down* pressbook.

STANLEY BAKER VS. PATRICK McGOOHAN in *Hell Drivers* (1957)

Hell Drivers is a nail-biting, fondly remembered film about law-breaking ballast drivers and the rivalry between brooding newcomer Stanley Baker and top dog Patrick McGoohan, who immediately sniffs out a challenging personality in the ex-convict. The two white-knuckle truckers have an excellent 90-second fight, cheered on by fellow drivers (including Sean Connery) as they uncork punches on one another's jaws. It's considered one of British cinema's best fights, with Rank Films' publicity playing up the exchange. American director Cy Endfield told the actors to go at it as realistically as possible without stuntmen, and much of the intense fight is unbalanced grappling. The tide turns on a painful kidney punch which gives Baker the upper hand. By the time they were finished, both men had multiple bruises and even a few loosened teeth, contributing to their "tough guy" images. Throughout the fight, McGoohan manages to keep a cigarette dangling from his lips. Biographer Robert Shail writes, "Baker and McGoohan reach a near demented level of aggression," while the *Sunday Times* praised "a pace and a muscular command of violent action uncommon in British cinema."

Stanley Baker, 5'11" and 190 pounds, worked in coal mines, then spent time as an amateur boxer and soldier with the Royal Army Service Corps. The hard-living actor was noted for his intense portrayals and preferred to do his own rugged screen fights after being shown how by stuntman Jock Easton. He battled Alan Ladd in *Hell Below Zero* (1954), Joe Robinson in *Sea Fury* (1958), Robert Mitchum in *The Angry Hills* (1959), John Crawford in *Hell Is a City* (1960) and Darren Nesbit in *Innocent Bystanders* (1972). The 6'1", 185-pound McGoohan boxed at Ratcliff College. He's best known for playing two-fisted John Drake on TV's *Danger Man* (1960–1961) and *Secret Agent* (1964–1966), winning fans with his willingness to perform many of his own rough-and-tumble

fights. On the big screen, he fought Ernest Borgnine in *Ice Station Zebra* (1968).

See: *Hell Drivers* DVD extras; *Hell Drivers* pressbook; Langley, Roger. *Patrick McGoohan: Danger Man or Prisoner?* Sheffield, England: Tomahawk, 2007; Shail, Robert. *Stanley Baker: A Life in Film.* Cardiff: University of Wales Press, 2008.

THE ARMY VS. NAVY BRAWL in *The Wings of Eagles* (1957)

Broadly played, entertaining nonsense. *The Wings of Eagles* features a massive brawl between Army and Navy units at a cake-cutting ceremony to celebrate who will be the first to fly around the globe. John Wayne is cast as real-life Navy leader Spig Wead, with Kenneth Tobey representing the Army. Both end up slathered in cake as their men carry on the slapstick fight. The John Ford–directed melee sees Wayne and several combatants run headlong into a swimming pool. Two scenes later, the antagonistic groups are at it again. *Variety* found the brawling to be "particularly entertaining," while *Harrison's Reports* commented that the free-for-all brawl "provokes many laughs." Ford claimed the fight was based on reality and he was an eyewitness who was forced to duck cake hurled in the air. The choreographic challenge for the director and cameraman Paul Vogel was fitting so many fighters moving at different angles into a confined area.

All the usual Ford stunt culprits are here including Cliff Lyons, Chuck Roberson, Fred Graham, Bob Morgan, Dale Van Sickel, Terry Wilson, Frank McGrath, Chuck Hayward, John Hudkins, Kermit Maynard, Paul Stader, Michael Dugan. Jack Williams, Paul Baxley, Wally Rose, George Robotham, Charles Horvath and Ronnie Rondell. Morgan lands a punch that dazes Wayne into eye-rolling silliness. Viewers will note that Morgan appears as two different Army men during the fight; one who gets punched inside by Wayne and one that gets punched outside by Dan Dailey. In the next fight, he's a Navy man. Graham also shows up as two different soldiers. These curious Ford casting decisions may have left editor Gene Ruggiero scratching his head when it came time to assemble the footage. Ford gave the golfer Ruggiero a new putter for his trouble

During the making of *Wings of Eagles,* Chuck Roberson and Cliff Lyons became involved in a real bar brawl with one another due to the excessive needling of Frank McGrath. It was not uncommon for both men to wind up engaging in semi-real fisticuffs on any given night. Usually Bob Morgan was Lyons' fight partner. When the bar's bouncer tried to break up the fight, Lyons knocked him out.

All the drinking and brawling both in the story and off-screen had repercussions. The Navy balked at approving the *Wings of Eagles* screenplay, specifically because of the fight and the emphasis on overly abundant alcohol consumption. A compromise was reached where Wayne's character makes reference to those rowdy days being a long time ago. However, there's little doubting it's a John Ford film: carefree and rollicking one moment; sentimental and tragic in the next.

Working from the screenplay, a director controls the set and imprints his or her artistic vision on the outcome. In regard to fight scenes, a director will discuss the scenario with his stunt coordinator to determine the fight routine and how much the actors can be expected to safely perform. The actors will be reminded to stay in character throughout the action and to place emphasis on certain beats or emotions. The director will choose his shots and angles with the director of photography and his cameramen. The best directors have the ability to edit in camera as they film, presenting the post-production team with a cohesive, nearly finished scene. Ford was a master at editing in the camera, a tactic giving him control over the studio and the assigned film cutter as there would be little if any alternative footage. Ford also had a definitive directorial style when it came to filming fights. He stripped away the violence and made them largely comic affairs, suggesting that the favorite pastimes of the men in his stories were competitive drinking and fighting. A John Ford fight was sure to feature a plethora of knockout haymakers and plenty of laughs.

See: "John Wayne Tells About Film Brawls." *Reading Eagle.* August 10, 1958; Roth, Lane. "Ritual Brawls in John Ford's Films." *Film Criticism.* Spring, 1983; Suid, Laurence. *Sailing on the Silver Screen: Hollywood and the U.S. Navy.* Annapolis, MD: Naval Institute Press, 1996; "Movie of the Month." *Argosy.* February, 1957.

John Derek vs. John Smith in *Fury at Showdown* (1957)

A genuine B-western sleeper from director Gerd Oswald and cinematographer Joseph La-Shelle, *Fury at Showdown* features a standout three-and-a-half-minute fight between John Derek and John Smith. It begins in a saloon and extends to the western street at Iverson Ranch, and doesn't end until the men are dragged away by a horse-drawn buggy. Derek is particularly enraged by the drink-confident Smith, calling the reformed gun-fighter "gutless." There's good stunt work by the anonymous doubles, but the stars do a great deal of fighting while co-star Nick Adams and towns-people look on. The bar's mirror is smashed, chairs are thrown, tables overturned, and both men go crashing out the front window. Derek tries to choke an unconscious Smith until Adams hits him over the head with a pistol. Publicity played up the fight's fury and the black eyes the characters had to sport through the rest of the story. An impressed *New York Times* called it "a humdinger of a fight."

The entire film was shot in a single week, benefitting from strong central performances and assured direction. Six-foot-two and 185 pounds, John Smith is cast against type as the bullying heel who spits a whiskey bottle's stopper into Derek's face to ignite the action. He first attracted attention for his ring scenes with pro wrestler Ivan Rasputin in *Friendly Persuasion* (1956). A 180-pound six-footer, John Derek was a paratrooper in World War II and worked closely with stuntmen David Sharpe and Jock Mahoney at Columbia to develop into a handy swashbuckling star. He fought Humphrey Bogart in *Knock on Any Door* (1949), Broderick Crawford in *The Last Posse* (1953), Jim Davis in *The Outcast* (1954) and Perry Lopez in *Omar Khayyam* (1957). On the TV series *Frontier Circus*, Derek battled Brian Keith in 1961's "The Smallest Target" and bested judo fighter Marc Marno in 1962's "The Inheritance"

See: *Fury at Showdown* film press kit; "John Derek Becomes Toughest Pretty Boy in Hollywood." *Deseret News.* March 4, 1949.

Jock Mahoney vs. Claude Akins and Lee Van Cleef in *Joe Dakota* (1957)

An intriguing fistic match-up is given a somewhat disappointing execution considering the tough guy players involved and publicity ads proclaiming, "He had to fight the whole town!" In a rehash of *Bad Day at Black Rock* (1955), mystery man Jock Mahoney arrives in a small town run by oil man Charles McGraw, who has a secret or two to hide in regard to the death of an old Indian. McGraw's formidable stooges are a pair of brawny brothers played by Claude Akins and Lee Van Cleef. They delight in playing a "game" where they sit opposite one another trading punches until one of them falls off their stool. At McGraw's urging, they entice Mahoney to join in on their fun. To their astonishment, Mahoney withstands their best blows, then knocks them both all over the wine shop. When the fists start flying, the slow-paced though visually appealing Richard Bartlett western receives a needed boost. However, the fighting lensed by cameraman George Robinson is over nearly as soon as it starts. The entire story was lifted for the 1959 *Wagon Train* episode "Alias Bill Hawks" with Terry Wilson stepping into Mahoney's role to fight Hal Baylor and Cliff Osmond.

Now that stunt ace Mahoney was a leading man, Universal was loath to put much action into his films as he insisted upon doing all his own stunts as a matter of pride. The Universal brass was afraid their investment would be injured, so the logical conclusion was to put him into films with a minimal amount of danger in the script. But danger was Mahoney's business and what made him most interesting as a performer. Although he proved a capable actor, audiences wanted to see him light up the screen in elaborate hair-mussing brawls the way he did on TV's *The Range Rider*. He does have a climactic fight with McGraw beneath a gusher and both men are covered in oil (actually a sticky substance known as Carbopole). Mahoney also fought Van Cleef on *The Range Rider* and TV's *Yancy Derringer* and had a fight with Akins on the latter show.

Six-foot-one, 210-pound Claude Akins was one of the era's most prolific bad guys, perhaps best known for trading punches with Dean Martin and getting rifle-whipped by John Wayne in *Rio Bravo* (1959). The World War II vet was a capable screen fighter who could impressively lay a punch into an opponent's bread basket. He was also expert at throwing a straight-on punch into the camera, a move he borrowed from John Wayne. Stuntmen liked working with Akins and made him an honorary Stuntmen's Association member. One of Akins' most memorable confrontations occurred in gorilla makeup when he dueled with Roddy McDowall in a treetop in *Battle for the Planet of the Apes* (1973). In *Timber Tramps* (1975), he played a lead and battled heavy Hal Baylor.

Notable fights include *Yellowstone Kelly* (1959), *Ride Beyond Vengeance* (1966) and *The Devil's Brigade* (1968) (see entries). On TV, Akins traveled from show to show menacing heroes, with many an episode ending with Akins punched out. He fought Lorne Greene in the 1960 *Bonanza* episode "The Mill," Guy Madison in the 1961 *Zane Grey Theatre* episode "Jericho," Peter Breck in the 1965 *Big Valley* episode "The Brawlers" and Rod Taylor in the 1977 *Oregon Trail* episode "Trappers' Rendezvous." His slugfest with Ralph Taeger in the 1967 *Hondo* episode "Hondo and the Gladiators" remains one of the small screen's best. Akins portrayed bare-knuckle boxing champion John L. Sullivan in the 1961 *Tales of Wells Fargo* episode "The Hand That Shook the World."

See: Buck, Jerry. "Claude Akins Gets Crack at TV Series." *Toledo Blade*. August 9, 1974; Collura, Joe. "Claude Akins: From Bad Guys to Good Roles." *Classic Images*. April 2014.

ELVIS PRESLEY VS. KENNETH BECKER in *Loving You* (1957)

Paramount's *Loving You* offers the first movie fight for the king of rock'n'roll Elvis Presley, and it firmly establishes his smoldering young punk persona. He is tough, sneering and sarcastic. The six-foot, 170-pound Presley was the nightmare of every 1950s parent with a teenage daughter. His image softened throughout the 1960s, but in 1957 his hips were as dangerous as his fists and Presley excelled at motion picture fighting. The Hal Kanter–directed film was based on Presley's own experience as a young rockabilly singer whose career exploded overnight. The film's café fight was a combination of a Memphis gas station fight and a Toledo hotel fight Presley had during his early whirlwind days of touring.

The screen tussle with Kenneth Becker was choreographed by Joe Gray, a former professional middleweight boxer. The tall, angular Becker goads "Sideburns" into performing a song in a juke joint full of teenagers. Presley accepts the challenge and launches into a scintillating "Mean Woman Blues," shaking his legs spasmodically and gyrating in front of the rapt females to drive them wild with squeals of delight. Presley flaunts his sexuality as much at Becker as he does the girls. When Becker can take it no more, the bully launches a meaty fist into Presley's curled lip. Presley is quickly on his feet and exchanging a series of blows, wowing the females even more. Becker is knocked unconscious and collapses onto the jukebox. Presley swipes his legs out from under him and stands insolently before Charles Lang's appreciative camera, dripping with makeup artist Wally

Westmore's sweat and blood. Presley and Becker also fight in *G.I. Blues* (1960) while "Blue Suede Shoes" plays on a jukebox, and Becker takes a drunken swing at Presley in *Girls! Girls! Girls!* (1962). The *Loving You* fight was broadly recreated in the 1988 comedy *Heartbreak Hotel* with David Keith portraying Elvis and Chris Mulkey taking on the Becker role.

Notable Presley fights include *Flaming Star* (1960), *Blue Hawaii* (1961), *It Happened at the World's Fair* (1963) and *Live a Little, Love a Little* (1968) (see entries). Fights of interest came against John Daheim in *Jailhouse Rock* (1957), Walter Matthau and Vic Morrow in *King Creole* (1958), Gary Lockwood in *Wild in the Country* (1961), Richard Devon and Jeff Morris in *Kid Galahad* (1962), Jeremy Slate in *Girls! Girls! Girls!* (1962), Alejandro Rey in *Fun in Acapulco* (1963), Steve Brodie, Norm Grabowski and Glenn Wilder in *Roustabout* (1964), Red West in *Tickle Me* (1965), Don Collier in *Paradise Hawaiian Style* (1966), Ross Hagen in *Speedway* (1968) and Warren Vanders in *Stay Away, Joe* (1968). On *Kissin' Cousins* (1964), Presley fought himself (as doubled when needed by Lance LeGault). Presley did every one of his own screen fights, only allowing bodyguard Red West to take his place in rehearsals. On *Kid Galahad* (1962), he worked with Mushy Callahan, who came away impressed with Presley's boxing ability.

See: Scott, Vernon. "Ex-Boxer Mushy Callahan Calls Elvis Presley Natural Athlete." *Beaver County Times*. December 5, 1962.

THE BACK ALLEY BRAWL in *Designing Woman* (1957)

This enjoyable MGM romantic comedy from Vincente Minnelli features Gregory Peck and Lauren Bacall clashing with one another and with a crooked boxing promoter's mob thugs. Peck is a mild-mannered sportswriter aware of a fix, while Bacall is a fashion designer whose colorful world proves alien to Peck. Punchy boxer Mickey Shaughnessy and Peck come to blows with Chuck Connors and his men in a three-minute back alley

Kenneth Becker is stiffened by a straight right from Elvis Presley in Paramount's *Loving You* (1957).

brawl *Variety* called "a rousing smash" and the *Village Voice* praised as "brilliantly choreographed." The *Montreal Gazette* went so far as to call it "the funniest fight scene ever" as Shaughnessy comically swings at everything that moves including dapper Tom Helmore and stagehands Chuck Hayward, Frank McGrath and Roy Jenson. Minnelli treats it as a fantastical stab at traditional images of male toughness and virility, finding humor in an alternative skill set. The protagonists are not faring well until Bacall's spirited hoofer pal Jack Cole arrives to turn the entire melee into a dance routine. Cole's dance kicks are as effective as karate blows as Connors and stunt thugs Terry Wilson, Bob Morgan, Charles Horvath, John Hudkins, Boyd "Red" Morgan, Michael Dugan and Sol Gorss are left dazed and confused at the end of the memorable sequence. Dave Sharpe coordinated the fight action.

The role was a departure for Peck, who was used to serious material. Minnelli cast the 6'5", 215-pound Chuck Connors because he needed someone who could believably intimidate Peck. In the end, it's Peck who knocks out Connors and sends him sprawling over a cart. Cole immediately jumps on the cart and sends Connors flying for John Alton's camera. Former professional athlete Connors did his own stunt, placing his hand against the cart to protect his face, then throwing himself backwards when he felt Cole hit the cart. Even star Peck was open to taking his own pratfalls during the fight sequences. Cole was a noted dance choreographer with MGM. The fight was the last scene filmed as Minnelli didn't want any of his actors injured early in the production.

Mickey Shaughnessy, six feet tall and 210 pounds, briefly cornered the market on playing tough Irish lugs. While serving as an Army drill instructor in World War II, the Golden Glover coached the boxing team. The ex-longshoreman was often called upon to play former fighters. He is best known as the jealous cellmate turned manager of Elvis Presley, who endangers both their livelihoods when he punches the singer in the throat in *Jailhouse Rock* (1957). Shaughnessy appeared in *North to Alaska* (1960) (see entry) and squared off against Glenn Ford in *The Sheepman* (1958) and Cornel Wilde above the Grand Canyon in *Edge of Eternity* (1959). On TV Shaughnessy wrestled Aldo Ray on the 1962 episode of *The Virginian* titled "Big Day, Great Day."

Gregory Peck, once an oarsman on the rowing team at U.C. Berkeley, was a solid leading man with a stalwart presence. He received multiple Academy Award nominations for his varied performances, and tight-lipped tough guys was one of his specialties. As a screen fighter, the six-three, 190-pound actor had effective reach, though the majority of his fights realistically ended up on the ground. Peck didn't shy away from letting more experienced stuntmen do what they did best, but he continued to take on action parts into his later years.

Peck had notable fights in *The Big Country* (1958) and *Cape Fear* (1962) (see entries). Fights of interest came against Forrest Tucker in *The Yearling* (1946), Robert Preston in *The Macomber Affair* (1947), John Russell in *Yellow Sky* (1948), Michael Ansara in *Only the Valiant* (1951), Anthony Quinn in *The World in His Arms* (1952), George Kennedy in *Mirage* (1965), Omar Sharif and Robert Phillips in *Mackenna's Gold* (1969), Nathaniel Narcisco in *The Stalking Moon* (1969), Ralph Meeker in *I Walk the Line* (1970) and Laurence Olivier in *The Boys from Brazil* (1978).

See: Carroll, Harrison. "Hollywood." *Lethbridge Herald.* December 7, 1956; Fishgall, Gary. *Gregory Peck: A Biography.* New York: Simon & Schuster, 2002; Kaplan, Peter W. "Mickey Shaughnessy

Dead; Comedian and Movie Actor." *New York Times.* July 26, 1985.

MICHAEL LANDON VS. TONY MARSHALL in *I Was A Teenage Werewolf* (1957)

A cult teen-horror film from American International Pictures and director Gene Fowler, Jr., *Teenage Werewolf* headlines a young Michael Landon in the title role. He's a troubled young man who opens the picture in a two-minute fistfight with fellow Rockdale High School student Tony Marshall. The latter is more muscular, but Landon fights with a chip on his shoulder and resorts to dirty tactics such as swinging a shovel and throwing dirt in Marshall's eyes. They throw effective punches directly into Joseph LaShelle's camera and grapple in the dirt in front of a shouting horde of fellow students before the police arrive to break them up. Veteran cinematographer LaShelle worked the quickie as a favor to first-time director Fowler, and his experience improves the fight immensely. The low-budget ($85,000) film was finished in six days. Tony Marshall was the stage name of stuntman Chuck Willcox, so he was able to do his own stunts and choreograph the fights.

The 5'8", 160-pound Landon, a javelin thrower at USC, does all the roughhousing without the benefit of a stuntman. He excelled in fights on the long-running TV series *Bonanza* (1959–1973). Fans of the show loved the way his character Little Joe threw himself into the action, hurdling over tables, flying through windows and even headbutting opponents. His double Bob Miles taught him to screen fight like a stuntman and became so confident in Landon's abilities he let him do everything. On a lark, Miles even allowed Landon to double actor DeForest Kelley in a short fight with Dana Andrews for *Town Tamer* (1965).

Two of his best known *Bonanza* fights came against his on-screen brothers Pernell Roberts and Dan Blocker in 1959's "A Rose for Lotta" and in 1961's "Springtime." All three brothers united to take on bodybuilder Cal Bolder in 1960's "The Ape," though it was big Dan Blocker who handled the bulk of the fight. For *Little House on the Prairie* (1974–1983), Landon stepped into the ring to box Moses Gunn in 1977's "The Fighter." As a TV guest, in 1958 he fought Steve McQueen in the *Wanted—Dead or Alive* segment "The Martin Poster" and Rory Calhoun in *The Texan* episode "The Hemp Tree." On film he took part in a brawl in *High School Confidential!* (1958) and fought Jack Hogan in *The Legend of Tom Dooley* (1958). In the early 1970s, Landon studied karate with Chuck Norris.

See: Greenwald, Charles. "Chuck Willcox: A True Valley Character." *Santa Ynez Valley Journal.* March 1, 2012; Lewis, Richard Warren. "Michael Landon: He Plays Cowboys and Indians for $13,000 a Week." *TV Guide.* July 22, 1967.

CAMERON MITCHELL vs. ALAN HALE, JR., in *All Mine to Give* (1957)

A tearjerker set in 1850s Wisconsin about hard-working Scottish immigrant Cameron Mitchell butting heads with tough boss Alan Hale, Jr. The latter thinks Mitchell is Scandinavian and derisively calls him Norski, keeping him from seeing his wife and kids because hiking back and forth to their cabin is draining his energy for cutting timber. Hale delights in testing Mitchell's mettle until the man can take it no more. Mitchell quits the job and stands up to Hale in a two-minute battle stretching around the snow-covered perimeter of their logging camp (actually an RKO set decorated by art director Albert D'Agostino). They grapple in the snow and atop wood piles, and Mitchell punches Hale through a stair railing. Both men are bloodied in the exhausting fistic exchange. Hale concedes defeat, then surprises the audience by joking that Mitchell knocked out his bad tooth and saved him a dreaded trip to the dentist. Hale offers to rehire Mitchell with a promotion and begins affectionately calling him Scotty.

The fight is well-mounted with uncredited stuntmen assisting in the long shots for William Skall's camera. Max Steiner provides the jaunty ethnic score, memorably striking slashing strings in synchronized time with Mitchell's biggest punches. Made in 1956 as *The Day They Took the Babies Away*, the film was picked up by Universal after RKO ran into financial difficulties. Publicity called the fight "a wild slugging match." Director Allen Reisner had directed a 1955 TV version under the original title as an episode of the anthology series *Climax*, with Leif Erickson in the lead role.

Air Corps bombardier Cameron Mitchell had an athletic background and a reputation for immersing himself in his roles. Five-eleven and 180 pounds, he portrayed boxers in *The Mighty McGurk* (1947) and *Leather Gloves* (1948). Mitchell

later won critical accolades as opiate-addicted ring champ Barney Ross in *Monkey on My Back* (1957). He had a strong straight right but a weakness in choosing his roles. European Viking films and low-budget domestic horror pics sullied his acting reputation. He is best known as the charismatic, two-fisted Buck Cannon in the western series *The High Chaparral* (1967–1971), where he had notable fights against a gang of stuntmen in 1968's "Shadow of the Wind" and French savate fighter Dave Sharpe in 1969's "The Last Hundred Miles."

Fights of interest came against James Millican in *Adventures of Gallant Bess* (1948), Dale Robertson in *The Outcasts of Poker Flat* (1952), Gary Cooper in *Garden of Evil* (1954), Chris Alcaide in *Monkey on My Back* (1957), Jeffrey Hunter in *No Down Payment* (1957) and Richard Burton in *The Klansman* (1974). One of his best fights came as a TV guest against John Anderson in the 1960 *Bonanza* episode "A House Divided."

See: Del Valle, David. "Cameron Mitchell: Star of Tomorrow." *Psychotronic Video.* #19, 1994; Raddatz, Leslie. "Straight Talking with Cameron Mitchell." *TV Guide.* April 27, 1968.

GARY MERRILL vs. LEE MARVIN in *The Missouri Traveler* (1958)

This wholesome coming-of-age story focuses on teenage drifter Brandon DeWilde, who affects citizens of a small Missouri town in 1915. They grow more emotionally during the story than young DeWilde, who finds a competitive mentor in well-to-do farmer Lee Marvin and a less demanding one in ex-boxer turned newspaper man Gary Merrill. The two adults are at odds and come to fisticuffs in the town square after a crowd-drawing Fourth of July horse race. The four-minute fight in front of the entire town of Delphi is straight out of *The Quiet Man* (1952), with the sweat-soaked participants and several surrounding townsmen comically hitting the ground, crashing carts and smashing through store windows. By the end of the fight, photographed by Winton C. Hoch, Marvin has attracted the attention of leading lady Mary Hosford and earns a kiss. The *Pittsburgh-Press* thought Merrill's tough guy casting was unbelievable but called the fight itself "tremendous." *Newsweek* termed it "a corking good fist-fight," and *The Hollywood Reporter* found it "a classic free-for-all battle."

"Crackling action," proclaimed the ads, and in the last reel the film delivers. Many of the townspeople were stuntmen hired to catch the actors and stunt doubles. Several citizens break into a battle royal of their own. Marvin was a more than capable screen fighter and does most of his own fighting here. Among the stuntmen taking falls and throwing punches are Cliff Lyons, Paul Stader, Terry Wilson, Harvey Parry, Chuck Hayward, Sailor Vincent, Whitey Hughes and Roy Jenson. Filming of the fight on the Warner Bros. lot was part of a promotional bit entitled *Hollywood by Helicopter* hosted by Bob Crane. Over 20 years later, the street location became familiar as the town square on the TV series *The Dukes of Hazzard* (1979–1985). *The Missouri Traveler* was produced by John Ford's son Patrick and directed by Jerry Hopper.

See: *Missouri Traveler* pressbook.

PETER CUSHING VS. CHRISTOPHER LEE in *Horror of Dracula* (1958)

The pulse-pounding climactic fight in Count Dracula's castle between the Lord of Darkness (Christopher Lee) and fearless vampire hunter Van Helsing (Peter Cushing) remains their most famous match-up. They battled through more than a decade and a half in Hammer horror films, with *Dracula, Prince of Darkness* (1966) featuring recycled footage from the *Horror of Dracula* fight. It's by no means a typical fistfight and is aided greatly by James Bernard's spine-tingling string score that sounds like a swarm of bees in flight. The battle begins as a foot race against time as Lee's Dracula tries to make it to the safety of his tomb before the sun rises. When Cushing catches up to him, the 6'5" Lee uses his superior strength to choke the breath from his foe. Cushing plays possum and when Lee attempts to bite his neck, Cushing is able to break away, run the length of a table and dive onto a curtain. He pulls it down, letting in the morning sun. Lee attempts to hide but is caught in the rays. Cushing ingeniously forms a cross with a pair of candle holders to drive Lee further into the sunlight and turn the screaming vampire into dust.

The nearly four-minute sequence is perfectly realized by director Terence Fisher. It's filmed in glorious color on Bernard Robinson's impressive castle set by Jack Asher. *The Dracula Book* calls it "one of the most breathtaking sequences in the genre." Character great Cushing is surprisingly young and agile here and appears to do his own run and leap onto the curtain. He added that bit

of action on set with stunt coordinator Peter Diamond's approval. Lee often did his own fights, although his depth perception was hindered on this film by the blood-red contact lenses he had to wear. The Royal Air Force veteran entered films as a stunt actor and belonged to three different stuntman unions. He and Cushing became lifelong friends after making this film. Their other standout fight is the one atop a speeding coach that begins *Dracula, A.D.* (1972).

See: Glut, Donald F. *The Dracula Book*. Metuchen, NJ: Scarecrow Press, 1975; Lee, Christopher. *Lord of Misrule*. London: Orion, 2004; Miller, Mark A. *Christopher Lee and Peter Cushing and Horror Cinema: A Filmography of Their 22 Collaborations*. Jefferson, NC: McFarland, 2010.

JOHN WAYNE VS. RYUZO DEMURA AND RINTARO KAGA in *The Barbarian and the Geisha* (1958)

A major East-meets-West misfire from John Wayne and director John Huston covering the story of early U.S. diplomat Townsend Harris in 1856 Japan. Wayne trades in his cowboy hat and boots for a kimono robe and looks ill at ease. What made him even more uncomfortable was a fight calling for him to be thrown several times by a smaller man using jujitsu.

Filmed on location in Kyoto, Japan, by 20th Century-Fox, it's colorfully shot by Charles G. Clarke and designed by art directors Walter M. Scott and Don B. Greenwood. None of the crew was Wayne's usual buddies, save for Chuck Roberson who accompanied him to coordinate stunts. The fight involves Wayne confronting both a big man and a small man. Wayne cuts the big man Ryuzo Demura down to size easily enough with his patented haymakers, but takes the little man Rintaro Kaga for granted and ends up on the ground. The scene ends with a comic tone as Kaga leads his partner off and an incredulous Wayne merely sits there as surprised as he is dazed. Roberson sought help in staging the martial art fight. U.S. Marine Donn Draeger was working in the Japanese film industry and was recruited to double Wayne because of his ability to take jujitsu falls. George Kerr, a Scottish judo student working as an extra, was recruited to double as Wayne's opposition.

The Barbarian and the Geisha was an odd film for Wayne and one he was unhappy making. He clashed with director Huston, whom Wayne began to believe was mocking his carefully established screen image. Wayne later confessed to grabbing Huston by the shirt collar while rearing back his fist. He didn't let it fly. It wouldn't have been the first time he took a swing at a director. In the early 1950s, he threw a punch at director Budd Boetticher in the latter's kitchen during a drinking argument. Former boxer Boetticher slipped the punch, which put a huge dent in his refrigerator. Boetticher had no fear stepping into a boxing ring with John Wayne but confessed that in a "no rules" fight, Wayne likely would have killed him. They all had a laugh about it later with Boetticher giving the marred appliance to character actor pal Walter Reed as a memento.

After the shock delivered by Spencer Tracy to Ernest Borgnine in *Bad Day at Black Rock,* seeing the great John Wayne toppled in *Barbarian* helped reinforce the mystical power of martial arts to western audiences. A short time later, Samuel Fuller's *The Crimson Kimono* (1959) featured Kendo and also served to pique interest in the Asian fighting arts. The 1960 TV episode "Karate" of the Robert Taylor series *The Detectives* boasted Bruce Tegner, and the syndicated 1960–1961 Rick Jason series *The Case of the Dangerous Robin* used the talents of Kenpo artist Ed Parker. Efrem Zimbalist, Jr., was taught judo for *77 Sunset Strip* (1958–1964) by Warner Bros. production manager Oren Haglund, a World War II hand-to-hand combat instructor. The judo chop and flip were soon being incorporated into the popular films of Elvis Presley, the James Bond franchise and the English TV series *The Avengers* (1961–1969). Martial arts continued to gain traction with audiences.

See: Bogdanovich, Peter. *Who the Hell's in It? Conversations with Hollywood's Legendary Actors.* New York: Random House, 2010; Nurse, Paul. "The Life and Times of American Martial Arts Pioneer Donn F. Draeger." *Black Belt.* February 2015; Smith, Aidan. "Interview: George Kerr, Scotland's Mr. Judo." *The Scotsman.* October 19, 2013.

Gary Cooper vs. Jack Lord in *Man of the West* (1958)

Man of the West is a bleak, textured and high-quality Anthony Mann western featuring Gary Cooper as a reformed outlaw whose train is robbed by a sadistic gang of old cohorts, among them Lee J. Cobb and Jack Lord. Cooper tries to protect fellow passenger Julie London and revisits his own violent past as the gang plans another heist. When Lord degradingly forces London to disrobe, Cooper does something about it in a violent, gritty, exhaustingly drawn-out fight that lasts too long (four minutes). D.P. Ernest Haller nicely captures the rugged Thousand Oaks, California, landscape they fight on, but the inability of Cooper to carry the action load works to the scene's detriment. Editor Richard Heermance would have been wise to trim it. A few punches miss their mark, but enough are spot-on to make it a memorable exchange. Doubles Jack Young and Jack Williams are obvious, but it's apparent that the principals were having a long day as well. They wrestle among rearing horses, pull hair, claw faces and try choking the life from one another. Lord swats Cooper with branches from a tree and tries jumping on the older man with both boot heels.

The most notorious aspect of the deadly serious fight has Cooper knocking Lord into submission, then announcing he's going to undress him the way the outlaw did London. Cooper begins tearing clothes off the howling, hysterical Lord. In its day, the dehumanizing action was shocking and unprecedented, and even viewing it now, it's hard to forget. The *New York Times* called it "one of the meanest fist-scrounging duels we've seen in years," and *Variety* declared it "superbly staged, bringing fresh value to one of the most hackneyed sequences in frontier films." *Newsweek* felt the aging Cooper was still "able to hold his own in a rousing fist fight," and the *Los Angeles Times* wrote that the fight, "for length and realism, rivals any seen on screen for moons."

Cooper, too old for the role as written, was bothered by his usual physical maladies. These included a chronic bad back and a shoulder injury. He looks appropriately pained throughout the fight and died of cancer two years after the film's release. Lord and Cooper were on friendly terms in real life. Lord considered Cooper his idol. He had originally met the star while working in New York as a Cadillac salesman, and Cooper later helped him land his first important part, in 1955's *The Court-Martial of Billy Mitchell.*

The six-foot, 180-pound Lord played football at New York University and served with the Merchant Marine during World War II. He starred in the rodeo-circuit TV series *Stoney Burke* (1962–1963) and then played criminal-hating policeman Steve McGarrett in the cop drama *Hawaii Five-O* (1968–1980). Frequently clad in a pressed leisure suit and tie as the island's perfectly coifed top cop, he fought Andrew Duggan and Bill Saito in 1968's "Cocoon," Nephi Hannemann in 1970's "Run, Johnny, Run" and Ron Feinberg in 1971's "No Bottles, No Cans, No People." In 1980's finale "Woe to Wo Fat," he fought arch-nemesis Khigh Dheigh, though the payoff was a disappointment. His best *Stoney Burke* fight was a barroom brawl with John Milford in 1963's "Web of Fear."

As a TV guest, Lord had a door-busting, furniture-toppling fight with Robert Bray on the 1961 *Stagecoach West* episode "House of Violence." He also fought Richard Boone on *Have Gun—Will Travel,* George Maharis on *Route 66* and David Janssen on *The Fugitive.* On the big screen, Lord tangled with Robert Taylor in *Tip on a Dead Jockey* (1957), Aldo Ray and Lance Fuller in *God's Little Acre* (1958), Gene Evans in *The Hangman* (1959) and James Shigeta in *Walk Like a Dragon* (1960).

See: *Man of the West* pressbook; Raddatz, Leslie. "How an Ex–Rodeo Rider Went West to Enjoy the Good Life as a Hawaiian Cop." *TV Guide.* January 4, 1969.

GREGORY PECK VS. CHARLTON HESTON in *The Big Country* (1958)

The decade's most epic fight scene remains a western classic. *Screen Savers* declares it "the fistfight to end all fistfights," and *Legendary Westerns*

Charlton Heston (left) and Gregory Peck stage one of the cinema's best-known fights in United Artists' *The Big Country* (1958).

names it among the best cowboy fights. Gregory Peck biographer Gerard Molyneaux calls it "perhaps the most memorable scene in the film"—director William Wyler's *The Big Country.* The opus clocks in at almost three hours, so that's saying something. In *Charlton Heston's Hollywood,* the actor proudly said it was "one of the best bare-knuckle fights on film," and he had fought his share. The *Toronto Star* calls it "a classic manly jaw-breaker" and includes it among their list of the ten greatest fights of all-time. In 1958, most critics overlooked the brawl, but it did have one major fan: President Dwight D. Eisenhower declared it his personal favorite.

The film's driving force is a long-standing land squabble between ranchers Charles Bickford and Burl Ives, with the latter's wild son Chuck Connors creating all kinds of trouble for visiting easterner Peck. A subplot sees Peck pitted against Bickford's foreman Heston in a much-anticipated fight over Peck's wife-to-be Carroll Baker. Throughout the film, Baker keeps telling Peck to take a stand against the bullying Heston, who wants her for himself. Misplaced seaman Peck opts to leave the ranch, but first pays a late night visit to Heston's quarters. The two agree that Heston's room isn't big enough to settle their differences, so they head to open range.

The monumental action takes place in a pre-dawn battle on a rolling field in Stockton, California's 3000-acre Drais spread, subbing for Texas range. No props, only two men. Wyler and cinematographer Franz Planer mix close-up action with extreme long shots, emphasizing the vastness of the wide open land and man's place in it. Wyler's staging makes the men's struggle seem futile and insignificant in comparison. And yet they keep fighting against one another to the point of exhaustion. The four-minute fight begins with mighty punches, flips and charges. Time elapses as the men struggle on in the darkness. Jerome Moross' iconic score doesn't creep in until well into the fight. Both men are on their knees, still launching punches with all the energy they can muster. Their faces are punched raw. In between blows, they paw at one another for an advantage. Each time it looks as if one is out, he finds the will to continue. And for what? The effectively drawn-out marathon ends in a stalemate, with Peck at least earning the grudging respect of Heston. Peck intones, "Now tell me, what did we prove?" Heston replies, "Nothing."

The scene took three days to film, with one entire day devoted to the principals from morning until night—a total of 14 hours. Wyler was infamous for demanding many takes and covering action from several camera angles. This created on-location conflict between Wyler and Peck, who not only was a tiring participant in the action but was a co-producer with a financial interest in staying on schedule and within budget. To make matters worse, temperatures during the day were in the 90s. Heston and Peck sustained many real bumps and bruises. Heston missed a mark and landed on a rock, injuring his back. When shooting wrapped, Heston rewarded himself with a well-earned beer in the limo on his way back to the hotel.

Stunt doubles Chuck Roberson (Peck) and Bob Morgan (Heston) put on a great fight in *The Spoilers* (1955) and had their own battle going on behind the scenes. In the early 1950s, both men vied for the attention of actress Yvonne DeCarlo. Morgan married her, but there remained a sense of competition between them. They were both 6'4", meaning they often came up for the same assignments. Both men doubled John Wayne. When one landed a stunt job over another, it meant they were competing financially as well. When it came time for the fight, the natural antagonism between the two channeled itself into their routine. The punches were thrown harder; the heads snapped back with greater ferocity. They threw each other and hit the ground with greater force than their norm. The stubborn nature of each man added greatly to the overall realism of *The Big Country* and its famous fight. In his autobiography, Roberson proclaimed, "Some of the best fight scenes ever put on film were made while Bob and I were hating each other's guts."

The 225-pound Roberson collected his fair share of battle scars playing henchmen in the B-westerns of Charles Starrett and Allan Lane. In the earliest days of TV, he could be seen throwing punches regularly against Clayton Moore (on *The Lone Ranger*), Gene Autry and Roy Rogers. One of his best doubling assignments came working a fight with fellow stuntman John Cason in the western *Rimfire* (1949). World War II vet Rober-

son was working as a studio cop when he met stuntman Fred Kennedy, who suggested he might find movie work. Roberson was schooled in fight action by Kennedy and Allen Pomeroy, emerging as enough of a screen presence to tangle on-camera with James Stewart in *Winchester '73* (1950), Robert Mitchum in *The Wonderful Country* (1959) and Peter Breck in *Shock Corridor* (1963) (see entry). From the early 1950s on, Roberson worked the majority of John Wayne's films, setting up fights and taking falls for The Duke where needed.

See: Herman, Jan. *A Talent for Trouble: The Life of Hollywood's Most Acclaimed Director, William Wyler.* New York: De Capo, 1997; Heston, Charlton, and Jean-Pierre Isbouts. *Charlton Heston's Hollywood: 50 Years in American Film.* New York: G.T., 1998; Molyneaux, Gerard. *Gregory Peck: A Bio-Bibliography.* Westport, CT: Greenwood, 1995.

ROBERT RYAN VS. JACK LAMBERT in *Day of the Outlaw* (1959)

Weather-beaten Robert Ryan makes a fine anti-hero in this stark Andre De Toth western effectively filmed on snow-covered Bend, Oregon, locations with Mount Bachelor rising in the background. Screenwriter Philip Yordan's tense scenario plays out in a suspenseful fashion. At the outset, Ryan is about to have it out with Alan Marshal over the man's wife Tina Louise, but former Army captain Burl Ives and his gang of cutthroats arrive in the tiny town. As the injured Ives loses his control over the men, it becomes apparent to Ryan that he will need to take action to save the town. He proves his worth to the gang by taking on their toughest bully, Jack Lambert, then claims he can lead them safely from the territory. He really intends to lead them into the wilderness and certain death for them all. United Artists publicity emphasized the physical action.

The one-minute fight with Lambert is a good one, with both men slipping on the icy street and struggling for superiority against the white backdrop. Ryan is able to pin Lambert's arm against his body and land a series of damaging blows. After several back-and-forth exchanges, Ryan lands a knockout punch that puts Lambert down for good. The camera was able to move in on the action as both men do their own fight, save for a couple of extreme distance shots that echo William Wyler's *The Big Country* (1958). For these long shots, stuntmen Al Wyatt and Boyd "Red" Morgan filled in. They also coordinated the fight for the actors. Aware of every image he and D.P. Russell Harlan were capturing, De Toth fought the producers to shoot the film in cold black-and-white instead of color. The film is a visual triumph and today highly regarded.

The role of the D.P. in a fight scene is vital. He is responsible for numerous decisions affecting how the action is captured on film. Working closely with the director and stunt coordinator, the D.P. chooses what distance and angle to shoot from as well as the lighting and background composition. He may use a stationary camera, a moving dolly shot, an overhead crane or even a handheld model allowing him to get in close with the actors. Depending on how involved or dangerous an action scene is, he may opt to employ multiple cameras to catch the same action from different angles in one take. Technically he and the director choose what type of lens to use and what speed to film. He may even opt for close-up point-of-view (POV) shots showing punches being thrown or received. Great care is taken to showcase impact punches in a fight and eliminate open space between a fist and its intended target. Obtaining a master shot of the entire routine to provide coverage for the editor is most important. This is usually done with professional stunt doubles. Establishing shots give a feel for the overall fighting area and the relationship of fighters to one another within the scene, framing the characters within the camera's borders.

Don Murray takes a big right cross from Richard Egan in 20th Century-Fox's *These Thousand Hills* (1959).

See: *Day of the Outlaw* pressbook; Grant, Ila S. "Ila Finds That Movie Making Is Hard Work." *Bend Bulletin*. November 22, 1958.

DON MURRAY VS. RICHARD EGAN in *These Thousand Hills* (1959)

A well-made 20th Century-Fox Richard Fleischer western from an A.B. Guthrie novel, *These Thousand Hills* features an excellent, long-forgotten screen fight in the tradition of *The Spoilers*. Producer David Weisbart publicly declared it the roughest fight ever put on film, while *Variety* termed it "superbly staged."

Ambitious Montana cowboy Don Murray and town bully Richard Egan build up great tension between the lead characters, who hate one another with a passion. The violence erupts inside a poker palace after Egan has manhandled female lead Lee Remick and caused the hanging death of Murray's friend Stuart Whitman. Murray throws whiskey in Egan's face, and the latter swiftly clears the table and launches a powerful right cross. It's a wall-crashing, face-clawing, bottle-smashing battle, featuring excellent grunt and punch sound effects and exemplary work from Ted White and Roy Jenson doubling the actors. The fight ends up on a muddy street where the men throw exhausted punches and wrestle with one another on the ground for Charles G. Clarke's camera. A desperate Egan pulls a gun and is shot in the belly by Remick for his action. The four-minute fight took over two days to film and cost the production $60,000. Hugh Fowler cut it together in excellent fashion.

In real life Egan was a war hero while Murray was a conscientious objector. During filming, the 6'2", 180-pound Murray missed a cue and took an Egan fist to the chest. The mighty blow knocked the wind out of him and he collapsed to the floor. An apologetic Egan helped the actor to his feet. Director Fleischer had the unfortunate job of telling Murray the take was no good and needed to be shot again, as the actor paused too long before falling. Murray also fought Robert Bray in *Bus Stop* (1956) and Alan Ladd in *One Foot in Hell* (1960). On TV, he had a couple of racially charged quarrels with co-star Otis Young on the western *The Outcasts* (1968–1969).

Richard Egan (six feet, 200 pounds) carried a sterling tough guy reputation. He was an Army judo instructor and did solo missions on a Japanese-held island during World War II. Built like a bull, he sported nearly 18" biceps, a 17" neck and a 48" chest. He had a black belt and boxed regularly with ring pro Jimmy Casino. Egan was an honorary member of the Stuntmen's Association. When Egan threw punches, his fists looked like they could do serious damage if they connected.

He fought Tyrone Power in *Untamed* (1955), Michael Pate in *The Revolt of Mamie Stover* (1955), John Pickard and John Dehner in *Tension at Table Rock* (1956), Walter Matthau in *Slaughter on Tenth Avenue* (1957), Khigh Dheigh in *Fanfare for a Death Scene* (1964) and Robert Mitchum in *The Amsterdam Kill* (1977). On his TV series *Empire* he fought John Dehner in "Echo of a Man" and on *Redigo* he battled James Best in "Little Angel Blue Eyes."

See: Johnson, Erskine. "Hollywood Today." *Park City Daily News.* July 17, 1958; Oppenheimer, Peter J. "Movie Mayhem." *Lakeland Ledger.* October 10, 1958; "Richard Egan of *Empire*." *TV Guide.* April 13, 1963.

STEVE REEVES VS. PRIMO CARNERA in *Hercules Unchained* (1959)

Following the international success of the Italian-made *Hercules* (1957) came *Hercules Unchained* (1959), again starring rugged American bodybuilder Steve Reeves. The 6'1", 215-pound Reeves was a Mr. America and Mr. Universe noted for his fantastic physical symmetry. He makes a perfect square-jawed bearded hero and even brings humor to his portrayal. The Army veteran is athletic and did the majority of his own stunt work in this and many sword-and-sandal films that followed. Here his greatest task is to take on the laughing giant Antaeus, played by former World Heavyweight Boxing champion Primo Carnera. The two-minute battle plays like a pro wrestling heave-and-ho match; the *New York Times* found it to be "an amusing episode." Every time Reeves thinks he has vanquished this giant guardian of Thebes, the son of the earth goddess rises with a grin. Reeves solves this problem by hoisting him over his head and depositing him in a body of water. Publicity played up the audience anticipation to see these two strongmen fighting on the screen.

The 6'6", 270-pound Carnera was in his 50s

during filming and had lost the heavily muscled frame that made him a feared heavyweight in the early 1930s. Max Baer beat him in 1934 and Carnera never regained the title. He went into the world of professional wrestling and made a few films along the way. The basic story of his life in boxing served as the inspiration for the sobering film *The Harder They Fall* (1956) with pro wrestler Mike Lane in the role. As for Reeves, when the peplum genre died out in the mid–1960s, he made one Spaghetti Western and then retired from acting, much to the disappointment of his legion of fans. He had notable fights with Gordon Scott in *Duel of the Titans* (1961) and Wayde Preston in *A Long Ride from Hell* (1968).

See: Helmer, George. *Steve Reeves: His Legacy in Films.* Malibu, CA: Classic Image, 2003; Page, Joseph S. *Primo Carnera: The Life and Career of the Heavyweight Boxing Champion.* Jefferson, NC: McFarland, 2011.

CLINT WALKER VS. CLAUDE AKINS in *Yellowstone Kelly* (1959)

In this Gordon Douglas western, rough-hewn Clint Walker fights burly screen tough Claude Akins and a half-dozen bullying cavalry soldiers over a two-minute period. The towering Walker bests them all in believable fashion. One he throws through a window; another he smashes into a water tank. A third receives a knee to the face. Walker was opposed to filming static fights and welcomed fresh and original choreography. For him, the more opponents, the better. They come at him from all directions but Walker, a one-man wrecking crew, weathers the storm in stalwart fashion. *Variety* called the fight sequences "excitingly staged."

Coming to the defense of young Edd Byrnes at the cavalry's fort, legendary trapper Walker plows through Akins, Warren Oates and stuntmen Roydon Clark, Dick Hudkins and Clyde Howdy with his superior punching power. Tom Hennesy was hired as Walker's double, but Walker does the fight. Loudmouth Akins is opposed to Walker's perceived Indian blood, but he's definitely barked up the wrong tree. As they later battle a Sioux tribe on the warpath led by John Russell, Akins is moved to make amends, a nice touch from screenwriter Burt Kennedy. The Warner Bros. film was effectively shot by Carl Guthrie on location in the Coconino National Forest of Arizona, subbing for the Wyoming and Montana locale. Co-star Ray

Danton, playing an aggressive Indian brave, begged off doing a fight with Walker when he saw the actor's real strength. Walker could tear the Los Angeles phone book in half and repeatedly fold a *Los Angeles Times* newspaper until it fit into his giant fist.

Standing 6'6" and weighing in at 245 pounds of rugged muscle, the square-jawed Walker had perhaps the most impressively muscled physique to ever flash across the screen. Seemingly chiseled from granite, Walker was ideally cast as a strong and silent western hero. He had worked a myriad of physical jobs before acting, among them construction worker, oil field roughneck, Merchant Marine, cowboy, private detective and Las Vegas sheriff's deputy. He was plucked from obscurity by the sheer impressiveness of his physical presence. In his earliest Hollywood days, he was a bar bouncer at the Ragdoll before winning the role of the wandering title character in the Warner Bros.

TV western *Cheyenne* (1955–1963). Audiences responded instantly to this new action hero.

Walker had a great talent for enacting fights on the show, putting on fantastic battles against heavies Mickey Simpson, Hal Baylor, Charles Horvath, Lane Bradford, Buddy Baer, Mike Lane and Leo Gordon. His screen fights with Gordon are legendary. When Walker threw a punch, it looked like it would take an opponent's head off. His selling of the intensity and power of his punches was unparalleled. He threw convincing punches from both sides, and occasionally featured a back hand rivaling that of James Arness. When it came to fights, he was his own stuntman. He could do fight action as well as any pro, and it was tough to find large stuntmen who moved in his manner. He was no lumbering giant but an agile big man who moved fluidly across the screen. Fans loved how his hair became mussed during a fight and fell over his forehead. One drawback to doing his own fights, Walker discovered, was he often ended up with splinters on his hands and arms from taking broken balsa wood chair shots.

Walker had notable fights in *The Night of the Grizzly* (1966) and *More Dead Than Alive* (1969) (see entries). Fights of note, often brief, came against Brian Keith in *Fort Dobbs* (1958), Brad Dexter in *None but the Brave* (1965), Lee Marvin, Gerry Crampton and Terry Richards in *The Dirty Dozen* (1967), Pedro Armendariz, Jr., in the TV movie *Hardcase* (1972), Glenn Wilder in the TV movie *The Bounty Man* (1972) and Bruce M. Fischer in *Baker's Hawk* (1976). In *Sam Whiskey* (1969), four stuntmen tried toppling him in a comic fight, and Walker engaged in a saloon brawl with Robert Conrad and stuntmen Ted White and Tony Epper on the TV

Clint Walker delivers a high knee to a stuntman in Warner Bros.' *Yellowstone Kelly* (1959).

mini-series *Centennial* (1978). On a 1963 appearance on *The Jack Benny Show,* Walker was an observer for the classic sketch "The Tall Cowboy," watching Sol Gorss audition for a part by getting beaten by stuntmen Clyde Howdy, Paul Baxley and Ronnie Rondell.

See: "It Was a Tough Fight Mom, but We Won." *TV Guide.* August 31, 1957; Thomas, Bob. "Clint Walker Refuses to Conform to Hollywood." *Ludington Daily News.* January 5, 1960; Williams, Tony. "Tall in the Saddle: An Interview with Clint Walker." *Shock Cinema.* #40. June 2011.

THE POOL HALL FIGHT in *The Crimson Kimono* (1959)

The Asian martial arts culture is given an in-depth look in Samuel Fuller's Los Angeles detective story *The Crimson Kimono.* The black-and-white picture is highlighted by two fight scenes in Little Tokyo. Cops James Shigeta and Glenn Corbett engage drunken judo expert Fuji Nozawa in a pool hall, teaming up to take him down in under 30 seconds with karate chops flying left and right. The Korean War veterans also engage in a Kendo sparring session with one another, made especially intense by their growing feelings for female witness Victoria Shaw. The sparring session opens a racial divide which the Japanese-American Shigeta and his best friend Corbett didn't know existed. Fuller's story explores many interesting themes, and the action is as hard-hitting as one would come to expect from the director. Each punch and kick from opposing angles is presented with rapid-fire Jerome Thoms editing and emphasized with a percussive smash by composer Harry Sukman. According to *The Cinema of Hong Kong,* the film "boasts the most detailed imaging of both karate and Kendo yet done in American cinema."

Fuller brought professional wrestler George Okamura in to work as his martial arts technical advisor and handle the stunts for Sam Leavitt's camera. Okamura wrestled as the Great Togo and insisted that when it came to the punches, he wanted Shigeta and Corbett to make contact with the body. Fuller was reluctant but ultimately agreed. Stuntmen Allen Pinson and Stacy Morgan were on the film for the fight sequences as doubles for the stars, who were both making their film debuts. Fuller found that the fight looked genuine, and by sharply cutting the film together he created a memorable scene. Fellow pro wrestler Fuji Nozawa was soon making the TV rounds to fight the likes of Richard Boone on *Have Gun—Will*

Travel and Rod Taylor on *Hong Kong.* On film he battled Dean Martin in *The Wrecking Crew* (1969) and Jim Brown in *Slaughter's Big Rip-Off* (1973) *(see entry).*

See: Fu, Poshek, and David Desser, *The Cinema of Hong Kong: History, Arts, Identity.* Cambridge: Cambridge University Press, 2002; Fuller, Samuel. *A Third Face: My Tale of Writing, Fighting, and Filmmaking.* New York: Hal Leonard, 2004.

GORDON SCOTT VS. JOCK MAHONEY in *Tarzan the Magnificent* (1960)

Gordon Scott took over the Tarzan role from Lex Barker in the mid–1950s and continued with substandard Sol Lesser back lot efforts. However, his last two films, *Tarzan's Greatest Adventure* (1959) and *Tarzan the Magnificent* for new producer Sy Weintraub, were shot on location in Africa with high-quality stories and intelligent dialogue. There was no Jane, no Boy and no Tarzan yell. They are considered the best Tarzan films with Scott nearly perfect in the role. In this story, Tarzan transports prisoner Coy Banton (Jock Mahoney) across the jungle until their inevitable confrontation. Director Robert Day handles the action well, and the climactic fistfight ranks as one of the best put on film. No stunt doubles were used, and the action is brutal. Mahoney's shirt is ripped off in the battle. It's a truly outstanding fight and a highlight of the entire Tarzan canon. *The Hollywood Reporter* called it "a fine slugging match." According to Tarzan chronicler David Fury, "the violent climax is definitely the highlight of the film."

This was Scott's last Tarzan film. The producers decided to move away from the muscleman look. Scott's successor in the Tarzan role was none other than Jock Mahoney, whose action movie experience proved invaluable in coordinating this film's fight. Mahoney may not have had Scott's pumped-up muscles, but his agility and coordination made him every bit as tough. The action was superbly shot on location in Kenya by Edward Scaife. Underwater footage was performed in a Brighton Beach swimming pool while the rolling in the sand was done on a soundstage at England's Sutherland Studios. While filming at the studio, Mahoney had Scott's arm in a tight vise-grip when Scott let out a scream. Mahoney immediately released him, and realized that in the course of their struggles an embarrassed Scott's Tarzan loincloth had come off in front of the crew.

A physical education major at the University of

Oregon, the 6'3", 230-pound Scott was a hand-to-hand combat instructor while serving as a military policeman in the Army. The athletic bodybuilder was working as a lifeguard at the Sahara Hotel in Las Vegas when film agents noted his husky build and nearly 19" biceps. After his Tarzan tenure, Scott journeyed to Italy to star in sword-and-sandal flicks. The fight choreography in these peplum films was often lacking, but Scott proved in his final two Tarzan films that he could be a believable man of action. Notable fights came against Woody Strode in *Tarzan's Fight for Life* (1958), Sol Gorss in *Tarzan and the Trappers* (1958), Anthony Quayle in *Tarzan's Greatest Adventure* (1959), Steve Reeves in *Duel of the Titans* (1961), Gordon Mitchell in *Kerim, Son of the Shiek* (1962) and Mario Brega in *Buffalo Bill* (1965).

See: Ferrante, Tim. "Twice Upon a Tarzan." *Starlog*. November 1988; Rothel, David. *Opened Time Capsules: My Vintage Conversations with Show Business Personalities*. Albany, GA: BearManor, 2010; Warren, Bill. "Tarzan the Magnificent." *Starlog*. February 1993.

Gordon Scott has the advantage over Jock Mahoney in Paramount's *Tarzan the Magnificent* (1960).

KIRK DOUGLAS VS. WOODY STRODE in *Spartacus* (1960)

Primarily a weapons battle, the famous gladiatorial duel between producer-star Kirk Douglas and Woody Strode in Stanley Kubrick's epic *Spartacus* remains one of the cinema's best-known fights. *Action Films* includes it among filmdom's best, and *Fight Choreography* states, "The fight still holds its own after repeated viewings and remains a classic fight scene to this day." For a 1991 special restoration re-release. The *Los Angeles Times* called it "one of the most famous movie fights ever filmed." Strode proudly called it "my most famous moment on the screen." He is especially memorable as the towering Ethiopian Draba, bringing great depth and dignity to his small part. Dalton Trumbo's script has the two slaves respect one another, reluctantly forced to fight for the entertainment of the Roman elite.

There's relatively little hand-to-hand combat or body contact to warrant inclusion here, save for a few shoulder blocks, uppercuts and a knee to the face. Plenty of athleticism is displayed by both participants as Douglas ducks and jumps Strode's net and trident and Strode eludes Douglas's short sword and small buckler shield while slogging around in heavy sand. Douglas puts up a brave fight but Strode is simply too strong, pinning the Thracian against the arena wall with his trident. Countess Nina Foch gives a thumb down, meaning for Strode to kill Douglas. However, the proud warrior Strode is aware that Douglas' charismatic Spartacus is the man most capable of leading the slaves in revolt against their Roman captors. He spares Douglas' life, then in defiance hurls his trident at the emperor's seat in the viewing box. He makes a tremendous leap towards Laurence Olivier's General Crassus only to be speared in the back and cut in the neck.

Douglas insisted on realism and insisted on doing his own stunts and using real steel weaponry without rubber tips. He and the original director Anthony Mann picked principal stuntmen to train for three months under stunt coordinator John Daheim and second unit director Yakima Canutt for the gladiator scenes. Among them were Richard Farnsworth, Loren Janes, Russ Saunders, Joe Wishard and Al Carmichael as doubles for Douglas.

Six-foot-four, 210-pound Strode was cast in part because he was strong enough to hurl the trident as well as perform the leap up the 12-foot wall. The UCLA track and football player was a gridiron star in Canada and wrestled professionally. Over 180 Hollywood stuntmen worked on the film, but none could believably double for the uniquely muscled Strode. To minimize the great difference in height between Douglas and Strode, the latter fought from a crouch position and Academy Award winning cinematographer Russell Metty shot from low angles. Legend has it that Douglas also had lifts built into his sandals.

Woody Strode overcomes Kirk Douglas in Universal's *Spartacus* (1960).

Filming of *Spartacus* lasted 16 months. The actors and stuntmen rehearsed for three weeks, and the main fight itself took 12 days to film on the Universal back lot. Kubrick covered the fight with many camera angles until it became a running bet among the stuntmen to see how many new set-ups Kubrick could use to cover the action. Kubrick shot a high ratio of takes from each angle and printed them all. The fight lasted an incredible 15 minutes in Kubrick's original six-hour cut. In the final version edited by Oscar-nominated Robert Lawrence, the fight sequence still clocked in at around three minutes of screen time. A few minor continuity quibbles exist, but overall it's fast-paced and entertaining. The fight is aided immeasurably by Alex North's varied and exciting Oscar-nominated score, a classic of its type. The gladiator arena design helped set decorators Alexander Golitzen, Eric Orbom, Russell A. Gausman and Julie Heron win an Oscar.

The fight staging has much in common with Kubrick's *Killer's Kiss* (1955), where Jamie Smith and Frank Silvera fight with an axe and a steel pole in a mannequin factory. Strode's trident was 25 pounds of wood and iron, but the one that drew blood was made of hard rubber and filled with fake karo syrup. As Strode slashed it across Douglas' chest, he pushed a button on the trident, ejecting a spurt of artificial blood, making for a great effect. When it was all over, an exhausted Douglas and Strode shared a bottle of whiskey in the star's dressing room.

Not everyone on the film was as enamored with the powerful star as Strode. Douglas also has fights with fellow slave Tony Curtis and bullying gladiator chief Charles McGraw during the revolt. The latter fight resulted in a real injury for McGraw. Douglas was to drown McGraw in a vat of soup, but he pushed McGraw's head down too forcefully and banged the actor's jaw on the bowl. Douglas blamed McGraw for putting up too much resistance. This didn't sit well with the stuntmen on the set, many of whom were close friends of McGraw. Stuntman Louie Elias completed the scene for McGraw. Douglas wasn't any gentler. Elias needed four stitches to sew up his chin. He diplomatically claimed his own foot slipped, causing the accident. Douglas also cracked one of stuntman Bob Hoy's ribs during a battle scene when he jabbed him forcefully with a fake sword. Strode had no complaints and was grateful to Douglas for his chance.

Strode was always up for a fight scene and even studied Kenpo karate in the late 1970s. He had fights of interest with Johnny Weissmuller in *Jungle Man-Eaters* (1954), Gordon Scott in *Tarzan's Fight for Life* (1958), Jock Mahoney in *Tarzan's Three Challenges* (1963), Mike Mazurki in *Seven Women* (1966) (see entry), Eddie Little Sky in *The Professionals* (1966), Sean Connery in *Shalako* (1968), Joe Namath in *The Last Rebel* (1971), Aldo Giuffre in *Loaded Guns* (1975), Paul L. Smith in *We Are No Angels* (1975), Pepper Martin in the TV pilot *The Outside Man* (1977), Jay T. Will in *Jaguar Lives!* (1979), Harold Sakata in *Invaders of* the Lost Gold (1981) and Sandy Alexander in *Vigilante* (1983). On TV, he fought Clint Eastwood in the 1961 *Rawhide* episode "Incident of the Buffalo Hunter," Cal Bolder in the 1966 *Daniel Boone* episode "Goliath" and Ron Ely and Jock Mahoney in the 1966 *Tarzan* episode "The Deadly Silence."

See: Douglas, Kirk. *I Am Spartacus*. New York: Open Road, 2012; Epstein, Dwayne. "Woody Strode: With the Best." *Filmfax*. February–March 1999; LoBrutto, Vincent. *Stanley Kubrick: A Biography*. New York: De Capo, 1999.

The Saloon and Street Brawl in *North to Alaska* (1960)

John Wayne's penchant for broad comedy took an even sillier turn in this entertaining Henry Hathaway gold rush comedy about prospecting partners Wayne and Stewart Granger and their encounters with French beauty Capucine and a bevy of claim jumpers. Point Magu, California, and 20th Century-Fox's back lot stand in for Nome, Alaska. The picture boasts two big fights, one in a beer-drenched saloon and one in a muddy street, both featuring cartoon-like sound effects. The latter even involves a herd of goats ramming heads as the men exchange fists and a seal applauds the action. The genuine nonsense seems especially disconcerting in a Wayne movie. The brawls are sprawling and riotous, with no one getting hurt and all the participants having a rollicking good time amidst the kegs of flying beer and the mud. *Variety* called the fights "classics of the cinematic art of make-believe," while the *Los Angeles Times* praised the "hilarious free-for-alls." *Time* referred to it as "a belly-busting burlesque of the standard barroom brawl," with the *New York Herald Tribune* finding the brawls "satirically fine." *The Big Damn Book of Sheer Manliness* includes it among cinema's best barroom brawls.

Richard Fleischer was originally assigned to direct but balked as it literally had no screenplay with an imminent start date. Hathaway was quickly brought on board. A former second unit director, he had a reputation for toughness and a straightforward shooting style. Richard Talmadge was his inventive stunt coordinator. Co-stars Fabian and Mickey Shaughnessy are heavily involved in the comic fisticuffs with Wayne also punching out Roy Jenson at a logging competition. Stuntmen and action actors working the fights include Boyd "Red" Morgan, Loren Janes, Fred Graham, Kermit Maynard, Sol Gorss, Harvey Parry, Tom Hennesy, John Epper, Cliff Lyons, Jack Tornek, Tap Canutt, Pat Hogan, George DeNormand, Ray Spiker, Jimmy Noel, Mike Lally, Chet Brandenburg, James Dime, Al Bain, Cap Sommers, Jack Gordon and Jack Perkins.

In a scene such as the two-minute Palace Saloon brawl, Talmadge designed the fight and had the stuntmen run through it with Bob Morgan and George Robotham substituting for Wayne and Granger. They'd add or subtract bits as they saw fit until they had a presentable routine. At this point, Wayne showed up to see what the stuntmen had created. He'd be briefed on his proposed actions and make suggestions of his own. The stuntmen would incorporate Wayne's suggestions into the routine if viable and rehearse for a couple of hours. With Leon Shamroy's cameras rolling, Wayne would do as much of the fight as he could, with Morgan stepping in for long shots or stunts deemed too dangerous for the star.

At this time of his career, Wayne was beginning to play into the larger-than-life qualities of his screen image. Though at 6'4" he towered over most of his co-stars, he began to wear lifts so he'd appear even taller on screen and in person. He was also wearing a hairpiece, which leads into one of this film's most notorious on-screen bloopers left in by editor Dorothy Spencer. At the end, in the three-minute street brawl, Wayne takes a punch from Ernie Kovacs and his wig literally flips off his head with his hat. Further evidence of poor editing and continuity occurs as Kovacs is muddy then clean during the fight. But the stunt work itself is top-drawer. *North to Alaska* typified Wayne's subsequent fights with heavy doses of humor and many participants so the aging Duke doesn't have to carry the load. Gone were the days of epic *Spoilers* and *Quiet Man* fights. Now he was merely content to throw an occasional big right and perform his fan-friendly rolling-eye punch-take.

See: *North to Alaska* pressbook; Scott, John L. "There's Lots of Punch in *North to Alaska*." *Los Angeles Times*. November 24, 1960.

Elvis Presley vs. Tom Reese in *Flaming Star* (1960)

One of Elvis Presley's best films features little singing but plenty of western drama and action. Don Siegel directed a story originally written for Marlon Brando with Presley cast as a Kiowa half-breed torn between allegiance to his father's white family and his mother Katy Jurado's tribe. Midway through the film (photographed by Charles G. Clarke), shifty cowpoke Tom Reese shows up to accost Presley's mother, and Presley fends him off with a vengeance. The star displays great energy in an outdoor fight that sees Presley throw a stool, knock Reese off a barn roof and mercilessly beat his head against a wall until Reese is begging him to stop. Editor Hugh Fowler and composer Cyril Mockridge rise to the occasion in complementing Presley's vigor. *Variety* called the fight "realistically staged," while Presley biographer James L. Neibaur claims the sequence is one of the film's "most stirring, emotional scenes." The exchange afterward with Jurado is priceless. She notes that her son is bleeding, and he replies he tripped in the dark. "You landed awful hard on your knuckles," she says knowingly.

Elvis Presley prepares to unload a punch on Tom Reese in 20th Century-Fox's *Flaming Star* (1960).

Stuntman Tom Sweet was on hand to double Presley, but the star ended up doing the entire fight at his own insistence. This impressed Reese's double Charles Horvath, a Marine Corps hand-to-hand combat instructor, who offered to give Presley judo pointers. While filming the fight, Presley accidentally made contact with Reese, whom he respectfully referred to as Mr. Reese throughout the filming. Presley was apologetic, as he left a temporary imprint of his fist on Reese's face and nearly knocked the much bigger man out. Reese was overwhelmed by Presley's sincerity and the respect he showed the actor. On the set, Presley worked out every morning doing karate with bodyguards Red West and Sonny West before the cameras rolled, much to the horror of the filmmakers who had so much money invested in the star and feared an injury. One morning Presley played a practical joke on director Siegel and producer David Weisbart when he showed up with a fake cast on his arm.

Six-foot-three, 230-pound Tom Reese was a Marine and military policeman whose slit-eyes, thick nose and menacing manner helped him become a prolific and surly heavy. When he arrived in Hollywood, Reese felt obliged to do his own fights until he realized he was keeping stuntmen from their checks. Reese injured his back doing a comic fight with Woody Allen in *Sleeper* (1973). He received 12 weeks of worker's compensation for the injury which ended up paying far more than the bit part itself.

Reese had notable screen fights with Roy Jenson in *Marines, Let's Go!* (1961), Tony Curtis in *40 Pounds of Trouble* (1962), Glenn Ford in *The Money Trap* (1966) and Dean Martin in *Murderers' Row* (1966). On TV, he sized up James Arness on *Gunsmoke*, Doug McClure on *The Virginian*, Chuck Connors on *Branded* and Mike Connors on *Mannix*. His best fights came against John Cassavettes in 1959's *Johnny Staccato* episode "The Return" and George Maharis in 1960's *Route 66* episode "The Strengthening Angels."

See: "Tom Reese." *Bonanza Gold*. April 2007; Worth, Fred L., and Steve D. Tamerus. *Elvis: His Life from A to Z*. Chicago: Contemporary Books, 1988.

EARL HOLLIMAN VS. BURT REYNOLDS in *Armored Command* (1961)

A World War II drama about Army recon squad holed up in a French village near the Siegfried Line with beautiful espionage agent Tina Louise causing friction between G.I.s Earl Holliman and Burt Reynolds. This leads to a nicely staged fistfight between sergeant Holliman and hot-headed private Reynolds that ends in a snow bank. It was one of Reynolds' first films and shows off his generous talent for screen fighting. Publicity tagged the fight the film's "high spot of drama." The *Springfield Union* called it "one of the better screen brawls," while *Variety* tagged it "a beaut of a no-holds-barred brawl."

The movie was filmed on location in Munich, Germany, where, a week earlier, a deadly fight had broken out in a beer hall and left locals in a testy state. When the American film crew moved in to facilitate romance with the local ladies, the men of the city were not amused. Co-star Marty Ingels claimed Reynolds came to his rescue, putting three local bruisers out of commission in a tavern by swinging into them from a hanging light before uncorking punches and spiriting Ingels to safety. Ingels' description sounds like something from a movie itself, but it's a story Reynolds often retold.

A running back at Florida State, Reynolds was forced to quit football because of injuries received in a car wreck. He headed for New York City, where he found jobs as a bar bouncer and stuntman on live television broadcasts. Reynolds (5'9", 170 pounds) put his all into filming fights. Few actors, or stuntmen for that matter, brought as much gusto and seeming disregard for their bodies as Reynolds did. His energy in these type of scenes gained him notice, and once he was established, it became a matter of pride for him to put on a good fight. He did running drop kicks into opponents, threw his body into boxes and over tables, took chair shots, and fell down stairs if needed. On *City Heat* (1984), he took a real chair to the jaw and

suffered a hairline fracture that caused TMJ and constant pain. It affected his ability to eat and resulted in a severe weight loss, with industry speculation about his health severely affecting his career. Stuntmen presented him with a Taurus World Stunt Lifetime Achievement Award for his contributions to action scenes.

Notable fights include *100 Rifles* (1969), *The Man Who Loved Cat Dancing* (1973), *Nickelodeon* (1976), *Hooper* (1978), *The Cannonball Run* (1981) and *Sharky's Machine* (1982) (see entries). Fights of interest came against George Hamilton in *Angel Baby* (1961), Bill Catching in *Operation CIA* (1965), Aldo Sambrell in *Navajo Joe* (1966), Eddie Nicart in *Impasse* (1969), Ossie Davis in *Sam Whiskey* (1969), Glenn Wilder and Charlie Picerni in *Shamus* (1973), Bo Hopkins and R.G. Armstrong in *White Lightning* (1973), Gene Hackman in *Lucky Lady* (1975), Jerry Reed in *Gator* (1976), Dar Robinson in *Stick* (1985), Joe Klecko and Pete Koch in *Heat* (1986), Dennis Burkley in *Malone* (1986), Nils Allen Stewart in *Cop and a Half* (1993) and Roddy Piper and Gene LeBell in *Hard Time* (1998).

On TV, he brawled with John Ireland in the 1959 *Riverboat* episode "The Fight Back" and engaged in a humorous fight against Don Megowan in the 1964 *Gunsmoke* episode "Comanches Is Soft." Reynolds spent three seasons on the show as half-breed blacksmith Quint Asper. His short-lived 1966 New York City cop drama *Hawk* saw him fight Ramon Bieri in "H Is a Dirty Letter" and Scott Glenn in "Wall of Silence." On *Dan August*, he squared off against William Smith in 1971's "The Meal Ticket." As a guest, Reynolds fought a karate-chopping Charles Aidman in 1960's *Johnny Ringo* episode "The Stranger" and George Maharis in 1962's *Route 66* episode "Love Is a Skinny Kid." He put on a barroom brawl for the 1983 TV special *Celebrity Daredevils*.

Earl Holliman (center) and Burt Reynolds clash (as James Dobson, left, watches) in Allied Artists' *Armored Command* (1961).

See: *Armored Com-*

mand pressbook; Jones, Shirley, Marty Ingels and Mickey Herskowitz. *Shirley & Marty: An Unlikely Love Story.* New York: Morrow, 1990; Scott, Vernon. "Burt Reynolds Likes a Bloody Barroom Brawl." *The Dispatch.* July 31, 1964.

ELVIS PRESLEY VS. STEVE BRODIE in *Blue Hawaii* (1961)

Norman Taurog's colorful *Blue Hawaii* is significant as the first of star Elvis Presley's popular travelogue formula musicals. It was also the earliest film to display his penchant for using martial arts in fight scenes. Due to his Southern upbringing, Presley and his characters were quick to step in and protect a lady's honor and virtue. Cast here as an island tour guide, he comes to the defense of young client Jenny Maxwell at a restaurant luau when drunken Steve Brodie gets fresh. Brodie tries to punch Presley and a one-minute brawl breaks out among the party guests for Charles Lang's camera. Presley takes care of Brodie with his fists but resorts to karate chops and a kick to flatten Red West. One stunt fighter is Hawaiian martial artist Daniel Kane Pai. *Blue Hawaii* was shot on location in Kauai at the Coco Palms Resort's Island Inn restaurant. *Hollywood Surf and Beach Movies* remarked, "Elvis' obligatory fight scene is well-staged."

The six-foot, 180-pound Brodie had an amateur boxing background and a notable screen fight with Robert Mitchum in *Out of the Past* (1947) on his résumé. Going into *Blue Hawaii,* he had lost 16 straight movie fights, but he considered this one a moral victory. He excels as the obnoxious lecher and returned to be punched out by Presley at a carnival in *Roustabout* (1964). *Blue Hawaii*'s success led to Presley making *Paradise Hawaiian Style* (1966), where the *Blue Hawaii* fight scenario was recreated with Don Collier taking on the Brodie part in *Paradise* as the drunken blowhard. To pass time between takes, Presley practiced his karate by breaking boards and bricks with his hands and feet.

Presley's incorporation of martial arts into his fights undoubtedly helped spread their popularity to the western world. He worked most often on screen fights with his bodyguard Red West, as they were familiar with one another and knew how to effectively present their moves. Most stuntmen were leery of working with karate and were learning on the fly how best to stage moves and reactions for the movie cameras. The easiest martial arts move to stage was the knife-hand strike or, as it became more commonly known, the judo chop. Most Presley fights featured the judo blow, a cinematic move of dubious effectiveness that became a staple for William Shatner on TV's *Star Trek,* Robert Culp on *I Spy* and Anne Francis on *Honey West.* One mere judo chop as delivered on film to the neck or shoulder area could instantly render an opponent helpless or unconscious.

There was one difference when it came to Presley. He was a legitimate black belt highly devoted to the discipline. He began studying martial arts with Jurgen Seydal while stationed with the U.S. Army in Germany in 1959. By early 1960, he had earned his brown belt training at Murakami Tesuji's club Yoseikan in Paris. He soon earned a Shotokan black belt from 1956 World Karate Champ Hank Slomanski. In 1960, Presley met Hawaiian Kenpo artist Ed Parker, with whom he trained throughout the 1970s. During that decade's martial arts craze, Presley and Parker developed an idea for Presley to be cast as a karate villain in an *Enter the Dragon*–inspired epic titled *The New Gladiators.* Presley's manager Colonel Tom Parker nixed the idea although footage surfaced in a documentary showing training and competition footage they filmed. In Memphis, Presley studied Tae Kwon Do with Korean master Kang Rhee, who awarded him a 7th degree black belt. That was seen as largely a ceremonial move, but there was no denying that Presley had earned his original belts through Slomanski and Parker with intense and dedicated training.

See: "Character Actor Finally a Victor." *Toledo Blade.* October 22, 1961; Lisanti, Thomas. *Hollywood Surf and Beach Movies.* Jefferson, NC: McFarland, 2012; Parker, Ed. "The King and I." *Black Belt.* March 1990.

GEORGE HAMILTON VS. CHARLES BRONSON in *A Thunder of Drums* (1961)

This solid western from director Joseph Newman depicts the rivalry between cavalry sergeant Richard Boone and young West Point lieutenant George Hamilton. The film's fisticuffs occur between the six-foot, perpetually tan Hamilton and rough-around-the-edges trooper Charles Bronson. Hamilton doesn't like that Bronson has been snooping around secret girlfriend Luana Patten's window and confronts him in the horse stables. Credibility is lost when Hamilton begins knocking the muscular Bronson around, although the stone-faced actor does land his share of blows. Bronson is great at selling the effect of Hamilton's punches for William Spencer's camera. A highlight has Bronson knocking Hamilton into a horse trough, then spitting on him. He even throws a horseshoe. Hamilton knocks Bronson unconscious with a series of head-turning punches. MGM publicity called it a "slam-bang, knockdown drag-out fight." *The Hollywood Reporter* chose to comment on the rhythmic background music: "Harry Sukman's score avoids the clichés of the genre and is often quite brilliant, his use of a guitar against a brawl for instance, being witty counterpointing."

It was through star Richard Boone's insistence that athletic stuntman Hal Needham received this early film break doubling Hamilton. Needham does almost the entire fight with actor Bronson, who is always watchable when engaging in fights. Editor Ferris Webster does the best he can to disguise this fact, but it's a rough go given Hamilton's ineptness at any type of action. Burt Reynolds fought him the same year in *Angel Baby* (1961) and often razzed Hamilton for his awkwardness. At any rate, a fight between Bronson and stunt legend Needham is definitely worth checking out.

The six-foot, 180-pound Needham was emerging as one of the top young stuntmen in the business. A former Army paratrooper, he excelled at fights, throwing great punches and tumbling over every prop available. He began to make his name setting up the stunts and doubling for Boone on TV's *Have Gun—Will Travel.* Needham would later become associated with the films of Burt Reynolds, both as stuntman, coordinator and full-fledged director. Writing about his friend Needham in his memoir *But Enough About Me,* Reynolds recalled: "He did everything with style. In a fight you could always recognize him because he had a unique way of throwing a punch then coming back across his chest with the same hand. Stuntmen called it a Needham."

During the early 1960s, Needham and equally athletic stunt partner Ronnie Rondell, Jr., fought countless battles on TV for heroes and heavies, especially at Universal. Needham was also the preferred fight partner of rough'n'tumble actor Robert Fuller, often filling in for the heavies on the classic TV series *Laramie* and *Wagon Train.* Needham was action director Andrew McLaglen's preferred stunt coordinator, and even John Wayne took a liking to the way Needham put on a fight.

See: Long, Mary. "The World's Greatest Stunt-

man." *Boca Raton News.* June 19, 1977; *A Thunder of Drums* pressbook.

GREGORY PECK VS. ROBERT MITCHUM in *Cape Fear* (1962)

This classic J. Lee Thompson suspense film was adapted from a John D. MacDonald novel about a vengeful ex-con, and ends with an outstanding fight sequence. *Cape Fear* showcases Robert Mitchum as Max Cady, a terrifying human monster who finishes a prison stretch and preys on the family of North Carolina lawyer Gregory Peck. Mitchum blames Peck's poor defense for his incarceration and is determined to see him squirm. Mitchum uses the law to his advantage, menacingly stalking the family while provoking Peck to operate outside legal means. When a desperate Peck hires strong-arm men to convince Mitchum to leave town, Mitchum beats up the toughs and then goes after Peck and his family with intent to harm. The *New York Times* called the climax a "perilous, agonizing showdown" and *Variety* termed "a forthright exercise in cumulative terror."

Peck is waiting along the Cape Fear River with his wife Polly Bergen and daughter Lori Martin aboard a houseboat. Peck and Mitchum battle in the water and on the shore in a sequence that editor George Tomasini intentionally drew out in contrast to the brisk pace of the rest of the film. Cinematographer Sam Leavitt shot the swamp sequence in shadows, taking advantage of the decision to film in black-and-white to accentuate Mitchum's slimy qualities and ability to blend into the night. Composer Bernard Herrmann contributes a memorable dramatic score. Mitchum nearly drowns Peck when he applies a rear naked chokehold and puts him underneath the water, but the mild-mannered Peck finds a reserve of strength and adrenaline to protect his family. Chuck Roberson doubled Peck while George Robotham doubled the shirtless Mitchum when he charges through the water and barrels into Peck. *Time* commented, "Mitchum, as usual, makes a nice shiny reptile, and it's gory good fun to watch Peck cut him up into handbags."

Peck and Mitchum were complete contrasts on the set. Peck studied his role and always arrived prepared for a day's filming. Mitchum spent long nights drinking and winged everything, using his uncanny intuition and photographic memory for quickly picking up lines. Producer Peck knew the Cady role was the showier of the two, but couldn't help but feel Mitchum was stealing the picture. Mitchum knew it and took delight in rubbing salt in Peck's self-imposed psychological wounds. In the fight, Peck accidentally punched Mitchum for real, a blow Mitchum acknowledged he felt days afterward. When holding Peck underwater, the two devised a signal where Peck tapped Mitchum's leg when he couldn't stay under any longer. On one take, Mitchum, caught up in the explosive Cady menace, held Peck under longer than planned and had to be pulled off him by crew members. Censors thought the drowning scene was violently unsettling and demanded it be reduced. Although location shooting was done in Savannah, Georgia, the fight was shot on the Universal back lot. The film was remade in 1991 with Nick Nolte and Robert DeNiro recreating the fight.

Robert Mitchum applies a "rear naked choke" on Gregory Peck during the climax of Universal's *Cape Fear* (1962).

See: *Cape Fear* pressbook; Chibnall, Steve. *J. Lee Thompson*. Manchester: Manchester University Press, 2001; *The Making of Cape Fear*.

THE BUFFALO HUNTER BRAWL in *Sergeants 3* (1962)

A three-minute fight between cavalry soldiers and buffalo hunters in the Antler Saloon is pervaded by comic mugging from Rat Pack stars Frank Sinatra, Dean Martin, Peter Lawford and Sammy Davis, Jr., in this *Gunga Din* update. It's played broadly for laughs as the three sergeants rescue bugler Davis from bullying Mickey Finn. The stars appear to be having fun engaging in the slapstick action. Two hundred forty–pound Finn, a professional wrestler turned actor, pairs up with Sinatra. Finn takes several wild swings-and-misses that Sinatra counters with jabs. The three sergeants execute a timing routine during which Sinatra hits Finn over the head with a spittoon. Dean Martin was handy in a fight while Peter Lawford amusingly breaks a chair down to kindling knocking it over heads. Stuntmen Charles Horvath, Henry Wills, Al Wyatt and Boyd "Red" Morgan comprise the primary bearded buffalo hunters. Minimal contributions are needed from the stars' doubles Buzz Henry, Joe Gray and Bill Catching.

Much of the film was shot on location in Kanab, Utah, by veteran cinematographer Winton C. Hoch, but the brawl was filmed in Hollywood on a Goldwyn Studios stage.

The *New York Times* said the fight "has the speed, comedy, and improbability of a Mack Sennett set-to," while *Variety* praised "the amusing fistic choreography." However, the content seen on screen hardly seems worthy of an effort from the normally serious-minded director John Sturges. The *Dallas Morning News* complained that Sturges "tries so much new stuff in the film fights that much of it looks ludicrous." During filming, Sturges had to deal with the power and ego of Sinatra, a disruptive force that could negate preparation and budget because of his unavailability and penchant for ad-libbing. The director was so affected by the making of this film that he demanded complete control on his next outing. That film turned out to be the classic *The Great Escape* (1963).

The fight is expertly edited by Ferris Webster. The editor's role in putting together a fight is crucial. In addition to concealing the use of doubles, the fight's rhythm and pacing must not drag or lose the audience's attention. Editors typically use a master shot of a fight for a source of structure. Cutting to different camera angles or perspectives keeps the audience engaged, but it must not be excessive. It's important for the editor to match action in the scene. There must be clarity and a sense of scope for the surroundings and the combatants. The audience should be able to tell what is going on and who's involved. Some editors make instinctive cuts, reacting as if they are the audience watching the film and flinching at the thrown punch. There must be a sense of excitement in the mix of cuts to keep the viewer slightly disoriented and on edge. A three-minute fight with multiple cuts is a lengthy undertaking, suggesting the brawl is a centerpiece. Editors bring fights in at 30 seconds or one minute—time-honored traditions for effectiveness. *Sergeants 3* is an exception.

Five-foot-seven, 140-pound Frank Sinatra had a great tough guy reputation for a slightly built man. He was an amateur boxer in his youth and fought public scraps throughout his career. He trained regularly with ring ace Al Silvani to keep his skills sharp and was known for his tenaciousness as well as his influential connections. Pal Robert Mitchum once claimed he wouldn't want to fight Sinatra. With age and added weight, Sinatra was convincing as tough Miami Beach detective Tony Rome in a pair of films.

Notable fights include *The Manchurian Candidate* (1962) and *4 for Texas* (1963) (see entries). Fights of interest came against Ernest Borgnine in *From Here to Eternity* (1953), Robert Mitchum in *Not as a Stranger* (1955), Tony Curtis in *Kings Go Forth* (1958), Ric Roman in *Some Came Running* (1958), Dan Blocker in *Come Blow Your Horn* (1963) and *Lady in Cement* (1968), Alf Kjellin in

Assault on a Queen (1966) and Babe Hart in *Tony Rome* (1967). On TV, Sinatra had a barroom brawl with Branscombe Richmond in the 1987 *Magnum P.I.* episode "Laura."

See: Carroll, Harrison. "Sergeants 3 Whoop It Up in Barroom." *The Dispatch*. July 29, 1961.

KIRK DOUGLAS VS. BILL RAISCH in *Lonely Are the Brave* (1962)

A nasty fight highlights this somber modern cowboy film from director David Miller about the changing of the West. Dalton Trumbo scripted, based on Edward Abbey's novel *Brave Cowboy*, with Philip Lathrop effectively filming in black-and-white. Kirk Douglas encounters bullying one-armed drunk Bill Raisch in a small New Mexico bar and tries his best to avoid a confrontation with the war veteran, though Douglas is looking for a reason to be thrown in the local jail (he has a friend there he's foolishly determined to break out). It all seems so simple and noble a cause until Raisch throws a bottle next to his head and kicks his chair out from underneath him. Douglas relents when Raisch spits out that he's a coward. Douglas wants to make the fight fair so he keeps an arm behind his back. However, Raisch is such a dirty fighter that Douglas is constantly tempted to bring his dominant arm into play, especially when Raisch pins him against the wall with a chair, tries choking him to death with a shirt sleeve, and cracks him over the skull with a pool stick. The scene is so plot-integrated that it served as a teaching tool for both future writers and directors. A retrospective review by the *Los Angeles Times* declared, "Their knockabout brawl is a remarkable feat of brute choreography, both genuinely dangerous and infinitely enthralling, and a showcase for director David Miller's unobtrusive, observational style."

There's great intensity throughout, enhanced by Jerry Goldsmith's up-tempo percussion score, a woman calling the police in Spanish, and the tavern regulars who appear ready to jump in against Douglas and finally do. Makeup artists Bud Westmore and Dave Grayson supply the

Bill Raisch (left) and Kirk Douglas clash in Universal's *Lonely Are the Brave* (1962).

blood on Douglas' face. Lathrop's camera zooms in for close-ups to heighten the sense of danger as the audience fears for the brave and honorable cowboy's safety. Editor Leon Barsha cuts the scene superbly, maintaining tension from beginning to end. The local police arrive and throw Douglas in jail, where he is beaten by sadistic guard George Kennedy.

It's the total mean-spiritedness of the Raisch character and his "handicap" that make the bar encounter unique and memorable. Although producer-star Douglas clashed creatively with director Miller, he considered it the personal favorite of his own films. Seeking realism, Douglas does all his own fight with Raisch, a former bodybuilder who lost his arm in World War II. Douglas knew Raisch as Burt Lancaster's longtime stand-in. Raisch attained even greater notoriety as the one-armed man eluding David Janssen on the TV series *The Fugitive* (1963–1967). The fight was performed on a closed set at Universal with Douglas emerging with real bruises, a minor wrist injury—and ultimately a piece of cinematic history. It's one of the best one-on-one bar fights ever done.

See: Adams, Sam. "Trampling Boundaries in *Lonely Are the Brave.*" *Los Angeles Times.* July 5, 2009; "He Is the Man Hunted by Dr. Richard Kimble." *Tuscaloosa News.* March 1, 1964; *Lonely Are the Brave* pressbook.

FRANK SINATRA VS. HENRY SILVA in *The Manchurian Candidate* (1962)

This classic from director John Frankenheimer concerns a Cold War sleeper (Laurence Harvey) brainwashed by the Communists while in Korea and now programmed to be a political assassin. The film has frightening dramatic intrigue laced with touches of satire and absurdity. The fight between star Frank Sinatra and Korean servant Henry Silva literally comes out of nowhere and jolts the audience to attention. It was one of the first extended karate scenes in an American film and took viewers by surprise with its violent furniture-smashing martial arts display. It was nevertheless disconcerting for many to

see skinny crooner Sinatra performing intense chops and open-palm strikes. For those who remember when it originally came out, it remains an all-time great fight. For those who didn't discover the long out-of-circulation film until decades later, the fight has the potential to be unintentionally hilarious. In many ways, it now resembles the comic fights between Peter Sellers and Burt Kwouk in the *Pink Panther* films.

The polished post-production work of Ferris Webster contributes greatly to the film's success as it drives the action forward. He was nominated for an Oscar for Best Editing. The fight took two days to film and credit for the on-screen action is spread in many directions. Stunt coordinator John Indrisano was in the mix. Buzz Henry doubled Sinatra while a heavily made-up Al Wyatt stood in for Silva. Hawaiian-born martial artist Gordon Doversola, a master of Okinawa-Te, was brought in to coordinate the fight with Beau Van Den Ecker assisting. Hollywood judoka Bruce Tegner was said to be involved in setting up the fight's judo aspects. David Chow, a Chinese stuntman and judo champ with a Hollywood dojo, also worked on the film and likely had input. Kenpo master Ed Parker's name pops up often. Both Sinatra and Silva trained with Parker before the film, although it's undocumented if Parker had any input on the set. He auditioned for Silva's part but frightened Frankenheimer with his size and the ferocity of his Kenpo movements.

Sinatra, who usually loathed preparing for film

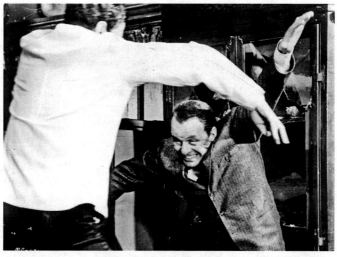

Henry Silva (left) and Frank Sinatra engage in the famous martial arts fight in United Artists' *The Manchurian Candidate* (1962).

work, looked forward to filming the fight. He and Silva ended up doing significant action, although Silva later incorrectly recalled they had done it all. One problem plaguing the choreography: Silva was left-handed while Sinatra was right-handed. Sinatra's cross-block of Silva's kick was a real unplanned reaction. Silva accidentally kicked with the opposite foot he had used in rehearsal. When Sinatra chopped a pre-scored table, he broke a finger but kept filming. The digit bothered him the rest of his life. Their toil was worthwhile as *Action Films* ranks it among filmdom's greatest fights. In his book on the movie, Greil Marcus calls it a "great karate fight."

Six-foot, 180-pound Henry Silva was a longshoreman before embarking on an acting career. A weightlifting proponent, he boasted nearly 17" arms before slimming down. A trained judoka, Silva studied kung fu with Jimmy Woo. He had the title role in *The Return of Mr. Moto* (1965) and engaged in a martial arts fight as the lead in *Assassination* (1967). However, he usually played menacing bad guys of various ethnic persuasion. In European cinema he impressively knocked heads alongside Woody Strode in *The Italian Connection* (1972). Fights of interest came against Audie Murphy in *Ride a Crooked Trail* (1958), Robert Taylor in *The Law and Jake Wade* (1958), Anthony Perkins in *Green Mansions* (1959), Hal Baylor and Kelly Thordsen in *Johnny Cool* (1963) and Steven Seagal in *Above the Law* (1988) (see entry). On TV, Silva battled Robert Bray in the 1961 *Stagecoach West* episode "The Raider" and Stuart Whitman in the 1967 *Cimarron Strip* episode "Journey to a Hanging."

See: Coppola, Louis A. *C.B.S. the Chucklehead Broadcasting System: Celebrating 44 Years of Insignificance.* Bloomington, IN: Author House, 2008; Marcus, Greil. *The Manchurian Candidate.* London: BFI, 2002; "Okinawa-Te: Forerunner of Modern Karate." *Black Belt.* March 1965; Warren, Bill. "Exerting Influence." *Starlog.* September 1990.

THE POKER FIGHT in *It Happened at the World's Fair* (1963)

Pilot Elvis Presley bails partner Gary Lockwood out of a gambling debt at Charlie's Garage by paying off the poker players (John Daheim, Red West, Saul Gorss and Troy Melton) in knuckle sandwiches. Director Norman Taurog and the stuntmen set a frenetic pace with Presley in the foreground taking on as many as three men at a time while Lockwood exchanges punches behind him. Cinematographer Joseph Ruttenberg and editor Fredric Steinkamp capture a perfect combination of varied shots, with just enough close-ups of Lockwood to remind the audience he's present. Presley mixes in karate kicks, a back heel trip and a reverse chop. One of the best moments has Daheim run into a Presley punch that stops him cold. West is knocked out the garage window and is followed by Lockwood's stunt double Bennie Dobbins after a double-punch from Daheim and Melton. Outside, Lockwood and West continue battling. A dazed Lockwood even swings wildly at Presley. Before they leave, Presley decks mechanic John Indrisano (the fight's coordinator) for good measure. The *Pittsburgh Press* called the one-minute battle "a lively all-out fight scene," while *Variety* referred to it as "elaborately spirited." Participant Red West recalled the brawl as "a great fight scene."

The MGM film, impressively set at Seattle's 1962 World's Fair, concludes with a bristling 45-second fight between Presley and fur smuggling heavy H.M. Wynant. Presley is in fine form exchanging lefts and rights with Wynant against boxes and shipping crates. Presley's furious punches overwhelm Wynant, who puts his hands up and begs for the barrage to end. When Presley does let up, Wynant takes a breath and sucker punches him. Presley finishes Wynant off quickly, memorably holding him up by his tie for the knockout blow. Presley rouses Lockwood, who once again comes up comically swinging at the star. Wynant does the majority of the fight with the electric Presley, and it ranks as another superior showcase for the singer to show off his fluid moves. Publicity touted the presence of "two spectacular free-for-all brawls."

Six-foot-one, 185-pound Lockwood entered films as a stuntman and customarily did his own fights. He had a real reputation as a brawler, having hospitalized a man in a frat house fistfight when he was playing football at UCLA. Boxing and karate training were two of his interests. He played one of his first acting roles opposite Presley in *Wild in the Country* (1961), with Presley's punches proving fatal to Lockwood's character. There was some brief tension between Presley and Lockwood because they were both dating Tuesday Weld, but the men settled their differences amicably.

Screen fights of interest came against James Best

in *Firecreek* (1968), Leslie Nielsen in *Project: Kill* (1976) and Tony Epper in *Bad Georgia Road* (1977). Lockwood starred in his own TV series *The Lieutenant* (1963–1964) as a tough Marine; fighting James Shigeta in 1964's "To Kill a Man." As a guest on *The Lloyd Bridges Show*, Lockwood stepped into the boxing ring against the star in 1963's "My Daddy Can Lick Your Daddy." He was in the squared circle again vs. Chuck Connors on the 1972 *Night Gallery* episode "The Ring with the Red Velvet Ropes."

His most memorable TV clash came against William Shatner in the 1966 *Star Trek* pilot episode "Where No Man Has Gone Before."

See: Clayton, Rose. *Elvis Up Close: In the Words of Those Who Knew Him Best.* Atlanta: Turner, 1995; *It Happened at the World's Fair* pressbook; Lockwood, Gary, and R.A. Jones. *2001 Memories: An Actor's Odyssey.* Cowboy Press, 2001; Taylor, Tim. "It Started with a Fist Fight." *Evening Independent.* December 3, 1961.

JOHN WAYNE VS. LEE MARVIN in *Donovan's Reef* (1963)

Donovan's Reef is a colorful, occasionally surreal John Ford film featuring John Wayne and Lee Marvin as Guns Donovan and Boats Gilhooley, annual participants in a Pacific island bout of fisticuffs at Donovan's Reef Tavern on their shared birthday. Mike Mazurki is the seen-it-all local police officer and *de facto* referee. They've carried on the fight for over 20 years, so long that neither can remember why they're fighting other than it's become a tradition. The fictional island Halekealoha anticipates the brawl much the way the Irish hamlet looked forward to Wayne and Victor McLaglen squaring off in *The Quiet Man.* Wayne and Marvin start their fight out of the gate and continue off and on throughout the Frank Nugent–James Edward Grant–scripted film. The intriguing star match-up might be better regarded had they fought one lengthier, epic bout.

The events appear to be a Hawaiian vacation for the cast and crew, with the filming of a motion picture an afterthought. The film suffers due to this, as well to Marvin's funny though broad mugging as the friendly antagonist. An aging Ford

seemed content to fall back on one of his favorite plot devices in staging the abundant punch-related pratfalls. The *Los Angeles Times* referred to it as merely "slam-bang hokum," although the book *In the Footsteps of* The Quiet Man calls it "a tremendous fight scene." According to *The Hollywood Reporter*, the film benefited chiefly from its casting: "Wayne and Marvin are well matched as the brawling buddies." It's remembered by most Wayne fans as another rollicking good time.

The fights involve lots of clowning around as the participants heartily mix booze with their brawling. The first encounter is the best thanks to the built-up tension and Wayne and Marvin's cat-and-mouse tiptoeing around one another to see who will make the first move. Wayne turns his back for a second as Marvin contemplates smashing a bottle over his head. A bemused Mazurki watches it all unfold. Marvin hauls off and punches Wayne in the jaw, sending him over a table. Marvin grabs a bottle to throw only to have Wayne command, "Not the brandy, you dope!" Marvin gently puts the bottle of brandy down and hurls a beer in its place. Wayne promptly smashes a chair over Marvin's head for the first knockout. However, the film loses any sense of potentially interesting menace once Marvin becomes less of a threat and partners up with the star.

As the picture unfolds, they trade punches when the other least expects it, including during a battle with members of Dick Foran's Australian Navy in the biggest barroom brawl. This was shot on a Paramount stage by William H. Clothier and

Lee Marvin (left) and John Wayne add comic touches to the traditional fistfight in Paramount's *Donovan's Reef* (1963).

assembled by Otho Lovering. Among the stuntmen and action actors taking part are Cliff Lyons, Chuck Roberson, Hal Needham, Tom Steele, Tom Hennesy, Jerry Gatlin, Wally Rose, William Burnside, Boyd "Red" Morgan, Eddy Donno, Frank Hagney, Jack McClure, Ralph Rowe, Riley Hill, Dave Armstrong, Guy Way, Hubie Kerns, Ron Nyman, Duke Green and Frank Baker. Both Wayne and Marvin used doubles for part of the fighting. Wayne missed an uppercut and tumbled over a breakaway table, injuring his back. Lyons coordinated the action. *USA Today* includes this battle among the Top 10 all-time fights, and *The Big Damn Book of Sheer Manliness* calls it one of filmdom's best barroom scuffles.

A local Arizona legend involves Wayne and Marvin getting into a fight at the Copper Queen Hotel in Bisbee and breaking a window. It's hard to say if it was with each other, third parties, mere drunken roughhousing, or rehearsal for a screen fight. Wayne and Marvin fought briefly once before in the western *The Comancheros* (1961) and stared one another down in *The Man Who Shot Liberty Valance* (1962). The two became deep-sea fishing buddies and drinking pals during the filming of *Donovan's Reef*. One night they became so inebriated that Marvin found his way to the airport and caught a flight back to Los Angeles. Upon arrival on the mainland, he went to the house of pal Keenan Wynn and climbed into bed with Wynn and his wife. They called Marvin's agent, who immediately came to whisk him back to Hawaii before his absence affected the picture. Admittedly, there wasn't much for Marvin to do besides punch and be punched by Wayne.

Motivation for screen fights should stem logically from the script. A screenwriter is the creator of the characters and the architect of the storyline. It's their responsibility to provide a valid reason for the fight as well as to punch up the pace of a film by avoiding too much reliance on dialogue. The easiest way to insert action into a plot without maxing out the budget is to put in a fistfight. Screenwriters typically eschew too much text in describing the details of a fight outside the verbal lines and emotional cues. It's enough to simply say the men fight and let the professional stuntmen take over the physical choreography. However, the characters' intellect, physical condition and background should be kept consistent with the plot. They shouldn't break out martial arts moves or stamina alien to the characters' background and training. Screenwriters Nugent and Grant were both veterans of previous John Ford and John Wayne excursions and knew how to tailor their script for their employers. *Donovan's Reef* is the quintessential brawling Wayne-Ford film, peppered throughout with good-natured fistic exchanges.

See: Carroll, Harrison. "Slam-Bang Brawl Recalls the Past." *Dispatch.* September 24, 1962; Klein, Doris. "Lee Marvin Tells Secrets of Movie Filming Fights." *Reading Eagle.* September 26, 1962.

PETER BRECK VS. CHUCK ROBERSON in *Shock Corridor* (1963)

A wild, sensationalistic cult film from director Samuel Fuller, *Shock Corridor* stars Peter Breck as a reporter who has himself admitted to an insane asylum to try to unravel a murder. As the over-the-top story unfolds, all the craziness begins to rub off on Breck, who must solve the case before he goes off the deep end. The climax is a two-minute fight between Breck and Chuck Roberson, here playing an orderly. They battle in a hydrotherapy chamber, into a kitchen and out onto the long corridor of the title. Highlights are Roberson knocking Breck into a water tank occupied by an oblivious patient, Breck dragging Roberson over a long table full of servings in the kitchen, and Breck pounding Roberson's head on the floor until he confesses. *Variety* claimed that Breck "really gets his lumps and earns his pay." The film was shot on the cheap, and a blooper occurs in the kitchen. When they crash against the table, a leg is knocked askew, yet when Roberson is dragged, the table leg is in its original position. Nevertheless, the fight was a favorite of director Martin Scorsese, who showed it to film students at New York University as he was enamored with the tracking shots of Fuller and cameraman Stanley Cortez.

Roberson did his own stunts, and the fight benefits from his experience and reactions for the camera. An energetic if unconvincing Buzz Henry stands in for Breck during the fight in the spa. He looks little like Breck, for whom Hal Needham or Chuck Bail usually doubled. The entire film was done in ten days, so it's understandable those stuntmen might have been tied up on other projects during that small window of opportunity. It's surprising Breck didn't do more of his own fighting, as the six-foot, 180-pound Navy vet became known for his fisticuffs as a TV cowboy on *The Big Valley* (1965–1969). Breck learned screen fighting from Needham and became comfortable throwing punches. He was easy to spot doing his own fights because his dark hair had a habit of vigorously flying around his forehead.

Breck's most notable cinematic fight came against Audie Murphy in *The Wild and the Innocent* (1959). He starred in two TV westerns: *Black Saddle* (1959–1960) as a gunfighter turned lawyer and *The Big Valley* as hot-tempered, two-fisted Nick Barkley. On the former, he had three fights against co-star Russell Johnson, the best coming in 1960's "The Apprentice." On *The Big Valley*, he had a bunkhouse brawl with co-star Lee Majors (playing Breck's half-brother) in the opening episode, one of the best fights put on television. The two also battled in 1966's "By Fires Unseen." He had other notable *Big Valley* slugfests against Claude Akins in 1965's "The Brawlers," Robert Fuller in 1967's "A Flock of Trouble" and Larry Pennell in 1967's "The Price of Victory." As a TV guest, Breck fought Doug McClure in the 1970 *Men from Shiloh* episode "Hannah."

See: Breck, Peter. "Cut 'Em Off at the Pass." *Wildest Westerns.* #3, 1999; Lousararian, Ed. "Peter Breck: TV's Toughest Cowboy." *Wildest Westerns.* #2, 1999; Raymond, Marc. *Hollywood's New Yorker: The Making of Martin Scorsese.* Albany, NY: SUNY, 2013.

Sean Connery vs. Robert Shaw in *From Russia with Love* (1963)

The intense, vicious confrontation between Sean Connery and Robert Shaw in a cramped Orient Express train compartment remains the best fight in the entire James Bond series and one of the top brawls ever. *Variety* called it "a glorious slap-up fight to the death." *The Complete James Bond Film Encyclopedia* went further, labeling it "probably the best fight ever choreographed on film." According to *Action Films*, it is "one of the best, if not the best close-quarters fights ever filmed." *The Spy Who Thrilled Us* declares it "hands down the best fight in the entire Bond canon," while *James Bond in the Cinema* opines, "[It] comprises one of

the best staged fights ever shown on the screen." *Kiss Kiss, Bang Bang* calls it "surely among the hardest-hitting of fistfights ever committed to film" and *The Films of Sean Connery* tags it "one of the screen's great fight sequences." Film critic Leonard Maltin declares it "one of the longest, most exciting fight scenes ever staged," and the *Toronto Star* writes that it is "a true benchmark in close-quarter bruising."

The outstanding choreography and innovative Peter Hunt editing make the two-minute fight a breathtaking and unforgettable hand-to-hand combat experience. It's violent, exciting and a jolt of espresso for a heretofore slow-paced spy film. Nothing that came before this fight had the sustained brutality or deadliness exhibited here. These two men aren't trying to knock one another out. They're trying to kill or be killed. For many years, the version shown on TV was edited because of violence and tone. Peter Perkins served as stunt coordinator with Bob Simmons doubling

Sean Connery delivers a right cross to Robert Shaw during the famous train compartment fight in United Artists' *From Russia with Love* (1963).

Connery and Jack Cooper doubling Shaw. The actors, however, did most of the fight and give terrific action performances. Only one shot in the finished product involved doubles. Director Terence Young, an ex-boxer and rugby player, forced Connery and Shaw to watch from the sidelines while the doubles repeatedly ran through the scene, allowing his actors to build a hefty head of steam when called upon. They filmed on a small set at Pinewood Studios and took two days to complete the fight. Two stationary and one free camera were used by Ted Moore. Intermittent dark blue light and tear gas effects (courtesy of special effects man Albert J. Luxford shooting oil smoke through a hidden pipe attached to the briefcase) added to the claustrophobic sense of time and space. The soundtrack featured no music, only the intensified train wheels on the track.

Young asked the 5'11", 180-pound Shaw, also a rugby vet, to bleach his hair a then-shocking blond, wear lifts and build up his physique to portray the ice-cold assassin Red Grant. Shaw took it upon himself to begin wrestling a trio of Turks to toughen up for the job. Shaw didn't pump up to a bodybuilder's physique, but he did succeed in making Grant a menacing presence and more than worthy adversary for Connery with his exceptional acting skill. Red Grant is acknowledged as one of the best Bond villains. The Richard Maibaum-scripted dialogue exchange before the fight is near-brilliant in its sustained tension. The audience thinks Bond might be done for, and Shaw literally promises a slow and painful death. What follows are sharp punches, kicks, stomps and bone-crunching slams into the compartment walls. There's a rib-cracking bear-hug and a full-nelson wrestling maneuver before Shaw produces a garrot to choke the life from Connery. A knife to Shaw's arm allows Connery to reverse that situation. In the end, an exhausted Connery realizes he has come within seconds of losing his life. He slowly adjusts his tie, buttons his jacket and smooths his hair; a solid bit of actor's business on Connery's part as he composes himself.

Six-two, 200-pound Connery was a merchant seaman and a Royal Navy veteran who fought on the outfit's junior boxing team. Upon his discharge, he worked as a bouncer and played football for the Bonnyrigg Rose. In 1953, he entered the Mr. Universe contest representing his native Scotland. His first break came on British TV in 1956 as boxer Mountain McClintock in *Requiem for a Heavyweight*. However, it was a short pub fight

with Kieron Moore in *Darby O'Gill and the Little People* (1959) that attracted the attention of Bond producer Albert Broccoli. As a screen fighter, Connery was quick, agile and deadly efficient. His aura suggested an element of danger and threat. Stuntmen noted that Connery took on a slight grin when he was performing fights. Although he toned down his weight workouts, a lithe Connery still carried enough size to be believable taking on even the biggest foes. His Bond characterization wasn't the cartoon character the role became during the Roger Moore years. When Connery's Bond was faced with a dire situation, the audience expected him to fight his way out. He also acquired a real tough guy rep after punching out mobster Johnny Stompanato.

Notable fights include *Goldfinger* (1964), *Thunderball* (1965), *You Only Live Twice* (1967), *Diamonds Are Forever* (1971) and *Never Say Never Again* (1983) (see entries). Fights of interest came against Joseph Wiseman in *Dr. No* (1962), Woody Strode in *Shalako* (1968), Ian Bannen in *The Offence* (1973), Ian McShane in *The Terrorists* (1974), Tony Brubaker in *The Next Man* (1976), Marc Boyle in *Outland* (1981), Richard Bradford in *The Untouchables* (1987), Rick Zumwalt in *The Presidio* (1988) and Tony Ganios in *Rising Sun* (1993). Connery and Shaw had an extended sword fight with one another in *Robin and Marian* (1976).

See: Carmean, Karen, and Georg Gaston. *Robert Shaw: More Than a Life.* Lanham, MD: Madison Books, 1994; *From Russia with Love* DVD special features; Yule, Andrew. *Sean Connery: From 007 to Hollywood Icon.* New York: Fine, 1992.

THE FILLING STATION BRAWL in *It's a Mad Mad Mad Mad World* (1963)

Stanley Kramer's classic star-studded comedy about human greed is full of memorable set pieces and inspired visual gags, many fantastically designed by stunt coordinator Carey Loftin. It was filmed by Ernest Laszlo and assembled by Oscar-nominated editors Gene Fowler, Jr., Robert C. Jones and Frederic Knudtson. Perhaps no sequence is funnier than hot-headed truck driver Jonathan Winters' destruction of a brand new filling station with meek attendants Marvin Kaplan and Arnold Stang attempting to fight and then merely escape the madman. With the aid of John

Hudkins' expert doubling, Winters busts through walls and garage doors, knocking over every prop imaginable as the terrified attendants literally become human torpedoes. They had earlier tried wrapping Winters in duct tape and beating him with wrenches to no avail. It only made him angrier. He's like a bull in a China shop, breaking everything in its path. Every action has a reaction, and here it's another segment of the weak building collapsing. When the attendants try hiding in the outside lavatory, two big punches bring that flimsy structure down. *Variety* called it "a devastating sight gag sequence."

An improvisational comedic genius, the thickly built Winters was a former Marine who ironically was recovering from a series of nervous breakdowns when cast in the part of an everyday guy who loses all sense of fair play when a fortune is at stake and he feels others are trying to swindle him. Winters was originally intent on performing his own stunts until he strained his back. The slightly built Stang was suffering from a broken left arm which he keeps immobile and gloved throughout the scene. Stang was a late replacement for comedian Jackie Mason, who was forced to bow out due to a prior commitment. For the action sequences, Stang is doubled liberally by Janos Prohaska. Kaplan is doubled by Bill Maxwell.

Weeks of pre-production went into the planning and rigging of this scene, which was completed in two days on location near Palm Springs at a specially constructed building. When Winters leaves, he backs his truck into a water tower that falls and takes out the station's last standing piece. The entire sequence was a triumph of creativity, but in filming this last bit the timing was slightly off and the last wall began falling before the tower hit. Special effects technician Linwood Dunn was able to correct this error without needing a retake. He merely split the screen, slightly slowing one side of the frame until when joined together with an optical printer the event appeared to take place in regular time and in logical order.

See: DVD extra *Something a Little Less Serious: A Tribute to* It's a Mad Mad Mad Mad World (1991).

THE MUDPIT BRAWL in *McLintock!* (1963)

An entertaining Andrew McLaglen–directed comedy-western, scripted by James Edward Grant,

McLintock! re-teams John Wayne and Maureen O'Hara as a long-separated though still warring couple intending to divorce but ultimately coming together by film's end. Producer-star Wayne is larger than life cattle baron G.W. McLintock, a role that fits him like a glove. At this point of his career, Wayne knew what his fans wanted, and he delivers his patented formula to a tee. The cast and crew are full of Wayne's family and friends, and the highlight is a giant slapstick battle between cowboys and homesteaders around a pit of mud. Cinematographer William Clothier was expert at filming colorful outdoor action scenes, and Otho Lovering synchronizes the footage superbly. Costumer Luster Bayless aids their effort by dressing his principals in bright, distinctive clothes so they will be easier to pick out of the large crowd of fighters. It's justifiably become one of the movies' most famous fights. *Time* wrote, "The highlight of the season is apt to be a free-for-all that ends with half the territory slugging it out hip-deep in a mud hole." *Cinema Retro* says the "highlight of the film is the famous mud pit fight scene which is amusing despite being predictable," while film historian Leonard Maltin adds, "There was never a brawl quite like the one in *McLintock!*"

Wayne gets the fight started by having a confrontation with an irate Leo Gordon, who keeps sticking a rifle into Wayne's belly while issuing threats. When Wayne can stand no more, he takes the gun from Gordon and intones, "Somebody ought to belt you in the mouth, but *I* won't. *I* won't." Wayne turns to leave, then declares, "The hell I won't." He rears back and launches a giant left cross that upends Gordon and sends him tumbling down the muddy hill into the water pooled at the bottom. It's one of filmdom's most iconic punches. In fact, *The Big Damn Book of Sheer Manliness* declares it "the greatest roundhouse in history." Chill Wills, Jack Kruschen, Patrick Wayne, Edward Faulkner, Strother Martin and many more get into the fight, and most end up riding down the hill into the mud.

The fight was filmed south of Tucson, Arizona, near the Mexican border town of Nogales. A clay pit with a 50-foot decline was first prepared by laying down gunite, a mixture of cement, sand and water that's customarily used to line swimming pools. Two tons of bentonite was brought in and put atop the gunite. The bentonite was absorbent aluminum silicate clay formed from volcanic ash, slippery in texture and resembling chocolate syrup. It was regularly used in oil well drilling to reduce friction. It provided the filmmakers an appropriate sliding surface (actual mud was too sticky for a smooth descent). O'Hara thought the concoction resembled bird poop while Wayne likened it to snot. The scene's total cost was $50,000.

United Artists publicity claimed the fight featured the largest collection of stuntmen ever gathered for one motion picture, with over 100 including stunt extras. Cliff Lyons coordinated the action with assistance from up-and-coming Hal Needham. Even Wayne had a hand in setting up and choreographing the punches. Among those taking part were Chuck Roberson, Chuck Hayward, Boyd "Red" Morgan, Roy Jenson, Loren Janes, Dean Smith, Jerry Gatlin, Jim Burk, Tom Steele, Harvey Parry, Paul Stader, Buddy Van Horn, Charles Horvath, Joe Canutt, Tap Canutt, Billy Shannon, Roy Sickner, Buzz Henry, Chuck Courtney, Rudy Robbins, Bob Harris, Jerry Summers, David Cass, Eddy Donno, Quentin Dickey, Jack

Young and Bill Hart. Tom Hennesy throws Strother Martin into an ore car and takes a hat pin in the backside from O'Hara. Aspiring Arizona locals Terry Leonard, Stacy Newton and 17-year-old Neil Summers got their start on the film. Summers, weighing 135 pounds, was paired up with Red Morgan, who was able to fling him like a rag doll down the hill.

Not everyone was eager to take the plunge. The scene was shot over a one-week period in November, and an unusual cold spell moved in on the Sonoran desert location. The first morning was windy and a layer of ice formed on the pool of water. Heaters were brought in to thaw out the ice while cast and crew huddled by gas fires to keep warm. Taking the first trip down the hill and into the icy water was stuntman Roy Jenson, who was doubling for Leo Gordon. Jenson split his head open with his backward flip when he landed hard on the gunite. He required 15 stitches and a trip to the hospital. Jenson's spilled blood sent an immediate shock wave around the set. The stuntmen began clamoring for additional hazard pay and stunt adjustments to make the fall. Since so many were scheduled to enter the mud, Wayne, as producer, saw his budget skyrocket if appropriate action wasn't taken. He boldly announced there was no danger in doing the stunt and to prove his point, both he and Maureen O'Hara would take the plunge. O'Hara, a legendary trooper, immediately approached her trusted friend Chuck Roberson for advice. He assured O'Hara the slide was safe if one slid down on their backside and kept their head raised. A sufficiently satisfied O'Hara promptly took the plunge to the amazement of everyone around. The Indian extras bowed in her presence. Against the wishes of the insurance men, Wayne quickly followed suit. Gordon took the next spill. At that point the stuntmen were shamed into going into the mud without any additional money paid out. Jenson's fall was the only injury incurred, although Strother Martin's double Dean Smith suffered an ear infection from the cold water.

The mass brawl continues atop the hill as John Wayne slides into the mud to join Maureen O'Hara in United Artists' *McLintock!* (1963).

Although she did the fall into the mud herself, O'Hara had a stuntwoman on the set named Lucille House. Wayne had stuntman Loren Janes dress in O'Hara's clothing and do an additional take of the fall due to the many heavy bodies thrashing about in the thick of the fight. A protective Wayne warned all the stuntmen he'd personally throw anyone into the mud who so much as touched O'Hara during the action. A common joke on the set was the phrase, "Here's mud in your eye!" At one point, a glob of mud landed on the lens of Clothier's camera.

See: Johnson, Erskine. "Wayne, Maureen O'Hara Prove Top Filming Mudders." *Times Daily.* December 5, 1962; *McLintock!* DVD extra *A Good Ol' Fashion Fight; McLintock!* pressbook.

THE BEER LOUNGE BRAWL in *Soldier in the Rain* (1963)

Ralph Nelson's *Soldier in the Rain* is an odd mix of comedy and drama about friendship between upstart dreamer Steve McQueen and career military man Jackie Gleason. Effective in parts, bewildering in others, it's best-known today for the all-out beer lounge brawl between McQueen and soldiers Ed Nelson and Lew Gallo, who tease him about his dog dying. *Variety* called it "as brutal a fight scene as may ever have been staged on celluloid." *Cinema Retro* declares it "one of the screen's best brawl sequences, rivaling even that great poolroom scene in Clint Eastwood's *Coogan's Bluff.*"

When the unfair double-team of Nelson and Gallo begin to overpower McQueen, huge Gleason comes to the rescue, using his strength to literally hoist Nelson over his head and slam him to a table, tumbling to the floor himself. All the actors' bodies contort at odd angles throughout the furniture-smashing fight, including an impressive end-over-end flip of Nelson's stuntman Howard Curtis. The fight concludes with McQueen delivering a now-famous running side jump-kick and putting Nelson into a headlock. All the action is too much for the overweight Gleason as he suffers a heart attack from the strain.

Dick Crockett was stunt coordinator of this unconventional two-minute fight, which took three days to film. Director Nelson, D.P. Philip Lathrop

and editor Ralph Winters keep the participants' identities well concealed. Vince Deadrick and Loren Janes were McQueen's stuntmen, although McQueen takes several surprisingly rough bumps. Guy Way was the heavyset Gleason's regular double. A wire was rigged up to aid them in hoisting Curtis into the air. Nelson ended up with plenty of bumps and bruises and a strained back, while McQueen received a slightly blackened eye.

An honorary member of the Stuntmen's Association, 5'10", 165-pound Marine Steve McQueen had few extended fights on film, ironic considering his screen image as a tough guy. Even on his TV western *Wanted—Dead or Alive* (1958–1962), he often turned his bounty hunter Josh Randall's fight action over to his doubles. One of his most noteworthy fights was the brief one he had with Nick Adams and Michael Landon in 1958's "The Martin Poster." In 1960's "Black Belt," he fought karate expert Robert Kino. McQueen studied martial arts with Ed Parker, Bruce Lee, Chuck Norris, Bob Wall and Pat Johnson, becoming proficient but never testing for a black belt. His thinking was, if he had a real fight, black belt status could be used against him in a lawsuit.

The short-tempered McQueen had many street fights, and the real-life experience flavored the choreography of his movie fights. He often fought dirty or tried to find a quick equalizer such as the razors he pulled on Ron Soble in *The Cincinnati Kid* (1965) and Fred Lerner in *Papillon* (1973). It brought a sense of danger and realism often lacking in the traditional heroic screen brawl.

Steve McQueen (center) battles Ed Nelson (left) and Lew Gallo in Allied Artists' *Soldier in the Rain* (1963).

McQueen's fights often had life-or-death conse- quences such as his knife fight with Martin Landau in *Nevada Smith* (1966). His best fights came against John Daheim and Roy Jenson in *Baby, the Rain Must Fall* (1965) and Karl Schueneman in *The Hunter* (1980).

See: Nelson, Ed, and Alvin M. Cotlar. *Beyond Peyton Place*. Tarentum, PA: Word Association, 2008; Sydenham, Richard. *Steve McQueen: The Cooler King: His Life Through His Films*. Birming- ham: Big Star, 2013; Terrill, Marshall. *Steve Mc- Queen: Portrait of an American Rebel*. New York: Dutton, 1994.

CARY GRANT vs. GEORGE KENNEDY in *Charade* (1963)

An enjoyable light suspense thriller from direc- tor Stanley Donen, *Charade* concerns mystery man Cary Grant acting as protector for widow Au- drey Hepburn while her husband's ex-accomplices close in on the whereabouts of a $250,000 World War II heist. Hulking, trenchcoat-clad menace George Kennedy, complete with metal claw for a right hand, is the most threatening bad guy. He corners Grant atop the American Express building in Paris and orders him to step off. Grant has other ideas. What follows is a riveting one-minute fight atop a slippery and slanted rooftop that sees Kennedy throwing menacing blows with his hook that look like they will rip Grant's head off. The entire sequence is superbly edited by James Clark. *Variety* termed it "a real gasper." According to *Mag- ill's*, the fight "stands as a perfect example of the combination of suspense and wit which makes *Charade* such a delight to watch."

The 61-year-old Grant, a former acrobat, sur- prises with his agility and use of kicks as the two push each other around the building's neon sign, and Grant almost goes over the edge. Grant suf- fered a few minor injuries during the fight, which according to him was par for the course through- out his career. The 6'4", 240-pound Kennedy rips a bloody and painful swath across Grant's back as the film deftly mixes violence with its comedy. Kennedy ultimately loses his balance with one of his Henry Mancini–punctuated swings and goes sliding down the roof with sparks flying from his metal hand. His hook catches the eave, allowing him to exchange witty barbs with Grant from Peter Stone's screenplay. Oscar-nominated composer Mancini intentionally left the entire fight sequence unscored, but in his final cut Donen opted to use a tiny bit of suspenseful vibraphone from an earlier scene.

The fighting style the 6'1", 180-pound Grant employs is known as Savate. It's a French martial art utilizing the feet and hands in the form of graceful kicks and open-handed slaps. It was a common streetfighting technique in Paris since the 19th century, popular because it avoided using a closed fist. Basque Zipota, a variation of Savate, could previously be seen in *Thunder in the Sun* (1959). Unfortunately, Donen felt the French stuntmen on *Charade* were using it too much and American audiences wouldn't accept the unfamil- iar idea of two U.S. men slapping and kicking. Iron- ically, savate was effectively showcased as the fight- ing style displayed by Robert Loggia on the TV series *T.H.E. Cat* (1966–1967). Paul Stader was brought from the States to Americanize the fight and double Grant over French stuntman Yvan Chiffre. Stader recruited a French professional wrestler familiar with both fighting styles to dou- ble Kennedy. The rooftop itself was a studio set built 30 feet above the stage floor. It was the most fisticuffs Grant had engaged in since *Gunga Din* (1939), where he took a mighty Victor McLaglen uppercut to the jaw that knocked him out cold. He had earlier engaged in one of the screen's first ju- jitsu throws with Dell Henderson in *The Awful Truth* (1937).

George Kennedy's imposing size landed him tons of work in the early 1960s as a fight partner with TV heroes such as Clint Walker on *Cheyenne*, Richard Boone on *Have Gun—Will Travel*, James Arness on *Gunsmoke* and Fess Parker on *Daniel Boone*. World War II combat veteran Kennedy was eager to please and often did his own fights for the camera. He was proud he never made contact with any actors he worked with. When James Stewart needed a sarcastic mouth to punch in *The Flight of the Phoenix* (1965) or John Wayne needed a mean face to clobber with an axe handle in *The Sons of Katie Elder* (1965), Kennedy was their man. He was still working to better himself on his fight technique even into the 1970s when he began studying Gosoku-ryu karate with Tak Kubota.

Notable fights came in *Lonely Are the Brave* (1962), *Cool Hand Luke* (1967) and *The Good Guys and the Bad Guys* (1969) (see entries). Fights of interest came against Gregory Peck in *Mirage* (1965), Peter Graves in *The Ballad of Josie* (1967), James Garner in *The Pink Jungle* (1968), Clint Eastwood in *Thunderbolt and Lightfoot* (1974), Dave Cass in *Earthquake* (1974) and Thomas

Hunter in *The Human Factor* (1975). His best TV battles came against Darren McGavin in 1960's *Riverboat* episode "River Champion," Dan Blocker in 1961's *Bonanza* episode "The Infernal Machine" and Charles Bronson in 1965's *Virginian* episode "Nobility of Kings."

See: Caps, John. *Henry Mancini: Reinventing Film Music*. Urbana: University of Illinois Press, 2012; Kennedy, George. *Trust Me: A Memoir*. New York: Applause, 2011; Nelson, Nancy. *Evenings with Cary Grant*. New York: Citadel, 2003.

FRANK SINATRA VS. DEAN MARTIN in *4 for Texas* (1963)

The satiric western *4 for Texas* is the best opportunity to see Rat Pack leaders Frank Sinatra and Dean Martin beat up one another on the big screen. They seem to be having fun doing so, although much of the tongue-in-cheek action in the finale is handled in long shot by stunt doubles in what the *Jersey Journal* termed "a great fight."

The cool crooners play wisecracking rivals vying for control of a gambling boat in 1870s Galveston, Texas. The movie manages to be entertaining enough, but is far from director Robert Aldrich's best work. Aldrich wasn't happy making the picture as he continually clashed with Sinatra's ego. Sinatra would only film one take and was sometimes gone for days. The two weren't even on speaking terms as the shoot progressed. Aldrich figured Sinatra spent 80 working hours as the star of a film that shot for 37 days.

Given those figures, it is likely Sinatra winged much of the fight without extensive rehearsal time. At least a few minor injuries were incurred. Martin forgot to duck and took a Sinatra punch to the jaw that put him on his back. Sinatra reached down to help him up but Martin good-naturedly bit Sinatra's ankle. It wasn't only the principals and stuntmen who were in danger. When director Aldrich attempted to show how he wanted Sinatra to be knocked through a warehouse door, he backed into an exposed nail on the door. It pierced his shoulder, requiring a nurse and a precautionary tetanus shot. Veteran cameramen Joseph Biroc, Carl Guthrie and Burnett Guffey assisted D.P. Ernest Las-

zlo with the second unit photography. Editor Michael Luciano was tasked with cutting together the reels of footage while Nelson Riddle provided the score.

The fight becomes a huge rumble on the wharf between dozens of men who unite to take on bad guy Charles Bronson and his gang. John Indrisano coordinated the large-scale action. At Sinatra's invitation, a great crowd of onlookers showed up at Warner Bros. to watch the battle. Stuntmen and former boxers included Hal Needham, Ronnie Rondell, Jr., Paul Stader, Chuck Roberson, Chuck Hayward, Roy Jenson, Chuck Hicks, Gene LeBell, Clyde Howdy, John Hudkins, Bennie Dobbins, Charles Horvath, Fred Carson, Jack Perkins, Charlie Picerni, Marvin Willens, Bill Catching, Leroy Johnson, George Orrison, Stephen Burnette, Larry Duran, Victor Paul, Richard Geary, Joe Brooks, Sol Gorss, Tom Steele, Joe Yrigoyen, Ray Spiker, Charles Sullivan, Gil Perkins, Victor Romito, Joe Ploski, Mike Lally, John Roy, Matty Jordan, Harry Wilson, Noble "Kid" Chissell, Mushy Callahan, Al Bain, Ralph Volkie, Sammy Snatch, Jack Gordon and George DeNormand. Character greats Mike Mazurki and Richard Jaeckel take part in the riverboat melee, as do diminutive Nick Dennis and towering Edric Connor. In an earlier comic fight, Dennis and Connor come to the aid of Martin against Mazurki and goons Harvey Parry, Gil Perkins and Fred Scheiwiller. Martin also has a fight with Jaeckel, knocking the tough guy off a second floor balcony.

Frank Sinatra reacts to a Dean Martin punch in Warner Bros.' *4 for Texas* (1963).

Mazurki had the opportunity to body slam one of Martin's men and chose a professional wrestler named Gene LeBell. The problem was that LeBell was already playing one of Sinatra's men, so he switched costumes and can be seen fighting on both sides throughout the action. Mazurki slammed LeBell to the ground, and when the assistant director asked the respected veteran how he liked the take, Mazurki said that he didn't. They did another take and again Mazurki didn't like it. On the third take, Mazurki was satisfied with the slam. In private, LeBell asked Mazurki what was wrong with the first slam. "Nothing," replied Mazurki as he lit up a cigar. LeBell realized that Mazurki had made him an extra $300 for each slam. LeBell sent Mazurki a box of cigars every year for his birthday.

Dean Martin (5'11", 175 pounds) boxed as welterweight Kid Crochet in his teens to a 1–11 record. Although his fight career was undistinguished, the experience served him well for his future in Hollywood. Legend has it that no one informed Martin he was supposed to fake punches in his first screen fight and he knocked out Don DeFore's tooth in My Friend Irma (1949). Martin later picked up some martial arts moves, from Bruce Lee no less, for his series of Matt Helm films in the 1960s. Martin played up the public image of being a boozer, but in reality he was a strict professional well-liked by stuntmen and crews for his humor and generosity. When a nervous Chuck Norris, in his film debut, accidentally kicked him in the shoulder on The Wrecking Crew (1969), Martin simply shrugged it off and was quicker to duck on the next take.

Notable fights include Sergeants 3 (1962), The Sons of Katie Elder (1965), Rough Night in Jericho (1967) and The Cannonball Run (1981) (see entries). Fights of interest came against Jeff Morrow in Pardners (1956), Ric Roman in Some Came Running (1958), Claude Akins in Rio Bravo (1959), Tom Reese in Murderers' Row (1966), Alain Delon in Texas Across the River (1966), Roy Jenson in The Ambushers (1967), Roddy McDowall in 5 Card Stud (1968), Pepper Martin in The Wrecking Crew (1969), Brian Keith in Something Big (1971) and Thalmus Rasulala and John Quade in Mr. Ricco (1975).

See: Alpert, Don. "One-Punch Martin: Color Him Unconcerned." Los Angeles Times. July 21, 1963; "On the Star View Screen." Southeast Missourian. May 22, 1964; Tosches, Nick. Dino: Living High in the Dirty Business of Dreams. New York: Delta, 1992.

ALAN LADD VS. GEORGE PEPPARD in The Carpetbaggers (1964)

Harold Robbins' popular novel is turned into an entertainingly trashy soap opera from director Edward Dmytryk. The film climaxes with a 90-second fight in an exquisite suite between cold, ruthless George Peppard and mentor Alan Ladd. Variety warned that it "will make the audience wince." According to The Films of Alan Ladd, it is "one of the most viciously realistic fights in Ladd's long tally of screen brawls," while Films and Filming agreed that it was "one of the goriest Ladd had ever endured." USA Today ranks it among the ten greatest fights ever filmed.

However, the fight isn't without its negatives. The furniture-smashing, glass-breaking and lip-bloodying gets so brutal that stuntmen Glenn Wilder and Paul Baxley are clearly visible throughout. Their obvious presence threatens to take the viewer out of the film. For that, Frank Bracht's editing must be faulted. Lapses in continuity occur. Wilder reaches for a fire poker with his right hand, but the film cuts to Peppard picking it up with his left. Dmytryk and Duke Callaghan's camera staging even catches a few missed punches with accompanying sound effects signaling bullseyes. There's an oddly missed punch where Peppard hurts his hand that makes the viewer wonder what exactly he was aiming at as Ladd is dazed and makes no effort to move away. Other than that, the fight routine put on by the stuntmen is enthusiastically staged.

The actors portray thinly disguised versions of multi-millionaire Howard Hughes and cowboy film star Tom Mix. An ailing Ladd appears a shell of his former handsome self. He died of an alcohol and barbiturate combo shortly after finishing this movie. Nevertheless, he gives a good performance as the aging movie star and is still up for throwing punches. One of the best touches has Ladd locking the door to the suite before the fight in anticipation of the action to follow. Highlights include Ladd (Baxley) flipping over tables and couches, Peppard swinging the fire poker, and Ladd laying Peppard out on a dining table. He pulls the tablecloth over Peppard and pummels him for the win. Ladd, with a bleeding cheek and shirt drenched in sweat applied by makeup artist Wally Westmore, pours a stiff drink at the fight's conclusion as Elmer Bernstein's score is cued up.

The role of the makeup artist isn't always apparent in a fight. Outside a bit of fake blood applied to the lip and a mist of sweat from a spritzer bottle, some films get by with minimal contribution from this department. Their expertise is more apt to be called upon for the fight's aftereffects such as bruises, swelling and the presence of fresh or healing cuts. For this reason, basic medical knowledge aids in authenticating the injuries. Stage blood can be manufactured in a variety of ways but is most commonly Karo corn syrup and red food coloring. Thick Ketchup is an old standby but can stain wardrobe. In black-and-white days, it was simply red, blue and black greasepaint. Perspiration is typically a mixture of water and glycerine.

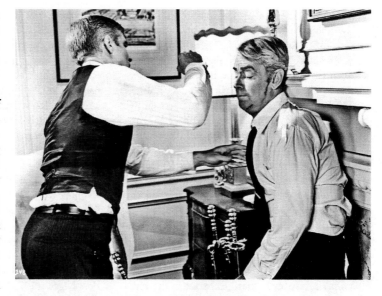

George Peppard takes a swing at Alan Ladd in Paramount's *The Carpetbaggers* (1964).

Six-foot, 175-pound George Peppard was a former Marine making a run at movie stardom. The former construction worker was considered one of the bright stars of tomorrow before settling into second-tier features as a quick-with-his-fists leading man. His reputation for surliness and fighting with producers undermined his career. He was the man originally cast as Blake Carrington on the early 1980s TV series *Dynasty*. He had filmed fights with co-star Bo Hopkins before the network opted to replace the testy star with John Forsythe. The fight scenes were redone with Hopkins and a stuntman filling in for the older Forsythe.

Peppard fought George Hamilton in *Home from the Hill* (1960), Arte Johnson in *The Third Day* (1965), Rock Hudson in *Tobruk* (1967), Slim Pickens in *Rough Night in Jericho* (1967) (see entry), H.B. Haggerty in *P.J.* (1968), Robert F. Lyons in *Pendulum* (1969), George Baker in *The Executioner* (1970), Don Gordon in *Cannon for Cordoba* (1970) and Steve Sandor in *One More Train to Rob* (1971). His best role came in the enjoyable TV mystery *Banacek* (1972–1974) where in 1973 Peppard outwitted giant Ted Cassidy in a junkyard in "Ten Thousand Dollars a Page" and proved agile enough to elude a Don Stroud kick aimed at his head in "No Stone Unturned." Peppard later starred in the silly action TV series *The A-Team* (1983–1987), dirtying his leather gloves with the occasional punch-up.

See: "George's Violent World." *Beaver County Times.* February 26, 1970; Henry, Marilyn, and Ron DeSourdis. *The Films of Alan Ladd.* Secaucus, NJ: Citadel, 1981; "Movie Makeup Men Have to Know How to De-Glamorize." *Nebraska State Journal.* May 14, 1944.

THE SALOON BRAWL in *Mail Order Bride* (1964)

Writer-director Burt Kennedy's slight but picturesque MGM western comedy *Mail Order Bride* features the kind of good-natured cowboy brawl in which everyone present in the bar Kate's Place gets in on two minutes of spirited fisticuffs no matter whether they are friend, foe or complete stranger. Kennedy felt it was nearly obligatory for a western to include a saloon brawl and his film doesn't disappoint. It's professionally done by the best stuntmen in the business. The *Anniston Star* wrote that Kennedy "kept the action at a fast pace with plenty of excitement in such scenes as a free-for-all chair-flying saloon brawl." There are few comic sight gags, including a man with a broken chair fitted over his head and a cowboy who forms a tower on another's shoulders only to be punched onto a table.

Retired gunfighter Buddy Ebsen sets events in motion while observing a card game involving Keir Dullea and his drinking buddy Warren Oates. Fulfilling a promise to Dullea's dead father, Ebsen wants the irresponsible young man out of the bar so he can provide him with both a land deed and a new wife. Through the power of suggestion, Oates is soon walloping on Dullea. Stunt actor Chuck Roberson announces "Fight!" and smashes a chair into the mirror behind the bar.

Cattle thief Oates' rowdy friends William Smith, Tony Epper, Billy Shannon and Jack Coffer begin punching everyone in the bar as well as each other. Smith does his own fighting while the three supporting players were all stunt actors. The 5'11", 175-pound Oates was a Marine and reveled in doing as much fake fighting as Kennedy would allow. Among the stuntmen taking part in the comic action are Hal Needham, Henry Wills, Roy Jenson, Bill Hart, Al Wyatt, Cliff Lyons, Pete Kellett and stunt coordinator Buzz Henry. The film is similar in look and feel to Sam Peckinpah's lyrical *Ride the High Country* (1962), which was made by this film's producer Richard E. Lyons in the High Sierras. Composer George Bassman (who provided a whimsical score for the fight) and editor Frank Santillo were also employed on both films.

As a screen fighter, former Air Force boxing and weightlifting champion William Smith had few peers. He could throw punches and sell emotional reaction shots with the best of them. A superb physical actor, Smith registered great anger on his face during a fight and never failed to verbally enhance a scene with his guttural fighting roar and throaty punch-induced gasps. His expert timing and quickness for a big man took him to another level. Instead of throwing the traditional roundhouse haymaker, the 6'2", 210-pound Smith delivered short, straight blows that appeared to hit dead-on but in actuality pulled up a fraction short of their target. Tutored by Jock Mahoney, Smith mastered the technique on the fight-heavy Universal TV Western *Laredo* (1965–1967), which employed many top stuntmen. Smith worked with them closely and was able to do all his own fighting without the need for a double. Despite his rippling muscles, the former semi-pro football player moved with an assured and explosive athleticism recalling Errol Flynn. Although he possessed leading man looks, Smith was a tremendous screen heavy. He was also a world-class arm-wrestling champ; his 18" arms looked like they could tear off limbs and instantly struck fear in many an opponent.

Smith studied martial arts extensively during the 1960s, working on San Soo Kung Fu with Jimmy Woo and Kenpo with Ed Parker. Smith often used devastatingly powerful knees and elbows in his fights. He nearly starred in both *Enter the Dragon* (1973) (see entry) and TV's *Kung Fu,* filming a test pilot fight with stuntman Paul Nuckles. Wearing prosthetic eye makeup, he was so convincingly menacing that the producers feared he would frighten audiences away. He had a starring role as a karate-fighting U.S. Marine in *Tiger Cage* (1974) which went unreleased. In *Blood and Guts* (1978), Smith played an aging pro wrestler and did all his own ring action. He was an honorary member of the Stuntmen's Association.

Notable fights include *Darker Than Amber* (1970), *C.C. and Company* (1970), *Grave of the Vampire* (1972), *Black Samson* (1974) and *Any Which Way You Can* (1980) (see entries). Fights of interest came against Tony Randall in *The Mating Game* (1959), Michael Haynes in *Chrome and Hot Leather* (1971), Peter Brown in *Piranha* (1972), Fred Williamson in *Hammer* (1972) and *Boss Nigger* (1975), Mickey Caruso in *Invasion of the Bee Girls* (1973), Richard Harris in *The Deadly Trackers* (1973), Yul Brynner in *The Ultimate Warrior* (1975), Cesare Danova in *Scorchy* (1976), Jude Farese in *Hollywood Man* (1976), Gary Busey in *Eye of the Tiger* (1986) and Dan Haggerty in *Spirit of the Eagle* (1991). He was memorable portraying Arnold Schwarzenegger's sword-wielding father in *Conan the Barbarian* (1982). On TV, he portrayed the hated villain Falconetti on the groundbreaking mini-series *Rich Man, Poor Man* (1976) and had an unforgettable fight with Nick Nolte in the cargo hold of a ship. Other TV fights of note came against James Arness in the 1972 *Gunsmoke* episode "Hostage," David Carradine in the 1973 *Kung Fu* "The Chalice," James Naughton in the 1974 *Planet of the Apes* "The Gladiators," Jack Palance in the 1975 *Bronk* "Wheel of Death," Mr. T in the 1983 *A-Team* "Pros and Cons" and Sam Elliott in the final episode of 1984's *The Yellow Rose.* On the 1985 *Simon and Simon* episode "Quint Is Out," he beat star Gerald McRaney to within an inch of his life.

See: Compo, Susan. *Warren Oates: A Wild Life.* Lexington: University Press of Kentucky, 2009; Liederman, Earl. "Hollywood He-Man: Bill Smith." *Strength & Health.* June 1961; Stout, Jerry. "What Do You Say to a Naked Lady?" *Fighting Stars.* June 1974.

SEAN CONNERY VS. HAROLD SAKATA in *Goldfinger* (1964)

This justifiably famous James Bond fight has Sean Connery taking on the prototypical subordinate villain Harold Sakata as Goldfinger's mute Korean henchman Oddjob. The four-minute battle sees the two squaring off in the gold environs of Fort Knox, with the grinning, massively built Sakata utilizing his deadly steel-rimmed bowler derby as a Frisbee aimed at Connery's head (a skill that took Sakata several weeks to master). This time, unlike *From Russia with Love*, Connery is without a doubt the underdog. Sakata's immense strength has been established earlier by screenwriters Richard Maibaum and Paul Dehn when he lifted a couch and hurled it at Connery. Nothing Connery does fazes Sakata, and he is tossed around like a rag doll by the composed killer. Connery's punches are repeatedly countered by Sakata chops, nerve holds and throws. Even a gold brick to the chest doesn't bother Sakata. He is one of cinema's first seemingly unstoppable killers.

Sean Connery uses everything at his disposal to fend off Harold Sakata in United Artists' *Goldfinger* (1964).

Despite the absence of a background score, the exciting fight is one of the Bond series' most popular segments, and Guy Hamilton's *Goldfinger* is often regarded as the most classically entertaining Bond film. Peter Hunt's fast-paced cutting brought a definitive visual sense to the Bond films by eliminating all wasteful movement and was a key component to their success with audiences. *The Films of Sean Connery* declares that Hunt's deft editing "continues to amaze, with the fight scenes in particular cut with astounding technique." The *New York Times* called the *Goldfinger* fight "spinningly staged and enacted, dripping in cliffhanging suspense." *The Complete James Bond Movie Encyclopedia* termed the fight "legendary," while *Kiss Kiss, Bang Bang* referred to it as "extremely hard-hitting." *James Bond in the Cinema* declared that the fight "must rate as some kind of cinematic landmark," and *The Manly Movie Guide* described it as "a thrilling bout of hand-to-hand combat."

The Fort Knox vault room fight took place on an elaborate Pinewood Studios set built by production designer Ken Adam and art director Peter Murton. The filmmakers were never allowed to see inside the real Kentucky gold depository for

reference. Stuntman Bob Simmons doubled Connery and coordinated the fight, with an assist from Gerry Crampton. Simmons was shorter than Connery and matched up better with Sakata when it came to height in the long shots. Sakata performed all his own stunts, including the impressive unbroken final fall onto his chest. The electrocution scene required two takes, a close-up and a medium shot. The pyrotechnics were achieved with the use of fireworks, and Sakata received painful burns on his hand in the close-up. He wouldn't release his grip because director Hamilton had not yet called cut. Sakata was offered an asbestos glove for the medium shot, which he refused to wear. In that shot, a spark went into the seat of his pants, making the agony he showed on camera real. Connery received a back injury which briefly delayed filming. He used the injury to his financial advantage in negotiating for the next film in the series, *Thunderball* (1965).

Of Japanese descent, the 5'10", 225-pound Sakata was a Hawaiian weightlifting champion turned professional wrestler billed as Tosh Togo. After *Goldfinger*, he incorporated the moniker Oddjob into his professional name for all future film roles and wrestling appearances. Connery also engages in a memorable pre-credits fight sequence with British stuntman Alf Joint who portrays the assassin Capungo. Connery throws Joint into a bathtub, where he is electrocuted and Connery quips, "Shocking." *The Spy Who Thrilled Us* calls this fight one of the best in the Bond series. Connery and co-star Honor Blackman received judo training from Joe Robinson. The judo flip Blackman exhibits on screen proved so popular with audiences that it became a regular move for stuntmen in their fight routines. In honor of her character, they commonly referred to it as the Pussy Galore. Blackman even appeared on *The Tonight Show* in 1966 with Johnny Carson specifically to flip the host.

See: Chick, Bob. "Derby Opened Door." *Evening Independent.* June 8, 1973; *Goldfinger* DVD special features; "Interview: Sean Connery." *Playboy.* November 1965; Kyriazi, Paul. *How to Live the James Bond Lifestyle.* Amazon, 2012.

THE BROTHERS BRAWL in *The Sons of Katie Elder* (1965)

In the fall of 1964, John Wayne fought the greatest fight of his life … against cancer. A golf ball–sized tumor was discovered in his left lung, requiring the total removal of the organ during a six-hour surgery in October. Wayne's handlers thought his career was over, but Wayne was determined to prove them wrong. An unknowing public believed Wayne was simply having fluid removed from a lung due to an old football injury. When he left the hospital, Wayne found the strength to rise from his wheelchair despite his weakened condition and the painful scar along his left side. Walking under his own power to the waiting limo, he stopped to shake hands with fans and smile for the reporters. Inside the limo, an oxygen tank was waiting for the exhausted star. Wayne's latest scheduled western, Henry Hathaway's *The Sons of Katie Elder* (1965), was pushed back indefinitely. The doctors told Wayne to engage in no strenuous activity for six months. However, he was itching to shoot the film after four. He was also ready to come clean with the public and let them know he had licked the Big C in hopes that others would realize that the diagnosis wasn't an automatic death sentence. The announcement that Wayne had conquered cancer increased his larger-than-life status with fans and made him more myth than man.

The screen fight with Dean Martin, Earl Holliman and Michael Anderson, Jr., would prove to the public and the industry that Wayne could still handle action. He was determined to do as much as possible without stunt double Chuck Roberson

and was prodded along by director Hathaway. Oxygen was always close by, particularly since much of the film was shot in the high elevations of Durango, Mexico. Wayne came through the humor-filled fight with flying colors, as the bickering brothers turn on one another over breakfast after Wayne refuses to be suckered into a poor-odds gunfight with George Kennedy. Martin was doubled by Henry Wills in the fight more than Wayne by Roberson. Loren Janes was there for Anderson and Jerry Gatlin on hand for Holliman in rehearsals, but those two actors do all their own fight for Lucien Ballard's camera. The slightly built Anderson spends a great portion of the fight on Wayne's back. A double punch from the floor memorably sends Wayne (actually Roberson) crashing out the front door. Martin also fights Jeremy Slate in the film while Wayne drops Kennedy with an axe-handle to the face. Roberson took the hit for Kennedy. *The Michigan Daily* termed the fight "exciting," while *Stage Combat* calls it "a great brawl."

See: Didion, Joan. *Slouching Toward Bethlehem.* Zola, 2013; Leydon, Joe. "Gritty Effort." *Cowboys & Indians.* April 2015; Wayne, John. "True Courage: Now I Know What It Means." *Lewiston Daily Sun.* February 22, 1975.

THE BORACHO SALOON BRAWL in *The Great Race* (1965)

Blake Edwards' large-scale Warner Bros. extravaganza went wildly over-budget in bringing its madcap zaniness to the screen. Everything about the two-and-a-half-hour film is done to the max, especially the comic saloon brawl in the western town of Boracho that *Film Daily* described as "a bruising brawl staged with force and exaggeration," and the *Los Angeles Herald Examiner* remarked was "a saloon fight the like of which has never been seen on the screen." *Action Films* writes it's "one of the great all-out western bar fights," while *Westways* declares it "the barroom brawl to end all barroom brawls." The scene took two weeks to film and is meant not only to parody *Dodge City* but rival it as dozens of stuntmen and stuntwomen punch their way across the camera. Tony Curtis and Jack Lemmon are the opposing stars with comedian Larry Storch figuring prominently as the droopy-mustached heavy Texas Jack. Everyone in the scene winds up with a black eye except Curtis. He plays The Great Leslie, immaculate in a white suit and gleaming teeth. None of set decorator

Larry Storch takes one on the chin from Tony Curtis in Warner Bros.' *The Great Race* (1965).

George James Hopkins' furniture remains intact. Later there's the largest pie fight ever filmed with over 2500 pies heaved about the screen. Miraculously, Curtis manages to keep his white suit spotless until the end.

Stunt coordinator Dick Crockett put the saloon brawl together. It's an inspired creation, full of whimsy, expert timing and mass destruction. Two men behind the bar throw slow-motion punches at one another that miss by more than a foot, an obvious in-joke created by Edwards and cameraman Russell Harlan and left intact by editor Ralph Winters. The entire fight is a tribute to Republic's crack stunt team of the 1940s, and many fondly remembered Cousins are employed including Dave Sharpe, Dale Van Sickel and Tom Steele. Stunt doubles for the action include Sharpe for Curtis, Van Sickel for Keenan Wynn and Jerry Summers for Larry Storch. Stunt actors Charles Horvath, Jack Perkins and Alex Sharp figure prominently as mustached henchmen. Roy Jenson delivers one of the fight's first punches and can be spied playing another character later on. Even Blake Edwards can be spotted slugging someone who bumps into him near the bar. Assistant director Mickey McCardle, a former stuntman, also shows up during the fight as a cowboy.

Highlights include Robert Hoy, Richard Farnsworth, Troy Melton and Dean Smith having a balcony cut out from underneath them and Summers taking a high fall after stepping out a door where a balcony used to be. Hal Needham takes a leap into a pile of stuntmen, but Dave Sharpe steals the show with a fantastic dive over a railing onto Gil Perkins, Joe Yrigoyen and Reg Parton. It's the equal to the great leaps he was performing 25 years earlier. Other stuntmen in the scene include Chuck Hicks, Paul Stader, Al Wyatt, Boyd "Red" Morgan, Sol Gorss, Bill Catching, Bill Hickman, Bobby Rose, Dick Geary, Wally Rose, Jerry Catron, Ronnie Rondell, Jr., Howard Curtis, John Hudkins, Dick Dial, John Moio, Joe Canutt, Walter Wyatt, Danny Sands, Bill Couch, Larry Duran, Paul Nuckles, Rod McGaughy, Joe Ferrante, Carl Sklover and Carey Loftin. Stuntwomen on hand as saloon maidens and dancehall girls who join the fighting are Helen Thurston, Sharon Lucas, Donna Hall, Stephanie Epper, Mary Statler and Patti

Saunders. They're all at the top of their game in this classic. Dick Crockett made his name as the stunt supervisor on Edwards' weekly detective series *Peter Gunn* (1958–1961). Every episode featured top fisticuff action with star Craig Stevens taking on what would become the entire roster of the Stuntmen's Association.

Tony Curtis, 5'9" and 160 pounds, was groomed for stardom by Universal in the early 1950s. It was there the spry Navy veteran was taught boxing by trainer Frankie Van for *Flesh and Fury* (1952). He was also trained in fencing for swashbuckling roles and had judo training under Ramon Ancho. His best fights were performed with a light-hearted gleam in his eye and tongue in cheek. He showcased his comic brawling ability in *Not with My Wife, You Don't* (1966) (see entry).

Curtis fought Lyle Bettger in *Forbidden* (1953), Patrick O'Neal in *The Black Shield of Falworth* (1954), Arthur Kennedy in *The Rawhide Years* (1955), Burt Lancaster in *Trapeze* (1956), Kirk Douglas in *The Vikings* (1958) and *Spartacus* (1960), Frank Sinatra in *Kings Go Forth* (1958), Sidney Poitier in *The Defiant Ones* (1958), James Franciscus in *The Outsider* (1961), Yul Brynner in *Taras Bulba* (1962), Tom Reese in *40 Pounds of Trouble* (1962), Eddie Albert in *Captain Newman, M.D.* (1963) and Charles Bronson in *You Can't Win 'Em All* (1970). On TV, he had entertaining battles with co-star Roger Moore on the *Persuaders* (1970–1971) episodes "Overture" and "Someone Like Me."

See: Malone, Aubrey. *The Defiant One: A Biography of Tony Curtis.* Jefferson, NC: McFarland, 2013; Scott, Vernon. "Crockett Is First Stunt Man to Get Credit on Screen." *The Milwaukee Journal.* February 25, 1961.

Tom Tryon vs. Harve Presnell in *The Glory Guys* (1965)

A tough two-man fight between cavalry officers Tom Tryon and Harve Presnell over female lead Senta Berger takes a backseat to an extended three-minute saloon brawl between troopers and a shady saloon proprietor's burly bouncers in this Arnold Laven western.

Cast as a rapscallion soldier, a young James Caan does all his own fight action. Six-foot-three and 215 pounds, Michael Forest, a boxer at the University of Washington and San Jose State, is cast as a heavy and also performs his own fighting. Another actor allowed to brawl is Slim Pickens,

who was familiar with the stuntmen as he had been one. Being able to place so many actors front and center greatly enhances the highly destructive action as bottle after bottle is smashed over heads. The two-minute head-shaking, leg-wobbling Tryon-Presnell fight won critical praise, with *Films and Filming* declaring it "a splendid fist fight," and *Film Daily* calling it "a bruising brawl, staged with force and exaggeration."

After extensive rehearsal, stunt coordinator Paul Stader oversaw the week-long filming of the saloon brawl featuring stuntmen Jack Perkins, Gil Perkins, Bill Catching, Whitey Hughes, Billy Hughes, Ronnie Rondell, Jr., Bill Coontz, Archie Butler, Sailor Vincent and George Robotham. Working closely with cinematographer James Wong Howe, Stader compared the action to the execution of a well-designed football play. The participants and camera operators had to have their timing down to the split second. Howe used three hand-held cameras to move in close, and found interesting camera placements during the two-man fight. This enabled the 6'4", 190-pound Presnell and the 6'2", 190-pound Tryon to do the bulk of the impressive fisticuffs. Walter Scott and Chuck Bail were available for doubling duties, but the stars were game for the action save for a tumble down the stairs. On several occasions there's emphasis on garnering an audience laugh as both men deliver titanic punches, sending the other backing up nearly 20 feet into fireplaces and closets. The leading roles were originally earmarked for Lee Marvin and James Coburn, a more intriguing screen match-up in a film scripted by the legendary Sam Peckinpah. Hardly anyone remembers the Tryon-Presnell fight, but they put on a fine show.

See: "Dance of Violence." *Deseret News.* July 17, 1965; Wong Howe, James. "Wong Howe Photographs *The Glory Guys.*" *American Cinematographer.* August, 1965.

The Dream Brawl in *Love and Kisses* (1965)

Weekends in early 1960s Hollywood often saw games of touch football played between a team commandeered by Elvis Presley and a squad led by teenage music idol Rick Nelson. They played a competitive game utilizing many athletic actors, stuntmen and college players. Taking the friendly rivalry between the team captains one step further, TV star Nelson tried starring in his own film and outdoing Presley at what he did best: staging a martial arts fight. Nelson's starring debut *Love and Kisses* was written and directed by his father Ozzie Nelson and co-starred Rick's wife Kristin. All were accustomed to portraying themselves weekly on the wholesome family show *The Adventures of Ozzie and Harriet* (1956–1966). Here Rick and Kristin play a young married couple who are forced financially to move in with his parents. Light situational comedy ensues in a film that has a sweet innocence about it until late in the picture when Nelson has a nightmare that his wife has become a stripper. This bizarre scene is something else entirely.

Within the dream, Nelson enters a Tiki bar strip club. He finds his scantily clad wife about to go on stage and protests. This brings about a warning from floor manager Angelo Brovelli and a summons for beefy bouncers Gene LeBell, Bruce Tegner, Guy Way and Fritz Ford. Over the next frenetic two minutes, Nelson executes judo flips, kicks and punches on the bouncers and anyone else who gets in his way. LeBell takes the best bumps as the

Judo expert Gene LeBell (left) is about to be tossed by Rick Nelson in Universal's *Love and Kisses* (1965).

men keep coming back for more. The entire bar gets into the swing of things with stuntmen John Hudkins, Victor Paul, Richard Elmore, Howard Curtis, football player Jim Boeke and stuntwoman Sharon Lucas all contributing. At one point, Nelson swings from a light fixture. Rick's brother David Nelson and Skip Young (Wally on the family's TV show) make quick comic cameos as bystanders watching the brawl. Bartender Jack Ellena joins the fight against Nelson and brings out a broken bottle and a knife. Nelson uses his martial arts to disarm Ellena and heave him through the bar's mirror. Ellena was Nelson's real-life bodyguard and a former professional wrestler and Los Angeles Ram. With no one else to fight, a dazed and bleeding Nelson wakes up from his crazy dream by falling out of bed.

Presley didn't have to worry much when it came to putting on a better fight. He was a far more skilled martial artist. Five-foot-eleven, 180-pound Nelson is energetic and gamely does all his own fight, but the action staging is technically subpar

despite the presence of qualified stunt personnel. They keep elements moving but are unable to account for the other side of the camera. Ozzie Nelson was using a crew from his TV show including D.P. Robert Moreno and editor Newell Kimlin. They were simply not up to the task of staging a superior action scene. Most of the stunt performers had appeared on the TV show and previously engaged in fights with Rick. The most noteworthy fighting episode was 1961's "The Manly Arts."

Nelson was a student of Bruce Tegner and had recently been awarded a controversial black belt in Tegner's jukado style. In his books, Tegner described Nelson's ability to learn and perform a fight as outstanding. However, detractors felt Nelson's black belt was honorary and not earned through the years of discipline commonly required. Many voiced their displeasure at Tegner's celebrity training. It was around the time of the release of *Love and Kisses* that Tegner began to catch heat within the growing Asian-American martial arts community for his cross-training practices. The 6'1", 205-pound judoka was writing and marketing numerous books introducing karate to the masses, often on styles on which he was less than expert. In 1967, he sold his Hollywood self-defense studio and largely disappeared from the public eye. He died in 1985.

See: Bashe, Philip. *Teenage Idol, Travelin' Man: The Complete Biography of Rick Nelson*. New York: Hyperion, 1992; Tegner, Bruce. *Judo: Beginner to Black Belt*. Ventura, CA: Thor, 1982; Tegner, Bruce. *Self-Defense: A Basic Course*. Ventura, CA: Thor, 1979.

Sean Connery vs. Bob Simmons in *Thunderball* (1965)

The fourth film in the James Bond series features a pre-credits teaser involving a memorable fight between Sean Connery and a man in drag among grandfather clocks in the Chateau d'Anet. The female impersonator is masquerading as the grieving widow of SPECTRE agent Jacques Boitier, but in fact is Boitier. The 90-second fight is made even more novel by the casting of Connery's regular stunt double Bob Simmons as Boitier, meaning Connery gets to do all his own power-punching stunts for the slightly undercranked sequence. Stuntman Harold Sanderson doubled Connery when the star is upended and lands on his back. The audience is thrown by the fact that attractive actress Rose Alba plays the Black Widow in the opening shots until the moment Connery knocks her wig off and both men

Bob Simmons takes a mighty punch from Sean Connery in United Artists' *Thunderball* (1965).

begin launching vicious punches. It's a bizarre tongue-in-cheek moment that gets swept away by the fury of the furniture-smashing action that follows. The two men knew how to work with one another on blocking out a fight for the cameras. *Kiss Kiss, Bang Bang* calls it "a good old-fashioned brawl."

The fight took two days to film with three prior days devoted to rehearsing the punches and swings of a fire poker. Special effects maestro Albert J. Luxford was called in for the bit where Simmons throws a knife and pins Connery's sleeve to the wall. The film was shot in reverse with Luxford pulling the knife from the wall with a strand of piano wire. The trickiest part of the shot was Connery needing to act in reverse, as if he were being pinned rather than released. Connery ultimately breaks Simmons' neck with the poker before tossing flowers on the body in a gesture showcasing Bond's sardonic sense of dark humor courtesy of screenwriters Richard Maibaum and John Hopkins. Connery makes his escape via jetpack and the credits roll with the expected Bond theme from composer John Barry.

Dynamic editor Peter Hunt once again assembled director Terence Young's action sequence superbly, but it is stuntman Simmons who's allowed to shine the brightest. His rough and violent Bond fight choreography mixed judo moves with fisticuffs and took fight scenes to a new level. The Bouvier fight was his personal favorite. Connery and Young had some humor at Simmons' expense, taking great delight in assisting with the application of his female makeup, much to the macho stuntman's chagrin.

See: *Thunderball* DVD special features.

Woody Strode vs. Mike Mazurki in *Seven Women* (1966)

Former professional wrestling titans Woody Strode and Mike Mazurki meet for a pitched torch-lit grappling scene in John Ford's final picture. Ford's favorite stock company players are improbably cast as Mongolian warriors who fight a duel to the death in front of a horde of Chinese extras for the right to deflower Anne Bancroft and the rest of the missionary women of the title. Unfortunately, the dream match-up comes a decade too late to sustain any real interest, and it's all over in less than half a minute. The two giants stalk one another, clinch and immediately go into a double choke for Joseph LaShelle's camera. After brief jockeying for position, warlord Mazurki breaks Strode's neck. Neither actor required a stunt double for the limited theatrics. It was something they could have performed in a ring any day of the week. Ford's longtime editor Otho Lovering constructed it with a minimum of camera cuts. Despite the apparent lack of interest behind the scenes, MGM called it "exciting" and "savage" in their publicity campaign and released several photos of them fighting to the death.

Mazurki did manage to convince the filmmakers that professional wrestler Gene LeBell was an expert on Mongolian wrestling and the lone man who could coordinate a fight between himself and Strode. Sensing a con when he was called for the job, LeBell agreed that he knew all about Mongolian wrestling, which in his mind soon resembled standard Greco-Roman wrestling. A ring was erected on the set and a week afforded for rehearsal time. LeBell quickly realized that Mazurki didn't intend to rehearse at all, but sit around in his bathrobe, smoking cigars and taking home an easy paycheck for his time. Strode kept himself occupied by performing push-ups in the corner to maintain his physique. He would do 1000 in a typical day. On the day of filming, Mazurki agreed to put the fight together, with LeBell working out a quick and fierce routine. When all was said and done, Mazurki reminded LeBell to send him a box of his favorite cigars for his birthday.

See: *Seven Women* pressbook.

JAMES COBURN VS. ROBERT GUNNER in *Our Man Flint* (1966)

This popular secret agent spoof was tall, lithe character actor James Coburn's first starring role.

He's well cast as superspy Derek Flint, master of everything under the sun including martial arts. He's introduced in his karate gi performing katas. Throughout the colorful Daniel Mann–directed film, the 6'2", 175-pound Coburn moves with grace and athletic assurance. Later he visits his superior Lee J. Cobb at headquarters and surprisingly unleashes his karate skills on Cobb's beefy guards Roy Jenson and Chuck Hicks in the corridor. He uses his feet, open hands and elbows to dismantle the stunt actors in 20 impressive seconds. Cobb thinks he's gone nuts until Coburn reveals that the guards are imposters. *Our Man Flint* was the first example of an American leading man fully adopting the Eastern kung fu philosophies. Previously audiences saw a smattering of judo chops or flips in Elvis Presley films, but here Coburn is kicking away with abandon. *Variety* noted that Coburn was an actor who "seems to thrive on physical exertion of the karate kind," while the *New York Times* called Flint's action prowess "fantastic and thoroughly flamboyant."

It's an entertaining mid–1960s romp from 20th Century-Fox that pokes fun at the James Bond films, especially when Coburn stages a karate-chopping nightclub fight in France with 0008, played by 6'4", 200-pound Sean Connery lookalike Robert Gunner. Buzz Henry coordinated the action with former Marlboro Man Gunner appearing to do his own fighting for Daniel L. Fapp's camera. *Fight Choreography: The Art of Non-Verbal*

Roy Jenson takes a high-flying kick from James Coburn in 20th Century-Fox's *Our Man Flint* (1966).

Dialogue calls this clever fight "very well-choreographed for the day." Coburn also fights bald-headed Michael St. Clair in a men's room and chief villain Edward Mulhare in the type of industrial factory these films always seemed to feature. Bruce Tegner is one of the men engaging Coburn in martial arts exercise at the beginning.

Coburn returned in an entertaining gymnasium fight for *In Like Flint* (1967), and several years later comically broke out his old moves against Bruce Willis in *Hudson Hawk* (1991). Coburn was a serious student of the arts, although he admitted publicly that what he displayed in the Flint films was little more than choreographed showmanship and he had never been in a real fight. Coburn went from Tegner and Ed Parker to befriending and training with Bruce Lee. Coburn formed a lasting friendship with Lee. Together they created the story "The Silent Flute," which became the martial arts action film *Circle of Iron* (1979) (see entry).

Army veteran Coburn also had fight action in *What Did You Do in the War, Daddy?* (1966) (see entry). Fights of interest came against Mario Adorf in *Major Dundee* (1965), Michael Blodgett in *The Carey Treatment* (1972), Charlton Heston in *The Last Hard Men* (1976) and Jack O'Halloran in *The Baltimore Bullet* (1980). On TV, he and co-star Ralph Taeger fought on the short-lived *Klondike* (1960). As a guest, Coburn battled Michael Landon in 1959's *Bonanza* episode "The Truckee Strip," Chuck Connors in 1961's *Rifleman* "The High Country" and Glenn Corbett in 1964's *Route 66* "Kiss the Monster—Make Him Sleep."

See: *Our Man Flint* DVD special features; *Our Man Flint* pressbook; Worth, Robert F. "James Coburn, 74, Is Dead." *New York Times*. November 19, 2002.

CHUCK CONNORS VS. CLAUDE AKINS in *Ride Beyond Vengeance* (1966)

This revenge western from director Bernard McEveety and writer-producer Andrew J. Fenady is notable for a violent three-minute saloon fight be-

Chuck Connors (left) and Claude Akins stage a furious fight in Columbia's *Ride Beyond Vengeance* (1966).

tween buffalo hunter Chuck Connors and deranged bad guy Claude Akins, whom Connors blames for the loss of his bride Kathryn Hays. There's also the past matter of Akins having had Connors held down for a hot branding iron. The *Fort Worth Press* claimed the action "makes previous screen brawls look like taffy-pulls," while the *Houston Post* called it "one heckuva scrap" and "worth the price of admission." Connors biographer David Fury termed it "a tremendous fight sequence," while famed director William Wyler told the press it was one of the greatest fights he ever saw.

All kinds of nastiness occurs as Akins goes after Connors with a broken beer mug and a sharp deer antler. Connors lifts Akins over his head and throws him over the bar into a mirror, smashing broken glass everywhere. The cable assisting him in doing so is clearly visible, but that's a minor quibble when the action is coming so fast and furious. Akins quickly takes a ride across the bar, smashes through a stair railing, and both men go out the saloon window. Bartender William Bryant keeps trying to step in with a gun but is understandably reticent to move between these men. Stunt coordinator Bill Catching was responsible for putting the scene together and doubled Connors, though both stars did the majority of their stunt work. Roydon Clark doubled Akins in a couple of the rougher sections, with his presence well-concealed by D.P. Lester Shorr and editor Otho Lovering. Richard Markowitz provided the perfunctory score.

Connors and Akins had worked together on TV's *The Rifleman* and were friendly before filming. They had even done a previous fight on *The Rifleman* and practiced for several days at Connors' house before filming this fight. However, once on the *Ride Beyond Vengeance* set, Connors opted to take a Method approach and work himself into a state of hatred toward Akins. Much of the struggle was notched up on account of Connors with Akins responding in kind. It took two days to film the tooth-and-nail action. The two actors were not on speaking terms during this period. After filming was done, they resumed their friendship. The on-screen results speak for themselves.

Six-foot-five, 215-pound Chuck Connors was a fine athlete playing both basketball and baseball at Seton Hall. After World War II Army service, he had professional careers in both sports with the Boston Celtics, the Brooklyn Dodgers and the Chicago Cubs. While with the AAA farm team the Los Angeles Angels, Connors began pursuing work in Hollywood. His imposing size and hatchet face led to work as a heavy before finding everlasting fame as the single father Lucas McCain on TV's *The Rifleman* (1958–1963). His series *Branded* (1965–1966) saw him cast as disgraced cavalry officer Jason McCord, unjustly accused of cowardice. Nearly every episode was built around a fight.

Connors' long arms generated plenty of explosive punching power. He enjoyed fight scenes and often wanted to perform the action. However, a fight injury once shut down *Branded* production for a week so doing his own stunts was a point of friction with the producers. He did let Fritz Ford step in for top fights on *The Rifleman* such as the ones against Dan Blocker in 1958's "The Sister" and Sean McClory in 1961's "I Take This Woman." On *Branded,* he entered the bare-knuckle ring to take on Chuck Hicks in 1965's "The Greatest Coward on Earth." On film, Connors fought Burt Lancaster in *South Sea Woman* (1953), Peter Graves in *Death in Small Doses* (1957), Rory Calhoun in *The Hired Gun* (1957), Gregory Peck in *Designing Woman* (1957) (see entry), Alex Cord in *Synanon* (1965), Charlton Heston in *Soylent Green* (1973) and Richard Harris in *99 and 44/100% Dead* (1974). He wore three-inch lifts for the 1956 *Gunsmoke* episode "The Preacher" to make him bigger than James Arness, but he still lost their bare-knuckle fight. Although he towered over Robert Horton, he lost again in the 1957 *Wagon Train* episode "The Charles Avery Story."

See: "Action Up." *Grand Prairie Daily News.* August 18, 1967; Anderson, Bob. "Ride Beyond Vengeance Interview with Andrew J. Fenady." *Trail Dust Magazine.* Spring 1996; Fury, David. *Chuck Connors: The Man Behind the Rifle.* Minneapolis: Artists Press, 1997.

MARLON BRANDO VS. RICHARD BRADFORD in *The Chase* (1966)

Small town Texas sheriff Marlon Brando gets the martyr treatment as he is beaten to within an inch of his life by angry local citizens on the hunt for escaped prisoner Robert Redford. At the same time, black prisoner Joel Fluellen is beaten in his jail cell with an overmatched Brando unable to prevent it. Screenwriter Lillian Hellman and director Arthur Penn effectively present author Horton Foote's original hotbed story of racial hatred, adultery and impulsive violence, drawing out the punishment over three minutes of excruciating screen time. Do-right Brando is accosted in the sheriff's office by the trio of Richard Bradford, Steve Ihnat and Clifton James while his helpless wife Angie Dickinson beats on the door and screams for help. Sound supervisor Charles J. Rice's work is particularly noteworthy recording the shuffling of feet on the floor and fists hitting flesh. Composer John Barry's cue is held off until the fight's end, rising as Brando's spent body collapses. Fueled by liquor, Bradford is in control throughout and effectively blocks Brando's every effort to mount a defense. It's a memorable moment which *USA Today* ranks among the cinema's greatest fights.

In his quest for Method realism, Brando asked that stunt coordinator Paul Baxley let him take the entire beating. Brando had Ben Lane's makeup department apply a liberal amount of fake blood, then kept adding to it as chief assailant Bradford battered him around. Cameraman Joseph LaShelle filmed in slow motion so Bradford could make contact, burying his fist deep into Brando's belly. Brando told Bradford not to hold back, and Bradford complied as Brando was his acting idol. Bradford jumped atop a desk, swinging at Brando so furiously that the other actors in the scene had to pull him off. Brando let his body go limp and fell off the table. The censors immediately took their scissors to the bloodiness, although a great deal of violence still comes through. *Hollywood Hellraisers* calls the beating "one of the most savage in cinema history."

Stocky, prematurely grey Bradford was a native Texan who played football on scholarship at Texas A&M University. After filming *The Chase*, the 5'10" Bradford accepted an offer to go to England to star in the cult series *Man in a Suitcase* (1967–1968). He was perfect as the two-fisted ex–CIA agent McGill, registering with audiences with his ability to dish out and receive punishment. He always emerged from a bout of fisticuffs realistically battered and exhausted. Unfortunately, Bradford couldn't capitalize on his early successes. He became a respected character actor, best known for fighting Sean Connery to the death in *The Untouchables* (1987).

See: Lyons, Leonard. "Asking for More Blood." *Times-Picayune.* July 3, 1965; "Marlon Brando Prompted Bradford Acting Career." *The Ottawa Journal.* June 8, 1968; Sellers, Robert. *Hollywood Hellraisers.* New York: Skyhorse, 2013.

CLINT WALKER VS. LEO GORDON in *The Night of the Grizzly* (1966)

This fondly remembered family outing from director Joseph Pevney is one of TV star Clint Walker's best known films and his own personal favorite. The towering Walker matches up with the glowering Leo Gordon as a nasty bounty hunter out for a $1000 reward for the death of a famed grizzly. Scripter Warren Douglas has given the characters a contentious history as Walker once had Gordon sent to jail for his transgressions. Veteran heavy Gordon was one of the few men who could believably go against the broad-shouldered Walker one on one. He did that on TV's *Cheyenne* in 1955's "The Outlander," 1956's "Death Deals the Hand" and 1962's "Vengeance Is Mine." The latter fight, clocking in at four minutes, earned a reputation as the best set of fisticuffs to ever appear on the small screen. Walker and Gordon did the entire exhausting fight without doubles.

On *Cheyenne,* Walker and Gordon talked movements out beforehand and told doubles Russ McCubbin and Boyd "Red" Morgan to sit down and watch. The same thing happened on *Night of the Grizzly* for Loyal Griggs and Harold Lipstein's camera, although McCubbin did double Walker in a couple of brief shots. Gordon appears to do the entire one minute–plus fight. Gordon's character is nursing an injury as he caught his ankle in a bear trap. A knowing Walker heaves Gordon's scarred boots into Cedar Lake, which sends Gordon into a knife-drawing, bear-trap swinging rage. During the fight, Gordon threatens, "I'm going to cut you up into bear meat." Walker fends him off with a series of powerful and well-placed punches that deposits Gordon face first into the water to the backing of Leith Stevens' dramatic score. Close-ups were filmed on the Paramount lot.

Variety found other fistfights in *Night of the Grizzly* to be "weakly motivated" in comparison to the great Walker-Gordon fight. Walker twice makes quick work of future TV Tarzan Ron Ely, the first with a simple backhanded swat. Later Ely teams up with Med Flory to take on Walker in a supply store. Both Ely and Flory stood 6'4" and along with Walker managed to inadvertently break up store parts not meant to be broken. The scene had to be shot a second time. Walker accidentally popped Ely on the nose, bloodying it and necessitating ten minutes of applied ice before

Leo Gordon attacks Clint Walker with a knife in Paramount's *The Night of the Grizzly* (1966).

Ely declared himself fit and ready for another round of fisticuffs.

See: Anderson, Bob. "Vengeance Is Mine." *Trail Dust.* Summer 1997. "Ely Followed by Disasters." *Trenton Evening Times.* December 16, 1965; "Grizzly Provides Match for Walker." *Big Spring Daily Herald.* December 18, 1966; *Night of the Grizzly* pressbook.

PAUL NEWMAN VS. WOLFGANG KIELING in *Torn Curtain* (1966)

One of the lesser efforts from the Master of Suspense Alfred Hitchcock, this Cold War spy film is nevertheless remembered for a torturous battle to the death between Paul Newman and menacing East German agent Wolfgang Kieling. In a German farmhouse, the two struggle at one another's throats while the house's occupant Carolyn Conwell tries to help Newman by breaking a kitchen knife off in Kieling's chest and pounding his legs with a shovel. The outcome of the drawn-out fight is unconventional to say the least as Newman and Conwell drag a still fighting Kieling across the floor and place his head in a gas oven. The reference to Auschwitz and Nazi death camps is obvious. Still, the *New York Times* called the scene the film's "strongest episode."

Intending to show how hard it is to kill a man, Hitchcock and cinematographer John F. Warren elected to film everything in close-up with no musical accompaniment and no stunt doubles. Hitchcock and stunt coordinator Dave Sharpe created a montage effect for the scene, shooting in bits and pieces over four days. They allowed Bud Hoffman's editing to establish the suspense of a pulled gun flying from a hand, the knife plunging and breaking, a shovel thudding on Kieling's shin, and the men grunting and groaning with hands squeezing necks. Hitchcock had taken a similar approach to the climactic fight between James Stewart and Raymond Burr in *Rear Window* (1954), which he also covered in long shot. Comparing the two approaches, he realized the montage version was much more effective on screen. That fight was accompanied by Bernard Herrmann's famous score. Herrmann began scoring *Torn Curtain* but was fired and replaced. Hitchcock opted this time to go with William Russell and Waldon Watson's sound effects.

Navy veteran Paul Newman played football for Kenyon College but was kicked off the team for getting into a bar fight. The 5'9", 160-pound actor

emerged in Hollywood portraying boxer Rocky Graziano in *Somebody Up There Likes Me* (1956), training for his ring action with Mushy Callahan and Al Silvani for his on-screen fight with Courtland Shepard. He later studied judo with sensei Joe Robinson. Newman quickly realized that his looks were integral to his success and kept fit throughout his illustrious career as an Oscar-winning leading man. Newman never pretended to be a big screen tough guy and took severe beatings in *The Hustler* (1961) and *Harper* (1966). He even allowed himself to be knocked out by stuntwoman Jeannie Epper in *The Life and Times of Judge Roy Bean* (1972).

However, he could also dish it out, striking an astonished David Canary in the jaw with a rifle in *Hombre* (1967) and engaging in memorable beefs in *Cool Hand Luke* (1967) and *Sometimes a Great Notion* (1970) (see entries). Fights of interest came against Rip Torn in *Sweet Bird of Youth* (1962), Don Kennedy in *Hud* (1963), Laurence Harvey in *The Outrage* (1964), Robert Wagner in *Winning* (1969), Tony Franciosa and Richard Jaeckel in *The Drowning Pool* (1975), Paul D'Amato in *Slapshot* (1977), James Franciscus in *When Time Ran Out* (1980) and Danny Aiello in *Fort Apache the Bronx* (1981). Most viewers fondly recall a comical kick between the legs of giant Ted Cassidy in *Butch Cassidy and the Sundance Kid* (1969).

See: Gottlieb, Sammy. *Hitchcock Interviews.* Jackson: University Press of Mississippi, 2003; Kleiner, Dick. "Alfred Hitchcock Puts Fight on Film." *Park City Daily.* December 6, 1965; Levy, Shawn. *Paul Newman: A Life.* New York: Harmony, 2009.

THE PUB BRAWL in *Alfie* (1966)

This Lewis Gilbert–directed British comedy made a star of Oscar-nominated Michael Caine, cast here as the title womanizing cad with nary a hint of morals in his being. In real life. the 6'2", 180-pound Michael Caine was a working class Cockney who served with the Royal Fusiliers during the Korean War, but in this film he is cast as a lover, not a fighter. The *Alfie* narrative has him moving from woman to woman while offering narration directly to the camera. His bedroom adventures rub even his male colleagues the wrong way, including Sydney Tafler, who takes a swing at him in Brixton's Black Horse Pub, starting a chain reaction brawl. Some viewers complained that the fight felt tacked-on and was the movie's weakest moment. *The New Yorker* called the barroom brawl "gratuitous" and "cinematic." Likewise, *The Milwaukee Journal* said the scene "smacks of self-indulgence—a tavern brawl that becomes a parody of tavern brawls."

The two minutes of action as filmed by cinematographer Otto Heller are pure John Ford slapstick brawl with an English bent. Mirrors are broken and furniture is smashed as a black-eyed Caine slinks away from a fight dominated by 6'8", 270-pound Ronald Rich, a giant impervious to being hit in the back with chairs. Stuntmen Johnny Morris (Caine's double), Eddie Stacey, Peter Brayham Del Baker, John Clifford, Billy Cornelius, Steve Emerson, Terence Maidment, Mark McBride, Manny Michael, Terry Walsh and Peter Diamond are among the many participants, with Diamond working as the stunt arranger. Among the stunt extras are Phil Joste, Bill Hibbert, Jim Payne, John Triplett and Steve Donahue. The set was an actual bar scheduled for demolition so everyone involved was given free rein to break whatever they came in to contact with during a wild single take. At least one badly choreographed swing-and-miss occurs that's left intact by editor Thelma Connell. Singer Queenie Watts and her band continue playing throughout the fighting.

See: Hall, William. *Arise, Sir Michael Caine.* London: John Blake, 2000; Joste, Philip S. *What Sort of a Job Is That?* Lulu, 2008; Palmer, Scott V. *British Stunt & Action Performers on Film and Television.* Brooklyn: Cypress Hills, 2017.

THE BAT BRAWLS in *Batman* (1966)

The campy TV series *Batman* (1966–1968) was a tremendous hit and spawned this big-screen Caped Crusader extension filmed between the first and second seasons by director Leslie H. Martinson. One of the joys of the series and this Lorenzo Semple, Jr.–scripted film are the energetic fights, which contain cartoon letter superimpositions such as POW, BAM and WHAM exploding onto the screen after a punch lands. The words are two-fold, as their screen placement also helps to obscure missed punches in the multiple-opponent fight choreography. D.P. Howard Schwartz and second unit camera operator Jack Marta film everything at slanted angles against art director Serge Krizman and Jack Martin Smith's colorful backgrounds, giving the fights the fresh and original look of a comic book come to life. Editor

Harry Gerstad's pacing is most effective, and Nelson Riddle's iconic score is perfect. Batman and Robin stars Adam West and Burt Ward do a great deal of their own screen fighting, but are doubled in some instances by stuntmen Hubie Kerns and Victor Paul. Kerns choreographed the action.

Villains Joker, Riddler, Penguin and Catwoman (Cesar Romero, Frank Gorshin, Burgess Meredith and Lee Meriwether) employ veteran stuntmen Gil Perkins, Dick Crockett and George Sawaya as their main henchmen. Others participating in fight action include stuntmen Louie Elias, Eddie Hice, Charlie Picerni, Wally Rose, Guy Way, Al Bain, Cap Sommers and Fred Stromsoe. Four main brawls are featured: an early seafront fight at Ye Old Benbow Taverne, Batman's alter ego Bruce Wayne's attempted escape from the villain's lair, a group of henchmen invading the Bat Cave and the climactic all-out fight on the deck of the Penguin's submarine. The finale was shot in a studio lake at 20th Century-Fox with three cameras, two positioned in rafts and one on a crane. Stuntman Ace Hudkins was injured after hitting his head on a submerged post diving off the submarine.

As for the episodic TV show, the most excitingly staged fisticuffs came in 1967 fighting the Mad Hatter (David Wayne) and his goons (including Lennie Bremen, Charlie Picerni and Roger Creed) on a water tower in "The Mad Hatter Runs Afoul" and battling the Joker and the Penguin (with henchmen Hal Baylor, Guy Way, Charlie Picerni, Eddie Saenz and Gil Perkins) in the Bat Cave in "The Zodiac Crimes." A fan favorite: "Batman's Satisfaction" where Batman and Robin briefly battle their crimefighting counterparts the Green Hornet and Kato (Van Williams and Bruce Lee) to a draw.

See: *Batman* DVD commentary; Garcia, Bob. "Batman: Making the Original Movie." *Cinefantastique.* 24/25. No. 6/1. 1994; Konow, David. "Holy Screenwriter, Batman! An Interview with Lorenzo Semple, Jr." *Shock Cinema.* #19, 2001; West, Adam, and Jeff Rovin. *Back to the Bat Cave.* London: Titan, 1994.

JAMES GARNER VS. AL WYATT, JOHN DAHEIM AND BOYD "RED" MORGAN in *Duel at Diablo* (1966)

High-energy fisticuffs highlight this offbeat oater shot on a western town set in Kanab, Utah. James Garner stars in an atypical tough guy performance and shows his weather-beaten mettle when he rescues Bibi Andersson from a group of unsavory miners in the local horse stables. The bearded bad guys are played by stuntmen Al Wyatt, Boyd "Red" Morgan and John Daheim, guaranteeing that the action will include plenty of hard rights to the chin and brutal face-gouging. *Duel at Diablo* was noted for its violence, including that coming from its leading man. The *New York Times* called it "a vicious film—grim, tough and taut." With the odds stacked against him, Garner is forced to fight dirty, biting a finger and head-butting Daheim in the nose. It's a refreshing change from the image of the prototypical vanilla cowboy hero. Fights are not clean and emotions can rise dramatically. With his nose busted, Daheim grabs a pitchfork to stick Garner, but Sidney Poitier hits him over the head and allows Garner to finish off Wyatt and Morgan with his fists.

Garner's longtime double Roydon Clark subs for the star when the going gets too rough and earns his reputation as one of the stunt business' top fight men. This includes crashing through a fence, collapsing a lean-to filled with hay and, most impressively, knocking over a horse as all four men take a collective tumble. Fred Steinkamp cuts away quickly during the action so the audience is unable to focus on Clark, although Garner does the majority of the fight. It's clearly Garner struggling on the ground with Wyatt when the remaining horses stampede from the stable. Wyatt and Morgan coordinated the solid action for director Ralph Nelson, who envisioned a fight to rival *The Spoilers*. Garner also gets knocked around by 6'6" Bill Travers and fights John Crawford in the sheriff's office. Garner had earlier done that fight with Timothy Carey, who was replaced in the role by Crawford for unspecified reasons. The eccentric Carey had a reputation for getting booted from projects.

Six-foot-two, 205-pound Garner served with the Army in Korea, earning a Purple Heart. As the star of TV's *Maverick* (1957–1962), he engaged in a top-shelf fight with guest star Clint Eastwood in 1959's "Duel at Sundown." Garner fought Leo Gordon in the show's pilot, earning that tough guy's respect when Gordon buried his fist into Garner's belly and Garner responded in kind. Gordon liked that from a leading man. Garner had a bare-knuckle battle against pro boxer Pat Comiskey in 1957's "Stampede," but normally used his smarts to elude dangerous situations. This was best exemplified by his suckering of martial arts legend Bruce Lee into taking a flying kick off the

Occidental Building in *Marlowe* (1969). He repeated that scenario against William Smith in the pilot to *The Rockford Files* (1974), suckering the muscleman into trying a karate kick on a pre-soaped floor. When Smith lands on his back, Garner sucker-punches him in the jaw with a palmed roll of quarters.

Garner was solid throwing a screen punch, but where he excelled was taking one. He could sell absorbing punishment as well as anyone in the business and was made an honorary member of the Stuntmen's Association. Garner engaged in fights with stunt actors on nearly every episode of his popular detective show *The Rockford Files* (1974–1980) and customarily came out on the losing end. He fought Tab Hunter in *The Girl He Left Behind* (1956), Tony Franciosa in *A Man Could Get Killed* (1966), George Kennedy in *The Pink Jungle* (1968), Lou Gossett in *Skin Game* (1971) and a bar-full of toughs in *Victor/Victoria* (1982). On his series *Nichols* (1971–1972), he had a big fight with Steve Forrest in 1971's "Away the Rolling River."

See: Garner, James, and Jon Winokur. *The Garner Files*. New York: Simon & Schuster, 2011; Kleiner, Dick. "Heartland of Big Westerns." *Racine Journal Times Bulletin*. November 7, 1965; Penton, Edgar. "*Duel at Diablo*: Surprise Western." *El Paso Herald-Post*. May 21, 1966.

HUGH O'BRIAN VS. MARIO ADORF in *Ten Little Indians* (1966)

George Pollack directed this mystery from the popular Agatha Christie novel, set in a snowy Alpine village. Rugged Hugh O'Brian is effectively cast in the lead, trying to get to the bottom of the killings. Chief suspect Mario Adorf engages in a fistfight with O'Brian beginning in the inn's kitchen. When it looks like the fight has come to a standstill, the beefy butler gets in a cheap shot. "Now you've asked for it, Buster," says O'Brian, who breaks out karate moves as he thrashes Adorf across the marble floor and up and down the staircases. The two men choke one another's necks and gouge at their eyes, tumbling down the stairs and knocking over a suit of armor. Repulsed by the brutality, spectator Wilfred Hyde-White declares, "Disgraceful!" English stuntman Terry Yorke doubled O'Brian for the impressive stair fall with Larry Taylor doubling Adorf. It was filmed on location at Kenure House in Rush County, Dublin, Ireland. *Time* remarked, "Mod sex appeal is dragged in by Shirley Eaton, fisticuffs by Hugh O'Brian."

Six-foot, 175-pound O'Brian was the youngest drill instructor in the Marine Corps. An excellent all-around athlete, he played football and boxed in the service before becoming a household name as the TV star of *The Life and Legend of Wyatt Earp* (1955–1962). The square-jawed O'Brian presented a macho image to the public and was proud of his masculine virility. Whenever possible, he showcased the hand-to-hand combat skills he picked up from the Marines both on the show and on the publicity trail. He staged a knock-down drag-out stunt fight for *The Ed Sullivan Show* and battled English stuntmen at the Odeon Theatre in London in 1958.

O'Brian fought Gene Autry in *Beyond the Purple Hills* (1950), Sidney Poitier in *Red Ball Express* (1952), Rock Hudson in *Back to God's Country* (1953) and *Seminole* (1953), Glenn Ford in *The Man from the Alamo* (1953), Alan Ladd in *Saskatchewan* (1954), Robert Evans in *The Fiend Who Walked the West* (1958), Nigel Green in *Africa—Texas Style* (1967), Peter Fonda in *Killer Force* (1975) and Bruce Lee in *Game of Death* (1979) (see entry). He had one of his best TV fights with James Drury on 1962's premiere episode of *The Virginian*, "The Executioners." On *Wyatt Earp*, O'Brian had a bare-knuckle brawl with Morgan Woodward in 1958's "The Manly Art."

See: O'Brian, Hugh, and Virginia O'Brian. *Hugh O'Brian: Or What's Left of Him.* Book Publishers Network, 2014; Wilson, Earl. "O'Brian's Proud of Wyatt Earp." *Milwaukee Sentinel.* November 8, 1957.

The Valerno Fountain Brawl in *What Did You Do in the War, Daddy?* (1966)

Director Blake Edwards followed up *The Great Race* (1965) with another comic farce featuring a wild one-and-a-half-minute set piece brawl with dozens of stuntmen in action. This time the setting is World War II, as an outfit of U.S. soldiers makes an on-again, off-again truce with Italian soldiers in the town of Valerno (actually a Lake Sherwood, California, set courtesy of production designer Fernando Carrere). As scripted by William Peter Blatty, it's a situation rife with comedic possibilities. In between drinking and gambling, they try to convince their superiors they are in a dire fight for life with one another. Aiding in this endeavor is aerial reconnaissance footage of a huge brawl

breaking out around a fountain square over gambling wagers. Bodies fly right and left and stars James Coburn and Aldo Ray become heavily involved. Character actor William Bryant is also in the thick of the action. Ray gets events started by belting Olympic boxer Vincent Barbi, while Coburn engages with stuntman Reg Parton. When fighting becomes too tough, Coburn pauses for a cigarette.

United Artists publicity declared it one of the largest free-for-alls ever filmed, with the donnybrook employing 25 stuntmen and nearly 400 extras. The Ralph Winters–edited fight is played for laughs and is well-orchestrated by stunt coordinator Richard Geary and cinematographer Philip Lathrop. Henry Mancini contributes a typically light and breezy score with "I've Been Working on the Railroad" backing the fight. Mickey McCardle served as the assistant director while stuntman Dick Crockett was an associate producer. Among the stunt artists are Dean Smith, Ronnie Rondell, Jr., Chuck Hicks, Gene LeBell, Charlie Picerni, Dave Sharpe, Ted White, Larry Duran, John Moio, Robert Hoy, George Sawaya, Bob Herron, Sol Gorss, Jerry Catron, Carey Loftin, Dale Van Sickel, Carl Saxe, Chuck O'Brien, Jesse Wayne, Budd Albright, Ken Del Conte, Glenn Wilder, Carol Daniels and Sharon Lucas.

Six-foot, 200-pound Aldo Ray was a Navy frogman during World War II before starring in football at Vallejo Junior College. He played semi-pro for the Petaluma Longhorns before arriving in Hollywood as a crewcut-sporting, thick-necked leading man specializing in tough war films. An early highlight was his hard-hitting boxer in *Pat and Mike* (1952). A drinking problem and cement-mixer voice dropped Ray into the tier of gruff character actors. His powerful physicality can best be seen as he destroys everything in his path playing the frightening heavy in *Welcome to Hard Times* (1967). Fellow actors were wary of Ray missing his mark with one of his mighty punches.

Ray led a bar brawl in *Battle Cry* (1955) and fought Rudy Bond and Brian Keith in *Nightfall* (1957), Jack Lord and Vic Morrow in *God's Little Acre* (1958) and James Caan in *Gone with the West* (1969). In *Riot on Sunset Strip* (1967), he serio-comically beat up a room-full of hippies. As a TV guest, Ray fought Dan Blocker in the 1964 *Bonanza* episode "The Wild One," Fess Parker in the 1965 *Daniel Boone* "The Trek" and Harry "Turk" Varteresian in the 1966 *Virginian* "Jacob Was a Plain Man."

See: Folkart, Burt A. "Aldo Ray; Raspy Voiced Actor Played Toughs, Soldiers in Wide Range of Films." *Los Angeles Times*. March 28, 1991; *What Did You Do in the War, Daddy?* pressbook.

THE NOISY BAR BRAWL in *Not with My Wife You Don't* (1966)

This enjoyably silly 1960s comedy features a two-minute brawl in a military officer's club choreographed to the song "The Stars and Stripes Forever" blaring from a jukebox. Warner Bros. publicity tagged it the noisiest fight of the season. The score was provided by John Williams, with Stanley Jones heading the sound department. Editor Aaron Stell synchronized the audio and visual elements and kept the action flowing. The film was written, produced and directed by Norman Panama. The plot has friendly rival Air Force officers George C. Scott and Tony Curtis lead a dozen stuntmen through the fight routine as each tries to spirit away pretty Betty Bresler while the other is occupied. Scott gets the action started by rallying the soldiers around the flag, claiming it has been spit on by Australia. Fred Krone and Chuck Hicks are highlighted as a pair of Aussie soldiers while Dave Sharpe, Roydon Clark, Bob Herron, Bennie Dobbins, Wally Rose, Bill Couch, John Macchia and Alex Plasschaert fill out the ranks. Sharpe stands out with a leap onto a pile of bodies and a flip onto a table.

The brawl hospitalizes Curtis' character, and he falls for his nurse Virna Lisi. After they are married, he is shipped off to Antarctica per orders. He later realizes that those orders were manipulated by serial womanizer Scott. Curtis makes a mad dash for Italy in an attempt to stop Scott from putting the moves on his wife. In the Quirt and Flagg tradition, Scott and Curtis engage in fisticuffs with one another in a Rome hotel room in front of Lisi. The concerned object of their competitive affection runs around the room with pillows to place beneath the men each time they fall. Publicity declared this "the softest fight in film history." A general (Carroll O'Connor) is in the room next door so the two combatants try to be quiet during their brawling. It's all played for uproarious laughs, a style Curtis was accustomed to, but former Marine Scott (six feet, 185 pounds) was treading new water here in outright comedy. One notable gaffe occurs when Scott knees Curtis in the face and the latter tumbles over a chair. Cameraman Charles Lang's angle is straight on and clearly shows the powerful blow is an obvious miss. Scott would go on to fight Gary Graham in *Hardcore* (1979).

See: "Comedy Set for Sunday at Aircaflia." *Colorado Springs Gazette-Telegraph*. August 17, 1968; Scott, John L. "Quiet Please—Combatants at Work." *Los Angeles Times*. April 24, 1966; Sheward, David. *Rage and Glory: The Volatile Life and Career of George C. Scott*. New York: Applause Theatre & Cinema Books, 2008.

JOHN WAYNE VS. ROBERT MITCHUM in *El Dorado* (1967)

What *could* have been a top action match-up came a decade too late to be significant. It's not helped by the fact that Robert Mitchum's character is an out-on-his-feet drunk, and his fight with John Wayne is over with a smattering of punches thrown. Still, it's enjoyable for fans of the two stars to see them swinging at one another in this pleasant Howard Hawks reworking of *Rio Bravo* (1959). The stars are old buddies caught in a range war, and Wayne needs to get Sheriff Mitchum off the booze to make a difference. Mitchum wants to stay on the sauce, and the two have it out with their fists in Mitchum's office. Most of the film was done on location at Old Tucson, but this interior was shot on Stage 16 of the Paramount lot by veteran

Robert Mitchum delivers a big punch on John Wayne in Paramount's *El Dorado* (1967).

cinematographer Harold Rosson. There's fine physical comedy, particularly as Wayne belts Mitchum on the head with a copper spittoon, and the latter gives a classically dazed facial expression. Another highlight has Mitchum trying to smash a chair over Wayne's head, but he hits the top bars over the jail door instead and takes himself out in the process. Chuck Roberson doubled for the falls. Mitchum later finds the intestinal fortitude to become tough with bad guy Ed Asner and his henchman Jim Davis, memorably clobbering them both with his rifle. Wayne and Mitchum hit it off with one another making *El Dorado*, and in the late 1960s occasionally got together to empty a bottle.

See: *El Dorado* pressbook; Heffernan, Harold. "Two Huskies Stage Big Fake Fight." *Toledo Blade.* December 29, 1965.

THE SALOON BRAWL in *The War Wagon* (1967)

This entertaining, star-powered western from director Burt Kennedy plays up the on-screen contrast between rivals John Wayne and Kirk Douglas, who join forces to steal villain Bruce Cabot's gold-laden war wagon. There's a saloon brawl started by Howard Keel in which both leads participate, although neither throws a punch at the other. It's one of those fights where cowboys come out of the woodwork to whale away with their fists, and the highlight is a piano being pushed through the front window. Stuntman Jim Burk calls out "Fight!" Others taking part include Hal Needham, Boyd "Red" Morgan, Jerry Gatlin, Gary McLarty, Everett Creach, Jack Williams and Eddy Donno. Tom Hennesy appears as the bartender, and Terry Wilson shows up as the sheriff who walks in the door, takes a fist to the face and stumbles back out. Wayne's longtime double Chuck Roberson worked on the film, while Needham doubled Douglas swinging on a chandelier. The sequence benefits from the cutting of Harry Gerstad, who keeps his two stars front and center in the action. The film was shot in Durango, Mexico, and the fight was done over several days at Churubusco Studios in Mexico City. *Film Bulletin* commented that Kennedy "excels at staging brawls," while *The Milwaukee Journal* found the brawl "worth half the admission price itself."

Wayne has an earlier fight with Don Collier, Sheb Wooley and Boyd "Red" Morgan, dispatching Cabot's three toughs in a matter of seconds.

This minor brawl had significance to Wayne's career. Wayne had kept a tally of his many fights and determined this was his 500th screen skirmish. Collier was on the receiving end of Wayne's punch and recalled at film festivals that the faked blow was the mightiest he ever saw cross his face. Although Wayne had limited energy and was taking nips from an oxygen tank, he was involved in all facets of the saloon brawl. He was in the forefront of the action slugging away and helped set the fight up with Kennedy, coordinator Needham, second unit director Cliff Lyons and cameraman William H. Clothier. Wayne even threw chairs into the melee off-camera and provided the fist that sent Terry Wilson out the door. Gary McLarty takes a chair over the head from Wayne. The young stuntman filled his hat with elbow pads in case Wayne hit him with the base instead of the more easily breakable legs. Wayne assured McLarty he had been doing this for years. When the call came for action, Wayne came down with the base atop McLarty's head and gave the stuntman a goose-egg despite the added protection. McLarty, a novice, told his boss the chair shot was perfect. McLarty is also the stuntman who takes the flying leap and crashes into the mirror behind the bar.

See: Garvin, Allen. "What in the World." *Times Daily.* October 15, 1967; Rose, Bob. "For Movie Brawls Call John Wayne." *Salt Lake City Tribune.* March 20, 1967; Schickel, Richard. "Duke Packs a Mean Punch." *Life.* August 4, 1967.

ROD TAYLOR vs. ERNEST BORGNINE in *Chuka* (1967)

Chuka, a different western from director Gordon Douglas, involves title gunfighter Rod Taylor's attempts to convince a fort full of Army misfits to leave before they are attacked by rampaging Arapaho Indians. It's well-acted but suffers from erratic execution and budget constraints. There's not enough contrast between the artificial studio fort and real expansive vistas for it to be considered a great western. Today it is best known for the showstopping fight between Taylor and Ernest Borgnine that ranks with the big screen's best. Paramount publicity described it as "one of the most brutally vicious man-to-man battles ever seen." *Variety* termed it "one of the most effective brawls in recent years," while *Motion Picture Herald* labeled it "a dandy of a fistfight." *Western Clippings* includes it among their "great screen fights."

Contributing to its effectiveness is the great tension built up between Taylor and Borgnine, as a soldier loyal to commander John Mills to a fault. Issues come to a head in front of the entire Army outfit as Taylor and Borgnine square off in the horse stables and out on the windblown street until they are both sporting makeup artist Wally Westmore's blood on their faces. The two exhausted men end up throwing punches on their knees, until they come to admire one another's guts. They become allies throughout the rest of the picture. The Leith Stevens score is near-perfect, remaining in the background except to rise and punctuate each mighty punch from sound effect technicians Garry Harris and John Wilkinson. Harold Stine's camerawork and Robert Wyman's editing contribute greatly, as does set decorator Robert Benton's straw-laden horse stable. The two-minute battle is nicely justified by the Richard Jessup plot, and the two stars give it their all. Stunt doubles originally had an entire routine mapped out, but Taylor and Borgnine were both eager to make it look as rough and realistic

Ernest Borgnine lands a solid blow to Rod Taylor in Paramount's *Chuka* (1967).

as possible. Bob Herron doubled Borgnine in a couple of spots while Billy Shannon and Louie Elias were on hand for Taylor. The star performs all his own stunts, including rolling underneath a horse and having his head smashed through a board. Taylor's bodyguard Fred Hakim was credited as stunt coordinator.

Standing 5'10" and weighing in at 185 pounds, Rod Taylor was a successful middleweight boxer in his native Australia. When he arrived in the States, Hollywood wasn't sure what to make of the brawny, broken-nosed actor. They screen-tested him for the leading role of boxer Rocky Graziano in *Somebody Up There Likes Me* (1956); the part went to Paul Newman but Taylor's test drew raves. His first Hollywood work was a fight with Alan Ladd in *Hell on Frisco Bay* (1955), where he reputedly became the 100th man to be beaten by Ladd on screen. He won many admirers fighting the Morlock creatures in *The Time Machine* (1960). By the time he was starring on the short-lived adventure series *Hong Kong* (1960–1961), the macho Taylor was doing all his own fights at his insis-

tence. His best battles came against Roy Jenson in 1960's "Pearl Flower," Charles Horvath in "Freebooter" and Teru Shimada in "Colonel Cat."

In real life, the gutsy Taylor knocked back the brew and was regarded as one of the toughest men in Hollywood. He carried with him a reputation from early Australian pub fights and translated that into playing two-fisted Irish poet Sean O'Casey in *Young Cassidy* (1965). At the height of his fame, he made headlines for getting into a brawl in a London nightclub. His hard-hitting fists became legendary after a real encounter with feared football pro Jim Brown. While making *The Deadly Trackers* (1973) in Durango, Mexico, he beat up co-star Richard Harris so severely that the latter had to miss several days of filming. The drinking and notoriety played havoc with the trajectory of Taylor's career.

As a screen fighter, Taylor went all-out, throwing teeth-baring hooks and crosses with great gusto. It's been said that his screen punches didn't always miss, but the results on screen were undeniably exciting. Notable fights include *Dark of the*

Sun (1968) and *Darker Than Amber* (1970) (see entries). Fights of interest came against Lloyd Berrell in *King of the Coral Sea* (1953), Henri Cogan in *The Liquidator* (1966), Gerry Crampton in *The High Commissioner* (1968), Harry Guardino in *The Hell with Heroes* (1968) and Dick Butkus and Gene LeBell in the pilot film *A Matter of Wife ... and Death* (1976). He took a big punch from John Wayne in *The Train Robbers* (1973). On TV's *Bearcats* (1971), he fought William Smith in "The Return of Esteban." On the short-lived *The Oregon Trail* (1977), he had an on-the-knees punchfest with co-star Charles Napier in "The Waterhole" and a bare-knuckle battle with Claude Akins in "Trappers' Rendezvous." As a guest star, Taylor punched out Robert Forster in the 1997 *Walker, Texas Ranger* episode "Texas vs. Cahill."

See: *Chuka* pressbook; Davidson, Bill. "Why Can't Rod Taylor Be a Pussycat?" *TV Guide.* February 23, 1971; Rane, Jordan. "Borgnine: On Saddling Up on Westerns." *Cowboys & Indians.* October 2012.

SEAN CONNERY VS. PETER MAIVIA in *You Only Live Twice* (1967)

The most underrated fight of the entire Bond series sees Sean Connery engage in a fantastic one-minute office struggle with a Samoan chauffeur (played by Peter Maivia, a professional wrestler and grandfather to future pro wrestling superstar The Rock aka Dwayne Johnson). *Kiss Kiss, Bang Bang* calls it "a terrific set-to," while *James Bond in the Cinema* opined, "This is definitely the best staged fight of the film and reminds one of the good old Oddjob days."

Bond is in Japan to save the world once again, but first he has to protect his own hide from the assassin, who gleefully withdraws a sword and tries to slice Connery in half. Several flips and incredible bumps are taken on the hard floor as Connery fends off the 6'1", 295-pound wrestler with an assortment of office furniture. He even makes use of a small leather couch, holding it up and jabbing Maivia with its end to keep distance between them. Connery sidesteps and clubs a charging Maivia with a statue, sending the agile villain end over end into unconsciousness. Maivia, who helped choreograph the fight, was popular on the English wrestling circuit and had a reputation as a true tough guy.

The final battle occurs in the volcano missile silo headquarters of villain Blofeld (Donald Pleas-

ence), with Connery taking on a hundred mysterious black-outfitted ninjas. He also has to deal with Blofeld's huge blond bodyguard Hans, portrayed by Ronald Rich. After a tense one-minute struggle with Rich in which he's largely manhandled, Connery flips the giant into a moat filled with piranha. Rich is an impressive henchman, but the film would have benefited tremendously by introducing and establishing him earlier as a potential threat. Romo Gorraro and Joe Robinson were doubles in this fight's long shots. Bond veteran Bob Simmons was stunt coordinator. His energies were largely spent on the film's large-scale action climax, filmed on a special set at Pinewood Studios. Martial arts technical advisor Donn Draeger lent a hand in the fight-blocking and doubled for Connery's Asian scenes.

The Bond series was beginning to show the strain of trying to be grand spectacle and suffers from indifferent direction by Lewis Gilbert and an inconsistent screenplay by Roald Dahl that simply employs too much sci-fi gadgetry. Despite the presence of esteemed cinematographer Freddie Young and the exotic location, the film doesn't always show the unparalleled money spent by production designer Ken Adam. An early rooftop fight in Japan's Kagoshima Seaport and Kobe Docks with multiple attackers is unwisely filmed in an aerial long shot, which robs it of its dramatic power and fails to showcase Bond's strengths as a fighter. The scene begs for more close-up action to be incorporated by editor Thelma Connell. Peter Hunt had resigned from the production team when he was bypassed as director, but producer Albert Broccoli persuaded Hunt to return as supervising editor and second unit director with the promise he'd direct the next adventure. Hunt's skills are most evident in the Maivia and Rush fights, with *The Spy Who Trilled Us* stating that they represent "a great example of the Bond team's genius at staging entertaining and suspenseful fight sequences."

You Only Live Twice is considered one of the lesser Connery Bonds, and the star declared it was his last. The character had become so big that he felt the need for distance from the role. Filming in Japan didn't help as the press hounded him relentlessly, even following him into the rest room to snap photos. Connery has been accused of being soft and out of shape for the role, though the Maivia fight hardly shows evidence of this. In addition to training with Draeger, Connery studied briefly with Shohitsu Nakajima and martial arts legend Mas Oyama, who trained him for a week in the privacy of a room in Tokyo's Hotel New Otani. Oyama awarded his pupil an honorary black belt for spreading the popularity of martial arts around the globe. However, the honorary award met with controversy from Japanese martial artists.

See: Adams, Andy. "007's Newest Gimmick." *Black Belt*. August 1967; Solomon, Brian. *WWE Legends*. New York: Simon & Schuster, 2010.

LEE MARVIN VS. TED WHITE AND JERRY CATRON in *Point Blank* (1967)

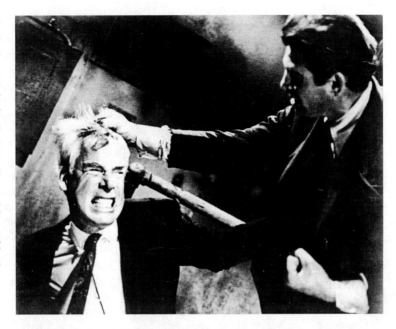

Ted White grabs a fistful of Lee Marvin's hair in MGM's *Point Blank* (1967).

This stylish and influential John Boorman–directed revenge movie provides audiences with the ultimate Lee Marvin violent killer performance. It also gives cinema the first groin punch, and as administered by Marvin to Ted White, it's a brutal, leg-doubling doozy. The MPAA relaxed restrictions on screen violence in 1967, and films immediately began striving for reality in their fights. Reacting to the sudden increase in screen violence, *Life* pointed to this moment specifically, stating it "summarizes in microcosm what's wrong with American movies at the moment." *Orange Coast Magazine* includes the *Point Blank* fight among the most brutal in screen history. Punching someone between the legs may seem unsporting, but any real fighter knows it's an opponent's most vulnerable area and the quickest way to end a fight. Notable genital-crunching fights include Paul Newman's kick to Ted Cassidy in *Butch Cassidy and the Sundance Kid* (1969), William Devane using his hook hand on Luke Askew in *Rolling Thunder* (1977), Charles Bronson grabbing and twisting giant Miguel Angel Fuentes in *The Evil That Men Do* (1984) and Clint Eastwood utilizing an axe handle on Richard Kiel in *Pale Rider* (1985).

The one-minute fight itself, with Marvin taking on thugs White and Jerry Catron backstage in a

psychedelic nightclub, is a triumph of editing, sound and composition. These come courtesy of Boorman's crew of editor Henry Berman, recording supervisor Franklin Milton and D.P. Philip Lathrop. Strobe lights flash, go-go girls gyrate, Bottechelli and Ruben nude images come and go, and singer Stu Gardner yelps from the stage as Marvin smashes a bottle over Catron's head, spills a shelf full of reels on White, then delivers a flying karate kick to White's midsection. The infamous crotch wallop is Marvin's final blow. The fight was shot on a soundstage with off-screen mattresses available for the men so they could make soft landings. Stunt coordinator Carey Loftin and stand-in Boyd Cabeen were available as doubles, but Marvin does as much of his own fighting as possible. The stuntmen rewarded him with a stunt check at the end of filming.

Despite his experience in fight scenes, Marvin could become loose in his choreographed movements. He mistimed a blow and knocked one of Catron's teeth loose. Both the 6'4", 215-pound White and the six-foot, 175-pound Catron were stuntmen. Former Marine White had a tough guy rep having played football at the University of Oklahoma and once winning the Southwest Heavyweight boxing title. It wasn't just the stuntmen Marvin was dominating on screen. One famous scene has female lead Angie Dickinson flailing away at an unemotional Marvin. She hits him until she can swing her arms no more and collapses to her knees in exhausted defeat. Marvin casually sits down and begins watching television. Existentialist viewers see Marvin's character as a dead man walking, a dream ghost of vengeance with this moment their proof. In rehearsal for another scene, Marvin slapped character actor John Vernon so hard that the latter began crying real tears. The film was based on Richard Stark's novel *The Hunter* and is a classic of its kind.

See: Bayouth, Michael. *In the Shadows of Giants.* Palm Avenue, 2014; Carroll, Harrison. "Lee Marvin in a Vicious Film Brawl." *New Castle News.* March 18, 1967; "Lee Marvin Gets Paid for Stuntman Chores." *Ottawa Citizen.* November 3, 1967.

Paul Newman vs. George Kennedy in *Cool Hand Luke* (1967)

One of the screen's most famous confrontations involves the use of gloves but hardly resembles a boxing match. The four-and-a-half-minute Southern prison grudge match between non-conformist Paul Newman and bullying top dog George Kennedy proves to be a pivotal point. It's a gross mismatch that sees the much larger Kennedy knock Newman down approximately 15 times. Underdog Newman's punches barely faze Kennedy. He has nothing behind them. Newman won't quit, and we see Kennedy gradually change during the bout as he begins to lose his anger and enthusiasm for doling out punishment. Even the audience of chain gang convicts loses interest as Newman refuses to stay down. It's a superb transition from co-screenwriters Frank Pierson and Donn Pearce and a fitting metaphor for life. Kennedy's Dragline becomes a devoted admirer of Newman's stubborn character Luke. The warden Strother Martin and guards, however, realize they have a problem on their hands in the fiercely independent Newman.

Director Stuart Rosenberg's *Cool Hand Luke* features what is arguably Newman's most famous

Paul Newman is knocked down by a George Kennedy right cross in Warner Bros./Seven Arts' *Cool Hand Luke* (1967).

performance: He was Oscar-nominated as Best Actor while Kennedy won a Best Supporting Oscar for his fine work. (Kennedy beat out Aldo Ray for the part.) The fight in the yard took four shooting days to complete on the Stockton, California, location which ably substituted for the Deep South after the set was dressed with moss and ivy by art director Cary Odell. Action coordinator Chuck Hicks can be glimpsed as a convict watching the fight. James Arnett was on hand to double Newman, but the star did the shirtless, sweat-soaked fight. The point-of-view shots, punches into the camera, and ground level action were considered cutting edge for the day. The scene was expertly photographed by Conrad Hall, edited by Sam O'Steen and scored with a lone acoustic guitar by Lalo Schifrin. All deserve as much credit for the scene's lasting reputation as the director and on-screen participants.

Mention should be made of the physical demands required to film a fight. A 190-pound man will burn between 10 and 15 calories a minute fighting, depending upon the intensity of the situation. The filming of a master shot can take significant rehearsal time and several takes until the scene is in the can, and one can see the potential for burning several hundred calories an hour. Sometimes filming of an extended fight can take up to a full week of production time. The elements and the environment can come into play. The participants may be outdoors under the blazing sun or inside beneath hot studio lights in heavy costumes. In either scenario, the effort can be physically and mentally draining. Bumps and bruises are commonplace. In *Cool Hand Luke*, Newman and Kennedy are shirtless with no padding to provide protection in case of a slip or a fall. Although they are both acting, a significant amount of their strain and toil in this scene is genuine.

See: Murphy, Myatt, and Mike Mejia. *The Men's Health Gym Bible*. New York: Rodale, 2006; "Screen Fights Are Fantasy, Says Professional Villain." *The Dispatch*. July 20, 1967.

MIKE HENRY VS. RAFER JOHNSON in *Tarzan and the Great River* (1967)

The Tarzan films often featured great fights and the newest Ape Man, 6'3", 210-pound pro football player Mike Henry, showed he could punch on par with his predecessors. To prove he's a hip and more modern Tarzan, Henry breaks out judo chops and throws. In director Robert Day's *Tarzan and the Great River*, Henry has a four-minute struggle on a narrow wooden bridge with 6'3", 200-pound Olympic decathlete Rafer Johnson, who plays a fanatical cult leader responsible for the death of Tarzan's friend. The two fight in and out of a jungle river and through a native village in what Tarzan chronicler David Fury describes as "a vicious picture-ending battle to the death." *Film Daily* found the hand-to-hand combat "fairly exciting," and the fantastic fight proved worthy of a follow-up. The identical Brazilian set was used for the next film *Tarzan and the Jungle Boy* (1968) where Henry and Johnson put on nearly 90 seconds of rough fisticuffs. No stuntmen were used, and Henry has claimed that they choreographed the fight action. It's an accomplishment considering the physical struggles Henry had to overcome in making the picture.

During filming of *Tarzan and the Great River*, Henry was bitten on the chin by a chimpanzee. The wound required nearly 20 stitches and Henry became sick with fever and delirium. For three days, he was in a near-coma. He suffered on the location from food poisoning, dysentery, an inner ear infection and a liver ailment from all the toxins in his body. Muscular animal trainers Dan Haggerty and Rockne Tarkington stood in for Henry in as many shots as possible, but the production had to be shut down for three weeks so Henry could regain his strength. Rafer Johnson suggested that Olympian Don Bragg could replace Henry, but Bragg was in litigation with Sy Weintraub over making a Tarzan knockoff film. Henry returned but announced he was done with the role after his three-film commitment. Weintraub filmed the third picture immediately instead of after a planned layoff, partly because of impending bad weather and for fear that if Henry returned to the States he might never come back. The third film was shut down by a typhoon and severe flooding, but Henry stuck it out. Henry originally planned to star in the *Tarzan* TV series but bowed out due to the demands of the location and Ron Ely took over the role. Henry recovered and had notable fights on *The Green Berets* (1968) and *More Dead Than Alive* (1969) (see entry).

See: Johnson, Rafer, and Philip Goldberg. *The Best That I Can Be*. Thorndike, ME: G.K. Hall, 1999; Petkovich, Anthony. "James Bond of the Jungle." *Filmfax*. May and August 2011.

GEORGE PEPPARD VS. SLIM PICKENS
in Rough Night in Jericho (1967)

A well-mounted Arnold Laven oater filmed in Kanab, Utah, Rough Night in Jericho pits drifting gunfighter George Peppard against cruel town boss Dean Martin. Arriving to help aging Marshal John McIntire, Peppard doesn't like the odds stacked against him but is intrigued by the notion of taking on the powerful Martin. The presence of Jean Simmons determines his fate. The highlight is a nasty two-and-a-half-minute fight between Peppard and henchman Slim Pickens. The latter is known for his humorous and drawling good ol' boy portrayals, but here he's in full brutal, villainous mode. Peppard comes to the rescue of Simmons and the two men battle around a livery stable. There's bullwhip-cracking and hair-pulling, nifty camerawork by Russell Metty, crisp editing from Ted Kent, and excellent use of sound effects. It's considered perhaps the most violent of the late 1960s throat-grabbing western fights and ends with Pickens' death by clubbing. Henry Wills was stunt coordinator with Bobby Clark and Jay Jones filling in for Peppard and Pickens.

Variety termed the movie "as bloody and violent a western as has played the screen," while Films and Filming declared, "What Rough Night in Jericho lacks in the way of suggesting time and place, it makes up for the realism of its scraps which manage to pack a considerable punch despite the irritating red paint we are supposed to accept as blood." Martin, cast against type as the villain, also has a saloon fight with trapper Med Flory that culminates with Flory's head repeatedly being bashed against the bar.

Army Air Corps veteran Slim Pickens (6'3", 230 pounds) was a well-known rodeo clown who tussled with his share of mean bulls. He also fought the occasional cowboy, with a fistfight against steer wrestler Phil Stadtler at San Francisco's Cow Palace becoming legendary. Pickens entered films as a stuntman and sidekick to cowboy star Rex Allen. He often played humorous characters, but those who knew him considered him to be one of the toughest men alive. He had broken nearly every bone in his body.

Notable fights include The Glory Guys (1965), Blazing Saddles (1974) and Mr. Billion (1977) (see entries). Fights of interest came against Percy Helton in Down Laredo Way (1953), Marlon Brando in One-Eyed Jacks (1961), Bill Bixby in The Apple Dumpling Gang (1975) and Christopher Connelly in Hawmps (1976). On TV, Pickens had a major fight with Brian Keith in an episode of The Westerner, "Line Camp" (1960), and a pair of comic black-and-blue battles with Dan Blocker in the Bonanza episodes "Half a Rogue" (1963) and "King of the Mountain" (1965).

See: "Slim Pickens Still Known for Drawl, Availability for Very Tough Roles." Colorado Springs Gazette. December 17, 1975; "Sober Mr. Martin Plays Film Heavy." Lima News. October 30, 1966.

BURT LANCASTER VS. OSSIE DAVIS
in The Scalphunters (1968)

The Scalphunters is an entertaining Sydney Pollack western that has an amusing interplay between erudite runaway slave Ossie Davis and fur trapper Burt Lancaster that manages to say much about topical 1960s race relations. Tensions between the pair mount as they outwit a group of Kiowa Indians and a marauding band of scalpers led by Telly Savalas who lay claim to Lancaster's pelts. Throughout the violent yet tongue-in-cheek William Norton–scripted film, Duke Callaghan films the leads at odd angles to accentuate the characters' sense of opposition. Composer Elmer Bernstein emphasizes the men as diametric opposites with their individual themes. Davis and Lancaster come to blows at the climax, and it's a lengthy serio-comic exchange of punches winding up in a mud hole. Variety called the fight "dynamic." Both participants become caked in mud and, theoretically, colorless to one another. The sight is so amusing that the Indians erupt in laughter. It might seem overly silly, but in 1968 comedy was one of the safest ways to address the subject of racial tension while still offering a primal cathartic effect by viewing the men inflicting pain upon one another. At one point they both swing and miss wildly and lose their balance. It's subtly symbolic of both sides' standing on the issue that they are both off-base.

In regard to the mud bath, United Artists publicity took a play on words and called the fight the dirtiest in screen history. The fight was filmed on a high mountain mesa in Mexico where temperatures were reported to reach over 100 degrees. For the mud hole, they needed to pump the water from a lower elevation, and it was ice cold. Between takes, Lancaster and Davis were huddled in blankets while the crew was sweating from the heat. Stunt coordinator Tony Epper doubled Lancaster, who claimed credit for choreographing the fight.

Editor John Woodcock does a fine job concealing Epper's involvement. The 6'2", 195-pound Davis also appears to do the fight though Chuck Roberson was on location and ready for an always controversial "paint down." At this time it was still common practice for a white stuntman to put on dark makeup to double a black actor as there were not yet firmly established black stuntmen. That would change.

Tony Epper had a reputation as one of the toughest men in Hollywood. A feared bar fighter, he inadvertently killed a man with a punch during an altercation in Nogales, Arizona, while making *Ulzana's Raid* (1972). Epper was outnumbered and it was determined that he acted in self-defense, and the unfortunate incident added to his already formidable reputation. At 6'4" and 220 pounds, he was a top fight man often recruited to portray heavies and throw his weight around. Fights of interest came against Gary Lockwood in *Bad Georgia Road* (1977), Marc Singer in *The Beastmaster* (1982), Tommy Lee Jones in the TV mini-series *Lonesome Dove* (1989) and Warren Beatty in *Dick Tracy* (1990). On TV, he fought everyone from Adam West on *Batman* to David Carradine on *Kung Fu*. His fight with Jan-Michael Vincent on the 1985 *Airwolf* episode "Annie Oakley" won a stuntman's award for best fight sequence of the year.

See: "Actor-Stuntman Tony Epper Dies at 73." *Variety*. July 30, 2012; "Ossie Davis Is Delighted with *Scalphunters* Role." *Pittsburgh Courier*. April 6, 1968; *The Scalphunters* pressbook.

THE SALOON BRAWL in *The Devil's Brigade* (1968)

Director Andrew McLaglen cast several rough-and-tumble actors and athletes in the uneven but nonetheless entertaining story of this real World War II unit, a combination of elite Canadians and U.S. soldiers that became the First Special Service Force. Much of the film concerns their rigorous Montana training and the conflict and prejudices that develop between the Yanks and the Canucks. Claude Akins on the U.S. side and Jack Watson on the Canadian side appear ready to come to blows, with Akins vowing to do his nastiest work. Their differences, however, become a common bond when they encounter a loudmouthed group of bullying lumberjacks led by Don Megowan and engage them in a wild five-minute saloon free-for-all. The joint is torn apart with upended tables and broken windows. The actors cast as soldiers perform their own limited stunt work for the fight, among them Akins, Watson, Richard Jaeckel, Luke Askew, Tom Stern, Andrew Prine and Jeremy Slate. The latter portrays the Canadian hand-to-hand combat expert training the men in the art of Defendu, a close quarters fighting system based on elements of Kodokan judo and W.E. Fairbairn's teachings. Slate's character was based on Dermot "Paddy" O'Neill. The arrival of M.P. Norman Alden adds to the mess. Akins and Watson end up arm-in-arm buddies.

McLaglen begins the scene with a fair amount of credible tension but intentionally allows it to devolve into outright comedy. *Films and Filming* praised the fight as "energetic," while *Variety* called it "well-staged." Studio publicity didn't shy away from declaring it "a screen brawl to rival the great film fights of all time." *The Big Damn Book of Sheer Manliness* includes it among their best barroom brawls.

The impressive fight was

Burt Lancaster (left) squares off against Ossie Davis in United Artists' *The Scalphunters* (1968).

completed over a continuous 24-hour period as
the film company was losing the location, a Salt
Lake City, Utah, gin mill. By the end of the
marathon filming session, the participants were so
tired and sore they could barely turn their heads.
It was an expensive day for producer David
Wolper. The stuntmen were on overtime and the
brawl cost nearly $3000 in prop supplies alone.
McLaglen ordered 25 tables, 24 chairs, 50 beer
mugs, 75 whiskey bottles, 25 shot glasses, 80 beer
bottles, five large beer kegs, 25 cases of bottled
beer and 45 cartons of cigarettes. Hal Needham
coordinated the action with D.P. William H.
Clothier and used nearly 30 stuntmen for the fight.
It's an achievement given the time constraints.
Stuntmen Ronnie Rondell, Jr., Fred Krone, Glenn
Wilder, Roydon Clark, Jerry Gatlin, John Hudkins,
Jim Burk, Chuck Hayward, Bill Couch and Budd
Albright worked in the melee. Krone is all over the
place. Some participants were former football
players and professional boxers, adding a few new
faces to the usual suspects. Among these were
Green Bay Packer standout Paul Hornung and
professional boxers Rex Layne, Don Fullmer and
his brother Gene Fullmer as the bartender. Professional wrestler and boxer Wilhelm Von Hom-
burg has a short fight on the battlefield with Akins.

Jeremy Slate, a 165-pound six-footer, served
with the Navy in World War II and played football
for St. Lawrence University. Taking advantage of
his beach boy good looks and physical handiness,
he landed the co-lead in the underwater TV adventure *The Aquanauts* aka *Malibu Run* (1960–
1961). He had a solid run in 1960s Hollywood
playing both good guys and bad guys, memorably
providing menace for Tom Laughlin's Billy Jack in
The Born Losers (1967). Slate fought Elvis Presley
in *Girls, Girls, Girls* (1962), Dean Martin in *The
Sons of Katie Elder* (1965) (see entry), Ross Hagen
in *The Mini-Skirt Mob* (1968), Adam Roarke in
Hell's Belles (1969) and Tom Stern in *Hells Angels
'69* (1969). Frankie Avalon hit him with a guitar
in *I'll Take Sweden* (1965). On TV, Slate faced
George Maharis in 1962's *Route 66* episode "Ever
Ride the Waves in Oklahoma?," Ryan O'Neal in
1963's *Empire* episode "The Loner," Robert Stack
in 1963's *Untouchables* episode "A Taste for Pine-
apple" and Michael Landon in 1968's *Bonanza*
episode "The Passing of a King."

See: Basden, Nelson. "Jeremy Slate." *Psychotronic Video.* #36, 2002; *The Devil's Brigade* pressbook; "Producer Tags Top Pros for Barroom Film
Brawl." *Times-Picayune.* January 14, 1968.

ROD TAYLOR VS. PETER CARSTEN in *Dark of the Sun* (1968)

Dark of the Sun (aka *The Mercenaries*), a gritty,
highly suspenseful Jack Cardiff jungle-action film,
is widely considered to be Rod Taylor's best and
has garnered a host of admirers over the years
(among them Martin Scorsese and Quentin
Tarantino). Taylor and Jim Brown play mercenaries in the Congo squaring off against rebels, diamond smugglers and other soldiers of fortune with
varying agendas as they try to rescue a kidnapped
Yvette Mimiuex. Taylor has disgust for former
Nazi mercenary Peter Carsten. Working from a
Wilbur Smith novel, screenwriter Quentin Werty
(a pseudonym for Ranald MacDougall) gave the
characters a past conflict that propels the plot forward. When the German knifes Brown, Taylor
goes after him with a vengeance in a thrilling,
white-knuckle Jeep chase that turns into one of
the era's most violent fistfights. Taylor literally
bulldogs Carsten from his Jeep and begins unloading vicious punches on his adversary as Jacques
Loussier's score pounds away. Carsten climbs
down a sheer rock face and a series of vines with
Taylor in hot pursuit until the fight concludes in
a small river.

There's great footage of stunt doubles Louie
Elias and Gerry Crampton fighting while hanging
from the vines. The fighters end up back on level
ground among the rocky edges of a river, as an animalistic Taylor savagely breaks Carsten's arm and
stabs the villain to death. It's a shocking moment
that audiences had never experienced from a film's
nominal hero. Then again, it was Rod Taylor, and
he was ticked off over his friend's death. Taylor
and Carsten had an earlier fight near a train with
Carsten brandishing a chainsaw; the battle ended
with Taylor pressing Carsten's head onto a train
rail. Ironically, Brown saves Carsten by plowing
into Taylor and wrestling him to the ground. *The
Milwaukee Journal* wrote there were "a couple of
brawls between Taylor and Carsten that for inven-
tiveness and excitement could not be improved
upon." The *Toledo Blade* called the action "so exceptionally brutal and violent that it makes grid
contests look like Sunday school picnics."

Despite the presence of stunt arrangers Elias
and Crampton, Taylor once again did the overwhelming majority of his stunts while nursing an
injury throughout filming. He tore tendons in the
knee when he landed awkwardly after jumping
from a balcony into the back of a Jeep. There were

fears that production would be shut down until the leading man healed, but Taylor opted to tough out the pain and returned to action after two days. There was little the star shied away from, and the film is literally wall-to-wall fighting with fists and guns. It's all thrilling and superbly edited by Ernest Walter. Elias, doubling Taylor for the rope fight, called the picture the most difficult he'd ever worked on. Elias and Crampton were 150 feet above the ground, swinging back and forth trading punches. Whenever they met in the middle, it ultimately knocked them back against the cliff face. The Nazi character portrayed by the stone-faced Carsten was based on an actual German in the Congo who wore an Iron Cross. D.P. Edward Scaife, veteran of the superior Tarzan films, gets the jungles of Jamaica to effectively stand in for the African Congo.

Dark of the Sun is notorious for the real animosity existing between the stars. To the press, Taylor heaped praise upon his co-star Brown, but behind the scenes he and the pro football player were at odds. In his memoir, co-star Kenneth More noted that they appeared to hate each other, and Taylor fancied his chances of knocking out the much bigger Brown. Taylor was around 5'10" and a solid 185 pounds. Brown was 6'2" and over 230 pounds of sculpted muscle; few pro football linebackers could bring him down in an open field tackle. Most thought Taylor had more guts than brains. Their brief fight in the film took five punishing takes of a shoulder block and increased the tension between the two. The bad blood carried over when filming was done. The two reportedly came to real blows during a major altercation at Hugh Hefner's Playboy Mansion.

See: Bowyer, Justin. *Conversations with Jack Cardiff: Art, Light, and Direction in Cinema*. London: Batsford, 2003; *Dark of the Sun* pressbook; McDaniel, Marlene. *Mr. Louie Elias: A Tribute*. Self-published, 2010; Munn, Michael. *Hollywood Rogues*. Oxford, England: Isis, 1992.

The Pool Hall Brawl
in *Coogan's Bluff* (1968)

Six-foot-four, 200-pound Clint Eastwood, a former lumberjack, lifeguard and Army swimming instructor, had already established himself on screen as a formidable presence with a gun on his hip, but Don Siegel's fish-out-of-water story *Coogan's Bluff* showed what the rising star could do with his fists. As a modern Arizona cop trailing killer Don Stroud in New York City, Eastwood faces ten men armed with pool cues in this terrifically created action scene. *The Motion Picture Guide* labels it "one of the best fight scenes ever," and *Orange Coast Magazine* includes it among the most brutally realistic hand-to-hand encounters. Eastwood's superstardom was cemented with his first devastating punch against the cocky, bespectacled Jerry Summers. He's descended upon by the entire bar, made up of Dick Crockett, Loren Janes, Larry Duran, Allen Pinson, Troy Melton, Fred Stromsoe, Andy Epper and stunt coordinator Paul Baxley. Eastwood smashes pool cues and throws eight balls at his assailants as he jumps atop the tables and kicks Pinson in the face. Kudos must go to Siegel and D.P. Bud Thackery who shoot from Eastwood's point of view as he leaps onto a pool table. In fact, at one point Eastwood filmed with a hand-held Arriflex camera while braced by a camera assistant. Composer Lalo Schifrin builds great suspense, and editor Sam E. Waxman cuts it together for maximum effect. The only false note is the fake-looking blood smeared on Eastwood's face.

Eastwood does the majority of the fight on a Universal soundstage (double Clyde Howdy takes over briefly for a fall off the table into a chair). He acquits himself well but is overcome by the multitude of fists and boots. The men flee at the sound

Clint Eastwood punches David Doyle in Universal's *Coogan's Bluff* (1968).

of police sirens, save for observer David Doyle, already established as a Stroud accomplice. Doyle comes over to give the prone Eastwood a final kick, only to have the bloodied star rise to his feet and knock Doyle flat onto a pool table. Eastwood delivers several short sledgehammer punches into Doyle's face as he demands to know the whereabouts of Stroud. This particular style of punch became an Eastwood trademark, as did his habit of rising up from near death to vanquish his foes. Stroud receives the punch after a climactic motorcycle chase.

Eastwood enjoyed doing fights. Instead of throwing from a wide angle for the camera to see, he favored pulling his fist straight back with his eyes glued on his opponent in close-up. This allowed him a certain intimacy with the viewer, who felt they were the target of Eastwood's teeth-clenching wrath. He seldom delivered the traditional John Wayne follow-through, instead often pulling up just short of his target which made his punches unique. Doing his own fights made his action scenes more believable, and he became the big screen's most identified bare-knuckle brawler with his comedy hits *Every Which Way but Loose* (1978) and *Any Which Way You Can* (1980).

Screen fighting was an art Eastwood developed over time. He lost his first encounter, suffering a one-punch knockdown from Scott Brady in the low-budget western *Ambush at Cimarron Pass* (1958), an experience Eastwood regarded as an overall embarrassment. He could be proud of a 1959 guest shot on TV's *Maverick* in which he had a great fight with James Garner in "Duel at Sundown." On his own series *Rawhide* (1959–1966), Eastwood's Rowdy Yates had a standout fight with Woody Strode in 1961's "Incident of the Buffalo Soldier." Fights of interest came against Fred Graham and Hal Baylor in 1961's "Incident of the Black Sheep," Mickey Finn in 1961's "Incident of the Wager on Payday," Bill Travers in 1963's "Incident at Two Graves" and Timothy Carey in 1965's "Encounter at Boot Hill." As he learned from various experienced directors and cameramen on *Rawhide,* Eastwood began to foster his own fighting technique. After success making Sergio Leone Spaghetti Westerns in Italy, he formed his own company Malpaso and his screen fights and tough guy image grew into legend.

Eastwood's toughness wasn't all movie show. Producer Fritz Manes claimed that in the 1950s, Eastwood cleared out a bar with six sailors when one took a cheap shot at his friend. He hoisted iron at Vince's Gym and possessed a natural inclination toward streetfighting moves such as disabling kicks to the lower legs that set up his strong fists. He trained with martial artist Donnie Williams for his fights in *The Gauntlet* (1977). Rangy and lithely muscled, he built a reputation as a quiet tough guy with a feared temper that he usually kept under control. He was one laconic star nobody wanted to rile. His rage could boil to the surface in an instant, and that was part of his screen appeal and physical presence.

Notable fights include *The Eiger Sanction* (1975), *Every Which Way but Loose* (1978) and *Any Which Way You Can* (1980) (see entries). Fights of interest came against Jose Marco in *For a Few Dollars More* (1967), Bruce Dern in *Hang 'Em High* (1968), Don Stroud in *Joe Kidd* (1972), Bill McKinney in *Thunderbolt and Lightfoot* (1974), Chuck Hicks and Robert Hoy in *The Enforcer* (1976), Roy Jenson and Dan Vadis in *The Gauntlet* (1977), Bruce M. Fischer in *Escape from Alcatraz* (1979) and *City Heat* (1984), Eugene Lipinski in *Firefox* (1982), Russ McCubbin and Robert Sutton in *Sudden Impact* (1983), Pete Koch, Everett McGill and Nicholas Worth in *Heartbreak Ridge* (1985), Clive Mantle in *White Hunter, Black Heart* (1990), Tommy Lee Jones in *Space Cowboys* (2000) and Sonny Vue in *Gran Torino* (2008).

See: Pope, Norris. *Chronicle of a Camera: The Arriflex 35 in North America, 1945–1972.* Jackson: University Press of Mississippi, 2013; Siegel, Don. *A Siegel Film: An Autobiography.* London: Faber & Faber, 1993.

ELVIS PRESLEY VS. RED WEST AND SONNY WEST in *Live a Little, Love a Little* (1968)

Norman Taurog's formula Elvis Presley comedy has Presley playing a fashion photographer who can fight and muss his hair. After being fired, he is accosted at a printing press by two workers, played by Presley's real-life bodyguards Red and Sonny West. The West cousins coordinated the energetic 90-second fight with Presley at the *Hollywood Citizen-News,* and it's arguably the best fight the singer ever did on screen. Despite stuntman Bob Harris being on the film, Presley performed all his own stunts for Fred Koenekamp's camera, mixing in karate kicks, chops and flips. There was excellent use of the obstacles found at the printing press. Sonny West displays great athleticism diving through a moving cart to hit Presley in the chest. Taurog was able to get his master shot in one take and was pleased with the realism of the action. He gave both Red and Sonny $600 apiece bonus for their day of work.

No discussion of the toughest men in Hollywood could be complete without mention of Red West. The six-foot, 200-pound Tennessean played football at Jones Junior College, boxed in Golden Gloves and served in the Marine Corps. He entered Hollywood as a stuntman and toiled as a bouncer at a San Fernando Valley bar, the Crossbow. West worked on nearly all Presley's films as his preferred fight part-

Elvis Presley (center) fights Sonny West (left) and Red West in MGM's *Live a Little, Love a Little* (1968).

ner, with noteworthy battles coming in *Wild in the Country* (1961) and *Tickle Me* (1965). The Memphis native had known Presley since high school and became his chief bodyguard on tour. West earned a black belt in Kenpo karate and later owned his own dojo. He was a regular stuntman on TV's *The Wild Wild West* and put on many outstanding fights with series star Robert Conrad. The best came in 1967's "The Night of the Running Death" (with West doubling Ken Swofford) and 1968's "The Night of the Vipers."

There was real friction between Presley and Red West, courtesy of both Red and Sonny being left off the guest list to Presley's marriage to Priscilla Beaulieu. It was a significant slight as both cousins were loyal and closer to Presley than anyone else in the Memphis Mafia. Red had not spoken to Presley for several months before being hired by Taurog for this film's fight. As Presley's use of prescription medication escalated to dangerous levels in the 1970s, he had Red and Sonny fired for intervening in his medicine's delivery. The bodyguards responded by writing the controversial *Elvis—What Happened?* The book was intended as a wake-up call in hopes they could shock Presley into stopping his substance abuse. It was too late to do any good. Presley died of polypharmacy in 1977, weeks after the book's release. Fans refused to believe the sensational informa-

tion in the book and saw Red and Sonny as money-hungry Judases. In reality, Presley tried to pay them not to write the book, but they refused the money.

See: Hoey, Michael A. *Elvis' Favorite Director: The Amazing 52-Year Career of Norman Taurog*. Albany, GA: BearManor, 2015; *Live a Little, Love a Little* pressbook; West, Sonny. *Elvis: Still Taking Care of Business*. Chicago: Triumph, 2008.

JIM BROWN VS. ERNEST BORGNINE in *The Split* (1968)

It's the super-cool late 1960s sex symbol versus the veteran movie brute as formidable NFL great Jim Brown tests heist recruit Ernest Borgnine early in Gordon Flemyng's caper film *The Split*. They have a punishing no-holds-barred fight behind a locked door in a gym's office. It's a ridiculous reason for a fight, but there's no denying it's the best moment in a stylish film equipped with heavy-hitting character actors, a hip Quincy Jones score and a plot lifted from a Donald Westlake novel centering on ripping off the take from a Los Angeles Rams football game. Editor Rita Roland put together a solid one-minute sequence of the stars exchanging powerful blows. The grinning Borgnine passes his test, but the loot comes up missing and everyone points a finger at Brown. MGM publicity played up the fight's martial arts and suggested karate school tie-ins to exhibitors for promotional purposes.

The presentation of a strong black male beating up a white man was notorious and took Sidney Poitier's famous slap from *In the Heat of the Night* (1967) several degrees further. To the film's credit, race is a non-issue among the characters. Clad in designer leather, a tight-lipped Brown is effective as the gang leader, while Borgnine is an old pro at bone-crunching physicality. The two had a brief buildup to an exchange earlier in the year in *Ice Station Zebra* (1968), and here they have the audience-pleasing match-up they should have had in that Cold War thriller. Novice movie fighter Brown connected for real with Borgnine. The latter wasn't happy but didn't complain. Paul Baxley served as fight coordinator, incorporating a Brown dropkick and a Borgnine throw that sent Brown end over end into a wall. Both highlight moves were performed by stuntmen Jimmy Casino

(Borgnine) and Calvin Brown, although cinematographer Burnett Guffey was able to move his camera in close on the action without being too revealing. Brown shattered his leg working on the film, an injury that derailed a promising career as the industry's first professional black stuntman.

Six-two, 230-pound Jim Brown was a phenomenal athlete and genetically gifted specimen of machismo with a deeply focused intensity suggesting a great capacity for inflicting violence. Coming out of Syracuse University as an All-American, he was offered a contract to become a professional boxer. Brown opted for pro football, where he became a nine-time Pro Bowler and a four-time MVP during his nine seasons as a fullback running over opponents for the Cleveland Browns. When he retired before his 30th birthday, he was the all-time rushing and touchdown leader and held 15 individual NFL records. Brown was legendary for his ability to break tackles, particularly with his use of stiff-arms and a devastating forearm blow that often knocked defenders dizzy. The powerfully built Brown had a 50" chest, a 32" waist, nearly 18" biceps and 28" thighs without the benefit of ever seriously touching a weight. Anatomists were literally studying his bone structure and muscle attachments.

Notable fights include *Dark of the Sun* (1968), *100 Rifles* (1969) and *Slaughter's Big Rip-Off* (1973) (see entries). Fights of interest came against Gerry Crampton and Terry Richards in *The Dirty Dozen* (1967), Charles Horvath in *Kenner* (1969), Bernie Casey in ... tick ... Tick ... Tick... (1970), Lee Van Cleef in *El Condor* (1970), Robert Phillips in *Slaughter* (1972), Bruce Glover in *Black Gunn* (1972), Ted Cassidy in *The Slams* (1973), Fred Williamson in *Three the Hard Way* (1974) and *Take a Hard Ride* (1975), and Arnold Schwarzenegger in *The Running Man* (1987). In *Mars Attacks* (1996), he played a legendary boxing champion, comically punching out the space invaders. On TV, he traded

Ernest Borgnine judo chops Jim Brown in MGM's *The Split* (1968).

punches with Bill Cosby on the 1967 *I Spy* episode "Cops and Robbers" and William Shatner on the 1983 *T.J. Hooker* episode "Raw Deal."

See: Carroll, Harrison. "Behind the Scenes in Hollywood." *New Castle News*. February 16, 1968; *The Split* pressbook.

THE MALAYSIA BAR BRAWL in *Hellfighters* (1968)

By 1968, it seemed unlikely any John Wayne-Andrew McLaglen film could pass muster without a barroom brawl. Never mind that this wasn't a western, or that the brawl clocked in at barely over a minute. Screenwriter Clair Huffaker was known to insert a fight whenever his people-plotting bogged down. *Hellfighters* is about modern oil well fire crews with Wayne's screen character based on the real-life fire ace Red Adair. Wayne and his hot-shot group are dispatched to Malaya where they are quick to have a fistfight with a rival bunch of Australians at Madame Lu's Bar (actually a Universal set). Seconds after being introduced to antagonistic John Alderson, Wayne is punching him out in a fight the *Salina Journal* called "a lulu." Co-stars Jim Hutton, Ed Faulkner and Bruce Cabot join Wayne to battle Alderson's men. The 6'2", 200-plus-pound Alderson was a member of the British Army whose nickname was "Basher."

Chuck Roberson was there to double Wayne, but did little more than help set up the action for Wayne to perform. Stunt coordinator Hal Needham does a fantastic job with the choreography. After years of working with Cliff Lyons and his crew of stuntmen, Wayne was familiarizing himself with Needham's new group of athletic danger men. Roydon Clark, Jim Burk, Mickey Gilbert, Stan Barrett, Dick Bullock, Everett Creach, Rock Walker, Alan Gibbs, Gary McLarty, Chuck Courtney and Ronnie Rondell, Jr., were relative newcomers in the eyes of Wayne, but they threw their bodies around the set with great energy. Wayne likely found solace in the fact that gray-haired crony Cabot was still right beside him throwing punches. However, both were beginning to show their age. Although the fight is exceedingly well-filmed by D.P. William Clothier, scored by Leonard Rosenman, and tightly edited by Folmar Blangsted, it remains one of the Duke's lesser recognized barroom brawls. The *Buffalo Courier Express* referred to it as "less than spectacular."

Much of the film was lensed in the Houston, Texas, area with local performers awarded bit parts. Baytown weathercaster Chris Chandler was given the small role of an obnoxious newscaster who gets on Wayne's bad side during an interview about a blown-out oil well. Wayne promptly knocks the man out. The casting of Chandler's on-screen character was close to home. When the movie had its local premiere, the audience erupted in cheers when Wayne decked their hometown celebrity.

See: Hines, Marilyn. "Wayne and Cast Battle Raging Oil Well Fires." *Salina Journal*. December 29, 1968; Holcomb, Henry. "He Conquers Baytown ... Big John Wayne." *Baytown Sun*. March 19, 1968.

CHARLES BRONSON VS. ALAIN DELON in *Farewell, Friend* (1968)

A finely choreographed fight in a high security office vault highlights this mystery thriller that cemented Charles Bronson's European stardom. He's especially good here as a charismatic soldier of fortune. As colleagues in the French-Algerian war, Bronson and co-star Alain Delon are evenly matched anti-heroes with different agendas who become trapped in a safe they've reluctantly joined to crack. They are soon at one another's throats. No doubles were used in the two-minute fight, unique in the sense that both men are dressed alike in white shirts and dark slacks. A marked effort to engage in blocks and body punches is displayed, a skill in which Bronson had few cinematic peers. Director Jean Herman and co-writer Sebastian Japrisot fashioned a slick and interesting film, allowing its leads to carry the Antoine Baud–coordinated action. The French-Italian production was retitled *Honor Among Thieves* for American consumption.

There's a moment when Bronson acts as a pimp of sorts to a wealthy clientele. However, when they become too nasty with the girl, Bronson emerges as her protector. He has little trouble with the rich man's bodyguards, dispatching them with an economy of kicks and well-placed chops. It's similar in staging to a fight in *Rider on the Rain* (1970) against multiple opponents that also perfectly illustrates how Bronson entered the pantheon of mythical tough guys. In this, he saves Marlene Jobert with a fluid explosion of fists, feet and lightning-quick reflexes. He had been a formidable screen fighter in the past, but now he was a European star and able to mow through five bodyguards in a few seconds without one landing a blow. Bronson repeated the action by taking on a bar full of cowboy toughs in *Chino* (1974).

Five-foot-nine and 165 pounds, Alain Delon served as a paratrooper with the French military and was a French-Indochina War veteran. He was as slick and graceful as he was handsome and consistently impressed audiences with his action abilities. He became a huge star in Europe portraying dangerous gangster characters in films like *Le Samourai* (1967). Delon fought Renalto Salvatori in *Rocco and His Brothers* (1960), John Davis Chandler and Tony Musante in *Once a Thief* (1965), Dean Martin in *Texas Across the River* (1966) and Jean-Paul Belmondo in *Borsalino* (1970) (see entry). At 50 and still fit, Delon impressed with several extended fights in 1985's *Cop's Honor* (aka *Parole de Flic*).

See: Chiesi, Roberto. *Alain Delon*. Rome: Gremesi, 2002.

CLINT WALKER VS. MIKE HENRY in *More Dead Than Alive* (1968)

More Dead Than Alive is an offbeat western with Clint Walker cast as a recently released convict trying to re-establish himself in society. He catches on with Vincent Price's traveling road show, but his past comes back to haunt him in the form of outlaw Mike Henry. The latter seeks vengeance on Walker for foiling his brother's attempted prison break. Henry bushwhacks Walker early in screenwriter George Schenck's plot. A laughing Henry improbably decides to let Walker live, setting up the climactic one-and-a-half-minute fight between the men. Both stars eschew the use of stunt doubles as they go all-out slugging and grappling in and around a barn. Hay on the ground provides a soft landing spot for their falls. Feedbags and supplies are hurled, wooden beams are swung at heads, and the two crash recklessly through a barn door. Walker also goes through a window in what is obviously him doing his own stunt. In the end, a vicious right cross from Walker knocks Henry out. "Laugh now," says Walker.

Fred Carson coordinated the action. Unfortunately, much of the fight's latter half is lost in the darkness of a poorly lit barn. Fault for this must be leveled at director Robert Sparr and cinematographer Jack Marquette. Sparr was coming from the TV ranks and had a reputation for shooting fast. Walker had worked with Sparr on *Cheyenne,* and they were accustomed to setting up screen fights in less than 15 minutes. The difference on bigger

features was that sometimes an entire day would be set aside for total preparation of an action scene. *More Dead Than Alive* falls somewhere in between. Editor John F. Schreyer cut it together the best he could considering the sometimes barely visible footage provided.

Walker always said he needed big guys to fight, and in rugged former NFL player and movie Tarzan Mike Henry he got his wish. Ironically, Henry started as a background player on Walker's series *Cheyenne,* with Warner Bros. signing him to a contract as a potential "Clint Walker Type." The stars did their job in exemplary fashion, putting on a savage and believable fight. However, a blooper is left intact for the sharp-eyed viewer. At the fight's beginning, when Walker burst through the window to tackle Henry, the latter momentarily forgot his gun was supposed to go flying for the men to scramble after. To save the shot, Henry flings away his own gun.

See: *More Dead Than Alive* Blu-ray special features; *More Dead Than Alive* pressbook; "Option Grid Pro." *Toledo Blade.* October 1, 1961; "TV Highlights." *San Antonio Express.* July 4, 1965.

JIM BROWN VS. BURT REYNOLDS in *100 Rifles* (1969)

The selling point of this Tom Gries western was the hot and notorious pairing of Jim Brown and Raquel Welch, although co-star Burt Reynolds walked away with the acting honors as a charismatic half–Yaqui bandit. Reynolds becomes Brown's prisoner, but the bickering duo are forced to unite for a big climax against Mexican soldiers led by Fernando Lamas. Halfway through the film, there's a solid 90-second fight between the shackled pair that has Reynolds landing a surprise kick. After some rolling around, the much larger Brown begins tossing Reynolds about and heaves him right over a 400-foot ledge. Reynolds hangs on the side as the bad guys approach, and Brown is forced to pull him back up via their chain. When Reynolds reaches the top, he lands another sucker punch on Brown. There were several inches in height and about a 60-pound weight difference between the combatants, but they make it work for the screen with camera angles and other time-worn tricks.

The film was shot in Almeria, Spain, with Chuck Roberson serving as the second unit director. Gries was originally going to have Roberson or Terry Leonard put on blackface to double

Brown, but the actors balked. Leonard said he did do portions of the film's horseback stunts in black-face. Reynolds injured his neck during the fight and had to wear a neck brace throughout the rest of filming. He also suffered a gashed head and a sprained wrist and knee. He said that being hand-cuffed to Jim Brown in a fight was like being chained to a Ferrari going 80 miles per hour down the highway. Character player Aldo Sambrell took Brown to task for being too rough in fights, terming it unprofessional. Roberson recalls Hal Needham being there to double Reynolds in the long shots hanging off the cliff, although in his au-tobiography Reynolds takes credit for doing his own stunts and choreographing the entire fight as well. He claims Brown had a fear of heights, and that's why he took advantage of setting the fight on the ledge overlooking the wide-open Spanish vista. Taking a potshot at his own career, Reynolds joked that if they fell off, the headline would be "Jim Brown and Unknown Actor Die."

See: Conley, Kevin. *The Full Burn*. New York: Bloomsbury, 2008; "Making a Movie with Jim Brown Can Be a Risky Operation." *Detroit Free Press*. October 10, 1968.

THE FOURTH OF JULY PICNIC BRAWL in *The Undefeated* (1969)

Andrew McLaglen's post–Civil War saga *The Undefeated* features the intriguing pairing of John Wayne and Rock Hudson, although they are more or less bystanders during the rip-roaring five-minute melee be-tween members of Wayne's Yan-kees and Hudson's Rebels at a Fourth of July picnic. Wayne and Hudson sip whiskey from their coffee tins and comment on the spirited fighting, which begins as a representative challenge be-tween Union member Jim Burk and Confederate Merlin Olsen, the giant-sized defensive tackle for the Los Angeles Rams. Stunt-man Burk has a showcase for his talents, bringing a healthy dose of charisma to his part and even doing double-duty as a stuntman for football player Roman Ga-briel during the brawl. Events es-calate after a minute of humorous fighting as the overmatched Burk

begins hitting other Johnny Rebs. Everyone gets in on the comic action, including cast members Bruce Cabot, Jan-Michael Vincent, Edward Faulkner, Harry Carey, Jr., and Don Collier. The 6'5", 275-pound Olsen upends a wagon with sev-eral stuntmen on it and lifts Jerry Gatlin over his head.

Familiar character actor Dub Taylor generates the most laughs during the good-natured fight as he eats chicken and mashed potatoes amidst the action. Comic relief bits often found their way into John Wayne's brawling scenes as he knew his au-dience appreciated the levity. Ben Johnson and Robert Donner are seen fishing by the river as a parallel pairing to Wayne and Hudson. Both tandems realize they need to contribute to the fighting as part of their duty. Donner and Johnson reluctantly take swings at one another, with the latter taking a nicely executed fall into the river. A grinning Wayne and Hudson set down their cups and each administer a knockdown blow, with Wayne enacting a comic spinning double take as the fight closes as a draw.

Wayne and McLaglen used a crew familiar to them. Cameraman William H. Clothier did exem-plary work shooting the outdoor action footage, filming Olsen from low angles to accentuate his size. Scriptwriter James Lee Barrett was responsi-ble for the humor while Hugo Montenegro con-tributed a whimsical score. Editor Robert Simpson assembled action coordinator Hal Needham's ex-tensive footage into an entertaining segment that

Rock Hudson lands a left cross on John Wayne in 20th Century-Fox's *The Undefeated* (1969).

sees both bruised and battered groups parting amicably. *The Milwaukee Journal* called it "a humorous interlude," and the *Pittsburgh Press* said the sequence "has all the fun of pure slapstick comedy." However, Wayne biographer Allen Eyles compared it unfavorably to the work of John Ford, saying it is "all surface knockabout with no sense of the shape and delight Ford brought to his mass fights."

Wayne does less fighting here than usual: He had suffered injured ribs and torn shoulder ligaments after falling from a horse early in the shooting. He was now in his early sixties and still taking hits of oxygen due to the high elevation of the Durango, Mexico, location, so his reluctance to join the heavy action is understandable given he was operating with one lung. Some have suggested that Wayne was homophobic and made it difficult on Hudson, but interviews of both actors and crew present a more pleasant picture. Wayne appreciated Hudson's professionalism on the set after he stepped in as a late replacement for James Arness. Hudson and Wayne played chess and bridge together, suggesting an amicable and comfortable set. The actors and crew were so familiar with one another that practical jokes were played. McLaglen took delight in waiting until the river's spring current was sufficiently cold before putting Johnson and Donner into the water. Stuntman John Hudkins also found humor at the expense of Burk, a Los Angeles Rams fan. Burk was looking forward to meeting both Olsen and quarterback Gabriel. However, he was dismayed to find both players giving him the cold shoulder on the set. Hudkins had told them Burk hated the Rams. Eventually they were all let in on the joke.

Needham drew silence from the crew when he dared to show Wayne how to execute a punch for the camera. The next take was good, and Wayne gave Needham his stamp of approval. Chuck Roberson and George Robotham were on hand to double Wayne and Hudson respectively but were not needed for the stars' brief contribution. In addition to Fred Krone, Roydon Clark, Tap Canutt, Bill Couch, Chuck Couch and Kent Hays, oldtimers in the mix include Gil Perkins, Wally Rose and Danny Sands. Needham liked using his young stuntmen including Glenn Wilder, Mickey Gilbert, Alan Gibbs, Stan Barrett, Gary McLarty, Billy Burton, Paul Nuckles, Bob Orrison, Dick Ziker, Walter Wyatt, Denny Arnold, Fred Waugh, Dick Bullock, Chuck Parkison, Jr., and J.N. Roberts.

See: Mat, Florence. "Rams Olsen and Gabriel."

Los Angeles Times. February 7, 1969; Royce, Brenda Scott. *Rock Hudson: A Bio-Bibliography.* Westport, CT: Greenwood, 1995.

GEORGE LAZENBY VS. IRVIN ALLEN in *On Her Majesty's Secret Service* (1969)

Faced with the unenviable task of following Sean Connery as James Bond, newcomer George Lazenby starred as 007 in this film only. Fan and media reaction was less than kind to the new Bond, and for two decades Lazenby became the answer to a trivia question. Then something interesting began to happen. Audiences and critics rediscovered and re-evaluated Lazenby's *On Her Majesty's Secret Service* and decided he wasn't so bad after all. Based on his looks, manner, humanity and especially his skill at fighting, many now consider Lazenby to be a decent Bond, who might have eclipsed Connery had he remained in the role. He was expected to take a few lumps as he found his feet in front of a movie camera. He is aided by a superior screenplay by Richard Maibaum and the by-now iconic Bond theme music from John Barry.

One thing that came naturally to Lazenby was fighting, and the fisticuff action he put onto the screen *sans* stuntman was excellent. *Kiss Kiss, Bang Bang* wrote that this film contains "easily the hardest-hitting of all Bond's film fights…. Every punch is overdubbed hard—a hefty, bonesplintering crack being called upon most often." The *Village Voice*, however, felt the fights were "sheer hyperbole" and complained they "sound like they were recorded from inside a punching bag." Lazenby is introduced with a solid fight on a Portugal beach, but it's a later one-minute furniture-knocker with burly thug Irvin Allen that's the show-stopper, superbly edited in director Peter Hunt's fast-paced frame-removing style by John Glen. Lazenby and Allen go at each other with fists, feet, forearms, elbows and knees as they smash a Monte Carlo motel room. Lazenby even employs an arm-bar. Bond veteran George Leech was stunt coordinator.

Six-foot-two, 190-pound Lazenby, a hand-tohand combat instructor in the Australian Army's Special Forces, won the Bond role based on a fight scene screen test. Producer "Cubby" Broccoli and director Hunt were impressed with his potential but wanted to see how he fought on camera. Leech hired Russian wrestler Yuri Borienko to serve as

Lazenby's opponent and put the men through the paces of the motel fight for three weeks of rehearsal. Lazenby needed to learn how to fake a fight, and to remember *not* to flinch beforehand when he knew a blow was coming. When it came time to roll film, they had a great routine worked out, but Lazenby accidentally connected with the wrestler and broke his nose. Broccoli and Leech liked the toughness they saw from Lazenby, and Hunt was so impressed he wanted to use the exciting footage of the test itself. Lazenby ended up recreating the fight with Allen while a recovering Borienko was rewarded with another part.

George Lazenby rears back for a double axe-handle blow on Irvin Harris in United Artists' *On Her Majesty's Secret Service* (1969).

For the two-minute pre-credit Guincho Beach sequence, Leech chose oars, nets and grappling hooks as props to add interest to the fight between Lazenby and stunt players Terry Mountain and Bill Morgan. The sea was cold and director Hunt gave Lazenby and Mountain a bottle of brandy to fortify them for the shoot. The water moves were first worked out on a mini-trampoline hidden in the sand for a couple of high jumps. The fight moved into the sea at sunset and it proved to be a particularly effective shot as the figures are silhouetted against the seascape. The beach scenes took approximately five days to film. Vic Armstrong was on hand to double Lazenby if needed. Lazenby had notable fights in *Stoner* (1974) and *The Man from Hong Kong* (1975) (see entry).

See: Graham, Sheilah. "Newcomer George Lazenby Starts from Scratch." *Toledo Blade.* November 10, 1968; Helfenstein, Charles. *The Making of* On Her Majesty's Secret Service. Spies, 2009.

ROBERT MITCHUM VS. GEORGE KENNEDY in *The Good Guys and the Bad Guys* (1969)

In this enjoyable comedy western from director Burt Kennedy, aging lawman Robert Mitchum and aging criminal George Kennedy are passed over by progress in the early 1900s. Both stars are delightful in their roles. Before they join forces to take on young David Carradine's gang, they have a fistfight in the Chama River to settle a decades-old score. The picturesque New Mexico locations enhance the comic huffing and puffing of the two stars. Parts of the fight were fought on a sandy river bank created on the Warner Bros. back lot. David Cass doubled Mitchum with Bob Terhune doubling Kennedy for an impressive fall into the river. Cinematographer Harry Stradling, Jr., takes advantage of the fall season and creates a beautiful composition of the out-of-breath men struggling in a literally changing land. Otho Lovering cut the long shots together with the close-ups of the principals superbly. *The Milwaukee Journal* called it "a brilliantly staged fight."

There's a comic street brawl early in the picture as the local ladies of the evening are led out of the town of Progress for political reasons. They throw their garter belts to the local townsmen, who begin a mass scrum for the mementos. Stunt actor Jack Perkins is featured most prominently here as an inebriated local. Director Kennedy humorously cuts to a pair of dogs having a tug of war over a garter belt, animalistic behavior not far removed from that of the town's citizens. Stunt actor Richard Farnsworth hollers "Fight!" when the fracas begins—a Burt Kennedy trademark. Kennedy and his stuntmen were still staging western brawls in *Support Your Local Sheriff* (1969) and *Support Your Local Gunfighter* (1971).

The phasing-out of the cowboy by modernization became a familiar theme in the 1960s cinema and ushered in the eventual death of the western itself. With a clamp-down on TV violence, many small-screen action oaters were cancelled. The concurrent collapse of the traditional studio system meant there was no longer functional western sets or livestock with wranglers readily available. The western became expensive to produce while the time-honored fistfight or gun showdown to resolve differences became pat and clichéd. Urban action introduced car chases and machine-gun fights to enthrall audiences, as did special effects–laden disaster films. More actors were coming to Hollywood from the East Coast, unable to ride a horse. *The Good Guys and the Bad Guys* is a perfect example of the end of a Hollywood era and a change in the way fisticuffs were presented on screen.

See: *The Good Guys and the Bad Guys* press-book; Heffernan, Howard. "There's Honor in Villainy." *The Palm Beach Post.* December 22, 1968.

Robert Mitchum (left) and George Kennedy stage an "old school" fight in Warner Bros.' *The Good Guys and the Bad Guys* (1969).

RICHARD HARRIS VS. ART LUND in *The Molly Maguires* (1970)

This is an overlooked Martin Ritt drama about violence among Irish miners and the owners they toil for in 1850s Pennsylvania. Undercover detective Richard Harris receives a rocky reception when he arrives in the town where the workers have a secret society known as "The Molly Maguires" that fights back against their oppression. At the behest of top miner Sean Connery, burly Art Lund greets Harris with a pub fistfight, and it's a fine one as coordinated by Roger Creed and lensed by James Wong Howe. Over in roughly a minute of screen time, the brawl features no stunt doubles and is most impressively done featuring kicks, broken furniture, eye-gouging, belly punches and beer thrown in the face. Originally it was to last five minutes of screen time, but Frank Bracht tightened it down to its current form.

The 6'4", 235-pound Lund, a Broadway actor in the early 1960s *Donnybrook*, was making his film debut. The World War II Navy veteran was a heavyweight Golden Gloves boxing champion in his youth and an All-American college football player for Westminster and Eastern Kentucky. He played football professionally for the Brooklyn Dodgers and his real toughness comes through on screen. The *Pittsburgh Post-Gazette* called him "impressive as a burly miner whose saloon brawl with Harris indicates that Lund might be a good, tough character actor in the Victor McLaglen–Ward Bond–Lee Marvin tradition."

The Molly Maguires' centerpiece is a game of rugby that ends in a slugging match between both mining teams and the police force overseeing the sport. Real teams were imported to the Eckley, Pennsylvania, location to take part in the action alongside actors and stuntmen Gil Perkins, Nick Dimitri, Chuck Hicks, Carl Saxe and John MacDonald. The ballsy actors did all their own stunt work, but didn't escape injury. On the first day alone, Harris sustained sore ribs and a bruised cheek, Connery a twisted knee, and Lund a cut ear. Not all the injuries occurred on the film set. Harris was punched out in a Hazelton bar by a local who didn't cotton to the actor putting the moves on his lady.

Six-foot-one, 205-pound Irishman Richard Harris was a noted drinker and volatile hellion. He competed successfully in rugby as a young man and laid claim to having broken his nose nine different times, often away from the sports field. He was a notorious brawler and pub fighter, and was known to fight in the stands at Munster matches. The charismatic Harris most famously fought alongside Robert Mitchum in a much publicized melee while filming *Night Fighters* (1960) in Ireland. Harris had a running feud for decades with English actor Oliver Reed, whom he referred to as his "slugging partner." Harris did resort to fisticuffs with Rod Taylor during the making of *The Deadly Trackers* (1973) and paid the price. Harris also clashed with Marlon Brando while making *Mutiny on the Bounty* (1962) after Brando offered what Harris considered a weak slap.

Harris had a reputation for getting carried away in fights, and most actors stayed on their toes when working with him. Notable screen fights came against Derek Turner in *This Sporting Life* (1963), Charlton Heston in *Major Dundee* (1965), Kirk Douglas in *The Heroes of Telemark* (1965), Max von Sydow in *Hawaii* (1966), Terry Leonard in *A Man Called Horse* (1970), William Smith in *The Deadly Trackers* (1973), Chuck Connors in *99 and 44/100% Dead* (1974), Bill Lucking in *Return of a Man Called Horse* (1976), Anthony James in *Ravagers* (1979), Christopher Plummer in *Highpoint* (1984) and Tom Berenger in *The Field* (1990). Gene Hackman gave him an especially memorable thrashing in *Unforgiven* (1992).

See: Callan, Michael Feeney. *Richard Harris: Sex, Death & the Movies*. London: Robson, 2003; Heffernan, Harold. "Guns Are Out, Fists Are In." *Milwaukee Journal*. July 11, 1968; Lincoln, Ivan M. "Ex-Utahn Art Lund to Star in Pops Concert." *Deseret News*. July 9, 1985.

CHARLTON HESTON VS. JAMES FRANCISCUS in *Beneath the Planet of the Apes* (1970)

This rushed sequel to the hugely popular sci-fi film *Planet of the Apes* (1968) features a novel premise for a fight on the eve of a major battle between the apes and human mutants living underground. Telepathic mutant Don Pedro Colley uses mind control to force astronauts Charlton Heston and James Franciscus to fight to the death in a cage with spiked bars. Both actors are game for the action, with Heston dwarfing the superbly fit Fran-

ciscus. Stuntmen Tony Epper and Loren Janes handle the long shots, but Heston and Franciscus are right in there punching, biting, clawing and kicking away barefoot for much of the grueling fight's three minutes. Franciscus turns psychotic thanks to the mind control. When it looks like they may need some deadly assistance, Colley introduces a spiked club which Franciscus swings at Heston's head. Colley's concentration is broken momentarily by slave girl Linda Harrison, and Heston and Franciscus seize the chance to take out the mutant and do battle with the attacking apes. *Movie Maker* referred to it as "an extremely well filmed fight sequence."

Ted Post directed with Chuck Roberson handling the second unit and Paul Stader coordinating the stunts. Like its predecessor, it's a triumph of production design from art directors Jack Martin Smith and William Creber and set decorator Walter M. Scott. However, Paul Dehn's script is weak and there's evidence of cost-cutting. The cell is particularly noteworthy given the medieval spikes jutting from the bars and the cold slabs of flowing stone that exist at odd angles. D.P. Milton Krasner has the scene lit to show the shadows of the menacing spikes on the walls behind the actors, creating added tension. Composer Leonard Rosenman provided a worthy follow-up to Jerry Goldsmith's groundbreaking score from the original. Background music doesn't accompany the fight: The lone noise (besides the combatants' grunts) is the buzzing drone of Colley inside their heads.

The film ends famously with Heston taking out the entire planet with an atomic bomb. It was the only way Heston agreed to return in the role for an extended cameo: if he could destroy everything and wipe out any chance for further money-grubbing sequels. Of course, 20th Century-Fox maneuvered around that. Heston originally wanted to appear in one scene at the beginning and be killed off, but agreed to disappear and return for the finale. Franciscus was nursing a badly sprained ankle acquired playing tennis before shooting began.

Five-ten and 165 pounds, Franciscus was a football captain at Taft prep school but a knee injury prevented him from continuing the sport at Yale. With his finely chiseled features, he made a solid and cerebral hero-type on screen, yet he was also capable of playing slick, egotistical and conniving villains. He was dedicated to his craft, including performing fight routines. He is best known as blind insurance investigator Mike Longstreet on the series *Longstreet* (1971–1972). In 1971's "Way of the Intercepting Fist," he is taught Jeet Kune Do by Bruce Lee. By episode's end, he puts his martial arts and extrasensory training into use during a fight against heavy John Milford. Fights of interest came against Tony Curtis in *The Outsider* (1961), Aldo Reggiani in *Cat o' Nine Tails* (1971) and Paul Newman in *When Time Ran Out* (1980).

See: "James Franciscus Mixes Brains and Brawn in Role." *Fairbanks Daily Miner.* October 24, 1964; Russo, Joe, Larry Landsman, and Edward Gross. *Planet of the Apes Revisited.* New York: St. Martin's, 2001.

JOHN WAYNE VS. FORREST TUCKER in *Chisum* (1970)

In *Sands of Iwo Jima* (1949), macho he-men John Wayne and Forrest Tucker had a strong buildup to a confrontation, which culminated with a far too brief exchange of punches between the stalwarts. The punches were great haymakers, but one wishes the two evenly matched actors would have traded a few more blows. Over 20 years and about 30 added pounds later, the bare-knuckle veterans did it right. They have a grand fight to the finish in the Andrew McLaglen western *Chisum*.

McLaglen was assistant director on the earlier film and made sure this one was a rousing audience pleaser with a Dominic Frontiere score rising to the occasion. He wanted his two aging stars to film as much of the fight as possible, although Chuck

Roberson and Jim Burk are in there for the dangerous stunts. Roberson broke his wrist taking a stair fall for Wayne. The two-minute slugfest was coordinated by Cliff Lyons and Hal Needham amidst burning buildings and a street full of stampeding cattle. Their *Sands of Iwo Jima* fight took two hours to film. The *Chisum* fight took over two days to complete, ending on a chilly Durango morning. At its conclusion, Wayne and Tucker joked they should be getting too old for this.

The fight begins with Roberson riding his stunt horse Cocaine through a glass window and leaping onto Tucker. Wayne and Tucker crash into a stove and begin uncorking huge punches, many punctuated by Tucker's inspired grunts. The fight goes up the stairs and onto a balcony as a longhorn display is tossed to the ground below. With flames licking at their bodies, they go off the edge of the second story and Tucker is impaled on the horn.

McLaglen had some fun with Burk before the fall. He replaced the special rubber longhorns with a real pair that Burk naturally discovered during his preparation. As the stuntmen take the fall, an aerial shot exposes the outline of their stunt mat beneath the dirt. This is a minor quibble in an otherwise well-done fight. However, Wayne was mildly upset with editor Robert Simpson upon seeing the film because Roberson was too visible to the audience. When Roberson falls off the stairwell, a dazed Wayne pops up into the camera frame, suggesting he was the one who had taken the fall. This old-time movie subterfuge is known as a Texas Switch. Even at the age of 62, Wayne still wanted fans to think he was doing all his own fights. When Wayne and Tucker exchange blows upstairs in two-shots, the fight is pure cinematic gold.

Wayne biographer Allen Eyles called the fight "a splendidly protracted free-for-all," while *Western Clippings* includes it among the "great screen fights." Most reviews respectfully took into account the passing years. The *Los Angeles Herald Examiner* called the fight "a classic" although it likened the stars to "two near extinct buffaloes." *The Hollywood Reporter* remarked, "The fist fight between Tucker and Wayne which caps off the action is well done as the two

Old pros Forrest Tucker (left) and John Wayne put on a memorable fight in Warner Bros.' *Chisum* (1970).

seeming behemoths slowly battle." The *Pittsburgh Press* noted of Wayne, "There are a couple of big fight scenes that he pulls off quite well for a guy of his years."

See: *Chisum* DVD extras; *Chisum* pressbook.

ROD TAYLOR VS. WILLIAM SMITH in *Darker Than Amber* (1970)

A landmark two-man fight punctuates this violent big screen version of John D. MacDonald's fictional tough guy of print, Travis McGee. It has widely been touted as one of *the* greatest screen fights, made all the more spectacular because no stunt doubles were used. Rod Taylor is well-cast as the Florida salvage expert who can't resist helping a damsel in distress. The girl is pretty Suzy Kendall, who's in deep with criminal bodybuilders William Smith and Robert Phillips. Taylor first takes out the six-foot, 185-pound Phillips in a tense fight on the beach that sees Taylor swinging a shovel. Phillips was a real tough guy, having played pro football and serving as a self-defense instructor with the Marines. He became a bodyguard for Governor Adlai Stevenson and an undercover cop. Once in Hollywood, he was often hired for Lee Marvin films to keep the star out of after-hours fights. The macho Taylor could sometimes throw choreography to the wind and connected with Phillips, breaking a bone in the supporting actor's hand. Taylor's inability to hold back in fights was a harbinger of the action to come.

Smith, with peroxide blond hair, and Taylor play cat-and-mouse games with Smith's girlfriend Ahna Capri as the bait aboard a cruise ship bound for Nassau in the Bahamas. Part of Taylor's plan is to send the dangerously psychotic Smith over the edge. When he goes, all hell breaks loose with a thrilling jolt and a blood-curdling battle cry. The three-and-a-half-minute fight starts in Taylor's cabin and ends up on the Prince George Dock with Smith belting and tossing aside anyone who gets in his way.

The first 90 seconds in the cabin between Taylor and Smith is mind-blowing. It looks like the two actors are trying to kill one another. There has never been a more blisteringly ferocious movie fight. Director Robert Clouse's hand-held camera gets in on the action, and John Parker's jazzy score keeps pace with the flying fists. Editor Fred Chulack put the exciting footage together creatively.

Because of the limitations of the set and the close proximity of the camera, the use of doubles would have been difficult, so the actors gamely agreed to do all they could. Before the fight began, Taylor offered Smith a challenge, and Smith became determined to prove his toughness. Roger Creed was on hand as stunt coordinator, but the fight became an ad-libbed free-for-all with both Taylor and Smith beating the hell out of one another for the camera's benefit. Much of the blood on screen was real and all Taylor's courtesy of a broken nose. At some point, the two lost track of their planned choreography, and Smith belted Taylor on the proboscis. Taylor kicked Smith hard across the set and demanded that Clouse keep Frank Phillips' cameras rolling as he proceeded to pound away. He smashed Smith with a breakaway lamp, and Smith smashed him with a real lamp. Clouse wisely kept the camera on as the two men improvised some of the best action ever committed to film. During the fight, Smith literally knocked Taylor out of his shoe with one punch. Taylor tasted his revenge on the film's last shot on the dock, when he is to hit Smith in the knee with a busted-up board. Taylor missed Smith's kneepad and cracked him in the shin.

Doubles Louis Elias and Nick Dimitri were on hand throughout the entire week of filming for the

William Smith (left) and Rod Taylor get carried away with the action in National General's legendary *Darker Than Amber* (1970).

extended fight but never participated in the action. Taylor and Smith were determined to do every single punch and fall. The actors paid the price for smashing one another so convincingly against the walls. Both had glazed eyes and were dizzy, barely able to walk away at the end of shooting. A doctor needed to tend to both. Luckily, the fight was the last scene scheduled. In addition to his broken nose, Taylor suffered a hand injury. Smith injured three ribs and strained muscles in his back and shoulder. Stuntman Jesse Wayne broke his heel playing a bystander heaved through the air by Smith. Utility stuntman Tom Edwards injured his back when he was slammed into a fence. Transportation captain Frank Lassiter had to be taken to the hospital after Smith threw a stuntman so far he landed on Lassiter off-screen and broke six of his teeth.

Critics then and now realized it packed a visceral punch. The *New York Times* termed it "a bone-cracking wind-up," while the *Chicago Sun Times* called the fights "beautifully choreographed." The *Montreal Gazette* wrote of Taylor: "His forte has always been the prolonged, ultra-bloody fist fight, and here he outdoes all his previous efforts." *Time* declared that the final fight "has not been matched for pure furniture-smashing gusto since Frank Sinatra took out after that Korean guy in *The Manchurian Candidate*," and *Motion Picture Herald* acknowledged, "[T]he fist-fights turn out to be some of the most savage to be seen in a movie for a long time."

Many reviewers were overwhelmed by the violence. The *Los Angeles Times* wrote, "Sadly, *Darker Than Amber* had so much going for it that it didn't need the hype of such huge quantities of blood and guts spilled all over it. The ultimate effect is the spoiling of what might have been a very good show." The film's reputation continues to grow with the passage of time. *Action Films* places it among the top of their rankings of all-time greats, writing it is "right up there with the train fight in *From Russia with Love*." The *Psychotronic Video Guide* calls it "an incredible arm-breaking fight on a ship, done without stuntmen," and *The Manly Movie Guide* praises it as "one of the all-time great climactic brawls." *Tales from the Cult Film Trenches* calls it "one of the most grueling and realistic-looking fight scenes ever captured on film," and *Orange Coast Magazine* includes it among the screen's most violent exchanges.

It was one of the first extended fights done entirely without stunt doubles. For their devotion, both actors were made honorary members of the Stuntmen's Association. Even decades later, industry stuntmen acknowledge it as perhaps the best fight ever put onto film. They weren't the only ones taking notice. *Darker Than Amber* became known as the film that convinced Bruce Lee to hire Clouse as the director of *Enter the Dragon* (1973) because the martial artist was so impressed with the filming of the fight. The *Amber* fight also gained a level of notoriety and mystique due to the violence and the cutting of a portion of the fight by TV censors. For years that TV print, with jumpy edits and music score, was the only one in circulation. It even surfaced as a VHS release. This made viewers who remembered the original version begin to trumpet its virtues and lament its apparent loss. Gone were many of the hardest punches, the smashing through a closet door, and Smith's sadistic breaking of a wine bottle over Taylor's head. In interviews, Taylor and Smith bemoaned the missing footage. Finally, a bootleg copy with Dutch subtitles surfaced with the fight and Ahna Capri's briefly nude corpse on the bed intact. Clips began to circulate on the internet, allowing a new generation to discover this action gem.

Smith has said *Darker Than Amber* is his single favorite of the dozens of screen fights he has done. He took great pride in getting knocked around by Taylor, a close friend Smith labeled as one of the toughest men he's ever encountered. Smith claimed Taylor's punches were the hardest he's taken from an actor. For his part, Smith upped the intensity of his weight workouts and came into the film with nearly 220 pounds of rippling steroid-free muscle on his 6'2" frame. His body fat was measured at four percent. To show the vanity of the character, who's supposed to be wearing a blond toupee that gets ripped off in the bloody climax on the dock, Smith bleached his hair. This was a shocking action for the day. Only professional wrestlers or campy fruitcakes bleached their hair. Smith took ribbing and catcalls from locals about his appearance. Taylor instructed his personal bodyguard Fred Hakim to look out for Smith and persuade anyone giving him a hard time to reconsider their teasing. Smith made guest appearances on Taylor's TV shows *Bearcats, The Oregon Trail* and *Masquerade*. On the 1971 *Bearcats* episode "The Return of Esteban," the two have a fight rolling down a hillside and into the brush. On this they let Louie Elias and Nick Dimitri do a portion of the fight in the sharp sticks. On the 1984 series

Masquerade, they have a brief fight on a cruise ship, an obvious ode to *Darker Than Amber.*

Unending praise must be heaped on Taylor and Smith for the lengths of their physical acting. Taylor especially gave his body up for the sake of art. Rarely has a man's body been seen flying through the air with such violent force. It is amazing that Taylor didn't break his back when Smith slams him against the wall the first time. Both men went above and beyond the normal call of duty and into an area of uncharted machismo. Each came off this film with a legitimate tough guy reputation that endured for decades. Smith became the preeminent movie and TV villain of the 1970s. In commenting on the fight in newspaper accounts, Taylor noted, "Movie fights have been a part of the business since silent days, but I must say that the one Bill and I have is the toughest I've ever seen."

See: *Darker Than Amber* pressbook; Scott, Vernon. "Gory Movie Fight for Real." *Seattle Daily Times.* April 26, 1970.

JOE NAMATH VS. WILLIAM SMITH in *C.C. and Company* (1970)

"Loving, brawling, and bustin' it up!" proclaimed the trade ads for Seymour Robbie's *C.C. and Company* (1970). Super Bowl–winning football quarterback Joe Namath stars as C.C. Ryder opposite love interest Ann-Margret in this goofy motorcycle film. It is different than anything else in the biker genre, playing like an Elvis Presley movie as clean-cut motorcyclist Namath tangles with scruffy gang leader William Smith, who gives a remarkably charismatic, scenery-chewing performance. Smith was a late replacement for Bruce Glover, who after arriving on set was thought to be too short to be a convincing rival for Namath in a fight. Ironically, Namath is an unconvincing rival for the muscular Smith, but it at least made the football star a tremendous underdog instead of a bully. The two have a high-energy one-minute fight alongside the wooded Santa Cruz River near Tucson, Arizona, while Mitch Ryder's "See See Rider/Jenny Take a Ride" effectively blares on the soundtrack. A barefoot Smith fights dirty, utilizing a spinning kick and a chain, but the 6'2", 195-pound Namath doesn't back down and fights gamely. Smith triumphs, but ends up the bloodier of the two combatants.

Namath is doubled in the fight by Nick Dimitri. The New York Jets wouldn't let him ride a motorcycle for fear of injury. Smith does the entire fight, including hurling his body through the air, with reckless abandon. Paul Nuckles was stunt coordinator with Charles Wheeler behind the camera and Fred Chulack responsible for editing the footage. The actors were ready to hate the football player but wound up befriending him. Namath's Jets teammate Mike Battle, renowned for his crazy fearlessness, also has a part. He's the one Smith pushes immediately before the Namath fight. When Smith pushed harder than he had in rehearsals, the football player punched Smith in the mouth. Battle had already been running at cast members and throwing footballs at their heads, so Smith immediately knocked Battle back down. The power of the punch convinced Battle, who loved to fight, to quickly give up any notion of pursuing the conflict further. The two wound up friends for the remainder of the shoot.

Playing a bike gang leader was nothing new for Smith. He was quickly gaining a reputation as the King of the Motorcycle Movies. Hollywood actors were rarely accepted by the real gangs, but after a few bumps in the road Smith proved an exception. He even received a letter of commendation from Hells Angels president Sonny Barger. After making a never-completed film with the Bandidos of Texas in 1968, Smith was made an honorary member of that outlaw club. During the making of *Run, Angel, Run!* (1969), Smith was in costume at a Santa Monica hamburger stand when he was accosted by five members of Satan's Slaves. Smith put three members of the motorcycle gang in the hospital with his real-life fight skills. While attending the New Jersey premiere of *The Losers* (1970), he landed in a skirmish with a gang who attacked him at the theater. Another real-life biker club, the Knight Riders, interfered with the making of *Angels Die Hard!* (1970) in Kern County, California. Smith fashioned that experience into the autobiographical biker film *Hollywood Man* (1976).

See: "Falconetti Character Disguises Many Talents of William Smith." *The Hollywood Reporter.* January 7, 1977; Garmon, Ron. "King of the Bikers: William Smith." *Worldly Remains.* #4, 2001.

DON STROUD VS. BILL MCKINNEY in *Angel Unchained* (1970)

Two of the 1970s' great psycho bad guys square off in this hippie vs. biker flick from director Lee Madden and AIP. Playing a rare good guy, lead Don Stroud runs afoul of fellow gang members when he shacks up with hippie girl Tyne Daly at an Arizona commune near the Superstition Mountains. Bill McKinney, one of the filthiest of the bikers, presses himself upon Daly, whom Stroud defends in a realistic one-minute assault of punches and spirited grappling in the mud of a garden. While filming the fight, Stroud thought McKinney was trying to kill him, but the two had lunch together when they were done. Stroud later claimed he thought it was one of the best fights put on film, and it's unique that bad guy McKinney ends up with the upper hand with an axe-heel raised above his head. He drops it with a smile, adding an interesting wrinkle to his bad guy characterization.

The low-budget film has an intriguing opening scene, a comic biker brawl set in the abandoned amusement park Legend City. The actors and stuntmen mixed in with real members of the Dirty Dozen Motorcycle Club from Mesa, Arizona, to ride the park's rides as they fight. Stroud rescues pal Larry Bishop at the top of the rollercoaster. As often happened on these low-budget biker flicks, there was a fair amount of actual partying going on behind the scenes. McKinney and a real outlaw biker got loaded while waiting for the set-up and proceeded to punch one another for real. Neither could feel any damage being done. The film ends with Stroud and the bikers protecting the hippies from dune buggy–riding cowboys who hate them both. Hal Needham and Bud Ekins coordinated the action while Billy Burton, Allan Gibbs, J.N. Roberts, Jerry Randall and Michael Haynes served as stuntmen.

Don Stroud (6'2", 200 pounds) was a surfing champion hired off the beach in Waikiki to double Troy Donahue on the TV series *Hawaiian Eye*. He had studied Kajukenbo karate and earned a black belt at age 16. When he moved to Los Angeles, he became the bouncer at the popular Whisky a Go Go on the Sunset Strip. Stroud had no acting training but excelled at playing violent villains and quickly gained notice. Given his size and martial arts background, he earned a reputation as a real tough guy. In 1990, the former lifeguard came to the aid of a mugging victim and fought six assailants for nearly ten minutes, receiving multiple knife wounds resulting in the loss of an eye. In 2004, he was inducted into the Black Belt Hall of Fame.

Stroud was an aggressive screen fighter throwing punches fast and furious. He administered terrifying screen beatings and could sometimes become carried away fighting in films like *Bloody Mama* (1970) and *The Killer Inside Me* (1976). He

impressed early in his career by launching stuntmen over a bar counter during a saloon brawl in *Journey to Shiloh* (1968). Notable fights include *Coogan's Bluff* (1968), *Slaughter's Big Rip-Off* (1973) and *Sudden Death* (1975) (see entries). Fights of interest came against Clint Eastwood in *Joe Kidd* (1972), Kirk Douglas and Neville Brand in *Scalawag* (1973), Park Jong Soo in *Search and Destroy* (1981) and Dennis Quaid in *The Night the Lights Went Out in Georgia* (1981). On TV, Stroud's best fights came against David Janssen in the 1972 *O'Hara, U.S. Treasury* episode "Operation: Smokescreen," Don Galloway in the 1972 *Ironside* "Nightmare Trip," George Peppard in 1973's *Banacek* "No Stone Unturned" and Joe Lando in the 1993 *Dr. Quinn, Medicine Woman* "Running Ghost." Stroud engaged David Carradine in a brief martial arts fight in the 1974 *Kung Fu* episode "Cry of the Night Beast."

See: "Don Stroud." *Psychotronic Video*. #38, 2003; Poggiali, Chris. "*Shock Cinema* Talks with the Incomparable Don Stroud." *Shock Cinema*. #13, 1998.

THE MORMON CAMP FIGHT in *They Call Me Trinity* (1970)

Handsome blue-eyed Terence Hill and burly Bud Spencer teamed up as unlikely brothers Trinity and Bambino for this innovative Spaghetti Western spoof made outside Rome by Italian writer-director Enzo Barboni (aka E.B. Clucher). The slapstick comedy launched an entertaining new genre known in America as Fagioli Westerns due to Hill's penchant for eating beans on screen. The two kind-hearted outlaws become reluctant heroes by taking on a greedy land developer (Farley Granger) who's pressuring a Mormon camp with his hired muscle. Hill and the bearded Spencer are a great combination of finesse and power, nonchalant in their methodical fighting pace and never doubting they will be victorious over a small army of bad guys including Remo Capitani's Mexican bandits in a climactic six-minute brawl. The whole thing plays like farce as Hill and Spencer toss their guns aside before the action begins. The carefree Hill swings windmill punches with a smile on his face while the irritable Spencer's signature move is a hammer-like fist atop his opponent's heads. Their punches occasionally have superhuman results: Bodies fly right and left across the screen and through the framework of an uncompleted Mormon structure as a result of kicks, punches and incredibly loud slaps. Hill does gymnastic routines on the wooden beams, and there's even some anachronistic pro wrestling–type moves and karate. Sometimes Spencer takes two heads in his huge hands and bangs them together.

"Genuine brawling entertainment!" promised the trade ads. It's cartoon-like in its violence with little if any bloodshed, but nevertheless a triumph of fight choreography the *Chicago Sun Times* called "highly stylized." *The A to Z of Westerns in Cinema* declared there are "amazing stunt falls in every which direction." *Action Films* called it "one of the funniest fights ever filmed" and included it on their

Bud Spencer (left) fights Remo Capitani in Avco Embassy's *They Call Me Trinity* (1970).

list of the all-time great screen fights. Barboni said he was inspired by the barn-raising sequence in *Seven Brides for Seven Brothers* (1954).

Hill and Spencer do all their own fights, working with a team of 30 veteran Italian stuntmen who were well-practiced in acrobatics. Among the stuntmen on this film were Miguel Pedragosa, Paola Magalotti, Riccardo Pizzuti, Fortunato Arena, Omera Capanna, Pietro Turrisi, Alberto Dell'Acqua, Roberto Dell'Acqua, Augusto Funari, Gilberto Galimlerti, Getano Imbro, Emilio Messina, Osaride Pevarello, Lorenzo Fineschi, Giancarlo Bastianoni, Sergio Smacchi, Marcello Verziara, Artemio Antonini, Oscar Giustini, Mario Dionisi, Paolo Figlia, Roberto Alessandri, Bruno Ukmar and Franco Ukmar. Assistant director-action coordinator Giorgio Ubaldi was largely responsible for putting the elaborate fight together for the camera. Nearly ten days were devoted to its filming. Fistfights in a general store and a saloon also make an impact. In the latter fight, the eternally relaxed Hill sits back and watches Spencer wipe out the entire roster of bad guys.

The duo first incorporated slapstick stuntmen fights in *Ace High* (1968) and *Boot Hill* (1969) but not to the extent of their *Trinity* hit. The popular physical comedy team returned as Trinity and Bambino in *Trinity Is Still My Name* (1972) and in many films with varying settings including *All the Way Boys* (1972), *Watch Out, We're Mad* (1974) (see entry), *Turn the Other Cheek* (aka *Two Missionaries*) (1975), *Crime Busters* (1977), *Odds and Evens* (1978), *I'm for the Hippopotamus* (1979), *Who Finds a Friend Finds Treasure* (1981), *Go for It* (1983), *Double Trouble* (1984), *Miami Supercops* (1985) and *Troublemakers* (aka *The Fight Before Christmas*) (1994). The films were so popular that lookalikes Michael Coby (aka Antonio Cantafora) and 6'4", 320-pound Paul L. Smith were paired for a similar series of Italian action comedies beginning with *Carambola* (1974).

Terence Hill (formerly Mario Girotti) was a rowing champion with a gymnastics background that served him well in action scenes. When ducking a punch, the spry Hill would go into a quick full squat, rising up explosively with a stinging jab. Five-eleven and 170 pounds, he was apt to hit an opponent with any part of his limber body, which kept his inventive action scenes consistently interesting. Sometimes sped-up camera tricks were used to make Hill appear impossibly fast, most notably when he repeatedly slaps Antonio Monselesan and Jean Martin in *Trinity Is Still My Name* and *My Name Is Nobody* (1973) before they can draw their guns. Hill said that fights were the favorite part of his films. He even took on Bud Spencer in *God Forgives, I Don't* (1967), dominating the fight with his acrobatics until Spencer unloads his signature "Hammer Blow" over his head. Hill chose to fall to the side like a dead pigeon, a great comic reaction. They fought again to a humorous stalemate into the closing credits of *All the Way Boys*. Hill also starred *sans* Spencer in *Man of the East* (1972) and *Mr. Billion* (1977) (see entries). Fights of interest came against Salvatore Borghese in *Super Fuzz* (1980) and Joe Krieg in *They Call Me Renegade* (1988).

See: Hughes, Howard. *Once Upon a Time in the Italian West: A Filmgoer's Guide to Spaghetti Westerns.* London: I.B. Taurus, 2004; Prickette, James. *Actors of the Spaghetti Western.* Xlibris, 2012.

THE BEACH BRAWL in *Sometimes a Great Notion* (1970)

The beer flowed freely on the Oregon location of the logging picture *Sometimes a Great Notion* (based on Ken Kesey's mammoth novel), creating a memorably fun film that became a local legend. One highlight is a beach picnic between rival logging interests in which a touch football game instantly becomes a rough game of tackle. Soon there's an all-out brawl in the sand and surf courtesy of a Jim Burk taunt that star Paul Newman takes offense to. In Kesey's novel, the characters fight in a bar, but screenwriter John Gay changed the setting to take advantage of the outdoor location. The men are at odds with one another because the independent Stamper family led by Henry Fonda never gives an inch and continues a logging contract, causing aggravation among the unionized locals who have been frozen out by the big companies during a strike.

The three-minute football game and resulting fight sequence were coordinated by stuntman James Arnett and filmed at Fogarty Beach between Newport and Lincoln City. Stars Paul Newman, Richard Jaeckel, Michael Sarrazin and Cliff Potts were up against stunt actors Jim Burk, Roy Jenson, Charles Horvath, Bennie Dobbins, Dick Hudkins, Stan Barrett, Fred Lerner, Dean Smith, Mickey Gilbert and Terry Leonard. Local loggers Ron Bernard and Gene Altemus also became involved, and all who partook ended up with a large amount of wet sand in their clothes. When the scene wrapped, two bottles of celebratory whiskey were broken out and passed among the actors and stuntmen.

By the time of the Fogarty Beach scenes, producer-star Newman had taken over from original director Richard Colla, who it was felt was spending too much time on overly artistic camera set-ups. The atmosphere on the film had been tense before the switch but now was far looser and resembled a Hollywood party on location. The previous day, Newman finished the crucial scene where Jaeckel is pinned under a log, a memorably heavy dramatic moment that led to an Oscar nomination for Jaeckel. Everyone on the crew was in the mood for levity which the beach fight beer fest provided over the next three days despite temperatures reaching nearly 100 degrees. Since Newman was involved as a principal, second unit director Michael Moore and assistant Mickey McCardle took on more responsibility with cinematographer Richard Moore.

The son of a champion amateur wrestler, 5'7", 170-pound Richard Jaeckel had a boxing background and served with the Merchant Marine during World War II. He was well-known among the California beach crowd for his skill on a surfboard and in the water. An exercise fanatic, he became one of the first Hollywood actors to sport a bodybuilder's physique. The stout character player was well-liked by film crews, especially the stuntmen whom he counted among his closest friends. Jaeckel was often effectively cast as tough soldiers and cowboys and didn't shy away from doing his own fight stunts, beginning with juvenile delinquent brawls in *City Across the River* (1949). He was a devotee of the Japanese martial art Kendo.

Notable fights include *4 for Texas* (1963) and *The Devil's Brigade* (1968) (see entries). Fights of interest came against Billy Murphy in *Sands of Iwo Jima* (1949), Dick York in *Cowboy* (1958), Charles Bronson in *When Hell Broke Loose* (1958), Mickey Rooney in *Platinum High School* (1960), Robert Horton in *The Green Slime* (1968), Henry Duval in *The Kill* (1973), Paul Newman in *The Drowning Pool* (1975), Harold Sakata in *Mako—The Jaws of Death* (1976) and Frankie Avalon in *Blood Song* (1981). On TV, Jaeckel fought Nick Adams in the 1960 *Rebel* episodes "The Rattler" and "Run, Killer, Run," Richard Boone in the 1962 *Have Gun—Will Travel* "The Predators," and Michael Higgins in the 1963 *Gunsmoke* "Two of a Kind."

See: Freese, Gene. *Richard Jaeckel: Hollywood's Man of Character.* Jefferson, NC: McFarland, 2016; Love, Matt. *Sometimes a Great Movie.* South Beach, OR: Nestucca. 2012.

ALAIN DELON VS. JEAN-PAUL BELMONDO in *Borsalino* (1970)

French film stars Alain Delon and Jean-Paul Belmondo, as 1930s gangsters in Marseilles, team up to form their own crime ring. They are at odds when they meet in the opening scene of Jacques Deray's film. Delon has been released from prison and arrives at Belmondo's bistro to look up former girlfriend Catherine Rouvel. She is now attached to the swaggering Belmondo, who takes umbrage at suave Delon's attempt to spirit her away. The two cocksure men trade punches back and forth for over three drawn-out minutes. Both actors do the entirety of the fight with stuntman Yvan Chiffre coordinating the action. The fight strives to be realistic with the effect of its punches, including many body blows. The men sweat, bleed, bruise and lose their footing. By fight's end, they have gained one another's respect and shake hands, prior to collapsing to the floor.

There was finagling going on behind the scenes because of star egos. They are so evenly matched because it was part of their contract. Neither wanted to be seen as the fight's loser. They also had to have the same number of close-ups. However, since Delon was a producer, he made it a point to have his name appear first on screen under that guise, though their contracts stipulated billing on equal grounds. Belmondo later sued over this issue. The fight is well-mounted by Deray and lensed by Jean-Jacques Tarbes, paying particular attention to the period detail. *Film Editing* calls it "spectacular." But the *New York Times* wasn't impressed, remarking that the fights "manage to be both dull and unusually brutal at the same time."

Five-foot-ten, 160-pound Belmondo was a professional soccer goalie and a successful amateur boxer, accounting for his trademark broken nose. The ugly/handsome look helped propel him to stardom as a New Wave Humphrey Bogart in Jean-Luc Godard's *Breathless* (1960). In a pair of entertaining action films, *That Man from Rio* (1964) and *Up to His Ears* (1965), Belmondo earned a reputation for doing his own fights and risky stunt work. He was still pulling off the smiling tough guy daredevil act nearly 20 years later in *The Professional* (1981) and *The Outsider* (1983). Comedy action star Jackie Chan called him an influence. In real life, Belmondo was known to accommodate those who wished to test his toughness. He fought Lino Ventura in *Greed in the Sun* (1964) and made a fight cameo in *Casino Royale* (1967).

See: Chelminski, Rudolph. "Kids Want to Be Like Him—or Belt Him." *Life.* November 11, 1966; Orpen, Valerie. *Film Editing: The Art of the Expressive.* London: Wallflower, 2003; "The Perils of Jean-Paul: Belmondo Declines Doubles Nearly Hits the Fin." *People.* August 22, 1977.

THE TOWN SQUARE SHOWDOWN in *Billy Jack* (1971)

Five-foot-ten, 180-pound filmmaker-star Tom Laughlin, former halfback for Marquette University's football squad, scored with audiences when he introduced his anti-establishment foot-fighter Billy Jack in the crude but watchable biker film *Born Losers* (1967). It was an intriguing role due to its many contradictions. Billy Jack was a half-breed Indian and former Green Beret who set aside his own pacifistic preaching when forced to stick up for the little person. After killing in Vietnam, he wanted peace, but when push came to shove he could kick tail. For the low-budget sequel, titled simply *Billy Jack*, Laughlin amped up the social activism and the karate while replacing the seedy bikers with bigoted cowboys and turn-the-other-way lawmen. The most famous scene, and the one that contributed to the martial arts boom that helped make Billy Jack an early 1970s cultural phenomenon, is the town square fight against ten local rednecks, which publicity trumpeted as "the most exciting karate fight ever filmed."

Mostly shot on location in Prescott, Arizona, the scene leading up to the fight occurs in Dent's Ice Cream Parlor when four locals led by David Roya and John McClure harass a group of young Indians and pour white flour over their heads. Laughlin arrives and announces intensely that such senseless violence makes him go berserk. He beats up the bullies in a matter of seconds with Hapkido karate moves, and knocks McClure out the front window. He knows the rest of the town will want to take him down, so he removes his cowboy boots and walks out to the town's courthouse square barefoot. He is quickly surrounded by a group of toughs and faced down by town boss Bert Freed. Realizing he will be forced to fight, Laughlin famously tells Freed, "I'm going to take this right foot, and I'm going to wop you on that side of your face," as he indicates Freed's right cheek. "Really," smiles Freed. "Really," says Laughlin, and he kicks Freed as he said he would. The rednecks descend on Laughlin, who dazzles them with his jumps, kicks, leg sweeps and spinning back kicks over the next 30 seconds. He is clubbed over the head and beaten up before Sheriff Kenneth Tobey arrives to put a halt to the violence. But in those 30 seconds, a superstar was born. *Cult Movies* calls this fight "spectacular."

The tremendous popularity of the fight is undoubtedly due to the presentation of the martial arts on display and the anticipation Laughlin creates through his dialogue and situations. American audiences had never seen anything like this style of footwork performed by a Caucasian, or here a white actor pretending to be half–Indian. In actuality, many of Laughlin's moves were done by his stunt double, Korean martial arts technical advisor Master Bong Soo Han. Laughlin came across Han in the summer of 1969 presenting an exhibition of his Hapkido in Pacific Palisades, California. He approached him about doing *Billy Jack* and the two trained together for the next six months. The Korean martial art of Hapkido is known as a "combination art" as it incorporates Korean kicks, judo throws, the Aikido use of "ki" as well as pressure points, grabs and even weapons. It was Han's hope to showcase different techniques throughout the film while never making the same movement twice. The famous kick to Freed's face is known as an outside crescent kick. Hundreds of karate students repeated the move in dojo studios around the country over the next several years as martial arts became all the rage.

The popular shedding of Laughlin's cowboy boots wasn't a realistic Hapkido necessity but a caveat of the filmmakers to insure greater safety for the stuntmen. Martial arts movements were frowned upon by the majority of stuntmen, who didn't like the risk involved with flying feet and unfamiliarity. Because of budgetary constraints, Arizona locals were used rather than professional stuntmen. Han insisted upon the use of bare feet

Tom Laughlin (left) became famous for the town square martial arts fight seen in Warner Bros.' *Billy Jack* (1971).

and generous padding beneath the men's clothes. Nevertheless at least two of the would-be stuntmen suffered mild injuries, one who took a Han foot to the mouth and another who took a roundhouse kick to his bicep. Han's wish was to display the movements in the most favorable light and for that he needed to make contact. He had hoped to segue from one movement into another and thought multiple cameras would capture the movements the best. The producers nixed any notion of going to the expense of extra cameras. On the point of filming continuous movements, the neophyte Han clashed with the director Laughlin (using the pseudonym T.C. Frank) and cameramen Fred J. Koenekamp and John M. Stephens. They had their own styles and comfort level and insisted they could present Han's fighting style effectively. What the filmmakers did was take a cue from Sam Peckinpah's use of slow-motion in *The Wild Bunch* (1969) and incorporate slow-mo in the beginning of a Han movement that became regular speed as the kick or punch was completed and the opponent fell. When edited by Larry Heath and Marion Rothman, the effect worked beautifully and became a regular feature of martial arts action for the *Kung Fu* series that followed in the early 1970s. The quick-cut editing is so good that the naked eye is unable to detect the presence of Han executing the kicks and advanced Hapkido techniques.

Laughlin began filming *Billy Jack* in the fall of 1969, but American International Pictures pulled the plug before it was picked up and completed by Warner Bros. After six weeks of location work, it took Laughlin over a year to finish the picture, with parts being completed in Santa Fe, New Mexico. When it was released in the spring of 1971 in the traditional regional method, it found little more than a cult audience. Laughlin stuck by his picture and gained control of a re-release from the studio after threatening a lawsuit. He rented over 1000 theaters and used a releasing technique termed four-walling: opening the movie simultaneously with a huge ad campaign. The film became a massive hit and made Laughlin tens of millions. He quickly followed with another sequel, *The Trial of Billy Jack*

(1974) (see entry). Thirty-five years later, Laughlin included nearly a minute of extra fight footage as a bonus on the DVD release.

Critics were not as enamored with the overlong, preachy, anti-establishment film as audiences, who embraced the Billy Jack character and the statement Laughlin was making about fighting injustice and corruption. In regard to martial arts, the *Chicago Sun Times* called the action scenes "first-rate," while *The Cleveland Press* cited it as "one of the most exciting brawls ever put on film." It was well-received by the martial arts community and the appreciative public. *Black Belt* praised the use of Hapkido as "realistic" and "well-executed." *The American Martial Arts Film* termed the karate "crude, if not effective," calling the fight itself "a doozey." *The Ultimate Guide to Martial Arts Movies of the 1970s* commented, "Anyone watching this film was taken aback by the simplicity and effectiveness of the fight." According to *Chasing Dragons*, "The scene is well-executed and Laughlin keeps the camera angles low and wide to capture the action, a technique that most American directors still seem unable to grasp."

See: *Billy Jack* DVD special features; Chawkins, Steve. "Filmmaker Behind the Hit *Billy Jack* Series." *Los Angeles Times*. December 16, 2013; MacLaughlin, Bob. "Those Fabulous Fight Scenes in *Billy Jack*." *Black Belt*. March 1972.

ROBERT FULLER VS. TONY RUSSEL in *The Hard Ride* (1971)

Burt Topper's *The Hard Ride* is an interesting biker film starring two-fisted TV Western mainstay Robert Fuller as a Vietnam vet returning home with the body of his buddy. He intends to give his pal a proper burial but runs afoul of the man's biker friends who want possession of his beautiful chopper named Baby. The main conflict comes in the form of gang leaders William Bonner and Tony Russel as an Indian motorcyclist. Russel also wants to take possession of Fuller's girlfriend Sherry Bain. Fuller has a two-minute fight in a sandpit with Russel in which Topper gets in close with a hand-held camera. Towards the end of the brawl, Topper utilizes slow-motion photography and sounds of the Vietnam War on the soundtrack. Despite the pretentiousness of these post-production bits, it's still considered to be one of the better fights in the biker genre. *Variety* praised the film for having "good brawl sequences."

Fuller choreographed the fight and neither

actor used a stuntman as they toppled over a picnic table. Fuller wears riding gloves, which served to protect his hands. At one point he throws an elbow to Russel's face. Fuller had no idea the filmmakers were going to use slow-motion in the scene, which might have changed the way he put the fight together. Russel was a star in Italian gladiator, spy and sci-fi films of the 1960s, often cast in leading parts because he was willing to do his own stunts. The film concludes with a battle between biker gangs filmed in California's Fifteen Mile Valley. In this impressively mounted Pier Six brawl, Fuller and Russel fight side by side against Bonner's gang.

One of the highlights of any *Laramie* (1959–1963) episode was the fights, which the 5'11", 175-pound former stuntman Fuller enthusiastically did without a double in his portrayal of Jess Harper. The Korean War vet patterned his fighting style after *Range Rider* hero Jock Mahoney and could throw a great screen punch and a mean backhand. He set an energetic pace in his fights and his timing was superb. Hal Needham was Fuller's favored fight partner and often doubled the show's guests since the two worked so well together. One of their best fights had Needham doubling Russell Johnson during a table-smashing saloon brawl in 1963's "Badge of Glory." In 1961's "Dragon at the Door," Fuller engaged in a battle with judo expert Robert Kino. Another top fight came against Arch Johnson in 1963's "No Place to Run." On *Wagon Train* (1963–1965), Fuller's Coop Smith fought co-star Denny Miller in 1963's "The Sandra Cummings Story." As a TV guest, Fuller had memorable fights with Peter Breck in the 1967 *Big Valley* episode "A Flock of Trouble" and Doug McClure in the 1967 *Virginian* episode "A Welcoming Town." On the big screen, Fuller fought Chuck Courtney in *Teenage Thunder* (1957), Denver Pyle in *Incident at Phantom Hill* (1966) and Seighardt Rupp in the German *Mittsommernacht* (1967). During the 1960s, Fuller and stuntman pal Chuck Courtney staged fight exhibitions for live audiences on a multi-city rodeo tour.

See: Barnum, Michael. "Tony Russel–Our Man on Gamma 1: The Wild, Wild Interview." *Video Watchdog*. #128. February 2007; Raddatz, Leslie. "The Gentle Brawler." *TV Guide*. December 1963.

CHARLES BRONSON VS. TOSHIRO MIFUNE in *Red Sun* (1971)

East meets Old West as cowboy Charles Bronson reluctantly joins forces with samurai warrior

Toshiro Mifune in a quest to recover a stolen sword. In anti-hero Bronson's case, he's also out to settle an old debt with former partner Alain Delon. After much whimsical verbal sparring in a foot trek across the Almeria, Spain, location, there's a short comic fight in which Bronson bushwhacks Mifune with a branch that's repeatedly halved in his hands. Bronson quickly deduces he's no match for Mifune and his sword, at which point Mifune sheds his weapon for a one-on-one fight. Bronson assumes a fighting stance and urges Mifune to take a swing. Bronson feels forced to take on the role of aggressor. A bewildered Bronson endures half a dozen judo tosses before diplomatically deciding Mifune must be getting tired. Bronson has been unable to land a single punch. In all the throws, he never loses his cowboy hat (the better to hide the identity of the Spanish stuntman). Later, Bronson does get the upper hand on Mifune after a sneak attack and holds him underwater, proving that sometimes old-fashioned brawn can win out over superior training. By the climax the two are a tandem fighting against Delon and his outlaws.

Director Terence Young and cinematographer Henri Alekan capture the sun-drenched battleground well, and editor Johnny Dwyre cuts optimally in what National General's advertising promised was "the greatest fighting machine the west has ever known." The stars are an intriguing pair and gradually gain a measure of trust and respect for one another. Although critics attacked it, *Red Sun* helped to solidify the charismatic Bronson's success as an international star. Bronson biographer Brian D'Ambrosio praised the film's "excellent fight scenes" and calls the Bronson-Mifune clash "terrific." *The Independent Film Journal* wrote, "Audiences will probably respond best to the scenes in which Bronson is constantly getting thrown on his ass."

The idea of mixing cowboys and martial artists wasn't new. It had been explored on numerous episodic TV westerns with cowboy heroes such as *Have Gun—Will Travel*'s Richard Boone improbably bettering trained martial artists with traditional punches. The most notable presence of martial arts in a western setting came from Robert Conrad displaying his karate skills against multiple Asian attackers in the first season of *The Wild Wild West* in 1965. Conrad returned to more traditional fisticuff action during the ensuing seasons. Chinese labor helped build the transcontinental railroad throughout the American west and Japanese began migrating to California after the 1868 Meiji

Revolution, so an Asian presence during this period wasn't out of place. The most famous example of a martial artist in the Old West came when David Carradine took on the part of wandering Shaolin priest Kwai Chang Caine in the 1971 TV movie *Kung Fu* and the highly popular series that ensued. Following the lead of *Red Sun*, Chen Lee took on Klaus Kinski and Gordon Mitchell in *The Fighting Fists of Shanghai Joe* (1973) and Lo Lieh and Lee Van Cleef teamed up for *The Stranger and the Gunfighter* (aka *Blood Money*) (1974). Tom Laughlin starred as a western swordsman in *The Master Gunfighter* (1975) while karate champ Jim Kelly made a supporting appearance in *Take a Hard Ride* (1975).

Toshiro Mifune was a member of the Imperial Japanese Army Air Force during World War II and then became a legend as the forceful ronin star of Akira Kurosawa's *Rashomon* (1950), *The Seven Samurai* (1954) and *Yojimbo* (1961). Despite being of average size (5'9", 160 pounds), he could project a powerful presence and had the grace of movement to make his action scenes believable. Mifune learned Kendo and Lai for his films from 8th degree black belt Dr. Juzo Sasamori, as well as judo from Kenjutsu master Yoshio Sugino who choreographed sword moves for the Kurosawa films. Mifune was never a master but became proficient at enacting martial arts and swordsmanship for the camera. He memorably fought Lee Marvin in *Hell in the Pacific* (1968) and battled alongside Scott Glenn in *The Challenge* (1982).

See: Hunter, Stephen. "Mifune Embodied Growling, Unkempt Machismo." *Deseret News.* January 2, 1998; "Inquiries About Actor Mifune." *Black Belt.* May 1964; *Red Sun* pressbook.

SEAN CONNERY VS. JOE ROBINSON in *Diamonds Are Forever* (1971)

An older and heavier Sean Connery returned to play James Bond in the successful if too-cartoonish *Diamonds Are Forever*. Plagued by a bumpy Richard Maibaum-Tom Mankiewicz script trying to transition Bond into the 1970s, it's one of the weaker Bonds but still delivered top thrills when it came to the fights. The *Evening Independent* declared that the film occasionally dragged a bit, "although the fight scenes do seem to more than make up for the slow spots." In the Bond tradition, early in the running time we're treated to a two-minute fight between 007 and diamond smuggler Peter Franks (Joe Robinson) in a Amsterdam elevator leaving little room for either big man to maneuver. There's plenty of grunting and broken glass. Exiting the elevator, Connery turns a fire extinguisher on Robinson and flips him over a balcony to his death. Bob Simmons was stunt coordinator and Connery double, with George Leech serving as assistant coordinator. John Barry's score effectively kicks in midway through the fight with Ted Moore shooting the cramped quarters superbly.

Director Guy Hamilton came up with the claustrophobic idea of placing the fighters in a tiny lift after seeing a friend's antiquated elevator. He liked that the two large men didn't have the room to throw traditional punches and would be crashing into the up and down buttons and breaking glass with their elbows. The elevator was built as a four foot square box model at Pinewood Studios. Connery's judo instructor Robinson was signed to play his opposition thanks to his stunt background, grappling skills and familiarity with the star. Ironically, since it was a featured role, Robinson was savvy enough to insure that his contract stipulate that a stuntman would be used for the sequences where the elevator was traveling fast.

Joe Robinson (left) and Sean Connery fight in an elevator in United Artists' *Diamonds Are Forever* (1971).

The principals and stunt team spent three weeks rehearsing this scene. On one take, Robinson accidentally pulled off Connery's toupee. On another take, the supposedly dead Robinson opened his eyes with female lead Jill St. John bending over him dressed in a skimpy outfit. Connery took the logistics all in stride, joking that the next Bond fight would likely be in a phone booth. Interestingly, Connery's Bond errs in breaking the glass with his elbow as he draws back to strike Robinson, alerting his foe to the impending danger. It's a rare case of Bond being an aggressor instead of a reactor. For this reason, some fans had a problem with the death of the Peter Franks character. There's also a continuity error from editors Bert Bates and John W. Holmes involving a crowbar that's dropped but reappears in Robinson's hand when Connery blasts him with foam.

Another popular encounter occurs later with a pair of limber females known as Bambi and Thumper. Bambi is played by Lola Lawson, although stuntwoman Donna Garrett erroneously receives on-screen credit. Professional singer-dancer Trina Parks was recruited to portray Thumper. The girls use their gymnastic skills to kick Connery all over a cutting-edge Las Vegas mansion (the scene was actually filmed in Palm Springs). The tables are turned when they end up in a swimming pool and Connery is able to use his muscle to hold the girls underwater. There's a notable moment during the battle when Parks kicks Connery between the legs. Parks kept holding back during rehearsals for fear of injuring Connery, despite his claims of being adequately protected. With the cameras rolling, Parks nailed Connery perfectly. Paul Baxley coordinated this sequence. However, the Joe Robinson fight remains the confrontation worthy of inclusion with the top Bond fights. *The Spy Who Thrilled Us* compared it favorably to the battle Connery had with Robert Shaw in *From Russia with Love* (1963), saying it "has some of the same viciousness and fight-to-the-death qualities." *Kiss Kiss, Bang Bang* called the Robinson set-to "wonderfully barbaric."

Joe Robinson, 6'2" and 220 pounds, won the European heavyweight championship wrestling as Tiger Joe Robinson. A judoka, he attempted to try out for the Tokyo Olympics but was denied due to his professional standing as a wrestler. Robinson was involved in a controversial late 1950s judo match-up against the legendary Kenshiro Abbe, with both claiming victory. Tape surfaced showing the much smaller and older Abbe dominating the early going but Robinson staying with him until his opponent tired. After injuring his back, Robinson left wrestling to pursue an acting career, winning the lead in *A Kid for Two Farthings* (1955) where he fought Primo Carnera. He failed to become a movie star despite putting on judo exhibitions on the beaches of Cannes. Robinson used his bodybuilder physique and 50" chest to star in a series of Italian muscleman films in the early 1960s.

With brother Doug he became a popular stunt arranger on TV's *The Avengers* (1961–1969) and ran a martial arts studio in Brighton. The brothers co-authored a book with series star Honor Blackman, *Honor Blackman's Book of Self-Defence*. Robinson trained Connery in judo for several of the Bond pictures and was in the running for the Red Grant role in *From Russia with Love*. He also trained Kirk Douglas, Frank Sinatra, Paul Newman, Albert Finney, Terence Stamp and Oliver Reed. In 1998, Robinson fought off eight muggers in Cape Town, South Africa, with martial arts. After he broke one man's arm, the others fled. He was 70 years old.

See: "Joe Has the Eye of the Tiger." *The Visitor.* August 10, 2004; "Trina Parks: The Girl Who Zaps James Bond." *Ebony.* March 1972.

THE GANG FIGHT in *A Clockwork Orange* (1971)

A stylized, disturbingly violent black comedy based on the futuristic Anthony Burgess novel, writer-director Stanley Kubrick's *A Clockwork Orange* was unlike anything that came before it in its artistic glorification of wanton free will. It originally received an X rating.

Malcolm McDowell is the charismatic young criminal Alex who leads his followers into acts of gleeful sexual deviance and brutal mayhem for amusement. Their archenemies are Billy's Boys,

led by Richard Connaught, whom McDowell doesn't think has "the yarbles" to take him in a fight. Alex and his droogs (Warren Clarke, James Marcus, Michael Tarn) encounter the rival gang on a stage at the demolished Karsino hotel on Taggs Island, and the chaotic action that follows includes a dazzling array of flying bodies, tables and chairs that explode into pieces upon impact. Window panes are upraised and come smashing down over heads with malicious intent. Yet Kubrick and McDowell make it entertaining in its own way, riding a fine line between thrilling and repulsing their audience with the repetitive assault. Billy's Boys are encountered in the midst of a rape, which makes McDowell's unruly thugs the fight's anti-heroes in the audience's eyes. As the story progresses, an attempt is made by society to rehabilitate McDowell, opening the film to debate the origins of criminal behavior and the ability to incur lasting change. Ironically, McDowell's science-based rehab involves physical torture known as the Ludovico Treatment, suggesting that his violent acts are not so much his own free will being acted upon as they are a conditioned response to the environment in which he has been brought up.

The Billy's Boys fight is a perfectly edited 90-second crescendo of violence matched effectively to Gioacchino Rossini's "The Thieving Magpie" by cutter Bill Butler. The classic music contrasts remarkably with a level of violence that hadn't previously been seen on screen. When it came to the fight action, Kubrick waived control of the scene to stunt coordinator Roy Scammel, but the cinematic camera style and overall weird tone is all Kubrick. The fight was shot over six days during the last of six months of filming. The most memorable moment is perhaps the serio-comic cane beatings that cinematographer John Alcott shot from a distance, creating a voyeuristic affect for the audience. Kubrick biographer Stuart Y. McDougal found the rhythmic images and swelling score "sexual and phallic."

Fights in film are often unrealistic, going far past the point of normal human resilience. Hand bones are unbroken and faces are too often free of blemishes in the next scene. It's part of the cinematic license given to Hollywood to entertain its audience with action scenes. Kubrick presents the most violent aspects of fights but he also presents it in an over-the-top manner that takes the violence into a different direction: brutality that inspires guilt-laden laughs. *Fight Choreography* referred to the brawls as "extremely lively and stylized," while *Action Films* included it among their greatest fights of all time, calling it "an ultraviolent little fight that has power."

See: *A Clockwork Orange* DVD special features; McDougal, Stuart Y. *Stanley Kubrick's* A Clockwork Orange. Cambridge: Cambridge University Press, 2003; Moorhead, Rory. "Roy Scammell: Stuntman Extraordinaire." *Harrow Times*. February 27. 2013.

John Wayne vs. Bruce Dern in *The Cowboys* (1972)

"I've broke my back once, and my hip twice," John Wayne tells Bruce Dern in Mark Rydell's *The Cowboys*, "and on my worst day I could still beat the hell out of you." Wayne does exactly that over the next three minutes as he gets the better of their exchanges and slams the long-haired cattle rustler against a tree. As the Duke walks away, a bloodied and beaten Dern, his nose broken, draws his gun and shoots Wayne in the back and legs. The scene shocked audiences. After all, the *New York Times* described Wayne as "marvelously indestructible" and the *Chicago Sun Times* kidded that Wayne "can absorb lead like nobody since *The Thing from Another World*." The on-screen killing of an icon was a moment Wayne told Dern audiences would hate him for, and he couldn't have been more correct. The actor received death threats after the film's release. Fully aware of Wayne's stance on the war in Vietnam, Dern joked to Wayne that the war protesters in Berkeley would love him.

Bill Catching was on hand to double Dern in the fight but not enough for the actor's taste. Wayne knew that the 6'1", 180-pound Dern was a Method actor so told him to come at him with everything he had. However, Wayne was simply too strong for Dern. The younger actor recollected Wayne walloped him in the fight, and Dern was bothered by a bad back from then on. His pain became a point of pride as he received the injury from getting beaten on screen by John Wayne. Dern didn't get any relief when Wayne's double Walter Wyatt stepped in for a few shots. The 6'2", 230-pound Wyatt was a champion steer wrestler who manhandled Dern as well. Wayne humorously chided Dern from off-camera to make a fight of it, but Dern was helpless in the vice-grip hands of the rodeo cowboy.

The fight was shot both on location at Pagosa Springs, Colorado, and in Burbank at the Warner Bros. studio where close-ups were done. Robert Surtees' nighttime camerawork is excellent. Buzz Henry served as stunt coordinator, and makeup man Dave Grayson provided the fake blood and bruises. Wayne was long opposed to graphic depictions of violence on screen, and everyone knew he'd be reluctant to have the bloody makeup applied. Grayson jokingly told Rydell he might need three assistants to hold Wayne down. Henry tried to bring up the subject but couldn't, too fearful of a volcanic reaction upon the request. When Grayson brought it up, he was surprised Wayne was agreeable to it, realizing that times were changing and audiences demanded realism. *Show* called the fight "savage, brutal, and very real." When it aired on ABC-TV in prime time the following year, censors left in the violence but deleted Wayne calling Dern "a son of a bitch."

The coming-of-age drama from William Dale Jennings' novel, about the ramrod of a cattle drive being forced to recruit a bunch of school age children, was a departure for Wayne. It had few of his regular crew working on it. Nevertheless he is perfectly cast as the boys' teacher of life lessons. One of those lessons occurs when two bulls square off.

John Wayne clobbers Bruce Dern in Warner Bros.' *The Cowboys* (1972).

Wayne shows the boys how the old bull has more experience and fends off the young bull. The moment foreshadows the later fight between Wayne and Dern.

See: Dern, Bruce, and Christopher Fryer and Robert Crane. *Things I've Said, but Probably Shouldn't Have: An Unrepentant Memoir*. Hoboken, NJ: John Wiley & Sons, 2007; Shepard, Donald, Dave Grayson, and Robert F. Slatzer. *Duke: The Life and Times of John Wayne*. New York: Citadel, 2002.

JAMES CAAN VS. GIANNI RUSSO in *The Godfather* (1972)

Widely regarded as one of the cinema's greatest achievements, Francis Ford Coppola's gangster saga *The Godfather* is nevertheless ridiculed by nitpicking fans for a single missed punch thrown by James Caan during the one-minute street fight where Caan's Sonny Corleone beats the tar out of abusive brother-in-law Gianni Russo. Caan misses the punch by what looks like a foot, yet there's an accompanying sound effect. In Coppola's defense, it's a continuous medium shot from D.P. Gordon Willis with Caan throwing a quick sequence of punches. There's no alternative camera angle to cut to in editing (William Reynolds and Peter Zinner were nominated for an Oscar in that department). The flaw lies in the post-synching, not in Coppola or stunt coordinator Paul Baxley's staging, which required extensive rehearsal and for the actors to hit 37 marks.

The fight is vitally important to the story as it shows the temper of Caan's Sonny Corleone character, half-brother of Al Pacino's Michael and son of Vito Corleone (Marlon Brando). His short fuse will be his undoing, and his enemies use Russo for that purpose. Caan is incensed that Russo has physically abused his sister Talia Shire. Russo is seen hanging out on a crowded street with children (two of them Coppola's) playing in an open fire hydrant when Caan pulls up. Russo tries to run but Caan tackles him and throws him against a wall. What follows are approximately two dozen unanswered punches and kicks, leaving Russo lying beaten to a pulp in the hydrant's spray. Caan smashes Russo with a garbage can and hits him with the lid. He even takes off Russo's shoe, beats him with it, and bites his hands when Russo holds onto a railing and refuses to let go. Giving a final kick, Caan warns, "You touch my sister again, I'll kill you."

Las Vegas club owner Russo had never acted on film before but had influential connections. He auditioned but wasn't initially cast. Brando took a liking to Russo's moxie after Russo confronted him. Caan, however, did not. Legend has it that Caan didn't hold back during the fight. Coppola resisted using stunt doubles. He couldn't film the missed punch from a different angle because Russo was injured when Caan connected with a few spirited body punches and kicks, cracking two of Russo's ribs. Russo also suffered a nicked elbow and wasn't pleased with Caan's physicality.

James Caan goes crazy on Gianni Russo in Paramount's classic *The Godfather* (1972).

The fight was shot on location on Pleasant Avenue in East Harlem.

James Caan grew up an athletic, streetwise kid who boxed and briefly played football at Michigan State. Five-foot-ten and 165 pounds, the brashly energetic Caan carried himself with an exaggerated bravado, but he was one of the more physically capable actors in Hollywood. His tough talk and swagger wasn't all show. He took an interest in competitive rodeo, becoming a member of the Professional Rodeo Cowboys Association. The martial arts also became a lifelong passion, and Caan was one of the few actors who did more than dabble. He studied kung fu in the 1960s and continued training with Emil Farkas and Tak Kubota. Caan focused on Gosoku-ryu karate, earning a black belt. Notable fights include *The Glory Guys* (1965), *The Killer Elite* (1975) and *1941* (1979) (see entries). Fights of interest came against Bing Russell in *Journey to Shiloh* (1968), Robert Duvall in *The Rain People* (1969), Christopher Morley in *Freebie and the Bean* (1974), Jim Davis in *Comes a Horseman* (1978) and Arnold Schwarzenegger in *Eraser* (1996).

See: *The Godfather* DVD special features; Lebo, Harlan. *The Godfather Legacy*. New York: Simon & Schuster, 2005; Seal, Mark. "*The Godfather* Wars." *Vanity Fair*. March 2009.

WILLIAM SMITH VS. MICHAEL PATAKI in *Grave of the Vampire* (1972)

This extremely low-budget horror film was shot in 11 days for $50,000. Nevertheless it gained a cult reputation for its striking atmosphere, eerie Jose Mendoza-Nava score, intelligent script by future *Sopranos* creator David Chase, and the solid lead performances by genre vets Michael Pataki and William Smith as father-and-son vampires. Smith is half-bloodsucker, conceived illegitimately as the result of a Pataki rape. He vows revenge for the death of his mother, who was forced to feed the baby her own blood. Thirty-odd years later, Smith finds Pataki teaching occult history at a university. The two have a cat-and-mouse game around female lead Lyn Peters, but when Pataki bares his fangs at a group séance, he's shocked at the strength and power Smith displays. Smith heatedly announces he's Pataki's son: "And I'm going to destroy you!"

Their resulting battle is one for the ages, a nearly five-minute wall-smasher featuring hair-

pulling, eye-gouging and nose-ripping action. *Fight Choreography* calls it "a lively brawl to the death." According to *Monster Rally*, Smith plays his part "with brooding intensity and his characteristic impressive physicality, the latter displayed in his climactic down-and-dirty fight to the finish." Director John Hayes and D.P. Paul Hipp join the battle with their camera as Smith and Pataki pound away at one another. Smith's back is lit on fire after he is knocked into a fireplace, and he launches his body end over end into a wall. He performs a double axe-handle blow and a clean and jerk with overhead press of Pataki's body. Unfortunately, the glass doorway Smith throws Pataki's body through is too obviously made of a thin paper-like material, detracting from the effectiveness of the scene. In the highlight of the fight, Smith wraps a chain around Pataki's neck and literally jerks him off the ground from his back onto his stomach. With Pataki dangling over a balcony by the chain, Smith karate chops a table leg and uses it as a makeshift stake to plunge into Pataki's heart.

Stunt coordinator Joe Pronto did much of the fight for Pataki, understandable considering the abuse Smith inflicts. The overhead lift was achieved by filming in reverse with Smith lowering Pronto. Smith allowed the use of stunt double Nick Dimitri's services for the fire gag and a convincing fall over a balcony into an open stairwell. The film was shot in downtown Los Angeles, with the climax taking place in a large manor. During the fight, Pataki's cheap fangs kept falling from his mouth, which threatened to give the actors the giggles. Pataki is best known as the Klingon aggressor in the humorous brawl highlighting the 1967 *Star Trek* episode "The Trouble with Tribbles."

See: *Grave of the Vampire* pressbook; "Interview: William Smith." *Fangoria*. #324, June, 2013; Wilson, S. Michael. *Monster Rally*. West Orange, NJ: Idea Men, 2008.

TERENCE HILL VS. RICCARDO PIZZUTI in *Man of the East* (1972)

Man of the East is an entertainingly silly Spaghetti Western from writer-director Enzo Barboni and the makers of the popular *Trinity* films. It is highlighted by an epic slapstick saloon brawl-street brawl between odd aristocrat Terence Hill and Italian stuntman Riccardo Pizzuti. The tenderfoot star's punches are often unorthodox, and he throws them with a glowing smile on his face. Pizzuti grins and laughs as he takes the punches. This is one of the happiest brawls ever committed to film. The only thing missing is Hill's usual co-star Bud Spencer. The uncanny Yugoslavian-shot action was coordinated by stuntman Giorgio Ubaldi, who considered his lengthy fights like dance routines. He counted out tempo and beat as the combatants landed punches on one another. Each of Ubaldi's fights took up to ten days to film. Cinematographer Aldo Giordani was behind the camera. The composing duo Guido and Maurizio De Angelis (aka Oliver Onions) provided a whimsical if seemingly neverending score.

There's another big saloon brawl where Pizzuti primarily squares off against American character actor Gregory Walcott. A recurring comic motif has characters' heads smashed through tables. Several Italian stuntmen handle the brawls with Hill and Walcott, among them Salvatore Borghese, Giovanni Cianfriglia, Bruno Arie, Giancarlo Bastianoni, Roberto Alessandri, Omero Capanna, Franco Daddi, Paolo Figlia, Osiride Pevarello, Renzo Pevarello, Franco Ukmar, Emilio Messina, Pietro Torrisi and Marcello Verziera. These stuntmen worked often with Hill and had their slapstick fight routines down to a science. Hill's fights paralleled those found in the martial arts genre as they often involved Hill taking on several fighters at once. He approached these fights with a sense of humor, a tack that worked in the face of the ridiculousness of the situations.

Often cast as a henchman, the shaggy, gray-bearded Pizzuti excelled at taking punches and throwing his rangy acrobat's body through the air with arms flailing and hair flying for comic effect. In *Man of the East*, his biggest role, he repeatedly dives into the dirt, rolls across tables or flips over Hill's back after a full-steam charge. He was a perfect cartoon complement to Hill and his fighting partner Bud Spencer, dating back to repeatedly taking a frying pan to the face in *They Call Me Trinity* (1970) (see entry) and getting his teeth knocked out in both *All the Way Boys* (1972) and *Odds and Evens* (aka *Gambling for High Stakes*) (1978). The fighting duo continued to beat on him for the next decade, most notably in *Trinity Is Still My Name* (1971), *Turn the Other Cheek* (1974), *Crime Busters* (1977) and *Go for It* (1983).

See: *Profession—Acrobat: An Afternoon with Ricardo Pizzuti*; Terence Hill 2002 Perugia interview transcript.

Lieh Lo vs. Hsiung Chao in *Five Fingers of Death* (aka *King Boxer*) (1972)

An influential Hong Kong martial arts film from producer Run Run Shaw and director Chang-Hwa Jeong, *Five Fingers of Death* was the first to be picked up, redubbed and distributed theatrically in both the United Kingdom and the United States by Warner Bros. Its success with western audiences paved the way for Bruce Lee and the flood of chop-socky flicks that followed. *Five Fingers of Death* (aka *King Boxer* in its native land) has all the ingredients necessary: rival martial arts schools and tournaments, snarling villains, violent revenge, screaming battle cries, the one-against-many theme and a very capable action lead in Chinese star Lieh Lo. The martial arts action as coordinated on theatrical backdrops by Chuan Chen and Chia Yung Liu is captivating, even featuring fantastical flying leaps as the combatants engage one another. Sometimes trampolines are used. At other points, the film is reversed to achieve the innovative stunts. It all leads to a five-minute showdown with sword-wielding Japanese warrior Hsiung Chao that concludes with Lo literally punching his foe through a wall.

The fighting is extremely violent, which was part of the appeal to U.S. audiences. When contact is made, dust flies from the costumes or the floorboards to show off the power of the blow. Decapitation and eyeball-plucking are everyday occurrences in this fantasy western from the East, which American audiences were quick to ooh and aah over. There are even kitschy nuggets such as an overactive zoom lens and Lo's glowing red palms announcing his Iron Fist technique while accompanied by Quincy Jones' iconic squealing siren score from the American TV cop show *Ironside*. Quentin Tarantino used this same memorable bit to great effect in *Kill Bill* (2003). *Five Fingers of Death* is one of his favorite films and an inspiration for his own production *The Man with the Iron Fists* (2012). Lo Lieh followed with *The Stranger and the Gunfighter* (aka *Blood Money*) (1974) where he fought heavyweight boxer Gregorio "Goyo" Peralta.

Publicity declared it "a masterpiece of martial arts" which was pure hyperbole but made people want to check it out. *Variety* was quick to note the film's merits, writing that the picture represented "a whole new era of bruising, battering savagery that should appeal to action audiences." According to the *Village Voice*, "The action sequences, as usual, are well handled, but are limited to the superhuman rather than the supernatural." The *New York Times* called the fighting "flashily spectacular" but noted that it all seemed more for show than actual skill. The *Pittsburgh Post-Gazette* wrote, "None of the film's absurdities matter apparently because audiences care only for the fight scenes which come every three or four minutes." The *Pittsburgh Press*: "Cinematographer Wang Yung-Lung's principal accomplishment is the mastery of slow motion, which is incorporated into all action sequences and blended with plenty of vrapps and fwoops." *The Ultimate Guide to Martial Arts Movies of the 1970s* has nothing but praise for "the incredible action and martial arts expertise of Lo Lieh." Martial arts had truly arrived, essentially replacing the time-honored western and forever altering the traditional notion of a fight scene.

See: Lucas, Charles. "Profile of a Great American Fad." *Black Belt*. October 1974.

BRUCE LEE vs. ROBERT BAKER in *The Chinese Connection* (aka *Fists of Fury*) (1972)

Despite his determination, innovative martial artist Bruce Lee's career in America stalled after the cancellation of the TV series *The Green Hornet* (1966–1967), where he had opened many eyes as Van Williams' supremely skilled cohort Kato. Lee couldn't manage much other than an impressive supporting role in *Marlowe* (1969) opposite James Garner where he famously destroys Garner's office only to be suckered into trying an ill-advised kick atop a building. Lee had a few undistinguished assignments as fight coordinator on *The Wrecking Crew* (1969) and *A Walk in the Spring Rain* (1970), as well as a couple of TV appearances on *Longstreet* (1971–1972), where he played blind investigator James Franciscus' karate instructor. He had hoped to star in what became the TV series *Kung Fu* but lost the role to Caucasian actor David Carradine. There was also a personal screenplay titled *The Silent Flute* which he hoped to co-star in with James Coburn. They scouted locations together in India, but that project kept getting pushed back.

Although he had reservations, Lee accepted an offer to go to Hong Kong and star in martial arts films for Golden Harvest and director Wei Lo. The first was *The Big Boss* (aka *Fists of Fury*) (1971) followed by *The Chinese Connection* (aka *Fists of Fury*) (1972). The former builds deliberate suspense by not having Lee fight until midway through, and then he was only allowed to personally choreograph a single fight in an ice factory against opponents who were not established as worthy adversaries. The latter film has wall-to-wall fighting with Lee and his own Jeet Kune Do front and center.

The Chinese Connection highlights the 5'7", 140-pound Lee's incredible speed and precision. In a fantastic four-minute fight in a Japanese dojo against multiple opponents, he uses his hands, feet and a pair of nunchaku (aka nunchucks). *Action Films* and *Black Belt* include this among the greatest fights of all-time. *The Ultimate Guide to Martial Arts Movies of the 1970s* calls it "one of Hong Kong cinema's most important fight scenes." It's one of the best examples of the often implausible one-against-many screen fights that dominate the genre. In one sequence, Lee expertly takes on nine attackers with not a single miss. As the star and choreographer, he gets to accentuate his own strengths, showing himself to be physically fit with tremendous screen presence and camera awareness. Audiences had never seen a star so powerful, fast to strike, and adaptable to more than a dozen opponents coming at him from all directions. Lee was so fast, he'd often pause and hold a pose for a moment after a series of movements so the audience had time to digest what occurred. Then it was on to the next attack. By the end of the fight, his opponents are so whipped they cringe like mistreated dogs at Lee's slightest movement.

The film is reputed to be the first Hong Kong martial arts film featuring a Caucasian villain, the mustached Russian character Petrov (Robert Baker). Baker had been Lee's student and the recipient of his famous "one-inch strike" during an exhibition at the Long Beach Invitational in 1967. He was big enough to be a believable threat to Lee on screen. When they were out on the town In Hong Kong, Lee jokingly told people that Baker was his bodyguard. In the movie, Lee and Baker spar with one another for three minutes, although Lee is toying with the bigger man. Baker's kicks and punches are no match for Lee's defense and counters. His size and strength are factors in his favor. Baker traps Lee in an arm-bar and locks his legs around Lee's neck. Lee breaks the hold by biting his opponent's leg. When Lee rises, he shows his humor by wiping his mouth as if he has feasted on a tasty morsel. After Lee has worn a bloodied Baker down, the fight ends with a slow-motion side-kick to the head and a deadly strike to the throat.

Profiled in the 1992 documentary *Deadliest Art: The Best of the Martial Arts Films, The Chinese Connection* also boasts future martial arts star Jackie Chan as a stuntman. Chan distinguished himself on the film by doubling the villain Suzuki (Riki Hashimoto) in the climactic scene where Lee kicks him 15 feet through the wall of a building. The stunt, which only Chan volunteered for, was a record-setting movement that gained Chan notoriety within the Hong Kong stunt community. He worked with Lee again on *Enter the Dragon* (1973) (see entry). These credits enabled Chan to become a renowned stunt coordinator and star.

On the crimefighting series *The Green Hornet*, Lee amazed the show's professional stuntmen with his quickness. Stunt coordinator Bennie Dobbins had to convince Lee his movements needed to be slowed down so the camera could follow them. When Lee balked, Dobbins countered by having Van Williams take on multiple opponents while Lee spent his time with one. Lee quickly got the message and learned more about fighting for the camera. The stuntmen in turn began to train in martial arts, realizing that Lee and his rapid-flying kicks were the wave of the future. Lee's best fight came against Mako Iwamatsu (doubled by Danny Inosanto) in 1966's "The Preying Mantis."

Lee was considered a one-in-a-million athlete when it came to his unique combination of skill, coordination, inner drive and physical attributes complimentary to his chosen sport. His Jeet Kune Do system utilized his dazzling speed and timing while designed to throw off an opponent's offense by beating them to the punch. Lee theorized that when an opponent was striking, he wasn't defending and could be vulnerable. He studied boxer Cassius Clay (Muhammad Ali) and fencing master Julio Martinez Costello to see how they closed the distance on an opponent or hit on half-beats to disrupt the other's style. Lee began utilizing snap punches to give extra power to his blows. His striking speed from three feet away was timed at five one-hundredths of a second. Many marveled at his ripped physique with a three percent body fat percentage and a miniscule 26" waist measurement. He pushed himself in training to grow as a man and as a fighter, continuously testing the levels of his body's strength and endurance. Notable fights include *Way of the Dragon* (1972), *Enter the Dragon* (1973) and *Game of Death* (1979) (see entries).

See: Lee, Bruce, and John R. Little. *Jeet Kune Do: Bruce Lee's Commentaries on the Martial Way.* Boston: C.E. Tuttle, 1997. Lee, Bruce, and John R. Little. *Words of the Dragon: Interviews, 1958–1973.* Boston: C.E. Tuttle, 1997.

THE BARROOM BRAWL in *Junior Bonner* (1972)

Director Sam Peckinpah, the former Marine noted for the bloody violence in *The Wild Bunch* (1969) and *Straw Dogs* (1971), offered a change-of-pace character study with this interesting Steve McQueen rodeo drama. Set in a changing Prescott, Arizona, it features an ambling, often humorous four-minute brawl inside the famed Palace Bar on Whiskey Row. Peckinpah and cinematographer Lucien Ballard took a week and a half to film the complicated scene, which involved a bar full of local extras amidst a bar full of local extras, several stuntmen, and a band playing on stage. Frank Santillo and Robert Wolfe's razor-sharp editing perfectly establishes the character and mood as McQueen and beautiful Barbara Leigh lock eyes with one another. Her escort Charles Gray is none too pleased when McQueen asks her to dance. Sensing that Gray is about to explode, McQueen takes advantage of his friendly rival Bill McKinney's interest in Leigh and lets him cut in. Gray confronts McKinney, and the venerable Ben Johnson steps in to knock Gray down with the first punch of the fight. Joe Don Baker, as McQueen's brother, also throws a punch while McQueen and Leigh slink off to an isolated spot to get to know one another better.

The action as written by screenwriter Jeb Rosebrook is raucous and full of local color; capturing the life of a beer-swilling rodeo cowboy. The Palace brawl wasn't part of the original script but a suggestion by Peckinpah, who retained Rosebrook on location. Tough guy McQueen doesn't throw a single punch in the brawl. A surprisingly engaging McKinney proves to be the most spirited fighter in the saloon and dominates the action. A highlight is a slow-motion McKinney leap into the ruckus. A small Indian local named Curly provides humor as he drunkenly ogles the girls and follows them into the rest room. The crew had to bail him out of jail most mornings. Peckinpah wanders through the scene at one point. Huge local James Shreeve begins cleaning up the mess and puts an end to the fisticuffs when he tells the band to play "The Star Spangled Banner." The fight ends with everyone having had a good time, with the exception of Gray. *Variety* wrote, "Audiences that consider such rough-and-tumble as innocuous, vicarious ventilation will get their fill."

Mickey Gilbert was stunt coordinator while the "Ward Brothers" stunt team (Autry, Steve and Troy), Denny Arnold and Wayne McLaren are featured in the action. Due to needing footage of the Prescott Rodeo Days in July of 1971, the film was rushed into pre-production and was over-budget as a result. The producers wouldn't let Gilbert have the 20 Hollywood stuntmen he requested, so he recruited Prescott locals at $5 a day and trained them at the local YMCA. When they stepped before the cameras with Gilbert's handful of professional stuntmen, the locals nervously rushed through the scene. Gilbert discussed the problem with Peckinpah and opted to roll camera on the next rehearsal. Not realizing the camera was on, Gilbert's trained locals performed perfectly.

Bill McKinney served with the Navy during the Korean War before cornering the early 1970s market for crazy villains and redneck ruffians with his deranged mountain man in *Deliverance* (1972). A professional tree-topper with guts to spare, he had an amateur boxing background and kept fit. Five-eleven and 170 pounds, he was able to handle his own screen brawling. Notable fights came in *Angel Unchained* (1970), *Every Which Way but Loose* (1978), *Bronco Billy* (1980) and *Any Which Way You Can* (1980) (see entries). He also skirmished with Tamara Dobson in *Cleopatra Jones* (1973), Clint Eastwood in *Thunderbolt and Lightfoot* (1974) and David Carradine in *Cannonball* (1976).

See: Gilbert, Mickey, and Roberta Rockwell. *Me and My Saddle Pal: My Life as a Hollywood Stuntman.* Outskirts Press, 2014; *Junior Bonner* DVD commentary; Loretti, Nicanor. "Bill McKinney: You Done Taken a Wrong Turn." *Shock Cinema.* #23, 2003.

BRUCE LEE VS. CHUCK NORRIS in *Way of the Dragon* (aka *Return of the Dragon*) (1972)

Considered by many to be the greatest movie fight ever, Bruce Lee against Chuck Norris in the Roman Colosseum delivers high thrills. *Cinema Retro* refers to it as "one of the greatest fight scenes ever filmed," and it's showcased in *Deadliest Art: The Best of the Martial Arts Films* (1992). Lee biographer Bruce Thomas calls it "one of the best fight scenes that Bruce Lee ever put on film." *The Ultimate Guide to Martial Arts Movies of the 1970s* claims it is "Norris' best fight scene to date." *Chas-*

ing Dragons writes, "Norris' duel with Lee is a classic." *Films of Fury* calls it "the most realistic empty-handed martial art fight ever filmed to that date." *Action Superheroes* and *Action Films* rank it as one of the top fights of all time. This match-up of karate legends literally changed the face of fight scenes as martial arts began to overtake traditional slugfests. Lee not only starred in the film but wrote, produced, directed and choreographed all the amazing fights. *Way of the Dragon* was originally intended for Chinese audiences, but after Lee's 1973 death and the overwhelming success of that year's *Enter the Dragon*, there was a U.S. release. According to *Variety*, "The highlight is the exciting climax," while the *Village Voice* said it "was worth seeing for the fabulous fight scene at the end."

The fight takes up nearly nine minutes of screen time, including two minutes of the men simply warming up with vertebrae-crunching stretches and karate kata. Throwing a curve in the face of tradition, bad guy Norris wears white while hero Lee wears black. They face off like gunfighters, while Lee gives ample screen time to an innocent kitten observing the action. The fighters are evenly matched with Norris the stronger of the two but Lee the quicker. Norris uses his high round-kick to advantage while Lee features a low heel-sweep. The choreography is intricate and all the technique advanced. Midway through, Lee changes tactics and begins dancing, his sudden fluidity throwing off Norris' timing. In a humorous moment, Lee pulls off a clump of Norris' chest hair. At one point, the two fighters smile knowingly at one another. The wordless fight is treated as poetry, with the action occasionally turning to slow-motion to emphasize the form of the fighters in long, unbroken takes. Norris suffers blurred vision, and the camera briefly becomes his eyes. Lee breaks Norris' arm and leg, but Norris gamely fights on. Lee is forced to snap Norris' neck to end the fight. In a somber moment uncharacteristic of Chinese kung fu films, Lee places Norris' gi and belt over his body in a show of respect for his fellow warrior.

Lee originally intended to have heavyweight karate champion Joe Lewis play his opponent, but Lewis declined. Lee then offered the role to middleweight champ Norris. This fight would potentially legitimize his standing among martial artists, seeing as he had chosen not to be a tournament fighter and was frowned upon in certain circles. Lee felt that tournament karate was too restricted by rules and regulations, hindrances to his instinctive style of Jeet Kune Do. Lee devised 20 pages of choreography for the final fight in the Colosseum, the oldest gladiatorial arena in the world. He began blocking the action in his home den with his wife Linda playing the Norris role. Special permits were arranged for the Colosseum itself while a replica set was built in Hong Kong. When the 5'9" Norris arrived in Italy, he weighed 162 pounds in comparison to Lee's 145. Lee asked Norris to put on close to 20 pounds in a week as he wanted him to appear much bigger than Lee on screen. Norris obliged and made it to a weight of 180 for the fight. An entire day was devoted to choreography with Lee trying to see if what he had on paper could be put on screen with Norris. The actors agreed to make light contact. The next three sixteen-hour days were devoted to the fight itself. Lee studiously checked the dailies for any sign of a missed punch or kick. If he saw anything questionable, they filmed it again.

Norris wished that he could have devised some of the choreography to make it even better, but it was Lee's show. When later questioned whether he could have beaten Lee for real, Norris took the high road and remained noncommittal. Some claim the two fighters were antagonistic toward one another because Lee had once shown Norris up after viewing Norris compete in a late 1960s karate tournament. In actuality, Norris was interested in studying with Lee and they began training together. Both realized the advantage of not being bound to one strict style. In Hong Kong, the film was censored for excessive violence (Lee landing five consecutive kicks to Norris' head). U.S. audiences were able to see the footage of Norris' noggin knocked about in its entirety.

Fellow karate champion Bob Wall accompanied Norris on location and trained with both Norris and Lee (*and* played a small role). More importantly, he ran interference for challenges toward Norris from the Chinese. Norris was besieged with threats and felt he should meet them. Instead, Wall stepped in by appearing on Chinese television and announcing that anyone who wanted to challenge Norris would have to go through Wall first. Wall had a legitimate tough guy reputation and claimed he'd fight anyone to the death. Wall demonstrated his tremendous ability to take punches and kicks from both Norris and Lee on TV. Nobody came forward to follow up on the challenges. Norris was then able to concentrate on the film fight with Lee.

Norris began studying judo while serving with the Air Force in Korea but switched to Tang Soo Do after injuring his shoulder. He quickly found he favored the high-flying kicks of the Tae Kwon Do offshoot. He earned his black belt in the art before heading back to the States and opening a karate studio. To drum up publicity for his school, he entered karate tournaments and made a name for himself; he became the World Professional Middleweight Karate Champion in 1968. Norris remained undefeated as a champion, retiring from competition in 1974. As Norris made a name in competition, his karate studios began to expand; he took on celebrity students Priscilla Presley and Steve McQueen. Bruce Lee offered Norris a small role in *The Wrecking Crew* (1969) fighting Dean Martin. McQueen was the first to suggest that Norris could have a career in movies, and Norris sold off his schools.

Although limited in his emotional expressiveness as an actor, Norris' martial arts skills were solid and provided enough high-kicking flash to dazzle audiences. His Nordic looks helped Americanize the arts and suggest that with proper training and commitment, elite black belt status didn't

Chuck Norris (left) and Bruce Lee square off for the legendary fight in Warner Bros.' *Way of the Dragon* (1972).

have to be exclusive to Asians. Norris became a tremendous influence to burgeoning martial artists and one of the top action stars of the 1980s. Nearly every one of his starring roles featured his trademark spinning back kick, and his status as a tough guy took on legendary proportions. Rarely did Norris face one man in a fight. Often he was taking on entire gangs with his speedy roundhouse kicks and well-aimed back fists. The fight in the biker bar in *Silent Rage* (1982) and the pub battle in *Code of Silence* (1985) are his best.

Notable fights include *A Force of One* (1979), *The Octagon* (1980) and *Lone Wolf McQuade* (1982) (see entries). Fights of interest came against Don Wong in *Slaughter in San Francisco* (1974), Ron Cedillos in *Breaker! Breaker!* (1977), Soon Taik Oh in *Good Guys Wear Black* (1978), Professor Toru Tanaka in *An Eye for an Eye* (1981), Seiji Sakaguchi in *Forced Vengeance* (1982), Richard Lynch in *Invasion USA* (1985), Robert Forster in *The Delta Force* (1986), Sonny Landham in *Firewalker* (1986) and Jack O'Halloran and Branscombe Richmond in *Hero and the Terror* (1988). Norris kicked butt weekly as the star of the hugely popular TV series *Walker, Texas Ranger* (1993–2001), tangling with everyone from boxer Randall "Tex" Cobb to UFC champ Frank Shamrock. He even fought such venerable character actors as Gary Busey, Michael Parks and Don Stroud. His best fights came against frequent guest Marshall Teague.

See: Ortiz, Sergio. "Duel to the Death in the Colosseum: Bruce Lee vs. Chuck Norris." *Fighting Stars.* October 1975; Thomas, Bruce. *Immortal Combat: Portrait of a True Warrior.* Berkeley, CA: Blue Snake, 2007.

Joe Don Baker vs. Corruption in *Walking Tall* (1973)

Walking Tall was a popular rural action hit from director Phil Karlson and producer-screenwriter Mort Briskin. It concerns the real-life heroics of pro wrestler and Marine turned Tennessee sheriff Buford Pusser, who took on corruption in the South. Big, raw-boned Joe Don Baker is perfectly cast as Pusser, and the highlight has him violently clubbing a bar full of thugs with a big stick of wood. The bad guys in question ganged up on him earlier during a bloody 90-second battle at the Lucky Spot Bar that Karlson and cinematographer Jack Marta filmed in red neon light. In that fight, Baker catches the pimps, bootleggers and confi-

dence men cheating his friend out of money during a dice game and turns his fists on them. He puts up a great fight against bouncers Gene LeBell, Gil Perkins and Victor Paul, as well as Arch Johnson, Dominick Mazzie, Del Monroe and Werner Venetz, a judoka brought in by LeBell. Baker delivers a double crotch punch. However, their numbers prove too much for him. They hold him down while Monroe cuts him with a knife and leaves him for dead. After Baker recuperates, he wields the hickory stick equalizer and later runs for sheriff to continue his ongoing battle. *Variety* wrote, "Phil Karlson's slaughter staging is far superior to his dramatic direction." *The New Yorker* called it "a heartbreaker as well as a gut-cruncher." The *Daytona Beach News Journal* claimed simply, "*Walking Tall* packs a punch."

Gil Perkins and Carey Loftin were stunt coordinators while Roydon Clark was on hand to double Baker. The star learned judo from Gene LeBell over a five-week period. The wooden club was made of rubber. It wasn't a weapon Pusser carried around, and he didn't single-handedly take on the bad guys. In the real roadhouse fight, two pals helped him. Pusser was often on set as a technical advisor watching Baker and later declared that the movie was "80 percent real." When it became a huge hit, plans for a sequel were immediately put in motion. This time Buford Pusser intended to star, but he was killed in an automobile accident. Baker had a feud with the producers and didn't want to continue in the role, so Bo Svenson was brought in to star in the sequels *Part Two, Walking Tall* (1975) and *Final Chapter, Walking Tall* (1977). Brian Dennehy played Pusser in a TV movie titled *A Real American Hero* (1978), and Svenson returned for the short-lived 1981 TV series *Walking Tall.* Dwayne "The Rock" Johnson took over the role for a 2004 reboot followed by two Kevin Sorbo direct-to-video releases.

Baker was a believable screen fighter, throwing punches with heavy grunts and bad intentions. He was the star of Robert Clouse's 1974 martial arts film *Golden Needles*, providing a brawling counterpoint to the high-flying kickers. But the beefy former Texas football player and Army veteran had a tendency to pack on the pounds and his days as a leading man were few. He settled into a career as a character actor. It looked like movie fights were the extent of his working out, so they took on a believably sweaty desperation with Baker's hair always mussed. To his credit, he did the bulk of his own on-screen fighting, seldom reliant on a stuntman to cover the action. Impressed by the 6'2" Baker's brutish size and natural strength, TV critic Gary Deeb wrote that he could "probably fight a Sequoia tree to a stand-off."

Notable fights include *Junior Bonner* (1972) and *Framed* (1975) (see entries). Fights of interest came against Bernie Casey in *Guns of the Magnificent Seven* (1969), Del Monroe in *Adam at 6 A.M.* (1970), Andy Robinson in *Charley Varrick* (1973), Merlin Olsen in *Mitchell* (1975), Timothy Carey in *Speedtrap* (1977) and Bud Davis in *Shadow of Chikara* (1977). One of his best roles came as a brutal hit man in the TV movie *Mongo's Back in Town* (1971), and he starred for a single season as the title character, a tough New York City cop, in *Eischied* (1979–1980). As a guest, Baker fought Dan Kemp and Harry Lauter in the 1969 *Big Valley* episode "Lightfoot" and Harry Swoger in the 1970 *Lancer* episode "Shadow of a Dead Man."

See: Buck, Jerry. "Joe Don Baker Getting Tired of Typecasting." *Daytona Beach Morning Journal.* May 27, 1978; Crist, Judith. "Hick, Hack, Hokum, Ho-Hum." *New York.* February 18, 1974; Deeb, Gary. "TV's Biggest Superstars." *Star-News.* June 11, 1979.

LEE MARVIN VS. ERNEST BORGNINE in *Emperor of the North* (1973)

A great action drama by director Robert Aldrich, *Emperor of the North* was originally developed as a Sam Peckinpah vehicle. Veteran tough guys Lee Marvin and Ernest Borgnine square off as a Depression era hobo and a sadistic railroad cop who wants to keep bums off his train at all cost. Marvin is no ordinary bum; he's A No. 1 and equally determined to ride Borgnine's rail. Cocky youth Keith Carradine is along for the ride, but this drama is focused on the cagey Marvin and the bloodthirsty Borgnine. Both men are ready to put their reputations and lives on the line. The climax is a masterful triumph of staging on an open flatcar as the Oregon scenery races past cinematographer Joseph Biroc's camera. It's apparent both aging actors are doing all the fighting. Borgnine declared *Emperor of the North* (aka *Emperor of the North Pole*) his personal favorite role.

The grueling five-minute battle involves fists, a hammer, a chain, a two-by-four and an axe. At one point Marvin knocks Borgnine off the car. As Borgnine hangs from the edge, he realizes his fate is in Marvin's hands. Marvin has him measured for a shot with the board, and a sudden sense of hurt appears in the helpless Borgnine's eyes. It's not that he fears being hit in the nose, it's that he's unready for the fight to end. Marvin feels the same way and lifts Borgnine up so they can resume the brawl with the declaration, "I promised you a fight, now get your ass up, you dirty miserable son of a bitch!" Borgnine literally cackles at the delight of continuing. The two delve deeper into their hatred for one another as Marvin introduces the axe into the savage battle. Marvin sinks the blade into Borgnine's shoulder, and Borgnine begins to bleed copiously. He realizes he is the loser. Marvin has him measured for a kill, but relents and pushes him off the train. He hears, "You haven't seen the last of me!" Carradine steps up to share in Marvin's glory, and the elder bum throws the annoying youth off the train. "You got no class," he explains.

Marvin claimed that the fight took 14 days to film. Both actors ran through the fight routine numerous times for the cameras, even doing the fight with Aldrich's camera on Carradine to capture his reaction shots. Marvin and Borgnine are only doubled at the

Fight scene vets Ernest Borgnine (left) and Lee Marvin put on a great battle atop a train in 20th Century-Fox's *Emperor of the North* (1973).

outset when Marvin jumps off a boxcar onto Borgnine, and the two fall over Carradine onto the flatcar. For that, Walter Scott doubled Marvin, Jerry Gatlin doubled Borgnine, and Jim Kingsley doubled Carradine. Gatlin doubled Borgnine for the outstanding back-fall off the train that ends the fight. The editing of Michael Luciano is superb throughout.

The *Chicago Sun Times* called it "a masterpiece of action direction by Robert Aldrich," while the *New York Times* wrote that Aldrich "staged the action sequences with a dizzying vividness and accuracy." *Variety* chimed in with, "The film has several outstanding sequences of the top action class as Aldrich makes the most of Christopher Knopf's screenplay in building them to a fever pitch." *The New Yorker*, turned off by the graphic violence, called the fight "positively disgusting." The *Los Angeles Times* was also put off by the gore but came away impressed by the film: "While the savagery that marks A No. 1 and Shack's final clash undeniably grows logically out of their characters, Aldrich depicts it so graphically that all that has been so admirably expressed is in danger of being blotted out by a reaction of sheer revulsion." Time has been kind to Aldrich's classic tough guy match-up with both *Action Superheroes* and *Action Films* including it among the greatest fights of all time.

See: *Emperor of the North* DVD commentary; *Emperor of the North* pressbook.

BRUCE LEE vs. BOB WALL in *Enter the Dragon* (1973)

Many have called *Enter the Dragon* the greatest martial arts action film ever. While that may be debated, there's no denying that many of the genre's most famous fights appear in the film. It's so iconic, it was lampooned in *The Kentucky Fried Movie* (1977). The karate-spy hybrid starring the legendary Bruce Lee is the most influential film of its kind. It was the first martial arts film to be given major U.S. studio backing, in this case Warner Bros., although most of it was lensed in Hong Kong over 13 weeks by visionary producers Fred Weintraub and Paul Heller. Technically the film rises well above the genre. Robert Clouse was the director and Gilbert Hubbs the innovative cinematographer, using slow motion particularly well in key spots to highlight martial art moves that would otherwise be imperceptible to the naked eye. Zooms are also employed to zero in on the intensity painted across Lee's face when he makes

a kill and lets rip with his famous war cry. Editor Kurt Hirschler uncharacteristically went on location with the film so he'd have a better feeling for the fights when he and George Watters hit the editing room. Several sequences were left uncut because they came across so perfectly. Michael Allin worked up a functional script while art director James Wong Sun concocted a colorful and interesting lair for the villain and the climactic fight. Lalo Schifrin provides a bouncy, memorable score flavored with sounds of the Orient.

As for the fights, Lee against Bob Wall and Lee against Kien Shih (aka Shek Kin) in the Hall of Mirrors are highlights. However, they are no match for Lee's incredible battle in the underground cave against dozens of charging opponents. Lee also fights Sammo Hung in the prologue. Charismatic Jim Kelly shows off his fancy moves against cocky Peter Archer and Shih, although he comes out the loser thanks to the latter's tiger claw attachment. Archer was a real-life Lee friend who ran a Hong Kong dojo. Angelo Mao, as Lee's ill-fated sister, fights off several of Wall's attackers via flashback in a running battle. Then there's venerable character lead John Saxon going against the heavily muscled Bolo Yeung (aka Tang Sze) in the tournament climax. Many would have preferred to see Lee squaring off against the formidable Yeung. The much-anticipated showdown that didn't happen is one reason some consider *Enter the Dragon* imperfect. Most are enamored with the overwhelming action and the legend of Lee, who died mere weeks before the film's release. All the major fight sequences were staged by the star. The *New York Times* was impressed: "The picture is expertly made and well-meshed; it moves like lightning and brims with color." According to *Variety*, "Lee socks over a performance seldom equaled in action." The *Los Angeles Times* called it "quite a few cuts above the usual kung fu epic," while *Fighting Stars* lauded "some of the most exciting and exacting fighting action ever filmed."

Lee's first memorable fight is a 90-second tournament match with Kin's scarred bodyguard Wall. Avenging the death of his sister, a spirited Lee beats the bigger Wall to every punch and kick. Wall is quickly frustrated and opts to fight dirty by grabbing Lee's foot during a front kick. Lee flips backward to release the hold and snaps his other foot into Wall's face as he goes end over end and lands on his feet. In reality, the incredible flip wasn't performed by Lee but by his acrobatic double Yuen Biao (aka Yuen Wah). Biao also performed Lee's series of flips over the monks at the beginning of the film. Wall next tries a spinning back kick, but Lee kicks him in the crotch before he can complete his move. Losing control, Wall grabs two bottles and smashes them together with intent to kill. Lee knocks the broken bottles away and delivers a devastating sidekick that sends Wall flying into the tournament onlookers. With his signature primal scream, Lee leaps in the air in slow motion and comes down on Wall with a death blow.

Wall and Lee were friends, but a controversial incident occurred during filming of this fight. Because of budgetary limitations and the Hong Kong location, sugar glass prop bottles were unavailable. Wall was forced to break real bottles together instead of fake ones. They filmed the fight seven times before the fighters made a timing mistake. Lee cut his hand on the broken glass and began to bleed. Filming had to be halted as assistant stunt coordinator Lam Ching Ying drove Lee through the mountain roads to the nearest hospital. The cut required 12 stitches, and filming with Lee had to be halted for a week. This is where the legend

comes in and much of it's attributed to director Clouse. When Lee returned to finish the fight, the Chinese stunt extras surrounding the action whispered that Wall had deliberately held onto the bottle in an effort to hurt Lee. To save face, Lee would have to kill the Caucasian. Lee had been having problems with the Chinese stunt extras throughout filming. More than one had challenged him, to see how good a martial artist he was. Lee answered most of their challenges with a few quick moves that put them in their place. Lee was now put into the position where he was expected to kill Wall or lose all respect with the Chinese. It's Clouse's recollections fueling the hyperbole. Clouse claimed Lee was ready to kill Wall, but Clouse convinced him that Wall was still needed for footage to be shot in the United States. Lee approached the extras with this information and was able to save face. Nevertheless, he went at Wall full-speed and made contact without holding back his power. Wall claimed this was how he and Lee had prearranged it anyway. Wall was famous for being able to take a hit. The side-kick administered

Bruce Lee scores a kick against Bob Wall in Warner Bros.' iconic *Enter the Dragon* (1973).

to a defenseless Wall was performed eight times and broke the arm of the man who was unfortunate enough to catch Wall as he fell into him. Wall was sore but uninjured. He had been close friends with Lee since 1963 and they remained friends until Lee's untimely death.

The three-and-a-half-minute underground cavern battle known as the "Tunnel Fight" involved 50 men charging at a shirtless Lee, who uses his hands and feet, a Bo Staff, Escrima sticks and a pair of nunchaku with blinding speed. The use of the nunchaku—Two short pieces of hard wood attached by a rope or chain—Sparked a craze for the weapons. Would-be martial artists around the world were soon bopping themselves in the head and groin as they tried to emulate Lee's rapid-fire moves. Some of the assailants came at Lee a dozen at a time and certain sequences took 14 takes to perfect. Lee was understandably tired out by the taxing fight, which required perfect timing and choreography. He was bothered by a slight groin pull during the scene, the result of having to alter his kicks to avoid full contact. He also had to be careful not to knock any of the stuntmen into the tunnel walls, as they were nothing but mud caked onto chicken wire and wooden frames. If a fake wall was hit by a body, it likely would have collapsed. One of the stuntmen was future martial arts film star Jackie Chan, who gets his neck snapped by Lee toward the beginning of the fight. He later charges again during the nunchaku sequence. Chan expected Lee to make light contact as rehearsed, but with the cameras rolling Lee accidentally hit Chan hard in the cheek. Lee finished his fighting pose for the camera, then rushed to check on the injured Chan. The apologetic Lee continued to look in on Chan during the remainder of the day. The future star wound up with a swollen cheek and a moment of cinematic history.

The nearly six-minute climactic battle against Shih as the evil Han ends in the secret Hall of Mirrors, a great sequence that shows off Clouse's technical expertise. Shih draws blood across Lee's chest with his clawed hand attachments. Lee famously tastes his own blood and defiantly unleashes a flurry of kicks and high-pitched wails on his foe. This two-room set was made up of $8000 worth of mirrors, reflecting reflections of reflections. To ensure that the camera crew was not seen, a six foot by eight square foot tall box was constructed in the middle of the room and covered with mirrors. The camera was placed in the box. Three shallow bays were built against one wall in the larger room and lined with narrow vertical mirrors creating a concave depression. This set of mirrors broke up any image into a dozen more images and greatly aided the suspense of the scene. Shih could attack at any time, and Lee could never be sure from where. The idea was so popular that it was appropriated by the James Bond franchise for the following year's *The Man with the Golden Gun* (1974). For the staging of one kick, Lee needed to stand six inches away from Shih and deliver a kick reaching three feet behind him. When captured in the mirrors, it looked like a perfectly placed hit. Stuntman Lam Ching Ying doubled Shih during portions of the fight with Lee.

The mature Chinese character actor Shih performed much of his own karate action, particularly in the earlier one-minute battle with Jim Kelly. After Kelly easily dispatches a few of the bad guy's thugs, Shih attaches his tiger claw and Kelly famously likens him to a comic book villain. Kelly got a brief shot at stardom in *Black Belt Jones* (1974) and *Three the Hard Way* (1974), but critics complained that he was mimicking Lee. Steve James skewered those performances with his Kung Fu Joe character in the spoof *I'm Gonna Git You Sucka* (1988).

Enter the Dragon was filmed under the title *Blood and Steel*, but Lee preferred *Enter the Dragon*. Warner Bros. thought U.S. audiences would be confused and offered the title *Han's Island*. International Middleweight Karate champ Kelly was a last-minute replacement for Rockne Tarkington, who had an argument with the producers and backed out. The character of Williams was originally intended to live and fight alongside Lee during the climax in the tournament yard. John Saxon's agent negotiated to have Saxon's character Roper survive since Saxon was an established actor and Lee's perceived co-star. The original choice for the part of Roper was Clouse's *Darker Than Amber* villain William Smith, and it's even been suggested that Rod Taylor was under consideration as well. Lee was a fan of the *Amber* fight and despite Smith's 6'2" height, he was enthusiastic about having Smith co-star with him. But Smith's part ran over on another film, and he was forced to give up the *Enter the Dragon* role. Fans denied a Lee–Bolo Yeung match-up must savor the notion of a Smith-Yeung finale, or even a Kelly-Yeung match. Instead they watched Saxon take on the Chinese Hercules, a 5'6" Mr. Hong Kong bodybuilding champ. Yeung played many martial arts bad guys, most notably against Jean Claude Van

Damme in *Bloodsport* (1988) and *Double Impact* (1991). He even played a good guy battling evil *Karate Kid* sensei Martin Kove in *Shootfighter* (1993). Saxon nearly didn't make the part as he tore a leg muscle performing a leaping kick on the first day of rehearsals. He's decent as Roper, the gambler who sandbags in fights to increase the betting odds against him, and handles the martial arts capably. The golf course fight between Saxon and Pat Johnson, Mike Bissell and Darnell Garcia was coordinated by Bob Wall and shot in the States. The scene was attempted with stuntmen but completed with martial artists.

Black Belt ranks *Enter the Dragon* as the best choreographed martial arts film in history. *Inside Kung Fu* calls the tunnel fight the greatest fight ever. The *Toronto Star* includes it in their top ten all-time fights. *Action Films* also lists it as having the greatest fights, and *The Psychotronic Video Guide* claims it "has some of the best fight scenes of all time." *The Ultimate Guide to Martial Arts Movies of the 1970s* feels Lee "single-handedly gave Chinese martial arts cinema legitimacy and the Chinese people an identity."

However, *Enter the Dragon* is far from perfect: Many criticize the poor fight staging of the background players during the climax. Others take issue with Clouse's positioning of the camera for Lee's fights. According to *Chasing Dragons,*

> There are several scenes where the martial arts direction is excellent. Yet Clouse failed to understand the most basic rule in the filming of fight sequences—if you shoot a fight in a medium shot or medium close-up, then the audience can't see the movements of the performers. In many sequences Clouse opted to shoot Lee in a medium close-up, negating the impact of the fight choreography by keeping many of Lee's actions effectively off-screen. When the film works it's because of Lee's presence. His animal magnetism and explosive choreography are the only interesting ingredients in the movie.

Five-ten and 170 pounds, fitness fanatic John Saxon avoided many of the vices plaguing his contemporaries. He has had a long and interesting career as a dependable character actor in all types of genres. Saxon first took judo lessons with Gene LeBell in 1957 at the Hollywood Judo Dojo when he was a brooding juvenile lead and later studied Shotokan karate and tai chi chuan with Hidetaka Nishiyama and James Wing Woo. The varied train-

ing gave him a leg up when it came time to co-star in *Enter the Dragon*. Although he was no expert, Saxon often incorporated martial arts into his fights and served as a narrator for the 1992 karate documentary *Deadliest Art: The Best of the Martial Arts Films*. He released the 2005 photo book *Twelve Weeks in Hong Kong* about his time with Lee.

Saxon fought Sal Mineo in *Rock, Pretty, Baby* (1956), Jody McCrea in *The Restless Years* (1958), Burt Lancaster in *The Unforgiven* (1960), Richard Widmark in *Death of a Gunfighter* (1969), David Janssen in *The Swiss Conspiracy* (1975), Reb Brown in the TV movie *Strange New World* (1975), Rosey Grier and Larry Duran in *The Glove* (1978) and Julio Cesar in *The Bees* (1978). He took a great punch from William Smith in *Fast Company* (1978). As a TV guest, Saxon battled David Carradine in the 1972 *Kung Fu* episode "King of the Mountain" and James Garner in the 1976 *Rockford Files* episode "A Portrait of Elizabeth." He had a memorable slow-motion fight with Lee Majors in the 1974 *Six Million Dollar Man* episode "Day of the Robot."

See: Bayne, Rick. "John Saxon." *Psychotronic Video.* #40, 2004; Clouse, Robert. *The Making of Enter the Dragon.* Unique, 1987; *Enter the Dragon* DVD special features; Jacques, Stephen. "John Saxon's Greatest Challenge." *Black Belt.* August 1973. Jacques, Stephen. "The Making of *Enter the Dragon.*" *Fighting Stars.* October 1973.

BURT REYNOLDS VS. JACK WARDEN in *The Man Who Loved Cat Dancing* (1973)

Richard C. Sarafian's romantic western *The Man Who Loved Cat Dancing* contains a realistic two-and-a-half-minute life-or-death struggle between Burt Reynolds and villainous Jack Warden as they jostle for position in an abandoned café while Sarah Miles looks on. Few punches are thrown as the men predominantly go for one another's throats like feral animals. Throughout much of the savage fight, Warden maintains a chokehold on Reynolds as they wrestle for control of a gun. Reynolds dumps hot water on Warden and presses his face to a hot stove. The stars insisted upon doing the majority of their own stunts, banging against the walls of the building and even crashing through a window and a door. When Reynolds gets the upper hand, he seizes a pistol and shoots rapist Warden between the legs.

While doing the fight at the St. George, Utah,

location, Reynolds suffered a hernia that laid him up in a Los Angeles hospital for a week. Warden suffered a blackened eye and numerous bumps and contusions. He proudly told the press it was "the fight scene to end all fight scenes," while assistant director Les Sheldon proclaimed it "one of the greatest fight scenes of all time." *The Manly Movie Guide* agreed: "[It's] one of the most thrillingly brutal fights in Hollywood history." MGM built their entire publicity trailer around the fight. The actors are doubled briefly by Alan Gibbs and Louie Elias. Hal Needham was stunt coordinator and Harry Stradling, Jr., controlled the camera, emphasizing the contrast between dark and light between the interior and exterior locations. One interesting shot has Reynolds straddle the camera as he pushes against the wall with both legs for leverage against Warden.

The film became notorious for what happened behind the scenes when it was filming in Gila Bend, Arizona. Reynolds briefly became a high-profile murder suspect when co-star Sarah Miles' obsessive boyfriend–business manager David Whiting wound up dead in her motel room with a suspicious head injury. Miles later testified that a jealous Whiting had roughed her up after she returned late from a Reynolds birthday party. Rumors ran rampant that Reynolds and Miles were having an affair during the film. Miles admitted she was with Reynolds when Whiting died of what was deemed a suicidal overdose. Reynolds was adamant that he had no involvement, and he was cleared of any wrongdoing. Miles was still married at the time to writer Robert Bolt.

Five-foot-nine, 190-pound Jack Warden boxed professionally under the name Johnny Costello. He was a nightclub bouncer, a pro player in the American Football League and a veteran of the Merchant Marine and the Navy, serving on a gunboat on China's Yangtze River. During World War II, he was a paratrooper with the Army's 101st Airborne and saw action in the Battle of the Bulge. He became a tremendously versatile character actor. Warden had notable screen fights with John Cassavettes and Sidney Poitier in *Edge of the City* (1957), Keir Dullea in *The Thin Red Line* (1964) and Gerrit Graham in *Used Cars* (1980), the latter a memorably comic battle. On TV, he starred as tough no-nonsense cops on *The Asphalt Jungle* (1961) and *N.Y.P.D.* (1967–1969). As a guest, Warden portrayed a professional wrestler in 1962's *Route 66* episode "A Feat of Strength." His ring action was doubled by Gene LeBell.

See: "Good Guy Becomes Heavy." *Times-Picayune.* July 15, 1973; Miles, Sarah. *Serves Me Right.* London: MacMillan, 1994; Taylor, Tadhg. *Masters of the Shoot 'Em Up.* Jefferson, NC: McFarland, 2015; Theskin, Joseph. "TV Actor Warden Jack of All Trades." *Beaver County Times.* March 10, 1976.

JIM BROWN VS. GENE LEBELL AND FUJI NOZAWA in *Slaughter's Big Rip-Off* (1973)

Action star Jim Brown kicks butt from start to finish in this mean-spirited exploitation film from director Gordon Douglas, a violent sequel to Jack Starrett's *Slaughter* (1972). The AIP pic is full of fights as the former Green Beret takes on a white syndicate led by Ed McMahon. Don Stroud is in great villainous form as McMahon's hit man, and it becomes highly personal between Brown and Stroud after the latter lays a serious beating on Brown's cohort Richard Williams and kills Brown's girlfriend Gloria Hendry. Although Stroud's character is a martial arts expert, Brown makes quick work of him in the finale, smashing his head through a car window and pounding his bloodied face repeatedly. Stroud does his own stunts here, enhancing the effectiveness of the action. Brown does all his own fighting as well, allowing his stuntman Tony Brubaker to coordinate the fights. The action is well lensed by veteran cameraman Charles F. Wheeler. *Variety* praised the fierce fights and promised "an avalanche of physical action."

Despite the buildup to the finish between Brown and Stroud, the best fight is a highly energetic battle between Brown and judo experts Gene LeBell and Fuji Nozawa in the confines of a small bungalow. Both LeBell and Nozawa were professional wrestlers and their intense vocal effects are serio-comic. LeBell puts on a great show against Brown, who was known in Hollywood circles as rough when working fights. There was no one better to pair him against than LeBell, who by his own admission loved inflicting pain on others. The stuntman's knowledge of chokeholds and submission moves and his willingness to apply them was unparalleled. But LeBell was a professional, and the fight between the two came off without a hitch. At the end, LeBell acted as if Brown had broken his neck, putting a swerve on the star and the film crew as they frantically called for a doctor. LeBell leapt to his feet with a smile.

Five-foot-eleven, 215-pound LeBell's mother

Aileen Eaton owned the Olympic Auditorium in Los Angeles, so LeBell grew up around all the classic boxers and wrestlers such as Lou Thesz and Ed "Strangler" Lewis. He took an interest in judo and began training with Jack Sergel, earning a black belt before serving with the Coast Guard. LeBell won the AAU California Judo Championship and was twice crowned the AAU National Judo Champ before venturing into professional wrestling and movie stunt work. He became an instantly recognizable stunt actor whom many felt had earned the title of "the toughest man alive." In 1963, LeBell fought a heavily promoted mixed martial arts match against professional boxer Milo Savage and won with a rear single lapel tourniquet choke. In a 50-plus–year stunt career, LeBell's claim to fame was he never won a screen fight. Every well-known martial artist from Bruce Lee to Chuck Norris went to LeBell for specialized judo training. In the 1967 *Ironside* episode "Tagged for Murder," LeBell squared off on the judo mat with Lee.

See: *Slaughter's Big Rip-Off* pressbook.

THE POOL HALL FIGHT in *Mean Streets* (1973)

Martin Scorsese's energetic *Mean Streets* resonated with audiences thanks to its innovative camerawork, pop music cues, realistic Little Italy street talk and the performances of a new breed of urban tough guy in the personas of Harvey Keitel and a skinny Robert De Niro. The crazy two-minute pool hall fight was filmed particularly well with the Marvelettes' "Please Mr. Postman" playing on the soundtrack as perfect accompaniment while Keitel, De Niro and friends Richard Romanus and David Proval take on fat loan shark George Memmoli and his buddies. Everyone in the fight lands realistically ineffective blows and some such as Keitel look like they don't want to fight at all. De Niro is the main instigator, jumping on a pool table to swing a broken pool stick at anyone who comes too close. The fight starts after Memmoli calls Proval a mook, a Neapolitan slang term for a big mouth. No one in the scene even knows the definition. Bill Catching was stunt coordinator and the most visible stuntman going after De Niro. Billy Burton and Bob Orrison are also in there.

Keitel and De Niro played tough guys on screen for the next 30-plus years, although most of the time they had a gun instead of a closed fist. Keitel

did have a memorable stairwell fight with Tony Siricco in *Fingers* (1978). Keitel was a former Marine who served in Lebanon and kept fit lifting weights. De Niro earned an Oscar playing boxer Jake LaMotta in *Raging Bull* (1980), a performance that garnered him a reputation for taking drastic measures with his body for the sake of his art. He famously gained 60 pounds to play an up-in-years LaMotta, before taking it off to play a young and muscular middleweight boxer. He trained with pros Al Silvani, Jimmy Gambina and Jim Nickerson, even daring to step into the ring for sparring sessions with LaMotta.

The *Mean Streets* fight was based on a real incident at the New York bar Foxy's Corner on Sixth Street and Second Avenue. Due to budgetary limitations, much of Scorsese's ode to his New York upbringing was filmed in Los Angeles. The pool hall used was located in a rough Chicano section near downtown. Scorsese filmed the fight in one day with a mostly non-union crew, managing 36 set-ups. The most famous was a hand-held camera shot by cinematographer Kent Wakeford, following Burton and Orrison beating on Proval across the room. Scorsese used a hand-held camera because the production couldn't afford to lay down tracks. Wakeford built a special carrier rig for the Aeroflex BL camera that maintained an increased freedom of movement but kept it from getting bouncy. Despite having been storyboarded, much of the fight has a chaotic and intentionally improvised feel to it. Scorsese didn't want it to appear like a polished Hollywood stuntman brawl. He wanted to capture the fear, aggression and the crazy sense of motion in such an encounter.

See: Angard, Susan. "Kent Wakeford: Redefining American Cinematography in *Mean Streets.*" *Huffington Post.* March 5, 2009; Schickel, Richard. *Conversations with Scorsese.* New York: Knopf, 2011; Thompson, David, and Ian Christie. *Scorsese on Scorsese.* New York: Macmillan, 2003.

THE SALOON BRAWL in *Westworld* (1973)

Westworld was an influential MGM sci-fi western from writer-director Michael Crichton about a futuristic vacation resort called Delos that indulges customer fantasies—but then the robotic staff led by gunslinger Yul Brynner begins to rebel and pits man vs. machine. Before events go haywire, vacationing buddies Richard Benjamin and James Brolin join a large brawl in Miss Carrie's

Saloon, as does comedy-relief sheriff Dick Van Patten. It's a hoot for the resort's guests to be in the middle of a western fistfight with no consequences. Broken bottles, flips over tables and falls off balconies keep viewers' eyes glued to the screen over the course of two well-edited minutes. Sci-fi purists wonder how the robots were able to drink beer and not injure the guests in this fight, but the scene should be taken as nothing more than Crichton exploring a common western trope and pure escapism for the sake of entertaining the audience. One interesting, barely perceptible moment of foreshadowing is staged in the background as Brolin hits one of the robots and it fails to react to the punch.

Action coordinator Dick Ziker and cinematographer Gene Polito put the scene together expertly, resorting to slow motion to emphasize the best stunts. Buddy Joe Hooker must have had a particularly good payday, as the stuntman takes falls all over the place. Stuntmen participating include Louie Elias, Walter Wyatt, Fred Krone, Bill Catching, Chuck Hayward, Bobby Bass and Alan Oliney. Mindi Miller (aka Ty Randolph) is a saloon girl and breaks a chair over a back. Charlie Picerni was on hand to double Benjamin, but the star did his own fight work in a change-of-pace role. Benjamin enthusiastically hit a post so hard that he accidentally brought down a large portion of the set and technical rigging. Composer Fred Karlin contributed a lively western theme to compliment the action. One of the silliest moments is the sound of a cuckoo clock when Hayward takes a bottle over the head. Outside of this one scene, the film is on the serious and thought-provoking side. First-time director Crichton was on a short shooting schedule and edited-in-camera as he shot. *Films in Review* paid Crichton the compliment of calling the fight a "John Fordian barroom brawl."

James Brolin, 6'3" and 200 pounds, was sufficiently impressive in the action scenes that he was under consideration to take over the role of James Bond from Roger Moore for *Octopussy* (1983). The Bond producers had Brolin film a choreographed fight screen test with British stuntman Clive Curtis. Moore ultimately decided to continue with the part. Brolin spoofed the Bond image by portraying a Hollywood heroic version of man-child comic Pee-wee Herman fighting ninjas in *Pee-wee's Big Adventure* (1985). Brolin's best fights came against John Whitely in *The Cape Town Affair* (1967), Charlton Heston in *Skyjacked* (1972)

and psycho kidnapper Cliff Gorman in *Night of the Juggler* (1980).

See: Fischer, Dennis. *Science Fiction Film Directors, 1895–1998.* Jefferson, NC: McFarland, 2011; *James Brolin Screen Test Fight*; Szebin, Fred. "*Westworld:* Behind the Mask, Beneath the Skin ... the Making of a Sci-Fi Classic." *Filmfax.* #110, 2006.

FRED WILLIAMSON VS. KEN KAZAMA in *That Man Bolt* (1973)

Rising black action star Fred Williamson was a confident, charismatic and handsome man whose low-budget films cleaned up at the box office. A professional athlete, he came across well in movement and appealed to both black and white audiences by consistently pitting himself as an underdog in fights. With *That Man Bolt,* Universal tried to share in the wealth generated by both the emerging black action and kung fu genres. Publicity played up the fact that this rambling James Bond knockoff's crew boasted legitimate martial artists: Japanese kickboxing champion Kenji Kazama, light heavyweight world karate champ Mike Stone, European black belt champ Emil Farkas and California State judo champ David Chow. Despite the presence of double Bob Minor, Williamson performed his own fights for stunt coordinator Eric Cord.

That Man Bolt turned out to be one of the better showcases for Williamson's physical talents thanks to having a decent budget and production schedule. Martial arts coordinator Farkas was able to work with Williamson and the stuntmen to design the fights and place them before multiple cameras to the best advantage. Co-directors Henry Levin and David Lowell Rich were experienced and the scenes were sufficiently lit by cinematographer Gerald Finnerman. Cord developed an innovative helmet-cam that could be worn by the combatants to move in close to the karate action and offer a unique perspective. Even with all these elements in its favor, *The Ultimate Guide to Martial Arts Movies of the 1970s* noted, "The fights in this film are awful." Eyes unversed in martial arts were more easily impressed. *The Van Nuys News* wrote, "*Bolt* is short on plot, but long on fairly well-staged fight scenes." *Variety* praised the "fine technical action staging," and the *New York Times* declared there was "a display of martial arts sufficient, perhaps, to slake the tears of devotees of the late Bruce Lee."

Williamson signed to star in a trio of Jefferson Bolt films, but Universal was uncertain how to follow up. They ended up paying Williamson off for the two unmade films. After *Bolt*, Williamson began producing his own low-budget films, with the time and money crunch showing. His fights in many of these self-described "beat 'em up" films (including *Mean Johnny Barrows* [1976], *Death Journey* [1976] and *Blind Rage* [1978]) border on embarrassing due to poor staging and choppy editing. It was apparent that trying to cash in on the martial arts craze was detrimental to Williamson. He was best suited as a smooth boxer or a desperate brawler, not a high-flying kicker.

As a professional football player, the 6'3", 210-pound Williamson was known as "the Hammer" for his hard-hitting blows. He had boxed in Golden Gloves before being a multi-sport star at Northwestern and an All-Pro for the Oakland Raiders and the Kansas City Chiefs. Before filming *Bolt*, this casual martial arts student trained hard for three weeks with instructor Farkas and later laid claim to black belts in Kenpo, Shotokan karate and Tae Kwon Do. In 1974, Williamson gave a demonstration during a karate tournament at Madison Square Garden and expressed interest in entering tournament competition, but he never became known as a martial artist. Hollywood turned a cold shoulder and Williamson took his filmmaking talents to Italy in the late 1970s.

Williamson's best fights were with William Smith in *Hammer* (1972) and *Boss Nigger* (1975),

although both battles proved disappointingly brief. There were also two unfortunately abbreviated fights with fellow gridiron great Jim Brown in *Three the Hard Way* (1974) and *Take a Hard Ride* (1975). Extended bare-knuckle brawls with either of those co-stars had the makings of greatness. Fights of interest came against John Quade in *Hammer* (1972), Art Lund in *Black Caesar* (1972), Fred Lerner in *The Legend of Nigger Charley* (1972), Tony King in *Hell Up in Harlem* (1973), Frank Stell in *Black Eye* (1974), Nick Dimitri in *Adios Amigo* (1975), Thalmus Rasulala in *Bucktown* (1975), Tom Morga in *Joshua* (1976) and George Eastman in *1990: The Bronx Warriors* (1982). Quentin Tarantino provided a memorable showcase for Williamson's tough guy credentials fighting a bar full of vampires in *From Dusk Till Dawn* (1996). In 1976, Williamson displayed his singing talents on *The Dinah Shore Show* until stuntmen Nick Dimitri and Gene LeBell interrupted him to stage a fight. In 1994, Williamson fought Lorenzo Lamas on the TV series *Renegade*.

See: Jacques, Stephen. "Fred Williamson's Still About the Action." *Fighting Stars*. December 1973; McCormick, Barry. "Fred Williamson: The Hammer Strikes." *Psychotronic*. #10, 1991; Seagal, Sandra. "How to Ruin a Fight Scene." *Martial Arts Movies*. October 1981.

THE GYMNASIUM FIGHT in *Watch Out, We're Mad* (1974)

Terence Hill and Bud Spencer teamed up outside the Spaghetti Western genre for more spectacular fight choreography, this time appearing as modern race car drivers who square off against mob interests for the sake of a prized dune buggy. They take part in an extended three-and-a-half-minute fight in a gymnasium in which Hill showcases his acrobatic ability, mixing in work on the pommel horse, the parallel bars and the high bar as a club full of boxers and gymnasts prove comically ineffective in swarming the stars. Spencer uses his great strength as he rips heavy punching bags and rings from the ceiling and repeatedly tears boxing gloves from the men's fists, then smacks them with

Ken Kazama (left) and Fred Williamson exchange kicks in Universal's *That Man Bolt* (1973).

the leather. The catchy Oliver Onions song "Dune Buggy" proves an interesting background choice for the on-screen shenanigans. There are also battles with leather-clad motorcyclists and a climactic fight in a restaurant filled with balloons, creating further comic possibilities.

Although made in Madrid by director Marcello Fondato, the fight features Italian stuntmen Giancarlo Bastianoni, Giovanni Cianfriglia, Rocco Lero, Osiride Pevarello, Pietro Torrisi, Franco Ukmar, Vincenzo Maggio, Omera Capanna and Marcello Verziera. The fight coordinator was Jose Luis Chinchilla. This is inspired slapstick and some of the best choreographed fight work the screen has ever seen. It preceded the comic fight choreography Jackie Chan became known for. *Cinema Italiano* wrote, "The fistfights and bizarre sight gags are equal to their Western equivalents, including a scene where the duo takes on a gym full of boxers."

Bud Spencer (formerly Carlo Pedersoli) was a 6'3", nearly 300-pound mountain of a man with surprising agility for his size. He was a boxer and record-setting swimmer who competed for Italy in the Olympics. He did all his own fights on screen, although admittedly few people ever managed to knock him off his feet. Mostly he was required to stand his ground throwing powerful hooks and backhands against multiple opponents to set up his trademark crunching "hammer blow." His screen image was consistently the angry bear who looked as if someone had woke him up, but on occasion he flashed a bemused smile at the futility of his attackers. The extreme silliness of his fights undermined his impressiveness as a movie tough guy. He would have made a formidable opponent for any of the era's biggest stars.

Spencer's best fight showcases remain *They Call Me Trinity* (1970) (see entry) and the many sequels and knockoffs he made with Hill. Spencer had a one-on-one bare-knuckle fight with Leroy Haynes in *Ace High* (1968), fought alongside Jack Palance in *It Can Be Done, Amigo* (1972), and later played the brawling detective character Flatfoot in several films beginning with *The Knockout Cop* (1973). In later films including *Bulldozer* (aka *Uppercut*) (1978) and *Buddy Goes West* (1981), he matched up with European heavyweight boxing champion Joe Bugner. While making *I'm for the Hippopotamus* (1979), Spencer misjudged a punch and knocked Bugner out for real. In *Bomber* (1982), he fought South African heavyweight contender Kallie Knoetze.

See: Hughes, Howard. *Cinema Italiano: The Complete Guide from Classics to Cult.* London: I.B. Tauris, 2011; Spencer, Bud, and Lorenzo De Luca. *Altrimenti Mi Arrabbio.* Schwarzkopf & Schwarzkopf: 2011.

THE MEL BROOKS BRAWL in *Blazing Saddles* (1974)

Mel Brooks' zany *Blazing Saddles* is full of scatological humor and Hollywood in-jokes as it spoofs the clichés of the western genre, including the famous all-out *Dodge City* (1939) brawl during the four-minute fight climax between land-grabbing Harvey Korman's hired outlaws and the townspeople of Rock Ridge. Stunt extras galore fight stars Cleavon Little, Gene Wilder, Slim Pickens and Alex Karras. The celebrated "Fourth Wall" is broken as Joseph Biroc's camera pulls back to reveal that the action is being staged on the Warner Bros. lot. All the players go from being characters in a movie to actors playing characters in a movie. The fight spills onto an adjoining set where Dom DeLuise is directing an all-male Busby Berkeley musical number. Chief outlaw Pickens promptly socks the mincing DeLuise in the belly. The fight enters the Warner commissary, and the film is sped up and under-cranked in homage to the old Republic westerns while backed by John Morris' energetic score. A pie fight erupts. Karras punches Pickens and sends him sliding across the tray area to the cash register. The cashier nonchalantly charges him for the food lying across his chest.

Brooks' biographer Robert Alan Crick terms it a "great fever-pitch fight," but some thought the scene went too far. The *Los Angeles Times* called the brawl both "rousing and ridiculous," while *The Hollywood Reporter* wrote that Brooks "has overindulged himself in the broad comedy of the final scenes and lessens the effect of the film somewhat…. It's a funny slapstick bit but it also distracts from the main portion of the film."

Karras' big punch on Pickens isn't the most famous one he delivers. That blow came earlier when 6'2", 245-pound Karras, as the dreaded Mongo, hauled off and knocked out a horse with a single punch. Former pro football player and wrestler Karras didn't connect with the horse. The punch's success is as much the result of stunt rider Jerry Gatlin's timing in pulling the horse's head and laying him down for the camera as the force of the fist. This famous blow, once voted the greatest movie punch in history, has a basis in reality.

Slim Pickens prepares to punch Dom DeLuise in Warner Bros.' *Blazing Saddles* (1974).

Brooks knew that comedian Sid Caesar had slugged a horse after it threw his wife. The producers of *Blazing Saddles* wanted Brooks to remove the scene for fear of cries of animal cruelty, but Brooks left it in.

One thing Brooks was unable to get into his film: He wanted John Wayne in the fight. He approached the icon in the Warner commissary and offered him a cameo. Wayne read the script and passed, but claimed he'd be the first in line to see it. The brawl itself was coordinated by veteran stuntman Al Wyatt and featured dozens of stuntmen and women. Among those figuring into the fight action were Hal Needham, Tony Epper, Jack Lilley, Terry Leonard, Paul Stader, Bill Catching, Loren Janes, Regis Parton, Fred Scheiwiller, Troy Melton, George Sawaya, Bennie Dobbins, George Fisher, Boyd "Red" Morgan, Bob Herron, Bill Shannon, Tom Steele, Dave Sharpe, George Orrison, Denny Arnold, Fred Stromsoe, Ken Ferguson, Stephen Burnette, Steve Moriarty, Dick Crockett, Chuck Hayward, Harvey Parry, Hank Robinson, Frankie Van, Joe Yrigoyen, Jack Perkins, Dick Warlock, George P. Wilbur, Ronnie Rondell, Jr., Seamon Glass, Andy Epper, Rai Bartonious and Mickey Gilbert. Doubling for Wilder, Little and

Karras were Mickey Gilbert, S.J. McGee and Walter Wyatt. Other spoofs with inspired fights include *The Big Bus* (1976) and *Top Secret* (1984).

See: *Blazing Saddles* DVD commentary and special features; Crick, Robert Alan. *The Big Screen Comedies of Mel Brooks.* Jefferson, NC: McFarland, 2002; Karras, Alex, and Herb Gluck. *Even Big Guys Cry.* New York: Rinehart & Winston, 1977.

Rockne Tarkington vs. William Smith in *Black Samson* (1974)

Warner Bros. tried to cash in with a hybrid black action-martial arts film, this time toplining 6'5", 230-pound Rockne Tarkington, the man who would have been Williams in *Enter the Dragon* had he not backed out at the last moment. The former University of Kansas athlete is Kendo staff–carrying Samson, a downtown Los Angeles bar owner so proud of his African heritage he wears Dashiki shirts and travels with a lion at his side. In the poems of Paul Laurence Dunbar, the character Black Samson of Brandywine was a giant Negro who carried a scythe. Tarkington learned Kendo serving with the Air Force in Japan and was an animal trainer. *Black Samson* is one of the better entries from the black action genre despite being afforded a mere two-week shooting schedule. Tarkington was up against William Smith, in superb bad guy form as a white mobster muscling in on the neighborhood. Smith is so hotheaded that he beats up his own men and even has his blonde girlfriend Connie Strickland take a job as a stripper at Tarkington's club to keep tabs on him. When Smith senses that Strickland is becoming too cozy with Tarkington, he casually throws her from a moving car.

Joe Tornatore, Nick Dimitri and Gene LeBell are the most prominent hoods Tarkington bests throughout the story. It all leads up to an amazing showdown on a city block between Smith's gang of stunt hoods and the entire neighborhood, who rain debris and junk on them from the rooftops before Tarkington and Smith square off in a tense 90-second battle amidst the descending garbage. It's not a traditional "I punch you, you punch me" fight: It's a down-and-dirty tackling and wrestling match over Tarkington's staff with Smith swinging a chain and biting an ear. Tarkington flips Smith and allows his own body to come crashing down with the momentum. Tarkington beats Smith with the chain before ending the fight by impaling Smith with the staff. Stunt doubles Marvin Walters and Nick Dimitri did the long shot coverage but stepped aside while the actors did the majority. All had to be cognizant of their fighting area considering the trash and heavy appliances strewn about. The film was directed by stuntman Chuck Bail with action coordinated by Eddie Donno. The *Village Voice* called it "a deliciously apt one-on-one finale," while *Variety* termed it "as bloody a fray as the screen has seen." *Film Bulletin* wrote, "Samson wins all the fights, which erupt regularly every 15 minutes or so and are keyed to the thrill-seeking excesses of the genre's devotees."

Tensions ran high on the Pasadena city street set. Smith and Tarkington were friends. However, the rooftops were filled with local extras instructed to hurl garbage at Smith and his stuntmen, and there was definite black-white tension. Everything imaginable was thrown at Smith and the stuntmen, including pans, bottles, bricks and mattresses. Even a refrigerator and a TV set are seen crashing to the ground! Smith's anger on screen and the pointing of his finger at the rooftops isn't acting, but a natural reaction to being hit by the garbage. There was a brief flare-up between Smith and the director: When Bail told Smith he wanted the actor's shirt to be ripped off in the fight, Smith complained he was sick of showing off his muscles on screen. Bail responded by asking why Smith went to the gym every day. Smith stormed to his dressing room, with the moviemakers wondering if the tough guy star and 6'4", 230-pound director were about to come to blows. A composed Smith soon returned and apologized to the cast and crew for holding up production. Tarkington battled Ron Ely numerous times on TV's *Tarzan* and fought Steve Sandor in *The No Mercy Man* (aka *Trained to Kill, USA*) (1975).

See: Albright, Brian. "Chuck Amuck!" *Shock Cinema.* June 2008; *Black Samson* pressbook.

TOM LAUGHLIN AND MASTER BONG SOO HAN VS. THE REDNECK COWBOYS in *The Trial of Billy Jack* (1974)

The makers of the first *Billy Jack* film couldn't find any professional stuntmen willing to work martial arts scenes with Tom Laughlin, but this sequel from Warner Bros. was overflowing with stuntmen eager to take Laughlin and co-star Master Bong Soo Han's kicks. The stuntmen realized that kung fu fighting was the new craze and the sooner they showed off their ability to work within the genre, the more offers they'd get. In the climax, Billy Jack's action is ramped up with Laughlin and Han both taking off their footwear and joining forces to take down Riley Hill's redneck cowboys in a town hall setting. Arizona stuntmen Jason Clark and Ron Nix are the chief henchmen with Jim Burk, Louie Elias, Glenn Wilder, Gary Combs, Jim Connors, Archie Harrison and Walter Wyatt participating in the major three-minute fight. Phil Adams and Bernie Bersten served as Laughlin's doubles. Fight choreographer Han had to account for every one of the stuntmen's actions on paper before undertaking the scene.

Incredible bumps were taken by the stuntmen with Elias going off a second floor balcony end over end onto a car's roof and Burk doing a cable jerk into a fully stocked bar. Laughlin continues to advocate peaceful measures but once again is comfortable in doling out pain. After he has dislocated Nix's shoulder with a martial arts move, Laughlin kindly puts it back into place for the injured man. The fight ends with Hill shooting Han, with Laughlin retaliating with a deadly flying kick to the throat. The film was nearly three hours long by this point and was attacked by critics for self-indulgence and heavy-handed preachiness.

Laughlin's 19-year-old son Frank is the credited director, but it was once again the multi-talented star in charge. Jack A. Marta was the D.P.

The *Los Angeles Times* tore the film apart but managed to find praise for the fights: "You await them eagerly this time because for the moment everybody stops talking in flat platitudes or crying or singing." *Time* offered this backhanded compliment: "Shoddily as they are staged, Billy Jack's fights are the only portions of the film with the slightest life at all." The *Village Voice* made a comparison between Laughlin and Bruce Lee: "Tom Laughlin's fight sequences are not as beautiful to watch as Bruce Lee's—Laughlin doesn't have Lee's astonishing speed and precise, clean line of movement—but they're more exciting because they're showcased in a melodramatic situation." *Variety* wrote, "Adherents of the current cycle of martial arts films will find satisfaction in several sequences in which Billy Jack engages in Hapkido, the Korean form of karate, for exciting action." *Action Films* considers this sequence one of the all-time great fights: "[T]he brawl makes excellent use of slow motion and the stunt work is top notch." *The Ultimate Guide to Martial Arts Movies of the 1970s* was also impressed by the Hapkido displayed: "It's a pity Laughlin didn't do more fights in these Billy Jack films, but it seems appropriate that a film about non-violence with too much violence could detract from the messages he was sharing with audiences."

See: Martinez, Mike. "The Trial of Billy Jack." *Fighting Stars.* December 1974; *The Trial of Billy Jack* DVD commentary.

GENE HACKMAN VS. JOHN CRAWFORD in *Night Moves* (1975)

An ambiguous Arthur Penn–directed neo-noir mystery, *Night Moves* cast a rock solid Gene Hackman as pro football player turned private eye Harry Moseby. He's not good at the latter and is suffering from marital problems and a mid-life crisis. Professionally he gets deeply involved in a missing person turned murder case involving teenage nymphet Melanie Griffith. Toward the end he finds himself in a bloody nighttime fight with the girl's stepfather John Crawford, the boozing live-in of Jennifer Warren. During his investigation, Hackman and Warren have begun an affair. All the relationships throughout the movie are strained, and nothing is what it seems. The audience isn't sure if Crawford is fighting desperately because of Warren or because Hackman has found a dead body on his property and there's something to hide.

The one-minute battle on Sanibel Island in the Florida Keys starts on a boat, splashes into the water, and ends up on land where Crawford inadvertently rams his own head into the pier. Hackman performs a back-fist and hurls Crawford through a screened-in porch, but at no point does he have the upper hand. It's not so much Hackman wins the fight as he manages to last long enough not to lose it. Crawford repeatedly hits Hackman in the face with a conch seashell. It's a fitting metaphor for the ineffective detective, who still doesn't know how everything fits even after he's been hit over the head with clues. *Cinema Retro* called it "one of the unsung fight scenes of the '70s."

The fight's editing by Dede Allen and Stephen A. Rotter is fragmented, but the lack of fluidity conceals the use of stunt doubles. The 6'2", 185-pound Hackman's brother Richard Hackman worked as his stand-in, and Glenn Wilder doubled for the star. Chuck Hicks doubled beefy character actor Crawford, no stranger to on-screen fights. He was taught in the late 1940s by his distant relative Yakima Canutt. Cinematographer Bruce Surtees contributed to the scene's effectiveness with his varied camera set-ups.

Former Marine Gene Hackman had a real-life tough guy reputation. At the age of 71, the ex–construction worker fought off two men after a fender bender turned into an ugly situation. In his early acting days, he had a penchant for getting into bar fights. However, Hackman found it difficult to play the most violent aspects of his flawed characters. He paid strict attention to the stunt pros to make sure the scenes were carefully choreographed and he never took a scene over the artistic line. Hackman's signature role came in *The French Connection* (1971) and *French Connection II* (1975) as Popeye Doyle, a tough New York City cop not averse to roughing up criminals and drug pushers. Hackman administered some memorable beatdowns, dominating rapist Richard Lynch in *Scarecrow* (1973), racist deputy Brad Dourif in *Mississippi Burning* (1988) and overhyped gunfighter Richard Harris in *Unforgiven* (1992). In *Mississippi Burning,* he manhandled cocky tough guy Michael Rooker.

Hollywood's favorite angry Everyman had fights of interest with Gregory Walcott in *Prime Cut* (1972), Jan-Michael Vincent in *Bite the Bullet* (1975), Burt Reynolds in *Lucky Lady* (1975),

George Fisher in *The Domino Principle* (1977) and James B. Sikking and Nigel Bennett in *Narrow Margin* (1990). On TV, he clashed with Glenn Corbett in the 1963 *Route 66* episode "Who Will Cheer My Bonnie Bride?" and Burt Reynolds in the 1966 *Hawk* episode "Do Not Mutilate or Spindle."

See: Munn, Michael. *Gene Hackman*. London: Robert Hale, 1997; Walker, Beverly. "Interview: Gene Hackman." *Film Comment*. November-December 1988; Welkos, Robert W. "Still the Tough Guy." *Los Angeles Times*. December 16, 2001.

THE BRITISH PUB BRAWL in *Brannigan* (1975)

John Wayne uncorks one of his final screen punches on Peter Brayham in United Artists' *Brannigan* (1975).

Coming close on the heels of his modern cop drama *McQ* (1974), John Wayne followed with another Dirty Harry–styled policeman in the Douglas Hickox–directed *Brannigan* (a surname derived from a term for an Irish brawl). This time Wayne's a tough Chicago cop chasing a fugitive in London, and Wayne has gone for a real change of pace by eschewing his usual stunt team for a troupe of Brits, many of whom were veterans of the James Bond 007 films. The fight itself, a raucous brawl in Leadenhall Market's The Lamb Pub, owes much to previous Wayne brawls, but it's of interest due to all the new faces and such comic touches as having the song "Let the Sunshine In" playing on the jukebox. Veteran camera operator Gerry Fisher was the director of photography.

Richard Attenborough as a Scotland Yard inspector is involved in the action as Wayne's co-star, and the two fight back to back like Alan Ladd and Van Heflin in *Shane* chinning anyone who closes in. Stunt coordinator Peter Brayham staged a remarkably similar battle for the British TV show *The Sweeney* in the 1974 episode "Night Out." *Brannigan* stuntmen of note were Alf Joint, George Leech, Nosher Powell, Les Crawford, Steve Emerson, Frank Henson, Del Baker, Alan Chuntz, Rick Lester and Doug Robinson. The *Chicago Sun Times* called it a "nice saloon free-for-all," while Leonard Maltin said the film's "highlight is amusing brawl in pub." *Time,* however, called the fight "poorly motivated and feebly staged," and *Variety* opined, "A pub brawl seems almost like an inside-joke insert."

The brawl was placed into the film because of its star. This was the final bare-knuckle brawl in the career of John Wayne. At 67, the Duke was beginning to feel the years of wear and tear. During the fight, he strained a muscle in his left arm when pulling a punch short. He also remained bothered by the nagging cough that had plagued him for a decade. The moist London weather exasperated the problem, but Wayne liked the British stuntmen and enjoyed doing the fight. He also gets to toss motorcyclist Tony Robinson into the Thames and makes short work of Brian Glover (aka pro wrestler Leon Arras). Wayne had been punching away on screen for over 40 years, and *Brannigan* provided a fitting fight for the legend to bow out on.

See: McEwan, Ian. "Same Old John Wayne." *Brandon Sun*. August 23, 1974; Powell, Nosher, and William Hall. *Nosher*. London: Blake, 1999.

MAX BAER, JR. VS. FORREST TUCKER in *The Wild McCullochs* (aka *The McCullochs*) (1975)

Max Baer Jr., dim-witted Jethro Bodine on TV's *The Beverly Hillbillies* (1964–1971), proved his true wile by writing, producing and starring in the mammoth drive-in money maker *Macon County Line* (1974). The 6'4", 210-pound actor followed that *tour de force* with the earnest, though less well-received period piece *The Wild McCullochs* which he directed and starred in. The selling point of this anachronistic family melodrama (set in 1949) is a ten-minute brawl that an entire Texas town has been itching for and cheers on. Baer as a stand-up young man and Forrest Tucker as his whiskey-drinking, blustery employer punch each other across an entire town over Baer's love for Tucker's daughter. After starting in the bar Tony's Wharf, they end up in a river by the film's conclusion, theoretically washing away all their differences. The characters like to settle disagreements with their fists as a measure of earning respect. The movie opens with Tucker pounding on drinking buddy Mike Mazurki, who grins through every minute of his punishment. During the climactic fight, Baer politely addresses Tucker as "sir" or "Mr. McCulloch." At the end, both combatants end up smiling. The *New York Times* called it "a long and boring and lovable fight," while the *Daytona Beach Morning Journal* felt Baer "messed up a half decent fight sequence by trying to insert humor." The *Los Angeles Times* wrote, "The epic brawl that climaxes the film is good, clean fisticuffs in the *Spoilers* tradition, not just another foray into morbid violence."

Although the fight is directly inspired by *The Quiet Man* (1952), it's well-choreographed and oddly enough directly influenced the far better known brawl between Clint Eastwood and William Smith in *Any Which Way You Can* (1980). All three fights take a break for a beer (Schlitz in *The McCullochs*) before starting anew with a big punch. Other similarities in staging and execution occur. They both cut away to comedy relief characters, in this case bartender Vito Scotti, his employee Timothy Scott, priest William Demarest and Baer's gambling buddy Sandy Kevin. Chuck Hicks was stunt coordinator and saw plenty of screen time in a salt-and-pepper wig as the double for the 55-year-old Tucker. Hicks also shows up in a humorous cameo as an angry motorist who Tucker unloads a punch on. Jim Connors doubled Baer. Fred Koenekamp's camera is sometimes a split-second late in following the action, and David Berlatsky's editing tends to be on the choppy side, but overall it's decently realized in scope considering its limited budget.

The film was shot in Rio Vista, California, a small Bay Area community located along the Sacramento River's delta region in Solano County. It's an unconvincing double for the state of Texas, but then the long hair and clothing sported by nearly everyone isn't characteristic of the time period either. It looks like a 1970s film. There were approximately a half dozen bars in downtown Rio Vista, and in between shooting the fight Tucker ducked into each and every one for a quick drink and to hold court for the locals. The screen legend acquits himself well, but it was his last chance at headlining a theatrical release. His many years of boozing had taken its toll. It's interesting how Baer's camera holds the elder actor in awe and esteem. Tucker was an acquaintance of Baer's father Max Baer, the heavyweight champion of the world. This was his 35th year of partaking in notable screen fights dating back to *The Westerner* (1940), a span bested only by John Wayne. The younger Baer lettered in boxing at Santa Clara College and shows off a decent jab throughout the screen action.

See: Bacon, James. "Hollywood Hotline." *State Times Advocate.* January 22, 1975; *The Wild McCullochs* pressbook.

CLINT EASTWOOD VS. GREGORY WALCOTT in *The Eiger Sanction* (1975)

Director-star Clint Eastwood liked character actor Gregory Walcott because he was big, professional and could do his own fights. They had known each other since Eastwood's *Rawhide* days, with the two fighting for the first time in 1963's "Incident of the Gallows Tree." Eastwood laid his first film punch on the beefy supporting player in the western *Joe Kidd* (1972), a moment audiences appreciated because Walcott's sheriff came across as smug. Eastwood's characters typically had a short fuse for obnoxiousness and viewers came to expect the star to lay one on Walcott's kisser. The mountain-climbing espionage adventure *The Eiger Sanction* contains what is arguably their most memorable exchange. Its main competition comes in *Every Which Way but Loose* (1978) where Eastwood humorously wallops Walcott with a bass fish in the face. It's a credit to both actors they were consistently able to make their characters' fistic exchanges mildly amusing for the audience. In *The Eiger Sanction*, Walcott plays an irritating nemesis of Eastwood who haphazardly blows the star's cover. When Eastwood voices his displeasure Walcott warns the star he is a black belt in karate while assuming a fighting stance. Eastwood's five-knuckle response knocks Walcott all the way down a Swiss Alps hillside. Eastwood rushes down the hill to complete the clock-cleaning. It's all over in a matter of seconds.

Although he was entering his mid-forties, Walcott was loyal to Eastwood and agreed to do one fall for the cameras. He had been carried on salary for five weeks for a small supporting part and didn't want to disappoint. Walcott promptly borrowed elbow and knee pads from the stuntmen and surveyed the hillside he'd be rolling down for sticks, stones and broken glass. When all was set, Frank Stanley's camera focused on Walcott's face, and Eastwood threw his fist in front of the lens. Walcott reacted to the blow and took a great spill down the steep hill. Unfortunately, an assistant's knee ended up in the shot as the camera panned on Walcott's tumble.

Gregory Walcott suffers one of many screen beatings at the fists of Clint Eastwood in Universal's *The Eiger Sanction* (1975).

Although he had agreed to do the stunt once, Walcott did the fall a total of three times. Walcott's willingness to take the extended fall made it possible for Ferris Webster to leave the bit untouched as a sustained and effective single shot. Years later, Eastwood rewarded Walcott by shooting around him on *Every Which Way but Loose* so he could take a choice role in *Norma Rae* (1979).

Six-three, 215-pound Walcott served as an athletic instructor in the Army before playing football at Furman University. He had a commanding presence, was agile enough to do the bulk of his own screen fighting and rarely met a screen punch that didn't knock him off his feet. Walcott was the original choice to fight Rock Hudson on *Giant* (1956) but another film ran over and he lost the part to Mickey Simpson. Fights of note came on *Prime Cut* (1972) with Lee Marvin and Gene Hackman and *Man of the East* (1972) (see entry). On TV, Walcott fought Chuck Connors in the *Rifleman* episode "The Angry Gun," John Smith in the *Laramie* episodes "Drifter's Gold" and "Sunday Shoot," Michael Landon in the *Little House on the Prairie* episode "In the Big Inning," and Jameson Parker and Gerald McRaney in the *Simon and Simon* episode "The Cop Who Came to Dinner."

See: Roberts, Frank. "The Worst Piece of Celluloid." *Suffolk News Herald.* July 14, 2015; Walcott, Gregory. *Hollywood Adventures: The Gregory Walcott Story.* Wilson, NC: *Wilson Daily Times,* 2003; Wallison, Joe, and Ed G. Lousaraian. "Gregory Walcott: He Went West and Won." *Wildest Westerns.* #5, 2002.

RON ELY vs. PAUL WEXLER in *Doc Savage, the Man of Bronze* (1975)

This controversially campy interpretation of pulp fiction hero Doc Savage was producer George Pal's final film. Nearly everything about the Michael Anderson–directed release was ridiculed by diehard Savage fans who were eagerly anticipating the film. Even the announced casting of lanky 6'4", 210-pound TV Tarzan Ron Ely met with dissension. Chuck Connors was attached to the film in the 1960s, and later Mr. Universe Steve Reeves was connected with Pal and the Savage role. Those projects fell through. Bodybuilding actor Brad Harris returned from Europe to test for the role. Other muscular actors lobbying for or considered for the role of Doc Savage were karate champ Joe Lewis, William Smith, Denny Miller, Steve Sandor and Mike Henry. Even Los Angeles Dodgers baseball pitcher Don Drysdale was tested. All would likely have met with far greater approval than Ely, who to his credit went on a rigorous weightlifting program to add 25 pounds of muscle to his frame. He also began serious training in martial arts with Tak Kubota and Hank Hamilton for the two extended fights.

Supposedly two versions were prepared: a straight cut and the ultimately released campy one complete with John Philip Sousa marching music, silly stabs at humor, absurd subtitles and heroic eyes that literally twinkled on screen. Nearly a year and a half elapsed between the time the film was shot and released. Warner Bros. was unsure how a dated pulp hero would play with hip 1970s audiences and chose to go the camp route. They couldn't have been more wrong. *Variety* derided the film for its "dopey action," and immediately a Save Savage Society was formed by fans who began petitioning the studio to re-cut, rescore and re-release the film.

More than 30 years later, a fan edit excising over seven minutes of silliness began to circulate on the Internet. This notably affected the climactic fight between Ely and villainous Paul Wexler as Captain Seas. In this nearly five-minute fight as originally released, intrusive and ridiculous subtitles announced each fighting style as sumo, gung fu, tai chi chuan, karate, bo jujitsu and fisticuffs. In addition to taking out the subtitles and sumo bits, the revamped version benefitted from concentrating on the latter portions of the fight. The suspense of fighting next to a pool of boiling oil was diminished in the original by editor Thomas McCarthy's constant cutting away to Doc's Fabulous Five, disappointingly portrayed as a largely bumbling Brain Trust. Again, improved editing of the original could have made the fight much better, as the action on screen is decent enough to warrant praise. A platinum-haired Ely fits the part with his ripped shirt accenting his bulked-up physique, and his martial arts are impressive enough for a big man. A slow-motion dropkick is filmed effectively by cinematographer Fred Koenekamp as Wexler's double Tony Epper is knocked several feet backward with the aid of a jerk cable.

There's also a spirited and well-done two-and-a-half-minute fight aboard a yacht with Ely and the Fabulous Five taking on a band of Wexler's thugs, including stuntmen Dick Durock, Roydon Clark, Ted White, George P. Wilbur, John Hudkins, Kim Kahana, Bob Herron, Denny Arnold, Gary Epper, Andy Epper, Mickey Gilbert, Bill Lane, Larry Holt, Joe Canutt *et al.* Ely helped stunt coordinators Tony Epper and Dar Robinson stage and direct this fight, and despite the Sousa music it definitely has more snap and style to it. The highlight is a Durock cable jerk. *Films and Filming* recognized this brawl as "surprisingly nasty." The *Evening Independent* wrote that the fights were "the film's best scenes in which mock martial arts and slick fakery outdo brutal strength time and again."

A Texas oil field roughneck, Ely served with the Air Force before landing his signature role of Tarzan on the 1966–1968 TV series. He did the majority of his own stunt work for the physically demanding show, including many tough fights. Ely had trained as an amateur boxer and improvised a jungle version of martial arts, which tended to gain him a reputation for making unwanted contact with his screen opponents. His best fights came against former Tarzan Jock Mahoney in the 1966 episode "The Deadly Silence" and 1967's "Mask of Rona." On the big screen, Ely fought Clint Walker in *The Night of the Grizzly* (1966) (see entry). On the 1981 TV pilot *The Seal* and the 1988 *Sea Hunt* reboot, he fought another former Tarzan, Denny Miller.

See: Jacques, Stephen. "Tarzan Exchanges Loincloth for Karate Gi." *Fighting Stars.* February 1974; Murray, Will. "Remember the Doc Savage Movie Disaster." *Bronze Gazette.* Vol. 1, #6, March 1992.

KEN NORTON VS. DUANE ALLEN in *Mandingo* (1975)

This controversial film deals with slavery in the Deep South and the barbaric fights staged between slaves for their masters' entertainment. Producer Dino De Laurentiis hired top talent in the form of director Richard Fleischer and leading man James Mason, but the sordid story is blood-filled and unsettling. Critics attacked the nudity, graphic violence and overall subject matter dealing with interracial sex. Of course, it proved popular at the box office, but its disappearance from circulation thereafter led to a certain cult fascination with the film. Playing the top Mandingo slave is heavyweight boxing contender Ken Norton, the 6'3", 230-pound muscleman who famously broke Muhammad Ali's jaw in the ring. A champion boxer for the Marine Corps, Norton captured the WBC heavyweight title in 1978. His opponent in *Mandingo* is 6'4", 225-pound Duane Allen, a tight end for the Los Angeles Rams football team. Norton also fights Mr. Universe Earl Maynard.

Choreographed by stunt coordinators Joe Canutt and Alan Oliney, the six-minute Allen fight starts as a boxing match but quickly devolves into a life-or-death struggle featuring eye-gouging and flesh-biting. *Orange Coast Magazine* declared it one of the screen's most realistically violent affairs. Norton is repeatedly knocked into the cheering crowd as Richard Kline's camera follows the brutal action. Editor Frank Bracht often cuts to shots of the bloodthirsty crowd. Norton's master Perry King becomes so unsettled at seeing his prize slave beaten and bloodied that he tries to cede the fight and save Norton's life. But Norton rallies. The ending offers a moment of suspense as to who the winner is, but it's soon revealed Allen has had his throat bit open. It's as ugly as it sounds. First time actor Norton, who beat out O.J. Simpson for the part, looks realistically uncomfortable at the action he must perform. Norton returned in the sequel *Drum* (1976) where he fought Yaphet Kotto. Quentin Tarantino paid homage to *Mandingo* in *Django Unchained* (2012).

See: *Mandingo* pressbook; Norton, Ken, Marshall Terrill and Mike Fitzgerald. *Going the Distance*. Champaign, IL: Sports Pub, 2000.

Joe Don Baker vs. Roy Jenson in *Framed* (1975)

Director Phil Karlson and screenwriter-producer Mort Briskin's follow-up to star Joe Don Baker's huge hit *Walking Tall* (1973) contains a tremendously violent fight; the film was banned in Sweden due to this blood-soaked sequence. It's another rural revenge story as professional card player Baker is set up by authority figures as a fall guy. After a mystery person takes a shot at him, Deputy Roy Jenson shows up in Baker's garage and tells him they're "going to the morgue." Jenson keeps cuffing and jabbing Baker, and there's only so much Baker can stand before he turns on the anger button. Two of the biggest sides of beef in Hollywood go at it for the next 90 seconds in a tremendously effective life-or-death struggle. Gil Perkins co-ordinated the action, which was improved by both actors doing the bulk of the fight. The nearly 50-year-old stunt actor Jenson could still dole out brutal body blows. The use of Baker's double, George P. Wilbur, is kept well hidden by Jack Marta's camera placement and Harry Gerstad's editing. The *Chicago Sun Times* commented, "The soundtrack sounds like a Charles Bronson fight scene with the treble turned up." Well-regarded writer James Crumley penned, "Even in a low-rent rip-off of the *Walking Tall* sequence, Roy Jenson and Joe Don Baker staged

the best, most convincing, most horrifying in its realism, greatest fight I have ever seen on the screen." *Orange Coast Magazine* considered it one of the most brutal and realistic hand-to-hand fights in cinema history.

This isn't one of those common exchanges of harmless movie punches. These men do serious damage to one another with fists, elbows, palm strikes and kicks. There's choking and eye-gouging, and Jenson hurls Baker's body through the air and into his open car. Jenson even throws in a football block, sending Baker crashing into a shelf. Baker throws the shelf onto Jenson. They both wind up bloody, broken and exhausted. Jenson kicks Baker in the face, and as he tries it again Baker kicks him in the shin. This is accompanied by a sickeningly unprecedented bone-breaking sound effect. They go for the throat and eyes until Baker slams Jenson's head repeatedly into the pavement. Jenson dies from his skull fracture as Baker collapses in exhaustion next to him. Baker spends the next ten minutes of the movie recovering in a hospital bed before being hauled off to prison. Baker also beats up Paul Mantee.

Roy Jenson was one of the toughest men in Hollywood and threw perhaps the most powerful

Joe Don Baker has the advantage on Roy Jenson in the violent fight in Paramount's *Framed* (1975).

screen punch in the business. His pounding of Paul Newman in *Harper* (1966) made audiences wince and required that scene be trimmed from its original length. The Navy veteran played football at UCLA and professionally in the Canadian Football League while getting started as a stuntman. Six-two and 215 pounds, Jenson could clear out bars single-handedly, and often cleaned up fights that pals Lee Marvin and Neville Brand began in bars along the Pacific Coast Highway. Jenson was a character, and his hard-living ways made him one of the great weather-beaten presences in 1970s cinema.

Notable fights came in *Designing Woman* (1957), *The Missouri Traveler* (1958), *These Thousand Hills* (1959), *McLintock!* (1963), *4 for Texas* (1963), *Mail Order Bride* (1964), *The Great Race* (1965), *Our Man Flint* (1966), *Sometimes a Great Notion* (1970), *Every Which Way but Loose* (1978) and *Any Which Way You Can* (1980) (see entries). Fights of interest came against Tom Reese in *Marines, Let's Go!* (1961), Steve McQueen in *Baby, the Rain Must Fall* (1965), Dean Martin in *The Ambushers* (1967), Robert Conrad in *The Bandits* (1967), Charlton Heston in *Will Penny* (1968), Henry Fonda and Ben Johnson in *The Red Pony* (1973), Richard Harris in *99 and 44/100% Dead* (1974) and Clint Eastwood in *The Gauntlet* (1977). On TV, Jenson tested all the leading men on *Bonanza, Batman, I Spy* and *Gunsmoke*. He had memorable fights with Rod Taylor in the 1960 *Hong Kong* episode "Pearl Flower," Craig Stevens in the 1960 *Peter Gunn* "The Long Green Kill," Mike Connors in the 1967 *Mannix* "Catalogue of Sins," William Shatner in the 1968 *Star Trek* "The Omega Glory," Ossie Davis in the 1969 *Bonanza* "The Wish," David Carradine in the 1971 *Kung Fu* pilot film, Michael Landon in the 1972 *Bonanza* "Forever" and Robert Blake in the 1975 *Baretta* "If You Can't Pay the Price."

See: Crumley, James. *The Muddy Fork & Other Things*. Livingstone, MT: Clark City, 1991; *Framed* pressbook; McCoy, Heath. "Jenson Dove into Hollywood." *Calgary-Herald*. May 16, 2007.

JIMMY WANG YU VS. GRANT PAGE AND GEORGE LAZENBY in *The Man from Hong Kong* (aka *Dragon Flies*) (1975)

Pioneering martial arts movie fighter Jimmy Wang Yu toplines this intriguing Chinese-Australian production, filmed on location in Syd-ney. One of the highlights is a wild five-minute fight in the kitchen of a Chinese restaurant between stoic cop Yu and wiry stuntman Grant Page, who throws his body around with a reckless abandon seldom seen on screen. *The Ultimate Guide to Martial Arts Movies of the 1970s* describes the fights as "the smash, crash and bash variety." Page is kicked off a speeding motorcycle, breaks several tables in the restaurant, rips the seat of his blue jeans, and is thrown into a fish tank to end the fight. There's also an interesting climactic fight between Yu and bad guy George Lazenby involving a fire stunt gone wrong. The entertaining film was written and directed by the talented Brian Trenchard-Smith and has wall-to-wall action coordinated by Australian stuntmen Page and Peter Armstrong.

The fight between Yu and Page took a full week to film. The outside portion including the kick off the motorcycle was filmed in Australia while all the interiors were filmed in Kowloon at an actual Chinese restaurant. The location was available because the owners were planning to renovate and gave the filmmakers permission to tear the place apart. Editor Ron Williams combines the locations seamlessly. The props in the kitchen, such as the meat cleavers, hooks and broken bottles, were real. Yu made events even more interesting when he told Page to swing the props at him and he'd duck in time. Page did so with reservations as he needed to aim for the head to make it look effective for the cameras, but Yu proved to have quick reflexes and dodged each swing. The ripping of Page's pants was a mistake left in for the sake of continuity. The fish tank and its contents were real and could have been deadly considering the glass broke when Yu threw Page in. There was enough water in the tank to flush the broken glass out ahead of Page.

Chinese stuntman Sammo Hung appears on screen to fight Yu in a jail cell after Australian cop Roger Ward captures the drug smuggler in a fight atop the formidable Ayres Rock in Central Australia. Russell Boyd's outdoor cinematography and Noel Quinlan's triumphant score are highlights in this opening scene. Hung coordinated at least one other scene with Yu fighting Hung's stunt team of Yuen Baio, Corey Yuen and Ching-Ying Lam. Trenchard-Smith even appears for a fight with Yu in an elevator. The Asian star had a strong ego and was constantly at odds with the first-time filmmaker and his crew. He barely held back his punches on the director during the fight. Yu was credited as co-director for the Asian film market for Raymond Chow's Golden Harvest.

The Lazenby fight was supposed to involve the former James Bond's jacket catching fire. Trenchard-Smith wanted Lazenby to do the stunt, but the actor was reluctant. The director shamed the star into doing the stunt by demonstrating it on himself first. Lazenby gave in with reservations. Fire retardant gel was rubbed on his hands and arms as a protective barrier, giving him enough time to pull off the jacket after it was set aflame. However, during the fight with Yu, some gel was rubbed off Lazenby's hand. When the jacket was set ablaze, he felt the exposed skin on his hand burn and he panicked. He was unable to get the jacket off and began to run off camera with Page close behind carrying a heavy blanket. Yu was able to tackle Lazenby and bring him down so Page could smother the flames. There were reports that an enraged Lazenby threw a punch at the director, a claim backed up by many principals interviewed in the documentary *Not Quite Hollywood* (2008). Even Lazenby concedes it might have happened.

Jimmy Wong Yu (film publicity and credits erroneously credited him as Wang Yu) rose to the forefront of late 1960s Hong Kong action films as the star of *One Armed Swordsman* (1967), *The Chinese Boxer* (1969), *One Armed Boxer* (1971) and *Master of the Flying Guillotine* (1975). He was a solid actor but a methodical martial artist who fought in a straightforward, linear manner. *Films of Fury* calls his martial arts "laughably bad." The lack of flashiness kept him from achieving wider popularity in the States as he was eclipsed by the legend of Bruce Lee and all of Lee's high-flying imitators. In real life, the former swimming champion had a reputation as a street fighter and was known to take on all comers when provoked.

See: Birchard, Bob. "007 to Zero and Return: James Bond, No. 2 Hits the Comeback Trail." *Fighting Stars*. October 1975; *The Man from Hong Kong* DVD special features; Page, Grant. *Man on Fire: A Stunt of a Life*. Crows Nest, NSW: Allen & Unwin, 2009; Reid, Craig. "Jimmy Wong Yu: The Crippled Hero." *Kung Fu*. March 2005.

ROBERT REDFORD vs. HANK GARRETT in *Three Days of the Condor* (1975)

Sydney Pollock's tense espionage thriller has held up well over the years, with audiences especially remembering the excellent fight between CIA reader Robert Redford and assassin Hank Garrett in Faye Dunaway's New York City apartment. Garrett's mailman has already been established by Lorenzo Semple, Jr.'s script as one of the killers of Redford's co-workers, so when he shows up under the guise of delivering a package, audiences cringe when an unsuspecting Redford turns his back. Garrett wastes no time in drawing a gun, but Redford has gotten wise at the right moment, hurling a pot of coffee at the hit man. Garrett's reaction could be described as "going postal" as the two men have a nearly one-minute battle with the former revealing martial art skills. Don Guidice's Oscar-nominated editing is superb. His cuts come in a quick flurry but never at the cost of continuity or comprehension as Redford must use every available resource, including a camera's flash and a fireplace poker to ward off Garrett's deadly kicks. He even pulls the rug out from underneath Garrett. The best moment is a white-knuckle staredown with Redford holding the poker and Garrett in his karate stance, both weighing the repercussions of their next movement as Pollock and cinematographer Owen Roizman capture them in alternating close-ups. The fight becomes a race for a firearm, and ironically Redford the desk jockey is the one who gets off the coolest shot as Garrett allows himself to be distracted by Dunaway.

Redford (5'9", 170 pounds) did much of his own fighting for the scene, although stuntman Dean Smith doubled him in parts. Professional wrestler Garrett, a real black belt, used a stunt double for a flip over a table. To simulate hot coffee, the prop department began mixing up a chemical batch that would smoke without any heat. They erroneously were under the assumption the coffee would be thrown on Garrett's clothing instead of his face. Redford immediately nixed any chemical being thrown into Garrett's eyes, saving him from a potential blinding. Unfortunately, Garrett wasn't able to return the favor. During the fight, Redford slipped and Garrett connected with his nose. An important point is the non-regulation brown Adidas tennis shoes worn by Garrett that tip off Redford to his true identity. Ironically, the shoes were Redford's. He gave them to Garrett for the scene and they fit. Garrett held onto them as a memento. The fight received an award from the New York Film Critics as the best of the year.

See: Anderson, Nancy. "Redford's Nose Knows." *Daily News*. January 11, 1980; Dare, Angela. "I'm Sure I Know You from Somewhere but ..." *Fighting Stars*. October 1974; Tuska, Jon, Vicki Piekarski and David Wilson. *Close-Up: The Contemporary Director*. Metuchen, NJ: Scarecrow, 1981.

Charles Bronson vs. Robert Tessier and Nick Dimitri in *Hard Times* (1975)

When asked how he earns his money, Depression era drifter Charles Bronson declares simply, "I knock people down." Writer-director Walter Hill's debut film is a flavorful account of the illegal bare knuckle matches that provided diversionary entertainment and some men a livelihood in the 1930s. It's one of Bronson's most interesting roles and an ode to his uncanny physicality and striking ability. There has never been another 53-year-old body that looked as hard, as sharp, or moved as quickly across the screen. Bronson as Chaney commands the camera with his lined face and enigmatic presence, uttering spare yet effective dialogue as a quiet loner who arrives in New Orleans by rail. In his first fight, he floors Fred Lerner with one devastating knockout punch ranking among the best ever thrown for the screen. The movie is full of fights from stunt coordinator Max Kleven, and they are some of the best ever put on the big screen. The amazing Bronson performs all his own stunt work, snapping off cobra-quick punches while providing effective defense. The fights Bronson has with bald behemoth Robert Tessier and

icy ringer Nick Dimitri are the most memorable.

Hard Times has achieved cult status and been named the favorite film of any number of macho tough guys for decades. It's on many "Best Of" lists, including a top spot on both *Action Films* and *Action Superheroes* magazines' ratings of the greatest fights of all time. The *Toronto Star* puts it in their top ten, calling it "a diamond in the rough." *Cinema Retro* described the fights as "brutal affairs that will convince you that these men are actually beating each other up." *Orange Coast Magazine* included the fistic action among the most realistic in screen history. The *Los Angeles Times* wrote, "The fight scenes are crunchingly spectacular," while *The Hollywood Reporter* praised the film's "sensational action." *Variety* came away impressed with "the well-staged slugfests." Bronson biographer Brian D'Ambrosio wrote, "No one has ever seen movie fights more thrillingly depicted." According to *Films in Review*, "The fights are beautifully choreographed and brilliantly edited." *The Boxing Filmography* added that the fights are "a fine blend of boxing artistry and physical brutality, remaining one of Hollywood's most memorable contributions to fisticuffs."

Midway through the film, the Chartres Street warehouse battle with the formidable Tessier is fought in a cage in front of an enthusiastic mob of bettors. The fighters have contrasting styles. The hulking Tessier is methodical as he bends forward and moves in with his forehead, daring Bronson to break his hand on Tessier's skull as others before him have done. Bronson moves with lightning-fast speed, jabbing and moving out of the way of Tessier's biggest punches and kicks. The audience gets the sense that Bronson at one time might have been a professional boxer, but his past remains as mysterious as his present. As Tessier repeatedly leaves himself open, Bronson begins throwing a barrage of quick combinations that wipes the smile off the big man's face. The flurry wears Tessier down, until he is slumped against the cage and on his backside. Im-

Nick Dimitri (left) and Charles Bronson square off in one of cinema's best-choreographed fight scenes in Columbia's *Hard Times* (1975).

pressed, mobster Michael McGuire wants Bronson as his own fighter, a proposition made possible due to Bronson's shifty manager James Coburn's gambling debts. Bronson is ready to move on but is enticed by failed medical student Strother Martin to face a Chicago fighter named Street (Nick Dimitri) to save the undeserving Coburn's life.

Dimitri has a far more streamlined and functional physique than Tessier and, like Bronson, reveals a true boxer's style. This time Bronson is the one far more economic in his movement as he weighs Dimitri's skill. The men jab and feint, each looking for an opening as the fight moves fluidly through an oyster-filled warehouse at night. Both men try for kicks. Bronson goes for the body, but Dimitri brings his fists down on Bronson's back. Bronson goes to the ground for the first time in the film and a cut opens above his eye. Dimitri waits for him to rise to his feet. They clinch as Bronson pounds his fists into Dimitri's kidneys. When they separate, Bronson goes to work with the combinations. Dimitri goes to his hands and knees and Bronson waits. McGuire senses Bronson could take his hitter and introduces hand weights to elicit a heavy knockout blow. Dimitri brushes "the palmers" aside and gets to his feet, only to have Bronson nail him repeatedly with his clenched fists until the dazed man slumps against the grill of an auto, out on his feet.

One of the best themes is the unspoken code of respect shown by the top fighters. They are noble warriors, aware they are professionals fighting for money over any need to sadistically hurt the other man. These men let up when the other is down, and the fact that Dimitri refuses to fight dirty reveals tons about his character. Likewise, it is interesting that Tessier is the one to help Dimitri to his feet and offer a reassuring pat on the back. Reduced to carrying Dimitri's bag before the climactic fight, he knows what it feels like to be hit by Bronson's sledgehammer fists. In the *Hard Times* novelization based on the original screenplay, more background is given for Bronson's Chaney, although the way he is presented combined with Bronson's own tight-lipped mystery is near perfect. In the novel, Chaney is a farmer whose children have died of typhoid fever. He takes on the controlling business interests and winds up in jail. His wife dies of a drug overdose while he is incarcerated and he kills a guard while escaping. The original version of the Bryan Gindolph–Bruce Henstell story had the added suspense of the police closing in on Chaney as he

fought Street before co-writer Walter Hill began paring events down. The film was originally going to be called *The Street Fighter*, but a Sonny Chiba film appeared under that title during production and the original title of *Hard Times* was reattached.

The camerawork is superb, as is Roger Spottiswoode's editing. Philip Lathrop employed five cameras to catch the action, including one perched on a 14-foot platform. Outside his rippling muscles, Bronson isn't a big man in a film filled with them, yet he is never dwarfed on screen. At 6'1", the 230-pound Tessier stands taller and outweighs him by 60 pounds, but his crouching stance and Lathrop's camera angles nullifies the size difference. Tessier was also wise to let his bodybuilder muscles go soft to add believability to the era. In the latter fight, it is apparent Bronson is wearing heels to add a few inches of height while the 6'2", 200-pound Dimitri is in flats, yet the 30 pounds Dimitri has on Bronson is not apparent. Physically they appear evenly matched. Heavyweight champion Jack Dempsey never weighed more than 190 pounds in the ring yet he felled men who weighed 40 to 50 pounds more than he did due to his boxing skill and the power of his blows. It's been said that *Hard Times* was based on Dempsey's early pugilistic years. In this sense, Bronson's success is entirely believable. His punches look hard and come so fast that the viewer believes he could indeed take out both Tessier and Dimitri. *The Spokesman Review* wrote that Bronson's punches "sound like someone hitting an empty oil drum with a baseball bat." *The New Yorker* humorously wrote that "the walloping fists sound like rhinos crashing into trees."

The fights were filmed on location in New Orleans in the fall of 1974. Director Hill later commented that he worked Bronson hard on the film, but the star was game for all the action. One problem was that Bronson was a smoker and was winded after 30 to 40 seconds of fist-throwing. Bronson trained to improve his stamina by running the New Orleans streets and the motel's halls, logging two miles every morning and two miles every evening. Hill had originally written the screenplay with Jan-Michael Vincent in mind for the lead and Warren Oates in the Coburn role, but he had no problem with casting Bronson. Bronson's age and weather-beaten visage added nuance to the part.

The grueling Dimitri fight took a full week to film at a riverfront warehouse on Tchoupitoulas Street due to the complicated choreography and camera movement. The location placed many time-consuming demands upon the production as the actors repeatedly toiled under the hot lights and amidst the overpowering odor of oysters. Between takes, Dimitri and Tessier watched football games on a portable television set to pass the time. Bronson kept to himself in the corner, doing pushups and flexing his biceps to keep his arms pumped up for the cameras. Bronson warmed up for the action by literally running five feet up the wall and kicking off. Both actors had water and baby oil continuously sprayed on them between shots to simulate sweat and maintain continuity. As an aside, Dimitri's glassy-eyed stare after being knocked out is one of the most believable facial expressions ever put on screen. It's a shame that stuntman Dimitri didn't get better acting roles after this film as he is quite good, although the part itself gave him a lasting cult status.

In the fight with Tessier, Bronson accidentally connected with the big man, as he had an actor's habit of coming in too close with his punches. Stunt coordinator Kleven had to remind Bronson that the camera couldn't pick up all his blows as they were traveling beyond the camera's range. A trained stuntman and therefore more aware of the illusion of camera angles, Tessier never touched Bronson with a punch. Bronson broke Tessier's nose when he forgot the choreography and kicked with the wrong leg. Tessier was bent over and expecting the kick to come from the left leg instead of the right. The shot remained in the film. The star was apologetic and concerned. Tessier shrugged it off and otherwise praised Bronson for his conditioning and coordination. Kleven told the press that Bronson was accepted among the stuntmen as one of their own and could put on screen fights better than any other actor in Hollywood. An additional fight with stuntman Bob Minor was filmed but cut from the final print. The Tessier fight is treated as spectacle with a throng of noise generated from the masses. The Dimitri fight is intimate in comparison. There's no musical accompaniment, only the noise of shuffling feet and bone smacking bone.

See: "Bronson Does Stunts." *Aberdeen Daily News.* September 9, 1976; Cox, Billy. "Sarasota Stuntman Says His Profession Overdue for Recognition." *Herald Tribune.* June 12, 2011; Daniel, Gregg. "Bob Tessier: The Villain Who Turns Hero." *Easyrider.* December 1986; *Hard Times* pressbook.

RYAN O'NEAL VS. PAT ROACH in *Barry Lyndon* (1975)

Writer-director Stanley Kubrick's exquisitely detailed period piece of Irish rogue Ryan O'Neal infiltrating upper-class Britain from the low ranks of the Army took over two years to finish. It is full of interesting and memorable set pieces among Ken Adam's impressive production design. Chief among those scenes with artistic merit are a climactic duel with Leon Vitali and a bare-knuckle brawl with bullying bruiser Pat Roach, a real-life professional wrestler. The first fight elevates Lyndon's status, but the second fight proves his social undoing. The 90-second fight with Roach within a square of fellow soldiers looks like a complete mismatch until the six-foot, 170-pound O'Neal shows off his boxing finesse and makes mincemeat of the 6'4", 275-pound giant. In fact, Roach doesn't land a single punch in the fight, showing how confident and precise O'Neal's character is as he repeatedly knocks Roach back into the crowd. The boxing prowess comes as a surprise to the audience as O'Neal uses his speed and agility to elude Roach's headhunting blows. An intuitive boxer, he attacks the body before going to the head to finish Roach off.

The fact that Roach wasn't going to land a punch was news to both Roach and stunt arranger Roy Scammell, who had created a more traditional routine only to be thrown a curve by Kubrick before the cameras rolled. Much of the original fight choreography remained, the difference being that Roach's punches were now all misses. It ends up working well, and is far more believable than O'Neal withstanding repeated punches from a fighter who outweighs him by more than 100 pounds. As Roach and Scammell rehearsed the fight in a public area, the police were called because someone thought it was a real fight. Roach then took a dive for the much smaller Scammell, which seemed to satisfy the police and no arrests were made.

Roach trained with O'Neal during the extended shoot, and O'Neal impressed the wrestler with his level of fitness. They sparred, ran up to seven miles, and had push-up contests on the set. Kubrick's beautiful but painstakingly long film was photographed by John Alcott with the fight staged over several days at Castle Grace in the Comeragh Mountains. Kubrick avoided static point-of-view shots in this fight, shooting from low angles and intentionally creating a great deal of camera movement and lack of focus. Roach positioned a hand-held camera on his right shoulder while throwing jabs at O'Neal with his left hand, then alternated arms so it appeared that the punches were coming from the camera itself. O'Neal once connected with Roach, who acted as if he hadn't been hit at all while a momentarily distracted O'Neal stood looking at him.

The fights O'Neal had in films like *Wild Rovers* (1971) and *Nickelodeon* (1976) (see entry) were far less noteworthy than those he had off-screen. With a Golden Gloves boxing background, O'Neal had a reputation as one of the few actors in Hollywood who could actually fight. However, he also had a fiery temper and a penchant for solving problems with his fists, resulting in assault and battery arrests. In 1983, there was a much-publicized fistfight with his own teenage son Griffin over the latter's drug use that saw two of the boy's teeth knocked out. Over 20 years later, they had another fight resulting in the father's arrest.

See: *Barry Lyndon* pressbook; Fleeman, Mike. "Ryan O'Neal Arrested After Fight with Son." *People.* February 4, 2007; Levin, Eric. "The Fighting, Loving O'Neal Clan." *People.* August 15, 1983.

ROBERT CONRAD VS. DON STROUD in *Sudden Death* (1975)

Kung fu became the "in" thing in the early 1970s, and much of Hollywood began training. The magazine *Fighting Stars* contained articles on the celebrities who were into martial arts. On one cover was actor Robert Conrad, a man who had been legitimately training with John Leoning since 1957 in Kajukenbo and Shotokan karate and had displayed his moves with regularity on the TV series *Hawaiian Eye* (1959–1963) and *The Wild Wild West* (1965–1969). It seemed natural that Conrad was on the lookout for a karate film, and the Filipino-made *Sudden Death* from director Eddie Romero and screenwriter Oscar Williams was right up his alley. It gave Conrad a chance to show off his martial art skills in a 90-second kick-fest against hit man Don Stroud, another real black belt, in what the ads touted as "two masters with a thousand ways to kill."

The two have a great showdown in a slaughter-house with nifty use of slow motion to show that the men are fighting to contact, punctuated by bursts of acceleration as they react to the power of the kicks and punches. Despite being the star, Conrad gets his hindquarters kicked by the high-flying Stroud, who even seems to punish the air with his intense katas. After being kicked into a block of ice, Conrad seizes a meat hook and ends the fight less than heroically. Conrad and co-star Felton Perry also show off their moves against local thugs in a bar brawl and a street fight. Both fights are energetic and well devised by stunt co-ordinator Chuck Courtney.

Conrad and Stroud made the heist film *Murph the Surf* (1975) in Fort Lauderdale, Florida, and got along so well that they were searching for another project to do together. However, after completion of *Sudden Death*, Conrad complained to the press Stroud broke three of his ribs with a kick, and though they were friends he suspected it was intentional. *Sudden Death* was filmed in 1975 and received a limited U.S. release in 1977, by which time Conrad had reestablished himself as a high-profile TV star with the World War II show *Baa Baa Black Sheep*. He was also doing a famous tough guy commercial spot in which he set an Eveready battery on his shoulder and dared anyone to knock it off.

The 5'5", 160-pound Conrad was a boxing aficionado who trained with Mushy Callahan and had a tough guy reputation in Hollywood despite his small stature. He even fought professional boxing matches after attaining stardom. Conrad's healthy ego and cocky swagger sometimes rubbed others the wrong way, and he was known to engage in real fistfights at the Back Stage bar near CBS. The far-out western series *The Wild Wild West* showcased amazingly intricate fight choreography. Conrad was front and center doing all his own fight stunts as James West, even incorporating martial arts into the fast-paced action. He worked primarily with a stunt crew consisting of Whitey Hughes, Bob Herron, Red West, Dick Cangey, Fred Stromsoe and Tommy Huff. Their timing and teamwork was impeccable. He also worked fights with physical actors the likes of Robert Phillips and Mike Masters. On the publicity trail, he staged live fights with Cangey and Hughes. Conrad is one of the few actors to be awarded membership into the Stuntman's Hall of Fame based upon his superb work on the show.

On the series *Hawaiian Eye* (1959–1963), Conrad's most notable fight came against Robert Colbert in 1960's "Typhoon." Usually he worked fights with stuntman Bob Herron. On *Baa Baa Black Sheep* (aka *Black Sheep Squadron*), Conrad fought Charles Napier in 1976's "Best Three Out of Five" and Red West in 1977's "Devil in the Slot."

Conrad had his best role playing the French trapper Pasquiel in the excellent mini-series *Centennial* (1978), taking part in a bar brawl with Clint Walker and Tony Epper. In the TV reboot *Wild Wild West Revisited* (1979), he fought Red West and Chuck Courtney. On film, he fought Ty Hardin in *Palm Springs Weekend* (1963), Roy Jenson in *The Bandits* (1967) and Neville Brand in the TV movie *The Adventures of Nick Carter* (1972).

See: Schultz, Bob. "Bob Conrad Lays It on the Line." *Fighting Stars*. February 1974; Wilson, Earl. "Robert Conrad Had Three Ribs Broken Filming Last Movie." *Sarasota Herald Tribune*. June 16, 1975.

JAMES CAAN vs. NINJAS in *The Killer Elite* (1975)

Heavily anticipated by the martial arts community before its release, Sam Peckinpah's CIA espionage misfire *The Killer Elite* ultimately proved to be a great disappointment when it came to the fight action. Partly due to his runaway chemical consumption, the great action master Peckinpah had no real interest in trying to outdo Bruce Lee when it came to directing punches and kicks. In fact, he wanted to make an action satire that did big business at the box office while simultaneously thumbing its nose at the movie studios and producers he was constantly at war with. Prior to ever rolling a camera, the film was relocated from England to San Francisco at star James Caan's suggestion and went through numerous costly script changes, with former Lee student Stirling Silliphant the one responsible for adding all the trendy martial arts elements. Silliphant's wife Tiana Alexandra, also a student of Lee, was cast as a principal. Peckinpah veteran Whitey Hughes was hired as stunt coordinator with martial artists Tak Kubota, Hank Hamilton, James Wing Woo, George Kee Cheung, Johnnie Burrell, Emil Farkas, Larry Wikel, Eric Lee, Gerald Okamura, Brandon Pender, Kim Kahana, Kuo Lien Ying, Cherry Lau, April Castro, June Castro, May Castro, Teresita M. Luz, Howard Lee, Lance Fisher, Dennis Gee, Sam Hiona, Brian Fung, Raymond Solis, Simon Tam, Wilfred Tang, Leo Whang, Werner Venetz and Danny Inosanto all employed for their fighting skills. Hughes was at a loss, trying to handle all the karate black belts, and brought in stuntman and judo expert Gene LeBell to aid him in dealing with the different styles and techniques who all wanted to show off their abilities.

The most prominent showcase for martial arts occurs during an assassination attempt at San Francisco International Airport in which several hired killers try to take out the bodyguards of Japanese politician Mako. However, Peckinpah and cameraman Philip Lathrop opt to keep the action exchanges exceptionally short. With his footage completed, four editors tried to find the best way to put the scene together. Peckinpah brought in Monte Hellman (a noted director) to intercut the fights with a dialogue exchange between government shadow agency heads Arthur Hill and Gig Young. Cinematically it's an effective editorial choice but not something that endeared Peckinpah to those who wanted to see karate battles given their full attention by the camera. Hellman noted that a great deal of martial arts action from this sequence ended up on the cutting room floor.

Caan's character is "retired" by turncoat agent Robert Duvall early in the film as he is shot in the elbow and the knee. The rest of the convoluted story sees Caan rehabilitating via martial arts through training with Kuo Lien Ying and Johnnie Burrell, as he learns to wield a cane as a weapon while seeking revenge on his old pal. Caan realizes that Duvall is only a pawn. Caan and cohorts Bo Hopkins and Burt Young have a climactic showdown with ninja assassins on the Navy's mothball fleet located on Suison Bay. Peckinpah effectively sets up this ghostly scenario with an eerie mood and foreboding Jerry Fielding score, inserting the briefest glimpses of ninjas moving into position for an attack. However, when the battle commences, Peckinpah begins to lose his grasp. He has Hellman resort to frequent jump cutting intercut with the slow-motion action and balletic stunts of Hughes and his stuntmen falling from the ships. It's a jarring effect that maintains visual interest but does nothing for the display of martial arts. In fact, this is where Peckinpah's ideas of satire emerge. The skilled ninjas are rendered useless as they impressively fly through the air with their kicks only to be shot down by Hopkins' machine-gun. Caan briefly engages the ninjas with his cane, but it's the short, overweight, balding Burt Young punching out ninjas and tossing them overboard that thoroughly stretches believability. In real life, Young was at odds with his mumbling, slovenly screen image. He was a former Marine and a boxer who could take any number of people by surprise with his toughness. But not a trained ninja. A sword battle between Mako and Tak Kubota offers a chance for Caan and Young to trade wisecracks.

According to the *Delta Democrat*, "Peckinpah, apparently aware that the film was dragging, stages several of his customarily brilliant fight scenes, but they are not enough to pull the film through," while the *New York Times* called it all "ridiculously operatic." *The Ultimate Guide to Martial Arts Movies of the 1970s* tagged the finale a "major disappointment." Peckinpah's career never recovered.

See: *The Killer Elite* pressbook; Mather, Jim. "The Karate Training of James Caan." *Black Belt.* March 1991; Stevens, Brad. *Monte Hellman: His Life and Films.* Jefferson, NC: McFarland, 2003.

JEFF BRIDGES VS. R.G. ARMSTRONG in *Stay Hungry* (1976)

Director Bob Rafelson's cult favorite about bodybuilding in Birmingham, Alabama, gave Arnold Schwarzenegger his first big role as a Mr. Universe favorite who befriends the film's star Jeff Bridges. The latter is putting together a real estate deal involving Schwarzenegger's gym, owned and operated by a seriously weird R.G. Armstrong in a ridiculous toupee. Rich kid Bridges becomes distracted by the characters he encounters, begins training, and ultimately dates Schwarzenegger's ex Sally Field. The film is as quirky and charming as its characters, although the climax does feature a violent 90-second fight at the gym between Bridges and the terrifyingly comic Armstrong (high on amyl nitrate) after the latter has forced himself on Field. Rafelson sent the stunt coordinator and stuntmen home, opting to choreograph the action with the actors to surprise the audience and keep the action authentic. Despite the fear of injury, Rafelson found his actors receptive to doing their own fight. The action is especially impressive considering the fact that the 6'3", 225-pound Armstrong, a former steelworker who went to Chapel Hill on a football scholarship, was nearly 60.

Weight plates, dumbbells, barbells and even a bench press are thrown at the camera and clang resoundingly off the exercise machines. The much bigger Armstrong realistically slams the 6'1", 170-pound Bridges into a wall and smashes a mirror with a bar-

bell. Bridges jumps catlike down a stairwell (a nifty stunt) to escape the deranged gym owner. The two crash out the gym's front window. Many of the weights thrown were obviously real iron, with lightweight wooden discs mixed in. Bridges was allowed to punch to contact with Armstrong, who wore towels underneath his bathrobe to absorb the force of the blows.

In another interesting fight, Bridges and character actor Robert Englund (playing Armstrong's gym assistant) take on young toughs led by Dennis Burkley. Englund, who beat out Sylvester Stallone for the part, had a gymnastics background and was able to throw his body around with confidence. The pool cue he takes between the legs is especially wince-inducing. The odd humor and shifts in tone left many critics scratching their heads. The *Los Angeles Times* wrote that there is "a clanging, exciting but preposterous fight scene." *Film Bulletin* found the fights "excitingly staged," while *Newsweek* called the Armstrong encounter "a rousing fight scene in which Bridges is wonderfully athletic."

Burly character actor Armstrong greatly enjoyed doing fights and threw some of the screen's most vicious and powerful blows. Many fellow actors were leery of doing fights with him because he came across so frighteningly intense. Few could play righteous anger so effectively. Armstrong knocked a handcuffed Kris Kristofferson from his chair and halfway across the room in *Pat Garrett and Billy the Kid* (1973) and pressed a knife to Burt

R.G. Armstrong (left) and Jeff Bridges fight using gym equipment in United Artists' *Stay Hungry* (1976).

Reynolds' throat in *White Lightning* (1973). His best fights came against Tom Tryon in the 1960 *Texas John Slaughter* episode "A Holster Full of Law" and Pernell Roberts in the 1967 *Gunsmoke* episode "A Stranger in Town." Armstrong lifted weights for many years at Vince's Gym, and his son worked there as a trainer. Some have suggested that Armstrong's inspired gym owner portrayal was a knowing swipe at bodybuilding entrepreneur Joe Weider, Schwarzenegger's early benefactor and promoter.

See: Boyer, Jay. *Bob Rafelson: Hollywood Maverick.* New York: Twayne, 1996; Humphreys, Justin. *Names You Never Remember with Faces You Never Forget.* Albany, GA: BearManor, 2006; *Stay Hungry* DVD commentary; *Stay Hungry* pressbook.

CHARLES BRONSON VS. ARCHIE MOORE in *Breakheart Pass* (1976)

There's plenty of mystery and Alistair MacLean–scripted suspense aboard a snowbound train in the 1870s Old West with Charles Bronson heading a large cast of familiar faces in *Breakheart Pass.*

In this well-regarded Tom Gries adventure film, Bronson is a government agent masquerading as a prisoner and the entire cast are suspects, including tough guy favorites Ben Johnson, Roy Jenson, Ed Lauter, Richard Crenna, Charles Durning and Bill McKinney. Even the train's cook, pro boxing

Charles Bronson (left) and Archie Moore put on a thrilling fight atop a train in United Artists' *Breakheart Pass* **(1976).**

champ Archie Moore, isn't to be trusted, and this leads to the most memorable moment. Moore and Bronson face off atop the snow-covered train in an exciting, superbly filmed one-minute fight that sees both men hanging off the train's edge as the Bitterroot Mountain, Idaho, scenery whizzes past. No process shots in this sequence: It's all real and shot on location. Stunt legend Yakima Canutt set up the rousing scene and directed the second unit for his final screen credit with D.P. Lucien Ballard also meriting special mention. Stuntmen Howard Curtis and Tony Brubaker doubled the stars during the hairier segments, including a tackle, a dropkick and the final flip off the train that sees Moore fall to his death and Bronson nearly go over as well. The sequence is edited by Byron "Buzz" Brandt for maximum thrills, emphasizing the danger for both the stuntmen and the actors. Jerry Goldsmith's robust score is nothing less than phenomenal. *Films in Review* praised the film's "remarkably stunning action shots," while *Films and Filming* gushed over "the superb train-top fight." Leonard Maltin called the fight "incredible," while *Film Score Monthly* labeled it "one of the most spectacular fight scenes ever filmed."

Bronson and Moore were game for close-up shots of both men hanging off the edge one-handed while they kick away at one another over a trestle. The 61-year-old Moore decided to do the fight because the 54-year-old Bronson was doing it. At one point, Moore pulled himself up from the safety bar with both arms and was shocked to see Bronson lift himself back up with one arm. Canutt told writer Harry Crews that Bronson was the greatest natural stuntman he'd ever seen, and Crews came away convinced Bronson might be the best natural athlete. Canutt shot the action with a camera crane that was put atop a flatcar and could be extended out to a variety of angles to emphasize the great dropoff below the men. Both men wore safety belts under their shirts with flexible airplane cable, allowing enough slack for freedom of movement. As an added precaution, hidden steps were nailed into the train's side so the men could support their weight if they tired. Out of sight was a safety net that was built from the train's edge with four-by-fours and extended close to 15 feet to catch stuntman Brubaker when he performed his fall. The entire sequence took two days to film, with the actors accounting for four hours atop the moving train.

See: Crews, Harry. "Charles Bronson Ain't No Pussycat." *Playboy.* October 1975; *Stunts in Action Films* TCM featurette; "Untitled." *Time.* May 5, 1975.

LEE MARVIN VS. ROGER MOORE in *Shout at the Devil* (1976)

This rollicking adventure film, set in pre–World War I Mozambique, concerns boozing Irish con man Lee Marvin roping proper Brit Roger Moore into his latest moneymaking scheme. The two become friendly adversaries united against common German foe Reinhard Kolldehoff until Moore falls in love with Marvin's daughter Barbara Parkins; then it's no-holds-barred for a wild four-minute serio-comic fight. The two have opposing styles with Marvin showing fancy footwork and Moore fighting straight ahead as a former Eton boxing champ. "Footwork, my boy," Marvin intones throughout the boisterous fight whenever he gains the upper hand. Marvin mugs it up to great comedic effect as the two battle through a large house, onto the porch, in and out a hut, through a load of laundry, and ultimately into pig slop where they both pass out. Moore marries Parkins in the ensuing scene with both men sporting black eyes.

Director Peter Hunt, veteran editor from the James Bond films, puts it all together in an entertaining fashion with D.P. Michael Reed employing the occasional use of slow-motion to highlight the broadest actions. There's no musical accompaniment, only the laughs of the native villagers as the two buffoons wreck their village. Marvin keeps a running commentary going throughout the fight as he pulls dirty trick after dirty trick, and Moore tries to fight by the Marquess of Queensberry rules. The emphasis here is on humor with one of the best moments coming when Marvin tries to swing a kick from a small sapling but brings the tree branch down on himself. Marvin did a great deal of

his own comic pratfalls, though South African stuntman Reo Ruiters doubled him for the fall off the balcony. Larry Taylor also worked as a Marvin stuntman. However, both stars did the majority of their stunt work over the roughly five days devoted to the scene. John Glen served as the second unit director and Moore's double Leslie Crawford was the fight arranger.

Despite playing a drunkard, this was a rare occurrence where Marvin kept away from booze throughout filming with a few exceptions. The two stars enjoyed one another and shared sips of Jack Daniel's in the evening. Their close friendship wasn't always the case. Legend has it when Moore first arrived in the U.S. in the 1950s on a studio contract, he ran afoul of a boozing Marvin, who baited what he thought was a foppish Brit into a fight. Moore responded with a hard punch that flattened Marvin. When the drunken aggressor stood up, he had a new respect for Moore and sang his praises for all to hear. Marvin went on record saying that Moore threw a great punch and would never be underestimated again. In his autobiography, Moore wrote that Marvin liked doing his own stunts and occasionally became carried away with the action when he'd had too much alcohol. If Moore noticed Marvin's eyes go "red" during the choreography, he'd do his best to steer clear of him. Nevertheless, he had vivid memories of Marvin's fists zinging dangerously close to his face.

American International publicity promoted the film as a great African adventure but a length of

Lee Marvin reacts to a Roger Moore punch in AIP's *Shout at the Devil* (1976).

over two hours and abrupt shifts in tone kept audiences and critics from fully embracing the picture. *Variety* called the fisticuffs "a highlight reminiscent of the memorable battle in John Ford's *The Quiet Man*," while the *New York Times* merely described it as a "protracted and mock-comic fistfight." The *Sarasota Herald Tribune* tagged it "one of the movie's high points," and *The Brandon Sun* labeled it "glorious." Moore's biographers Gareth Owen and Oliver Bayan described the scene as a "wonderfully funny but cleverly choreographed bare knuckle fight." Moore himself proudly called it "one dilly of a fight scene."

Moore had recently tackled the iconic role of James Bond in *Live and Let Die* (1973) and *The Man with the Golden Gun* (1974). A Royal Army veteran active in Military Intelligence, he brought a much lighter touch to Bond. He had been exposed to boxing, judo, jujitsu and Kendo while playing Simon Templar on *The Saint* (1962–1969). For his second Bond film, he studied Mongolian kung fu with Hungarian sifu Lajo Jakab. Despite the fight training, 6'1", 180-pound Moore never seemed at ease as a tough guy on screen and lacked the hard edge Sean Connery brought to his Bond portrayal. Moore's fights had a tongue-in-cheek aspect to them with Moore (and his double) often batted around by a larger opponent.

Notable fights include *The Spy Who Loved Me* (1976) and *The Cannonball Run* (1981) (see entries). Fights of interest came against Julius Harris in *Live and Let Die* (1973), Yao Lin Chen in *The Man with the Golden Gun* (1974), Richard Kiel and Toshiro Suga in *Moonraker* (1979), John Wyman in *For Your Eyes Only* (1981), David Meyer in *Octopussy* (1983) and Christopher Walken in *A View to a Kill* (1985). He had one of his best fights opposing a trio of saw blade–wielding assassins in *Octopussy* (1983). Moore's most notable TV match-up on *The Saint* came against Oliver Reed in 1963's "The King of the Beggars." In 1965's "The Crooked Ring," he put on boxing gloves to go up against Nosher Powell. On the TV series *The Persuaders* (1970–1971), Moore memorably fought co-star Tony Curtis in "Overture" and "Someone Like Me."

See: Moore, Roger. *My Word Is My Bond: A Memoir*. London: It Books, 2009; Owen, Gareth, and Oliver Bayan. *Roger Moore: His Films and Career*. London: Robert Hale, 2002; Thien, Alex. "Superspy Actor Uncovers New Role." *Milwaukee Sentinel*. October 29, 1975.

RYAN O'NEAL VS. BURT REYNOLDS in *Nickelodeon* (1976)

This Peter Bogdanovich misfire takes an affectionate look at silent movies with plenty of slapstick and rat-a-tat dialogue from the writer-director. Ryan O'Neal, 1970s Golden Boy, headlines with co-star Burt Reynolds, who mugs it up comically while vying with O'Neal for the affections of Jane Hitchcock. Reynolds' cocky bravado is tiring, but he does make a worthy fisticuffs opponent for O'Neal in a four-minute fight that's played entirely for laughs. Shot on Modesto, California, flatlands, the fight occurs as O'Neal takes the helm for his first film as director and Reynolds shows up as a patent company stooge hired to sabotage the camera. After much bare knuckle hilarity involving a bucking bronco, a chicken coop, a feisty Jack Russell Terrier, a wagon full of hay, tangled legs and O'Neal's faulty suspenders, the fight concludes with the men gaining a mutual admiration for one another. Reynolds is offered the leading role in O'Neal's film.

Behind the scenes there was tension and competitiveness between the stars. Reynolds suffered numerous minor injuries performing slapstick pratfalls for Laszlo Kovacs' camera. They filmed the fight over two days in 100 degree heat, and Reynolds, suffering from chest pains, repeatedly passed out in his trailer. When his color took on a ghostly white, it was decided that stunt coordinator Hal Needham would complete the remainder with O'Neal's double Joe Amsler. Needham filled in for Reynolds for the next two weeks in long shots while Reynolds underwent a battery of tests and the film fell behind schedule. Reynolds was ultimately diagnosed with hypoglycemia and anxiety attacks. In the fight that appears on screen, Needham and Amsler show up crashing through a fence.

Critics were divided on the film's merits, with most of influence lambasting it. The *New York Times* wrote, "There is an endless fight between Mr. O'Neal and Mr. Reynolds. It is choreographed as a comic ballet. It is infinitely familiar, infinitely slick and not at all funny." The *Free Lance-Star* added, "There is one heck of a lot of fighting in this picture that seems to be drenched in digressions." The *Register-Guard* did say positively, "The movie breaks loose with a tremendously funny fight scene," and *Texas Monthly* chipped in with, "There's a terrific fight between Reynolds and O'Neal, which nicely parodies the overlong knockout brawls of the silent era." Few working on the picture cared for the demanding director, who unsuccessfully pushed Columbia to have the picture shot in black-and-white. Roughly a year after the release, O'Neal punched out Bogdanovich at the Hollywood nightclub Pips. Needham sent up the director's pompous image in his own film *Hooper* (1978), with Reynolds punching out a Bogdanovich-inspired director played by Robert Klein.

See: *Nickelodeon* DVD commentary; "Star." *San Antonio Express*. April 17, 1977.

ROY SCHEIDER VS. JAMES WING WOO in *Marathon Man* (1976)

A taut, well-made international spy thriller from director John Schleslinger. Dustin Hoffman stars as a grad student who becomes mixed up with deadly Nazi war criminal Laurence Olivier. The movie is most famous for the excruciating dental torture scene, but fans are also fond of a brutal one-minute fight on a Paris balcony and motel room between and Roy Scheider, playing Hoffman's mysterious brother, and assassin James Wing Woo. Stunt coordinator Everett Creach allowed the actors to do their own impressive stunt work. The scene is superbly staged for Conrad Hall's camera, but it's curious that Woo was hired given his extensive kung fu background. The highly realistic fight doesn't feature any martial arts outside of a Scheider karate chop that he delivers with an injured hand. Woo (not to be confused with San Soo Kung Fu master Jimmy H. Woo) was well-known as the owner of the Academy of Karate Kung Fu and the Chinese Martial Arts Association, both located on Hollywood Boulevard. The 5'9", 160-pound Scheider was a Golden Gloves boxer and a wrestler at Rutgers College.

There's a great deal of suspense built courtesy of editor James Clark as Scheider watches a parade while Woo sneaks into the room and his face appears behind the white sheer curtain. The fight still comes with a jolt as Scheider is standing on his high balcony wearing only his skivvies after performing a set of push-ups. Rarely has a heroic figure been exposed to such a degree as Woo raises a garrote to wrap it around Scheider's throat. Scheider's quick reaction is life-saving. He gets his palm in front of his neck, and blood goes flying as the wire digs into his flesh. This special makeup effect was created by the legendary Dick Smith. There's a nod to Alfred Hitchcock's *Rear Window* (1954) as a witness in a wheelchair across the

street is helpless to do anything but watch the men struggle behind an increasingly blood-stained curtain. Woo swings the garrote like a bola, but a bloody Scheider manages to move behind Woo, place his hands around his jaw, and press his knee into the small of Woo's back until his neck snaps. Scheider collapses in believable exhaustion. Increasing the scene's effectiveness is the lack of musical accompaniment. The viewer hears only the parade chants from below. The *Los Angeles Times* called the fight "spectacular," while *Movie Maker* termed it "hair-raising."

True to screenwriter William Goldman's source novel, the film originally introduced Scheider's character and a fellow spy at an airport. Scheider's colleague goes to the rest room and doesn't return. When Scheider investigates, he finds a pair of assassins whom he engages in hand-to-hand combat. This entire sequence lasted over eight minutes and was excised after an early San Francisco preview indicated that audiences were turned off by too much graphic violence. These introductory scenes were why leading man Scheider took a supporting role as they created a sense of vulnerability to his tough guy character. The undignified death on the toilet of his fellow spy was a key reason a mortally wounded Scheider later crawls to Hoffman's apartment. Olivier's dental torture of Hoffman is an attempt to extract perceived information Scheider was trying to relay; when in reality it was simply that Scheider was trying to die with dignity.

See: Goldman, William. *William Goldman: Four Screenplays with Essays*. New York: Applause, 1995; Kachmar, Diane C. *Roy Scheider: A Film Biography*. Jefferson, NC: McFarland, 2002; *Marathon Man* DVD special features.

PETER SELLERS VS. BURT KWOUK in *The Pink Panther Strikes Again* (1976)

Beginning with Blake Edwards' *A Shot in the Dark* (1964), a running gag in the classic side-splitting *Pink Panther* films became the spirited, highly destructive martial art battles between the klutzy, dimwitted Inspector Clouseau (Peter Sellers, in his greatest role) and his loyal servant Cato (Burt Kwouk). To keep fit and always on his toes, Clouseau has instructed Cato to attack him unannounced. Each successive film finds Cato lying in wait for Clouseau, and the damage they do to his home with their fights is comic genius. The three-minute fight in *The Pink Panther Strikes Again* is their masterpiece, managing to add new wrinkles to their previous battles and spoof the burgeoning kung fu genre at the same time. Dick Crockett doubles Kwouk while Sellers is doubled by British stuntman Joe Dunne.

The *Strikes Again* fight begins with Cato hiding atop the canopy of Clousseau's bed as the inspector lies down. Cato rips the canopy and both scream as Cato falls atop Clousseau and the bed collapses. They rush to their respective hidden weapons and put on a sped-up version of staff and nunchaku expertise. The fight switches to slow motion and hilariously slurred sound as Cato charges and Clousseau breaks his nunchaku over the back of Cato's neck. The two manage to hit everything but one another in the confines of Clousseau's apartment. Clousseau charges Cato and trips over his crazed commander Herbert Lom's periscope sticking up from the floor. Lom, on a ladder in the apartment below, falls to the floor. Clousseau and Cato next stalk one another through the apartment, somehow ending up back to back but oblivious to the other's presence. As they become aware of one another and scream warrior cries, they are interrupted by the telephone (a running motif). Doing his duty as Clousseau's servant, Cato moves to answer the phone. Clousseau whacks him over the head and wins the fight.

Director Edwards was a martial arts student, having trained with Kenpo master Ed Parker whom he often consulted. Sellers had taken judo classes in his younger days but by the 1970s was besieged by heart problems and had a pacemaker. He did as little action as possible, with stunt double Dunne ably filling in. Nimble co-star Kwouk called the series of fights "one of the great running gags in motion picture history," but admitted that neither he nor Sellers had any clue when it came to being true martial artists. Often they were making it up as they went along, encouraged by Edwards to improvise where they saw fit. Veteran stunt coordinator John Sullivan originally plotted the *Strikes Again* fight as a more traditional punchfest. Dunne argued that the comic essence of the Clousseau-Cato fights was that they hardly ever made actual contact. Edwards agreed

with Dunne, who became stunt coordinator for Edwards' films. The results in *Strikes Again* are golden, and *Action Films* includes it among cinema's great fights.

See: Parker, Ed. "Blake Edwards and the Martial Arts." *Black Belt*. June 1990; Rigelsford, Adrian. *Peter Sellers: A Life in Character*. Virgin, 2004; Salome, Lou. "Sellers Stunt Double Speaks: I Took Falls for Inspector Clousseau." *Action Films*. February 1983.

TERENCE HILL VS. BOB HERRON in *Mr. Billion* (1977)

Trinity star Terence Hill took a shot at stardom in the United States with the adventure comedy *Mr. Billion* (originally titled *Windfall*), about a simple Italian mechanic trying to collect an inheritance in America despite nefarious interests represented by banker Jackie Gleason. Writer-director Jonathan Kaplan's film is lighthearted and engaging enough, but lacks the essentials that made Hill a star in Italy. Specifically the fights feature none of the crazy comedy Hill was known for, as they

Terence Hill (left) and Bob Herron battle on the edge of the Grand Canyon in 20th Century-Fox's *Mr. Billion* (1977).

are filmed in the more traditional dramatic Holly-wood style. The disjointed picture was a commer-cial misfire. Nevertheless, there's an outstanding fight at the climax due to an inspired setting and fantastic aerial helicopter shots from high above: Hill and veteran stunt actor Bob Herron engage in a truly dangerous fight at the Grand Canyon's edge. There was no safety net and only a small ledge be-neath Herron and Hill's double Walter Scott. A slip or a fall could have meant death. "More action, excitement, romance and riotous adventure than money can buy," promised the ads.

Fred Stromsoe served as stunt coordinator and Nate Long directed the second unit, although hel-icopter pilot James Gavin was the aerial coordina-tor in charge of the dizzying shots that cinematog-rapher Matthew Leonetti captured. The Canyon had served as the backdrop for another memorable climax with Cornel Wilde and Mickey Shaugh-nessy dangling in an ore bucket over the gorge in *Edge of Eternity* (1959). Reviews of *Mr. Billion* tended to focus on the campy set-up to the action, which involved leading lady Valerie Perrine tied to a rock like something from a silent movie cliff-hanger. *Time* wrote, "The filmmakers have to be kidding—only they don't seem to know it." *Film Bulletin* did find the action sequence to be "well-staged."

Earlier there's a standard cowboy brawl in the Hog Leg Saloon in which Slim Pickens and stunt actor Neil Summers take part. Summers is bounced around like a pinball in the fight while Pickens takes his own stunt fall onto a table. Although Pickens is Hill's opposition in the fight, he be-comes an ally who helps even the odds at the Grand Canyon when a gunman gets Hill in his sights. Other stunt fighters in the Hog Leg include Fred Lerner, Chuck Hayward, Larry Holt and Norm Blankenship. Unfortunately the editing for the sequence by O. Nicholas Brown cuts away from the action too often to fully appreciate it. Stunt actor Dave Cass also engages Hill in a per-ilous fight in an open helicopter. On the TV series *Here Come the Brides*, Cass and Herron worked a notable fight together doubling Robert Brown and Mark Lenard in 1969's "His Sister's Keeper." At over five minutes in length, it was one of the longest fights ever done for TV.

See: Ivie, Mark, and John D. Ross. "Robert Her-ron: 80, Unbreakable ... and Still Going Strong!" *Inside Stunts.* Summer 2004; *Mr. Billion* press-book.

STUART WHITMAN VS. KUNG FU KICKING DRAG QUEENS in *Strange Shadows in an Empty Room* (aka *Blazing Magnums*) (1977)

This violent Italian-Canadian co-production was filmed in Montreal by director Alberto De-Martino. Craggy Stuart Whitman stars as a Dirty Harry–like cop out to catch the murderer of his sister. His investigation leads him to a penthouse apartment inhabited by three razor-wielding, karate-kicking men dressed as women. Most pub-licity and reviews refer to them as transvestites. Whitman's Tough Tony is kicked out a sliding glass door and winds up hanging from a ledge several stories above the street but pulls himself back up to finish off the trio. This two-and-a-half-minute brawl is well edited by Vincenzo Tomassi. Whit-man makes particularly nasty use of a hot curling iron, contributing to this audacious film's cult rep-utation. *Italian Crime Filmography* declared that the fight went "wildly over-the-top in a way no mainstream U.S. film would."

As bizarre as the scenario comes off, it wasn't unprecedented. James Caan beat up a transvestite in *Freebie and the Bean* (1974) and Jim Mitchum had a back alley brawl with three tranny hookers (among them pro boxer Tony Burton) in *Track-down* (1976). Whitman's fight, however, is far and away the best. Guilda, Gene Chandler and Vicki Lane are the kung fu combatants, while Whitman is doubled by American stuntman Tom Sutton. Publicity played up Whitman's gutsiness and the fact he did much of his own stunt work for cine-matographer Aristide Massaccesi's hand-held cam-era. The scene was shot atop a 26-story office building in downtown Montreal. Whitman hung 260 feet above the ground from the side of the building. Appropriate safety precautions were un-dertaken to guarantee the star's safety, but Whit-man should be commended for the lengths (the heights?) he'd go to for a low-budget feature.

Risk-taking was nothing new to the 190-pound six-footer, a light heavyweight boxing champion in the Army who played football at Los Angeles City College and worked construction jobs on the side. When it came down to a casting decision be-tween Whitman and Larry Pennell for a never-made biography of boxer Jack Dempsey, Whitman trained with pro John Indrisano and suggested that the producers put both actors in the ring and let them fight for the part. On *Sands of the Kalahari* (1965), he wrestled a real baboon, though it was sedated. Whitman trained with Bruce Lee and had a reputation as a man quick with his fists if challenged in a bar, factors in his later casting as the title detective in the Hong Kong–made Hammer film *Shatter* (aka *Call Him Mr. Shatter*) (1974) where he mixed it up with martial artists Chia Yung Liu and Pei Chi Huang.

Fights of interest came against Michael Pataki and John Indrisano in *Ten North Frederick* (1958), Claude Akins in *Hound Dog Man* (1959), Ken Scott in *The Fiercest Heart* (1961), John Wayne and Tom Hennesy in *The Comancheros* (1961), Reggie Nalder in *The Day and the Hour* (1963), Roddy McDowall in *Shock Treatment* (1964), Stanley Baker in *Sands of the Kalahari* (1965), Lee Van Cleef in *Captain Apache* (1971) and Robert Wagner in the TV movie *City Beneath the Sea* (1971). He led an old-fashioned saloon brawl in the TV movie *Once Upon a Texas Train* (1988). On the ambitious TV western *Cimarron Strip* (1967–1968), Whitman fought Telly Savalas, Richard Boone, Steve Forrest, Henry Silva and Victor French. As a guest star, he knocked out George Peppard in the 1983 *A-Team* episode "West Coast Turnaround." In 1994, Whitman played two-fisted Laredo Jake Boyd on the "Deadly Reunion" episode of *Walker, Texas Ranger*.

See: Curti, Roberto. *Italian Crime Filmography, 1968–1980.* Jefferson, NC: McFarland, 2013; Petkovich, Anthony. "They Made Me a Cult Film Star: An Interview with Actor Stuart Whitman." *Shock Cinema.* #44, June 2013; Scott, Vernon. "Actor Would Fight for Film Part." *Deseret News.* September 19, 1957.

ROBERT TESSIER VS. EARL MAYNARD in *The Deep* (1977)

Writer Peter Benchley's popular Bermudan scuba diving adventure features a pair of standout fights while serving to introduce a tough, hunky blond actor, Nick Nolte, to big-screen audiences as the hero.

It has been notoriously difficult to make underwater fights exciting for audiences so director Peter Yates wisely stages his two main battles on land. Midway through the film, the six-one, 185-pound Nolte squares off with six-two, 210-pound stunt actor Bob Minor 80 feet above the ground on a specially built cliffside elevator. It's a tense exchange of body positioning and punches reminis-

cent of the cramped fight in *Diamonds Are Forever* (1971). The Max Kleven–coordinated action has Minor travel down the elevator carriage while Nolte rides the counterbalance up with the two tangling in the middle. Yates filmed the exciting action in a basket suspended from a crane by steel wire at Marley Beach. Production designer Tony Masters conceived the elevator. Additional footage of this fight found its way into the extended TV broadcast.

Though stunt double Jim Nickerson did the second unit long shots, Nolte insisted on doing much of the fight. He and Minor were nearly injured when they accidentally hit a button during their struggle that caused the elevator to move unexpectedly. They stopped it an instant before the moving parts could have taken off Minor's arm. The climax of the fight has Minor plummeting to his death as the counterweights break loose, and Nolte reaches a perch. However, the broken cables snap past him and knock Nolte down the elevator shaft before he catches a handhold and climbs the rope. The thrilling scene was shot day-for-night with filters by Christopher Challis due to the problems of lighting an entire cliff. The lighting and the offbeat logistics left many viewers in the dark. The *New York Times* called it "a life-and-death fight on an outside elevator that I still can't figure out."

In a subplot, muscular Robert Tessier plays a rare good guy as dive-master star Robert Shaw's loyal friend. He is afforded the opportunity to have a great one-minute fight with 5'10", 225-pound professional wrestler Earl Maynard in a dive shop. Stunt coordinator Fred Stromsoe was suggested a prop outboard motor be used. Tough guys Tessier and Maynard insisted on a real motor and running blade, adding an extra sense of danger to the tense scene. *The Cavalier Daily* remarked that the fight was "so exciting you can scarcely watch them comfortably," while *The Michigan Daily* found it "memorable in its grisliness but so out of kilter with anything in the main storyline that the sequence looks like it could have been lifted from a completely different film." This isn't necessarily true. Keen viewers will note the foreshadowing in an earlier meeting where both actors mentally size one another up without saying a word. After that glare between them, it would have been disappointing had they not fought.

At one point in the fight choreography, Mr. Universe Maynard accidentally put his knee into Tessier's nose. Tessier shrugged off the injury and continued to film. As the fight climaxes, both men go to the neck and jockey for position, kicking at one another's legs as they each force the other's neck to the side. There's no music, only the eerily effective sound of the men's labored grunting. The scene fades with the sound of crackling bone. Shaw later finds Tessier's broken body hung against the wall, every bone and joint sadistically and grotesquely turned. Tessier and Maynard fought again in *The Sword and the Sorcerer* (1982) with Maynard emerging victorious after another gruesome battle.

Algonquin Indian Tessier, 6'1" and 230 pounds, served as a paratrooper during the Korean War before entering films as a stuntman in the 1960s. Tessier's break came opposing Tom Laughlin's Billy Jack as a menacing cyclist in *Born Losers* (1967). He is best known for shaving his head for *The Longest Yard* (1974) where, playing the toughest convict on the cellblock, he breaks Richard Kiel's nose with a karate blow and a sadistic grin on his face. Tessier famously fought Charles Bronson in *Hard Times* (1975) and took part in brawls in *Hooper* (1978) and

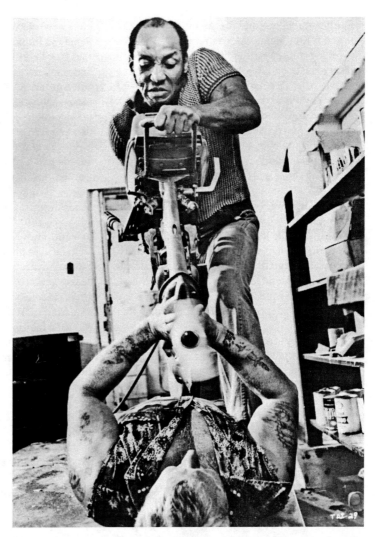

Earl Maynard (top) and Robert Tessier use a real running outboard motor as a weapon in Columbia's *The Deep* (1977).

The Cannonball Run (1981) (see entries). With 19" biceps and a 50" chest, Tessier had a reputation as one of the strongest and toughest men in Hollywood. He fought Ned Romero in *Last of the Mohicans* (1977), Dale Robinette in *The Billion Dollar Threat* (1979), and Marjoe Gortner in *Starcrash* (1979). As a guest he fought Robert Urich in the 1980 *Vegas* episode "Sudden Death" and challenged Mr. T in the *A-Team* episode "The Out of Towners."

See: Brownstein, Bill. "Top Gun Tessier Shoots Straight from the Hip." *Montreal Gazette.* April 20, 1985; Guber, Peter. *Inside the Deep.* New York: Bantam, 1977.

ROGER MOORE VS. RICHARD KIEL in *The Spy Who Loved Me* (1977)

Roger Moore hit his tongue-in-cheek stride with the third James Bond installment from director Lewis Gilbert and screenwriter Richard Maibaum. The film has spectacular action sequences courtesy of stunt coordinator Bob Simmons and perhaps the most memorable Bond villain yet in the form of giant, steel-toothed Jaws (Richard Kiel). Bond and Jaws have four fights, and the size discrepancy between the two borders on the comic as Kiel's huge hand literally covers all Moore's face as he manhandles him, first among Egyptian ruins and later in a train compartment, a Sardinian roadway and the Atlantis station. On the train, Kiel presses Moore repeatedly against the ceiling before he is shocked with an open lamp socket to his cobalt steel braces and kicked out the window. After each narrow Bond escape, the silent Kiel merely dusts off and goes about his business. Simmons and George Leech coordinated the fights with Martin Grace doubling Moore. Simmons and Grace both doubled Kiel, although they were a foot shorter. Action editor John Glen does well hiding the size discrepancy.

The 7'2", 330-pound Jaws character proved so popular that he was brought back for the next film *Moonraker* (1979), where he ultimately became a good guy and fought alongside Bond in the climax. The character enjoyed great cultural popularity. Kiel was director Gilbert's choice for the role, although boxer Jack O'Halloran, American Indian Will Sampson and British weightlifter Dave Prowse were under consideration. Even after Kiel had been signed for the role, the 6'7" Prowse was offered the opportunity to serve as Kiel's double. He declined, not wanting to be known as a stuntman instead of an actor. His greatest fame came embodying Darth Vader on *Star Wars* (1977), with James Earl Jones providing the distinctive voiceover for Prowse's physical actions.

For the stunt in the train compartment, Simmons opted to dive through real glass over the standard movie sugar glass. He thought the sugar glass looked fake and strived for realism, though he valued safety. Simmons perfected a method of punching through the glass as he dove, reasoning that stuntmen were only cut if they drew their hands in after making contact. The greatest difficulty posed to Simmons was that he had little room with which to get a running start for cinematographer Claude Renoir's camera. His first dive proved perfect. However, when standing up, he inadvertently pushed off from broken glass and cut his hand, requiring two minor stitches. Kiel worked closely with the stuntmen on a mock set before filming. For the part where Kiel pushes Moore against a wall, Simmons had to reposition a luggage cart to give them more room in which to work. They also determined that a shelf with a lamp needed to be moved closer so it was within Moore's reach when it came time to shock Kiel. Moore utilized mini-trampolines to get into the air so it looked like Kiel was effortlessly heaving him around. At one point, an articulated dummy was used in place of the star.

Moore also fights the burly, bald-headed Sandor (Milton Reid) on a Cairo rooftop. *The Spy Who Thrilled Us* cites this as one of the Bond films' better fights, but most fans consider it poorly realized and lacking intensity. Stuntman Jack Cooper doubled Reid for the 60-foot fall off the roof. Reid was a thickly built pro wrestler who had played a guard in the original Bond film *Dr. No* (1962), a credit that hindered his chances to be cast as Oddjob in *Goldfinger* (1964). He campaigned heavily, even going so far as to challenge fellow wrestler Harold Sakata to a winner-gets-the-role elimination match that was never realized.

A bar bouncer, Kiel didn't like to fight but enjoyed intimidating customers at both the Ragdoll and the Crossbow into behaving appropriately. In Hollywood he was often called upon to dwarf opponents in fights, none more so than Robert Conrad on TV's *The Wild Wild West*. He fought Ralph Taeger on *Klondike*, Chuck Connors on *The Rifleman* and Fess Parker on *Daniel Boone*. Kiel was limited in mobility, but to his credit did a great deal of his own fight work as he was difficult to double due to his immense size. Fights of interest came against Paul Mantee in *A Man Called Dagger* (1967), Carl Weathers in *Force 10*

Roger Moore (left) battles giant villain Richard Kiel in United Artists' *The Spy Who Loved Me* (1977).

from *Navarone* (1978) and Clint Eastwood in *Pale Rider* (1985).

See: Kiel, Richard. *Making It Big in the Movies*. Richmond: Reynolds & Hearn, 2002; Weaver, Tom. "Voltaire Talks." *Starlog*. #353. March 2007.

JACKIE CHAN VS. HWANG JANG LEE in *Snake in the Eagle's Shadow* (1978) and *Drunken Master* (1978)

In the wake of the violent chop-socky drivel filling the screens after the death of Bruce Lee came this groundbreaking back-to-back tandem of *Snake in the Eagle's Shadow* and *Drunken Master* starring Jackie Chan, previously thought to be no more than one of many Lee imitators. Rigorously trained in gymnastics and martial arts during his childhood at the Peking Opera's China Drama School, the 5'6", 150-pound Chan entered Hong Kong films as a stuntman opposite Bruce Lee in *The Chinese Connection* (1972) and *Enter the Dragon* (1973) (see entries) and had extreme acrobatic talent and fighting ability. However, the foremost trait setting him apart from the pack was his sense of humor. These are funny and highly entertaining action films with great extended fights against villain Hwang Jang Lee. The fight choreography is mind-boggling considering the intricate series of punches, kicks, blocks and flips filling the screen. Credit must also be given to first-time director and martial arts coordinator Yuen Woo Ping, who later contributed to fights in the *Matrix* and *Kill Bill* films. He was assisted by Corey Yuen (aka Yuen Kwai) and his brothers Yuen Chun-Wei and Yuen Shun-Yi. However, there's no denying the one person most responsible for making these films box office hits in his native country was Chan. The films proved so popular that Chan was brought to the U.S. and given a shot at stardom in *The Big Brawl* (1980). Eventually, he attained that lofty goal in America after becoming known for his oftentimes dangerous stunt work.

The plots of both films are remarkably similar. In *Snake in the Eagle's Shadow*, Chan plays a young man who apprentices from older master Simon Yuen (the director's father). He learns Snake Fist technique only to run into the flying feet of Hwang Jang Lee, an Eagle Claw master who wants to rid the world of all styles challenging his own. After taking much abuse throughout the film, Chan invents the superior Cat Claw technique to overcome his foe in an extended climactic showdown. In *Drunken Master*, Chan is once again taught by Simon Yuen, this time the legendary styles of the Eight Drunken Masters, who were great fighters because of unsteadiness and unpredictability in their fighting. The more alcohol Chan drinks, the better fighter he becomes. Chan plays the ridiculousness of the situation to the hilt, especially in the final showdown where he reveals to his master that he never bothered to properly learn the eighth drunken master's technique. He is forced to improvise on the spot to overcome the supremely evil Lee. The film is full of memorable fights. *The Ultimate Guide to Martial Arts Movies of the 1970s* called it "a landmark movie in the kung fu film genre and arguably one of Jackie Chan's best films." According to *Films of Fury*, the films are "brilliantly conceived and executed" and "perfectly designed for Chan's skills." *The Essential Jackie Chan Sourcebook* noted that *Drunken Master*'s 18-minute fight finale "literally sent kung fu aficionados hearts a-flutter."

Reasoning that no one could truly replace Bruce Lee, Chan opted to become the antithesis of the screen legend. Instead of kicking high and serious, Chan kicked low and with humor, often shaking his fist in pain after striking someone. Comedic facial expression played a great role in his ability to connect with audiences. The new

Jackie Chan (top) brings humor to his fight with Hwang Jang Lee in Seasonal Films' *Drunken Master* (1978).

genre of comic kung fu made inventive use of props and emphasized rhythm in the fights. Chan's tongue-in-cheek fighting style truly set him far apart from his contemporaries. However, pivotal to the success of these films is that Chan was facing a great fighter in the form of Hwang Jang Lee, a Tae Kwon Do instructor for the Korean Army and noted for the great power in his kicks. In martial arts magazines he was marketed as "the lord of leg combat." During his time in the service, he was challenged by a Vietnamese knife-fighting expert. Lee turned down the challenge, but when the aggressive opponent lunged at Lee with his knife, Lee delivered a roundhouse kick to the knife-fighter's head. The single kick killed the man; it was judged to be an act of self-defense. Lee began working in Korean action films in the early 1970s and achieved notoriety. This brought him to the attention of Hong Kong, who matched him up with Chan for these two films.

Friction between the two fighters first surfaced during the making of *Snake in the Eagle's Shadow*. This stemmed from a Lee kick that made contact with Chan and knocked out a tooth as evidenced on film at the end. Although Chan was angry about the injury, Lee was brought back for the second film. Lee once again made hard contact with Chan, and they never worked together again. Chan was also slashed on the arm by a sword, one of dozens of nicks, scrapes and major calamities that helped to define Chan as an action performer willing to take great risks to achieve big screen magic. In 1994, Chan made the official sequel *Legend of Drunken Master* (aka *Drunken Master II*) where he fought Kenneth Lo for 20 minutes in a fight that took four months to film.

By 1983, Chan had developed the Jackie Chan's Stuntman Association (employing up to two dozen members including his own bodyguards Ken Lo, Brad Allen and William Tuan), a group that worked on all Chan's films. Chan's fights and stunts became the films' focus, with months sometimes being devoted to completing a fight and hundreds of takes being filmed to perfect a stunt. Some of Chan's more famous set piece fights against his team of stuntmen were a bar fight and bicycle chase in *Project A* (1983), the mall melee in *Police Story* (1985), the playground fight in *Police Story 2* (1985), the prop-heavy fight against monks and amazons in *Armour of God* (1986), the factory fights in *Dragons Forever* (1987) and *Drunken Master II* (1994), the parlor fight in *Thunderbolt* (1995), the chairs and ladders fight in *First*

Strike* (1996), the runaway carriage fight in *Mr. Nice Guy* (1997), the saloon fight in *Shanghai Noon* (2000), a horseshoe fight in *Shanghai Knights* (2003), the art studio brawl in *Around the World in 80 Days* (2004) and the Lego Land fight in *New Police Story* (2004).

Chan had notable fights in *The Big Brawl* (1980), *The Cannonball Run* (1981), *Wheels on Meals* (1984) and *Twinkle, Twinkle Lucky Stars* (1985) (see entries). Fights of interest came against Dick Wei in *Project A* (1984), *My Lucky Stars* (1985) and *Heart of Dragon* (aka *First Mission*) (1985), Bill "Superfoot" Wallace in *The Protector* (1985), Andy Lau in *Island of Fire* (1991), Sam Wong in *Police Story 3: Supercop* (1992), Richard Norton and Gary Daniels in *City Hunter* (1993), Mark Akerstream in *Rumble in the Bronx* (1996), Nathan Jones in *First Strike* (1996), Richard Norton in *Mr. Nice Guy* (1997), Brad Allen in *Gorgeous* (1999), Ron Smoorenburg and Ken Lo in *Who Am I?* (1999), Donnie Yen in *Shanghai Knights* (2003), Andy On in *New Police Story* (2004) and Jet Li in *The Forbidden Kingdom* (2008).

See: Jackie Chan, *Drunken Master-Snake in the Eagle's Shadow*, Blu-Ray boxset; Kehr, Dave. "Chan Can Do." *Film Comment*. May-June 1988.

REB BROWN VS. THE PARTY CRASHERS in *Big Wednesday* (1978)

Writer-director John Milius' cult surfing movie tracks the lives of three Malibu surfers (Jan-Michael Vincent, William Katt and Gary Busey) from their irresponsible early 1960s youth through the 1970s. Despite the looming presence of Vietnam and personal problems along the way, the three reunite for one last mythical wave. In the early part of the film, Milius stages an entertaining three-minute fight between the surfer crowd and a group of party crashers led by Michael Talbot. The fun scene features a shirtless Busey, lathered in barbecue sauce, as the crazy Leroy the Masochist. A drunken Vincent wanders into the fight eating a watermelon and takes a fist through that melon from Al Wyatt, Jr. Robert Englund sprays a garden hose inside the house and Geoff Parks takes a tumble down the stairs (a stunt executed by Terry Leonard). When it looks like the crashers might be getting the better of Busey, the muscular Reb Brown comes down the stairs to the tune of Ray Charles warbling "What'd I Say?" The next minute is one of cinema's most convincing displays of screen fighting. The shirtless Brown cleans house on the crashers, destroying their tough guy Wyatt and taking out their karate man with great blocks and body blows. The crashers run into the night.

In throwing the first punch, Busey miscalculated a back-hand and broke Talbot's nose. Talbot understandably disappears for the remainder of the action. Stunt actor Wyatt miscalculated a punch and struck Brown in the jaw. The smile Brown gives on camera is genuine, and the subsequent body blows administered to Wyatt were not pulled according to Milius. Second generation stuntmen Diamond Farnsworth and John Robotham were uncredited crashers, while stunt actor Mike Raden represented the surfers. Busey and Brown did all their own fighting for Bruce Surtees' camera. There's another violent fight in a Tijuana bar started by Vincent. Stunt coordinator Leonard shows up as the bartender, and stuntmen Denny Arnold, Richard Epper, Ken Ferguson and a knife-wielding Thomas Rosales, Jr., take part.

Milius was a surfer in Malibu during the late 1950s and early 1960s and with co-writer Denny Aaberg based his characters on actual people from that era. Vincent's alcoholic surfer was fashioned after the talented nose-rider Lance Carson while Brown was based on Ray "The Malibu Enforcer" Kunze. The latter policed the beaches with his tough guy reputation. Fights between the Malibu crowd and the Valley kids were not uncommon, and on one occasion Kunze was said to have taken out a karate specialist. During the 1960s, Kunze moonlighted as a stuntman for the Beach Party flicks under the pseudonym Peter Proportion. He was on the *Big Wednesday* set to meet Brown and offer pointers. The fight shot for nearly one week on an MGM soundstage in August 1977. The young actors partied hard that week, although a somber mood came when it was announced Elvis Presley had died.

Reb Brown, 6'3" and 230 pounds, played football at USC and was discovered working as a bouncer at the Handlebar Saloon in Pasadena. He was intent on becoming a Los Angeles Sheriff's Deputy while embarking on a professional boxing career. With his handsome Nordic features and streamlined bodybuilder's physique, he epitomized the 1970s California beach lifestyle. Signed to a contract at Universal, he filmed two pilots as Captain America for a proposed 1979 TV series that fell through. He also starred as a bare-knuckle fighter in *Cage* (1989) opposite Lou Ferrigno.

Brown had his best fight with martial artist Steve James in *Street Hunter* (1990). TV audiences fondly remember him taking on Don Johnson in the 1987 *Miami Vice* episode "Viking Bikers from Hell."

See: *Big Wednesday* DVD commentary; Hernandez, Marjorie. "Captain America Is a Superstar in Camarillo." *Ventura County Star*. July 21, 2011; Ligon, Patty. "Stunt Filming Choreographed." *El Paso Herald Post*. July 22, 1977; Wharton, David. "To Protect and Surf." *Los Angeles Times*. June 7, 2005.

THE TRUCKSTOP FIGHT in *Convoy* (1978)

Legendary director Sam Peckinpah created a hit with the trucker film *Convoy*, but the runaway production was the nail in the coffin of his professional career. Indicative of the times, the trucks may have been fueled by diesel, but cocaine was what kept many cast and crew running with their chemically deranged leader on location in New Mexico. All but six crew members were fired from the film, which went so far over budget and time they had to take a break in shooting to allow musician star Kris Kristofferson to complete a prearranged concert tour. James Coburn came in as a second unit director and tried to keep his friend Peckinpah in check, but he was too far gone. The excessive care he had put into such personal and poetic westerns as *Ride the High Country* (1962), *Major Dundee* (1965), *The Wild Bunch* (1969), *The Ballad of Cable Hogue* (1970) and *Pat Garrett and Billy the Kid* (1973) paled in comparison to the time spent on what he knew in his heart was a piece of schlock created to cash in on the CB trucker craze. The producers were ready to fire Peckinpah, but Kristofferson stood up for his director and threatened to quit. Peckinpah later railed at Kristofferson for keeping him on the film.

An ill-prepared and indecisive Peckinpah had Harry Stradling, Jr., shoot reels of coverage with multiple cameras, hoping he and his small army of editors could salvage something in postproduction, but when it came down to it most of the B.W.L. Norton–scripted film consisted of Kristofferson and female lead Ali MacGraw sitting in the cab of a truck. Peckinpah doubled the $6 million dollar budget with his delays and lost all the clout he was once able to muster in butting heads with the studios. Peckinpah would die in a few years after being given one last chance with the interesting but failed thriller *The Osterman*

Weekend (1983). Despite his apathy toward *Convoy*, the anti-establishment film became a cult movie with its target audience. Critics lambasted it, save for the action and stunts. The *Los Angeles Times* called its fisticuffs "spectacular," while the *Montreal Gazette* wrote, "There are a few flashes of Peckinpah's talents, in a slow-motion fight scene, for example, and some pretty shots of trucks driving through blowing sand."

One set piece is a nearly three-minute diner brawl between the truckers and bad guy sheriff Ernest Borgnine's beefy deputies Jim Burk and Allen Keller. A catalyst for the plot, the 11-person fight was scheduled to be shot over three days early in the production but wound up taking Peckinpah a week and a half to film. The fight at the Silver Cloud diner in Algodones became half-slapstick in nature as Peckinpah utilized his penchant for slow-motion action to dwell on broken ketchup bottles, smashed glass, flying chairs and tumbling bodies. It's as if he was knowingly parodying himself. *Texas Monthly* felt, "The slow-motion brawl at the diner actually lessens the impact of the fight; it merely becomes an abstract lesson in technique." Kristofferson is involved in much of the action, although stunt coordinator Gary Combs fills in for one backward fall. Trucker Burt Young engages in the fight action with a bemused grin on his face. Bob Herron was on hand to double Borgnine, who's knocked out by a Kristofferson kick early in the fight. Jophery Brown doubled Franklyn Ajaye while Jadie David subbed for Madge Sinclair. Truckers Whitey Hughes, Billy Hughes and Tommy Huff were pro stuntmen.

Five-eleven and 165 pounds, Kristofferson was a Golden Gloves boxer and played football at Pomona College before joining the Army as an Airborne Ranger. He volunteered to fly helicopters in Vietnam but wound up working construction jobs while pursuing a career as a country songwriter in Nashville. The Rhodes scholar was a walking contradiction, his intelligence and literate ability seemingly at odds with his penchant for drinking and punching out problems. He was the toughest troubadour in town, but for years fought problems with alcohol. As a screen fighter he had grit and swagger and could work with the stuntmen but wasn't always good at pulling his punches. He sent Keith Carradine to the hospital with an errant blow on *Trouble in Mind* (1985). One of his more memorable fights came against celebrity heckler Robert Englund in *A Star Is Born* (1976).

See: Fine, Marshall. *Bloody Sam: The Life and*

Films of Sam Peckinpah. New York: DI Fine, 1991; Gallagher, Hugh. "*Convoy* Movie Filming Goes On." *Albuquerque Journal*. May 29, 1977; Miller, Stephen. *Kristofferson: The Wild American*. London: Omnibus, 2008.

THE PALOMINO BAR BRAWL in *Hooper* (1978)

Director Hal Needham and star Burt Reynolds called *Hooper* an ode to all stuntmen, although some interpret it to be autobiographical on both Needham and Reynolds' parts. Aging, broken-down Sonny Hooper is Hollywood's top stuntman, but he's being challenged for his title by young up-and-comer Jan-Michael Vincent. In many ways it parallels Needham's transition from bone-breaking macho man in front of the camera to the man calling shots behind it. The Vincent character has been said to be based on Stan Barrett, a Needham protégé who often worked with Reynolds. At the same time, Reynolds plays up his own love for stunts, even going so far as to watch footage of himself riding rapids in *Deliverance* (1972) under the guise of it being Hooper doing stunt work. What's more, Sally Field is the female love interest and her father is a legendary stuntman named Jocko, played by a crusty, scene-stealing Brian Keith. In real life, Field's stepfather was actor-stuntman Jock Mahoney, and some claim *Hooper* is based partly on his rambunctious adventures. Others say it's about Buddy Joe Hooker, arguably the top stuntman in town when *Hooper* was made. He worked on the film as Jan-Michael Vincent's double.

The film is full of great stunts and scant on character development, save for when Keith lands in a hospital bed and Reynolds sees his own future flash before his eyes. There's an interesting character to be found in a man who beats himself up for a living and reaches the end of his physical abilities, but Reynolds falls back too often on his familiar charming smile and self-amused laugh to add much substance to the part. This is never more apparent than in the three-minute bar fight at the Palomino Club, the legendary country music venue once located in North Hollywood. Reynolds and his stuntman pals are too loud for real-life Pittsburgh Steelers quarterback Terry Bradshaw and Robert Tessier, members of a S.W.A.T. team who complain they have money in the jukebox. Reynolds puts on a helmet and moronically smashes his head into the music machine to reimburse them. He then sucker punches Bradshaw, who spits out a tooth and smiles. It's obvious the violence will be played for laughs as Bradshaw's hand breaks the silly helmet with a punch.

A rowdy Keith has some humorous moments during the ensuing battle as he quips to James Best, "We're getting too old for this shit," and Field garners laughs as she finishes her meal amidst the flying bodies. Norm Grabowski distracts an opponent by lifting the Roman centurion skirt he's clad in. Tessier and Vincent square off, but they're given too little screen time to make an impact. Mostly it's a succession of stuntmen doing

Burt Reynolds (left) and Jan-Michael Vincent in a fight seen only on some TV prints of Warner Bros.' *Hooper* (1978).

their thing in the Bobby Bass–coordinated action, including Jim Burk, Tony Epper, Walter Wyatt, Jim Connors, Bennie Moore, Jophery Brown, Fred Schiewiller, Bob Orrison, Tommy Huff, Tom Elliot, Billy Hank Hooker, J.N. Roberts and Gary McLarty. Stan Barrett was Reynolds' double. Bradshaw's offensive lineman Sam Davis and former Philadelphia Eagles linebacker Tim Rossovich play bouncers. The latter lifts Reynolds over his head and tosses him out the back window before gallantly assisting Field out. Bradshaw, Vincent and Tessier follow, while Keith tosses himself out the window. Bradshaw injured his throwing elbow when he flew out the fake window. They all improbably bond in the trash and end up watching movies at Reynolds' home. Cut from the theatrical print but later shown on an expanded network TV telecast was a fistfight between Reynolds and Vincent. *Variety* called the Palomino brawl "skillfully executed," while *The Miami News* termed it "a classic Hollywood bar brawl."

Brian Keith served with the Marines during World War II as an aerial gunner. He attained the rank of sergeant but was busted down to corporal after getting into a barroom brawl. The former dockworker entered films as a stunt double for Victor Mature. Six-one and 195 pounds, he earned a reputation as a drinker and brawler, as well as a consummate character lead. One of his first parts came as the star of a *Mike Hammer* TV pilot. He gave an early glimpse of judo skill facing Chuck

Courtney in *5 Against the House* (1955). The rugged, plain-spoken Keith was a longtime iron lifter at Vince's Gym in Studio City. His strength was considerable, as was his punch. While guesting on the 1963 *Fugitive* episode "Fear in a Desert City," he accidentally broke star David Janssen's ribs with a mistimed punch.

Fights of interest came against Robert Ryan in *Alaska Seas* (1954), Fernando Lamas in *Jivaro* (1954), Aldo Ray in *Nightfall* (1957), Clint Walker in *Fort Dobbs* (1958), James Drury in *Ten Who Dared* (1960), James Stewart in *The Rare Breed* (1966), Dean Martin in *something big* (1971), Terry Leonard in *The Wind and the Lion* (1975) and Charlton Heston in *The Mountain Men* (1980). On the 1959 pilot to the short-lived TV classic *The Westerner* (1960), aired as a segment of *Zane Grey Theater*, Keith had a rough-and-tumble fight with villain Neville Brand and surprisingly came out the loser. On the series itself, Keith fought Slim Pickens in "Line Camp" and had a running brawl with John Dehner in "Brown," "The Courting of Libby" and "The Painting." One of his most memorable fights came against Geoffrey Toone in 1960's "Jeff."

See: Bradshaw, Terry, and Buddy Martin. *Looking Deep*. New York: Berkley, 1991; *Hooper* pressbook; "Brian Keith." *TV Guide*. May 26, 1984; Van Gelder, Lawrence. "Brian Keith, Hardy Actor, 75; Played Dads and Desperadoes." *New York Times*. June 25, 1997.

CLINT EASTWOOD VS. WALTER BARNES in *Every Which Way but Loose* (1978)

The hard-hitting back alley bare-knuckle brawls of *Hard Times* (1975) get a broad comic treatment from Clint Eastwood, who plays simple California mechanic Philo Beddoe. The truck-driving modern cowboy's constant companion is a scene-stealing orangutan named Clyde, with Eastwood's pal Geoffrey Lewis arranging the pick-up fights. In addition to jaw-cracking fights with George P. Wilbur, William J. Quinn and Walter Barnes in front of enthusiastic betting crowds, Eastwood has running fisticuffs with vindictive cop Gregory Walcott and John Quade's embarrassing motorcycle gang The Black Widows (consisting of Roy Jenson, Dan Vadis, Bill McKinney and Gene LeBell spoofing their tough guy images). He begins the James Fargo–directed film by knocking around Bob Golden over a handful of peanuts.

Hardly five minutes goes by without Eastwood punching someone.

The punches heard here are perhaps the loudest sound effects ever associated with a movie punch. Critic Roger Ebert noted it sounded like someone was whacking a Naugahyde sofa with a ping pong paddle. Cinematographer Rexford Metz used hand-held Panaflex and Eyemo cameras while assuming the position of the opposing fighter taking punches from Eastwood. Generalized lighting allowed him to look in any direction. The technique greatly enhanced the fights and made the audience feel they were a participant instead of an observer. Editors Ferris Webster and Joel Cox cut back and forth between these point-of-view shots and established a rhythm with the trading of punches. *Variety* wrote, "Action sequences are acceptably choreographed." According to *Knockout*, "[The film] establishes a new landscape for working-class culture in the fight film."

The climactic fight is the most memorable as

Clint Eastwood (center) takes on an entire motorcycle gang with his fists in Warner Bros.' *Every Which Way but Loose* (1978).

Eastwood meets up with bare-knuckle legend Tank Murdock, played by 6'1", 245-pound football pro Walter Barnes. Eastwood is shocked to find Murdock is gray, heavy in the gut, and wearing his old varsity sweater. Barnes is letter perfect in the role, portraying a true tough guy whose best days are far behind him. When they begin to trade punches, it becomes obvious to Eastwood that Barnes is riding on reputation alone. As he knocks his counterpart about, he begins to hear the crowd murmur he's going to be the new Tank Murdock. Feeling sympathy for the older fighter and pangs of doubt at becoming the new man to be taken down, Eastwood leaves himself open for a final desperation shot. After taking Barnes' Sunday punch, Eastwood stays down for the count. The moment lends a sudden sense of depth and character to what for much of the film had been the equivalent of a crude romp of cartoon violence.

The Murdock character was based on a real person who traveled around the country fighting for money. The script was submitted to Eastwood through a friend because they thought he could give it to Burt Reynolds. Eastwood took a shine to the unlikely project, seeing it as a vehicle to soften his own image and tap into the late 1970s "good old boy" market that Reynolds had so much success with via *Smokey and the Bandit* (1977). Eastwood, after all, was a bit of a California cowboy already familiar with the honkytonks that Philo Beddoe traversed. Everyone associated with Eastwood told him he was crazy to take on the movie, but he went ahead. When released, the movie became Eastwood's biggest moneymaker to date, proving all his naysayers wrong.

To train for the fights, Eastwood hired veteran boxing trainer Al Silvani, who had worked with Jake LaMotta and Rocky Graziano, among 20 world champs. Silvani was a longtime pal of Frank Sinatra, often traveling with the Rat Pack and playing minor bits or stunt parts in Sinatra's films. Here he appears as Murdock's manager. Eastwood also upped his weight workouts. Despite being 47, Eastwood never appeared more muscular. He did all his own fights, though George Orrison and stunt coordinator Buddy Van Horn were on hand if needed. Chuck Hicks doubled Barnes for a couple of knockdowns. The film ultimately gave Eastwood the image of a man who was tough with or without a gun at his side. Eastwood followed with a sequel, *Any Which Way You Can* (1980) (see entry), featuring an even bigger and better climactic fight with William Smith.

See: Anderson, Bob. "Walter Barnes Interview." *Trail Dust Magazine.* Winter 1995-Spring 1996; *Every Which Way but Loose* pressbook; Grindon, Legar. *Knockout: The Boxer and Boxing in American Cinema.* Jackson: University Press of Mississippi, 2011.

MASTER BONG SOO HAN VS. ED PARKER in *Kill the Golden Goose* (1979)

This intriguing match-up between the leading masters of Hapkido and Kenpo karate was promoted in martial arts magazines as one of the greatest film fights in history. Unfortunately, it's far from it because of marginal production values, bad acting, dated fashion trends, rushed choreography and ho-hum direction from Elliot Hong (aka Hong Eiu Bo). The film received a scant release. The foremost problem is Master Bong Soo Han as Captain Han, Los Angeles police detective who does all his fights in wide collar leisure suits. While his martial arts kicks are solid, his acting is hilariously bad and he gives the most wooden line readings imaginable. The film begs for an actual actor to be cast in this starring role. Fellow martial artist Ed Parker makes for an effectively menacing bad guy in the part of Mauna Loa, a hit man named after a Hawaiian volcano. The problem with Parker is his quick and direct Kenpo moves are difficult to capture for the cameras. The producers asked Parker for a rough and realistic streetfighting style before filming, so it may not be his Kenpo at fault. Parker's fights are exceedingly violent, and the camera often cuts away from his bare-handed beatings, giving the film a cheap and choppily edited feel.

When it comes time for the much anticipated two-and-a-half-minute Han-Parker warehouse battle (choreographed by the masters), the audience quickly realizes that neither martial artist is willing to show his own style as inferior. Instead, we're treated to lots of parrying and little actual contact. Han throws some fancy kicks that largely miss, while Parker gets to demonstrate his prowess twirling a chain, a staff and a light pole. Han breaks a board and Parker shows off his power smashing a chair Han wields as defense, but those are the few lively moments. It's a disappointment after the heavy hype that had people envisioning an epic fight along the lines of Bruce Lee and Chuck Norris in *Way of the Dragon* (1972). The moment Parker connects with the light pole and gains the upper hand, cop Brad Von Beltz shoots him with a powerful .454 Casule handgun. Parker, wearing a bullet-proof vest, moves toward Von Beltz, but Han lands a jumping kick from behind. Parker is pushed into an exposed industrial blade and dies.

The reality of the situation is the film was budgeted for $300,000 with half of that money in deferments, meaning the movie cost $150,000 to make. While Bruce Lee spent weeks plotting out his fights before they went before the cameras, Han and Parker did no preparation or blocking at all. They merely stepped into the warehouse the producers had secured for a 24-hour shoot, looked around for useful props and began to fight with whatever was at hand. Such a situation could pose many dangers, but Han and Parker had no problems. Unfortunately, since there were many other scenes to shoot in the location, they didn't have much time to perfect their moves. Then there was the matter of who'd be shown to have the upper hand at any given moment. As a result, the fight suffers. According to *The Ultimate Guide to Martial Arts Movies of the 1970s*, the viewer is "short-changed by what could have been a truly great fight scene."

The film was co-written and produced by noted writer and martial arts devotee Joe Hyams, who also plays one of Parker's victims. His co-writer and co-producers were western movie actor Von Beltz (aka Brad Weston) and Patrick Strong, who trained with Bruce Lee as far back as the early 1960s in Seattle. Strong has a brief parking garage fight with Han that's superior to the final battle. He is credited as a choreographer with Han for that fight. Another important behind-the-scenes figure is Russell Dodson, who served as an associate producer, 2nd unit director and stunt coordinator. Dodson was a martial arts choreographer for *The Kentucky Fried Movie* (1977) with Han and had worked with Parker in *Revenge of the Pink Panther* (1978). Dodson appears in *Kill the Golden Goose* as Parker's brother-in-law, a karate teacher paid a visit by Han. He and his muscular cohort A.J. Rosenthal are dispatched with ease by Han in a fight that's also superior to the climactic Han-Parker fight.

The six-foot, 210-pound Parker has a short fight with six-foot, 230-pound bodybuilder Ken Waller. The Mr. Universe was known as a tough guy in bodybuilding circles. He served in the Marines and played football collegiately at Western Kentucky and professionally in Canada. His presence was promoted through bodybuilding magazines.

He injured his elbow in the fight when he was knocked onto a table. His fight with Parker necessitated a second take because Waller's neck was so thick he couldn't effectively snap it back to simulate being hit. Noted Kenpo masters Larry Tatum and Rainer Schulte also show up *sans* billing to be dispatched by Parker.

Native Hawaiian Ed Parker was introduced to Kenpo in the late 1940s by Frank Chow, Adriano Emperado and William K.S. Chow. After serving with the U.S. Coast Guard during the Korean War, Parker opened his own influential studio. Parker's Kenpo used linear and circular motion with multiple strikes delivered in quick succession to vital parts of the opponent's body with the hands, elbows and knees. Instead of the traditional, one or two commonly taught movements, Parker advocated a series of powerful, continuously flowing movements designed to incapacitate and injure the opponent over simply allowing one to escape an attack. His system was flexible in thought and action, often a reaction to a particular situation or attack. Parker essentially added a strong offense to the art of self-defense.

To introduce his system, Parker typically arranged a demo at a gym and allowed the toughest guys to try landing a punch on him. None were successful. Parker was unique for a martial artist because he lifted weights for power. In 1956, he opened a dojo in Pasadena, California, and began taking on celebrity clients such as director Blake Edwards. This led to occasional film and television work as a technical advisor and stunt fighter. Parker met resistance from established stuntmen within the industry who felt he was taking work away from them. Parker's most famous celebrity client became Elvis Presley, who first met Parker in the early 1960s and trained with him periodically while making movies. By the 1970s, Parker became one of the singer's most trusted friends and often traveled on tour as a bodyguard. The two had hoped to make their own martial arts action film, *The New Gladiators*, but Presley's manager Colonel Tom Parker nixed the notion. Footage bankrolled by Presley of martial arts tournaments and personal training appeared as a *New Gladiators* (2002) documentary.

Parker had behind-the-scenes involvement in *The Manchurian Candidate* (1962) (see entry) and displayed his Kenpo skills as the formidable assassin Mr. Chong in *Revenge of the Pink Panther* (1978). Fights of interest came against Dean Martin in *The Wrecking Crew* (1969), Earl Owensby in *Buckstone County Prison* (aka *Seabo*) (1977) and Tino Tuisolega in *Seven* (1979), a Hawaiian-made action film starring Parker's student William Smith. Parker can be seen training with Smith in the pilot to *The Rockford Files* (1974). Parker's student Jeff Speakman debuted in *The Perfect Weapon* (1990), which remains the best showcase on film for Parker's Kenpo style. Credited as the film's technical advisor, Parker died from a heart attack before its release.

See: Kerr, Leslie-Ann. "Bong Soo Han in *Kill the Golden Goose*." *Fighting Stars*. April 1980; Parker, Edmund K., and M. Leilani Parker. *Memories of Ed Parker: Senior Grand Master of American Kenpo Karate*. Create Space, 2013; Roberson, Tim. "Ed Parker Rides the Waves of Martial Arts Films." *Fighting Stars*. December 1979.

JEFF COOPER VS. DAVID CARRADINE in *Circle of Iron* (aka *The Silent Flute*) (1979)

This mystical martial arts adventure was the brainchild of Bruce Lee, James Coburn and screenwriter Stirling Silliphant. Unfortunately, the final product is a misfire, especially hurt by poor casting and subpar fight choreography. It disappointed many, although the ideas and philosophy presented are of interest. Israeli locations add much to the look of the film, directed by first-timer Richard Moore, previously a D.P. who originally considered the script to *The Silent Flute* unfilmable. After Lee's untimely 1973 death, the project attracted new interest when it became attached to producer Sandy Howard and actor David Carradine, who had great name recognition thanks to the popularity of the early 1970s *Kung Fu* TV series. But Carradine wasn't a martial artist, merely an athletic actor who had some training. He was an interesting presence, though, and able to portray the multitude of parts Lee had originally envisioned playing. That left the role of Cord the seeker, who'd carry the bulk of the action.

Karate champion Joe Lewis was originally offered the role of Cord but turned it down largely because he didn't want to work fights with a non-martial artist like Carradine. Well-built blond actor Jeff Cooper was earmarked by Carradine from the beginning, despite the fact his martial arts skills weren't much better than his longtime friend Carradine's. The 6'3" Cooper, best known for opposing Tom Laughlin in *Born Losers* (1967), had been sparring with Carradine at Kam Yuen's.

He was a genuinely hard guy and a deep thinker, but the role of Cord didn't fit him. Nearing 40, he was far too old for the part despite being in fantastic shape. His greatest offense in the eyes of martial arts fans was the fact that his kicks lacked snap and height. *The Ultimate Guide to Martial Arts Movies of the 1970s* writes, "This film does not deliver on the martial arts fight scenes on any level." *Films of Fury* simply calls it "awful."

Stunt coordinator Terry Leonard had little to do with the martial arts choreography. That responsibility fell to Yuen, Carradine's trainer and the man who had taken over the fights of the final season of *Kung Fu*. Unfortunately, Carradine and Cooper, for all their enthusiasm simply didn't have the skill level needed to pull off the fights successfully either between themselves or with fellow fighters Earl Maynard, Anthony DeLongis, Mike Vendrell, Wilbur Chang, Tom Ascensio, Donnie Williams, James Watson, Bob Gardner, Milan Shelden and Leo Whang. Cinematographer Ronnie Taylor, despite a storied history as a cameraman, didn't have much experience doing fights outside *Barry Lyndon* (1975) and a few episodes of television's *The Avengers*. Joe Lewis was brought in at the end of production in an attempt to save the fights. Lewis doubled Cooper for some kicks and hired Mike Stone to double Carradine in pick-up scenes filmed near Los Angeles. The star took that as a great insult to all the training he had put in with Yuen, but Lewis was able to show Carradine kicks that looked much better on screen than what he had been doing. The same producers starred Lewis in *Jaguar Lives!* (1979), where he had a well-mounted climactic fight with Anthony DeLongis.

Before the arrival of Lewis, the fights were not going well. Some of that had to do with budgetary limitations and the extra time director Moore was spending trying to coax a passable lead performance from Cooper. The stars were hurting one another physically to the detriment of the film. Cooper had a tooth knocked out by Carradine on the first day of filming. Carradine broke his nose twice when playing the monkey man character. On the first occasion, Yuen broke it. Four days later, Cooper reinjured it. Carradine also gouged a toe and hurt his knee, which further hindered his ability to move gracefully on camera. Most critics attacked Cooper's performance and the film as philosophical nonsense, but the *Pittsburgh Post-Gazette* did write, "The fighting, surprisingly, is one of the best things in the film. It is violent, of course, but virtually bloodless and carefully cho-reographed and photographed so that at times it seems more a dance film than anything else."

Six-foot-one, 175-pound Carradine became a leading figure in the martial arts craze of the 1970s via *Kung Fu* (1972–1975) once he beat out real martial artist Bruce Lee for the role of half–Chinese drifter Kwai Chang Caine. Thanks to early dance training, the lanky Carradine had a strong pair of legs that served him well for all the jumping and kicking. Every *Kung Fu* episode had at least one or two confrontations in which pacifist Caine kicked the snot out of prejudiced cowboys with his bare feet. Due to censorship rules, the show was limited to four minutes of violence an episode. Those four minutes were undeniably the most popular with audiences. The choreography effectively used slow motion for the fights and became a huge hit.

Carradine had no martial arts background when cast but soon began sporadic training with Yuen. Many of his roles involved fights, and Carradine often incorporated kicks into his films whether he knew what he was doing or not. He looked passable enough to general audiences who readily accepted him as a real tough guy. However, the eccentric free spirit earned a Hollywood reputation for being undisciplined in fights. He often made contact with actors and stuntmen, and his open drug and alcohol use negatively affected his once promising career. Carradine's best *Kung Fu* fight came against a chain-wielding William Smith in 1973's "The Chalice." He also fought the likes of Roy Jenson, John Saxon, Robert Phillips, Don Stroud, Bo Svenson, Carl Weathers, Bill Saito and David Chow. He rebooted the Caine character for the 1986 telefilm *Kung Fu: The Movie*, fighting William Lucking and Bruce Lee's son Brandon. On his 1966 western TV series *Shane*, he fought Charles Grodin and Ross Hagen in "The Great Invasion."

Carradine fought Glenn Ford in *Heaven with a Gun* (1969), Sylvester Stallone in *Death Race 2000* (1975), Bill McKinney in *Cannonball* (1976), Charles Napier in *Thunder and Lightning* (1977), James Remar in *The Long Riders* (1980), Chuck Norris in *Lone Wolf McQuade* (1983) (see entry), Anthony DeLongis in *The Warrior and the Sorceress* (1984), Patrick Swayze in the TV mini-series *North and South Book II* (1986), Mel Gibson in *Bird on a Wire* (1990) and Chad McQueen in *Martial Law* (1990). In 2004, he was cast by Quentin Tarantino as the title character in *Kill Bill*. Carra-

dine trained for three months with Yuen Woo Ping in preparation for his brief sword battle with Uma Thurman.

See: *Circle of Iron* DVD commentary; "The Reincarnation of Bruce Lee's *The Silent Flute*." *Fighting Stars*. February 1977; Schimpff, Connie. "The Awakening of *The Silent Flute*." *Fighting Stars*. February 1978; Thomas, Bruce. *Bruce Lee: Fighting Spirit*. Berkeley, CA: Frog, 1995.

PETER HEHIR vs. STEVE RACKMAN in *The Last of the Knucklemen* (1979)

The Last of the Knucklemen was a critically acclaimed Australian indie about a group of rugged Outback miners held together by tough foreman Gerard Kennedy despite near-constant in-fighting. Their isolated environment leaves little opportunity for any distraction outside drinking and gambling. The graying hard-case Kennedy is front and center throughout writer-director Tim Burstall's impressive adaptation of John Power's play, although his authority as "the last of the knucklemen" is challenged at every turn by the manipulative Michael Preston. In the background is the quiet and mysterious Peter Hehir, who with his thin build and shaggy blond hair throws everyone a curve when he opts to step in and fight Preston's huge German stooge Steve Rackman in Kennedy's place. After laying down a significant wager on the outcome, Hehir makes his case that Kennedy's fight is with Preston, and Kennedy can see the wisdom in that argument. Hehir surprises everyone when he turns out to be a black belt who destroys Rackman with his powerful kicks both inside and outside the miner's desolate tin shed quarters in under two minutes. The end credits roll with Kennedy fighting Preston against the red desert landscape in long shot, their fight ultimately insignificant and never-ending with no clear winner. In scenarios such as these, men will always clash with one another.

Six-foot-one Gerard Kennedy was a popular star of Australian TV while the six-foot Michael Preston had briefly been a professional boxer in his native England. Steve "Crusher" Rackman was a popular professional wrestler in Australia and had a background as both a boxer and a bouncer. Rackman does his own stunts in the fight, including going through the wall of the shed and breaking a car window with his head. Hehir was doubled throughout by Aussie martial artist Richard Norton. His presence is well-concealed by cinematographer Dan Burstall. The fight was choreographed by Australian stuntmen Graham Mathrick and Matt Burns.

See: Murphy, Jim. "Mike Hits the Right Note." *Australian Women's Weekly*. March 11, 1981; Murphy, Jim. "The Secret Life: Gerard Kennedy." *Australian Women's Weekly*. November 12, 1980.

THE BASEBALL FURIES AND MEN'S ROOM FIGHTS in *The Warriors* (1979)

Director Walter Hill, the man behind the camera for the great Charles Bronson fights in *Hard Times,* returned with a no-name cast but plenty of stylized action scenes that stirred up real violence in theaters upon the film's release. In addition to vandalism, there were three deaths at screenings around the country. The fast-moving plot is based on a Sol Yurick novel from the Greek *Anabasis* and concerns the assassination of a charismatic street gang leader who had hoped to unify all the youth in New York City to rise together. The real culprit David Patrick Kelly pens the blame on the Warriors, whose small group must escape across town on foot at night to their own home turf in Coney Island. It becomes a tense, nightmarish world of fight after fight against all the rival gangs who are out to do them in. Two battles stand out from the rest: the Riverside Park fight against the Baseball Furies who dress in New York Yankee pinstripes and face paint while arming themselves with ball bats; and the men's room fight against the Punks.

Movie Maker called it "stylishly photographed with amazing fight sequences," while *The Stanford Daily* wrote, "Walter Hill directs the chase and fight sequences with a touch of genius." The *New York Times* was also impressed: "Mr. Hill stages some wonderfully looking encounters." The *Chicago Sun Times* termed it "a ballet of stylized male violence." *The Motion Picture Guide* added, "The fight scenes are brilliantly

choreographed, and instead of focusing on the violence Hill concentrates on pure movement." *Orange Coast Magazine* called the fights some of the most violent in screen history. *Action Films* places the bathroom fight among its all-time great battles: "[It's] a perfect blend of mixed fighting styles, fast editing and pulse-pounding rock soundtrack."

At Hill's direction, stunt coordinator Craig R. Baxley kept the fights realistic and grounded. They were so violent that much of the action didn't survive censors for its eventual television broadcast. Hill had Andrew Laszlo shoot from low angles, utilizing multiple viewpoints and quick cuts to achieve a flowing sense of energy and momentum with the constant movement on screen. The editing and overall presentation was slick with a young cast acquitting themselves well. Among the Warriors, Michael Beck as Swan and James Remar as Ajax stand out. Remar is a revelation as the cocky Ajax. When it comes time to rumble, he backs up every one of his boasts and proves to be a great fighter. Remar and Ajax became audience favorites

Michael Beck (left) goes to bat against Steven Chambers in Paramount's *The Warriors* (1979).

as the film took on a cult following. Remar is only around for the fight in the park, during which he cleans up on the opposition. Soon after, he tries to pick up Mercedes Ruehl but finds out she's a cop. Handcuffed to a park bench, he's last seen struggling against his bonds.

Due to budgetary constraints, the studio refused Baxley's request to bring highly paid Hollywood stuntmen with him to New York, so he used members of the recently formed Stunt Specialists and a variety of gymnasts and dancers adept at body movement. He put the main actors through an abbreviated stunt school so they wouldn't need to be doubled, a smart move that greatly aided the way the fights came off. The sinewy Beck, a football quarterback for Millsaps College, was able to handle the action requirements. He set the athletic pace for the rest of the cast, who had to do scene after scene of running throughout the film. Remar kept in solid muscular shape by lifting weights for the role, and the two young stars often performed push-ups between takes to keep their bare arms pumped for the cameras.

The two-minute Riverside Park fight occurs with the cleated Furies in hot pursuit of a fragmented group of Warriors on glistening streets as Barry Devorzon's synthesizer score builds superb tension. Swan and Cowboy (Tom McKittich) duck away from Ajax and Snow (Brian Taylor), leaving those two as the primary focus of the Furies. When Snow begins to tire from the chase, Remar announces he's sick of running. When the first Fury knocks out Snow and brandishes a baseball bat, Remar famously declares, "I'm going to shove that up your ass and turn you into a Popsicle." The fight was graphically written by Hill and co-scripter David Shaber and featured little musical accompaniment despite producer Lawrence Gordon's suggestion that a score might diffuse the impact of the violence. Hill made the Baseball Furies distinctive soldiers by having them run in single file with military spacing and stopping on a mark. There was so much running to do, the stuntmen tired and a group called the New York Roadrunners were brought in for a night of running scenes.

The Baseball Furies each had a different makeup scheme. Leader Jerry Hewitt had yellow face paint and a black eye. Steven Chambers had a purple and black face while Leon Delaney had an orange face with black eyes and lips. Others were Richard Chiotti, Tony Catham, Gene Bicknell, T.J. McNamara, Lane Ruoff, Harry Madsen, Bill Anagnos, John Gibson and Steve James. Rob Ryder served as a location scout but assumed the role of the black and blue Fury when the original stuntman blew out his knee. Ryder squared off against Beck in the fight. Real 36" baseball bats were used, and the fight was rehearsed for two weeks before going before the cameras. Hill hoped to achieve the feeling of a Kurosawa samurai film with this fight.

The 90-second Union Station subway men's room fight was the lone scene not shot on location. It was shot over a period of five days at the Astoria Studios in Astoria, Queens. Portraying the punks are Konrad Sheehan, Craig R. Baxley, Gary Baxley, A.J. Bakunas, Eddie Earl Hatch, Tommy Huff and Leon Delaney. Sheehan, on roller skates, is the most notable with his long hair and black shirt with yellow stripes; the role is often attributed to Craig Baxley. Again Hill builds great tension with the synthesizer score as Sheehan checks under the stalls for the Warriors, who ultimately burst out in a flurry of fists, elbows and bats appropriated from the Furies. Snow again distinguishes himself as one to be reckoned with as he lays into the Punks. Even the skinny Rembrandt (Marcelino Sanchez) proves to be a great fighter while Cochise (David Harris) breaks out impressive karate moves. Stuntman Gary Baxley doubled for Warrior Vermin (Terry Michos) when he is thrown into a mirror on the wall. Hill and his editors Dave Holden, Freeman Davies and Billy Weber do a superb job mixing the action. The editors nicknamed Hill "The Blanket" because he literally covered the action from every angle.

See: Kipp, Jeremiah. "The Quiet Cool of a Gypsy Actor: An Interview with James Remar." *Shock Cinema.* #19, 2001; "New York Mythology." *Fader.* #26, December 2004; Ryder, Rob. *Hollywood Jock.* New York: Harper, 2006; Talbot, Paul. "Swan Song: An Interview with Actor Michael Beck." *Shock Cinema.* #41, 2011; *The Warriors* DVD special features.

TONY GANIOS VS. THE SKINHEADS in *The Wanderers* (1979)

"Leave … the kid … alone," says the mysterious leather-jacketed hulk Perry (Tony Ganios). A group of bullying Bronx skinheads think they're tough and more than a match for one man in an alleyway in director Philip Kaufman's nostalgic coming-of-age film (set in 1963), based on Richard Price's novel about an Italian street gang of lovable losers. As "Hollywood cool" as any John

Wayne western character riding into town, Ganios repeats his solemn warning. With an everpresent toothpick between his teeth, Ganios annihilates the Fordham Baldies in a tremendously satisfying display of bare-knuckle prowess. The massive (-6'6", 400-pound) Baldie leader Erland Van Lidth gives Ganios a wide berth as they stare down with the tune "Pipeline" by the Chantays playing on the soundtrack. It's a memorable introductory scene, and defender Ganios soon becomes a vital member of Ken Wahl's gang of Tully High wannabe toughs named the Wanderers. Among the Baldies pounded on by Ganios are stunt actors Danny Aiello III, Nicholas J. Giangiulio, Joe Zimmardi and John Devaney.

The fights come often enough that *Newsweek* labeled the film "like *Grease* with brass knuckles." There's another violent five-minute brawl during a football game between assorted rival ethnic groups and the menacing short-statured Ducky Boys led by Mark Lesly and Alan Braunstein, numbering nearly a hundred strong pint-sized Irish toughs wielding knives and bats. This scene has a bizarre feel to it as Michael Chapman's camera speeds up and slows down with flying dust covering the field and droning music playing on the soundtrack. Although he has a cast on a broken arm, Ganios fights them off well, as does the Chinese martial arts gang led by Teddy Wong (Dion Albanese) and the black gang the Del Bombers led by Michael Wright.

Perhaps no one is more impressive than grayhaired Emilio (William Andrews), the abusive bodybuilding father of Perry's pal Joey (John Friedrich). Andrews is a hoot as he rips a park bench apart and wields a wooden plank in battle, then swings one of the Ducky Boys around in a circle, clearing all those in his way. Stunt coordinator Vic Magnotta put the scene together with dozens of extras and stunt fighters including Konrad Sheehan, Jerry Hewitt, Steve James, Frank Ferrara, Bill Anagnos, Eddie Earl Hatch and Tim Gallin. Kung fu master Lawrence Tan set up the martial arts for the camera and performed the kicks and sweeps. The battle took a full week of production days to film at Van Cortlandt Park (it was lensed intermittently throughout the movie based on the weather).

Six-foot-four Greek-Italian teenager Tony Ganios was powerlifting in a Manhattan gym when his bodybuilder uncle Pete Ganios convinced him to audition. He won the part of Perry in an example of perfect casting. He became better known as the character Meat in the 1980s *Porky's* films before his career petered out due to the inability of casting directors to see him as anything other than a tough ethnic character. He reprised his Perry role in the Phil Kaufman film *Rising Sun* (1993), toothpick still in mouth as he plays a doorman who confronts Sean Connery. His Perry could take on entire street gangs in *The Wanderers,* but Connery dispatches him with a simple swat. In real life Ganios trained in Brazilian jujitsu.

See: Goldberg, Robert. "The Hands of Tan." *New York Magazine.* September 15, 1986; Hannon, James. *Lost Boys of the Bronx: The Oral History of the Ducky Boys Gang.* Author House, 2010.

Bruce Lee vs. Kareem Abdul-Jabbar and Danny Inosanto in *Game of Death* (1979)

The 1973 death of Bruce Lee and the smashing success of *Enter the Dragon* unleashed a flurry of copycat martial art films. Several of these starred Bruce Lee clones, such as Bruce Li (Ho Tsung Tao) and Bruce Le (Huang Kin Lung). It came to light that before starring in the U.S.-produced *Enter the Dragon,* Lee had begun work on his own Hong Kong–made film, *Game of Death.* Various sources claimed that Golden Harvest had nearly 100 minutes of raw Lee footage, including completed fights with Danny Inosanto, Ing-Sik Whang and 7'4" basketball superstar Kareem Abdul-Jabbar. Director Robert Clouse failed to duplicate his Lee success with the martial arts films *Black Belt Jones* (1974), *Golden Needles* (1974) and *The Ultimate Warrior* (1975). He was commissioned to finish Lee's *Game of Death,* but his screenplay (written under the pseudonym Jan Spears) drastically changed Lee's original vision. Despite tremendous anticipation, Clouse's *Game of Death* release, five years after Lee's death, was considered an abomination.

The Lee character, now named Billy Lo, is a martial arts movie star who fakes his own death and alters his appearance after being pressured by a syndicate led by suave Hugh O'Brian and his muscle Mel Novak and Bob Wall. Though Clouse's film features decent production values, Sammo Hung stunt coordination and a solid John Barry score, there's a pathetic use of Lee doubles throughout, including ill-matching footage of the real Lee via footage fighting Chuck Norris in *Way of the Dragon* and a notorious shot of a cardboard cutout of Lee's face taped to a mirror. Worse, the new footage of the real Lee amounted to a mere 11 minutes of screen time. Those 11 minutes, however, contained fights in a multi-level Chinese restaurant with a yellow jumpsuited Lee battling both Inosanto and Abdul-Jabbar. For most Lee fans, this exciting new footage was enough to add to the Lee legend as the greatest fighter of all time.

Lee's original vision surfaced many years later in the documentary *Bruce Lee: A Warrior's Journey* along with the Whang fight and radically different footage. In this version, Lee was accompanied by fellow fighters James Tien and Chieh Yuan, who serve mostly as comic relief. The Chinese restaurant was instead a five-level Korean pagoda (the Beopussa Temple in Songgaison National Park, South Korea) featuring a different challenge at each level. It was Lee's intention to show different martial arts and their inferiority to his freeform Jeet Kune Do style. The first fight had Lee and his cohorts fighting Hung and ten black belts at the pagoda's base. Hapkido master Wang was on the first floor, besting Tien and Yuan but no match for Lee. The second floor, never filmed, was to have Lee's friend Taky Kamura as a master of Praying Mantis Kung Fu. The third level, named the Palace of the Dragon, would contain Ji Han Jae, another Hapkido fighter. The fourth level contained escrima weapons fighter Inosanto, while the top level contained Abdul-Jabbar, a freeform Jeet Kune Do fighter who strangles Tien but is bested by Lee when he discovers that the giant's weakness is an extreme sensitivity to light. In real life, Abdul-

Jabbar suffered from Corneal Erosion Syndrome, necessitating his trademark goggles on the basketball court.

Abdul-Jabbar, who originally studied Aikido, was a casual student of Lee while he was in Los Angeles playing basketball with UCLA in the late 1960s. After moving into the pro ranks, he continued to explore martial arts. While Abdul-Jabbar was on vacation in China in 1972, Lee hit upon the idea of hooking up with him and fashioning a fight for his new film. Abdul-Jabbar readily agreed, so Lee choreographed a fight between the two wildly different physical specimens. Lee was careful to inject not only his philosophy on fighting into the scene, but humor as well. This was evidenced by Abdul-Jabbar's first kick that leaves a huge footprint on Lee's yellow jumpsuit. The fight took five days to film and is a triumph for Lee as he vanquishes the giant. Detractors claim that Abdul-Jabbar's martial arts appear awkward, but there's no denying that Lee pulled off one of history's most interesting screen match-ups. Once again he was adding to his own reputation and legend by taking on a giant in battle, much as he had done by taking out karate champ Norris in *Way of the Dragon*.

Inosanto was a student of Lee, though for a brief period in the 1960s he served as Lee's instructor in Filipino martial arts. As so often happened with Lee, he quickly eclipsed his master, but the two remained good friends and sparring partners throughout the remainder of Lee's life. In *Game of Death*, the two engage in a weapons fight in which Lee gets to show his skill in those arts. He begins using a Chinese bako, a thin, reedy bamboo, before moving to escrima sticks. Inosanto breaks out a pair of nunchaku, swings them impressively, and smiles confidently, "How do you like that?" His smile vanishes as Lee produces his own nunchaku and manipulates them masterfully. Lee humorously smacks Inosanto on the nose and asks, "How do you like that?" Real nunchaku were used in the action, but foam rubber replacements were used for contact. Lee had originally intended to use the bako, but Inosanto kept breaking it in re-

Bruce Lee blocks a Kareem Abdul-Jabbar kick in Columbia's *Game of Death* (1979).

hearsal. During the fight, Inosanto was accidentally kicked a couple of times and landed hard on his back after doing a half-flip. Helpers were supposed to slide a mat under him for his fall but became caught up watching the furious action.

The various other fights against Inosanto, Novak and O'Brian were done by doubles (Bruce Li turned down that job). For the Wall fight, Kim Tai-Chung (Yuen Baio) doubled Lee. His other stand-in for the new fight footage was Chen Yao-Po. The O'Brian fight, though well-choreographed, suffers from being anticlimactic coming after the Abdul-Jabbar battle. Day-night continuity is a problem, and the audience knows this isn't the real Lee engaging in the final fight. O'Brian studied karate with Wall in preparation for the role, which both Steve McQueen and James Coburn turned down. Boxing champ Muhammad Ali and soccer star Pele were also approached by Golden Harvest. O'Brian met with the real Lee in 1973 about playing Steiner and was making preparations to fly to Hong Kong when Lee died. Lee intended to fight Bolo Yeung at some point in the finished film.

In 1993, *Black Belt* ranked this one of the best choreographed martial arts films in screen history, and it's showcased in the documentary *Deadliest Art: The Best of the Martial Arts Films* (1992). *Corsair* wrote that *Game of Death* had "some of the best fight scenes ever to be filmed in a kung fu–oriented movie." Leonard Maltin agreed that it contained "some of the most explosive fight scenes ever filmed." *Films of Fury* called it "a magnum opus of Bruce's kung fu—smart, humorous, effective, exciting, fascinating, and even deep." *Action Films* put it near the top of its all-time greatest battles: "It shows Bruce at his cocky best." *The Ultimate Guide to Martial Arts Movies of the 1970s* wasn't sold on the footage, feeling that had Lee lived, he likely would have tightened up or reshot some of the footage prior to release "to match his high expectations of quality and perfection."

See: Barden, Renardo. "Dan Inosanto's Hong Kong Sabbatical." *Fighting Stars*. September 1978; Barden, Renardo. "Kareem Abdul-Jabbar: A Remembrance of Bruce Lee." *Fighting Stars*. November 1978; Lucas, Charles, and Fran Colberg. "Duel to the Death with Bruce Lee." *Fighting Stars*. June 1975; "Western Hero to Eastern Bad Guy: Hugh O'Brian Changes Roles for *Game of Death*." *Fighting Stars*. November 1978.

CHUCK NORRIS VS. BILL "SUPERFOOT" WALLACE in *A Force of One* (1979)

When Chuck Norris retired from karate competition, his middleweight championship successor was Bill "Superfoot" Wallace. The latter was undefeated in the kickboxing ring for the next several years, prompting many fans to endorse a dream match between Wallace and the legendary Norris. Since Norris had moved on in his career and wasn't about to step back into active competition, he did the next best thing for karate fans. He cast Wallace as Sparks, the villain in his latest film while he starred as Matt Logan, a kickboxing champion who helps the police track down a murdering drug dealer who smashes the windpipes of narcotics officers. Through an unbelievably contrived coincidence, the killer of the cops and Norris' protégé Eric Laneuville happens to be none other than Wallace, Norris' opponent for the championship bout held during the climax.

Despite suffering from a routine plot and execution under director Paul Aaron, *A Force of One* features plenty of kickboxing in the ring and a final memorable slow-motion confrontation between Norris and the psychotic Wallace on a darkened country road. This climactic scene was shot at Malibu Ranch on a cold January night with both actors barefoot and shirtless. *The Ultimate Guide to Martial Arts Movies of the 1970s* said that it was shot completely in slow motion, "which instead of accentuating any particular piece of amazing skill or emotional beat, makes the final fight with Wallace more a downer than an upper." *Films of Fury* weighed in with, "*A Force of One* was superior to anything else that could have been termed an American martial arts movie at the time." Chuck's stuntman brother Aaron Norris was on hand to double the star and help choreograph the fights. He appears as Chuck's corner man, and before Wallace was signed was slated to play Sparks. Cameraman Brian Maeda was a martial artist and used pads and a hand-held camera to obtain unique point-of-view footage of Norris and Wallace delivering kicks and punches. Composer Richard Halligan slowed the tempo of his score down appropriately when the action switched to slow motion. The fight ends with a broken neck and a gruesome ratcheting sound effect.

Although they never faced each other in competition, Wallace fought several of Norris' black belts and once briefly sparred with Norris in 1975.

This occurred in an empty gym with only the two men present. Both diplomatically recalled that the other got the better of the exchange. The two were friendly and trained together in California for several weeks before the film, during which they'd work on the fights. Norris originated the idea for *A Force of One* as far back as 1972, at which time he attached the title *Good Guys Wear Black*. That title was appropriated for a 1978 Norris film with an entirely different plot, but black belt champ Pat Johnson had worked on Norris' idea and completed a story and eventual screenplay with Ernest Tidyman. Based on the success of *Good Guys Wear Black*, the new film was quickly green-lighted and became another cog in what would make Norris one of the 1980s' most popular action stars.

See: Barden, Renardo, "Bill Wallace: Superfoot as Bad Guy." *Fighting Stars*. June 1979; *A Force of One* DVD special features; Robertson, Tim. "Karate and Career: Balancing the Burden." *Fighting Stars*. December 1979; Stout, Jerry. "Brian Maeda: The Fighting Filmmaker." *Fighting Stars*. December 1979.

THE USO BRAWL in *1941* (1979)

This is an incredibly destructive Steven Spielberg comedy (scripted by Bob Gale and Robert Zemeckis) about the hysteric aftermath of the Pearl Harbor bombing on the West Coast in December 1941. The presence of a Japanese sub captained by Toshiro Mifune and German advisor Christopher Lee in American waters leads to plenty of spirited plot machinations. The loud and overly ambitious film was lambasted by critics but has its admirers for its non-stop sense of chaotic energy. Several jokes or characterizations miss the bullseye, but they come at a rapid-fire pace and some are undeniably inventive. A major set piece is a massive brawl between soldiers and sailors at a USO jitterbug dance contest hilariously emceed by Joe Flaherty. Fry cook Bobby Di Cicco is determined to win the contest with his girl Dianne Kay, but the male counterparts for the dance must be military only. Di Cicco's getting around the rules sets the fight in motion as hot-headed soldier Treat Williams also has his eyes on Kay and stalks the elusive Di Cicco through the dancers. Wendie Jo Sperber has her eyes on Williams, and all save for Kay seem oblivious to those around them in their single-minded pursuits. When the mercurial Williams lands a knockout punch on Di Cicco (who has donned a sailor's outfit to enter the con-

test), the battle lines are drawn between the military factions. Williams immediately takes three chairs over the head from the seamen.

Stunt coordinator Terry Leonard pays homage to *Dodge City* as multiple fighting bodies fly right and left across the screen at a frenzied pace while the house band plays on. The sprawling riot pours out onto Hollywood Boulevard, with the night action superbly captured by the Oscar-nominated lensing of cinematographer William A. Fraker. Pro football player Frank McRae gets involved wearing a baseball catcher's gear for protection as Zoot Suiters get in on the action. Tank commander Dan Aykroyd gains some semblance of control after firing a heavy machine-gun into the air, announcing that he hates seeing "Americans fighting Americans." At that point, crazy pilot Wild Bill Kelso (John Belushi) comes flying out of the sky in hot pursuit of what he incorrectly believes is a Japanese plane. Belushi also has a cameo during the fight as a Marlon Brando *Godfather*-inspired character eating spaghetti in a restaurant when the window is broken by a fire truck ladder. In another notable cameo, James Caan is a sailor who throws Di Cicco's pal Perry Lang over a railing and onto a table. Caan was visiting the Burbank set and decided to join the stuntmen for the action scene at Spielberg's request.

Few of the usual suspects are visible, which sets it apart from other films. Most of the stunt players are of a new generation which makes perfect sense given the bulk of the sailors and soldiers should be young men. The only readily identifiable screen fighters are Dick Durock and Jerry Brutsche as an MP and a soldier dragged across the dance floor by his fingernails. Vito Carenzo has a running part as a shore patrolman who lands another big punch on Di Cicco. Six-foot-six Brian Frishman is hard to miss as another seaman. Among the stars, 5'11", 185-pound Treat Williams, a football player at Franklin and Marshall College, was impressive enough throwing punches that he was later cast as legendary boxer Jack Dempsey in the TV movie *Dempsey* (1983).

Composer John Williams had the jazzy Benny Goodman song "Sing, Sing, Sing" played on the set throughout rehearsals and filming of the fight but opted to compose a Goodman-like original aptly titled "Swing, Swing, Swing" during postproduction. The original composition still managed to capture the era but gave him the latitude in scoring the film to specifically emphasize punches and falls with brass and woodwinds matched to Michael Kahn's editing. Snippets of the Irish tune "The Rakes of Mallow" from *The Quiet Man* are heard at the fight's beginning in an ode to that John Ford film.

Most reviewers appreciated the USO sequence. The *Chicago Sun Times* wrote that the brawl sequence "works wonderfully," while *New York* opined that Spielberg displayed "a muscular grace in his scenes of excess." The *Sun-Sentinel* added, "The USO number that turns into an epic brawl is actually well-choreographed and would perhaps be considered fair entertainment in a more appropriate film for such a scene, but is completely out of synch here."

See: Hettrick, Scott. "Fascinating New Look at Awful *1941*." *Sun-Sentinel*. July 5, 1996; *The Making of 1941* DVD special features; Williams, Christian. "The Tricks of Treat." *Washington Post*. December 29, 1981.

STACY KEACH VS. STEVE SANDOR in *The Ninth Configuration* (1980)

Writer-director William Peter Blatty's cerebral cult film about patients in a military psychiatric asylum during the Vietnam War concludes with one of the tensest scenes in screen history, a fight between military doctor Stacy Keach and a scary gang of outlaw bikers led by a memorable Steve Sandor. Set in a gothic castle in Northern California, the film is full of oddball characters, quotable dialogue, and arguments on the existence of God between the patients, some of whom may be faking their condition to avoid combat. Keach is revealed to be the infamous Killer Kane, a special ops combat warrior who spent his time in Vietnam cutting off the heads of the enemy on dangerous behind-enemy-lines missions. Mentally the Marine has cracked from all the killing, and it's hoped by his superiors that he can benefit from curing the assorted patients.

Keach takes an interest in God-denying Scott Wilson, an astronaut who refuses to go to the moon because he's afraid he might not return. As Keach begins to make headway with Wilson, new patient Don Gordon recognizes Keach and his dark past is revealed. A disappointed Wilson checks out of the hospital and drowns his sorrows in a cheap beer joint. Among the patrons are members of a biker gang led by Sandor and seedy Richard Lynch. When the bikers begin to play rough with Wilson, Keach arrives to intervene. The bikers turn their attention to Keach, taunting

him to the point where Sandor becomes angry at the pacifistic Keach's degrading the Marine uniform when he stoops to lick spilled beer off the floor. However, when Lynch tries to sodomize Wilson, Keach's Killer Kane persona emerges in full bloody regalia. Keach snaps, and so do the necks of an entire biker gang. Keach's fighting is deadly efficient, and he doesn't waste any moves in dispatching the gang. Sandor rises for a second try and is hurled through the bar window for his trouble. Blatty and cinematographer Gerry Fisher effectively film a lonely Keach standing over the destruction he has wrought.

The film was made in Hungary, the location of the castle used as the military asylum. The biker bar was a local film set with a real Viennese motorcycle gang as extras. The fight took three days to complete. Stunt coordinator Bobby Bass appears as a biker, as do Tim Rossovich, Gary Epper and Gary's sister Jeannie Epper, often regarded as the toughest stuntwoman in the business. Keach's real-wife Marilyn is a biker girl and takes a fake punch from Keach. Blatty's wife Linda plays the waitress who phones the police. The six-foot, 175-pound Keach does all the convincing martial art action, a testament to the work put in with judo expert Bass. Sandor, whom Blatty cast after seeing him play a theatrical pro wrestler in the TV movie *Mad Bull* (1977), made several suggestions that found their way onto the screen. These include the frightening eyeliner he wears, the slow split he slides into to reach Keach on the floor, tearing off his gloves after they've touched Keach, and the pausing between lines to build drama.

Leonard Maltin called it "an amazing barroom fight scene." *Variety* praised the film's "terrific series of concluding scenes." In his autobiography, Keach proudly called it "one of the great barroom fight scenes in movie history." This sequence has been discussed as a model for aspiring film directors on how to build tension within a scene. Everything from the dialogue to Barry Devorzon's background music and especially Blatty's editing contributes. Blatty's original cut of the fight was three-and-a-half minutes, but he later polished it to under a minute. Supposedly some 17 different versions found their way into circulation, all courtesy of Blatty's continued experimentation. In some markets, the film was released as *Twinkle, Twinkle Killer Kane*.

Six-foot-two and 200 pounds, Steve Sandor was a trainer of guard dogs in the Air Force. A dedicated weightlifting and martial arts enthusiast, he served as an especially formidable TV villain during the 1970s. On screen, he sought to make his fights as realistic as possible and displayed great agility for a big man. He did his own fight stunts and was noted for the savage intensity he brought to his portrayals. One of his most interesting assignments came as Frank Frazetta's animation model for the mysterious character Darkwolf, the fighting warrior in Ralph Bakshi's *Fire and Ice* (1983).

Fights of interest came against George Peppard in *One More Train to Rob* (1971), Rockne Tarkington in *The No Mercy Man* (aka *Trained to Kill: USA*) (1975), Alex Karras in *Mad Bull* (1977) and Mike Lane in *Stryker* (1983). On TV, Sandor fought William Shatner in the 1968 "Gamesters of Triskelion" episode of *Star Trek,* as well as Jack Palance on *Bronk,* Robert Urich on *Vegas,* Lee Majors on *The Fall Guy* and Mr. T on *The A-Team.*

See: Birchard, Bob. "A Champ in the Amen Corner." *Fighting Stars.* August 1975; Keach, Stacy. *All in All: An Actor's Life On and Off the Stage.* Guilford, CT: Lyons, 2013; *The Ninth Configuration* DVD commentary.

THE SALOON BRAWL in *Bronco Billy* (1980)

Having a saloon brawl in a Clint Eastwood action comedy about a modern cowboy seems natural, and *Bronco Billy* delivers with the star and his ragtag Wild West troupe engaging in fisticuffs with a bar full of toughs. It was memorable to the Boise, Idaho, locals who appeared in the scene filmed at the Big Pine Saloon. They saw a Hollywood fight choreographed up close with stuntmen going through the moves at half-speed in rehearsal while voicing "Pow, Pow!" for perceived hits. Chuck Hicks coordinated the fight because Eastwood's normal stunt coordinator Buddy Van Horn was unavailable. After the main brawl, two cowboys (Hicks and Robert Hoy) accost Sondra Locke in the parking lot. Eastwood makes quick work of them with his fists. This night scene was shot with a hand-held camera by cinematographer David Worth to emphasize the sense of urgency.

The bar brawl was filmed with three cameras set up at a variety of angles to capture the action. Worth lit the scene with strong natural overhead bulbs to limit wasted time. Country singer Merle Haggard and his band The Strangers play during the fight as entertainment, even as thrown beer bottles clang off the microphone stand. They lip-synched their song "Barroom Buddies" to a pre-recorded playback. The beer bottles were tossed from a few feet away so they'd have a greater chance of hitting the target. Twenty stuntmen were brought in for the location shoot with local extras hired to fill out the ranks.

Though he was directing the film, Eastwood did all his own fighting on screen. The man hired to double him, George Orrison, appears as a cowboy and throws the first punch against Bill McKinney. Six-foot-four, 225-pound bodybuilding actor Dan Vadis is in the melee pitching away alongside McKinney. At one point, McKinney punches his hook hand through the bathroom door. Eastwood's company redid the bathroom stalls, and the cast signed the door as a memento for the establishment. Producer Fritz Manes even gets involved and performs a stunt, taking a hit and going through dry-wall between a pair of 2 × 4s. Among the stunt fighters, six-foot-five Dick Durock paired up with five-foot-four Jesse Wayne to throw the little guy (Wayne) around the bar, and Norm Blankenship punches a beer mug from actor Sam Bottoms' hand. Others stunt artists include Tony Epper, Vince Deadrick, Ted White, Al Wyatt and John "Bear" Hudkins. Gene LeBell and Jim Burk's names are connected to the film, but they are not visible in the fight action. A good deal of fight footage ended up on the cutting room floor after editors Joel Cox and Ferris Webster trimmed the film down.

See: Accola, John. "Money, Memories Remain as *Bronco Billy* Departs." *Idaho Statesman.* November 11, 1979; Kershner, Sandy. *On the Trail of Bronco Billy.* Create Space, 2011.

CHUCK NORRIS VS. RICHARD NORTON in *The Octagon* (1980)

This film's influential martial arts choreography is considered by many to be Chuck Norris' best display of his skills on film as he takes on an army of ninjas in an octagon-shaped training center. The film started the 1980s fascination with ninjas on screen as the black-clad killers, led by weapons masters Tadashi Yamashita and Gerald Okamura, figure prominently in the training of a group of terrorists. The mysterious lethal ninja character Kyo has a nearly three-minute battle with Norris near the conclusion involving swords, long knives, feet and throwing stars. Australian martial artist Richard Norton portrays the hooded Kyo and also appears as the blond mercenary character Long-legs. In addition to that double duty, he appears as a stunt ninja in numerous action segments.

Director Erik Karson filmed the Norris-Norton fight with double camera coverage and no cinematic tricks, opting to let the powerful action speak for itself. The two fighters worked on the intricate choreography for more than a month in the Norris backyard and had their moves timed perfectly. Editor Eric Kann merely had to piece together the seamlessly flowing action. *Action Films* names this among its top 25 greatest screen fights, with the final fight against Okinawan karate champ Yamashita paling in comparison. Chuck and his brother Aaron Norris were the fight choreographers. Aaron also portrays the character Hatband, who takes a cowboy boot to the face. Like Norton, Aaron doubled several ninjas. It became a running gag on the *Octagon* set as stuntmen Aaron, Norton, Ben Perry, John Barrett and Eric De Pland would be knocked out on screen only to reemerge seconds later as a different ninja to do it again. Norton was killed eight times.

With the exception of Norton, the ninja stuntmen were Norris students who worked well with their boss. Unlike traditional fights, much of the action involved light physical contact to sell the blows for the camera. This was especially dangerous considering the fact that in some scenes, Norris is wearing cowboy boots which could do serious damage if a fighter missed his mark. To protect their faces, the stuntmen wore hockey masks underneath their ninja hoods. Norton added a comedic ad-lib to his first fight with Norris when he takes a boot between the legs and turns to the camera. John Belushi suggested the aside when Norton was serving as his bodyguard. Norris kicked to contact in the finale when he put a foot onto Norton's chest and knocked the latter through a flaming wall. Norton took the kick but another stuntman did the full fire burn. The eerie growling hisses Kyo uses throughout the fight were a form of deep-breathing in Sanchin kata. Norton tangled again with Norris in *An Eye for an Eye* (1981) and *Forced Vengeance* (1982), as well as the TV series *Walker, Texas Ranger* for which Norton served as fight coordinator for several seasons.

Earning a black belt at the age of 17 in his native Australia, 6'2", 190-pound Norton learned streetfighting from professional bouncer Bob Jones. The two developed a progressive and evolving martial art they called Zen Do Kai. Norton became the head bouncer at several nightclubs while simultaneously serving as the chief karate instructor for a growing chain of martial art schools. In 1972, Norton and Jones headed up security for a Rolling Stones tour and traveled on the road as bodyguards for such musical acts as Fleetwood Mac, David Bowie, James Taylor and Abba. Norton film-debuted as a stuntman in *Last of the Knucklemen* (1979) (see entry). He fought female karate champion Cynthia Rothrock in *Magic Crystal* (1987) and *Lady Dragon* (1992), though he often paired up with her to fight bad guys in her *China O'Brien* films. He proved a worthy adversary for Jackie Chan in *City Hunter* (1992) and *Mr. Nice Guy* (1997), as well as Chan and Sammo Hung in *Twinkle, Twinkle Lucky Stars* (1985) (see entry).

See: Brown. B.B. "Richard Norton: A Villain to Watch." *Fighting Stars*. April 1981; Coleman, Jim. "Meet the Villainous Richard Norton." *Black Belt*. March 1994; Loder, Kurt. "Richard Norton: Body Builder of the Stars." *Rolling Stone*. September 6, 1979; *The Octagon* DVD special features.

CHARLES BRONSON VS. DENNY MILLER in *Cabo Blanco* (1980)

This *Casablanca* retread with Charles Bronson in the Humphrey Bogart lead has its moments but was heavily edited upon release and disappeared quickly from theaters. Involving a hunt for Nazi gold, it's set in a seaside Peruvian town post–World War II but filmed in Barra de Navidad and the Bay of Tenactita, Mexico. The most interesting aspect is the fight between expatriate Bronson and sadistic German soldier Denny Miller, with Bronson coming to the rescue of Camilla Sparv when Miller slaps her around. The 6'4", 235-pound Miller towers over Bronson, but the latter is furious in his assault as he grabs a metal trash can and thrashes the taller man quickly. Miller is backed over a bed and flipped against a wall, knocking a marlin spear plaque off its mooring. The deadly decoration falls and a sharp point lands in Miller's eye, one of the gorier killings seen in a non-horror film. *The Cincinnati-Enquirer* called it "the strangest fight sequence ever filmed."

As his career went from respected character actor to craggy-faced superstar, the surly Bronson developed a testy reputation among film crews. This was especially apparent with the largely local crew on *Cabo Blanco*. Bronson consistently had problems with the script even as the cameras were ready to roll and created a great deal of unrest in regard to the fight. Bennie Dobbins was stunt coordinator, brought in after Bronson disapproved of his original double. Bronson insisted upon the actors doing the entire fight. The athletic Miller was game for the fight but didn't like the idea of taking the fall beneath the sharp marlin spear. Bronson called Miller's double Tony Epper fat, and the offended stuntman was ready to tear into the star. Dobbins had to send Epper back to Los Angeles, and Miller had no recourse but to do the scene. Local crew members privately told Miller to accidentally let his fists make contact with Bronson, but Miller had too much sense, professionalism and respect for the Hollywood star. He realized that Bronson was a shy, quiet man who preferred the company of his wife and kids. The delays he caused were because he was trying to make a good film and a memorable screen fight.

As they began their fighting, Bronson challenged the original choreography. He was supposed to pick up a breakaway drawer and beat Miller with it, but he decided a 20-gallon metal waste can with an octagon shape made a more interesting and lethal prop. Miller reluctantly agreed, putting several stunt pads under his long-sleeved shirt to absorb the blows. On the first take, Bronson cut three of his own fingers on the trash can and the pro–Miller crew erupted in applause. On the second take, with taped fingers, Bronson nailed the entire scene perfectly. The dropping of the marlin spear was done with a metal plate placed over Miller's off-screen eye. When the spear dropped, a tube with fake blood gushed its contents. When Miller asked the cameraman if the shot looked convincing, the man showed Miller the still-raised hairs on his forearm.

UCLA basketball player Miller made his name in Hollywood as the first blond Tarzan in the slapdash *Tarzan, the Ape Man* (1959). The Army veteran had more success on TV than in films, portraying genial trail scout Duke Shannon on the popular TV western *Wagon Train* (1961–1965); in his introductory episode "The Duke Shannon Story," he had a memorable fight with stunt actor Terry Wilson. Universal exec Lew Wasserman proclaimed that it was the best fight he'd ever seen. Wilson tutored Miller in the art of screen fighting which stood him in good stead for the remainder of his career as a physical actor capable of doing many of his own stunts. He fought co-star Robert Fuller in 1963's "The Sandra Cummings Story."

Memorable TV fights came against Richard Boone in the 1960 *Have Gun—Will Travel* episode "Saturday Night," Chuck Connors in the 1960 *Rifleman* "The Promoter," Jack Palance in the 1976

Bronk "Next of Kin" and Tom Selleck in the 1982 *Magnum P.I.* "Three Minus Two." Miller portrayed bare-knuckle fighters on episodes of *Dusty's Trail, Young Maverick* and *Magnum P.I.* On the 1980 series *When the Whistle Blows,* Miller slipped during a fight scene and took a real punch from pro football player Tim Rossovich; the injury called for extensive dental surgery. It didn't stop him from doing his own fights. Miller had fights of interest with Ron Ely in the 1981 TV pilot *The Seal* and 1987's *Sea Hunt* reboot, as well as Stacy Keach in the Mike Hammer TV movie *More Than Murder* (1983).

See: Anderson, Nancy. "The Hidden Man in Charles Bronson Is Revealed." *Bulletin Journal.* April 22, 1979; Miller, Denny. *Didn't You Used to Be What's His Name?* Las Vegas: To Your Health, 2004.

JACKIE CHAN vs. H.B. HAGGERTY in *The Big Brawl* (aka *Battle Creek Brawl*) (1980)

The Big Brawl is noteworthy as Jackie Chan's introduction to American audiences. In it, he plays a young Chinaman in 1930s Chicago forced by mobsters into a bare-knuckle fight event in Battle Creek, Texas (actually San Antonio and Floresville). Produced and directed by *Enter the Dragon* filmmakers Fred Weintraub and Robert Clouse, *The Big Brawl* wasn't a great theatrical success, although it found an audience on cable television and home video. Chan fans either love it or hate it. The con side opposes the Americanized fights against heavy and oftentimes theatrically plodding professional wrestlers. Those who love it see it as Chan's first attempt to reach American audiences with his special blend of martial arts humor and fantastic gymnastic displays.

The extended climactic brawl involves Chan taking on several wrestling types in a battle royal. Earl Maynard, Ox Baker, Tor Kamata, Paul Mercado and Jeep Swenson are some of the wrestlers who are eliminated early. Chan fights matches against Clarence "Sonny" Barnes and Steve Merjanian. The 6'1", 240-pound Barnes was Minnesota's amateur boxing champion and Merjanian was one of the strongest men in the world. Chan reaches the ten-minute grand finale against H.B. Haggerty, who earlier in the picture squeezed the life from Maynard and Gene LeBell. At first Chan isn't able to fight back against Haggerty because his mentor Mako has been kidnapped by gang-

Professional wrestler H.B. Haggerty (left) goes up against Jackie Chan in Warner Bros.' *The Big Brawl* (aka *Battle Creek Brawl*) (1980).

sters. When Mako escapes, Chan is able to unleash his quickness and multi-angled kicks on a frustrated Haggerty. Sensing a loss, the mobsters backing Haggerty lure Chan into an empty theater. There he takes on mob thugs Loren Janes, George Fisher, Tom Morga and Nigel Binns, as well as the knife-wielding lead heavy Ron Max, with a flurry of kung fu. Chan emerges from the theater to finish off Haggerty and claim the grand prize.

Chan also has a comic back alley fight worthy of Buster Keaton. Admonished by his father not to fight, Chan bests mob thugs Pat Johnson, Talmadge Scott and 6'5", 275-pound pro wrestler Lenny Montana by forcing them to fall over themselves while he eludes them with a series of pratfalls and "accidental" kicks. There are also several enjoyable training sequences with the well-cast Mako, a siege on the mob's lair, an audition fight against two Asian martial artists in an open air theater, and a roller-skating race in which Chan fights Donnie Williams. All in all, it's a great chance for Chan to show off his athleticism, which was per-

fectly complimented by a catchy Lalo Schifrin score. Clouse, the go-to man for helming such fare, continued with minor martial arts outings in *Force: Five* (1981), *Gymkata* (1985) and *China O'Brien* (1990).

There was some tension on the set as Chan struggled to learn English even as the cameras rolled. Stunt coordinator Pat Johnson clashed mildly with Chan, who felt stifled by the American filmmakers' insistence that he not coordinate his own fights. Johnson stressed to Chan what American audiences liked and expected. Chan found himself at certain points doing roundhouse punches over short and effective kung fu strikes. Clouse had confidence in Johnson's abilities, as they had worked together several times. The biggest problem for Chan was the pace of American filming. While the wrestlers and stuntmen were physically slow by Asian standards, the filming style was exceptionally fast, geared toward staying on budget and ahead of schedule to protect the bottom line. Chan was a perfectionist known to take weeks on a fight that would be the focus of an entire Chinese film. When he wasn't afforded the unending timetable to complete his fights, he felt his own physical performance suffer. Although Johnson was merely working in the American style, many Chan fans hold him personally responsible for this film's perceived shortcomings. In fairness to Johnson, he likely had little say in casting the slow wrestlers. Chan tried the U.S. again with *Rumble in the Bronx* (1996) and became a surprise sensation. After several more modestly successful U.S. releases, he struck box office gold with the *Rush Hour* franchise beginning in 1998.

The *Gadsden Times* wrote, "Forget the plot and watch the young Chan zip through a series of encounters with the athletic grace of Gene Kelly in his prime," but *The Essential Jackie Chan Sourcebook* found the *Big Brawl* action scenes "watered down by Chan standards." Surprisingly, an article in *Black Belt* ranked this as one of the best choreographed martial arts films. According to *Fight Choreography*, "The filmmakers were not able to capture the ingenuity, creativity, humor and intricacy of the fight scenes that made Chan stand out in his Hong Kong films because of *The Big Brawl's* emphasis on brute strength, power and size.... The cues were too much like one-step sparring, where everyone was reacting to a right-handed lunge punch, which also slowed down the pace and narrowed down the possibility of what could be done."

Don "Hard-Boiled" Haggerty had a tough guy reputation dating back to his pro football days with the Green Bay Packers. During the off-season, the Navy veteran toured the land as a pro wrestler, a vocation he continued full-time when his football days were over. Six-one and 265 pounds, the bald, snarling Haggerty became one of the best known heels in the business. He was also a man able to "shoot" in the ring if need be. To "shoot" is to throw away the script and wrestle for real when there's actual animosity existing between two wrestlers or someone new to a territory has to earn the right to headline. Nobody in the business wanted to "shoot" with Haggerty.

Haggerty found a place in Hollywood where his fearsome appearance made him a perfect casting choice when a script called for a giant menacing madman with a handlebar mustache to wreak havoc. The poolroom brawl in *Earthquake* (1974) is a fine example. Fights of interest came against George Peppard in *P.J.* (1968), Anthony Quinn in *A Dream of Kings* (1969), Pam Grier in *Foxy Brown* (1974), Richard Lawson in *Black Fist* (1974), Bo

Svenson in *Final Chapter—Walking Tall* (1977), David Carradine in *Deathsport* (1978), Gil Gerard in *Buck Rogers in the 25th Century* (1979) and Pepper Martin in *The Malay Trader* (1981). On TV, he fought James Garner in the 1971 *Nichols* episode "Fight of the Century" and Lou Ferrigno in the 1981 *Incredible Hulk* "Half-Nelson."

See: *The Big Brawl* pressbook; Oliver, Myrna. "Hard-Boiled Haggerty, 78; Wrestler, Stuntman, Actor." *Los Angeles Times*. February 3, 2004; Singer, Ben. "Jackie Chan: Welcome to L.A." *Fighting Stars*. April 1981.

SAM J. JONES VS. TIMOTHY DALTON in *Flash Gordon* (1980)

A colorful and campy sci-fi extravaganza from Italian producer Dino De Laurentiis and director Mike Hodges, *Flash Gordon* stars handsome unknown Sam J. Jones as the square-jawed football player turned space hero taking on Ming the Merciless (Max von Sydow). First he has to fight his way through Timothy Dalton's Prince Barin in a bullwhip battle to the death on a rotating tilted disc with spikes that intermittently rise and fall. During the three-minute battle, the two alpha males bond and gain a measure of respect for one another. It's an ingenious set-up for a fight and well-realized by stunt coordinator Terry Forrestal and second unit director Rocky Taylor. The fight was rehearsed for several weeks and there were three technicians on hand to operate both the disc and the hydraulic rubber-tipped iron spikes in conjunction with the worked-out fight moves.

During the London shooting, the stars lobbied fight director William Hobbs to let them do much of the difficult action themselves even though stuntmen John Lees, Jim Dowdall and Vic Armstrong were on hand to serve as doubles. Several times both actors fell nearly 30 feet into boxes surrounding the disc as they worked out the complicated choreography. There were several minor injuries incurred by both, and humorously their costumes kept showing silver spray paint from the dressed-up disc. In the original Lorenzo Semple, Jr., script, both characters were supposed to be stripped to the waist. In the finished product, the dashing Dalton wears a hunter green outfit evoking memories of Errol Flynn as Robin Hood. The 6'2" Dalton had been trained at the Royal Academy of Dramatic Art and was well-versed in stage combat. He was taught how to handle a bullwhip by stuntman Reg Harding.

The 6'3", 205-pound Jones, a Marine, saloon bouncer and semi-pro football player for the Burien Flyers, was discovered by De Laurentiis on *The Dating Game*. Jones proved to be a handful for the producer and landed in a fight on location with ten toughs in Leicester Square in which he received a gash on his face. De Laurentiis barged into the hospital to insure that the surgeons could save his leading man's face for the rest of the shoot. During Christmas break, Jones returned to California and never came back to finish the film. De Laurentiis used stand-ins, stunt doubles and voiceover artists to piece together what he needed for second unit and post-production work. Outside of fight-heavy B-films like *Fist of Honor* (1993), Jones never had a starring role in another major movie. He did show up spoofing his own bad boy image in a memorable cameo in *Ted* (2012).

See: Kezich, Tulio, and Alessandra Levantasi. *Dino: The Life and Films of Dino De Laurentiis.* New York: Miramax, 2004; Leftley, Nick. "Flash Gordon Speaks!" *Maxim.* December 2012; Scott, Vernon. "Sam Jones Got Lucky in Flash Gordon Role." *Schenectady Gazette.* December 20, 1980; Willson, Karen. "Sam J. Jones." *Starlog.* #41, December 1980.

CLINT EASTWOOD VS. WILLIAM SMITH in *Any Which Way You Can* (1980)

Inspired by the lengthy *Quiet Man* (1952) brawl, this action-comedy sequel to *Every Which Way but Loose* (1978) features what has been called the longest two-man fight ever seen on film. Clint Eastwood and William Smith (as a formidable but surprisingly friendly adversary) knock one another all over Jackson Hole, Wyoming, while the entire town cheers them on and makes bets on the outcome of what they call "the fight of the century." The two stars, old pros at screen battle, do nearly the entire 20-minute fight themselves while numerous cutaways from editor Ferris Webster address a variety of subplots. Eastwood is doubled by George Orrison only for a crash through a barn door and a restaurant window. His usual stuntman Buddy Van Horn was on the other side of the camera serving as the director, a solid choice for this assignment given his familiarity with screen fights and optimum camera angles. Smith, at perhaps his most heavily muscled, managed his own stunts despite Nick Dimitri being in costume and on the set ready to double him.

Shooting on location in Jackson Hole meant that the production needed the cooperation of local businesses, whose main street was roped off during the peak summer tourist season. Everything went without a hitch. The proprietors were paid handsomely and the filmmakers quickly repaired any damage their monumental battle caused. The community was excited to take part in an Eastwood film and interact with his established cast of familiar faces and beer-drinking simian sidekick Clyde. Producer-star Eastwood, long known for his efficient filmmaking, worked quickly. An entire week had been set aside for the fight but the action was accomplished in less time with hundreds of local extras cheering the fighters on. Legendary tough guy Smith was relieved to finish it quickly as his lifestyle was leaving him short of breath in the 8000-foot elevation. Despite the care he put into his body regarding nutrition and intense physical exercise, Smith was smoking too much and was lured to the infamous local Million Dollar Cowboy Bar for drinks by co-star Harry Guardino. He wasn't missing any weight workouts in the morning as his famed 18½" arms were as cut and heavily ridged as they'd been a decade earlier. When he doffs his outer shirt for the fight, there was a collective gasp in theaters around the country. Smith's impressive muscles instantly made Eastwood the underdog.

Eastwood and Smith were longtime acquaintances from Vince's Gym, and their matching up for a screen brawl seemed a natural at the time. The two actors enjoyed a friendly sportsman's rivalry like their characters Philo Beddoe and Jack Wilson (an apparent homage to Jack Palance's character from *Shane*, which was filmed in Jackson Hole). Eastwood was in top shape from regular running workouts, and at one point he and Smith take a jog together as part of their training. Eastwood's Beddoe runs in blue jeans while the money-backed Wilson has expensive jogging suits. *Any Which Way You Can* was made in the summer of 1980 with a presidential election looming on the horizon. The two actors engaged in playful banter since Smith was a Democrat while Eastwood was a Reagan-backing Republican. When Eastwood cracked a couple of Smith's ribs during the fight, Smith was reluctant to let the star know he'd hurt him and simply fought on. Smith regarded Eastwood as one of the toughest screen fighters he ever faced, on a par with Rod Taylor from *Darker Than Amber* (1970).

Some reviewers hinted that the idea of two men

Clint Eastwood (left) and William Smith put on an audience-pleasing donnybrook in Warner Bros.' *Any Which Way You Can* (1980).

pummeling one another with such macho mutual admiration had homosexual overtones despite the presence of Sondra Locke in the cast as Eastwood's girlfriend. Smith's character and the shading he brings to it is perhaps the most interesting aspect of the film. It would have been easy for his Jack Wilson to be nothing more than a fearsome and threatening presence, which Stanford Sherman's script alludes to by referencing that Smith's past opponents wound up dead or incapacitated. Yet Smith brings personality to the part and even becomes Eastwood's ally in fighting off the Mafia stooges to rescue Locke.

The fight is called off due to mob meddling, but Eastwood and Smith are too intrigued by the idea of who is best to let it go at that. The fight begins in a darkened barn and then stretches throughout the town square and pauses for an Olympia beer. With a smile and a quip, the two punch away again and crash through a restaurant window. Eastwood breaks his arm courtesy of a Smith kick, but Eastwood is determined to fight on one-handed. The two have kept a running tally throughout the film of favors owed, and a relieved Smith declares,

"We're even." Eastwood clenches his teeth and corrects him with, "No, I owe you." An iconic punch knocks Smith clean through a door, its hinges flying. Smith improbably punches air as a one-handed Eastwood rallies to knock him around beneath Jackson Hole's antler-lined town square. After landing a head-twisting punch in front of the camera, Eastwood finishes Smith with a rabbit punch to the neck. He's not out for long, but Smith awakes with a smile and an offer to take his pal to the hospital as the town erupts in adoration for the show the two men put on.

Warner Bros. publicity trumpeted the fight as "the most knuckle-bustin,' gut-wrenchin,' brain-scramblin,' butt-bruisin,' lip-splittin' brawl of all time!" It's a crowd-pleaser to be sure, and most professional reviewers fell in line in allotting the fight a place as one of the greats. The *Los Angeles Times* wrote that the brawl "proves to be enjoyable because it restores the good, clean fight of the once-hallowed *Spoilers* tradition." *Variety* called it "an epic," and *People* thought it was "a splendid bare-knuckle brawl." *The Big Damn Book of Sheer Manliness* called it one of the best one-on-one fights in film history, while *Action Films* ranked it one of the greatest of all time, declaring, "William Smith was a perfect choice to go head to head with Eastwood and their final fight does not disappoint." *The Hollywood Reporter* concurred: "It helps considerably that Wilson, engagingly played by Smith, is no stereotyped heavy; it's altogether proper that two strong stalwarts like Smith and Eastwood end up as friends." The *Washington Post* opined, "Though usually cast as a villain, Smith has always seemed one of the more engaging studs on the screen. In fact, his extroverted nature and imposing physique tend to make him a more likeable rugged presence and credible physical threat than the star."

As good as the fight is, much of the choreography consists of Smith and Eastwood taking head-snapping punches in front of the camera or swinging their own blows at the lens as the Foley Artists have a field day with the sound effects. David Worth followed the combatants around with a carbon arc lamp on a dolly to use as fill light in a nod to the way John Ford had filmed *The Quiet Man*. He also included a frame-within-a-frame of Smith at the Antler Park entryway evoking Ford. The bit with Clyde grabbing a fistful of spaghetti in the restaurant was an improvised moment left in to get a laugh. Eastwood also has a humorous fight with stunt actor Dick Durock.

The best fight is arguably the Palomino Bar cowboy brawl in which Eastwood and Smith join forces. It's a fight set up by Smith to gauge how good his opponent Eastwood is. Stunt actor George Fisher insults Locke's singing with Smith stepping in to defend her. Taking a punch from Fisher, Smith steps aside to watch Eastwood pound away at Fisher, Walter Scott, Vince Deadrick and Gene Hartline. However, Fisher becomes enraged to the point of drawing a knife and Smith re-enters the action with a ferocity that causes Eastwood to perform his patented squint and raised eyebrow. Smith breaks Fisher's knife-wielding arm, kicks Scott in the face, knees Deadrick in the nose, and chokes Scott down to a knee before putting him out with a short and powerful right hand. It's an interesting moment between Smith and Eastwood as they size one another up and the soundtrack cranks up the appropriate tune "The Good Guys and the Bad Guys" by John Durrill.

See: *Any Which Way You Can* press kit; Teymur. T. "William Smith: My Fight with Clint Eastwood Was the Longest Two-Man Fight on Screen." *BZ Film*. April 1, 2010.

CHRISTOPHER REEVE VS. PEPPER MARTIN in *Superman II* (1981)

This scene remains a lightning rod of debate among Man of Steel fans because Superman seemingly seeks revenge on a simple blowhard bully portrayed to perfection by Pepper Martin. Early in the film, Superman (Christopher Reeve) has lost his powers, and in the guise of Clark Kent is accosted by Rocky (Martin) in a diner over a seat. The tough truck driver mops the floor with Reeve in front of Lois Lane (Margot Kidder). He's such a louse, he even sucker-punches Reeve in the back of the head and knocks him through a glass partition. Reeve did his own stunt here despite Vic Armstrong being his assigned double. Later, after Superman has regained his powers and rid the world of super threats Terence Stamp, Sara Douglas and Jack O'Halloran, he meets up again with Martin at Don's Diner. This time Superman gives Martin his just deserts. Martin hurts his hand on Reeve's stomach and ends up being thrown the length of the diner into a pinball machine. Reeve explains to the astonished customers with a smile, "I've been working out." The amusingly brief fights were choreographed by Alf Joint with an assist from Armstrong.

Superman II began filming back to back with the original *Superman* in 1977 under the direction of Richard Donner. Due to finances, filming was suspended while the first film was completed in the editing room. During this period, the producers decided to go in a different direction than Donner's dark tone and hired Richard Lester to complete the sequel and bring a lighter touch. The release left some audience members scratching their heads as the evil villains now sought occasional laughs amidst their mass killing spree. Twenty years later, a full Donner release saw the light of day on DVD. The diner sequence was filmed by Donner on a London set.

The casting of the Man of Steel proved problematic. They ended up going with an unknown in the form of the handsome Juilliard-trained Reeve, who was chosen over 200 other hopefuls. The one problem: Reeve was non-athletic and weighed 180 pounds on a rangy 6'4" frame. The producers considered using a padded suit before hiring British bodybuilder David Prowse to bulk Reeve up in time for filming. Through an intense three-hour daily weightlifting regimen, Prowse added 30 pounds of muscle onto Reeve, including two whole inches onto his biceps. Reeve felt he wasn't getting big enough quick enough and Prowse was relieved of his duties before filming. Stuntmen Joint and Armstrong and co-star O'Halloran kept the young star on the weight workouts during production. In the guise of Superman, he opted to do many of his own stunts due to a confidence in his new body. However, Reeve let the sudden stardom go to his head and unwisely ran afoul of 6'6", 250-pound former heavyweight contender O'Halloran. His attitude was quickly adjusted. To Reeve's credit, he is nearly perfect in the dual role of Superman and Clark Kent.

When 6'2", 230-pound pro wrestler Pepper Martin arrived on the set, Reeve kept his distance. Martin picked up on this and began to stare menacingly at Reeve, which unsettled the star. Director Donner requested that Martin wear two-inch lifts and let him have a hand in the fight choreography which made Reeve even more uncomfortable. The star legitimately feared being hurt by the imposing Martin. Martin put him at ease by taking Reeve's place in the fight rehearsals to demonstrate how the moves could be performed safely. He puffed out Reeve's jacket and buried his fist into the cushioned material which effectively fooled the camera when combined with Reeve's reaction. Utilizing multiple cameras, they captured the first fight in one take. When it came time for the second fight, Martin did his own stunt wearing a jerk vest. At first Martin's pants created too much drag on the tabletop. This problem was solved by having him travel atop a tray of steaming food.

Martin served in the Royal Canadian Navy and played professional football for the Hamilton Tigers before embarking on a pro wrestling career (at one point, he held the NWA Pacific Northwest Championship). His wrestling friends Woody Strode and Harold Sakata introduced him to Hollywood. He was a fitting film and TV heavy, memorably taking a rifle stock to the jaw from John Wayne in *Cahill—U.S. Marshal* (1973). Given his mat background, many producers and directors allowed him to choreograph his screen fights, for which he never required a stuntman. He tangled often with Mike Connors on *Mannix* and James Garner on *The Rockford Files*.

Fights of interest came against Tom Stern in *Angels from Hell* (1968), Dean Martin in *The Wrecking Crew* (1969), Mike Lane in *Gone with the West* (1969), Hal Needham in *The Animals* (1970) and Woody Strode in the TV pilot *The Outside Man* (1977). Martin starred in the unreleased 1981 film *The Malay Trader* where he put on a fight with fellow wrestler H.B. Haggerty. On TV, he fought Walter Brennan in *The Guns of Will Sonnett* episode "Alone," Jerry Quarry in the *I Dream of Jeannie* "The Strongest Man in the World" and John Vernon in the *Bonanza* "Yonder Man."

See: Martin, Pepper, and Penny Lane. *Shrapnel of the Soul and Redemption.* Page, 2016; Prowse, Dave. *Straight from the Force's Mouth: The Autobiography of Dave Prowse.* Andrews, 2011; *Superman II* DVD special features.

HARRISON FORD VS. PAT ROACH in *Raiders of the Lost Ark* (1981)

Screenwriter Lawrence Kasdan's two-fisted character Indiana Jones (Harrison Ford) took part in all types of hair-raising adventures that made him hugely popular with audiences while simultaneously evoking fond memories of Republic action serials of the 1930s and 1940s. Producer George Lucas and director Steven Spielberg staged all the action on a grand scale with the backing of John Williams' iconic score, and several memorable set pieces are excitingly edited by Michael Kahn. Foremost among these is Ford's fight with a giant bald German airplane mechanic (Pat Roach), made all the more dangerous by the fact that a propeller plane is circling them and is about to go up in flames. Glenn Randall, Jr., coordinated the stunts with British stuntman Vic Armstrong standing in for Ford when the action became too hairy. It's a rousingly good fight and the most memorable of the entire franchise thanks in large part to the ingenious scenario and Ford's underdog status as he goes up against his huge opponent. Interestingly, Ford fights dirty from the outset, kicking, biting and throwing dirt into the eyes of the grinning, cocksure mechanic.

Roach, a professional wrestler turned stunt actor, was something of a good luck piece to the Indiana Jones franchise. He also played the main Sherpa who fights Ford during the Raven Bar fight and again went toe to toe with Ford as an Indian guard who ends up in the jaws of a rock crusher in *Indiana Jones and the Temple of Doom* (1984). He played a Gestapo agent and fought Ford on a dirigible in *Indiana Jones and the Last Crusade* (1989); the footage ended up on the cutting room floor. This fight resurfaced on special DVD extras.

The *Raiders* fight was shot in Tunisia. The gutsy star wound up doing much of the action with Roach. Both actors relied on one another to signal when it was time to move out of the way of the live propeller as they continuously circled one another while throwing punches, oftentimes unintentionally landing blows to the other's face. Ford never complained, even when he suffered a minor knee injury when a heat-softened tire ran over his leg. He was too busy watching Roach and his relationship with the blade to notice his own location to the plane's tires. Crew members had to rock the plane off the trapped Ford. A drive-chain is clearly visible on-screen as the means to turn the plane's undercar-

Pat Roach (left) and Harrison Ford fight around a moving propeller plane in Paramount's *Raiders of the Lost Ark* (1981).

riage. One of the greatest logistical hurdles for cinematographer Douglas Slocombe was the continuity of the shadows, necessitating the scene be shot at the same time each day. Photos from the set show Spielberg sparring with Roach to perfect the fight. Stuntwoman Wendy Leech doubles female lead Karen Allen as she and Armstrong run away from the plane in long shot. In real life, Armstrong and Leech married. Armstrong won favor with Spielberg by calling out that a Ford punch would appear as a miss on camera. Spielberg was ready to wrap the shot but filmed the punch again from a different angle. Armstrong was proven right when viewing dailies, saving the production from having to reshoot the costly scene again.

The Raven Bar fight was filmed first in a London studio. Roach was knocked out when he was smashed onto a table that didn't break. Matters were exacerbated by the fact that Roach was on fire in the scene. Stuntman Billy Horrigan ran into the shot to extinguish Roach, who was unable to signal that the fire was becoming too hot. Among the bits of the fight that didn't make the final cut: Roach press-slamming Ford overhead and throwing him against the wall. These later resurfaced in "Making Of" documentaries. Spielberg then cast Roach as Otto the German mechanic, necessitating that Roach shave his head and have a local police friend vouch for his identity when presenting his passport to leave the country.

Six-one, 185-pound Harrison Ford, a carpenter by trade, excelled as an action hero and enthusi-

astic screen puncher. However, little in his background suggested he'd be so skilled in this endeavor outside his working with wood. He had never participated in athletics and was a conscientious objector during the Vietnam War. Yet Ford took to the weight training he did for the part of Jones and quickly developed a reputation for being agile and able to do much of his own stunt work. He was especially good at acting while partaking in fights, which added to his popularity with audiences.

Many notice the disparity in fighting styles Ford creates dependent on the type of character he is playing. Indiana Jones is a great and resourceful fighter, though he is often overmatched physically by his opponents. Ford's Everyman heroes are far clumsier, stumbling and grimacing as they are unaccustomed to fisticuffs but still manage to obtain results. One of Ford's most popular moments came in the original *Raiders* when he is presented with expert swordsman Terry Richards in a marketplace. Ford and Richards were supposed to have an extended fight, but Ford was suffering from an upset stomach and dysentery. He suggested to Spielberg that he merely withdraw his gun and shoot the swordsman. The humorous gag got one of the biggest audience reactions. Ford's best fights came against Rutger Hauer in *Blade Runner* (1982), Michael Levering in *Witness* (1985), Sean Bean in *Patriot Games* (1992), Andreas Katsulas in *The Fugitive* (1993), Gary Oldman in *Air Force One* (1997), Paul Bettany in

Firewall (2006) and Igor Jijikine and Dimitri Di-atchenko in *Indiana Jones and the Kingdom of the Crystal Skull* (2008).

See: Duke, Brad. *Harrison Ford: The Films.* Jefferson, NC: McFarland, 2008; *Raiders of the Lost Ark* DVD commentary; Rinzler, J.W., and Laurent Bouzereau. *The Complete Making of Indiana Jones: The Definitive Story Behind All Four Films.* Del Rey, 2008.

THE BIKER BRAWL in *The Cannonball Run* (1981)

This silly, often absurd Hal Needham cross-country car race picture headlines the director's pal Burt Reynolds in yet another of his mugging, self-centered "good old boy" portrayals. Reynolds is partnered with Dom DeLuise in an ambulance with their main competition coming from Dean Martin and Sammy Davis, Jr., dressed as priests in a red Ferrari. Jackie Chan improbably plays a Japanese competitor in a Subaru. Roger Moore comes off the best as a dandy who thinks he's Roger Moore playing James Bond. Farrah Fawcett, Jack Elam, Bert Convy, Jamie Farr, Adrienne Barbeau, Tara Buckman, Rick Aviles, Michael Hui and Alfie Wise are all along for the ridiculous ride. The *Chicago Sun Times* called it "an abdication of artistic responsibility at the lowest possible level of ambition."

When the competitors are stalled by road work on a desert highway, they encounter a biker gang led by Peter Fonda. The bikers prove to be incredibly incompetent as the heavyset DeLuise dons the superhero persona of Captain Chaos for the four-minute fight, which seems to be aimed at entertaining 12-year-olds. Reynolds takes nothing seriously as he laughs throughout the punchfest. Martin is also guilty of taking the fighting too lightly, though the sight of a 60-year-old priest beating up bikers is a visual treat. At least Chan gets to show off his kicks. However, it's a poorly choreographed fight by his standards. Several of his kicks sweep past his foes without the appearance of contact. According to *Hick Flicks,* "[Chan's] fancy footwork is crowded out by the mugging and preening of his co-stars," while *The Essential Jackie Chan Sourcebook* admitted that the film is "difficult for some fans to watch." Chan does get a laugh when he executes a final double leg kick and splits his pants. Moore also gets laughs spoofing his image when he adopts a martial arts stance and announces he is Roger Moore. Biker Robert

Tessier, unimpressed, punches Moore in the jaw to the humorous sound effect of glass breaking.

Bobby Bass was stunt coordinator with Allan Graf, Dave Mungenast, Don Ruffin, Tom Harper, Richard Epper, Mike DeLuna, Jim Nickerson, Brad Orrison and Conrad Palmisano taking part in the fight action outside Tucson, Arizona. Bobby Sargent doubles star Reynolds when Chan is fighting in the foreground. Needham let Chan set up his own fighting but wouldn't acquiesce to the month of preparation Chan requested for the scene. The husky Graf, a USC football player who takes an extended series of Chan's punches and kicks, would become one of the more visible stunt actors of the 1980s and 1990s. His crowning achievement: his brutal fight with W. Earl Brown in the 2006 *Deadwood* episode "A Two-Headed Beast."

Overall the film proved great fun for the actors to make and was a huge box office hit thanks to undemanding audiences who simply sought a few laughs. It was followed in 1984 by *Cannonball Run 2* which was every bit as dumb and featured another climactic desert brawl at the Pinto Ranch. This one threw in Telly Savalas, Doug McClure, Tony Danza, Richard Kiel, Henry Silva, Joe Thiesmann and an orangutan, among other ingredients. Chan's fight choreography with stuntmen Branscombe Richmond, Rick Avery and Tom Elliott was at least improved in this second go-round. For all its flaws, these fun-filled fights still have a place in the hearts of those who saw them as kids.

See: *The Cannonball Run* DVD commentary; Von Doviak, Scott. *Hick Flicks: The Rise and Fall of Redneck Cinema.* Jefferson, NC: McFarland, 2004.

JAN-MICHAEL VINCENT vs. MICHAEL PARKS in *Hard Country* (1981)

Considered a knock-off of *Urban Cowboy* (1980), director David Greene's Texas-set *Hard Country* has its merits. Filmed in 1979, it provides an early look at Kim Basinger as a young beauty who wants to escape the dead-end life of her beer-guzzling boyfriend Jan-Michael Vincent but loves him all the same. It also features one heck of a fight between antagonistic brothers Vincent and Michael Parks. The blood vs. blood aspect makes this particularly interesting, and it's one of the best acted and most emotional fights ever put on film. Vincent and Parks engage in the brutal fistic exchange after the sleazy Parks senses Basinger's vulnerability and forces himself on her. The two knock one another all over a model mobile home office until each is a bloody, bruised, red-eyed mess. They are on the verge of tears but out of brotherly competition continue to take the fight one punch further to try to get the last word. Finally Vincent calls it quits and staggers off and Parks collapses into an easy chair. The 5'11", 170-pound Parks is especially good here. The actors do the majority of the physical exchange with doubles Mike Tillman and Mickey Gilbert seen in long shot for a couple of wall-slamming tumbles. John Moio served as stunt coordinator.

Five-foot-ten, 165-pound Vincent spent his youth soaking up sun on California's beaches. His Golden Boy good looks and sinewy build attracted attention as the hippie-turned-Marine in the TV movie *Tribes* (1970), and he immediately proved himself skilled in on-screen and off-screen fisticuffs. He once beat up Charles Manson follower Tex Watson and won the role of Robert Mitchum's son in *Going Home* (1971) by getting into a boxing ring to spar with the star. Charles Bronson likewise approved Vincent's casting as his hit man apprentice in *The Mechanic* (1972), and the young actor was especially good taking on multiple opponents in a poolroom fight in *Buster and Billie* (1974). Once heralded as the next Paul Newman, Vincent marred his reputation with substance abuse and a multitude of legal difficulties including barroom quarrels.

Vincent had notable fights in *The Undefeated* (1969), *Big Wednesday* (1978) and *Hooper* (1978) (see entries). Fights of interest came against Robert Mitchum in *Going Home*, Gene Hackman and James Coburn in *Bite the Bullet* (1975), L.Q. Jones and Martin Kove in *White Line Fever* (1975), Richard Gere in *Baby Blue Marine* (1976), Rudy Ramos in *Defiance* (1980), Lance Henriksen in *Hit List* (1989) and Dan Haggerty in *Abducted II: The Reunion* (1995). On TV's *Bonanza,* he fought Jim Davis in 1968's "The Arrival of Eddie" and Charles McGraw in 1969's "Unwanted." On *Gunsmoke,* he fought Ken Mayer in 1971's "The Legend." By the time he was starring on *Airwolf* (1984–1987), he was more reliant on stunt doubles for extended fights.

A few other 1980s fights flew under the radar and are worthy of mention, specifically for their unbridled brutality. Among these are Sean Penn against Esai Morales in *Bad Boys* (1983), Rutger Hauer taking on Brion James and John Dennis

Johnston in *A Breed Apart* (1984), Steve James laying a martial arts whooping on Willem Dafoe in *To Live and Die in L.A.* (1985), Tommy Lee Jones fighting Lee Ving and stuntmen Carl Ciarfalio and Don Pulford in *Black Moon Rising* (1986), Bryan Brown improvising with kitchenware on Tim Gallin in *F/X* (1986), Jeff Daniels trying to survive against a psychopathic Ray Liotta in *Something Wild* (1986), drunk Mickey Rourke goading bartender Frank Stallone into an alley fight in *Barfly* (1987), and Tom Selleck battling crooked cop David Rasche in *An Innocent Man* (1989).

See: *Jan-Michael Vincent: The E! True Hollywood Story*; Shapiro, Dana. "Jan-Michael Vincent." *Icon.* June 1999.

BURT REYNOLDS vs. DAN INOSANTO AND WEAVER LEVY in *Sharky's Machine* (1981)

After muddying his tough guy reputation with a flurry of comedic car crash films for stuntman pal Hal Needham, Burt Reynolds returned to gritty urban police fare as the director and star of *Sharky's Machine,* based on William Diehl's novel. Reynolds' role as Atlanta vice cop Sharky recalls the physical direction his career once seemed headed as the star of the TV cop shows *Hawk* (1966) and *Dan August* (1970–1971). The energetic film has many hard-hitting and memorable moments as Reynolds saves high-priced call girl Rachel Ward from crazed hit man Henry Silva; including a basement fight with a pair of Asian thugs (Dan Inosanto and Weaver Levy). The one-minute fight in partner Richard Libertini's home begins with a jolt and is superbly choreographed by Bobby Bass. It benefits from the gutsiness of Reynolds, who does all his own fighting for William A. Fraker's mobile camera despite Bobby Sargent being available for doubling duties. Atlanta-based Wing Chung instructor Francis Fong doubled Inosanto when Reynolds smashes him into a kid's playpen.

Although Reynolds puts up a valiant fight and swings a folding chair at his assailants, the speed of the martial artists' furious assault soon takes him down. Cal Poly football player Levy knocks him out with a pair of nunchaku. Plaudits go to Reynolds for being unafraid to lose a screen fight, setting himself up as an underdog for the audience to root for. This leads to an unforgettable scene where Reynolds is tortured on a boat by crooked cop Darryl Hickman and has his fingers cut off one joint at a time by Inosanto's balisong knife. Reynolds ultimately gets what's left of his hands on Hickman's gun and takes care of the Asian assassins before the final shootout with Silva in a highrise. Few reviews mentioned the Asian fight specifically, although *Time* wrote of Reynolds, "As a director he's good with violent unpleasantness."

When Inosanto auditioned for Bass, he was surprised to find Reynolds wanted to run through the fight with him to test his reactions to Reynolds' punches. A dull knife blade was used for the exchange and Inosanto inadvertently cut the star. Inosanto feared Reynolds would be upset, but the star didn't care. He simply asked Inosanto to throw him to complete the audition. After Reynolds hit the floor, he bandaged his hand and told Bass they had found their man. In the film, Bass allowed Inosanto to fully show off his martial arts, tweaking what didn't work well for the camera.

See: Oliver, Myrna. "Bobby Bass, 65: Legendary Hollywood Stuntman." *Los Angeles Times*. November 11, 2001.

Sylvester Stallone vs. The Police Station in *First Blood* (1982)

With regard to the boxing choreography seen in the original *Rocky* (1976), this is far and away the best fight of Sylvester Stallone's career based on a combination of technical expertise and audience involvement. At this point in his career, Stallone had the ability to rouse audience emotion with himself cast as the underdog. *First Blood* introduces movie audiences to one of Stallone's most famous characters, disillusioned Vietnam vet John Rambo, a killing machine struggling to adapt to life back in the U.S. The iconic character originated in writer David Morrell's 1972 page-turner of a novel of the same name. When Stallone's Rambo is unjustly railroaded by Pacific Northwest cop Brian Dennehy, he unleashes his pent-up frustration on the entire police station, taking down Dennehy and sheriff's deputies Jack Starrett, Chris Mulkey, David Caruso, Michael Talbott, Bruce Barbour, Alf Humphreys and David Crowley in a heart-pumping burst of adrenaline *Newsweek* called "astonishingly efficient." Diamond Farnsworth, Frank Orsatti and Don McGovern were all on hand to double Stallone, but the screenwriter-star did the majority of the fight action. Cinematographer Andrew Laszlo was able to keep his camera on Stallone throughout, aiding the verisimilitude of the fight immensely. Although he was opposed to actors doing their own fights on the principle of safety, Conrad Palmisano coordinated the action and handled the second unit for director Ted Kotcheff. Jerry Goldsmith's rousing score is especially memorable and fits the transition of the scene. Joan Freeman edits for maximum impact.

The film was shot on location in Hope, British Columbia, during the fall and winter, with Stallone parading around the frigid environment in a cut-off T-shirt. The police station was built in front of the town's District Hall on the corner of Wallace and Third Avenue, with the on-screen construction being

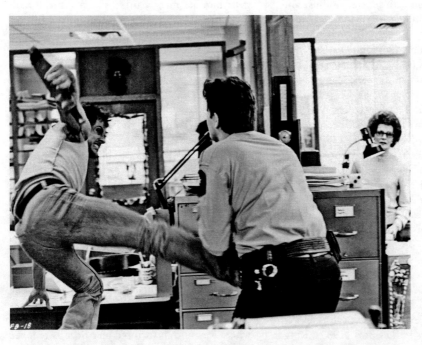

Sylvester Stallone takes out Michael Talbot in Orion's *First Blood* (1982).

worked into the plot as a remodel by production designer Wolf Kroeger. The actors playing the policemen were skeptical Stallone could best them in a realistic fight. Stallone's bodyguard Tony Maffatone was brought in as a technical advisor. A weapons expert, he demonstrated to the actors and stuntmen that a man of Rambo's training could indeed escape the situation by having them all take a whack at him. He dispatched the entire squad with ease. Filming ensued but not without Stallone taking his share of bumps and bruises. Stallone endured up to 14 takes being clubbed in the small of the back by character actor Starrett, who tended to get carried away with his performance. Stallone erred during the breakout and smashed a stuntman's nose with his elbow. Actors Dennehy, Mulkey and Talbott all waved away stuntmen and took falls to improve the footage. Stallone showed off his agility sliding across the floors and breaking out the Tiger Claw technique to dispatch a deputy. Stallone gave his all to the fight and the results are on the screen. According to *Fight Choreography*,

> Rambo's empty-handed fight scene against multiple attackers is a brawl, self-defense, and grappling in a very well-choreographed fight scene. Although a few of the moves and reactions in the fight were theatrically flashy, it still keeps the emotional core of the fight. What also made the fight/escape from jail so satisfying for the audience was the gradual set-up that led to the fight, so by the time Rambo emotionally explodes and fights back, the audience was already behind Stallone's character, and they are relieved of all the tension that was built up to that point.

Sylvester Stallone, 5'8" and 180 pounds, served as an athletic coach and worked odd jobs such as bouncer while trying to break into films. He made it as the screenwriter and star of *Rocky*, an inspirational tale about a simple-minded tough from the streets of Philadelphia who gets a chance to fight for the heavyweight title. Stallone's Rocky Balboa character won audiences over by doing one-armed pushups and punching raw sides of beef in a meat locker. As screenwriter, he insisted he play a part in the fight choreography in his bouts against Carl Weathers, although Jim Nickerson handled the more intricate aspects of the punches and camera angles. The Rocky role propelled Stallone to star status, and from that point forward he realized how his physique factored in

his success. Over the next several years he began adding increasing muscle to his 16" biceps by working out with bodybuilders Franco Columbu and George Pipasik. Stallone trained in the boxing ring with Ray Notaro for *Rocky* sequels and also endured martial arts workouts with Carter Wong and David Lea. As his muscles grew, he became an on-screen power-puncher, dropping the likes of obnoxious characters Martin Kove in *Rambo: First Blood Part II* (1985) and Andy Robinson in *Cobra* (1986) with one mighty blow.

Stallone fought David Carradine in *Death Race 2000* (1975), Voyo Goric in *Rambo: First Blood Part II* (1985), Brian Thompson in *Cobra* (1986), Terry Funk in *Over the Top* (1987), Harold Diamond and Randy Raney in *Rambo 3* (1988), Sonny Landham in *Lock Up* (1989), Robert Z'Dar in *Tango and Cash* (1989), Tommy Morrison in *Rocky V* (1990), Wesley Snipes in *Demolition Man* (1993), Mickey Rourke in *Get Carter* (2000), Steve Austin in *The Expendables* (2010), Jean Claude Van Damme in *The Expendables 2* (2012), Jason Momoa in *Bullet to the Head* (2012), Arnold Schwarzenegger in *Escape Plan* (2013) and Mel Gibson in *The Expendables 3* (2014).

See: *First Blood* DVD commentary; Sanello, Frank. *Stallone: A Rocky Life*. Edinburgh: Mainstream, 1998; Taub, Eric. *Gaffers, Grips, and Best Boys*. New York: St. Martin's, 1994.

Nick Nolte vs. Eddie Murphy in *48 Hrs.* (1982)

Writer-director Walter Hill's popular comedy-action flick memorably pairs beefy, perpetually hung-over cop Nick Nolte with flashy, sharp-tongued convict Eddie Murphy, who he has sprung from prison for 48 hours to help him track down brutal cop-killing criminals James Remar and Sonny Landham. The cop and con are at each other's throats from the get-go, with their acid remarks spilling into a riotous three-minute physical confrontation in an alleyway that begins with Nolte announcing, "I fight dirty." He slugs Murphy, who slams the car door into the unsuspecting Nolte's legs. It's a classic brawler vs. boxer situation, as Murphy scores early with his jabs and quickness, making the shambling Nolte swing wildly and stumble around. Nolte uses his superior brawn to tackle Murphy into the garbage and put a whooping on him with several unanswered punches. *Time* didn't think the mismatch would take that long, noting, "The brawny Nolte looks as if he could blow the willowy Murphy away with one punch." Both men are comically exhausted as the police arrive to break up the fight. Nolte shows his badge to the cops, who allow the fighters to leave in Nolte's beat-up sky blue Cadillac Deville convertible. As Nolte prepares to pull away, he lands a final blow on Murphy's jaw. The *Chicago Sun Times* remarked that Hill's films "almost always feature at least one beautifully choreographed, unbelievably violent fight scene."

Bennie Dobbins was stunt coordinator with Terry Leonard doubling Nolte and John Sherrod doubling Murphy over the three days it took for Hill to complete the scene. The major drawback is the too-obvious use of Sherrod as Murphy's double. It was Murphy's film debut, and he was unfamiliar with movie fights. Dobbins was able to use Nolte far more than he was Murphy in setting up the best punches and angles. Movie fight veteran Nolte's on camera for over 90 percent of the fight. Dobbins was constantly sparring with Murphy and throwing punches at him on the set to keep him loose for the fight. Hill and cinematographer Ric Waite shot over Nolte's back on Murphy and over Sherrod's back on Nolte, trying to keep Sherrod in shadow as much as possible. They had both actors throw punches at one another to give editor Freeman Davies the best footage possible. Nolte weighed over 220 pounds, while Murphy was closer to 150. In the sequel *Another 48 Hrs.* (1990), a much heavier Murphy gets revenge by throwing a basketball into Nolte's face.

Standing nearly 6'1" and tipping the scales at 185 pounds in top shape, Nolte was good enough as a football player to receive a scholarship to Arizona State but was loath to attend classes. He also played ball at Eastern Arizona College, the University of Omaha, Colorado State and Pasadena City College. On the side, he was an iron worker in Los Angeles. At this point, he came to the realization that he didn't have what it takes to become a professional football player. He was busted by the FBI for selling fake draft cards to underage drinkers and became a convicted felon, which kept him from Vietnam and turned him on to the life of an itinerant actor.

It was his star-making turn as good-hearted loser Tom Jordache in the groundbreaking 1976 mini-series *Rich Man, Poor Man* that made him a household name. Nolte was superb in the multifaceted role, playing a quick-fisted hellion who surprises NFL legend Dick Butkus with the power behind his blows in a street fight. Nolte becomes

a pro boxer on the run from the mob after he takes out champion George Maharis in a hotel brawl over Lynda Day George. As an adult hiding out in the Merchant Marine, he encounters the infamously evil Falconetti (William Smith) at sea. Tension between the men builds to the breaking point as Smith bullies Nolte's black friend Herbert Jefferson, Jr. Nolte and Smith have the most heavily anticipated fight in TV history in a cargo hold, and neither disappoints during the two minutes of action. Nolte did all his own fights with Smith, earning the respect of the industry's stuntmen.

Nolte was a physical actor known for obsessive preparation. He trained several months with pro boxer Sonny Shields for the *Rich Man, Poor Man* part and often transformed his body from role to role. He was huge and threatening in *Q&A* (1990), as scary to the audience as to Timothy Hutton when he decided to rough him up. In the comic *Three Fugitives* (1989), Nolte was like a bull in a China shop knocking over everything in his way. He opened eyes with the precision of his brutality in taking out Richard Masur and Ray Sharkey with martial arts in *Who'll Stop the Rain* (1978). He had trained in tai chi chuan for the role with Marshall Ho'o. Nolte fought Robert Viharo in *Return to Macon County* (1975), Bob Minor in *The Deep* (1977) (see entry), Dennis Hayden, Rex Pierson and Dave Efron in *Another 48 Hrs.* (1990), Robert DeNiro in *Cape Fear* (1991), Treat Williams and Daniel Baldwin in *Mulholland Falls* (1996) and Sean Penn in *U–Turn* (1997).

See: *48 Hrs.* movie press kit; Gast, Peter. "48 Hrs.: High Tension Stunts in Nick Nolte's Crime Thriller." *Action Films.* February 1983; "Nolte Had to Take Pounding for Role." *The Dispatch.* February 6, 1976.

CHUCK NORRIS VS. DAVID CARRADINE in *Lone Wolf McQuade* (1983)

A highly anticipated three-minute showdown between grizzled karate hero Chuck Norris and TV's *Kung Fu* stylist David Carradine had audiences rushing to movie theaters. Multiple black belt Norris is a tough Texas Ranger in modern-day El Paso and Carradine is a European martial arts champ heading a smuggling operation along the border. Both are involved with Barbara Carrera, and the film builds to the memorable climax that sees their contrasting styles meet in a dusty border town with pulsating Spaghetti Western music from composer Francesco De Masi heightening the tension. Not only are their styles different, but Carradine strangled Norris' mentor L.Q. Jones, shot his dog, and fights dirty one-on-one. He kicks Norris when he's down, tosses dirt in his face and, worst of all, he backhands Norris' teenage daughter to the ground. This sends Norris on a rallying comeback of flying reverse kicks and spinning backhands in a display of raw, unbridled power. Punishing elbow blows and sweaty slow-motion shots are displayed, as both actors impressively do the fight without the aid of stunt doubles.

Chuck Norris (left) and David Carradine engage in a highly anticipated showdown in Orion's *Lone Wolf McQuade* (1983).

John Barrett and Darwin Benjamin were on hand to stunt-double Norris with Charlie Skeen ready to step in for Carradine, but the actors were adamant they were doing everything. Cinematographer Roger Sherman did need to speed up the camera to make a few Carradine kicks appear more impressive. Norris choreographed the fight with the help of his brother Aaron Norris. Aaron plays one of the goons Chuck fights throughout the film, as do Gil Reyes, Richard Terschel, Russ Dodson, Rick McCallum and Kane Hodder. *Lone Wolf McQuade* was one of Chuck's most popular films and was later reworked into the long-running TV series *Walker, Texas Ranger* (1993–2001).

Publicity played up the fact that Carradine's contract stipulated he couldn't be seen losing a screen fight to Norris for fear of upsetting his *Kung Fu* fans. Carradine dominates the fight early, only to be pulled away from the action when he begins to lose. Norris and director Steve Carver solve the contract situation with a grenade. Carradine, battling a stagnant career, was energized by landing the film and trained with Rob Moses. Once he reached the set, he began a training program with Norris' stable of stuntmen. When Carradine grew bored with the rigor after the first day, he bought beers and shots of rum for the stuntmen. The next day he sailed through the workouts while the stuntmen struggled. It was decided that Carradine could do his own thing on the set.

Norris and Carradine avoided working out together to build up the tension between their characters. Stories surfaced that the stuntmen warned the star that Carradine was hitting and kicking too hard. Once filming began, Norris had to issue a warning to Carradine, emphasized with a moderate punch to Carradine's kidney. Reports of broken noses and Carradine kicks to Norris' jaw reached the media, but Carradine later recalled only a strained leg ligament on his part and a bulky groin for Norris as a result of the four days it took to film the battle. He claimed their fight went smoothly and that Norris was a total professional. *Black Belt* called the final fight "one of Norris' best," while the *Toledo Blade* regarded it as a "treat for barroom brawl fans."

See: Allen, Terence. "The Top Three Movies of Jean-Claude Van Damme and Chuck Norris." *Black Belt*. August 1994; "Chuck Norris Goes Troubleshooting." *Fighting Stars*. February 1983.

The Greasers vs. the Socs in *The Outsiders* (1983)

"Let's do it for Johnny!" announces teen heartthrob Matt Dillon before the Greasers rumble in the rain with the Socs (the preppy socials) in an empty lot in this Francis Ford Coppola adaptation of the popular S.E. Hinton novel about 1960s youth.

Johnny (Ralph Macchio) was knifed in an incident with Socs Leif Garrett and Darren Daulton, leading to the major showdown and plenty of heated emotion. Coppola said that the filming of this fight was harder than anything he'd ever done. There were approximately two dozen young men in front of Stephen H. Burum's camera all trying to capture the maestro Coppola's attention with their energetic fighting. After an establishing pan of the combatants, Coppola and his editors chose to keep the segmented shots brief and confined, maintaining visual interest and believability with a flurry of cuts. There were no sweeping panorama shots of the overall battle since there were a great deal of local extras filling the ranks.

Standing out among the cast of young up-and-comers during the brawl are Greasers Patrick Swayze and Tom Cruise. Both prove to be superior fighters and show their future potential as action stars. Swayze starred in *Road House* (1989) (see entry) while Cruise played a bare-knuckle scrapper in *Far and Away* (1992). Matt Dillon as Dallas also acquits himself well in the nearly four minutes of brawling. Rob Lowe, C. Thomas Howell, Emilio Estevez and Glenn Withrow register far lower on the scale of tough guy swagger. Howell's Ponyboy Curtis is knocked unconscious by the fight's first punch. Primarily representing the Socs in the rumble is stunt actor John Meier as a former football acquaintance of Swayze's Darrell Curtis. Those two square off throughout the fight, which was filmed at Crutchfield Park in Tulsa, Oklahoma.

As part of the auditioning process, the young actors were asked to improvise a fight on a soundstage, with everyone intent on impressing Coppola. Stunt coordinator Buddy Joe Hooker and Coppola took a chance once on location in Tulsa by hiring as fighters many locals, including Tom Hillman, Tom Patton, Joe Cervantez and Gene Bledsoe who were paired up as fighting partners with the stars for budgetary reasons. Intermixed with the locals were young professional stuntmen Reid Rondell, Tom Elliott, Steve Davison and Scott Wilder. Much of the brawl became an ad-libbed free-for-all, especially when rain began to fall on the first day of shooting. For continuity's sake and because the rushes looked so good, simulated "rain towers" were used for the remainder of the four-day shoot with a bonfire raging in the background. The battleground became a virtual mud pit with cast members slipping and sliding all over the place as they wrestled and punched at one another. Between takes, the cast members wrapped in blankets and drank hot chocolate. The chilly stars came away with some real injuries: a cut lip for Estevez, a black eye for Howell, a bloody nose for Lowe, and a broken thumb for Cruise. Cruise also had a cap removed from a tooth for the fight. When a local punched Swayze square in the face, Swayze responded by knocking the man out.

Hooker tried to build a spirit of unity among his young cast of Greasers by having them train together, running and lifting weights daily while he taught them to stunt-fight. Much of the actors' free time was spent gearing up for the fight and raising havoc in the hotel. They routinely donned boxing gloves, headgear and mouthpieces and sparred with one another in their hotel rooms. Cruise added nearly 20 pounds of muscle for the role. The young "Brat Pack" (as they were dubbed by the press) became like brothers. Throughout the shoot, the filmmakers intentionally maintained tension between the actors cast as Greasers and Socs, including a much-hyped football game between the groups. There was some real animosity between cast members. Cruise and Lowe had to be pulled apart when their rehearsals became too spirited.

See: Coppola, Francis Ford, and Gene Phillips. *Francis Ford Coppola: Interviews.* Jackson: University Press of Mississippi, 2004; Lowe, Rob. *Stories I Only Tell My Friends: An Autobiography.* New York: Henry Holt, 2011; Sheen, Martin, and Emilio Estevez. *Along the Way: The Journey of a Father and Son.* New York: Simon & Schuster, 2012.

Sean Connery vs. Pat Roach in *Never Say Never Again* (1983)

Never Say Never Again is a James Bond film made outside the franchise's normal production team by director Irvin Kershner from a Lorenzo Semple, Jr., screenplay. It therefore faced an audience of divided loyalties. The film is based on *Thunderball*, which was already made with Sean Connery in 1965. The new producers did manage to coax a graying Connery back to reprise his most famous role, despite him once saying he'd never again play the part. The movie is a mixed bag, but does boast a four-minute fight at a Shrublands health clinic, where an aging 007 has been sent to dry out and get back into fighting condition. He gets to do that when the huge SPECTRE henchman Lippe (Pat Roach) shows up to interrupt a Connery weightlifting session by pushing down on the bench press machine. "Heavy, Mr. Bond?" Roach asks, his sole line of dialogue.

The two fight all over the clinic, with Connery

Pat Roach (left) stalks Sean Connery in Warner Bros.' *Never Say Never Again* (1983).

doing everything possible to survive against his oversized opponent. Connery emerges victorious after throwing the contents of a lab beaker into Roach's face. With burning eyes, Roach backs into a shelf filled with glass objects. He falls to his knees and then flat on his face, revealing shards of glass and a long cylinder in his back. It's a curious end for a powerful bad guy in the Oddjob and Jaws tradition. When Connery looks at the container's contents, it's James Bond's urine sample. Supposedly the ammonia present in the specimen burned Roach's eyes, but some viewers like to think Agent 007 had a nasty case of the clap. *Newsweek* labeled the fight a "fun passage," while the *Pittsburgh Post-Gazette* found it "thrilling and well-choreographed."

Throughout the Douglas Slocombe–lensed fight, Roach takes delight in tossing Connery like a rag doll. Its broadly comedic staging is far more reminiscent of the Roger Moore–style Bond fights than those of Connery. More often than not, stunt coordinator Vic Armstrong fills in for the 51-year-old star. Stunt actor Roach does his own fight work. Connery punches with dumbbells and throws them at Roach. He even swings a chest expander, which Roach rips apart with one great pull. However, the fight suffers because we never discover anything about Lippe. There's no introduction before the fight to establish his lethalness or cruelty. He appears inconsistent throughout the fight as well. He displays great strength and can punch through doors. Other times Connery merely shakes off the punches. Roach keeps coming, but there's little sense of dramatic urgency as there was in the previous Connery Bond fights. Here it seems they're spoofing Bond. A disengaged Roach even stops to smile when he overhears a goal being scored from a soccer broadcast. Ironically, he has just kicked Connery in the head. An interesting weapon is used by Roach, a whip-like 44-inch metal belt he can snap to rigidity to break Connery's defenses such as the blade of a knife.

Roach was intrigued by the odd weight bench at the beginning of the scene, as was the audience.

When Roach cut the cable attached to the counterweights, the unattached bar became heavier. Roach bought the bench from the filmmakers and modified it. He placed it in his own gymnasium and advertised it as the bench from the film. It attracted great attention, and Roach was occasionally known to re-enact the Connery scene with lucky gym patrons. Since the film was made outside normal Bond production channels, some stuntmen caught flak. All was quickly forgotten and Armstrong once again resumed working on the Bond series. Armstrong blocked the action out on paper, but once on the set he went from visual memory and accepted suggestions from Connery and Roach. They spent three weeks putting the fight together. Aikido instructor Steven Seagal was hired to brush up Connery's martial arts skills. Instead, Seagal managed to break Connery's wrist during training. He wasn't around when the filmmakers filmed the fight at Luton Hoo in Bedfordshire. The filming was rushed as they were losing the location (the queen was scheduled to attend a dance the following day). They recreated the lab room at Elstree Studios in London. Ironically, the finished film features only the footage shot at Luton Hoo.

See: *Film '83: Never Say Never Again* special; *Never Say Never Again* press kit.

JACKIE CHAN VS. BENNY "THE JET" URQUIDEZ in *Wheels on Meals* (1984)

Jackie Chan has said that the mind-boggling five-minute kung fu vs. kickboxing battle in the Barcelona Spanish Old Castle in *Wheels on Meals* was his best, and there's little argument. *Inside Kung Fu* called the showpiece of this curiously titled action-comedy "one of the greatest fights of all time." *Jackie Chan: Inside the Dragon* said it was "one of the best fight scenes ever filmed." *Films of Fury* termed it "the most realistic martial arts fight in kung fu film history," and it's highlighted in the 1992 documentary *Deadliest Art: The Best of the Martial Arts Films*. The high praise is warranted as the screen is filled with some of the fastest action ever put onto celluloid. Speculation abounds that the film was slightly sped up, but Chan has denied that's the case. It's simply two great martial artists at the peak of their powers. The fighters make body contact with several kicks, sometimes reversing the other fighter's momentum and sending their body sprawling in the opposite direction.

Highlights are a Chan cartwheel kick and an Urquidez spinning back kick that misses Chan but extinguishes the flames of a series of six nearby candles. This was an amazing feat Urquidez repeated for the cameras on a second take. Despite the intensity of the action, Chan brings his patented humor, pausing a few times to rub a sore body part and breaking out of a hold by tickling Urquidez's armpit. These close-up humor breaks help the fight's pacing, so it's not merely a desensitizing assault on the viewer's senses. It also gives the fighters a chance to size one another up. Chan ends the fight with a flying knee to Urquidez's chin that knocks the latter out a high window.

The fight coordinator was *Wheels on Meals* director and co-star Sammo Hung, one of the popular "three brothers" consisting of Chan, Hung and the other co-star Yuen Biao. Chan and Biao both fight Keith Vitali. This was top-ranked American karate fighter Vitali's first experience with Hong Kong–style filmmaking and he was in awe at the skill and time put into the fights. He was confused, however, when Chan told him they were ready to do their on-screen fight as they hadn't yet rehearsed or worked out the choreography. Chan said that rhythm was more important than choreography and they'd find their on-screen tempo once they started sparring for the cameras. Chan told Vitali to throw some kicks, and he began beating a rhythm on his own thigh. When he had a cadence worked out, he began mixing in his own kicks. In his fight with Chan, Vitali accidentally kicked the star in the throat. Vitali immediately broke character to check on Chan's welfare. This drew the wrath of the crew since Hung had not called "cut." The ever-resilient Chan was okay. Vitali later kicked Hung during a fight. Hung told Vitali at the film's end that he'd be hit over the head with a vase in a fight scene for these transgressions. Hung held true to his word, and there's the trace of a smile on Vitali's face when the vase goes over his skull. The Vitali role was originally offered to Richard Norton, who was on tour as Linda Ronstadt's bodyguard and had to decline.

Behind the scenes, there was considerable tension observed between Chan and Urquidez. Chan challenged Urquidez to see who could do the most back-flips, but Urquidez had little interest in engaging in showboat acrobatics. It was decided they'd fight to contact on the body, and at times the contact was too hard. The Chinese stuntmen were amazed by Urquidez's fighting skill and ability to withstand Chan's punches and kicks, which had to play on Chan's ego. Some viewers believe Urquidez had padding on beneath his shirt, but Chan's light cut off T-shirt appears to provide him little protection. Some uncharacteristic grappling occurs, leading viewers to believe parts of the improvised fight might have been real. At one point, Chan hit Urquidez full force in the head. Urquidez merely smiled when Hung checked on him. When Chan was hit in return, he became angry, warning Urquidez he'd never work in Hong Kong again. Whether this was said in jest or in seriousness is unknown. Chan did repeatedly joke about putting on gloves for real with Urquidez, to which the kickboxer responded, "Any time, Jackie." That never happened, especially seeing as both men were tired by the end of the nearly 48 straight hours spent shooting the fight. Chan literally slept on the floor of the set instead of returning to his accommodations. Whatever the tensions were between them during this shoot, Chan was highly complementary of Urquidez in interviews. Urquidez was brought back to Hong Kong to fight Chan for *Dragons Forever* (1987). This fight, although shorter in length, is nonetheless an interesting companion to their *Wheels on Meals* masterpiece. Urquidez also impressed with an excellent fight against John Cusack in *Grosse Pointe Blank* (1997).

See: Logan, Bey. "Hong Kong Superstar Jackie Chan Owes as Much to Charlie Chaplin as He Does to Bruce Lee." *Black Belt.* January 1994.

MICHAEL PARE vs. WILLEM DAFOE in *Streets of Fire* (1984)

Director Walter Hill returns with one of the 1980s' most visceral and stylish fights in what was marketed as "a rock and roll fable" set in "another time, another place" as beautiful rock singer Diane Lane is kidnapped by a vicious biker gang. To the rescue comes Lane's former lover, 1950s-style loner Michael Pare. He memorably squares off against 1980s punk-rock biker Willem Dafoe with spike maul sledgehammers for the first half of the climactic four-minute fight, then fists and boots until Pare literally pushes a wobbly, out-on-his-feet Dafoe over. It's all backed by Ry Cooder's pulsating score.

The actors are perfect in their roles. There's an especially great moment when the impossibly pale Dafoe loses his hammer and his lips begin to quiver as he realizes Pare can smash him. The sporting Pare tosses his hammer aside and offers

to go bare-knuckle. Dafoe's fists clinch and he lets out a primal scream as he rushes Pare. Over the next two minutes, Pare gets to knock the heavy lacquer from Dafoe's hair, but not before some tense moments where Dafoe gets the upper hand.

Almost the entire fight is impressively done by the stars with Hill editing sharply for maximum impact. Stunt doubles Bruce Barbour and Diamond Farnsworth's presence is undetected in the finished product. The fight took more than nine days to shoot and was another triumph for stunt coordinator Bennie Dobbins. The fight is the only scene set during the daytime. Production designer John Vallone created an impressive neon color-filled world resembling the streets of Chicago beneath the elevated rail. Much of the movie was shot under a giant tarpaulin-covered set at Universal Studios, with painstakingly long periods of time spent by cinematographer Andrew Laszlo to light the rain-covered streets.

Pare's character Tom Cody is a cool hero and a great fighter. The audience first encounters him in a diner after he has been summoned to rescue Lane from the creepy clutches of Dafoe. In the diner, Pare's Cody encounters wannabe tough Paul Mones and his gang (stuntmen Vince Deadrick, Jr., Paul M. Lane, Bernie Pock, Spiro Razatos and Jeff Smolek). Taking off his jacket to reveal cut-off sleeves and ripped muscles, Pare takes Mones' butterfly knife, slaps him and gives him the knife back. "Try again," he insists. When Mones does try, Pare beats him and his entire gang up with ease and takes their 1951 Studebaker. All the vehicles are from this vintage era. He later rescues Lane from the bikers in a storm of fiery gas tank explosions with Dafoe promising it's now personal between the two. This sets up the final showdown where the two fighters deliver.

Hill cast the two actors because they were relatively unknown. In reality, the 6'1", 185-pound Pare, a former high school wrestler and football player, towered over the 5'7", 145-pound Dafoe, yet they appear evenly matched thanks to superb editing and Hill's variety of camera tricks. The sledgehammers they use were made of rubber. Pare wanted to take boxing lessons but Hill persuaded him not to, preferring that Pare stick to roundhouse punches for the camera. In post-production, the sound effects crew achieved their flesh-pounding results by purchasing a pig carcass they whaled on with fists and assorted objects. The *Chicago Tribune* found the fight "repulsive" while the *Los Angeles Times* called the action "noisy and empty." It nonetheless proved influential.

Cinematically, Streets of Fire is a transition fight, bringing in the 1980s and beyond at full-bore with its rapid-fire edits and Ry Cooder backing score. It's in line with the glossily produced music video approach raging across MTV at the time. There's still "old school" mixed in. The choreography is pure streetfighting with no elaborate spinning martial arts moves. Hill's camera is stationary with numerous long shots and pauses in the action informing the audience exactly what is going on. The actors are afforded a chance to register dramatically and play off one another. What people remember most about the fight are the comic book exchanges of hammers and fists flash-cut in time to match the rock music score. It's different enough from what came before to begin ushering in a new era.

See: Loretti, Nicanor. "Eddie Wilson Speaks! An Interview with Michael Pare." *Shock Cinema*. #25, 2004; Maslin, Janet. "At the Show." *New York Times*. June 8, 1984; "The Sound of Impact." *Wall Street Journal*. January 2, 2014.

ARNOLD SCHWARZENEGGER VS. VERNON WELLS in *Commando* (1985)

In *Commando*, we find perhaps the 1980s' corniest fight: Austrian bodybuilder Arnold Schwarzenegger as Special Forces agent John Matrix vs. rogue commando Bennett (Vernon Wells) after the latter kidnaps his daughter Alyssa Milano. The fact Bennett is an out-of-shape, flamboyant heavy dressed in a chain-mail tank top while looking like Freddie Mercury of the rock band Queen makes it all the more campy. Wells' hilariously over-the-top performance made Bennett a cult figure with audiences. The film itself is entertaining popcorn nonsense, despite being notoriously violent. Schwarzenegger kills almost 90 people and punches and kicks scores more, all the while delivering comic one-liners courtesy of screenwriter Steven de Souza. Wisecracking heroes would continue to strain action film creditability going forward.

Stunt coordinator Bennie Dobbins and fight coordinator Mike Vendrell were busy on this film, setting up major fights with Wells in a boiler room, Bill Duke in a motel room, and approximately 30 stuntmen at the Sherman Oaks Galleria Mall. *Variety* called the fights "sharp martial arts stuff." The Duke fight was shot in a day at the now-defunct Sunspot Cabaret Motel along the Pacific Coast Highway. It's good despite the fact that stuntman Jophery Brown is far too apparent as Duke's double. The mall fight is cartoon-like as Schwarzenegger dispatches guard after guard, even hurling a dozen off him at once. This fight took six days to film and was shot at night so the mall could remain open during the daytime. The final battle with the soldiers of the fictional country Val Verde was filmed at both the San Simeon Hearst Estate near Big Sur and the Harold Lloyd Estate in Beverly Hills. Joel Kramer and Jeff Jensen were assigned as Schwarzenegger's doubles, but the shirtless star would do the majority of his own action scenes due to his physique. George Fisher doubled Wells. Martial arts expert Vendrell worked out daily with Schwarzenegger on location or at the gym installed on the 20th Century-Fox lot.

Wells, having scored as the bad guy in *The Road Warrior* (1982), originally read for Bennett but didn't land the part and returned to his native Australia. Two days into production, Schwarzenegger, director Mark Lester and producer Joel Silver decided the actor who was cast as Bennett wasn't credible enough as a physical threat. They opted to recast the part and summoned Wells from Australia. Unfortunately, Wells had fallen out of shape and was recovering from a broken arm (he kept it in a sling when not filming). Even worse, the Bennett outfit he inherited was too small and accentuated the belly-weight he had gained. The contrast between Schwarzenegger and Wells is marked, and many consider this fight one of the greatest mismatches in screen history. Although they were roughly the same height and weight, Schwarzenegger's Matrix was all muscle and Wells' Bennett looked like a one-time athlete who hadn't been inside a gym in years. Odds were evened by Matrix suffering from a bullet wound in the arm and, one would surmise, exhaustion from killing 81 people in the ten minutes prior to the showdown.

One reason for the cult status is the perceived gay angle existing between Matrix and Bennett, which director Lester denies was ever screenwriter Steven de Souza's intention. Wells' mustached Bennett pines over Matrix like a lost love throughout the film with campy line readings. He refers to the object of his infatuation by his first name, while Schwarzenegger refers to his character as Bennett, the unfit soldier he kicked out of his unit for unspecified reasons. When they meet in the climax, the dialogue between the two goes way over the

1985

291

top as Schwarzenegger teases Wells with his knife and what he fantasizes doing with it, and the latter reaches ecstatic heights with his line readings.

The Matrix-Bennett fight was originally supposed to take place on the beach, but during filming it was decided to shoot in a boiler room on the 20th Century-Fox lot. The actors and stuntmen fought atop grates and received numerous cuts and scratches. Wells won admirers when he didn't flinch upon grabbing the hot furnace door as he tries to force Schwarzenegger inside. The latter

Vernon Wells (left) battles Arnold Schwarzenegger in 20th Century-Fox's *Commando* (1985).

trusted Wells not to push him too close to the fire. The nine-inch knives were custom-made by Texan knife expert Jack W. Crain. Schwarzenegger dominates the early part of the fight as Wells loses his blade. Midway through the battle, Wells is pushed into a transformer and is electrocuted. Miraculously, he makes a stunning comeback and begins to win the fight ("I'm feeling really, really good, John!"). Wells gets a gun and is about to shoot Schwarzenegger, but the hero rips a steam pipe from the wall and hurls it into Wells, pinning him to the wall as steam exits the pipe (actually condensed CO_2). Schwarzenegger ends the fight with the now famous line, "Let off some steam, Bennett."

Arnold Schwarzenegger was a seven-time Mr. Olympia and five-time Mr. Universe back when he was carrying roughly 20 more pounds of muscle on his physique. The 6'1" Austrian Army veteran worked hard on martial arts and agility training for *Conan the Barbarian* (1982), but it was arguably the display of his pumped-up muscles that turned him into the biggest action star of the 1980s and 1990s. When the shirt was off or the arms were bared, it was hard to believably double him. Schwarzenegger fought Rick Rossovich in *The Terminator* (1984), Jesse "The Body" Ventura in *The Running Man* (1987), Sven Ole-Thorsen in *Red Heat* (1988), David Efron in *Twins* (1988), Michael Ironside in *Total Recall* (1990), Richard Tyson in *Kindergarten Cop* (1990), Robert Patrick in *Terminator 2—Judgment Day* (1991), Ofer

Samra in *True Lies* (1994), James Caan in *Eraser* (1996) and Sylvester Stallone in *Escape Plan* (2013).

See: *Commando* DVD commentary; *Commando* movie press kit; Horsting, Jessie. "The Spectre of Wez." *Starlog*. #124. November 1987.

SAMMO HUNG VS. RICHARD NORTON in *Twinkle, Twinkle Lucky Stars* (1985)

This Sammo Hung–directed Hong Kong film, the third in the *Lucky Stars* series, opens with an incredible three-minute fight in a Pepsi bottling warehouse: Jackie Chan fights alongside Yuen Baio and Andy Lau against an army of thugs including Kar Lok Chin and Dick Wei. This is creative fight choreography at its finest, with the nimble Baio getting a showcase for his fighting skills. Outside the martial arts and acrobatics, the rest of the thinly plotted comic action film is no great shakes. It concludes with Hung taking on western villain Richard Norton in a grueling battle, and then Japanese assassin Yasuaki Kurata's deadly sais with tennis rackets. Chan has a brief alley fight with Norton during a chase and was originally supposed to have the fight with Norton for the climax. However, Chan hurt his back doing a stunt, and Hung stepped in to fight Norton.

The men fought to contact (the Hong Kong custom) in a banquet room setting for over three minutes, continually working in moments of levity. After a devastating Norton kick, Hung rubs his chest and Norton asks, "Painful?" Hung pretends it isn't, and the bit becomes a running gag. Two of the best moments have Hung being knocked through a glass door and doing a flip off a table to avoid a chair thrown by Norton. Hung shows us these moments in slow motion. Throughout the fight, the 5'7", 230-pound Hung hit Norton hard but expected to be hit in return. It was Norton's first Hong Kong film so he was obliged to accept whatever was dished out to make a good impression. Hung's side-kick was especially forceful and literally knocked Norton across the room. The lone precautionary measure taken: Norton used a small piece of cotton as a mouth guard. The fight was grueling under the hot studio lights, the temperature reaching upwards of 115 degrees (there was no air conditioning). The film crew shot 18 hours a day, seven days a week, for three weeks on the Hung-Norton fight to perfect it. When Hung's fist connects in slow motion with Norton's jaw for the final punch, it creates an explosion of moisture from Norton's hair. The fight is featured in *Deadliest Art: The Best of the Martial Arts Films* (1992). According to *Films of Fury*, "the brilliantly choreographed and executed fights save the day."

Roly-poly, surprisingly agile Hung specialized in Wing Chun kung fu, showing off both powerful blocks and strikes. After study at the Peking Opera, he debuted as a motion picture stuntman in his teens. Hung's fight choreography and overall film direction is noted for its frenetic pacing and his preference for fighting to flesh-smacking contact. He often made up the choreography on the fly, working on a few moves at a time before putting together a rough edit of the fight routine in the evening. He'd decide what the next day's moves would be and how much longer the overall fight should last and in which direction it should go. He understood the importance of camera angles and editing to complement his entertaining choreography.

Along with Chan, Hung was at the forefront of the comedy kung fu genre emerging in the late 1970s as he starred in *Enter the Fat Dragon* (1978), a film spoofing his girth. In the early 1980s, he created the comic horror kung fu genre and later starred in the popular American TV series *Martial Law* (1998–2000). Notable fights include *Enter the Dragon* (1973), *The Man from Hong Kong* (1975), *Game of Death* (1979) and *Wheels on Meals* (1984) (see entries). Fights of interest came

against George Lazenby in *Stoner* (1975), Lee Hoi San in *The Magnificent Butcher* (1979), Cynthia Rothrock in *Millionaire's Express* (1986), Billy Chow in *Eastern Condors* (1987), Lau Kar-Leung in *Pedicab Driver* (1988) and Donnie Yen in *SPL* (2005).

See: Cooper, Richard. *Enter the Fat Dragon: The Life and Films of Sammo Hung.* Screen Power Publishing, 2009.

MEL GIBSON VS. GARY BUSEY in *Lethal Weapon* (1987)

"Would you like a shot at the title?" Mel Gibson memorably asks Gary Busey.

"Don't mind if I do," replies the stone cold psycho.

The audience knows they're in store for a whale of a fight in a meeting of men who'd later ironically be perceived to be two of the most eccentric actors in Hollywood. *Lethal Weapon* is one of the first films to feature legitimate Brazilian jiu-jitsu and mixed martial arts, and was influential in the frenetic filming style it presented. Gibson and Busey fight all-out for nearly four minutes at night on a watery lawn in front of cops who uncharacteristically allow one of their own to partake in a vendetta match. Riggs (Gibson) and Mr. Joshua (Busey) are ex–special forces Black Ops warriors and therefore have fighting styles rarely seen in movies. Their realistic moves were a forerunner to pop culture interest in submission fighting, especially considering Gibson finishes Busey off with a triangle choke.

The box office smash from screenwriter Shane Black became the prototype for the "buddy cop" film thanks to the chemistry between the suicidal Gibson and his sympathetic though often exasperated partner Danny Glover. A lean Busey has never been better than as the chilling killer who impassively allows a flame to burn the skin on his arm. The original cut opened with a scene where Gibson impressively dispatches Jeff Imada and Miguel Nunez in a bar, but this was dropped in favor of the famous moment where a solo Gibson sticks a gun in his mouth and contemplates pulling the trigger. The film spawned three sequels, with Gibson unexplainably losing all the fighting knowledge he possessed in the first film. By *Lethal Weapon 4* (1998), he is kicked all over the screen by martial artist Jet Li and is incapable of mounting any defense.

Gibson, Glover and Busey were given two

months of extensive training in weapons, fighting and physical fitness with stunt coordinator Bobby Bass. Gibson worked out four hours a day for the role. Director Richard Donner let it be known that he wanted the climactic fight to be as original as possible. Assistant director Willie Simmons was into unusual martial arts and introduced Donner and Bass to three martial arts experts who brought fresh fighting styles to the film. Two styles had roots in the American penal system but could be traced back to Africa. Jailhouse Rock, represented by technical advisor Dennis Newsome, was a 19th century African art of self-defense involving head-butting, boxing and utilizing one's surroundings for defense. Capoeira was created by Angolans from West Africa to protect against slave traders. It features large circular kicks and flowing dance-like movements. Cedric Adams was the film's expert in this style. Brazilian jujitsu was a modification to traditional Japanese jujitsu perfected by the Gracie family in Brazil in the early 1900s. Rorion Gracie was the technical advisor in this style with an assist on the film from his brother Royce. Both were renowned ground fighters.

Stunt doubles Mic Rodgers and Shane Dixon worked through the fight routine, but they're mostly seen in long shots in the finished film. The bulk of the action is Gibson and Busey. The 5'8", 160-pound Gibson uses flashier elbows, kicks and leg sweeps. The six-foot, 185-pound Busey takes advantage of his size and strength, lifting Gibson off the ground and slamming him onto the top of a police cruiser. Both men trade vicious head butts, and Busey swings a pole at Gibson, who defends himself with a police baton. At one point Busey begs Gibson to kick him in the face. The fight was filmed over a period of four nights in studio-manufactured rain. The water source was a fire hydrant while a wind machine simulated a helicopter overhead. In the celebrated final sequence, Gibson goes for a failed arm-bar while Busey tries a rape choke. Gibson is able to apply the triangle choke with his legs and cinch it around Busey's neck as the latter makes it into his guard position.

It took Gibson several takes to apply the triangle choke correctly for Stephen Blatt's cameras. The intricacies of the various unfamiliar styles proved troublesome for both the actors and the stuntmen. They had such difficulty in presenting the non-traditional moves for the camera that Donner opted to film in an equally non-traditional manner. Donner went in close with a hand-held camera,

using herky-jerky movements and an overhead spotlight from the hovering helicopter to distort the on-screen movement. The film was edited by Stuart Baird in a quick, choppy style to make it difficult to tell what was going on. This fast-paced style where the camera is quicker than the eye became the norm in Hollywood's ensuing years, especially in such films as *The Bourne Identity* (2002) and its sequels where the viewer is in danger of becoming nauseated from all the on-screen motion. This type of fight can be counterproductive to both audience comprehension and the showcasing of offensive or defensive movements. There was a reason John Wayne and Yakima Canutt threw telegraphed roundhouse punches for the camera and the audience's benefit.

The *Chicago Tribune* wasn't impressed: "The final fight scene, billed as virtuoso of hand-to-hand combat, is so over-lit and over-edited the viewer can't see what's happening." The *Washington Post* was willing to overlook the flashiness and accept the fight for what it contributed to the storyline: "The release provided by the final confrontation is genuinely cathartic." In regard to director Donner, *Time* wrote, "Among movie bone-crackers he is the one who seems to have an advanced degree in chiropractic." The fight did impress the writers of *The Big Damn Book of Sheer Manliness* who call it one of the best one-on-one fights in film history.

See: *Lethal Weapon* DVD special features; *Lethal Weapon* press kit; O'Neill, Terry. "Terry O'Neill Interviews Mel Gibson." *Fighting Arts International*. #44, 1987; Taylor, Gerard. *Capoeira: The Jogo de Angola from Luanda to Cyberspace*. Berkeley, CA: North Atlantic, 2005.

TIMOTHY DALTON VS. ANDREAS WISNIEWSKI in *The Living Daylights* (1987)

By the 1980s, the James Bond franchise was pushing the envelope for extravagant stunts, and director John Glen's *The Living Daylights* doesn't disappoint. The climactic fight is between first-time Bond Timothy Dalton and towering blond assassin Necros (Andreas Wisniewski) on a cargo net hanging from the back of a Hercules 130 transport plane in flight over Afghanistan; it provides one of the series' most elaborate real-life gags in the days before CGI made anything possible. The net flaps back and forth in turbulence thousands of feet above the earth as the men struggle with one another while simultaneously hanging on for dear life. If the thrilling scenario presented by screenwriters Richard Maibaum and Michael G. Wilson isn't enough, there's a ticking bomb. And they're flying into a mountain. After years of being conditioned to the whimsical Roger Moore's take on Bond, audiences weren't sure what to make of the grim Dalton's serious and intense portrayal of 007. But once John Barry's iconic score kicks in, the audience is caught up in the drama.

Stuntmen B.J. Worth and Jake Lombard doubled Dalton and Wisniewski in the air over the Mojave Desert for the long shots. Skydiving specialist Worth served as the aerial coordinator. Although both were equipped with safety chutes, they were in danger of being knocked unconscious as they were whipped around on the net. Hidden spotters were on hand in the back of the cargo hold to dive off after them if they either lost their grip or were hit and flew away. When climbing in on the flapping net, Worth was nearly cracked against the plane. The close-ups were shot by Alec Mills at Pinewood with the actors on a mock-up net over a fake landscape approximately six feet above the ground. Even that was taxing as it took three days to complete the fight with Dalton and Wisniewski hanging on the ropes. *The Spy Who Thrilled Us* calls this the best stunt sequence in the entire Bond series. According to *The Motion Picture Guide*, "This is one of the most harrowing fight scenes in any Bond opus, or any recent action adventure film for that matter."

The Hercules fight is not even the film's best. That honor goes to the surprising "old school" fight in a kitchen between Wisniewski and a secondary character played by stuntman Bill Weston as an operative identified as Green Four. Wisniewski, disguised as a milkman, encounters butler Weston in the kitchen at the Stonor Park safe house where Jeroen Krabbe is under guard. Wisniewski kills to the song "Where Has Everybody Gone?" and he puts that on his portable cassette player as an especially odd touch. Their wild fight pulls out all the stops; an electric carving knife and frying pan are brought into play. It's refreshing to see a character other than Bond exhibit actual fighting skills, and Weston is nearly successful in eliminating the highly skilled assassin. Although he was a ballet dancer by trade, the athletic 6'2" Wisniewski did the fight with coaching from the stuntmen. However, he did inadvertently knock Weston unconscious. The stuntman also broke a finger. As a reward of sorts, Weston's Green Four

survives the fight coordinated by Paul Weston. *Time* humorously wrote that the film has "the best kitchen fight since the Gremlins got microwaved." Dalton played Bond again in *Licence to Kill* (1989), in which he took part in a major brawl in Bimini's Barrelhead Bar.

See: Glen, John. *For My Eyes Only*. Washington, D.C.: Brassey's, 2001; *The Living Daylights* DVD special features; "Timothy Dalton." *The Living Daylights* Official Poster Magazine. 1987.

STEVEN SEAGAL VS. HENRY SILVA in *Above the Law* (1988)

Aikido master Steven Seagal, in his starring debut, presented a unique new martial art for the screen and achieved instant popularity with audiences. The 6'4", 210-pound actor's brutal art of self-defense was an eye-opener. An offshoot of jujitsu, Aikido emphasizes joint locks and throws. Seagal had distinguished himself as the first Caucasian to run a dojo in Japan, and was introduced to the film world as fight coordinator in the action-packed film *The Challenge* (1982). Having powerful agent Michael Ovitz as a student opened more doors in Hollywood. It helped immensely that *Above the Law* had a decent budget and a skilled director in Andrew Davis to ensure that the fights were well-done. Seagal had his differences with Davis over where best to position the camera to showcase his streamlined streetfighting version of Aikido.

The cocky Seagal backs up his tough talk with quick and powerful moves and he shows no shred of mercy as he breaks bones and dislocates the joints of his opponents. Hardly anyone gives him a fight, and that became a common complaint about Seagal and his action scenes. Even when he was taking on someone as skilled as Danny Inosanto in *Out for Justice* (1991), his opponent was barely allowed to put up any kind of a fight. Branscombe Richmond was beaten to a pulp in *Hard to Kill* (1989), William Forsyth was annihilated in *Out for Justice* and Tommy Lee Jones fared horribly in an *Under Siege* (1992) knife fight. Audiences initially took to Seagal but his persona quickly wore thin. He slipped into a string of direct-to-video films as he gained a great deal of weight.

In *Above the Law,* Seagal plays former CIA agent turned Chicago cop Nico Toscani. A rogue CIA group headed by Henry Silva is funneling drug money to Central America and Seagal rises to the challenge. He takes on the criminal element in a bar fight, a street fight and a convenience store fight before clashing with chief bad guy Silva and his men in the basement kitchen of Chicago's Blackstone Hotel. The scene was filmed during the humid summer with the temperature reaching nearly 100 degrees. Silva, wearing a weighted glove and fighting poor eyesight, accidentally broke Seagal's nose in the scene. Seagal was rushed to the hospital and forced to stay up all night icing his nose to avoid swelling and black eyes. He took the blame for the accident, believing he should have used a foam glove or had a stuntman take the aging Silva's place.

The *Chicago Tribune* called the action sequences "sleek and strong." The *Boston Globe* wrote, "While there's no questioning Steven Seagal's authenticity in the fight scenes, these scenes never seem anything but set pieces." *Films of Fury* writes of Seagal's Aikido prowess, "It was the hand-to-hand equivalent of a wild-mouse rollercoaster, spinning the antagonists in tight, fast, vicious circles." Vern, author of *Seagology: The Ass-Kicking Films of Steven Seagal*, took a tongue-in-cheek approach to Seagal but wrote seriously about *Above the Law*'s fighting: "His Aikido looks convincing and the quickness of the fights make them stand out from other action pictures of the time. The fights are also more raw and brutal than many martial arts films, especially American ones. His style is not as much about looking cool as it is about dispatching opponents as quickly as possible."

See: *Above the Law* pressbook; Coleman, Jim. "One Tough Dude." *Black Belt*. February 1989; Goldstein, Patrick. "Steven Seagal Gets Shot at Stardom." *Los Angeles Times*. February 14, 1988; Vern. *Seagology: The Ass-Kicking Films of Steven Seagal*. London: Titan, 2008.

BRUCE WILLIS VS. ALEXANDER GODUNOV in *Die Hard* (1988)

In the testosterone-filled era of heavily muscled cartoon action stars named Schwarzenegger and Stallone came a decidedly different Everyman hero in the form of *Die Hard*'s John McClane (played by Bruce Willis). He had an average-guy body and talked himself through self-doubt into action, but when he took on a gang of terrorists in a Los Angeles high-rise, he connected mightily with audiences. *Entertainment Weekly* ranks this as the greatest action movie ever made. That might be a stretch, but there's no denying that the John

McTiernan film pushes many of the right buttons. The fact that Willis is playing a New York City cop gives him plausibility for his gun handling and fighting ability, highlighted by a fight against Alexander Godunov. Both men are given extreme motivation to hurt the other by Steven de Souza and Jeb Stuart's screenplay. Willis is trying to rescue his wife Bonnie Bedelia from lead terrorist Alan Rickman and an impending explosion, while Godunov is trying to avenge Willis' self-defense killing of his brother Andreas Wisniewski. Willis rubs salt into Godunov's mental wound by telling him how his brother screamed when Willis broke his neck.

Stunt coordinator Charlie Picerni put the fight together with an emphasis on the characters and their actions for cinematographer Jan de Bont's fluid camera. Picerni uniquely designed it so the 6'2" Godunov's menacing character Karl punches on a straight plane while Willis attacks from angles. Ballet dancer Godunov's martial arts kicks quickly put Willis at a distinct disadvantage, as does his pistol which puts Willis on the run. The fight transitions from a darkly lit, steam-filled room in the Nakatomi Plaza (actually the new Fox Plaza) to a bright open stairwell courtesy of production designer Jackson De Govia; the ever resourceful Willis makes use of his surroundings to continually harass and confound Godunov. A hanging chain puts what Willis thinks is a permanent end to Godunov. Throughout the loud four-minute battle, composer Michael Kamen's score is present but unobtrusive, rising to meet the fight's most suspenseful moments.

One flaw in the thrilling fight is the liberal use of easily identifiable stunt doubles (Keii Johnson for Willis, Don McGovern for Godunov). This was in the days before Hollywood began placing actors' heads on stuntmen's bodies through the use of computer effects, but for some fans it's an endearingly cheesy quality to an otherwise exciting action film. To some viewers it was the end of an era. According to the video essay *Chaos Cinema*, "The fight itself is frantic yet clearly understandable, both riveting and stabilizing, the M.O. of classic cinema."

Willis unfortunately made several increasingly ridiculous *Die Hard* sequels that saw his wisecracking McClane character become a hardened tough guy with the nearly superhuman ability to survive large-scale explosions. Willis, a 180-pound six-footer, had solid fights with Vernon Wells in *Sunset* (1988), William Sadler and John Amos in *Die*

Hard 2 (1990) and Karl Urban in *Red* (2010). He threw a killer punch at Kim Coates in *The Last Boy Scout* (1991). On TV's *Moonlighting* (1985–1989), his cocky David Addison character was deservedly punched out by Mark Harmon in 1987's "I Am Curious Maddie."

See: *Chaos Cinema* (2011); *Die Hard* DVD commentary; *Die Hard* movie press kit.

RODDY PIPER VS. KEITH DAVID in *They Live* (1988)

Writer-director John Carpenter's cult sci-fi film about aliens secretly invading our society features one of Hollywood's most famous screen fights. Upon its release, the *New York Times* called it "a noisy attenuated slugfest" and the *Los Angeles Times* labeled it "crazily protracted." Yet this fight has routinely made most Internet-era "Best Of" lists based on its length and sheer rugged tenacity.

The over-the-top fight is nearly six minutes of brutal back-and-forth back alley action as Roddy Piper tries to force his fellow construction worker Keith David to don special sunglasses that will allow him to see the aliens' subliminal messages in our everyday advertising, as well as the aliens sprinkled among the citizens. David wants nothing to do with the sunglasses, but Piper is relentless. So is the "old school" fight. Both actors take all their own incredible bumps in the Jeff Imada–coordinated action. Carpenter and D.P. Gary B. Kibbe shot with a Panaglide Steadicam, allowing them to smoothly follow the action. Editors Gib Jaffe and Frank Jimenez manage to maintain pace for one of the screen's most extended battles. There's enough variation in movement to maintain visual interest.

The fight has it all: punches, kicks, knees, a back suplex and even a 2 × 4 that Piper smashes into a car window. David chastises him with an expletive and Piper half-laughs an apology, one of the fight's more memorable moments. Many see it as an absurd reason for the friends to dole out violent punishment on one another. Why doesn't David just look through the glasses? Perhaps it's because David knows there's something out there he doesn't want to see, and his life will never be the same if he does. Piper finally forces David to don the sunglasses and see the world around him. The two join forces to take on the aliens, with a gun-wielding Piper famously proclaiming, "I've come here to chew bubblegum and kick ass, and I'm all out of bubblegum."

In the original script, the fight sequence was brief, but when Carpenter landed pro wrestler Rowdy Roddy Piper as his leading man he began to envision an epic battle to rival *The Quiet Man* (1952). Carpenter even had his actors watch that film for inspiration. Carpenter left it up to Imada and the actors to come up with the action, requesting only that three wrestling moves be used. These were a suplex, a clothesline and a sidewalk slam. When Carpenter gave the revised script to Imada, there were four blank pages reading, "The Fight Begins," "The Fight Continues," "The Fight Still Continues" and "The Fight Concludes." Imada's first order of business was toning down Piper, who was used to selling

Roddy Piper (left) and Keith David put on a fight for the ages in Universal's *They Live* (1988).

moves to a huge live audience. Piper and David rehearsed with Imada for three weeks in Carpenter's backyard before unveiling their work to the director. The fight itself was filmed in two and a half shooting days on a specially padded parking lot that looked realistic and rough. For years, the landmark punchathon was shown to new stuntmen entering the business as an example of how to put on a great fight. It was even spoofed on the animated *South Park* show as "The Cripple Fight," with the choreography copied in homage.

The six-foot Piper had a reputation as a fearless tough guy beyond the wrestling ring. He was a Golden Gloves boxer in his youth and earned a judo black belt training under Gene LeBell. Piper was over 220 pounds when Carpenter approached him at 1987's Wrestlemania III, but that weight could appear too bulky on film. At the director's request, Piper trained and dieted with the legendary Vince Gironda, who ripped him up for the cameras at 200 pounds. The 6'2", 220-pound David was a stage-trained actor with a certificate in Stage Combat. Piper claimed that David had a terrific punch but no idea of his own personal strength. Piper told David he could unload on him below the neck, but to pull his punches around the face. When the TV show *Entertainment Tonight* came on the set to cover the fight, a nervous David accidentally connected with Piper's face. Piper shrugged the blow off and told David not to worry about it. David occasionally clipped Piper in the eye when snapping back a punch, but the wrestler didn't mind when compared to what he usually experienced in the ring. David later recalled that he never felt intimidated working with the wrestler, as Piper insured his safety and was a complete professional. Piper had noteworthy fights with martial artist Billy Blanks in *Back in Action* (1993) and *Tough and Deadly* (1995).

See: Lethem, Jonathan. *They Live.* Soft Skull, 2010; Nashawaty, Chris. "*They Live:* John Carpenter on Why His Sci-Fi Classic Is as Timely as Ever." *Entertainment Weekly.* November 5, 2012; Piper, Roddy, and Robert Picarello. *In the Pit with Piper.* New York: Berkley Boulevard, 2002; *They Live* movie press kit; Wilson, D. Harlan. *They Live.* New York: Columbia University Press, 2015.

PATRICK SWAYZE vs. MARSHALL TEAGUE in *Road House* (1989)

Rowdy Herrington's cult favorite *Road House* is one of the decade's cheesiest yet most treasured films, containing enough fights to fill ten normal films. It's *The Rocky Horror Picture Show* for macho guys. Much of its lasting appeal is due to the Zen-like cool of philosopher–bar bouncer Dalton (Patrick Swayze), whose given to saying catchphrases like, "Pain don't hurt" when he's sliced open by a knife. The undersized Dalton is a well-dressed, long-haired NYU grad and the best "cooler" in the business. A cooler is the lead bouncer who makes everything fall in line. His reputation is transcontinental. When Swayze takes on a particularly tough bar called the Double Deuce in the small town of Jasper, Missouri, he runs afoul of local fat cat John Wesley (Ben Gazzara) and his thugs. The local law is so nonexistent Dalton calls in his mentor, the grizzled Wade Garrett (Sam Elliott), to lend a hand, thereby treating the audience to hand-to-hand combat nirvana. There's one problem with Dalton: He's haunted by a past incident in which he ripped a man's throat out, and strong evidence suggests our conflicted hero might be a serial offender when he faces flashy martial artist Jimmy Reno (Marshall Teague, playing a role Scott Glenn turned down).

Stunt coordinator Charlie Picerni put the fights together and kickboxing champion Benny Urquidez trained Swayze and made sure the martial arts were accurately presented on screen. Black belt stuntman Randy Hall was hired to double

Patrick Swayze (left) and Marshall Teague engage in a riverbank duel in United Artists' *Road House* (1989).

Swayze if the actor couldn't pick up all the moves. Teague was an accomplished martial artist and wouldn't require a double. Urquidez closely watched Swayze's movements for a full week before deciding on a specific martial arts style for him to adapt. As he began to teach Swayze cat-like fighting moves, he incorporated background music into their training because of Swayze's strong dance history. With a beat behind him, Swayze picked up the moves well enough to do his own fighting. Hall doubled him when he bull-dogged Teague off a motorcycle.

The cities of Fresno and Valencia, California, stood in for rural Missouri. When Teague arrived at the locale, he and the 5'9", 165-pound Swayze began testing one another. The ice was broken after Teague made physical contact with Swayze while blocking the fight and the latter absorbed the blow without complaint. Both were outfitted with hidden pads in target areas to absorb blows. They fought to contact the rest of the fight, which took five nights to film. The men performed the fight routine a total of 71 times for the cameras. Swayze, who was shirtless, had to have makeup cover the bruises that formed on his arms and ribs. When the fight was over, he had fluid drained from his left knee. At one point, Teague picked up a log in the heat of battle and hit Swayze with it. That shot remains, and Swayze later claimed his ribs were injured from the hit. The fight blocking and kicks are all done well, with sparse but memorable dialogue interspersed throughout the three-minute battle to heighten the drama and increase the tension between the men. Swayze goes for the throat when Teague brings a gun into the fight.

Director Herrington wanted to incorporate the infamous ripping-out of Teague's throat based on a second-hand story he was told. The actors were uncomfortable and felt it was too over-the-top, but they went through with it. Female lead Kelly Lynch later related that she almost laughed off-camera when it came time for Swayze to rear back and rip. Teague took the fall into the river, with the water recorded at a chilly 42 degrees. Teague did a perfect take, earning a $500 bet from a crew member who told him he'd "suck air" when he hit the cold water. Swayze and Teague became close friends and remained in contact with one another.

Herrington and cinematographer Dean Cundey shot much of the fight action with a Steadicam so they could move the camera as the action dictated. This insured better coverage of the overall choreography and that misses would appear to be hits.

What's more, it kept the audience involved in the flow of the action. And there's a ton of action. Swayze fights not only Teague but Gazzara in the climax. Given Swayze had been established as a super fighter and had torn out Teague's throat, the fight is evened out by having Swayze shot in the arm and Gazzara swinging everything available in his mansion (an actual Bel Air estate). When Swayze overcomes all the odds, his hand instinctively goes back into full trachea-ripping position. At that moment, none other than beleaguered auto store owner Red West arrives with a rifle to make his decision for him.

Along the way, Swayze has multiple fights against Terry Funk, Anthony Delongis, Gary Hudson, John Doe, Michael Rider, John Young and Tiny Ron Taylor. Actors Delongis and Hudson had started as stuntmen and were able to do all their own fights, as did professional wrestler Funk. A conflicted Swayze even takes a swing at Elliott, who catches the punch in midair. The streetfighting Elliott goes through most of the same henchmen Swayze has already walloped, including Teague in a bar brawl. Gazzara stops that interesting fight by firing a gun in the air. Entire fight sequences were cut due to the film's length. Actor Keith David, fresh from making *They Live* (1988), can barely be seen in the finished film though he gets prominent billing in the opening credits. He had a much larger role as a bar patron who helps the bouncers in a fight against the rednecks. David had a fight with Funk that was cut for time. The burly Funk, one of the legends of the wrestling ring for the brutal style he employed and the lengths he'd push his battered body, contributes greatly to the film as the Double Deuce's original bouncer who doesn't go quietly into the night. His presence and popularity in hardcore wrestling circles adds to the movie's macho cult appeal.

There's a slew of stunt personnel filling the ranks of the bar brawls, including Tony Epper, Jeannie Epper, Mic Rodgers, Henry Kingi, Allan Graf, Ted White, Glenn Wilder, Branscombe Richmond, Gary Combs, Tommy Huff, Gary McLarty, Jeff Imada, Bruce Paul Barbour, Leon Delaney, Frank Orsatti, Ron Stein, Patricia Tallman and Buddy Joe Hooker. About 40 other stunt performers receive credit and can likely be seen somewhere in the background of the fights. R.L. Tolbert served as Elliott's double, though Elliott appears to do all his own stunts. He'd staged memorable fights with David Soul and William Smith on TV's *The Yellow Rose* (1983–1984) and went on to have a noteworthy battle with Gavan O'Herlihy in the western *Conagher* (1991).

Critics lambasted *Road House*, but *New York Magazine* did find the multitude of fights "emotionally satisfying." Most reviewers were willing to accept the overall implausibility and count it as a guilty pleasure. However, more than a few thought the action stretched too far. The *Chicago Tribune* said the movie would have been "perfectly hilarious, were it not for the wide strain of sadism that underlies the action," while the *Washington Post* said that the film "lays out its story with the subtlety of a wrestling match." The *Los Angeles Times* wrote, "Melodramatic at best, Herrington is in his element in fight scenes, and out of it the rest of the time." *Road House* was followed by *Road House 2: Last Call* (2006), a Swayze-less sequel.

See: Holtzclaw, Mike. "*Road House* Role Lives On." *Daily Press*. February 2, 2003; *Road House* DVD commentary; *Road House* press kit; Wood, Jennifer M. "The Best Fight Scenes from *Road House*." *Men's Journal*. June 2014.

Epilogue

In many ways, *Road House* was the end of an era and an appropriate cut-off point for this text. Fight choreography changed drastically in the increasingly computerized world of the 1990s. Flashy kicks, at times anatomically impossible, permanently replaced the roundhouse punch as traditional slugfests became all but obsolete. Rapid editing, hyperactive camera movements, post-production digital altering, close-framing, and Wushu-influenced wire work seen in films like *The Matrix* (1999) forever altered what a fight scene looked like and how it was perceived by increasingly younger audiences with shorter attention spans. Screen fighters such as Jean-Claude Van Damme, Dolph Lundgren, Jet Li and Wesley Snipes enjoyed brief periods of popularity as screen kickers. New action stars the likes of Jason Statham and Michael Jai White needed to be well-versed in martial arts to effectively come across to modern audiences. Mention should be made of the occasional "old school" fight that snuck through during this time such as those seen in *Fight Club* (1999) and *Snatch* (2000), both starring Brad Pitt. There was still the occasional interesting match-up generating buzz such as the pairing of heavily muscled actors Vin Diesel and Dwayne "The Rock" Johnson in *Fast Five* (2011).

Road House is a modern western, a film that harkens back to an earlier time where men solved their problems using their fists. A highly trained fighter could remain calm and cool until it was time *not* to be cool, confident in his superior training that he could take on any type of situation. Times have changed, and the popularity of mixed martial arts (MMA) sporting events and even to a degree glamorized tough guy characters like Swayze's Dalton on cable broadcasts of *Road House* are largely responsible. The new century has seen MMA gyms spring up around the country with an increasing interest in Brazilian jujitsu and Israeli-based Krav Maga defense techniques. Small city bars and local road houses are now likely to have any number of clientele with some training in effective ground fighting.

The cinematic appeal of the muscular Schwarzenegger-Stallone action hero of the 1980s also created a nation of bicep-flexing testosterone junkies who have further clouded their rational thought with hormone-altering steroid use. This new generation has likely been raised on violent video games, extreme pro wrestling and rap music, seeking instant gratification in the sensory-overloaded Internet age. The general code of cowboy ethics first exhibited in the John Wayne B-western has changed. There used to be a time when a beaten man left with his head down and that was it. Now there's an emotional rush to seek retribution, repercussions be damned. Old-fashioned bar fights seen as recently as Clint Eastwood's early 1980s output have vanished. Now any real smash-up results in numerous arrests and lawsuits. Punch out a loudmouth troublemaker in today's day and age and you'd be running the risk of being shot, stabbed, arrested and sued. It's far easier to live vicariously through the cinema, fantasizing that we're in there throwing punches alongside Randolph Scott and the Duke in a different time and a different place.

301

Bibliography

Books

Aaker, Everett. *Encyclopedia of Early Television Crime Fighters.* Jefferson, NC: McFarland, 2006.

Aaker, Everett. *Television Western Players of the Fifties.* Jefferson, NC: McFarland, 1997.

Armstrong, Stephen B. *Andrew V. McLaglen: The Life and Hollywood Career.* Jefferson, NC: McFarland, 2011.

Armstrong, Vic, and Robert Sellers. *The True Adventures of the World's Greatest Stuntman.* London: Titan, 2012.

Atkinson, Barry. *Six Gun Law: The Westerns of Randolph Scott, Audie Murphy, Joel McCrea, and George Montgomery.* Midnight Marquee, 2015.

Barnes, Alan, and Marcus Hearn. *Kiss Kiss, Bang Bang! The Unofficial James Bond Film Companion.* London: Batsford, 2000.

Baxter, John. *Stunt: The Story of the Great Movie Stuntmen.* New York: Doubleday, 1974.

Bernardin, Matt. "The 25 Greatest Action Films Ever!" *Entertainment Weekly.* June 22, 2007.

Bertolino, Marco, and Ettore Ridoli. *Bud Spencer and Terence Hill.* Gremese Editore, 2002.

Blake, Michael F. *Code of Honor: The Making of Three Great American Westerns.* New York: Taylor, 2003.

Blottner, Gene. *Universal Sound Westerns 1929–1946: The Complete Filmography.* Jefferson, NC: McFarland, 2003.

Blottner, Gene. *Universal-International Westerns 1947–1963: The Complete Filmography.* Jefferson, NC: McFarland, 2000.

Borgnine, Ernest. *Ernie.* New York: Citadel, 2008.

Brosnan, John. *James Bond in the Cinema.* San Diego: A.S. Barnes, 1981.

Brown, Jim, and Steve Delsohn. *Out of Bounds.* New York: Zebra, 1990.

Cagney, James. *Cagney on Cagney.* Garden City, New York: Doubleday, 1976.

Canutt, Yakima, and Oliver Drake. *Stunt Man: The Autobiography of Yakima Canutt.* New York: Walker, and Co., 1979.

Carradine, David. *Endless Highway.* Boston, MA: Journey, 1995.

Cheng, Long, and Jeff Yang. *I Am Jackie Chan: My Life in Action.* New York: Ballantine, 1999.

Clark, Mike. "Fight Scenes with Punch." *USA Today.* February 2, 1989.

Cline, William C. *In the Nick of Time: Motion Picture Sound Serials.* Jefferson, NC: McFarland, 1984.

Clouse, Robert. *Bruce Lee: The Biography.* Unique, 1988.

Cooper, Richard. *More 100% Jackie Chan: The Essential Companion.* London: Titan, 2004.

Copeland, Bobby J. *Charlie King: We Called Him Blackie.* Madison, NC: Empire, 2003.

Copeland, Bobby J. *Roy Barcroft: King of the Badmen.* Madison, NC: Empire, 2000.

Corcoran, John. *The Unauthorized Jackie Chan Encyclopedia.* Chicago: Contemporary, 2003.

D'Ambrosio, Brian. *Menacing Face Worth Millions: A Life of Charles Bronson.* Lulu, 2012.

Darby, William. *Anthony Mann: The Film Career.* Jefferson, NC: McFarland, 2009.

Davis, Ronald L. *Duke: The Life and Image of John Wayne.* Norman, OK: University of Oklahoma Press, 2001.

Deadliest Art: The Best of the Martial Arts Films (1992).

DiLeo, John. *Screen Savers: 40 Remarkable Movies Awaiting Rediscovery.* Hansen, 2010.

DiLeo, Michael. *The Spy Who Thrilled Us: A Guide to the Best of the Cinematic James Bond.* New York: Limelight, 2002.

Dombrowski, Lisa. *The Films of Samuel Fuller: If You Die, I'll Kill You.* Middletown, Conn: Wesleyan University, 2008.

Douglas, Kirk. *The Ragman's Son.* New York: Simon & Schuster, 1988.

Epstein, Dwayne. *Lee Marvin: Point Blank.* Tucson, AZ: Schaffner Press, 2013.

Eubanks, I.E. "Fighting on the Screen." *Motion Picture.* September, 1917.

Everitt, David, and Harold Schecter. *The Manly Movie Guide.* New York: Boulevard, 1997.

Eyles, Allen. *John Wayne.* South Brunswick: Barnes, 1979.

Eyman, Scott. *John Ford: Print the Legend.* Baltimore, MD: John Hopkins, 1999.

Eyman, Scott. *John Wayne, the Life and Legend.* New York: Simon & Schuster, 2014.

Fagen, Herb. *Duke, We're Glad We Knew You.* New York: Citadel, 1996.

Fenin, George N., and William J. Everson. *The Western: From Silents to the Seventies.* New York: Penguin, 1973.

Flynn, Errol. *My Wicked Wicked Ways.* New York: Cooper Square, 2003.

Freese, Gene. *Jock Mahoney: The Life and Films of a Hollywood Stuntman.* Jefferson, NC: McFarland, 2013.

Freese, Gene Scott. *Hollywood Stunt Performers, 1910s–1970s.* Jefferson, NC: McFarland, 2014.

Fury, David. *Kings of the Jungle.* Jefferson, NC: McFarland, 2001.

Garnett, Tay, and Fredda Dudley Barling. *Light Your Torches and Pull Up Your Tights.* New Rochelle, New York: Arlington House, 1973.

Gentry, Clyde. *Jackie Chan: Inside the Dragon.* Dallas, TX: Taylor, 1997.

Goldrup, Jim, and Tom Goldrup. *Feature Players: The Stories Behind the Faces. Vol. 1–3.* Self, 1986–1992.

Gregory, Mollie. *Stuntwomen: The Untold Hollywood Story.* Lexington, KN: University Press, 2015.

Griffith, B. "25 All Time Great Movie Fights." *Action Films.* November 1992.

Gross, Edward. *Bruce Lee: Fists of Fury.* Pioneer, 1990.

Guttmacher, Peter. *Legendary Westerns.* New York: Metro, 1995.

Hagner, John G. *Dave Sharpe and Me.* Self, 1985.

Hagner, John G. *Falling for Stars.* El John, 1964.

Hanson, Patricia King, and Stephen Hanson. *Magill's Survey of Cinema.* Englewood Cliffs, NJ: Salem, 1980–1985.

Heston, Charlton. *In the Arena.* New York: Boulevard Books, 1997.

Horner, William R. *Bad at the Bijou.* Jefferson, NC: McFarland, 2000.

Hughes, Howard. *Aim for the Heart: The Films of Clint Eastwood.* New York: I.B. Tauris, 2009.

Jacobs, David Henry. "10 Greatest Fight Scenes of All Time." *Action Superheroes.* #4, 1992.

Jarlett, Franklin. *Robert Ryan: A Biography and Critical Filmography.* Jefferson, NC: McFarland, 1990.

Jones, J.R. *The Lives of Robert Ryan.* Wesleyan, 2015.

Joyner, C. Courtney. *The Westerners: Interviews with Actors, Directors, Writers, and Producers.* Jefferson, NC: McFarland, 2009.

Kaminsky, Stuart. *Coop: The Life and Legend of Gary Cooper.* New York: St. Martin's Press, 1980.

Kazanjjan, Howard, and Chris Enss. *The Young Duke: The Early Life of John Wayne.* New York: Lyons, 2009.

Kelly, Perry. *Dan Inosanto: The Man, the Teacher, the Artist.* Palladin, 2000.

Kennedy, Burt. *Hollywood Trail Boss.* New York: Boulevard, 1997.

Kirkland, J. Michael. *Stage Combat Resource Materials: A Selected and Annotated Bibliography.* Westport, CN: Praeger, 2006.

Kreng, John. *Fight Choreography: The Art of Non-Verbal Dialogue.* Thomson Course Technology, 2008.

Landesman, Fred. *The John Wayne Filmography.* Jefferson, NC: McFarland, 2004.

LeBell, Gene, and Bob Calhoun. *The Godfather of Grappling.* Santa Monica, CA: Self, 2004.

Lentz, Robert J. *Lee Marvin: His Films and Career.* Jefferson, NC: McFarland, 2000.

Lilley, Tim. *Campfire Conversations.* Akron, OH: Big Trail, 2007.

Lilley, Tim. *Campfire Conversations Complete.* Akron, OH: Big Trail, 2010.

Linet, Beverly. *Ladd: The Life, the Legend, the Legacy of Alan Ladd.* New York: Arbor House, 1979.

Lott, M. Ray. *The American Martial Arts Film.* Jefferson, NC: McFarland, 2004.

Lovell, Glen. *Escape Artist: The Life and Films of John Sturges.* Madison, WI: University of Wisconsin, 2008.

Luxford, Albert J., and Garreth Owen. *Albert J. Luxford, the Gimmick Man: Memoir of a Special Effects Maestro.* Jefferson, NC: McFarland, 2002.

Magers, Boyd, Nareau, Bob, and Copeland, Bobby. *Best of the Badmen.* Empire, 2005.

Maltin, Leonard. *Leonard Maltin's 2015 Movie Guide.* New York: Signet, 2014.

Marrill, Alvin H. *Robert Mitchum on the Screen.* New York: A.S. Barnes, 1978.

McBride, Joseph. *Searching for John Ford: A Life.* New York: St. Martin's Press, 2003.

McKay, James. *Dana Andrews: The Face of Noir.* Jefferson, NC: McFarland, 2010.

McNeil, Joe. *Arizona's Little Hollywood.* Sedona Monthly Books, 2010.

McNulty, Thomas. *Errol Flynn: The Life and Career.* Jefferson, NC: McFarland, 2004.

Meyer, William R. *The Making of the Great Westerns.* New York: Arlington House, 1979.

Meyers, Jeffrey. *Gary Cooper: American Hero.* NU: Cooper Square, 2001.

Meyers, Ric. *Films of Fury: The Kung Fu Movie Book.* Guilford, CT: Emery, 2011.

Meyers, Ric. *The Great Martial Arts Movies: From Bruce Lee to Jackie Chan—And More.* New York: Citadel, 2001. (updated as *Films of Fury*)

Miller, Don. *Hollywood Corral.* Burbank, CA: Riverwood, 1993.

Moss, Marilyn Ann. *Raoul Walsh: The True Adventures of Hollywood's Legendary Director.* Lexington, KY: Univ. Press of Kentucky, 2011.

Munn, Michael. *Clint Eastwood: Hollywood's Loner.* London: Robson, 1992.

Munn, Michael. *John Wayne: The Man Behind the Myth.* New York: New American, 2005.

Needham, Hal. *Stuntman! My Car-Crashing, Plane-Jumping, Bone-Breaking, Death-Defying Hollywood Life.* Little Brown & Co., 2011.

Neibaur, James L. *The Elvis Movies.* Lanham: Rowman & Littlefield, 2014.

New York Times Film Reviews 1913–1968. New York: 1970.

Nollen, Scott Allen. *Three Bad Men: John Ford, John Wayne, Ward Bond.* Jefferson, NC: McFarland, 2013.

Norris, Chuck, and Ken Abraham. *Against All Odds: My Story.* Nashville, TN: B&H, 2006.

Nott, Robert. *The Films of Randolph Scott.* Jefferson, NC: McFarland, 2004.

Nott, Robert. *Last of the Cowboy Heroes.* Jefferson, NC: McFarland, 2000.

O'Brien, Daniel. *The Frank Sinatra Film Guide.* Batsford, 1998.

Paul, Louis. *Tales from the Cult Film Trenches.* Jefferson, NC: McFarland, 2008.

Peary, Danny. *Cult Movies.* New York: Dell, 1981.

Pevere, Geoff. "Punch Drunk Love: The Top 10 Movie Fight Scenes." *Toronto Star.* October 6, 2007.

Pfeiffer, Lee, and Phillip Lisa. *The Films of Sean Connery.* New York: Citadel, 2001.

Pitts, Michael R. *Charles Bronson: The 95 Films and the 156 Television Appearances.* Jefferson, NC: McFarland, 1999.

Reid, Craig D. "The 10 Best and 10 Worst Choreographed Martial Arts Films." *Black Belt.* May 1993.

Reid, Craig D. *The Ultimate Guide to Martial Arts Movies of the 1970s.* Santa Clarita, CA: Black Belt, 2010.

Reynolds, Burt. *My Life.* London: Coronet, 1994.

Rhodes, Gary D. *Stanley Kubrick: Essays on His Films and Legacy.* Jefferson, NC: McFarland, 2008.

Rhodes, Scott. "25 All-Time Great Movie Fights." *Martial Arts Movies.* September 1992. (note: identical to the article attributed to B. Griffith in *Action Films.*)

Riva, Mario. *Marlene Dietrich.* Toronto: Knopf, 1992.

Roach, Pat, and Shirley Thompson. *If: The Pat Roach Story.* Studley: Brewin, 2002.

Roberson, Chuck, and Bodie Thoene. *The Fall Guy.* North Vancouver, BC: Hancock House, 1979.

Roberts, Jerry. *Mitchum: In His Own Words.* New York: Limelight, 2000.

Rode, Alan K. *Charles McGraw: Biography of a Film Noir Tough Guy.* Jefferson, NC: McFarland, 2008.

Romano, Frederick V. *The Boxing Filmography: American Features 1920–2003.* Jefferson, NC: McFarland, 2004.

Rovin, Jeff. *The Essential Jackie Chan Source Book.* New York: Simon & Schuster, 1997.

Rubin, Steven Jay. *The Complete James Bond Movie Encyclopedia.* Contemporary, 1990.

Rubin, Steven Jay. *The James Bond Films.* Arlington House, 1981.

Schickel, Richard. *Clint Eastwood: A Biography.* New York: Vintage, 1996.

Schiller, Ralph. *The Complete Films of Broderick Crawford.* Lulu, 2016.

Server, Lee. *Baby, I Don't Care.* New York: St. Martin's Press, 2001.

Server, Lee. *Sam Fuller: Film Is a Battleground.* Jefferson, NC: McFarland, 2003.

Silver, Alain. *Whatever Happened to Robert Aldrich?: His Life and His Films.* Limelight, 2004.

Simmons, Bob, and Kenneth Passingham. *Nobody Does It Better: My 25 Years with James Bond and Other Stories.* Sterling, 1987.

Simmons, Garner. *Sam Peckinpah: A Portrait in Montage.* New York: Limelight, 1998.

Siverio, Manny. "How to Throw a Movie Punch." *Curio.* Spring 1998.

Smith, Dean, and Mike Cox. *Cowboy Stuntman.* Lubbock, TX: Texas Tech, 2013.

Smith, Don G. *Lon Chaney, Jr.: Horror Film Star.* Jefferson, NC: McFarland, 1996.

Spencer, Gary. "Western Film Fights." *Blazing West.* #2, 1985.

Spicer, Chrystopher J. *Clark Gable: Biography, Film-ography, Bibliography.* Jefferson, NC: McFarland, 2002.

Stidworthy, David. *High on the Hogs: A Biker Filmography.* Jefferson, NC: McFarland, 2003.

Strode, Woody, and Sam Young. *Goal Dust.* Lanham, Madison, 1993.

Swayze, Patrick, and Lisa Niemi Swayze. *The Time of My Life.* New York: Simon & Schuster, 2009.

Talbot, Paul. *Bronson's Loose Again: On the Set with Charles Bronson.* BearManor, 2015.

Thomas, Tony. *The Best of Universal.* Rowman & Littlefield, 1997.

Thompson, Rod. "A Night at the Fights." *Orange Coast Magazine.* August 1989.

Tuska, Jon. *The Filming of the West.* London: Hale, 1978.

Udel, James C. *The Film Crew of Hollywood.* Jefferson, NC: McFarland, 2014.

Vagg, Stephen. *Rod Taylor: An Aussie in Hollywood.* BearManor, 2010.

Van Hoffman, Todd, Brand Van Hoffman, and Colby Allerton. *The Von Hoffman Bros. Big Damn Book of Sheer Manliness.* Santa Monica, CA: General, 1997.

Variety Film Reviews. New York: Bowker, 1986–1990.

Varner, Paul. *The A to Z of Westerns in Cinema.* Scarecrow, 2009.

Wagner, Rob. "Flickering Fists." *Collier's.* February 18, 1928.

Wallace, Stone. *George Raft: The Man Who Would Be Bogart.* BearManor, 2015.

Wasson, Sam. *A Splurch in the Kisser: The Films of Blake Edwards.* Middletown, CN: Wesleyan, 2009.

Wayne, Jesse. *Confessions of a Hollywood Stuntman.* Self, 2013.

Wayne, John. "Jimmie Fidler's Personality Parade." *Nevada State Journal.* January 23, 1955.

Weiner, David Jon. *Burns, Falls, and Crashes: Interviews with Movie Stunt Performers.* Jefferson, NC: McFarland, 1996.

Weldon, Michael. *The Psychotronic Video Guide.* New York: St. Martin's, 1996.

West, David. *Chasing Dragons: An Introduction to the Martial Arts Film.* London: Tauris, 2006.

Witney, William. *In a Door, into a Fight, Out a Door, into a Chase: Moviemaking Remembered by the Guy at the Door.* Jefferson, NC: McFarland, 1996.

Woodbridge, A.L. "Those Terrible Screen Battles." *Los Angeles Times.* February 11, 1925.

Wooley, John, and Michael H. Price. *The Big Book of Biker Flicks: 40 of the Best Motorcycle Movies of All Time.* Hawk, 2005.

Worth, David. *Zen and the Art of Independent Filmmaking: A Cautionary Tale.* Create Space, 2014.

Zolotow, Maurice. *John Wayne: Shooting Star.* New York: Allen, 1974.

Periodicals

Action Films, various issues

Aftra/SAG Newsletter: Arizona Branch. Various issues featuring Rodd Wolff's "Stunt and Safety" articles.

Black Belt Magazine, various issues.
Cinema Retro, various issues
Commonweal, various issues
Cue, various issues
Esquire, various issues
Falling for Stars. John Hagner, 1965–1981.
Fighting Stars Magazine, various issues.
Film Bulletin, various issues
Film Daily, various issues
Film Score Monthly, various issues
Films and Filming, various issues
Films in Review, various issues
Harrison's Reports, various issues
Hollywood Stuntman's Hall of Fame Newsletter. John Hagner, 1982–1993.
Inside Karate, various issues.
Inside Kung-Fu, various issues.
Life, various issues
Motion Picture Herald, various issues
Movie Maker, various issues
Newsweek, various issues

Punch, various issues
Show, various issues
The Spectator, various issues
Time, various issues
The Trail Beyond. Tim Lilley's "Those Fabulous Film Fights," 1999–2008.
Western Clippings. Boyd Magers, #1–

Websites

www.ancestry.com (newspaper archive)
www.b-westerns.com
www.genealogybank.com (newspaper archive)
www.googlenews.com (newspaper archive)
www.imdb.com
www.newspaperarchive.com (newspaper archive)
www.proquestarchives.com (newspaper archive)
www.tcm.com
www.terencehill.it
www.westernclippings.com
www.wikipedia.org

Index

Numbers in **bold italics** indicate pages with photographs.